IGNEOUS PETROLOGY

SECOND EDITION

ALEXANDER R. McBIRNEY
University of Oregon, Eugene

CBS Publishers & Distributors Pvt. Ltd.
New Delhi • Bengaluru • Chennai • Kochi • Kolkata • Mumbai
Hyderabad • Nagpur • Patna • Pune • Vijayawada

ISBN: 81-239-1412-1

First Indian Reprint: 1994

This edition has been published in India by arrangement with
Jones & Bartlet Publishers Inc., USA

Published by **Satish Kumar Jain** and produced by **Varun Jain** for
CBS Publishers & Distributors Pvt. Ltd.,
4819/XI Prahlad Street, 24 Ansari Road, Daryaganj, New Delhi - 110002
delhi@cbspd.com, cbspubs@airtelmail.in • www.cbspd.com
Ph.: 23289259, 23266861, 23266867 • Fax: 011-23243014

Corporate Office: 204 FIE, Industrial Area, Patparganj, Delhi - 110 092
Ph: 49344934 • Fax: 011-49344935
E-mail: publishing@cbspd.com • publicity@cbspd.com

Branches:
- ***Bengaluru:*** 2975, 17th Cross, K.R. Road, Bansankari 2nd Stage, Bengaluru - 70 • Ph: +91-80-26771678/79 • Fax: +91-80-26771680 E-mail: cbsbng@gmail.com, bangalore@cbspd.com
- ***Chennai:*** No. 7, Subbaraya Street, Shenoy Nagar, Chennai - 600030 Ph: +91-44-26681266, 26680620 • Fax: +91-44-42032115 E-mail: chennai@cbspd.com
- ***Kochi:*** Ashana House, 39/1904, A.M. Thomas Road, Valanjambalam, Ernakulum, Kochi • Ph: +91-484-4059061-65 Fax: +91-484-4059065 • E-mail: cochin@cbspd.com
- ***Kolkata:*** 6-B, Ground Floor, Rameshwar Shaw Road, Kolkata - 700014 Ph: +91-33-22891126/7/8 • E-mail: kolkata@cbspd.com
- ***Mumbai:*** 83-C, Dr. E. Moses Road, Worli, Mumbai - 400018 Ph: +91-9833017933, 022-24902340/41 • E-mail: mumbai@cbspd.com

Representatives:
- Hyderabad: 0-9885175004
- Patna: 0-9334159340
- Jharkhand: 0-9811541605
- Nagpur: 0-9021734563
- Pune: 0-9623451994
- Uttarakhand: 0-9716462459

Printed at:
J.S. Offset Printers, Delhi (India)

Contents

Preface to the Second Edition

The necessity of revising the first edition of this text so soon after writing it demonstrates very well the dramatic rate at which igneous petrology advances. In preparing this revision, I have often reflected on the amazing scope of the changes I have witnessed in my own time. When I emerged from graduate school in the early 1960s, I felt secure in the belief that I understood igneous rocks. Indoctrinated with a reverence for the work of Bowen, Daly, Wager, and their peers, I had little doubt that, armed with my powerful array of tools—rock hammer, microscope, phase diagrams, and chemical analyses—I could deal with most of the volcanic and plutonic rocks of the world. Now, thirty years later, I have more tools but far less assurance that I can use them to explain all rocks. Having seen so many cherished notions discredited or, at least, badly tarnished, my self-assurance is tempered with doubts and reservations.

I am sure that most petrologists sooner or later share this experience. In the course of a career, one greets each new petrologic development, be it a new isotopic relation, a thermodynamic calculation, or a sophisticated geophysical measurement, with the hope that at last he has the key that will unlock all his problems. More often than not these bursts of enthusiasm are followed by a realization that there is no magic solution, only an increasing complexity demanding broader and deeper understanding of the Earth.

What I find so remarkable is the accelerating pace we are witnessing today. One need only consider how many sections of the first version of this text have been outdated in the years since they were written. The most conspicuous advances have been in interpretations of oceanic volcanism and the geochemical relations of basalts to an evolving mantle. No less important, but still unresolved, are the questions raised by new studies of differentiated basic intrusions. Many of the most basic concepts of how magmas crystallize and differentiate are in a wild state of flux.

I cannot claim to have mastered all the arcane ramifications of these complex topics; I know of few who can. This, of course, is why it has become so difficult to maintain the balanced perspective needed in any textbook that is meant to be comprehensive. And yet, it seems to me that the trend toward increasing specialization makes it all the more important to do so. Otherwise, one tends to take a myopic view of one's own narrow interests and loses sight of the fundamental nature of the rocks one is dealing with. For this reason, I have relied heavily on the guidance of those who are much more at home in certain realms of petrology than I am. I am particularly indebted to Derek Bostok, Godfrey Fitton, Dennis Geist, Gordon Goles, Dana Johnston, Bruce Marsh, S.A. Morse, Adolphe Nicolas, Dean Presnall, Alberto Patino-Douce, and Mark Richards, all of whom have contributed expert advice on major sections of this new edition. Any shortcomings that remain cannot be due to a lack of good advice.

ALEXANDER MCBIRNEY
Eugene, Oregon
Summer, 1992

Preface to the First Edition

One of America's great petrologists, the late Frank Schairer, once remarked that, to understand igneous rocks, a geologist must first learn "to think like a molten silicate." I doubt if one can consciously design a book to achieve such an abstract end, but I am sure that to do so one must convey to the student a good deal more than factual information. The ideal book should, in my view, lead the student through the kinds of logic, speculation, and intuitive reasoning that are such central elements of petrologic thought. I have sought to do this by presenting petrologic principles, not as fixed dogma, but as ideas that evolve with each increment of information and insight.

Few fields of science are advancing more rapidly today than the study of igneous rocks, and, as happens in any field that is not stagnant, many petrologic concepts that are fashionable today are destined to be discarded tomorrow. Thus, advances in petrology demand a constant reassessment of a great store of geological and geochemical information. In doing this, special scrutiny is given to any persistent anomaly that fails to fit an accepted interpretation, for, more often than not, one learn less from all the examples that fit a popular concept than from a single observation that violates it.

It seems clear, I believe, that the direction of igneous petrology today is toward more rigorous analyses of physical magmatic processes. To interpret igneous rocks, it is just as important to understand the physics of heat and mass transfer as it is to know the phase diagram for plagioclase or the rules of trace-element fractionation. Equally important are the dramatic advances made possible by the modern computer. This powerful tool has already changed our way of dealing with complex petrologic problems, many of which could not be dealt with by older methods. In an effort to introduce the student to a few of the elementary types of computer techniques, a collection of useful programs has been prepared for use on a small personal computer. These can be obtained by means of the leaflet enclosed with this book.

The text is intended for a one-term course for students who already have an elementary background in petrography and petrology. I assume a basic knowledge of mineralogy, structural geology, and college-level chemistry, physics, and mathematics. In dealing with the principles of phase diagrams, for example, I have assumed that the student is already familiar with the elementary systems.

Likewise, if the student has had a modern course in inorganic chemistry, it can be assumed that he understands the fundamental aspects of solutions, chemical potential, and reaction coefficients. The book will have greater value, of course, if it is integrated with laboratory sessions that enable the student to examine examples of the petrographic suites discussed in the text.

A few illustrative problems are included, not so much as exercises to test the reader's understanding but rather to bring out certain principles that are shown more convincingly by having the reader demonstrate them to himself. These are supplemented by a second set designed for use with the computer programs already mentioned.

Of the many persons who made this book possible, I am indebted most to the late Howel Williams, who first awakened my interest in volcanic rocks; had he lived to contribute to it, this would be a far better book. I have relied on many friends, colleagues, and students for ideas and critical appraisal. Among those who reviewed various chapters and early drafts were Richard L. Armstrong, Brian H. Baker, Derek Bostok, Ralph Cristiansen, Julius El Dasch, Robert Decker, Gordon G. Goldes, Richard Jahns, Peter W. Lipman, Dennis Macaskie, Bruce D. Marsh, S.A. Morse, D.C. Presnall, and H.S. Yoder, Jr. Above all, my greatest debt is to the unnumbered students who have endured my lectures and from time to time confronted me with those unexpected questions that remind us that we seldom understand rocks as well as we think and never as well as we should.

ALEXANDER MCBIRNEY
Eugene, Oregon
Spring, 1985

COMPUTER PROGRAMS FOR
IGNEOUS PETROLOGY

A set of 15 integrated computer programs has been designed to accompany the text of the second edition of Igneous Petrology. These are professional level programs widely used by igneous petrologists and geochemists. They make it possible to store geochemical data in a set of uniform files that can be used to carry out a variety of petrologic functions on an IBM or Apple computer. The principal programs make it possible to do the following.

— compile, store, and edit up to 70 analyses for as many as 50 major and trace elements in a form that can be printed as tables or used for calculations in other programs in the same system;
— calculate molecular, CIPW, and alkaline norms and convert analyses from weight to molecular percentages;
— calculate averages and linear regressions of compositional trends;
— construct X-Y and ternary variation diagrams as well as various types of normalized plots, such as rare-earth and spider diagrams on linear or log scales;
— calculate mass-balances for major elements to test fractionation models; the same program allows for independent predictions of trace-element abundances for any postulated assemblage of minerals and distribution coefficients;
— calculate liquidus temperatures, viscosities, densities, heat capacities, and other physical properties of silicate melts and rocks;
— calculate the compositional trends of low-pressure differentiation by the method of Nathan and Van Kirk;
— convert chemical analyses to mineral formulas and vice versa.

A manual provides detailed instructions for use of the programs and a set of problems illustrating a variety of common petrologic calculations. The latter are designed to deal with the most common types of calculations used by igneous petrologists. Sample data files are furnished to show how the petrologic techniques explained in the text can be applied to real suites of rocks. Versions are available for the following types of computers.

— IBM PC or compatible equivalents
— IBM PS (hard disk)
— Apple Macintosh
— Apple II+ or IIe with disk drive
— Apple II+ or IIe with hard disk

The package can be purchased for $50 from:

Alexander McBirney
2780 Capital Drive
Eugene, OR 97403

IGNEOUS PETROLOGY

CRATERE DE LA MONTAGNE DE LA COUPE, AU COLET D'AISA,
Avec un Courant de Lave qui donne naissance à un pavé de basalte prismatique.

In 1763, Nicolas Desmarest traced a flow of columnar basalt to its origin in a volcanic crater near Clermont Ferrand in Central France. In so doing, he demonstrated that, contrary to a widely held belief, basalts are not precipitates from sea water but products of volcanic eruptions. This simple piece of field work, together with studies elsewhere in the Auvergne, marked the demise of the Neptunist doctrines and the beginning of modern igneous petrology. The highly idealized view shown here is from an illustration published by Faujas de Saint-Fond in 1778. (Courtesy of the Bibiothèque Nationale de Paris)

1

THE EARTH AND ITS MAGMATISM

MUCH OF WHAT we know about the composition, evolution, and internal workings of our planet has been learned through studies of igneous rocks. Drawing on many realms of science to integrate the results of field observations, geophysical measurements, and laboratory experiments, igneous petrology has enabled us to understand a host of complex natural processes, few of which can ever be directly measured or observed.

The earth is basically an enormous igneous rock, composite in form and covered with a thin, weathered surface. Its interior is a high-temperature assemblage of crystals and magmatic fluids, its crust a layer of volcanic and intrusive rocks and the products of their weathering, erosion, and metamorphism. Each year about fifty square kilometers of its surface are covered by new lava, while to its crust are added twenty to thirty cubic kilometers of mantle-derived magma. These igneous rocks may be weathered and reconstituted into new sedimentary and metamorphic forms, only to be buried and eventually returned to the crust as new magmas. Even the waters of the seas and the gases of the air we breathe have igneous origins; they have accumulated mainly through degassing of the earth's interior through prolonged periods of magmatic activity. Igneous petrology is the study of these rocks—their origins, compositional evolution, and relations to the tectonic processes shaping the earth and planets.

THE EARLY EVOLUTION OF THE EARTH

The lavas erupted by Kilauea volcano in Hawaii or by Mount Saint Helens in the Cascade Range represent only the latest products of a long, continuing process by which our planet has attained its present structure and form. Indeed, the igneous activity we witness today can only be understood in terms of much earlier processes through which Earth first took form, gained mass and heat, and proceeded to differentiate into a core, mantle, and crust. Like the other dense planetary bodies in orbits close to the Sun, Mercury, Venus, Mars, and the asteroids, Earth probably accreted from the hot inner part of a great disk-like cloud of gas and dust rotating slowly about the Sun. As separate bodies aggregated from their dispersed state into growing clots, they gained thermal energy, first from their inward falling mass, then from self-compression and decay of radioactive elements that were then far more abundant than today. The temperatures of parts of these "terrestrial planets" were high enough, even during their early stages of accretion, to vaporize many of the more abundant elements. Close to the Sun only the most refractory metals, aluminum, titanium, calcium, and their oxides, could condense. Farther from the Sun iron, nickel, and silicates were able to accumulate, and only at much greater distances could more volatile components, such as water, ammonia, and methane, condense as parts of the giant outer planets, Jupiter, Saturn, Uranus, and Neptune.

Meteorites and the composition of Earth

Much of our knowledge of the compositions and early stages of formation of the planets comes to us in the form of exotic fragments falling from space. Several thousand tons of meteorites, mostly dust-size particles, reach Earth each day. Though highly varied, this material can be divided into three broad types, known as *stones, stony irons,* and *irons*. Among specimens found on the ground long after their fall, stony meteorites are much less common than irons, because, having the appearance of common terrestrial rocks, they are less conspicuous and unlikely to attract the attention of the farmer who overturns one with his plow. They are also more fragile; they break up in the atmosphere or on impact and deteriorate quickly by weathering. Among meteorites seen to fall, however, they are much more important; they account for by far the largest fraction, roughly 94 percent. This great preponderance among observed falls must be a more accurate reflection of their original proportion in the bodies from which they come.

The iron meteorites, or *siderites,* consist of an alloy of metallic iron with about 11 percent nickel and minor amounts of other components, most notably the sulfide mineral troilite, a form of pyrrhotite found only in meteorites. The metal is a coarsely crystalline intergrowth of nickel-rich lamellae in a nickel-poor host. When polished and etched with acid, it reveals a characteristic structure known as Widmanstatten figures (Fig. 1–1).

Intermediate between irons and stones are the stony irons, or *siderolites,* containing about equal amounts of nickel-iron and coarse crystals of olivine and, less commonly, pyroxene. Stony meteorites are composed almost entirely of the same silicate minerals, plagioclase, pyroxene, and olivine, that are the most abundant constituents of the earth's crust and upper mantle. They are of two types, *chondrites* and *achondrites,* which are usually distinguished by the presence or absence of distinctive spheroidal aggregates known as *chondrules* (Fig. 1–2). Ranging up to a centimeter or so in size, these curious features are intergrowths of differing proportions of pyroxene and olivine that must have nucleated and grown at elevated temperatures in globules of liquid or glass (Fig. 1–3a). Most are thought to be droplets preserved from the original particles that accreted to form the asteroidal bodies from which most meteorites are derived, but some may have formed as impact melts, as have certain fragments with similar forms found on the surface of the Moon. The chondrules are set in a matrix of small crystals of

(a)

Figure 1–1 (a) A polished section cut through the Canyon Diablo iron meteorite, which fell near Holbrook, Arizona. The pattern of crystals, known as Widmanstatten structure, results from a slowly cooled intergrowth of two forms of nickel-iron. The rounded clots are troilite (FeS). (b) The Thiel Mountain siderolite of Antarctica consists of large crystals of olivine in a matrix of metallic nickel-iron. (Both photographs through the courtesy of Dr. Brian Mason, Smithsonian Institution, Washington, D. C.)

(b)

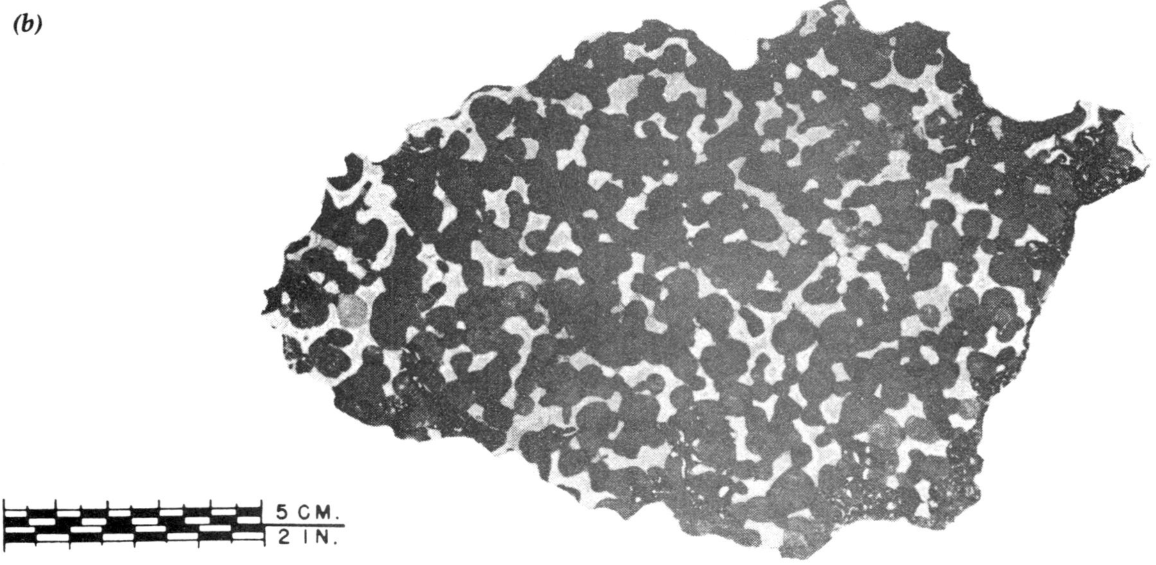

(a)

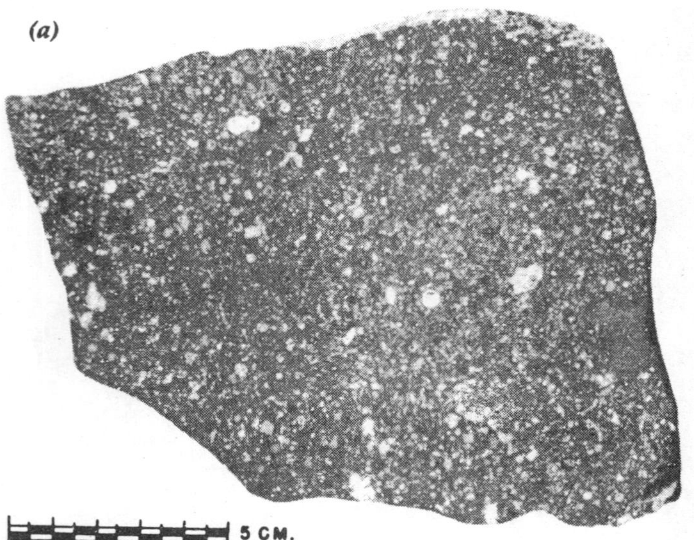

Figure 1–2 (a) The Allende chondritic meteorite of Mexico contains numerous round clots, known as chondrules. (b) The same features are seen here in a microscopic view of the Selma meteorite. The chondrules have an average diameter of about 1 mm and are made up mainly of olivine (white) and pyroxene (light grey). (Both photographs through the courtesy of Dr. Brian Mason, Smithsonian Institution, Washington, D. C.)

(b)

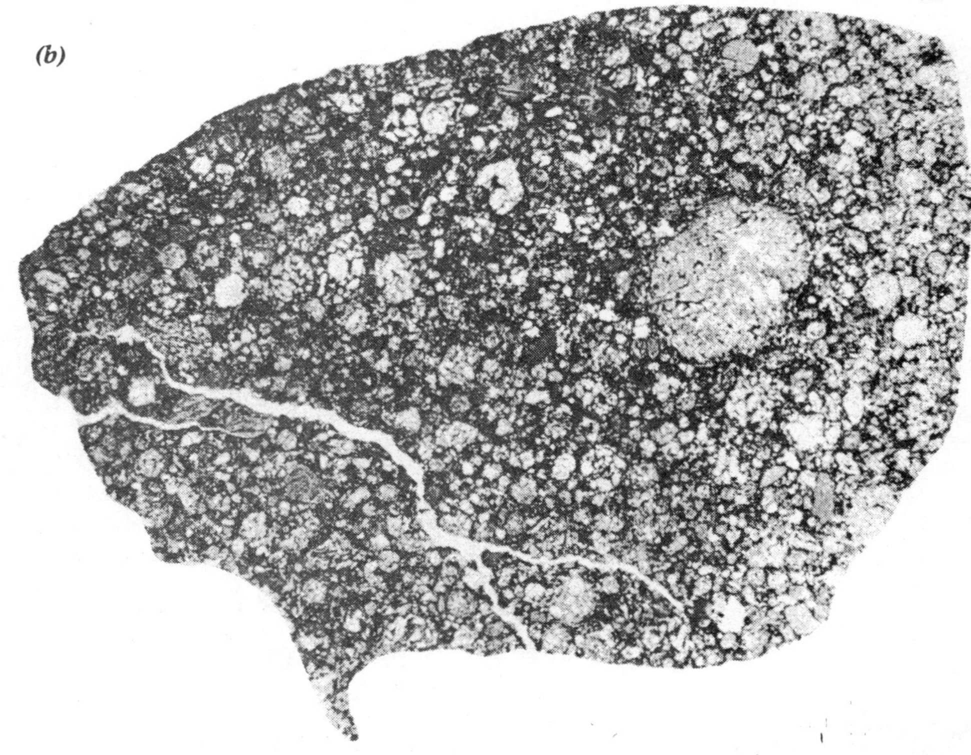

olivine, hypersthene, diopside, plagioclase, and rounded particles of nickel-iron and troilite.

Many chondritic meteorites have loose porous textures, and some contain small amounts of carbon or even water that seem to have condensed in the outermost layers of the accreting mass. These *carbonaceous chondrites* must represent the shallow parts of an early planetary body that for some reason escaped the strong surficial heating that affected the parental bodies of other meteorites.

About 10 percent of the stony meteorites belong to the group known as achondrites, which are distinguished, as their name implies, by an absence of chondrules. Achondrites are also depleted of volatile components and metallic nickel-iron, and some have large crystals that appear to have been formed at high temperatures under conditions of slow cooling (Fig. 1–3b). Where well preserved, their textures resemble those of gabbroic rocks formed at moderate depths in the earth's crust, but most are so severely crushed that their original textures are obliterated. This pervasive crushing attests to the violent deformation of the parental bodies that must have occurred at the time of their disruption; the effects are too strong to have been caused by impact with the earth. Some of the plagioclase crystals, for example, have an isotropic, vitreous form known as *maskelynite* that has also been found in terrestrial rocks subjected to an intense shock, such as that of a nuclear explosion (Fig. 1–3c).

Ages measured from decay of the radioactive elements in stony meteorites fall uniformly close to 4.6 billion years and are thought to be nearly as great as the solar system as a whole. If so, the compositions of chondritic meteorites may be close to that of the original earth. Although the exact relations of the different types of meteorites are still disputed, a convenient way of thinking of them is as parts of multiple bodies, smaller but compositionally like the earth, that were suddenly disrupted soon after differentiating.

By removing from chondrites their small clots of nickel-iron and recrystallizing the remaining constituents at moderate depths, it would be possible to pro-

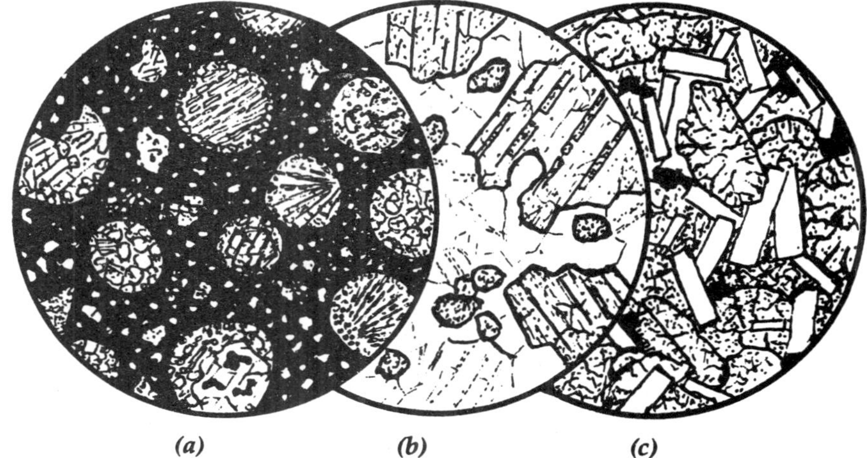

Figure 1–3 Typical textures of meteorites. (a) The Allende chondrite contains well-formed chondrules of olivine and pyroxene in an opaque, iron-rich matrix. (b) The Moore County achondrite consists of pigeonite and plagiolcase intergrown in a coarse, gabbroic texture. (c) The Shergotty achondrite contains crushed pigeonite and maskelynite, an isotropic form of plagioclase produced by intense shock. Diameters of fields are about 3 mm.

duce rocks with most of the features that are distinctive of achondrites. Thus the gross differences between the two classes of stony meteorites can be related to segregation of a crudely layered body with clots, or perhaps a core, of nickel-iron, a mantle of achondritic composition, and a thick chondritic crust. The chondrites, by this reasoning, are close to the original bulk composition of the terrestrial planets before they formed a core and acquired their present structures and evolved compositions.

This is not to say that all meteorites have come from a primitive planet close to the earth in size and position in the solar system. Apart from specimens recently discovered in Antarctica and shown to have come from the Moon, most are thought to be from the asteroidal belt between Mars and Jupiter. Being farther from the Sun, these bodies must have differed, at least in minor ways, from the inner planets. Nor could they have been as large as Earth, because the mineral assemblages of meteorites show no evidence of ever having formed under pressures even approaching that of Earth's mantle. Some of the common minerals in stony meteorites, most notably plagioclase, are stable only at shallow depths; no high-pressure forms, such as garnet or spinel, have been found to indicate that the mineral assemblages crystallized in the deep interior of a large body.

Though chondritic meteorites differ somewhat in their bulk compositions, proportions of chondrules, and oxidation states, their differences are not random. They can be related to various degrees of heating and metamorphism at differing depths within the outer layer of their parental bodies. Carbon, sulfur, and water contents, for example, vary inversely with the inferred original temperatures and relative depths of burial deduced from the textures and mineral assemblages of individual chondrites. The average composition of chondrites (Table 1-1, no. 1) is not far from that of the non-volatile parts of the inner solar system as a whole. Apart from certain deficiencies of the volatile elements, which may be due to the conditions under which the parental bodies of meteorites accreted, the individual elements have proportions not unlike those of the earth. The abundances of heat-producing radioactive elements, for example, are almost exactly those that would produce the observed surface heat-flow of the earth if they were distributed in the same proportions as they are thought to have in the earth's core, mantle, and crust. It is these remarkable consistencies that lead us to conclude that the initial bulk composition of the earth resembled that of chondritic meteorites and that the present abundances of elements in different parts of the earth resulted from their redistribution during formation of the core, mantle, and crust.

Formation of the earth's core and mantle

It is uncertain whether the earth's core formed during the initial process of accretion or at a slightly later stage after the temperature of the earth had been raised by meteoritic impact and decay of radioactive elements in its interior; the latter seems more likely. At some early stage, as the temperature of the earth rose during a period of intense heating, the melting temperature of nickel-iron and iron sulfides was exceeded, and molten metal began to gravitate toward the interior.

Table 1-1 The composition in column 1 (left) is that of an average bronzite chondrite and can be thought of as roughly equivalent to the bulk composition of a primitive earth. The composition in column 2 was obtained by subtracting from column 1 the composition of a core having a mass equal to 32 percent of the earth and a composition the same as that of iron meteorites. It can be compared with two types of rocks that are thought to be typical of the earth's mantle. Column 3 is the average composition of 9 garnet peridotites from African diamond pipes, and column 4 is an Archean ultramafic lava (komatiite) thought to have been produced by total melting of the mantle.

	1.	2.	3.	4.
SiO_2	36.57	48.0	46.5	45.23
TiO_2	0.10	0.13	0.3	0.20
Al_2O_3	2.30	3.0	1.8	3.66
FeO	9.67	13.0	6.7	10.98
MnO	0.33	0.4	0.1	0.22
MgO	23.69	31.0	42.0	32.16
CaO	1.77	2.3	1.5	5.28
Na_2O	0.86	1.1	0.2	0.44
K_2O	0.10	0.13	0.2	0.17
P_2O_5	0.26	0.34	0.02	0.02
Cr_2O_3	0.42	0.55	0.4	0.47
Fe	16.90			
Ni	1.64			
FeS	5.30			

Source: 1 and 2 from Mason, 1962, 3 from Bostok, pers. comm., and 4 from Nesbitt and Sun, 1976, *Earth & Planets. Ltrs.*, 31:433–453.

As it sank, it gained heat from its loss of potential energy and descended as an aggregated molten mass to the center of the earth.

If this is indeed what happened, one can calculate the composition that the mantle would have after separation of a core with a mass amounting to about 32 percent of an earth with an original composition close to that of the average chondritic meteorite. The resulting values, shown in Table 1-1, no. 2, fall within the range of certain types of exotic rocks brought up from below the crust in deep-focused, explosive eruptions (Table 1-1, nos. 3 and 4). Although the exact proportions of some components remain uncertain, this is our best estimate of the overall composition of the source region from which most igneous rocks are derived.

Formation of the crust

Important as it is in deciphering the early history of the earth, the evidence from meteorites is of little help in interpreting how the earth went on to form its crust. Notably absent from the thousands of meteorites that have been studied are any specimens resembling terrestrial crustal rocks, such as shale, granite, rhyolite, or schist. For some reason, possibly because they were small and lost heat too quickly to reach the required temperature, the parental bodies of meteorites ceased to evolve soon after their formation and failed to develop crusts like that of the earth.

We must turn instead to the Moon and planets to find the evidence needed to reconstruct a record of events subsequent to formation of the earth's core. The Moon may have passed through the same early phases of development that affected the earth, but it has long since dissipated much of its internal energy and is now cold and "dead" in the sense that it lacks volcanism and has had no tectonic activity for about three billion years. Even though its surface was bombarded by meteorites until all traces of early landforms were obliterated, petrologists have been able to deduce the form and composition of the Moon's ancient surface. It is divided into two distinct parts, the highlands, consisting of plagioclase-rich rocks called *anorthosites*, and the maria, which were vast expanses of basaltic lava. The scale of magmatism responsible for this division was so great that many lunar geologists believe that during the early accretionary stage of its history, when bombardment by meteorites was especially intense, the surface of the Moon was an ocean of basaltic magma some 400 km deep, in which great blocks of anorthosite floated like icebergs in the sea.

Though it is difficult to conceive of magmatism on this scale, we now have evidence that intense extra-terrestrial volcanism is in fact a reality. Pictures sent back by space probes passing the moons of Jupiter have shown that Io, a moon nearly as large as the terrestrial planets, is presently in a stage of volcanic activity surpassing anything known on Earth. Eight huge, active volcanoes have been detected, and the surface appears to be a vast plain of sulfurous lava. No record of such intense magmatism can be found on the earth today, but then it is not likely that it would be, for the earliest crust of the earth and the record it held are long since lost. We can infer, however, that the primitive crust of the earth was formed by magmatic processes not unlike those of the Moon and Io.

Today, Earth has by far the most volcanism of any of the inner planets. Mercury seems to have had none whatever since very early in its history; Mars shows evidence of volcanism in the recent past but less than that of Venus, which is second only to Earth in the scale of its volcanism. Much of the surface of Venus has been flooded by immense flows of basaltic lava; its average rate of production of magma is estimated at about nineteen cubic kilometers per year, compared to twenty to thirty for the earth. The rates for Mars and the Moon are thought to have been much less than one cubic kilometer per year.

The fact that Io, a moon of Jupiter, shows such vigorous activity today, and Mars, Mercury, and our own Moon do not, may tell us something about magmatic processes on Earth. The scarcity or total absence of volcanism on the innermost terrestrial planets today can logically be attributed to their compositions and sizes. When first formed in orbits close to the Sun, they retained only small amounts of volatile, heat-producing radioactive elements, and their small sizes allowed them to dissipate heat very quickly. But this cannot be the only factor. Being farther from the Sun, Io probably retains more heat-producing elements, but, in addition, the magnetic and gravitational forces due to its proximity to the enormous mass of Jupiter must continue to generate large amounts of thermal energy through tidal friction, thereby augmenting the internal heat available for melting.

If so, we must conclude that the earth's long and complex evolution results from an extraordinary combination of circumstances: its size, composition, and position in the solar system. Were it smaller or closer to the Sun, it would now be as barren as our Moon or Mercury. Were it farther from the Sun or close to a much larger body, it might still be as active as Io. Thanks to its unique setting, Earth has enough tectonic and volcanic activity to maintain a diversified continental crust and just the right conditions to develop oceans, continents, and, most important, an atmosphere with moderate temperatures capable of supporting life.

Formation of the crust was essentially a process of segregation by which the first partial melts produced during the initial heating of the mantle formed buoyant masses of magma that rose toward the surface. Chief among the components

Table 1–2 Contributions of the principal radioactive elements to the heat production of the mantle.

Isotope	Half life (10^9 yrs)	Heat production (cal/g/yr)	Abundance in Mantle (ppm)	Heat production per gram of mantle (10^{-6} cal/g/yr)
^{238}U	4.5	0.706	0.03–0.13	0.02–0.09
^{232}Th	13.9	0.202	0.12–0.52	0.02–0.04
^{40}K	1.3	0.211	0.05–0.22	0.01–0.05
				0.05–0.18

of these early melts were the large, oxygen-seeking "lithophile" elements, silicon and aluminum, along with lesser amounts of iron, magnesium, calcium, and alkalies. The elements segregated in this way are not necessarily light ones; many, like uranium, lead, and gold, are heavy metals, but because their compounds have low melting temperatures or high solubilities in silica-rich melts, they were scavenged from the mantle and concentrated in the continental crust. So effective was this process that, even though the crust accounts for less than one percent of the total mass of the earth, it contains most of the earth's lithophile elements. Potassium, for example, has an average abundance in the mantle of only seven or eight parts per million, but in the continental crust it accounts for about 25,900 ppm.

The consequences of this efficient concentration of lithophile components into the crust have been enormous. Without it, extraction of metals and industrial minerals from ore deposits would be virtually impossible. What is even more important, this same group of lithophile elements includes the radioactive isotopes of potassium, uranium, and thorium, and their segregation into the crust greatly reduces the rate of heat production in the mantle (Table 1–2). This in turn reduces the intensity of magmatic activity to a level that makes our planet habitable.

The rocks that formed the initial crust of the earth have long since been reworked or lost to erosion. The oldest preserved record of the earth's magmatic activity is found in Archean rocks formed less than three-and-a-half billion years ago, long after the continental crust had formed and the primitive oceans and atmosphere were well established. Geologists still debate whether magmatism declined abruptly following formation of the crust or whether it declined more gradually and in Archean time was still much more intense than today. Few doubt, however, that it resulted from steeper temperature gradients that generated hotter magmas at very shallow depths in the upper mantle. One reason for believing this is that the earliest Precambrian rocks include an unusual type of ultramafic lavas, the *komatiites,* that are all but unknown among younger rocks and must have been erupted at temperatures in excess of 1,700 °C, far hotter than any observed or even inferred in modern volcanoes. Moreover, many of the metamorphic gradients found in Archean rocks reflect unusually high temperatures at shallow depths, and it appears that crustal rocks began to melt at higher levels than they do today. With time, the continental crust seems to have cooled and thickened, and temperatures in the upper mantle also declined, so that today most magmas are produced by melting at depths well below the crust.

ISOTOPIC EVOLUTION OF THE CRUST AND MANTLE

The decay of radioactive isotopes of certain elements, such as rubidium, uranium, thorium, and samarium, provides a useful temporal perspective on the early history of the earth. As rubidium-87 decays to strontium-87, the ratio of the latter to the non-radiogenic isotope, strontium-86, increases with time. In a similar way, as the radioactive isotope of uranium, ^{238}U, decays to lead-206, and samarium-147 decays to neodymium-143, the ratios of these decay products to their non-radiogenic counterparts, ^{204}Pb and ^{144}Nd, change with time. Details of these isotopic systems are outlined in Appendix D, but for our present purposes it will suffice to note how the growth curves for the radiogenic isotopes enable us to trace major geochemical changes far back in time. All three systems have decay constants long enough to produce measurable effects on the time scale of the earth's history. Moreover, the elements were partitioned in different ways during development of the core, mantle, and crust, so that isotopic evidence of their redistribution provides a way of inferring the timing and effects of major geochemical processes.

Figure 1–4 shows how the isotopic ratios of Sr, Pb, and Nd are thought to have evolved since the planet first began to take its present form. Because the rates of change of these ratios are proportional to the relative abundances of the parent and daughter elements, any process that changed their proportions in any part of the earth has in turn affected the subsequent rate of change of the isotopic ratio.

Consider first the case of strontium (Fig. 1–4a). The Rb/Sr ratio of the earth as a whole was determined at the time of accretion of the solar nebula, but the original concentrations and ratio of the parent and daughter elements have not remained uniform throughout the earth. Both elements were strongly excluded from the Ni-Fe melt forming the core, so, although both were residually enriched in the mantle, their relative proportions were not affected, and the rate of increase of $^{87}Sr/^{86}Sr$ remained constant. But later events, such as those leading to formation of the continental crust, have had a quite different effect. Because Rb had a greater affinity than Sr for the first liquids produced by melting of the primitive mantle, it was more strongly partitioned into the crust, while, at the same time, the Rb/Sr ratio of the remaining mantle was significantly reduced. The subsequent increase of radiogenic ^{87}Sr and its ratio to the non-radiogenic isotope ^{86}Sr was therefore slower in the mantle than it was in the Rb-rich continental crust.

The present distribution of U and Pb in the earth is also the result of a series of events beginning with accretion of the planet and continuing through the various stages of evolution of the core, mantle, and crust. The mobility of the individual isotopes during the earliest stages is not well understood, but it is thought that formation of the core could have resulted in separation of Pb from U and

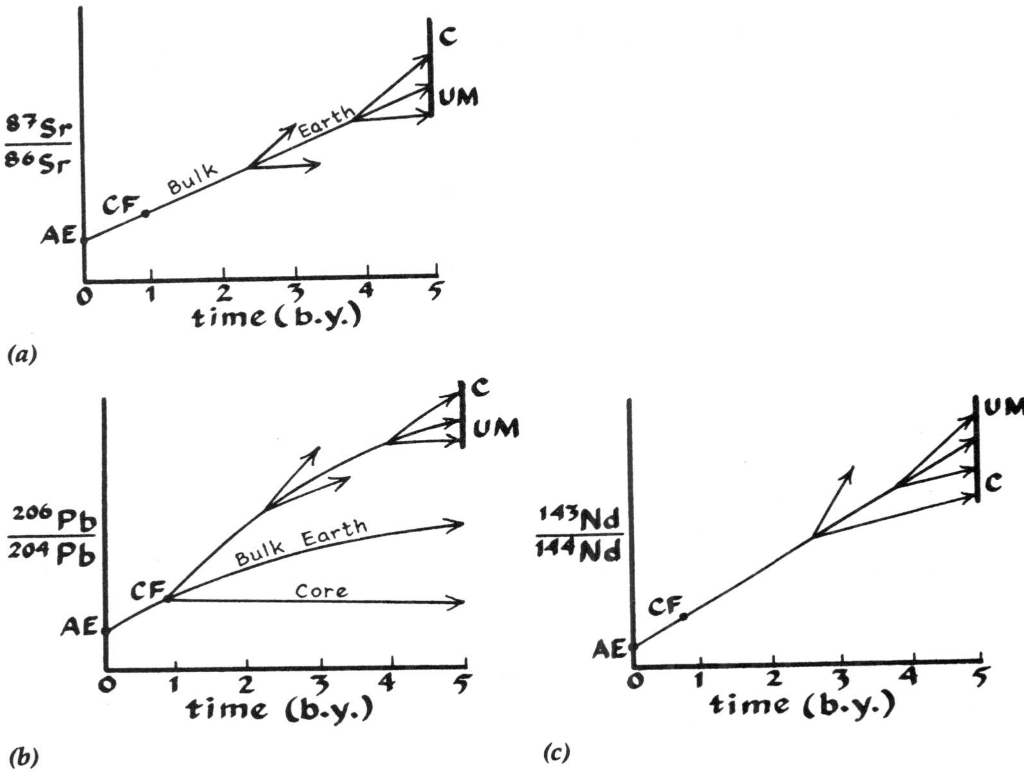

Figure 1–4 Each of the isotopic systems, Sr, Pb, and Nd, evolved through various stages starting with accretion of the earth (AE) and continuing at differing rates according to the partitioning of the isotopes at the time of formation of the core (CF) and separation of the continental crust (C) from the upper mantle (UM). Unlike Sm and Nd, which seem to have been concentrated by about the same amounts in both the upper and lower crusts, Rb and U are more strongly concentrated in the upper crust; their abundances in the lower crust are close to those of the mantle. The present ratios of ^{87}Sr to ^{86}Sr in the crust and mantle are related to that of the earth as a whole as shown schematically by the values at t = 0. (After D. J. De Paolo, 1981, *EOS*, 62:137–140.)

another radioactive parent of Pb, thorium, with much of the Pb going into the core, probably as a sulfide mineral. U and Th remained in the mantle to be later concentrated in molten silicates that were segregated to form the upper continental crust. The slope of the growth curve of the radiogenic isotope ^{206}Pb relative to the non-radiogenic form ^{204}Pb changed with each of these events, so that the present ratios of the isotopes in the crust and mantle differ, as shown schematically in Figure 1–4b.

Owing to the marked enrichment of U in the upper crust, continental Pb tends to be much more radiogenic than that of mantle-derived basalts, but neither is strictly uniform. Pb ratios have regional patterns that reflect the age and local history of the crust and mantle. It is thought, for example, that much of the crustal lead concentrated in the continents has been carried into the oceans by rivers and then cycled back to the continents by subduction. The erosion-averaged leads removed from the surface of the continents and deposited with sediments on the ocean floor have fairly uniform isotopic ratios, owing to global mixing in the oceans. This material is so rich in radiogenic Pb that when it is subducted and incorporated into the magmas of island arcs, it overwhelms the much smaller contribution of the lead-depleted mantle.

The development of the rare-earth system, Sm-Nd, resembles that of Sr and Pb but has important differences. The parent/daughter ratio, Sm/Nd, was not greatly altered by formation of the core, because all the rare-earth elements were equally excluded from the metallic melt. During subsequent evolution of the mantle, the ratio of ^{143}Nd to ^{144}Nd continued to increase as Sm decayed. The rate of increase, being a direct function of the relative abundances of Sm and Nd, corresponded to a parent-daughter ratio of about 0.31, the same as that of chondritic meteorites. This ratio is altered in magmas produced by partial melting, because Sm is partitioned less strongly into a silicate melt than is Nd. Thus, unlike Rb/Sr, the parent-daughter ratio Sm/Nd is reduced in magmas relative to the mantle from which they are derived.

Although the rare-earth elements, including both Sm and Nd, are strongly concentrated in the crust, the abundance of Nd in the crust is about twenty-five times that of the mantle, while that of Sm is somewhat less, about sixteen. Because this decreases the parent-daughter ratio, the rate of increase of ^{143}Nd/^{144}Nd has been slower in the continental crust than in the mantle from which crustal rocks are derived (Fig. 1-4c). Thus, even though the absolute abundances of the rare-earth elements are greater in the crust than in the mantle, the Nd isotopic ratio evolves more rapidly in the mantle than it does in the crust—just the opposite of ^{87}Sr/^{86}Sr. The Nd ratio differs according to the local age of the crust, but it is always less than would be expected for a chondritic parent-daughter ratio, while that of the mantle is greater by a complementary amount.

It is convenient to relate these ratios to those for the bulk earth, assuming the latter initially had a chondritic composition. Deviations from this average composition are expressed as ϵ_{Nd}, the fractional difference in units of 0.01 percent. For example, if the crust had not been formed and the mantle retained a chondritic Sm/Nd ratio, its ϵ_{Nd} would have a constant value of zero. The present ϵ_{Nd} value of the upper mantle, as shown by modern oceanic basalts, is about +12, whereas the average value for the continental crust is about −15.

Assuming these values are the result of differing amounts of separation of Sm and Nd from a mantle that initially had chondritic abundances of the REE, it is possible to use a simple mass balance to estimate how much of the mantle has been depleted of these lithophile elements by formation of the continental crust. If the mass of the continents is estimated from their areal extent and thickness, and the average Sm and Nd abundances are known for both the upper mantle and crust, one can easily calculate the mass of the depleted mantle. When this is done, one finds that the depleted part of the mantle would extend to a depth of about 600 to 700 km. If the entire mantle is not mixed by continual convection, depletion of these and other lithophile elements from the upper levels of the mantle would cause it to be compositionally layered on a global scale. Whether it is or is not is a question that will concern us later when we consider the origins of mantle-derived magmas.

COMPOSITIONAL EVOLUTION OF THE CRUST AND MANTLE

Following the early events that established the basic division of the earth into a core, mantle, and primitive crust, a much longer period elapsed before the continents took on a form similar to what they now have. Since no direct record of the first billion years has been preserved, the nature of the initial continental crust can only be inferred, but the subsequent history of the Archean can be deduced from remnants of deeply eroded continental regions, such as Greenland and the Canadian Shield, where the oldest rocks on Earth have survived more than three billion years of deformation and erosion. Although the record in these isolated remnants is fragmentary and may be far from complete, their remarkable similarity wherever they can be seen suggests that the conditions they record were broadly uniform throughout the early continents.

Following their initial formation, the continents continued to grow and evolve as magmatism added to their mass and surficial processes of weathering and erosion brought their composition into closer equilibrium with the atmosphere and hydrosphere. At the same time, the character of magmas added to the crust changed in response to the changing composition and thermal regime of the mantle, and by the end of Archean time, both the nature of magmatism and the average composition of the crust had approached what they are today.

Early evolution of the continental crust

The dominant character of volcanic and plutonic activity during the early history of the continents was quite unlike that associated with modern tectonic regimes. Because the mantle's greater radioactivity generated more heat at mantle depths, the thermal gradient was very steep, and advanced melting occurred at shallow depths. Certain types of magmas, such as very olivine-rich lavas, *komatiites,* and very plagioclase-rich plutonic rocks, *anorthosites,* have been confined almost exclusively to the Archean. The fact that these magmas could have been liquids only at exceptionally high temperatures suggests that they were products of melting in a geothermal gradient that was much steeper than it is today. Other types of magmas, such as a sodic variety of granite, *trondhjemite,* though not confined to the earlier periods, were proportionately more common than they are today. The rarity of true granites and other potassium-rich felsic rocks suggests that the relatively small potassium-sodium ratios of early felsic magmas reflect the immaturity of the Archean continental crust. Only after prolonged weathering and erosion had produced large amounts of mature sediments did their concentrations of potassium increase to modern levels, and the fact that the proportions of granites to trondhjemites increased during this same time implies that felsic plutonic rocks derive at least part of their composition from assimilation or partial melting of a crust that became more mature with time.

Not only was the early crust more primitive, the tectonic regime also seems to have been quite different. The record, of course, is incomplete and difficult to decipher. It is preserved in two main types of terranes, one dominated by high-grade metamorphic and plutonic rocks and the other by more weakly metamorphosed volcanic rocks and sediments of *greenstone belts*. The former consists mainly of gneisses, amphibolites, and granulites derived from metamorphism of older igneous rocks. Meta-sediments are much less common. The plutonic rocks are chiefly quartz-rich intermediate rocks, tonalites, or, more specifically, trondhjemites, that are notable for a strong dominance of sodic plagioclase over potassium feldspar. Dikes and layered sills were intruded into the gneiss and, along with everything else, were strongly deformed and metamorphosed. Some of these intrusions were ultramafic rocks (peridotites), while others were gabbros in which the plagioclase had an exceptionally calcic composition. The more feldspar-rich gabbros grade into layered anorthosites, but large anorthositic plutons did not become common until later in the Archean and Proterozoic.

Most of the rocks are multiply deformed, and many show signs of having been partly remelted, so that distinctions between igneous and metamorphic rocks became blurred. Much of the deformation is concentrated around circular or oval domes of partly melted and mobilized masses of gneiss, up to two or three hundred kilometers in diameter, that rose as diapirs, compressing the surrounding rocks into tight, complex folds.

The more weakly metamorphosed rocks of greenstone belts represent shallower parts of the crust that are thought to have developed by accumulation in down-warped linear or triangular basins (Fig. 1-5). The majority were formed between 3,500 and 2,300 million years ago. Opinions as to their origins differ widely. They have conventionally been regarded as fold belts caught between small, colliding plates of primitive crust; they have also been interpreted as impact structures, similar to those of the moon. The fact that many formed at the same time, 3,100 to 3,600 million years ago, when intense basaltic volcanism was flooding the lunar maria, may be coincidental but is at least consistent with a period of intense bombardment by meteorites. The generally accepted view today, however, is that the greenstone belts were caught and squeezed between diapiric intrusions of felsic plutonic rocks at the time of formation of the continental crust.

The stratigraphic sequences of greenstone belts are remarkably similar throughout the world. They have a thick, lower section consisting of komatiites, peridotites, and pillow basalts with only minor sedimentary interbeds. These mafic and ultramafic rocks grade into a sequence of more intermediate compositions, andesites, dacites, and rhyodacites, that tend to become more felsic and pyroclastic upward. In the uppermost units volcanic rocks give way to cherts,

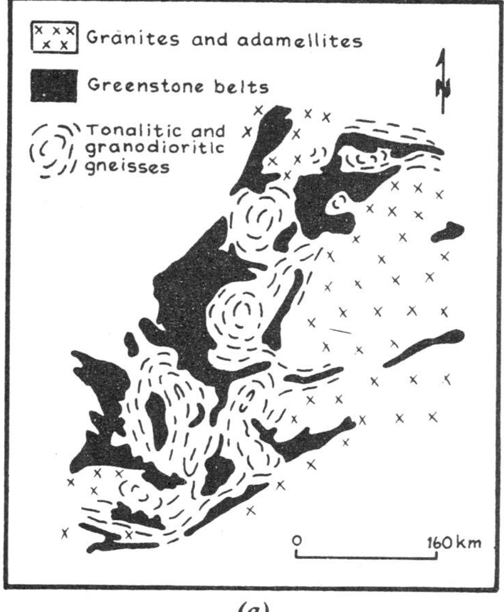

(a)

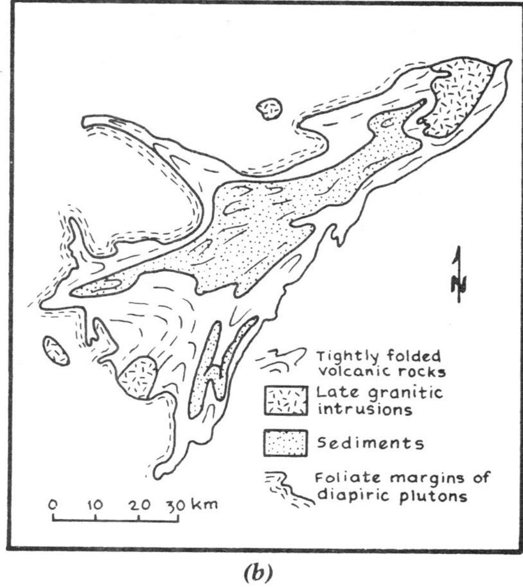

(b)

Figure 1–5 The characteristic features of Archean terranes. (a) shows the broad character of the Barberton Belt of South Africa comprising greenstone belts tightly compressed between islands of gneiss and diapiric felsic plutons. (b) is a closer view of a greenstone belt. In the latter, the volcanic and sedimentary beds form an irregular syncline. (Adapted from C. R. Anhaeusser, 1971, *Geol. Soc. Australia Sp. Pub. No. 3*, 103–120, and M. J. and R. P. Viljoen, 1970, in *African Magmatism and Tectonics*, T. N. Clifford and I. G. Gass, eds., 27–49.)

greywackes, shales, and conglomerates laid down shortly before the entire mass was strongly compressed and folded.

The Archean was clearly a time of intense tectonic and magmatic activity. Dynamic processes driven by strong, shallow convection of the mantle must have been very rapid; rates of spreading at divergent plate boundaries are estimated to have been about six times faster than they are today.

Despite the presence of andesites and other rocks common to modern island arcs, the geologic evidence for structures of the kind associated with modern subduction are hard to find. The continents were certainly mobile and continued to grow, both by marginal accretion and by addition of mantle-derived magmas to their interiors, but the tectonic relations and mechanisms of melting seem to have been quite different from those of later periods.

Plate motion was probably driven by the viscous drag of the convecting mantle with little if any contribution from the gravitational pull of subducted plates. Much of the driving force of modern subduction is thought to be the negative buoyancy of a descending basaltic slab that is converted to *eclogite*, a garnet-pyroxene rock with a density greater than that of the average mantle. If the descending basalt were remelted before reaching the depths where this transition occurs, it would not have the high density needed to pull the slab farther into the mantle. Not until the Proterozoic, about two billion years ago, did the basalt-eclogite transition become possible. By that time, the continents had become thicker and stronger, and plate tectonics took on a more modern aspect.

Most of the later growth of the continents resulted from addition of lighter magmas to the upper crust while denser, more mafic magmas remained at greater depths where they underplated the continents. Thus the crust tends to be more mafic and denser with depth. On average the total composition of the early crust was not unlike that of modern island arcs, but with time it became relatively richer in SiO_2, Al_2O_3, and K_2O (Table 1-3) as weathering and erosion concentrated these components in increasing volumes of sediments. By early Proterozoic time the composition of the continental crust had already attained a mass and average composition that have remained remarkably constant to the present.

Post-Archean magmatism

Although individual continents have changed shape and size, the simple fact that they have survived prolonged periods of erosion that should long ago have stripped away the upper crust suggests that the crust has been steadily renewed. Without some such process, nothing but the roots of continents would remain, and, since these deeper levels tend to be more mafic, the average compositions of sediments should have changed with time. The fact that modern products of erosion differ little from those laid down a billion years ago means that gains and losses are approximately in balance.

Part of the explanation for this apparent stability is that almost 60 percent of the sediments produced by erosion come from older sediments rather than from metamorphic and igneous rocks of the basement. When this material is deposited on the sea floor, part is scraped from the oceanic plates and accreted to the continental shelves at convergent plate boundaries. Another part is subducted and returned to the continents in the magmas of orogenic belts. Thus the products of erosion are largely recycled, and the rate at which the average composition of the crust can change is greatly reduced. Nevertheless, the igneous rocks added to the continents from the mantle cannot have an average composition

	1. Archean Crust	2. Modern Crust	3. Basalt-Rhyolite
SiO_2	57.0	60.3	60.2
TiO_2	1.0	1.0	1.1
Al_2O_3	15.2	15.6	14.7
FeO*	9.6	7.2	6.9
MgO	5.9	3.9	5.2
CaO	7.3	5.8	6.1
Na_2O	3.0	3.2	3.3
K_2O	0.9	2.5	2.1

Table 1-3 Average compositions of the Archean and modern continental crust. The average compositions of the rocks of island arcs are shown for comparison along with the composition of a 50-50 mixture of basalt and rhyolite. All iron is shown as FeO*.

Source: No. 1 from S. R. Taylor and S. M. McLennan, 1985, *The Continental Crust: Its Composition and Evolution*. Blackwell Sci. Publ. 312 pp. No. 2 from S. R. Taylor, 1964, *Geoch. Cosmoch. Acta*, 28:1273.

very different from that of the crust, for, if they did, the effect of their addition would gradually become apparent in a temporal change in the character of sediments.

The most conspicuous additions to the continents from the mantle have been the huge volumes of basaltic magma that have been erupted throughout Phanerozoic time. Unless this mafic contribution is balanced by additions of corresponding amounts of felsic material, it should result in a steady dilution of the lithophile elements and a steady basicification of the continents. The fact that this is not seen means that some other input of a complementary composition helps to maintain the balance of mafic and felsic components in the crust. Moreover, the proportions of these components must have remained approximately equal for much of geologic time.

Note that the average composition of the modern crust (Table 1–3) is roughly that of a 50–50 mixture of basalt and granite. If, as the increased potassium content of post-Archean granites indicates, most granites are derived largely from older crustal rocks, they do not constitute a net addition that could balance the effect of basaltic rocks coming from the mantle. Nevertheless, certain lines of geochemical evidence indicate that a large proportion of the granitic magma added to the continents is not recycled crust, but magma that is derived, though indirectly, from the mantle. Such magmas cannot be produced in any important amounts by simple melting of mantle peridotites, but we shall see (in chapter ten) that basaltic or amphibolitic rocks in the lower crust could provide a more fertile source.

The sizes of the great sheets of rhyolite covering large parts of the continents rival those of flood basalts, both in thickness and extent. Comparable volumes of granite are found in the deep interiors of most continents. If, as seems likely, a substantial part of this large volume comes from mantle-derived magmas and is not simply recycled crust, it constitutes a continued addition that helps maintain the nearly constant composition of the continental crust. It also means that the process of separation of lithophile components from the mantle did not end abruptly with formation of the primitive continents but has continued, though at a much slower rate, to the present.

Secular variations of igneous rocks

While the nearly constant average composition of continental sediments is well-established, it is more difficult, if not impossible, to say whether igneous rocks have also remained unchanged through Phanerozoic time. While stratigraphers have determined the proportions of different types of sediments during past geologic periods, igneous petrologists have failed to compile comparable data on the volumes or average compositions of igneous rocks. Without this information it is impossible to identify long-term trends in the geochemical exchange between the mantle and continents. A student hungering for international acclaim would do well to consider devoting a lifelong career to rectifying this shameful deficiency. Until someone takes up the formidable task, we can only speculate on broad, highly subjective impressions.

We have already noted the increasing potassium content of plutonic rocks in the early Precambrian. Basalts seem to show the opposite trend. Archean basalts resemble those of the modern ocean floor in most respects, but they have slightly more K_2O, .14 to .26 percent as compared to less than .10 percent for the basalts erupted at modern oceanic ridges. This difference is interpreted as evidence that the upper mantle from which these magmas have been derived has become more depleted with time. It is not clear, however, whether or not this has been a long-term, gradual trend.

There is little doubt that global rates of magmatism have varied widely through time. The best record, oddly enough, is found in the rise and fall of sea level that accompanies increases and decreases of spreading rates on oceanic ridges. Because the elevations and volumes of the ridges vary directly with the rate of seafloor spreading and hence the rate at which basalts are added to the crust, periods of high sea level are also times of increased magmatic activity, at least in the oceans. Although we can infer that increased spreading rates entail a comparable increase of subduction-related magmatic activity, there is no way of knowing how this correlates with magmatism in the interior of continents.

THE EARTH'S IGNEOUS ACTIVITY TODAY

The distribution of global magmatism today is largely confined to a small number of geologic settings (Fig. 1-6), where it is closely related to the motion of lithospheric plates. How long this pattern has prevailed is uncertain, and one must keep in mind the possibility that the relations seen today may be different from those of the past.

Nevertheless, the present pattern provides a convenient way of dividing Cenozoic magmatic activity into a small number of distinct types, each with its own compositional and eruptive characteristics. By far the most important focus of magmatism, at least in volumetric terms, is at spreading axes and divergent plate boundaries (Table 1-4). In most places, these are zones of seafloor spreading and separation of oceanic lithosphere, but they also include tensional regions of the continental crust, the great rift of East Africa being the most notable example. Perhaps the best place to observe this type of activity is in Iceland, where the Mid-Atlantic Ridge can be seen emerging from the sea, crossing the island, and descending again into the Arctic Ocean. At intervals of a few decades, eruptions of fluid basaltic lava pour from fissures to flood wide areas of the surface, while the feeder-dikes of these same eruptions solidify at shallow depths and add as much as a meter or so at a time to the lithosphere along the central axis of the island. In the same way, the ocean floor must be spreading laterally as new lava and dikes are emplaced along the oceanic ridges.

By far the greatest number of the world's active land volcanoes are concentrated along the lines of plate convergence where the oceanic lithosphere descends into the mantle. They form a "chain of fire" following, with few interruptions, the entire circumference of the Pacific Ocean. Other volcanic belts, such as those of the Antilles Arc and Indonesia, are in similar settings. Volcanism is notably rare at convergent boundaries where both plates are continental. A few

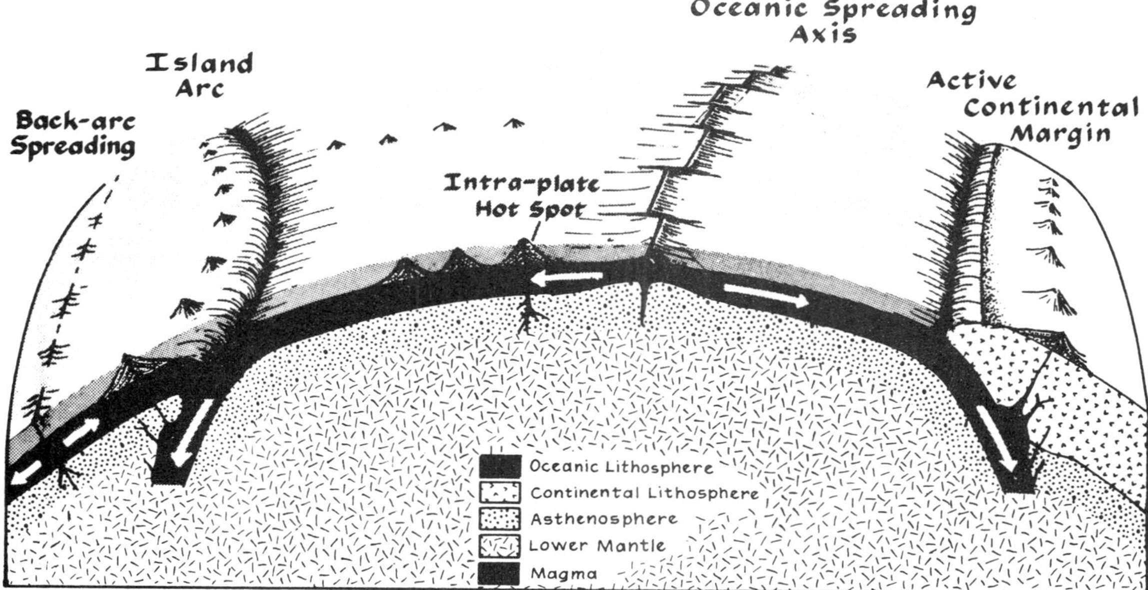

Figure 1–6 Modern igneous activity has been concentrated in three tectonic settings. The largest volume (about 21 cubic km per year) is produced at spreading axes (center). Lesser amounts (between 1 and 10 cubic km per year) are associated with converging plate boundaries in island arcs (left), where the overlying plate is oceanic, and continental margins (right), where it is continental. Subordinate amounts of magmatism are found in intraplate regions (left center) where moving plates pass over a persistent thermal anomaly in the mantle.

plutons have been intruded into these collisional zones, but only under very special circumstances.

Many of the great belts of batholiths were probably roots of volcanic chains like those seen today at convergent plate boundaries, but others are well within the interiors of continents in quite different tectonic settings. Some may have been related to great outpourings of rhyolitic ignimbrites, such as the siliceous

Table 1–4 Global rates of cenozoic magmatism.

Location	Rate (km^3/yr) Volcanic Rocks	Plutonic Rocks
Oceanic ridges	3	18
Convergent plate boundaries	0.4–0.6	2.5–8.0
Continental intraplate regions	0.03–0.1	0.1–1.5
Oceanic intraplate regions	0.3–0.4	1.5–2.0
Global Total	3.7–4.1	22.1–29.5

(*Source:* From estimates of J. A. Crisp, *Jour. Volc. Geoth. Res.*, 1983.)

pyroclastic flows that cover wide areas of North America. They are commonly associated with zones of continental rifting, but a few of the large centers, such the caldera complex of Yellowstone or the granitic ring-complexes of New England, may be continental manifestations of mantle hotspots equivalent to those forming long chains of volcanoes in intraplate regions of the oceans.

THE NATURE OF THE MANTLE

Our knowledge of the mantle comes from several sources, including geophysical measurements of its physical properties, samples brought up from deep sources in volcanic eruptions, and experimental studies of rocks at very high pressures. Here we will look briefly at the geophysical evidence and what can be inferred from it.

Geophysical properties of the mantle

The velocities of seismic waves transmitted through the crust and mantle vary with the mineralogical character, density, and temperature of the rocks through which they travel. In this way, they place broad but strict limits on the temperatures and compositions of the crust, mantle, and core (Figs. 1–7 and 1–8).

The sharp, step-like *Mohorovicic discontinuity*, or *Moho*, marks the base of the crust; it lies about 5 to 10 km below the oceans but ranges from 25 to 90 km or more below the continents. Below that level, the compressional wave velocities (> 7 km/sec) and densities (> 3.2 g/cm^3) correspond to rocks composed entirely of dense, mafic minerals, such as olivine and pyroxene. Except for a sharp decrease in the *low-velocity zone* at a depth of about 100 kilometers, seismic velocities increase downward as far as the core.

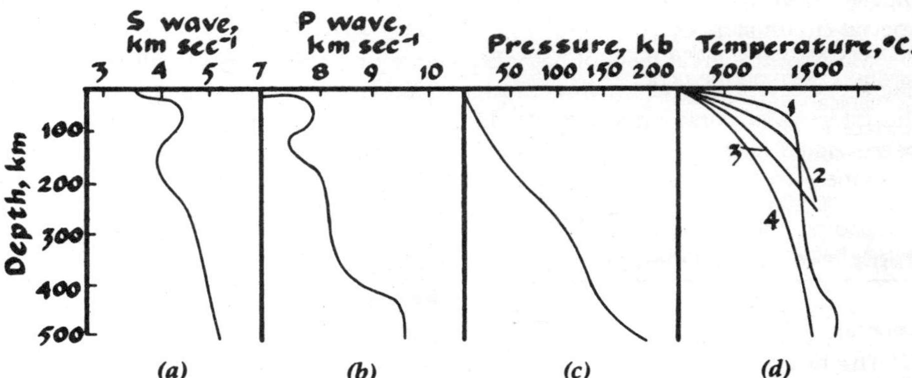

Figure 1–7 Some physical properties of the crust and mantle: (a) Compressional (P) wave velocities. (b) Shear (S) wave velocities. (c) Pressures assuming densities consistent with measured seismic velocities. (d) Some proposed temperature profiles. 1 and 2 are estimates for the mantle under the oceans; 3 and 4 are possible continental geotherms.

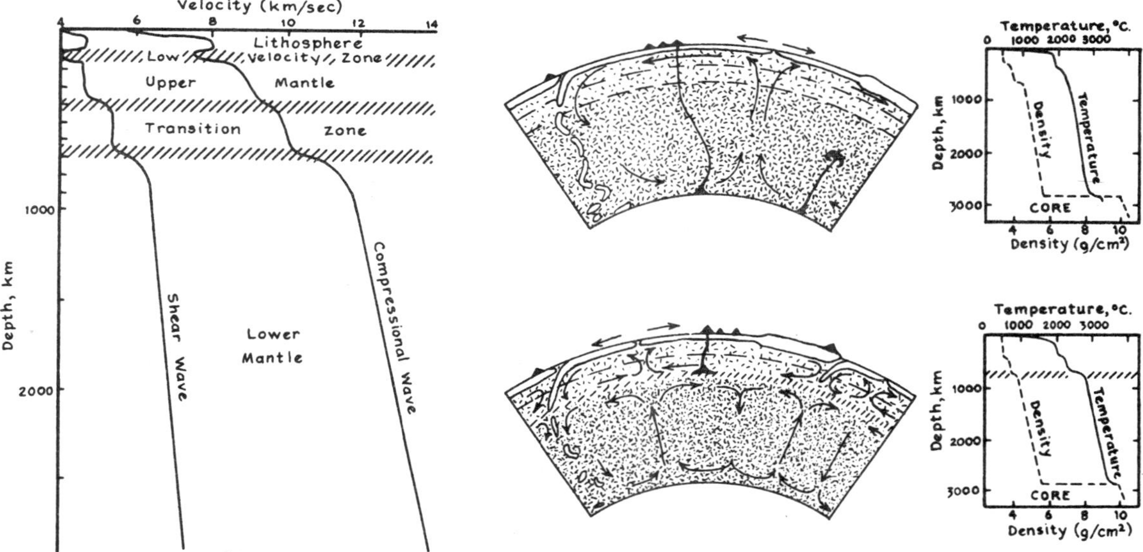

Figure 1–8 Two possible models for large-scale flow in the mantle. Interpretations of the structure of the mantle are based on the observed velocities of seismic waves, shown on the left. The marked discontinuities are thought to correspond to pressure-induced changes of the structure of olivine, first to a spinel-like structure at about 400 km and then to a denser perovskite-like structure near 670 km. The lower diagram shows two possible ways in which the upper and lower mantle could be coupled. In the ridge-subduction system on the right, the coupling is mechanical, and the sense of motion at the interface is the same. In the system on the left, the coupling is thermal; the heat transfer across the boundary drives the upper system and the directions of motion at the interface are opposed. The latter is thought to form a density barrier restricting convection and effectively separating the lower from the upper mantle. According to this interpretation, convection of the lower mantle transfers heat from the core-mantle boundary to the upper mantle. Convection in the upper mantle is the result mainly of upwelling at spreading ridges and descending slabs of oceanic lithosphere at convergent plate boundaries. The subducted material may continue to descend through the 670 km discontinuity and sink to the base of the mantle, where it contributes to the inhomogeneity of hotspot related magmas that may be generated at those depths. This interpretation is still tentative and far from being universally accepted. (Based in part on R. Jeanloz and S. Morris, 1986, *Ann. Rev. Earth Planet. Sci.*, 14:377–415 and G. F. Davies, 1990, *Earth Planet. Sci. Ltrs.*, 99:94–109.)

The low-velocity zone is nearly coincident with the base of the *lithosphere*. The latter includes both the crust and that part of the upper mantle that behaves as an elastic solid. The *asthenosphere* on which it floats has a viscosity low enough to permit isostatic adjustment and motion of the drifting lithospheric plates. The lithosphere is somewhat thicker under the continents than under the oceans, and in both places it slowly thickens as it cools. The lithospheric mantle is thought to change composition with time as it gains mobile components from the underlying asthenosphere.

The thermal gradient of the lithosphere is governed primarily by the rate at which heat is transferred by conduction. At greater depths, where heat is transferred more rapidly by convection, the thermal gradient is less steep. The depth at which the conductive gradient of the lithosphere intersects the convective gradient of the asthenosphere corresponds closely to the low-velocity zone where the mantle is close to the temperature at which it begins to melt. This cannot be a layer of totally molten rock, however. Since shear waves, which are not normally transmitted through liquids, are only slightly retarded as they pass through this zone, the molten fraction cannot be more than a percent or two.

Two worldwide seismic discontinuities, at depths of about 400 and 670 km, define the top and bottom of a *transition zone* separating the upper and lower mantle. They are thought to mark pressure-induced changes in the mineral assemblages of the mantle. At pressures equivalent to about 400 km, olivine takes on a denser, spinel-like structure, and at those corresponding to the 670 km discontinuity, it changes to an even denser form with the structure of perovskite.

Seismic information of this kind, if combined with precise satellite measurements of the configuration of Earth and measurements of its surface heat flow, make it possible to estimate the thermal regime of the mantle and identify broad zones of deep-seated magmatic activity. Beyond that, however, it is difficult to define the precise temperature and density of the mantle, even at the shallowest levels.

These conditions could be determined more accurately if we had reliable determinations of the thermal gradient of the lithosphere, but this is one of the most difficult physical properties to measure. The wide range of estimates is illustrated by the examples shown in Figure 1–7d. Direct measurements of Earth's thermal gradient in deep mines and boreholes indicate that temperatures near the surface increase with depth at rates of about 15 °C per km. It is clear, however, that these measured gradients cannot extend to much deeper levels, for, if they are projected downward, they rapidly reach and exceed temperatures at which any plausible mantle rocks would be largely molten. Hence, the rate at which temperature increases must decline rapidly with depth.

It might seem that a better way of estimating the thermal gradient in the lithosphere would be to measure the amount of heat reaching the surface from Earth's interior (between 1 and 2×10^{-6} cal cm^{-2} sec^{-1}) and, making due allowance for the distribution of radioactive heat sources, to calculate the thermal gradient required to produce the observed flux of heat through rocks of known thermal conductivity. Unfortunately, as we shall see in the next chapter, thermal conductivity is strongly dependent on temperature, and we find that in order to estimate its value we must first know the temperature of the rocks, which, of course, is what we are trying to determine from the conductivity!

Convection in the mantle

Even if a thermal gradient could be calculated in this way, it would be correct only if all heat is transferred by conduction and none by convection. This is probably a safe assumption when dealing with the lithosphere in regions remote from spreading axes and zones of subduction, but it is less likely to be valid for the mantle in the asthenosphere and below. Although most would agree that the mantle probably convects, the exact manner in which it does so is still a matter of dispute. The uncertainty stems mainly from a lack of knowledge of the effects of high pressure and temperature on the physical properties of the mantle, particularly its viscosity and thermal conductivity.

The mantle is thought to turn over slowly, transferring heat generated in the core and in the mantle itself to the asthenosphere and the lithosphere. The temperature within any convecting horizon is probably close to an *adiabatic* gradient. That is to say, the heat content of the rocks remains nearly constant while temperature varies with pressure, much as it does in the earth's atmosphere, where the temperature decreases as air rises and expands but increases as it descends and is compressed. And just as the temperature of air is buffered by the heat absorbed or released when water vaporizes or condenses, the temperature of the mantle must be moderated by the heat absorbed or released when minerals melt, crystallize, or change their crystalline structure in response to changes in pressure.

Figure 1–8 illustrates two conceptions of the mantle consistent with these principles. In one, the entire mantle convects as a single unit, while in the other the upper and lower mantle convect as essentially separate systems. In the latter, the pressure-induced structural change of olivine responsible for the seismic discontinuity near 670 km is thought to constitute a density barrier that impedes convection. The energy exchange required for light rocks to descend or their heavy equivalents to rise across this discontinuity could prevent the entire mantle from convecting as a unit and effectively isolate the lower mantle from the upper. If correct, this interpretation has important petrologic implications, for it implies that the two discrete layers could evolve independently toward quite different compositions. As we shall see in later chapters, this would have important consequences for the origins of magmas and for the long-term evolution of the earth.

SELECTED REFERENCES

Brown, G. C., and A. E. Mussett. 1981. *The Inaccessible Earth*. Unwin Hyman. 235 pp. An excellent summary of the origin and geophysical properties of the earth.

De Paolo, D. J. 1981. Nd isotopic studies: some new perspectives on earth structure and evolution. *EOS* 62:137–40.

Murray, B., M. C. Malin, and R. Greeley 1981. *Earthlike Planets*. W. H. Freeman & Co. 387 pp. An excellent summary of recently acquired knowledge of the solar system.

Windley, B. F. 1984. *The Evolving Continents*, John Wiley & Sons. 399 pp. A comprehensive, well-written description of the early history of the continents.

2

MAGMAS AND IGNEOUS ROCKS

BASIC TO ALL the diverse aspects of igneous geology is the nature of magma itself—its physical and chemical properties and its relations to its geologic environment. Magma can be defined as a completely or partly molten natural substance, which, on cooling, solidifies as a crystalline or glassy igneous rock. Most magmas are rich in silica and are capable of deforming by viscous flow under moderate stresses. They may have crystals in suspension, and most have volatile components that exsolve on relief of pressure.

The differences between magmas and crystalline rocks are not as sharply defined as are those between simpler liquids and solids. The temperatures through which solidification takes place may span as much as 200 °C, and within this range the physical properties of magma gradually change in response to the increasing proportions of crystals and the changing characteristics of the liquid in which they grow.

COMPOSITION

Igneous rocks are often divided into two broad groups according to their proportions of light or dark minerals. Granites, for example, are said to be *felsic* or *leucocratic*, because they consist almost entirely of the light-colored minerals quartz and feldspar, whereas gabbros, which contain abundant, dark, ferromagnesian minerals, are referred to as *mafic* or *melanocratic*, and rocks totally devoid of light minerals are said to be *ultramafic*. The corresponding terms *acidic* and *basic*, often found in older literature, were based on a long-since discredited concept. Although petrologists shun them, their use is so entrenched that they are difficult to avoid. No sharp boundary can be drawn between mafic and felsic rocks; the terms are loosely qualitative. A more precise measure is *color index* (CI), which is simply the volumetric proportion of ferromagnesium minerals.

Igneous rocks are either *intrusive* or *extrusive*, and, depending on their depth of emplacement and solidification, are divided into three broad groups: *plutonic* rocks that have cooled slowly at moderate to great depths in the crust or mantle, *hypabyssal* rocks emplaced in shallow, sub-volcanic conditions, and *volcanic* rocks erupted on the surface. Each plutonic rock has a volcanic equivalent, but on a broad scale the proportions of different chemical compositions in the two groups are not the same. Plutonic suites tend to have volumetrically greater proportions of felsic rocks, whereas volcanic suites tend to be more mafic, but, like most generalities, this one has many exceptions.

The chemical compositions of igneous rocks are usually considered in terms of two groups of elements—a fixed number of *major elements* that normally accounts for 98 to 99 percent of the total, and a variety of *trace elements* with much lower concentrations. Standard analyses, such as those in Tables 2-1 and 2-2, report the thirteen major components as weight percentages of oxides listed in a conventional order. The trace elements listed in analyses depend on the nature of the rock and the purpose of the analysis; they are reported, not as oxides, but as single elements in parts per million (ppm) and may be listed in any convenient order.

Petrologists attach so much importance to the compositional diversity of igneous rocks that they tend to overlook the basic regularities that characterize the abundances of their chemical constituents. Inspection of any compilation of chemical analyses, such as those in Tables 2-1 and 2-2, shows that compositions are neither limitless nor random. Each individual component accounts for a characteristic proportion of the rock. Silica is by far the dominant oxide; all other constituents are less abundant and have smaller ranges. Few igneous rocks are known in which alumina is not between 10 and 20 percent, and in virtually none is it more abundant than silica. Apart from a few exotic alkaline rocks, the alkalies Na_2O and K_2O rarely total more than 10 percent and normally are less than half that amount. Most components vary sympathetically in the sense that the abundance of each is usually linked to that of others. One would be justifiably suspicious of an analysis of an igneous rock with 70 percent SiO_2 in which CaO is more abundant than Na_2O, or MgO dominant over the iron oxides, even though the absolute abundance of each individual component is within its normal range for igneous rocks as a whole.

The fact that we recognize certain abundances or ratios of components as typically igneous and instinctively question compositions that violate these patterns shows that natural magmas are not randomly mixed solutions, but the products of systematic processes controlled by strict physical-chemical laws.

Equally important is the regularity with which certain rock types are found together in characteristic geologic settings. The lavas erupted in different tectonic environments are often distinctive and, in some instances, unique. The fact that granitic plutons, for example, are nowhere found within the deep oceanic basins, but only on continents, places severe limits on processes that could account for their formation. Throughout most of geologic time certain types of rocks have formed distinctive suites, and members of one of these suites rarely occur in others. The regularity of these natural groupings of rocks must reflect fundamental differences in their origins.

Nomenclature

The ostensible aim of igneous petrology is to understand these relations, and in order to do this one needs an orderly way of referring to igneous rocks and iden-

Table 2–1 Typical chemical and normative compositions of volcanic rocks in Figure 2–4.

	Sub-alkaline rocks							
	Tholeiitic series				Calc-alkaline series			
	Picrite basalt	Olivine tholeiite	Tholeiite	Icelandite	High alumina basalt	Andesite	Dacite	Rhyolite
SiO_2	46.4	49.2	53.8	61.8	49.2	60.0	69.7	73.2
TiO_2	2.0	2.3	2.0	1.3	1.5	1.0	0.4	0.2
Al_2O_3	8.5	13.3	13.9	15.4	17.7	16.0	15.2	14.0
Fe_2O_3	2.5	1.3	2.6	2.4	2.8	1.9	1.1	0.6
FeO	9.8	9.7	9.3	5.8	7.2	6.2	1.9	1.7
MgO	20.8	10.4	4.1	1.8	6.9	3.9	0.9	0.4
CaO	7.4	10.9	7.9	5.0	9.9	5.9	2.7	1.3
Na_2O	1.6	2.2	3.0	4.4	2.9	3.9	4.5	3.9
K_2O	0.3	0.5	1.5	1.6	0.7	0.9	3.0	4.1
P_2O_5	0.2	0.2	0.4	0.4	0.3	0.2	0.1	0.1
Q	—	—	6.7	14.9	—	12.3	22.8	28.8
Il	2.7	3.2	2.9	1.8	2.1	1.4	0.6	0.3
Mt	2.6	1.4	2.8	2.5	3.0	2.0	1.2	0.6
Or	1.7	3.0	9.2	9.6	4.2	5.4	17.9	24.5
Ab	14.0	19.8	28.0	40.0	26.3	35.3	40.7	35.5
An	14.8	25.0	20.8	17.8	33.5	23.7	12.5	5.9
Di	15.8	22.3	13.7	3.8	11.3	3.6	0.3	—
Hy	16.2	14.8	15.1	8.7	13.9	16.0	4.0	3.1
Ol	31.8	10.3	—	—	5.1	—	—	—
Ap	0.4	0.4	0.9	0.9	0.6	0.4	0.2	0.2
C	—	—	—	—	—	—	—	1.1

tifying their salient features. Unfortunately, igneous petrologists have been slow in reaching this simple goal. Until recently they were burdened with hundreds of rock names, many of which were used in a different sense from one country or institution to another. Many of these names have now been abandoned, and the remaining ones are more rigorously defined.

Although petrology is still plagued with conflicting systems of classification and nomenclature, a consensus is beginning to emerge. The one for plutonic rocks outlined in Figures 2–1 and 2–2 is as widely accepted as any is likely to be. The same is not true, unfortunately, for volcanic rocks. Volcanic rocks present a special problem, because two magmas of identical chemical composition can crystallize to very different mineral assemblages, depending on their rates and conditions of crystallization. The term *heteromorphism* is used to describe this phenomenon. Thus, a basaltic magma may form many heteromorphic rocks, including gabbro, dolerite (a medium-grained hypabyssal rock), various types of basalt, and sideromelane (a clear, brown basaltic glass). Because of the extreme heteromorphism of volcanic rocks, they are more difficult to define mineralogically than are their plutonic counterparts.

Table 2–1 continued.

	Alkaline rocks							
	Alkaline series							
	Ankaramite	Nepheline basanite	Alkali olivine basalt	Hawaiite	Mugearite	Benmorite	Trachyte	Phonolite
SiO_2	44.1	44.2	45.4	47.9	49.7	55.6	60.7	60.6
TiO_2	2.7	1.6	3.0	3.4	2.1	0.9	0.5	0.1
Al_2O_3	12.1	15.6	14.7	15.9	17.0	16.4	20.5	18.3
Fe_2O_3	3.2	4.4	4.1	4.9	3.5	3.1	2.3	2.8
FeO	9.6	6.1	9.2	7.6	9.0	4.9	0.4	1.2
MgO	13.0	8.9	7.8	4.8	2.8	1.1	0.2	0.1
CaO	11.5	9.7	10.5	8.0	5.5	2.9	1.4	0.8
Na_2O	1.9	4.0	3.0	4.2	5.8	6.1	6.2	8.9
K_2O	0.7	1.8	1.0	1.5	1.9	3.5	6.7	5.1
P_2O_5	0.3	0.7	0.4	0.7	0.5	0.7	0.1	—
Il	3.8	2.3	4.3	4.8	3.0	1.3	0.7	0.1
Mt	3.4	4.7	4.4	5.2	3.7	3.9	2.4	—
Or	4.2	10.8	6.0	9.1	11.5	21.5	38.9	22.1
Ab	12.5	13.2	22.2	37.7	41.2	57.0	47.0	44.4
An	22.6	19.6	24.1	20.6	15.1	7.3	6.2	3.9
Di	26.3	19.7	21.0	12.3	7.6	2.3	—	—
Hy	—	—	—	—	—	3.3	—	—
Ol	23.9	14.5	14.1	8.3	9.7	2.3	—	1.5
Ne	2.8	13.9	3.1	0.5	7.2	—	4.7	14.4
Lc	—	—	—	—	—	—	—	5.9
Ap	0.6	1.5	0.9	1.5	1.1	1.5	0.2	—
Ac	—	—	—	—	—	—	—	7.7

Source: Adapted from Irvine and Baragar, 1971.

In order to surmount this problem, modern petrologists tend to rely more on chemical than on petrographic criteria to characterize volcanic rocks. An important step was made in this direction when, in 1971, two Canadian geologists, Irvine and Baragar, published a statistical study of chemical analyses of large numbers of volcanic rocks and established compositional limits for the major types of natural associations. Their classification scheme (Figs. 2–3 and 2–4 and Table 2–4) corresponds closely to current usage, particularly in the English-speaking world. It has the virtue of not depending on any particular genetic interpretation; it merely groups rocks according to their observed compositions and geological associations.

Although one might wish that classification systems were based on sound genetic relations and that names could be made to fit neat pigeon holes, experience shows that most rock names are too deeply entrenched to be abandoned or redefined, no matter how logical the revision might seem to those who propose it. The ingenious system designed to classify rocks on the basis of "normative" minerals is an excellent example of this problem.

Around the beginning of this century four petrologists, Cross, Iddings, Pirs-

Table 2–2 Average Chemical and Mineral Compositions of Selected Plutonic Rocks

	Granite	Syenite	Granodiorite	Quartz Diorite	Diorite	Gabbro	Olivine Diabase	Diabase	Dunite	Lherzolite (Peridotite)
Chemical composition										
SiO_2	70.18	60.19	65.01	61.59	56.77	48.24	48.54	50.48	40.49	43.95
TiO_2	0.39	0.67	0.57	0.66	0.84	0.97	1.31	1.45	0.02	0.10
Al_2O_3	14.47	16.28	15.94	16.21	16.67	17.88	15.24	15.34	0.86	4.82
Fe_2O_3	1.57	2.74	1.74	2.54	3.26	3.16	3.06	3.84	2.84	2.20
FeO	1.78	3.28	2.65	3.77	4.40	5.95	8.88	7.78	5.54	6.34
MnO	0.12	0.14	0.07	0.10	0.13	0.13	0.21	0.20	0.16	0.19
MgO	0.88	2.49	1.91	2.80	4.17	7.51	8.08	5.79	46.32	36.81
CaO	1.99	4.30	4.42	5.38	6.74	10.99	9.38	8.94	0.70	3.57
Na_2O	3.48	3.98	3.70	3.37	3.39	2.55	2.69	3.07	0.10	6.63
K_2O	4.11	4.49	2.75	2.10	2.12	0.89	0.98	0.97	0.04	0.21
H_2O	0.84	1.16	1.04	1.22	1.36	1.45	1.35	1.89	2.88	1.08
P_2O_5	0.19	0.28	0.20	0.26	0.25	0.28	0.28	0.25	0.05	0.10
Density	2.667	2.757	2.716	2.806	2.839	2.976	2.970	2.965	3.289	3.330
Mineral composition										
Quartz	25	—	21	20	2	—	—	—	—	—
K Feldspar	40	72	15	6	3	—	—	—	—	—
Oligoclase	26	12	—	—	—	—	—	—	—	—
Andesine	—	—	46	56	64	—	—	—	—	—
Labradorite	—	—	—	—	—	65	63	62	—	—
Biotite	5	2	3	4	5	1	—	1	—	—
Amphibole	1	7	13	8	12	3	—	1	—	—
Orthopyroxene	—	—	—	1	3	6	—	—	2	15
Clinopyroxene	—	4	—	3	8	14	21	29	—	10
Olivine	—	—	—	—	—	7	12	3	95	71
Magnetite	2	2	1	2	2	2	2	2	2	1
Ilmenite	1	1	—	—	—	2	2	2	—	—
Apatite	tr	tr	tr	tr	tr	—	—	—	—	—
Sphene	tr	tr	1	tr	tr	—	—	—	—	—
Spinel	—	—	—	—	—	—	—	—	1	3

Source: After Daly and Larsen, *Geol. Soc. Am. Special Paper 36*, 1942 with modifications and reduced to 100%.

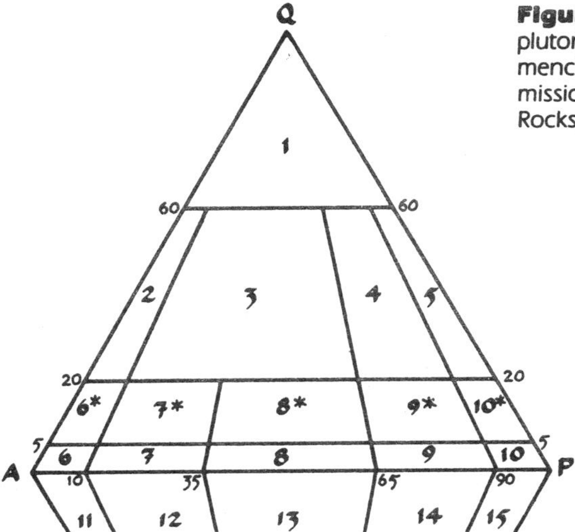

Figure 2-1 Classification of felsic plutonic rocks. See Table 2-3 for key to nomenclature. (Adapted from IUGS Subcommission on the Systematics of Igneous Rocks, *Geotimes*, October, 1973.)

son, and Washington, devised a thoroughly quantitative and logical scheme for the classification of volcanic rocks. They discarded all previous nomenclature and set up a new set of names based entirely on parameters that could be calculated from a chemical analysis. The nomenclature and classification system was received with admiration and acclaim, but was used by scarcely anyone except its authors and was promptly abandoned.

Normative composition and classification of igneous rocks

In contrast to the resounding failure of their classification scheme, the techniques Cross and his co-workers developed for relating chemical analyses of volcanic rocks to mineralogical assemblages proved to have more lasting value. They provide a convenient way of comparing diverse chemical compositions by recasting the analysis of a rock into a standard set of idealized, or "normative," minerals. They do this by transforming the weight percentages of the major components into minerals that might form with complete equilibrium crystallization under plutonic conditions in the upper crust. In this way, the nature of a rock can be defined independently of differing conditions of crystallization and equilibration. The calculation is designed to yield a mineral assemblage, known as a *norm*, which corresponds moderately well to the actual mineral assemblage, or *mode*, of a totally crystalline rock formed at low pressure under conditions of ideal equilibration. A number of variants of the basic norm calculation have been devised. The one used here and explained in Appendix A is referred to as the Barth-Niggli, or Molecular, Norm. It has an advantage over the older CIPW norm (named from the initials of the four petrologists who devised the original system) in that the resulting mineral assemblage is closer to the volumetric proportions observed in the mode. The CIPW norm yields an assemblage based on weight

Table 2–3 Determinative key for plutonic rocks with less than 90 percent mafic minerals and less than 60 percent feldspathoids (Fig. 2–1). A is alkali feldspar, P plagioclase, Q quartz, F feldspathoids, and M mafic minerals. The divisions on the A-P axis are at 10, 35, 65, and 90 percent plagioclase.

Field	Rock name
I. Q > 60% of light minerals	(1) Quartz-rich granitoids
II. Q = 20–60% of light minerals	
a. P = 0–10% of feldspar	(2) Alkali-feldspar granite
b. P = 10–65% of feldspar	(3) Granite
c. P = 65–90% of feldspar	(4) Granodiorite
d. P = 90–100% of feldspar	(5) Tonalite
(trondhjemites are leuco-tonalites (M = 0–10%) containing oligoclase or andesine)	
III. Q = 5–20% of light minerals.	
a. P = 0–10% of feldspar	(6*) Alkali quartz syenite
b. P = 10–35% of feldspar	(7*) Quartz syenite
c. P = 35–65% of feldspar	(8*) Quartz monzonite
d. P = 65–90% of feldspar	(9*)
An < 50	Quartz monzodiorite
An > 50	Quartz monzogabbro
e. P = 90–100% of feldspar	(10*)
An < 50	Quartz diorite
An > 50	Quartz gabbro
M = 0–10%	Quartz anorthosite
IV. Q = 0–5% of light minerals	
a. P = 0–10% of feldspar	(6) Alkali syenite
b. P = 10–35% of feldspar	(7) Syenite
c. P = 35–65% of feldspar	(8) Monzonite
d. P = 65–90% of feldspar	(9)
An < 50	Monzodiorite
An > 50	Monzogabbro
e. P = 90–100% of feldspar	(10)
An < 50	Diorite
An > 50	Gabbro
M = 0–10%	Anorthosite
V. F = 0–60% of light minerals	
a. P = 0–10% of feldspar	(11) Feldspathoidal alkali syenite
b. P = 10–35% of feldspar	(12) Feldspathoidal syenite
c. P = 35–65% of feldspar	(13) Feldspathoidal monzonite
d. P = 65–90% of feldspar	(14)
An < 50	Feldspathoidal monzodiorite
An > 50	Feldspathoidal monzogabbro
e. P = 90–100% of feldspar	(15)
An < 50	Feldspathoidal diorite
An > 50	Feldspathoidal gabbro

Source: Adapted from IUGS Subcommission on the Systematics of Igneous Rocks, 1973.

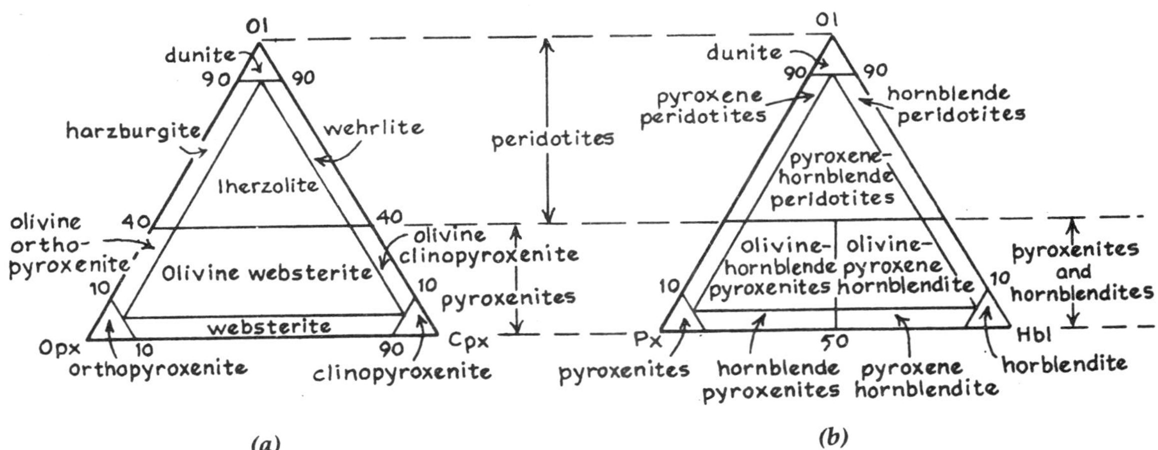

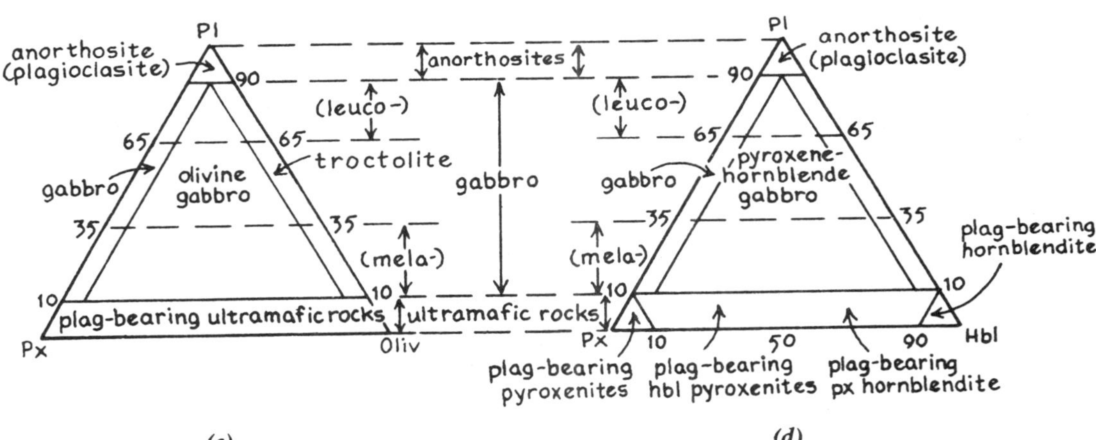

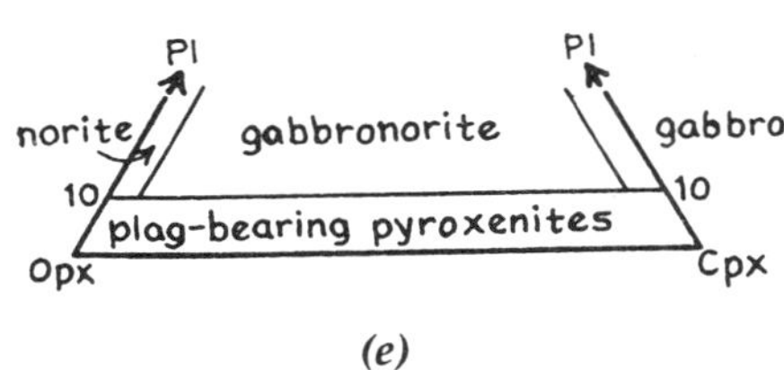

Figure 2–2 Classification of plutonic ultramafic rocks without hornblende (a) and with hornblende (b). Gabbroic rocks without hornblende are given in (c) and those with hornblende in (d). Gabbroic rocks with orthopyroxene are shown in (e).

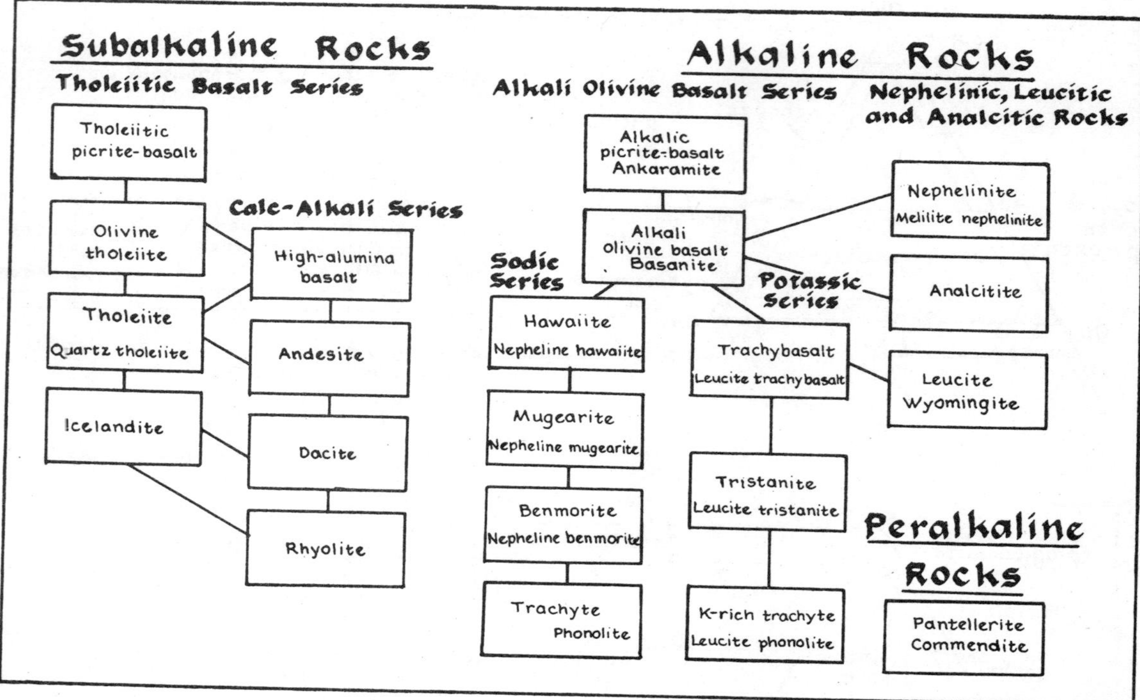

Figure 2–3 General classification of the common volcanic rocks. Lines joining boxes serve to outline common associations. Rock names in small print are variants of the main rock name in the box. (After Irvine and Baragar, 1971, *Can. J. Earth. Sci.*, 8:523–548.)

percentages and overemphasizes iron and titanium oxides. Moreover, the simple molecular proportions are easier to convert to alternative minerals in reaction equations.

Genetic classifications

The ideal classification system would, of course, be one that groups igneous rocks genetically according to the physical-chemical or tectonic factors governing their composition and mode of occurrence. Although far from achieving this ideal, some of the broad categories to which rocks are commonly assigned have developed because petrologists perceived a genetic link that caused certain suites of rocks to share particular chemical and mineralogical attributes in distinct geological settings. The most notable example is the division between alkaline and sub-alkaline rocks. The distinction between these two major groups can be traced back at least as far as the "Atlantic" and "Pacific" types proposed by Alfred Harker at the beginning of this century. Their basic compositional difference is mainly in their concentrations of silica relative to alkalies. Sub-alkaline rocks are "critically saturated" with SiO_2. That is to say, they have enough of that com-

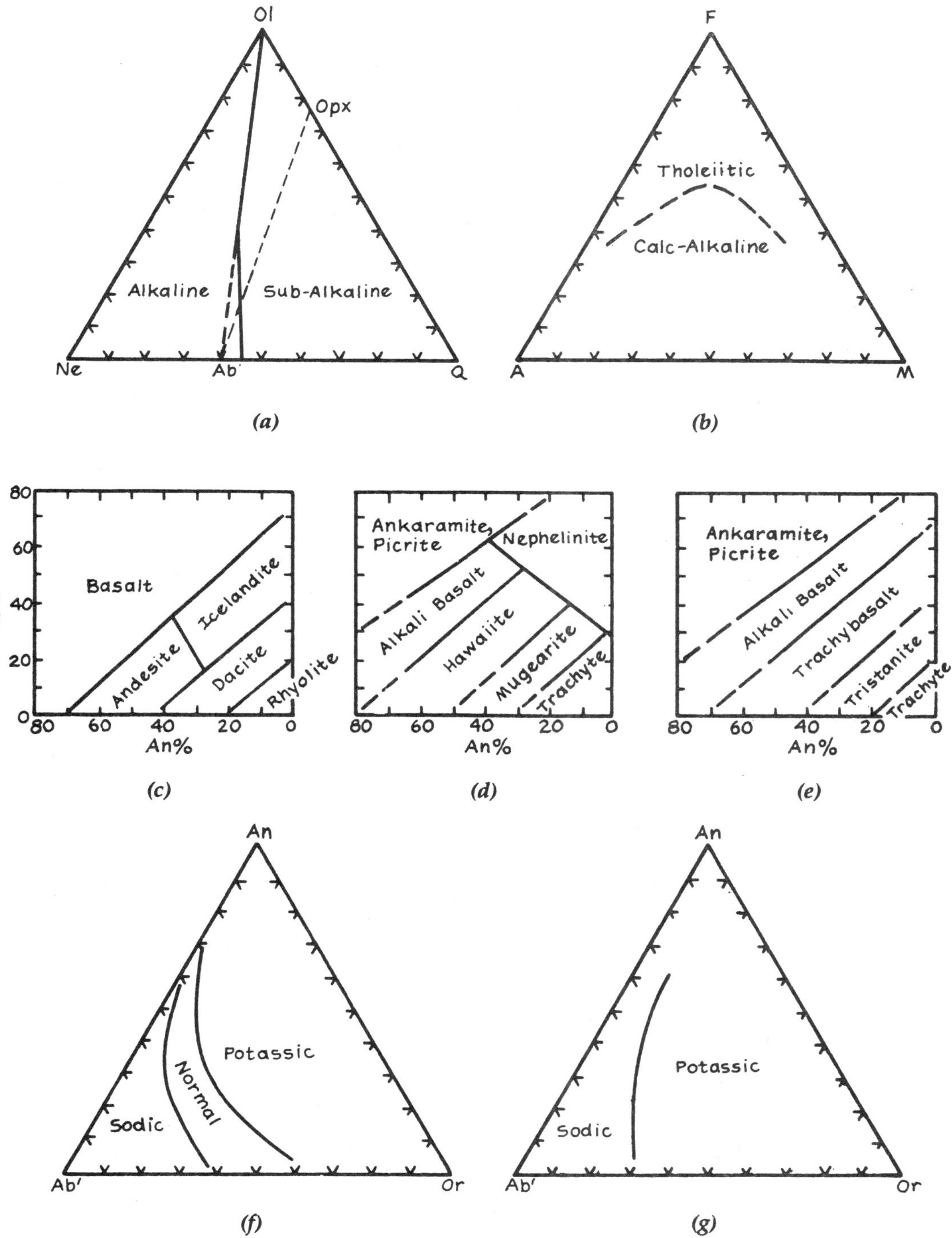

Figure 2–4 Compositional limits of the common volcanic rocks according to the classification system of Table 2–4.

Table 2–4 A volcanic rock may be classified on the basis of its chemical and normative composition according to the system of Irvine and Baragar (1971), depicted in Figs. 2–3 and 2–4. The procedure is as follows.

1. If the rock has normative acmite (Ac), it is probably peralkaline. Otherwise go to Step 2.

2. Classify as sub-alkaline or alkaline according to the boundary line in Fig. 2–4a and the criteria given in Chapter 7. If the rock is subalkaline, go to Step 3; if alkaline to Step 4.

3. (a) Classify as calc-alkaline or tholeiitic using the boundary lines in Fig. 2–4b. See Chapter 9 for details.
(b) If olivine (Ol) is greater than 25%, the rock is a tholeiitic picrite. Otherwise, classify as basalt, andesite, icelandite, dacite, or rhyolite according to Fig. 2–4c.
(c) Classify as potassic, "normal," or sodic according to Fig. 2–4f. Go to Step 5.

4. (a) Decide whether the rock is a nephelinite, leucitite, or analcitite on the basis of its petrographic character and the criteria in Chapter 11. Otherwise continue below.
(b) If olivine (Ol) is greater than 25%, the rock is an alkaline picrite. If modal olivine plus augite exceed 25% it is an ankaramite. Assign the rock to one of the two alkaline basalt series using Fig. 2–4g. Classify it further according to Fig. 2–4d or 2–4e as appropriate.

5. Check the result against analyses in Table 2–1 and elsewhere in the text. And, most important, check the result against the rock's petrographic characteristics. If the rock has been significantly altered or has an unusual composition, this step will help to avoid errors.

---

ponent to form a set of modal or normative minerals that does not include an alumina silicate with less silica than feldspar. The alkaline rocks are deficient in silica relative to other components, especially Na_2O and K_2O, and for this reason contain a normative feldspathoid, such as nepheline (Ne) or leucite (Lc). Alkaline rocks can be subdivided on the basis of how strongly they are undersaturated with silica and whether potassium or sodium is the dominant alkali. Rocks in which the molecular proportion of $Na_2O + K_2O$ exceeds that of Al_2O_3 are called *peralkaline* and, because all the alkalies cannot enter alumina silicates, they contain the sodic pyroxene acmite (Ac) in their norm. Their mode may include any of a number of sodic pyroxenes or amphiboles.

The sub-alkaline group has two major subdivisions, a *tholeiitic* and a *calc-alkaline* series, which differ mainly in their relative concentrations of iron and alumina. The mafic and felsic end-members are basalts and rhyolites that differ in only minor ways between the two series, but intermediate tholeiitic magmas are richer in iron, whereas calc-alkaline rocks tend to have more Al_2O_3 and, hence, more plagioclase.

Some rocks have more Al_2O_3 than can be incorporated in feldspar. In the norm, this results in corundum (C), and, in plutonic rocks, the excess Al_2O_3 normally enters muscovite. Such rocks are called *peraluminous*.

These major divisions correspond rather well to the tectonic association mentioned in the preceding chapter, and, for that reason, they form a logical basis for the system illustrated in Figure 2–3. Tholeiitic basalts and their differentiates are by far the most voluminous and ubiquitous group. Although they occur in almost every geological environment, they are most characteristic of the ocean floor and divergent plate boundaries; calc-alkaline rocks are associated almost exclusively with orogenic belts and convergent plate boundaries. Alkaline rocks are found in intra-plate regions of both the oceans and continents and only rarely at plate boundaries. Most oceanic rocks are sodic, in contrast to their continental counterparts, which tend to be more potassic. Although they seldom account for large volumes, the alkaline rocks are exceedingly diverse and include as many petrographic varieties as all other rocks series combined.

Volatile components

Even though volatiles constitute only a small weight fraction of magmas, their molecular weights are low, so that their mole fraction of a magma can be large. Moreover, they have disproportionately large effects on physical properties, such as viscosity, and on the composition, order of appearance, and form of crystallizing minerals. Though much of the volatile content of volcanic rocks is lost before minerals crystallize at low pressures, plutonic rocks retain more of their volatiles and incorporate them into stable minerals. Water, for example, enters the hydrous minerals amphibole and mica, and sulfur combines with iron or copper to form sulfides. Few igneous rocks contain carbonates or other CO_2-bearing minerals, but some, notably carbonatites, contain major amounts. Halogens are essential constituents of apatite, tourmaline, topaz, and some amphiboles.

All natural magmas contain dissolved water, carbon dioxide, and other volatile components that may be absorbed and exsolved in complex ways as magmas rise from their source to cool and crystallize at shallower depths. It is difficult to know what proportions of these gases were constituents of the original magma at its source. Recent studies of continental volcanoes indicate that CO_2 may be the dominant gas at depth and that much of the water released during eruptions is absorbed from the crust. The most reliable data on mantle-derived volatile components come from glassy lavas dredged from the deep ocean floor, where pressures are so great that little exsolution takes place before the lava is quenched. CO_2, H_2O, and lesser amounts of sulfur gases account for by far the greater part of the total volatile content and together amount to less than one percent by weight; chlorine and fluorine are present in smaller amounts.

The solubilities of gases in magmas vary with pressure, temperature, and with the compositions of both the gas and the liquid (Fig. 2–5). Every student is well aware (or should be) that warm beer foams more than cold beer and that uncapping a bottle results in an escape of bubbles. These simple observations illustrate the fact that solubility decreases when confining pressure on the gas is reduced and when temperature increases. The same principles hold for magmas. In addition, if the pressure of the gas alone is constant and less than the total load pressure on the liquid, solubility decreases as load pressure increases. The effect can be thought of as one of squeezing the gas from the liquid, because the volume of the liquid with dissolved volatiles is greater than the volume of the liquid alone. For this reason, the water content of columns of magma can be greater at the top than at depth.

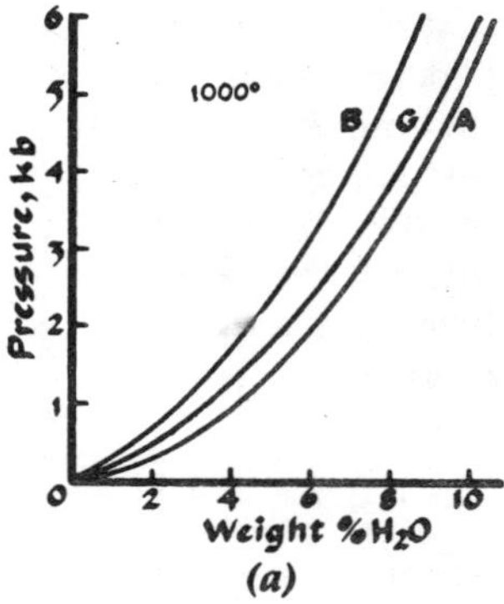

(a)

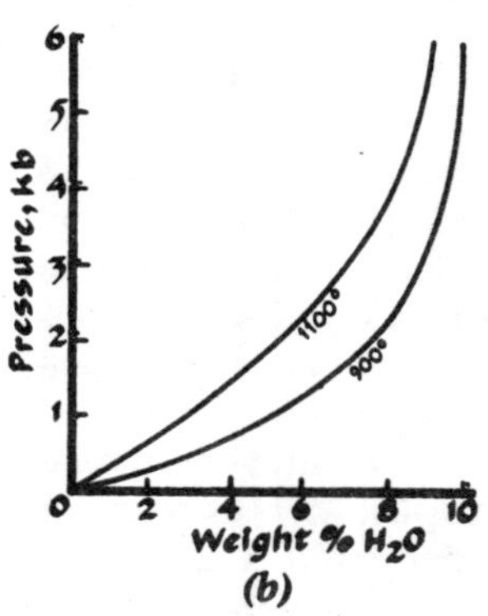

(b)

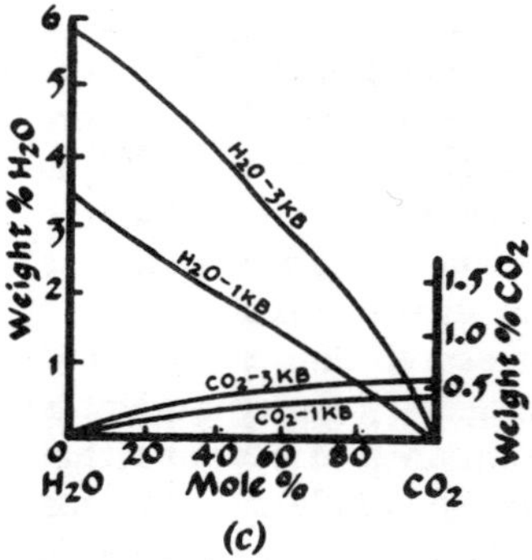

(c)

Figure 2–5 The solubility of volatiles in magmas is a function of pressure, temperature, and the compositions of the liquids and gases. (a) shows the solubility of H_2O in basalt (B), granite (G), and andesite (A), all at 1,100°C, as a function of pressure of H_2O. Note that although the three compositions have about the same solubilities at the same temperature, the three types of magmas are liquid at very different temperatures, and their solubilities under natural conditions will differ accordingly. As shown in (b), the solubility in granite increases with falling temperature; basalt and andesite show similar effects. Hence natural basalts have the lowest solubility as natural liquids and granites the highest. The pressure of another gas, such as CO_2, decreases the solubility of H_2O. (c) shows solubilities in a basaltic melt at 1,200°C and two different total pressures, one and three kilobars. (Data from Hamilton and Anderson, 1967, *Basalts* 1:445–482; Goranson, 1931, *Amer. J. Sci.*, 22:481–502: and Kadik et al., 1972, *Geoch. Internat.*, 9:1041–1050.)

Most silica-rich magmas can hold more water in solution than can more mafic magmas (Fig. 2–5a), and this effect is augmented by the lower temperatures of the former (Fig. 2–5b). If another gas, such as CO_2, is present, it reduces the solubility of water, as shown in Figure 2–5c.

PHYSICAL PROPERTIES OF MAGMAS

The wealth of data on the chemical and mineralogical nature of igneous rocks stands out in striking contrast to the meager information available on the properties of the liquids from which these rocks crystallized. Until recently, this deficiency has been a serious handicap for petrologic interpretations, but more studies are now being focused on physical aspects of magmas, and our knowledge of their behavior is rapidly increasing.

Temperatures and other thermal properties

Temperatures recorded for erupting lavas rarely fall outside the range between 800 °C and 1,200 °C. The lower values are observed in partly crystalline lavas and probably correspond to the limiting conditions under which magmas can flow. Magmas containing more than about 40 to 50 percent crystals are so viscous that they rarely erupt at the surface. The fact that low temperatures are observed in lavas with differentiated or felsic compositions, and high-temperature eruptions are confined to basalts, implies that few magmas have a wide enough range of crystallization to remain mobile at temperatures much below that at which crystallization begins.

Very few lavas are hotter than the temperature at which their first minerals crystallize. Basalts, for example, are rarely observed at temperatures above 1,200 °C, and, even at their highest temperatures, they have little or no superheat. That is to say they can cool through only a small temperature interval before crystals begin to nucleate and grow. This is a significant observation, for it tells us much about the manner in which magmas reach the surface.

When we consider that the melting temperatures of common igneous rocks increase with pressure at a rate of roughly 3 °C for each kilometer of depth, it is apparent that at depths where magmas are generated (at least 50 km) their melting temperatures must be at least 150° higher than those observed at the surface. The fact that erupting lavas are close to their crystallization temperatures at atmospheric pressure indicates that they must lose heat as they rise and that the temperatures observed at the surface cannot be those at which the magma formed at depth. Some of the consequences of these relations are discussed in later chapters.

Some rhyolites may have been exceptions to the rule that magmas erupt with little or no superheat. Estimates of temperatures of obsidian flows suggest that they may have been as much as one or two hundred degrees above their crystallization temperatures, but these estimates are subject to so many unknown factors that they are far from reliable. It is unfortunate that not a single rhyolitic eruption has been observed in which temperatures of the magma could be measured or even estimated.

One of the most distinctive thermal properties of magmas and igneous rocks is the great contrast between their heat capacity and heat of fusion or crystallization. *Heat capacity*, C_p, is defined by the relation

$$C_p = \frac{\Delta H}{\Delta T} \qquad [2\text{–}1]$$

in which ΔH is the amount of heat that must be added or removed to raise or lower the temperature of one gram by one degree centigrade. (The term *specific heat* refers to the heat capacity of a substance relative to water at the same conditions.) *Heat of fusion*, ΔH_F, is the heat that must be added or removed to melt or crystallize one gram that is already at the temperature where the liquid and solid coexist. For most rocks, C_p is about 0.3 cal g^{-1} deg^{-1}, whereas typical values for ΔH_F are around 65 to 100 cal g^{-1}. Because of this large difference, roughly the same amount of heat is involved in melting or crystallization of a rock as in raising or lowering the temperature of the rock or melt by 200 to 300°C.

Igneous rocks and melts are exceptionally poor conductors of heat. Their thermal conductivity (Fig. 2–6) is a function of two mechanisms of heat transfer,

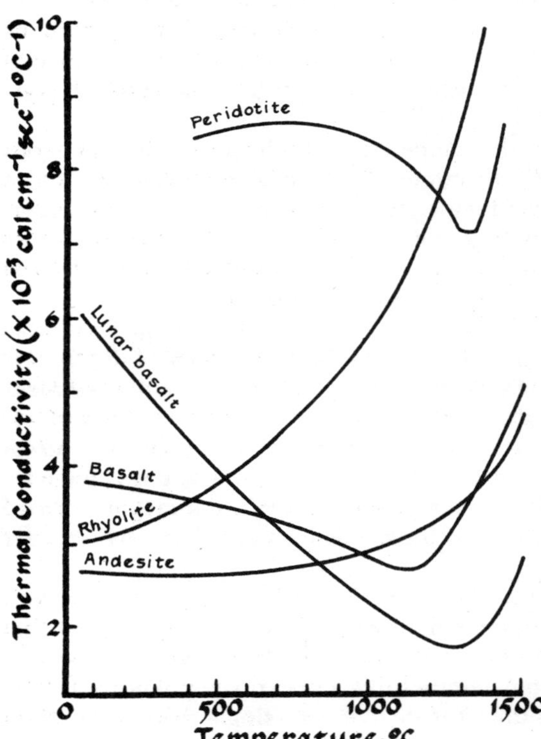

Figure 2–6 Thermal conductivities of some common igneous rocks. (After Murase and McBirney, 1973, *Geol. Soc. Amer. Bull.*, 84:3563–3592.)

ordinary lattice, or phonon, conduction and radiative, or photon, conduction. The first declines as temperature increases and the lattice structure expands, while the second increases owing to the increasing transparency for radiative heat transfer. The conductivity of most mafic rocks declines at a decreasing rate up to temperatures of about 1,200°C. Beyond that temperature, the opacity of the rocks decreases rapidly, so that radiative heat transfer increases and the total conductivity becomes much higher. Siliceous rocks, such as andesite and rhyolite, have lower opacities and hence greater thermal conductivity at lower temperatures than do mafic rocks.

The physical-chemical nature of silicate liquids

Several lines of evidence show that silicate liquids are not simple ionic solutions but have a degree of ordering that approaches that of minerals (Fig. 2-7). The small differences of densities and refractive indices between crystalline rocks and their glasses (rarely more than a few percent) indicate that the structural arrangement of atoms does not differ greatly in the two states. Moreover, the amount of heat involved in changing from the crystalline solid to the liquid state is small compared to that of vaporization and indicates that the crystalline structure undergoes relatively little disruption in passing from the solid to the liquid. The difference between the structure of the liquid and crystalline forms lies mainly in the extent of linkage of the atoms. The atoms in silicate melts seem to be bonded

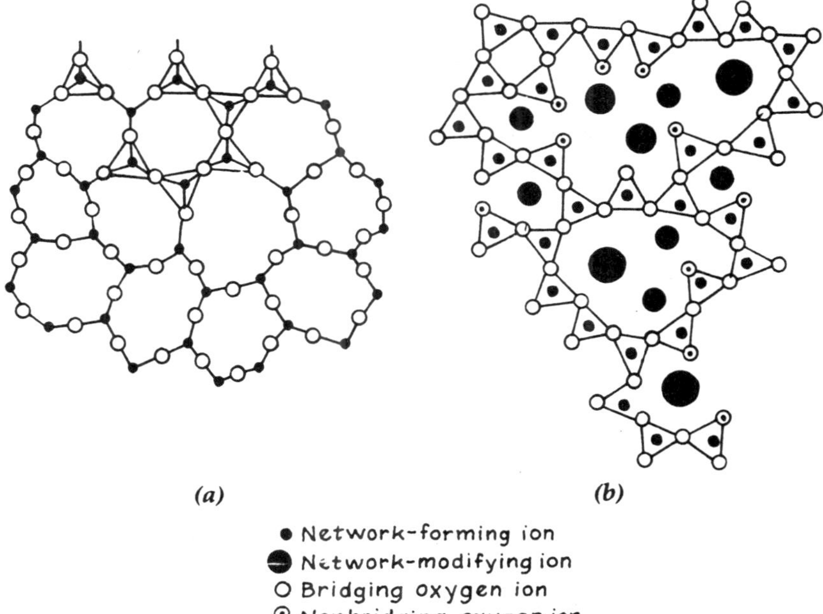

Figure 2-7 Schematic structural configurations of pure silica (a) in which an ordered silica mineral is shown in the upper part of the field and a less-ordered liquid or glass below. A silicate liquid containing network-modifying ions is shown in (b). (After Carmichael et al., 1974, *Igneous Petrology*, McGraw-Hill.)

by forces similar to those between the atoms of crystals but with less long-range order, probably on a scale of about 20 Angstrom units (Å) or 20×10^{-8} cm.

The nature of the silicon ion itself is responsible for many of the overall properties of magmas. Because of its high charge (+4), small radius (0.39 Å), and its coordination number with oxygen (4), its bonding with oxygen is much stronger than that of other common cations. Al, although not so strongly bonded to oxygen as Si, is nevertheless stronger than Ca, Mg, or Na, and, in some respects, Si and Al play similar roles in both liquids and crystalline solids.

In pure silica melts, silica tetrahedra are linked in three-dimensional networks with oxygen atoms, most of which are shared by two or more tetrahedra. Other cations can enter the melt in limited amounts as independent ions occupying spaces between the tetrahedra and thereby modifying the basic framework (Fig. 2–7b).

In this sense, Si and Al are often referred to as *framework-forming* elements. *Framework modifiers*, the ions occupying spaces within the basic framework structure, are Mg, Ca, Fe, Na, and most other metals. These components can be accommodated in amounts up to about 20 cation percent before the basic framework begins to break down into smaller geometric units. The basic network of tetrahedra in which Si is bonded to O atoms in a ratio of 1 to 2 is reduced to less extensive units with smaller Si/O ratios as other cations take the place of Si in sharing O atoms. In breaking the continuity of the structure into smaller units, the framework changes from extensive three-dimensional networks of tetrahedra, almost all linked by shared oxygens, to configurations with more non-bridging oxygens. When more than 66 percent of the cations are framework modifiers, the liquid takes the form of orthosilicates in which each Si atom forms a separate tetrahedron.

Viscosity

The effect of the proportion of Si atoms on the framework linkage of silicates is seen most clearly in the viscosity of their liquids. Viscosity, η, is a measure of the resistance to flow of any fluid substance. More strictly, it is defined as the ratio of the applied shear stress to the rate of deformation or shear strain (Fig. 2–8) and is expressed by the general relation

$$\sigma = \sigma_0 + \eta\left(\frac{du}{dz}\right)^n \qquad [2\text{–}2]$$

where σ is the total shear stress, applied parallel to the direction of deformation, σ_0 is the stress required to initiate flow, and du/dz is the gradient of velocity, dx/dt, over a distance z normal to the direction of shear, x. The exponent n has a value of 1.0 or less, depending on the nature of the specific fluid and the velocity gradient produced by shear strain. For so-called Newtonian fluids (curve A in Fig. 2–9), n is 1.0 and σ_0 is zero, but many "pseudoplastic" fluids and liquids with suspended solid particles have a non-linear relation of shear stress to strain rate, such as that depicted by curve B in Figure 2-9, for which the value of n is less than 1.0. Other substances, including many highly polymerized materials,

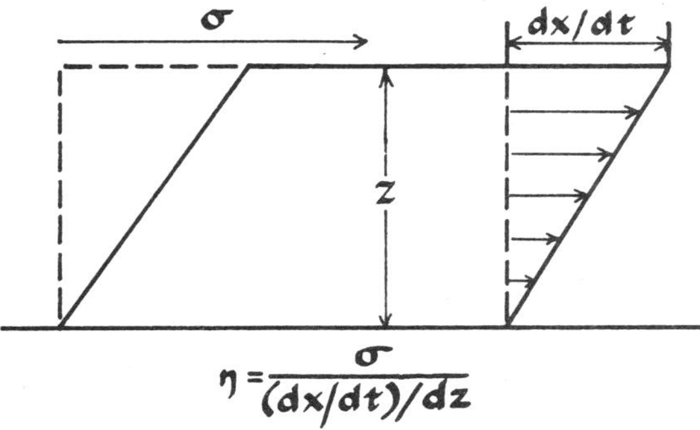

Figure 2–8 Viscosity is defined as the ratio of the shear stress applied to a layer of thickness z to the rate at which it is permanently deformed in a direction x parallel to the stress. See text for explanation.

have a finite yield strength that must be overcome before they deform permanently (curve C, Fig. 2-9). At stresses below σ_0 they have an elastic behavior, but at higher stresses they are visco-elastic.

Although the viscosities of most silicate melts can be explained, at least crudely, in terms of their proportions of Si/O bonds, we lack a comprehensive theory to account for the individual effects of all the major cations. It is possible to estimate viscosities of superheated liquids from their chemical composition (Appendix B), but the relations in the range of temperatures of natural magmas are so complex that it is difficult to predict their viscosity, except by analogy with compositions that have been investigated experimentally. Figure 2–9 shows the measured viscosities of some common igneous rocks in and above their melting ranges and illustrates the principal effects of composition and temperature. As one would expect, viscosities drop with increasing temperature and decreasing silica content. The effect of pressure is to reduce viscosity, because it causes ionic complexes to take on more compact structural configurations. Water and most other volatile components tend to reduce viscosity, because they break the continuity of framework structures in the melt. A small increase in H_2O results in a large decrease of viscosity, as shown for a granitic composition in Figure 2–10b. The effect on more mafic magmas is less dramatic. Suspended crystals have the

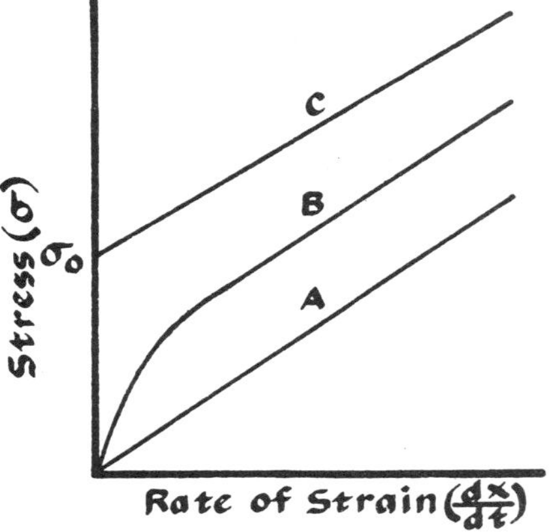

Figure 2–9 The physical characteristics of different types of liquids are illustrated by the relations between the rate at which they are permanently deformed by shear (dx/dt) and the stress (σ) parallel to the direction of shear. Newtonian fluids (A) have a linear relation with an origin at zero on both axes. Some non-Newtonian fluids have non-linear relations (B), while others (C) have a finite yield strength (σ_o) that must be exceeded before they are permanently deformed by viscous flow.

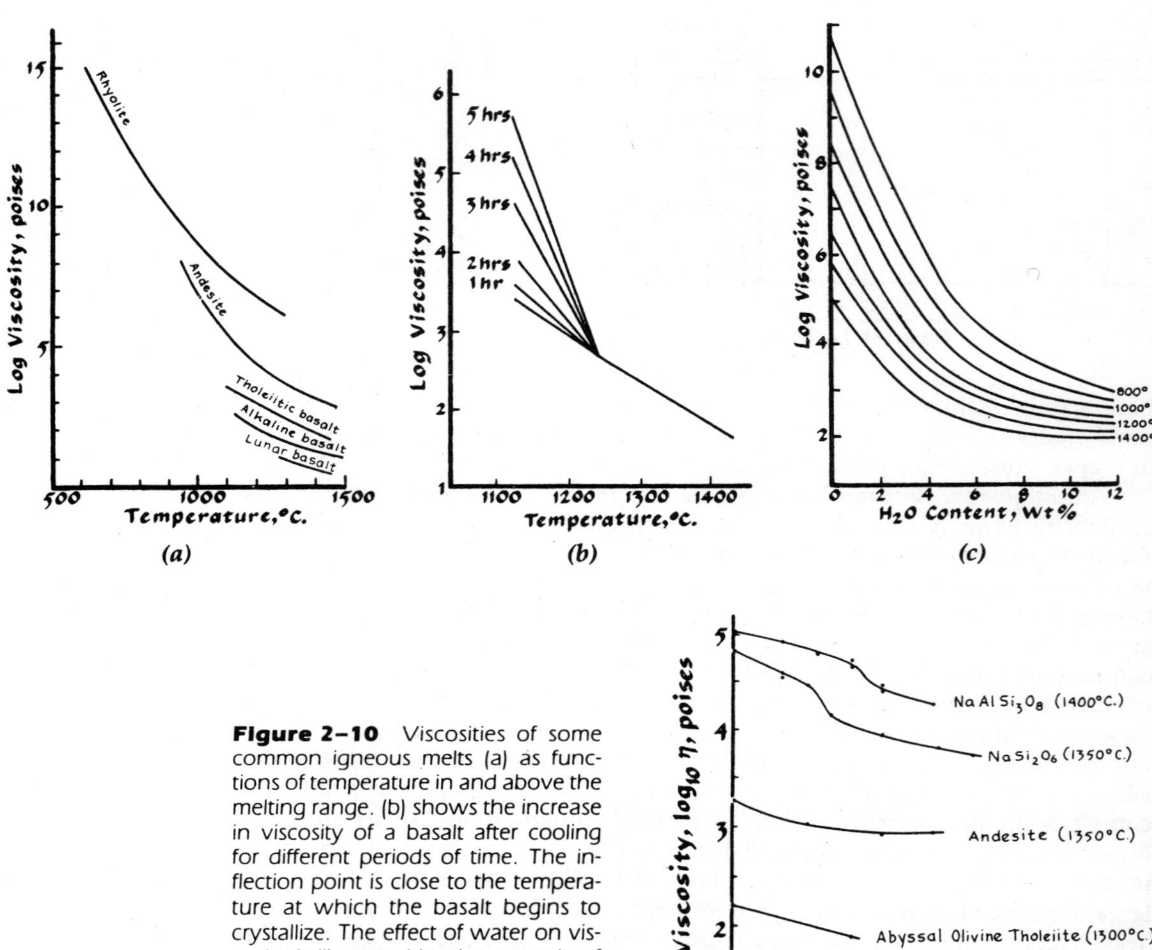

Figure 2–10 Viscosities of some common igneous melts (a) as functions of temperature in and above the melting range. (b) shows the increase in viscosity of a basalt after cooling for different periods of time. The inflection point is close to the temperature at which the basalt begins to crystallize. The effect of water on viscosity is illustrated by the example of a granitic liquid shown in (c). The effect of pressure is to reduce the viscosity of most silicate melts (d). (a, b, and c are from Murase and McBirney, 1973, *Geol. Soc. Amer. Bull.*, 84:3563–3592. d is from Scarfe, Mysen, and Virgo, 1987, *Geoch. Soc. Spec. Publ. No. 1*, 59–67.)

opposite effect; viscosity rises rapidly as crystals nucleate and grow in a basaltic melt.

The term *effective viscosity* is used to designate the viscosity of an inhomogeneous fluid, such as a magma with suspended crystals or bubbles. Its value can be estimated from the relationship:

$$\eta_{eff} = \eta_0(1 - 1.35\phi)^{-2.5} \qquad [2\text{–}3]$$

in which η_{eff} is the effective viscosity of a fluid having a crystal-free viscosity of η_0 and a fractional volume of solids, ϕ. The equation assumes crystals of spherical form and uniform size with a maximum concentration when closely packed of 1/1.35. For natural magmas containing crystals of different sizes and shapes the value of the coefficient of ϕ is closer to 1.7. The equation shows how the effective viscosity of a magma may increase by an order of magnitude or more when its crystal content approaches 50 percent; as ϕ approaches 1/1.35 the effective viscosity approaches infinity. At the same time, of course, the remaining liquid changes composition, so that the viscosity also changes by virtue of that factor as well. (Methods of estimating viscosities of such magmas are given in Appendix B.)

Density

Next to viscosity, density is probably the most important property affecting the physical behavior and chemical differentiation of magmas. The densities of most magmas range between about 2.2 and 3.1 g cm^{-3}. They vary with temperature, pressure, and composition.

The effect of temperature is expressed by the volumetric coefficient of thermal expansion, α, the proportional change of volume, V, per degree at constant pressure:

$$\alpha = \frac{1}{V}\left(\frac{\partial V}{\partial T}\right)_P \qquad [2\text{–}4]$$

α normally has a value for silicate melts of about 3.0×10^{-5} per degree. The corresponding effect of pressure, isothermal compressibility, often designated β, is defined as

$$\beta = \frac{1}{V}\left(\frac{\partial V}{\partial P}\right)_T \qquad [2\text{–}5]$$

and has a value of about 7.0×10^{-6} bar^{-1} for most silicate liquids. Thus, the effect of a one degree increase of temperature on a totally liquid magma with an original density of 2.7 g cm^{-3} would be a decrease of density of about .003 percent. This is equivalent to a difference of pressure of 4.3 bars or the weight of about 16.2 m of the same magma. The magnitudes of both thermal expansion and compressibility are lower for crystalline rocks, the respective values being about 2×10^{-5} deg^{-1} and 1.5×10^{-6} bar^{-1}. The values for partly crystalline magmas are, of course, intermediate between those of the liquid and solid.

The effect of composition on density is large relative to that of temperature and pressure. Figure 2–11 shows the densities of liquids with the compositions of common igneous rocks over a broad range of temperature; note that the decrease of density due to thermal expansion is much less than that of changing composition. The main component responsible for this large compositional effect is iron. In a given series of differentiated magmas, density may increase or decrease, depending on whether iron is enriched or depleted in the liquid as it evolves in composition from basaltic to more felsic magmas, such as rhyolite.

EFFECTS OF COOLING AND CRYSTALLIZATION

It can be seen from relationships such as these that the properties of magmas differ from those of simple solutions, in that no sharp boundary can be drawn between the liquid and the solid. Consider first what happens when a magma cools and crystallizes without changing its bulk composition. As it solidifies, it passes gradually through a succession of stages in which its density, viscosity, and yield strength increase with falling temperature. At the highest temperatures, where crystals are sparse, the magma can be permanently deformed by viscous flow, even under small stresses. Its behavior approaches that of a true Newtonian fluid, but with falling temperature and increasing proportions of crystals, viscosity increases abruptly.

When crystals make up as much as half the volume, the magma can still be deformed by viscous flow, but the stresses required for a given shear rate are higher, and an increasing yield strength must be exceeded to produce permanent strain. Short-term stresses lower than the yield strength produce recoverable elastic strain, whereas small stresses of long duration may be absorbed by various forms of creep in the crystal-liquid mush. When the proportion of crystals becomes great enough for grain-to-grain contact, the partly molten assemblage behaves like an elastic solid when subjected to small, short-term stresses. Very slow deformation can take place at low stresses by diffusion through the liquid fraction, but this mechanism decreases in importance with further cooling, so that when the last fluid disappears the rock behaves as a brittle solid for short-term stresses.

Consider next a magma that evolves in composition as it cools and differentiates. Because changing composition can affect the physical properties in different ways, depending on how the magma evolves, the variations of viscosity and density may be quite different from one igneous series to another (Fig. 2–11b). In calc-alkaline magmas, the effect of declining temperature is augmented by that of increasing silica content to cause a steady increase of viscosity throughout the entire range, from basalt to rhyolite. This increase would be even greater, of course, if the effect of phenocrysts, which are plentiful in these magmas, were also taken into account. Tholeiitic magmas show little increase of viscosity until the composition passes the point of maximum iron enrichment. The effect of the increased concentration of iron, a network-modifier, offsets that of falling temperature, and viscosity remains nearly constant through the early and middle stages of differentiation. An intermediate type of variation is seen in some alkaline magmas in which alkalies play a strong role as network-modifiers, especially in very silica-poor liquids.

Similar differences are found in the variations of density. Density declines throughout the entire calc-alkaline series, owing to the steady decrease in iron and increase in silica that characterizes the entire range, from basalt to rhyolite, in magmas of this type. Because tholeiitic and most alkaline magmas become progressively enriched in iron through most of their mafic and intermediate range of compositions, the effect of thermal contraction is reinforced by that of composition, and the liquids increase in density as they cool and differentiate.

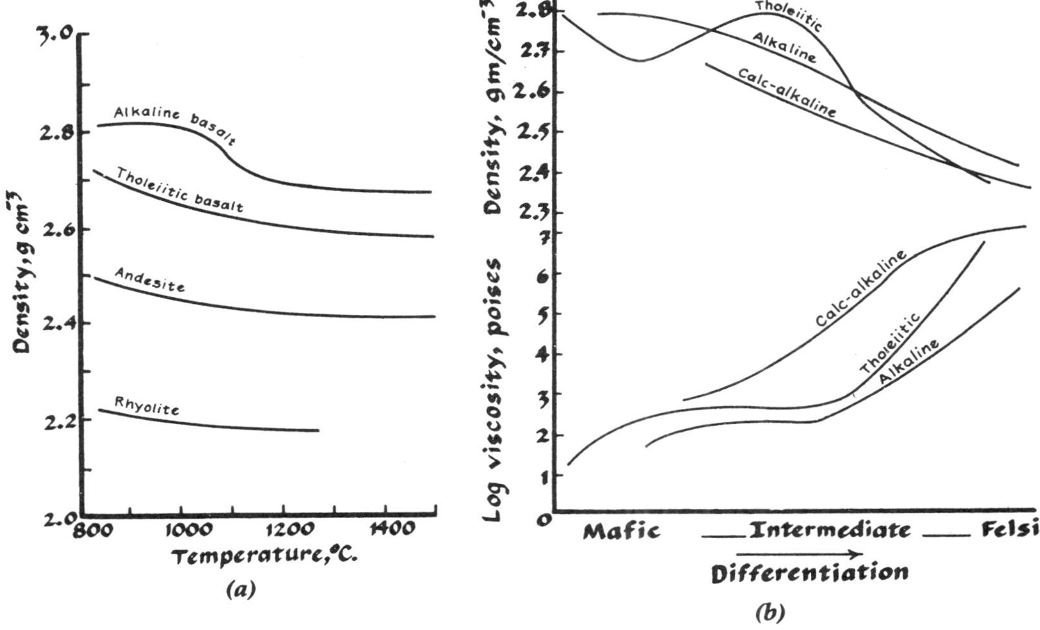

Figure 2–11 (a) Densities of some common igneous compositions in the liquid state as functions of temperature. (b) Variations of density (above) and viscosity (below) of the three main types of magmas as they evolve toward more felsic compositions. The differences result mainly from their differing rates of enrichment of silica, iron, and alkalies. The curves for tholeiites are based on lavas of Hawaii and the Galapagos Islands. The calc-alkaline curves are for rocks of the Cascade Range, and the alkaline ones are for the phonolitic series of Tahiti.

Beyond a certain point, however, iron enrichment reaches a maximum, and as silica and alkalies begin to increase more rapidly, density declines abruptly until it reaches a minimum in the most felsic end-members of the series.

TRANSFER OF MASS AND ENERGY BY DIFFUSION

Nearly all processes of igneous geology involve a transfer of mass or energy to approach a state of equilibrium at a lower energy level. When lava is discharged at the summit of a volcano and descends to lower elevations, it loses potential energy and gives up heat to its surroundings. Both forms of energy are transferred by virtue of a difference or gradient of energy level, in one case elevation and the other temperature, and the direction of transfer is always from the high to the low energy level. This is the essence of the Second Law of Thermodynamics, which simply states that heat flows from a hot body to a cold one, or, in a more general sense, that energy is always transferred from a higher to a lower level. In magmatic processes we are concerned mainly with the ways in which this principle governs processes of heat and mass transfer leading to different types of igneous rocks.

In the case of a descending lava flow, three types of processes are taking place simultaneously—transfer of heat, mass, and momentum, but the laws governing the rates of these processes have almost identical forms. Just as the rate of heat loss is related to the rate of change of internal energy, the rate of chemical diffusion between crystals and liquid is related to the rate of change of concentration of chemical components, and the rate of acceleration of velocity is related to the transfer of momentum within a viscous fluid.

We can understand the basic equations governing these processes if we consider those for heat transfer and bear in mind that the same principles govern chemical diffusion and transfer of momentum. The Fourier equation for heat conduction:

$$q = -K\frac{dT}{dZ} \qquad [2\text{–}6]$$

describes the rate of heat transfer, q, through a unit cross-sectional area of a layer of thickness, Z, by conduction between two bodies held at constant temperatures, such that $T_1 > T_2$. K is the coefficient of thermal conductivity in units, such as calories cm^{-1} deg^{-1} sec^{-1}, and the negative sign reflects the fact that heat flows in the direction of declining temperature. An identical relation, known as Fick's Law, describes the rate of tranfer of mass by chemical diffusion, and comparison with the equation for viscous flow of a Newtonian fluid (equation 2–2) shows the corresponding relations for transfer of momentum.

For most geological purposes we are not interested in the steady-state condition so much as the changes that take place with time, as, for example, when hot magma intrudes a cooler horizon or blocks of roof-rocks are incorporated into a pluton and equilibrate chemically and thermally with the magma. Under conditions such as these, the increase in temperature of the rocks to which heat energy is added will be a function of the total heat-flux, Q, into an element of volume, $A\Delta Z$,

$$Q = -A\Delta Z\frac{\partial q}{\partial Z} \qquad [2\text{–}7]$$

Since this flux must equal the rate of increase of heat content, H, with time, t, in the same element of volume, then

$$-A\Delta Z\frac{\partial q}{\partial Z} = \frac{\partial}{\partial t}(A\Delta Z\rho H) \qquad [2\text{–}8]$$

and, since $A\Delta Z$ and ρ are constants,

$$-\frac{\partial q}{\partial Z} = \rho\frac{\partial H}{\partial t} \qquad [2\text{–}9]$$

As we saw in an earlier section, the change of temperature is related to the change of heat content according to $C_p = dH/dT$ (from equation 2–1), and from equation 2–6.

$$q = -K\frac{\partial T}{\partial Z} \qquad [2\text{–}10]$$

Moreover, thermal diffusivity is defined as

$$\kappa = \frac{K}{\rho C_P} \qquad [2\text{–}11]$$

Therefore, by substitution we can obtain

$$\frac{\partial T}{\partial t} = \kappa\frac{\partial^2 T}{\partial Z^2} \qquad [2\text{–}12a]$$

which is the basic diffusion equation for the rate of change of temperature in a non-uniform thermal gradient. The corresponding equations for chemical diffusion and transfer of momentum are

$$\frac{\partial C}{\partial t} = D\frac{\partial^2 C}{\partial Z^2} \qquad [2\text{–}12b]$$

and

$$\frac{\partial V}{\partial t} = \nu\frac{\partial^2 V}{\partial Z^2} \qquad [2\text{–}12c]$$

in which C = concentration,
U = velocity,
D = chemical diffusivity, and
ν = kinematic viscosity (η/ρ).

Typical values of D, ν, and κ are given in Table 2–5. Note that the units of all three are identical: $cm^2 sec^{-1}$.

When integrated for different limiting conditions, these equations can be applied to specific problems of linear thermal, chemical, or mechanical diffusion. Here we need note only a few examples using the thermal case as illustrative of the general behavior. (The derivation of the equations given here, as well as others for different geometric configurations, can be found in references at the end of this chapter. A table of error functions [erf and erfc], given in Appendix C, will facilitate their numerical evaluation.)

The most simple case (Fig. 2–12a) is that of two semi-infinite bodies with the

Table 2–5 Some typical physical constants for igneous rocks and melts.

C_P	Heat capacity	0.25 to 0.30 cal g^{-1}
ΔH_F	Heat of fusion	65 to 100 cal g^{-1}
α	Coefficient of thermal expansion	3×10^{-5} deg^{-1}
κ	Thermal diffusivity	4×10^{-4} $cm^2 sec^{-1}$
η	Viscosity (poise)	10^2 to 10^5 g $cm^{-1} sec^{-1}$
ν	Kinematic viscosity (stokes)	10^2 to 10^4 $cm^2 sec^{-1}$
D	Chemical diffusivity	10^{-5} to 10^{-8} $cm^2 sec^{-1}$

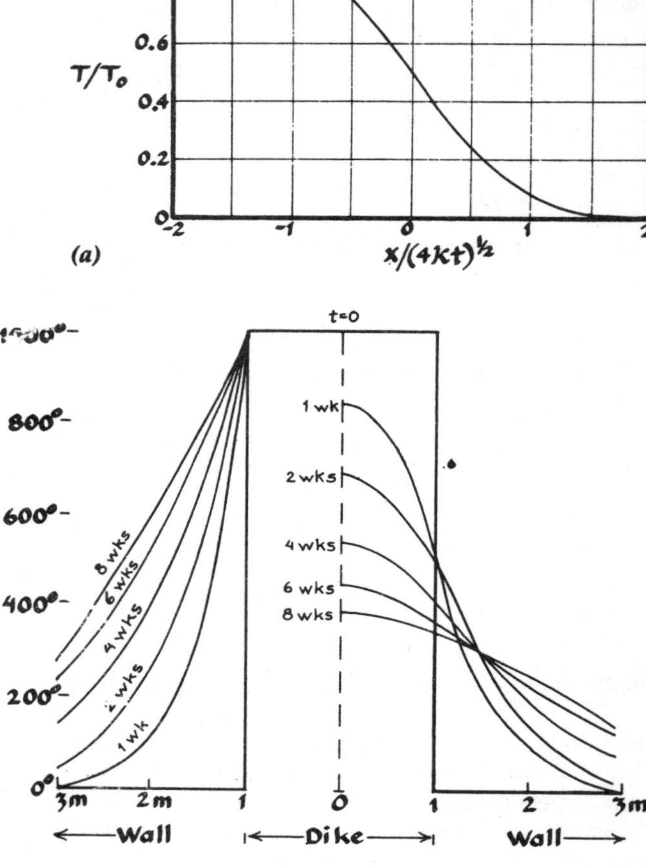

Figure 2–12 (a) The diffusion profile of temperature (T/T_0) across a contact between two semi-infinite bodies with the same thermal properties is a function of the square root of time and diffusivity, k. The distance x is measured from the contact at X = 0. The profile for concentration of a chemical component would differ only in that k would be replaced by chemical diffusivity, D. (After J. Crank, 1956, *The Mathematics of Diffusion*, Oxford Press, 347 pp.) (b) If one of the bodies has a finite dimension normal to the contact, as would an igneous intrusion, the temperature would decline, as shown by this example based on a suddenly emplaced dike. The left side of the section shows the temperature in the walls after various times if the magma continues to flow through the dike, as it would if it reached the surface to feed a large lava flow. In this case, the dike acts as a heat source of constant temperature, and the temperature in the walls can be calculated according to equation 2–15. The right side shows the temperature distribution if the magma is instantly emplaced and immediately ceases to flow. The temperature profiles are calculated from equation 2–13 or from the graph above.

same thermal diffusivity, κ, and each with an initially uniform temperature such that $T_1 > T_2$. The distribution of temperature, T, of either body relative to its initial temperature, T_0, is a function of the square root of (κt) and distance, X, from the contact at X = 0. It is given by:

$$T(X, t) = \frac{1}{2} T_0 \, \mathrm{erfc} \frac{X}{2\sqrt{\kappa t}} \qquad [2\text{–}13]$$

An example of a situation to which this equation might be applied would be that of two large bodies of rock with differing temperatures suddenly brought into close contact by faulting, so that heat flows from one to the other. It can also be applied to chemical diffusion between two bodies of different compositions. The general solution illustrated in Figure 2-12a shows the characteristic form of the temperature distribution with distance scaled to the square root of time and diffusivity. If the diffusivities of the two bodies differ, the scaling factors for each side of the contact will also differ accordingly. Figure 2-12b shows how the temperature distribution in and around a dike would change with time as heat is transferred from the dike into its walls.

The distance that the effects of diffusion extend beyond the boundary is a function of only time and diffusivity and is independent of the magnitude of the initial temperature contrast. A small contrast of temperature, composition, or momentum propagates its effect just as fast as a large one in materials of the same physical properties, the only difference being the amount that is transferred.

The assumption that diffusivity is the same on both sides of the boundary does not apply to the case of a crystallizing magma. As we have seen, the heat of crystallization of magmas is large compared to the heat capacity of either the liquid or solid, and the effect of this difference is to reduce the rate of cooling of the magma as it passes through the crystallization interval. The heat of crystallization, ΔH_F, given up during crystallization through a temperature interval, $T_1 - T_2$, can be allowed for by adding the proportional heat per degree to the heat capacity to obtain an effective heat capacity:

$$h = C_p + \Delta H_F/(T_1 - T_2) \qquad [2\text{-}14]$$

which can be substituted for C_p in equation 2-11 to obtain an appropriate value for thermal diffusivity.

In equation 2-13, transfer is assumed to be entirely by diffusion. If heat is being removed by mass transfer, as it would be, for example, at the top of a lava flow emplaced under rapidly convecting water, then the interface may be maintained close to a constant temperature, T_1, and the equation for the distribution of temperature in the semi-infinite source becomes

$$\frac{T - T_1}{T_0 - T_1} = \text{erf}\frac{X}{2\sqrt{\kappa t}} \qquad [2\text{-}15]$$

An example of a geological application of these principles is shown in Figure 2-13, which shows the predicted and measured temperature distributions in a cooling Hawaiian lava lake. The base of the lava cools by conduction to the ground, while the upper part loses heat to the air and to rainwater that falls on the surface and seeps down cracks in the crust. When the water vaporizes, it absorbs heat and tends to hold the temperature close to the boiling point of water. As long as the interior of the magma is still at least partly molten and able to convect, the temperature of the molten zone is nearly constant. In the solidified zones, the temperature distribution is governed by conduction to a zone of constant temperature above and to an essentially infinite body of rock below. The importance of the heat of crystallization of the magma can be seen by comparing

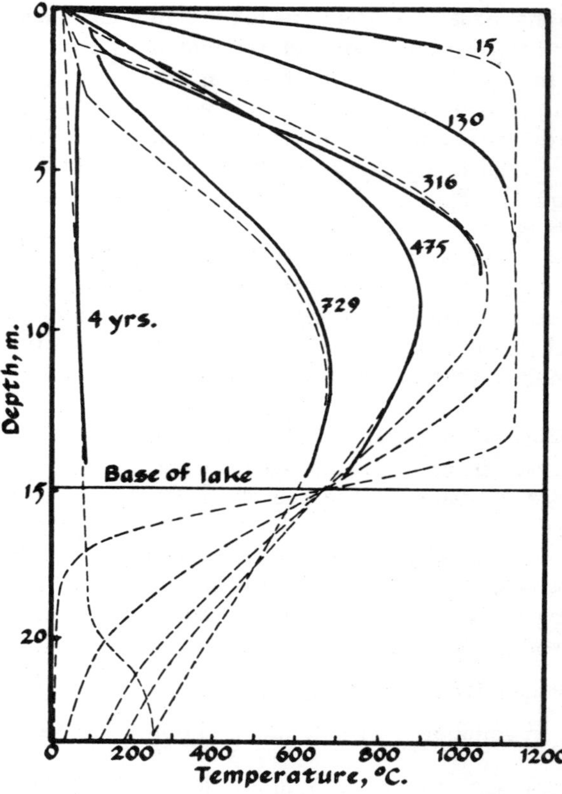

Figure 2–13 The calculated temperatures for a cooling lava lake are shown here (broken lines) together with temperature profiles measured in bore holes drilled after the number of days indicated by the numbers on each curve. The upper contact is at a nearly constant temperature of the atmosphere, while the lower one is governed by conduction to the underlying rocks. The average difference between the calculated and measured temperatures is less than two degrees. (Based on work of the U. S. Geological Survey.)

the slow rate of cooling while the magma is still above its solidus temperature (slightly above 1,100°C.) with the more rapid rate after it has crystallized.

FLOW OF MAGMA IN THE MANTLE AND CRUST

Under the conditions of high temperature and pressure that prevail in the mantle small amounts of liquid are probably able to infiltrate through intra-crystalline spaces, much as water flows through an aquifer. Judging from experimental studies of partly melted rocks at high pressure, it seems unlikely that a liquid fraction of more than 2 or 3 percent can be formed before the melt begins to migrate upward. Although the nature of this flow cannot be observed directly in the mantle, it can be inferred from the laws governing flow through porous media.

Flow through porous rocks

When rocks begin to melt at high pressures, small amounts of liquid tend to be concentrated where the edges of three mineral grains come together. Tube-like channels along these intersections form a network of interconnected passageways, and, if there is a pressure gradient on the liquid, it can migrate along these channels. So long as the dimensions of the channels are small compared to those of the system as a whole, the flow can be treated in terms of Darcy's Law for flow through a uniform porous medium:

$$q = \frac{k}{\eta}\frac{dP}{dz} \qquad [2\text{–}16]$$

where q is the volume flowing through a unit area, dP/dz is the pressure gradient in the direction z, k is the permeability, and η is viscosity. Thus, the rate of flow varies directly with the permeability and pressure gradient and inversely with viscosity. The units of k are cm^2 if η is in poise, and typical values range from about 10^{-6}, the permeability of sand, to 10^{-16} for a solid coarse-grained plutonic rock. The variation is particularly large where the liquid fraction is small.

Because the value of q is in units such as cm^3/cm^2 sec, it has the same dimensions as velocity, cm/sec, but because the area of the total cross section is much larger than that of the channels, its average velocity is much less than the actual velocity of the fluid in the channels. The permeability of partially molten rocks varies with the volumetric fraction of the pore space, also known as porosity, ϕ, and with the geometry and degree to which the spaces are interconnected in pathways through the solid. Pumice, for example, has a large percentage of void space but low permeability, because few of the voids are connected, whereas fractured basalt may have little porosity but great permeability.

The pressure gradient, dP/dz, may result from stress on the deformable crystalline matrix or from differences of density between one part of the liquid and another. As we saw earlier, the densities of silicate liquids can vary greatly as their compositions evolve, and this can result in a condition in which a light liquid is overlain by a relatively heavy one. In most instances, the liquid fraction will be less dense than the crystals, and, at high temperatures and pressures, the latter can be deformed by solid-state creep at rates that are rapid enough to cause the liquid to migrate upward under the force of gravity.

Diapiric rise

Density and viscosity also affect the manner in which magmas rise from their source and pass through the lithosphere (Fig. 2–14). The mechanism of intrusion of a particular magma depends mainly on its physical properties and those of the rocks through which it passes. At deep levels where rocks can be deformed plastically, many magmas are thought to rise as plumes or diapirs. The velocity of ascent of these buoyant masses is determined, at least approximately, by the general form of Stokes' Law

$$U = \frac{g\Delta\rho r^2}{3\eta_1}\left(\frac{\eta_2 + \eta_1}{\eta_2 + \frac{3}{2}\eta_1}\right) \qquad [2\text{–}17]$$

in which the velocity, U, of a spherical body is governed by its radius, r, density contrast, $\Delta\rho$, viscosity, η_2, and the viscosity, η_1, of the material through which it moves. Thus, the most rapidly ascending magmas would be those of large size and density contrast rising through rocks of low viscosity. Note that in the two

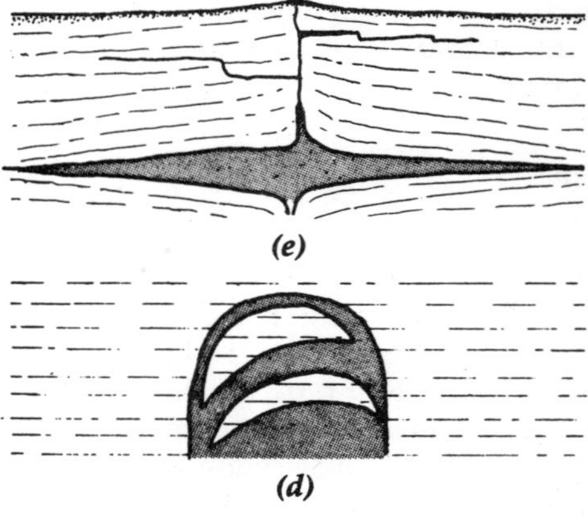

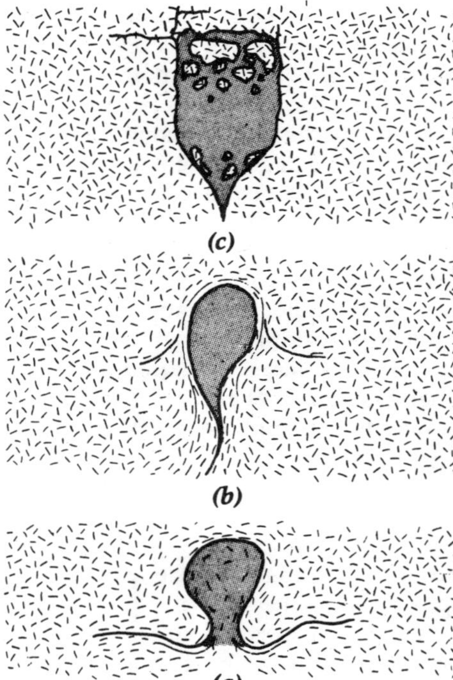

Figure 2–14 Magma generated in the mantle (a) is thought to rise when the buoyant mass of crystal-liquid mush becomes gravitationally unstable. It moves as plume-shaped diapirs through the plastic mantle (b) but on reaching more brittle rocks of the lithosphere, it may stope its way upward, either by dislodging blocks in a piecemeal fashion (c) or wedging its way upward in "bell-jar" shaped intrusions (d). At some stage in this sequence, the fluid part of the magma may separate from its crystalline residue. In the uppermost levels of the crust, magmas rise through dilational fractures that tend to become cylindrical conduits as they become established vents for surface eruptions (e).

limiting cases where the body has a viscosity, η_2, of zero or infinity, the numerical factor in equation 2–17 changes only from 2/9 to 1/3, so that the viscosity of the body has much less effect on its velocity of ascent than the viscosity of the material through which it rises.

In a few rare instances, earthquake epicenters have been observed to rise from mantle depths at rates of 500 to 2,000 meters per day prior to eruption of magma at the surface. This rate has been interpreted as that of a rising plume of magma fracturing and wedging aside the rocks through which it rises.

Because small, dense bodies rise more slowly than large, light ones, they tend to lose more heat and have a poorer chance of approaching the surface. They also tend to equilibrate more effectively with the rocks through which they rise. It seems probable, therefore, that these factors have a strong influence on the types of rocks we see in the earth's crust. Lavas can scarcely be an accurate sampling of all the compositions and volumes of magma coming from the mantle. One can think of the light, cool rocks of the lithosphere as a crude barrier that tends to filter out magmas that are much denser than the crust or too viscous to rise through narrow channels. It also impedes the rise of magmas that contain too little heat to survive strong cooling at shallow levels. The large increase of viscosity that comes with advanced degrees of crystallization severely limits the ability of crystal-rich magmas to rise through the crust. When the proportion of crystals reaches 40 or 50 percent, the rate of flow becomes so slow that the magma loses heat to the crust and solidifies before it reaches the surface.

In the upper levels of the brittle lithosphere, magmas rise by a variety of mechanisms, such as flow through fractures and stoping. The latter is a mechanism by which fracturing and wedging aside of roof rocks provides the space into which magma rises. Blocks stoped from the roof founder in the magma and may be assimilated or otherwise incorporated into the rising mass. In so doing, they alter its temperature and composition, and can have an important effect on the evolution of magmas in the crust.

Flow through fractures is probably confined to the upper few kilometers of the crust where the strength of rocks can support channels with rigid walls. The average velocity of flow, U, varies with the gradient of pressure, dP/dZ, and with the width of the fracture, W, or radius, R, of a cylindrical conduit and inversely with the viscosity of the magma, η, according to the relations

$$U = \frac{R^2}{12\eta}\left(\frac{dP}{dz}\right) \qquad [2\text{–}18a]$$

$$U = \frac{W^2}{8\eta}\left(\frac{dP}{dz}\right) \qquad [2\text{–}18b]$$

Because magmas passing through narrow fractures in cool rocks are so drastically cooled, there is a critical balance between the velocity of ascent and the rate of heat loss that determines how far a magma can rise.

The most efficient mechanism of fracturing brittle rock is by propagation of fissures, because the broad area of a planar surface results in the greatest total force for a given hydraulic pressure. Once magma begins to flow through such a channel, however, the shape tends to become less planar and more cylindrical. The reason for this change is that a cylindrical conduit is thermally and mechanically the most efficient channel for fluid flow. Because a smaller surface to volume ratio reduces heat losses and frictional drag, magma remains hotter and flows most rapidly in the widest part of a fissure so that, with time, it erodes its walls and establishes more equidimensional conduits. In thinner, less-efficient sections, it loses more heat, flows more slowly, and eventually freezes. For this reason, shallow conduits tend to become more pipe-like the longer flow continues.

Depending on the properties of the magma and the width of its channel, flow may be either *laminar* or *turbulent*. In laminar flow the stream lines or tracks of particles are smooth and nearly parallel, as they are, for example, in glaciers. Turbulent flow is characterized by random swirls, just as one sees in a rapidly flowing river in flood. For most fluids, the transition to turbulence occurs when the dimensionless Reynolds number,

$$\mathrm{Re} = \frac{\rho \mathrm{UL}}{\eta} \qquad [2\text{–}19]$$

reaches a critical value of about 2,000. In this expression, ρ is density, U is velocity, L is a characteristic dimension, and η is viscosity. The Reynolds number is the ratio of the inertial to the viscous or frictional forces in a moving fluid. In laminar flow, viscosity dominates, whereas in turbulent flow viscosity is less important than inertial forces.

The petrologic importance of this distinction lies in the fact that in turbulent flow, intimate mixing can take place between magmas of differing composition, and processes involving transfer of heat and mass are more efficient. In laminar flow, these processes are much slower, because they are more dependent on diffusion.

CONVECTION

Chemical and thermal diffusion play important roles in a number of important magmatic processes, not the least of which is convection. Although it has yet to be observed directly in a natural magma chamber, several indirect lines of evidence indicate that convection may be a major process affecting the ways in which magmas cool, crystallize, and differentiate.

When the margins of an intrusion give up heat to their walls, diffusional gradients of temperature, composition, and velocity develop in the *boundary layer* between the crystalline walls and fluid interior. Within this boundary layer, thermal and compositional gradients result from transfer of heat and chemical components across the margins of the cooling magma. The effect must extend into the interior for distances that are functions of time and diffusivity.

The boundary layer of a cooling body of magma can be divided into three parts, each having a width determined by the corresponding rate of diffusion of heat, chemical components, and momentum (Fig. 2–15). Just as loss of heat to the walls produces a thermal gradient into the magma, chemical exchange between the magma and crystals growing at the wall produces a *compositional boundary layer* with concentration gradients for each component of the magma. The *thermal boundary layer* tends to be wider than the compositional one, because, as we have seen, thermal diffusivity is so much greater than chemical diffusivity. The *momentum boundary layer* results from the velocity imparted to the

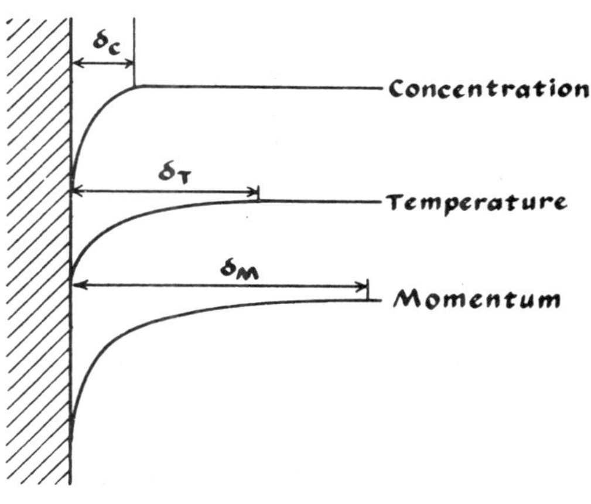

Figure 2–15 Three different types of boundary layers may form at the margins of a cooling body of magma. Their relative widths depend on their respective diffusivities. Because chemical diffusivity is very slow, the compositional boundary layer, shown by the concentration profile at the top, is normally narrower than the thermal boundary layer. Both temperature and composition affect the density of the fluid and cause it to sink or rise. The velocity imparted by gravitational forces is transferred farther into the mass of the fluid in the interior to form a broad momentum boundary layer. The wall depicted here is highly schematic; it is not necessarily the same for all three boundary layers but may extend different distances into a partly crystallized mushy zone.

magma by the changes of density in the thermal and compositional boundary layers. Gravitational energy that sets these two zones in motion is transferred by the viscosity of the magma in the form of momentum toward the interior of the body. Because momentum is transferred more rapidly than heat or chemical components, the momentum boundary layer tends to be the widest of the three layers. Under conditions of turbulent flow, mechanical mixing, not diffusion, governs the rates of transfer of heat and chemical components, and the widths of the compositional and momentum boundary layers are nearly equal.

Owing to the buoyancy forces produced by cooling and crystallization at the margins, any magmatic body with a horizontal temperature gradient will tend to convect with the boundary layer descending or rising, depending on the sign of density change induced by cooling. The magnitude of this driving force is related to the dimensionless *Grashof number,* which expresses the ratio of thermally induced buoyancy to viscous drag:

$$\mathrm{Gr} = \frac{g\alpha\Delta TL^3}{\nu^2} \qquad [2\text{–}20]$$

in which L is a characteristic dimension, usually the vertical thickness of the body, and ν is kinematic viscosity (η/ρ). The term α is the coefficient of thermal expansion.

A body that is cooled from the top and has a vertical rather than a horizontal temperature gradient may convect if the driving force, as expressed by Gr, is great enough to offset the viscous resistance of the magma and the rate at which the temperature contrast is reduced by diffusion of heat into the surroundings. The *Prandtl number,* Pr, expresses these latter properties in the dimensionless ratio of kinematic viscosity to thermal diffusivity,

$$\mathrm{Pr} = \frac{\nu}{\kappa} \qquad [2\text{–}21]$$

Thus, the criterion determining whether a magma with a vertical temperature gradient will convect or not is the product of these two parameters, the Grashof and Prandtl numbers, namely another dimensionless term, the Rayleigh number,

$$Ra_T = \frac{g\alpha\Delta TL^3}{\nu\kappa} \quad [2\text{–}22a]$$

A fluid cooled at the top or heated at the base will convect spontaneously when Ra_T exceeds a value of about 2,000.

In the case of magmas, which normally crystallize and change composition when they cool, any thermally induced change of density will entail a compositional change which, as we saw in an earlier section, can have an even greater effect on density than simple thermal contraction. A corresponding Rayleigh number can be defined for convection driven by a density contrast resulting from compositional differences:

$$Ra_S = \frac{g\beta\Delta SL^3}{\nu\kappa} \quad [2\text{–}22b]$$

where β is the change of density corresponding to a unit change of concentration of a chemical component, S. Unlike Ra_T, Ra_S may be either positive on negative depending on how the heavy components are fractionated between the liquid and crystals (Fig. 2–11b). Because composition and temperature cannot vary independently but are linked to strict crystal-liquid relations, it is possible to calculate the factor β in terms of the trend of differentiation with temperature for any particular magma. These two effects, one thermal and the other compositional, can be combined in an "effective" Rayleigh number

$$Ra_{eff} = -Ra_T + (Pr/Pr+1)Ra_S \quad [2\text{–}23]$$

which has been shown experimentally to have a critical value of about 2,500 at which convection is initiated by the combination of thermal and compositional density changes.

It is important to note that the Rayleigh number expresses the critical condition for initiation of convection by vertical gradients of density. For cooling on a side-wall, the critical Rayleigh number has no meaning; any liquid with a density contrast will rise or descend.

Because the form of convection depends on the size, shape, and other physical properties of a magmatic body and can be driven by both thermal and compositional effects on density, it can take a variety of forms.

Thermally driven convection

In its simplest form, thermally driven convection produces simple "Benard-type" cells, such as those depicted in Figure 2–16a. This could be the dominant regime in broad, sheet-like bodies soon after their emplacement. Convection could be either laminar or turbulent, depending on the size, shape, and physical properties of the magma. It would be turbulent in large equidimensional bodies

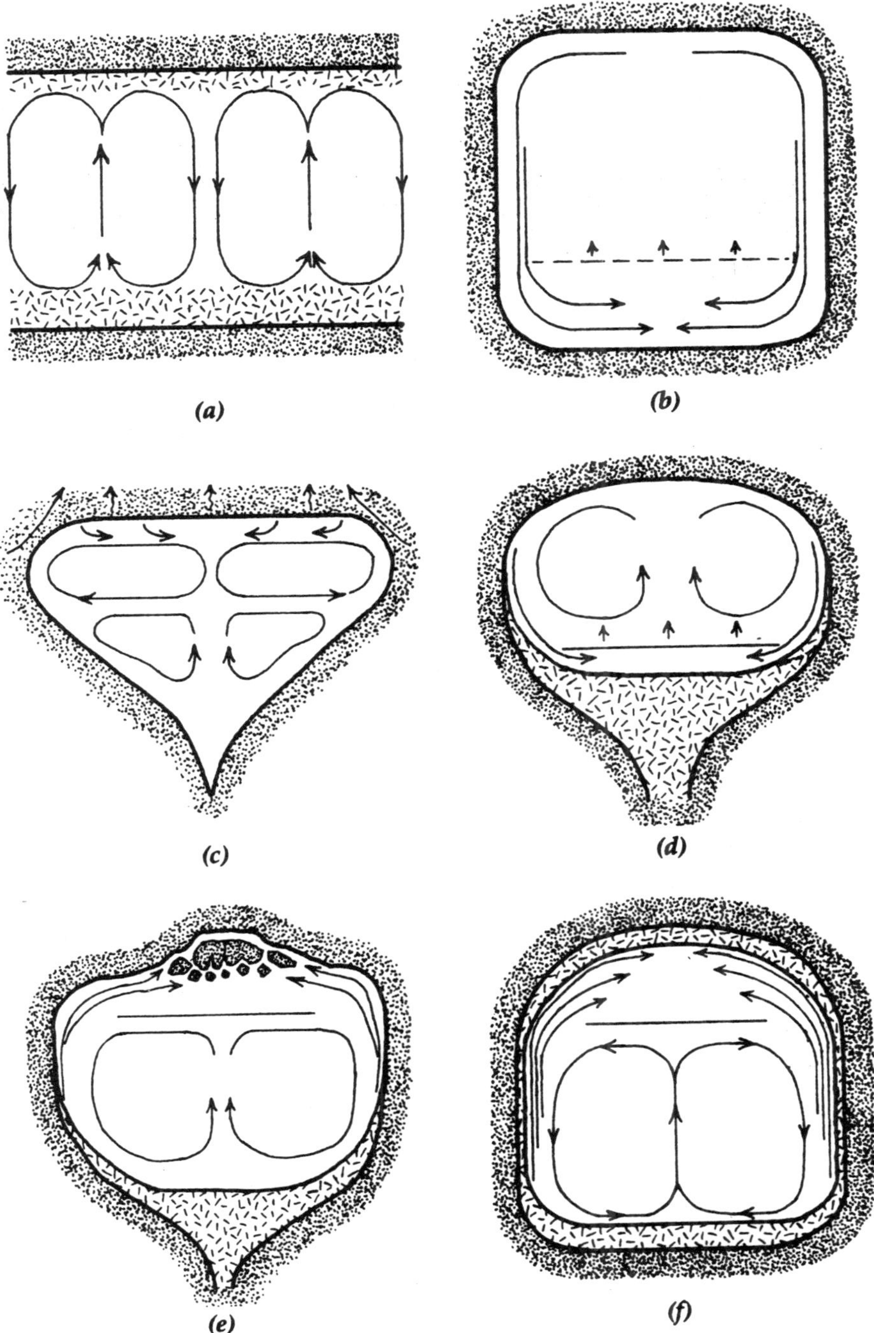

Figure 2–16 Different types of magmatic convection discussed in the text.

of hot magma, and laminar in narrower or flatter intrusions of more viscous magmas.

If cooling and crystallization is taking place at the roof, walls, and floor of a magma chamber, the temperature difference between the top and base may be so small that, instead of turning over as a unit, the cool boundary layer may descend to the base and remain there, causing the body to become thermally stratified, much as a room does when hot air rises to the ceiling and cool air accumulates near the floor (Fig. 2–16b). The body would not stagnate so long as the boundary layer is cooler than the interior of the intrusion, but the descending liquid may not circulate in the manner usually visualized for convective turnover.

Many shallow intrusions probably lose much more heat from their roof than they do from their walls and floor. This difference is due mainly to the rapid transfer of heat by shallow groundwater that sets up a system of hydrothermal circulation over the roof. Under such conditions, the cool magma under the roof may descend at one or more places near the center rather than at the margins. At the same time, cooling of the lower walls may cause deeper levels to convect in the opposite sense, so that the body separates into two independent systems, one above the other (Fig. 2–16c).

Combined thermal and compositional effects

A number of possible conditions can be visualized in which thermally driven convection is reinforced or opposed by compositional effects on density. Collectively, these are referred to as double-diffusive convection, because they depend on two diffusing properties, heat and chemical components. The simplest of these is that in which the compositional changes accompanying crystallization increase density and reinforce thermal contraction. In this case, the magma will descend along the walls, but, owing to its greater compositional density, it may pond on the floor, leaving the interior largely unaffected (Fig. 2–16d). The opposite may occur if the compositional effects oppose those of simple thermal contraction. This condition could result, for example, from melting of light felsic rocks in the roof and walls of a hot, dense, mafic intrusion. The buoyant boundary layer produced by melting may rise and accumulate under the roof as a separate zone that does not mix with the main body below (Fig. 2–16e). The same effect could be produced by cooling and crystallization of a magma that becomes much lighter as it evolves in composition (Fig. 2–16f). In both cases, the buoyant compositional boundary layer rises along the wall, even when the broad thermal boundary layer produces a descending counterflow in the interior.

An individual intrusion may pass through a number of these convective regimes during the course of cooling and solidification, and, as we shall find in later chapters, each may have a different effect on the way an intrusion crystallizes and differentiates.

Whatever its form, it is not the rate of convection of the magma but the rate of conduction through its wall-rocks that governs the rate of cooling of most intrusions. Just as the low conductivity of the vacuum of a thermos bottle limits the rate at which heat moves through its walls, the slow, conductive transfer of heat through dry rocks around an intrusion limits the rate at which heat is lost from the interior. Most magmas would need only a slow convective turnover to supply heat to the walls as fast as it is conducted away. Thus, it is the rate of heat transfer through the walls that governs the rate of convection, not vice versa.

Because of this and other limitations, it seems that thermal convection in most intrusions is probably sluggish. In fact, recent work has raised the question of whether cooling magmas convect at all. If the magma has started to crystallize, most if not all its heat losses to the walls may be absorbed by crystallization in a thermal boundary layer, so that the main mass of liquid in the interior may be thermally insulated from the effects of cooling at the margins. Although this crystallizing layer may become denser, owing to the combined thermal and compositional effects, its sharply increased viscosity tends to stabilize it. Tiny newly formed crystals settle too slowly to escape the advancing front of solidification and, instead, form a blanket that effectively locks up most of the buoyancy effects that would otherwise drive convection. Though still controversial, this interpretation provides a convenient explanation for certain sills that seem to have preserved inhomogeneities established at the time of their intrusion and never disturbed during subsequent cooling.

SELECTED REFERENCES

Irvine, T. N., and W. R. A. Baragar. 1971. A guide to the chemical classification of the common volcanic rocks. *Can. Jour. Earth Sci.* 8:523–548. A standard reference for the nomenclature of volcanic rocks based on their chemical compositions.

Jaeger, J. C. 1968. Cooling and solidification of igneous rocks, in *Basalts: The Poldervaart Treatise on Rocks of Basaltic Composition. Vol.* 2, H. H. Hess and A. Poldervaart, eds., 503–571. A simplified, but very useful, treatment of heat and mass transfer during cooling and solidification of magmas.

Turcotte, D. L., and Schubert. 1982. *Geodynamics: Applications of Continuum Physics to Geological Problems*. Wiley. 450 pp. A comprehensive treatment of physical processes with special attention to the mechanisms of plate tectonics.

Williams, H., and A. R. McBirney. 1979. *Volcanology*. Freeman, Cooper & Co. 397 pp. An advanced text on volcanoes with chapters devoted to the behavior of magmas.

3

CRYSTAL-LIQUID RELATIONS

TWO RECENT ERUPTIONS of Kilauea volcano, one in 1959 and the other in 1965, poured basaltic lava into pit-craters where it ponded, formed a solid crust, and slowly cooled. The rates of solidification, though rapid compared to those of plutonic rocks, were slow enough to permit geologists to drill through the crust and follow the crystallization of the lava as its temperature gradually declined. Figure 3–1 shows a series of samples recovered from the drill holes and quenched to preserve the liquid (now glass) and minerals that were growing from it at successive stages of cooling.

Solidification of this slowly cooled basalt illustrates how different the crystallization of natural magmas is from that of liquids that are compositionally simpler. First, crystallization did not occur at a single temperature, as ice does when it freezes at 0°C; instead it extended through at least 200 degrees of cooling. Second, the individual minerals began to nucleate and grow at temperatures well below those at which the same crystals would form from a liquid of their own composition. Augite, for example, began to crystallize at between 1,180 and 1,160°C, but the melting temperature of this mineral (in the absence of other components) is about 1,250°C; labradorite appeared at around 1,160°C, but in a liquid of its own composition this mineral starts to crystallize near 1,350°C. Once formed, these minerals continued to grow as the liquid slowly cooled (Fig. 3–2). Olivine, on the other hand, crystallized early but later ceased to grow and was partly resorbed in the cooler evolving liquid. Finally, and most important, the liquid changed composition throughout the course of crystallization. It first became more iron-rich until iron-oxide minerals began to crystallize; it then became poorer in iron but richer in silica and other components, so that the last liquid differed markedly in composition from the initial lava. In contrast to the original basaltic composition with about 50 percent SiO_2, the last liquid to crystallized contained more than 75 percent SiO_2 and had a composition close to that of rhyolite. Had the liquid fraction been separated at any stage of this process, it could have formed rocks with compositions very different from that of the original magma.

It is these characteristics of magmatic crystallization that account for much of the compositional diversity of natural igneous rocks. To understand these processes, we need first consider a few simple theoretical aspects of crystallization and then see how these principles apply to igneous rocks.

SOME BASIC THERMODYNAMIC RELATIONS

If we consider the behavior of a body in isolation from its surroundings, we speak of it as a *system*. Most of the systems we discuss are simpler than the lava lake, and they are studied under artificially controlled conditions that permit more precise observations. A part of such a system is referred to as a *phase*, if it has a particular set of homogeneous properties that make it mechanically separable from the rest of the system. A homogeneous liquid is an example of a single phase, and an assemblage of olivine crystals is another, but a mixture of olivine and pyroxene would constitute two phases, because these minerals have different physical properties, such as density or magnetic susceptibility, that can be used to separate them.

A crystallizing silicate liquid, like any other system capable of a physical or chemical transformation, has certain properties, such as volume, pressure, temperature, and composition, that define its chemical and physical nature. These properties, often referred to as *parameters of state*, are of two kinds, *extensive* and *intensive*. As their name implies, extensive parameters are those whose magnitude depends on the extent or amount of the system or phase. Intensive properties, on the other hand, have constant values in any part of a system, regardless of the mass or volume. Thus, pressure and temperature are independent of the mass of the substance they describe. The ratio of any two extensive parameters is also independent of the total mass and has a constant value in a homogenous system. Thus the ratio of weight or mass to volume is an intensive property, density, as are specific volume (the reciprocal of density), molar volume (the volume per unit molar weight), or molar energy content.

The properties of most value in describing an igneous phase or system are those that define energy states, because these determine whether a geological system is stable and how it tends to change. The total energy, E, of a geological system has three main components, thermal, mechanical, and chemical, each of which is the product of an intensive and an extensive property.

$$\begin{aligned} \text{Thermal energy (Q)} &= \text{temperature (T)} \times \text{entropy (S)} \\ \text{Mechanical energy (W)} &= \text{pressure (P)} \times \text{volume (V)} \\ \text{Chemical energy (U)} &= \text{chemical potential } (\mu) \times \text{mass (M)} \end{aligned}$$

so that

$$E = TS + PV + \mu M \tag{3–1}$$

The terms *entropy* and *chemical potential* are less familiar than temperature, pressure, volume, and mass and may require some explanation. Entropy, denoted S, is a measure of the amount of energy represented by the randomness or degree of disorder of the arrangement of atoms; as more energy is added to a substance, it becomes progressively less ordered. Thus, a gas has higher entropy than a liquid of the same composition and temperature, and a liquid has a higher entropy than the crystalline form of the same substance. When a system undergoes a change from one level of entropy to another, as from a liquid to a solid, the amount of that change is measured by the amount of energy given up or absorbed, dQ, divided by the absolute temperature.

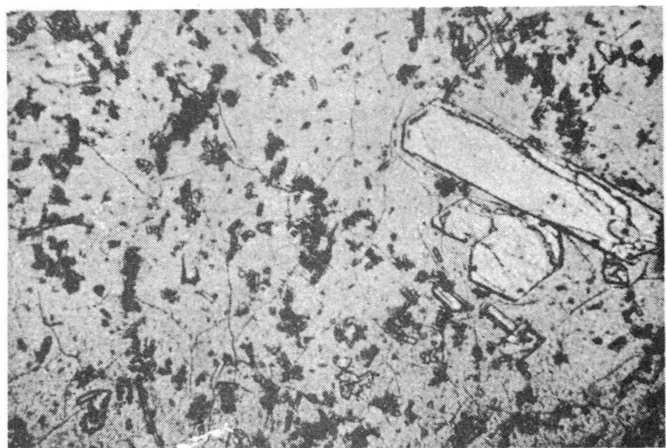

Figure 3–1 Photomicrographs of samples recovered from different depths in a crystallizing lava lake on Kilauea Volcano, Hawaii. Width of field in each photograph is 1.2 mm. (T. L. Wright, U. S. Geological Survey)

(a) A sample from the glassy crust quenched from a temperature of about 1,170°C. Euhedral phenocrysts of olivine grew at greater depths before the basalt was erupted. Pyroxene has just begun to nucleate from the matrix of clear basaltic liquid, now glass.

(b) At 1,130°, the pyroxene is larger, and plagioclase has appeared.

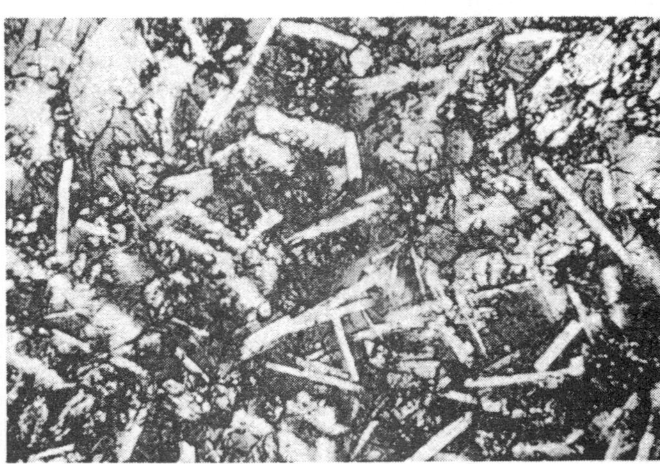

(c) At 1,075°, crystallization is well advanced. The dark reddish-brown color of the glass reflects its enrichment in iron and titanium.

(d) At 1,065° opaque minerals (magnetite and ilmenite) have nucleated when the liquid became saturated with iron and titanium. Note the rounded and embayed form of the olivine at the lower right. It shows signs of reaction with the liquid.

(e) At 1,020°C the lava is about 80 percent crystals. Small pools of iron-poor and silica-rich liquid remain in the interstices of the crystalline mush. Note the small needles of apatite that began to grow when the residual liquid became enriched in phosphorus. Crystallization of magnetite and ilmenite has reduced the iron and titanium contents of the remaining liquid to low levels.

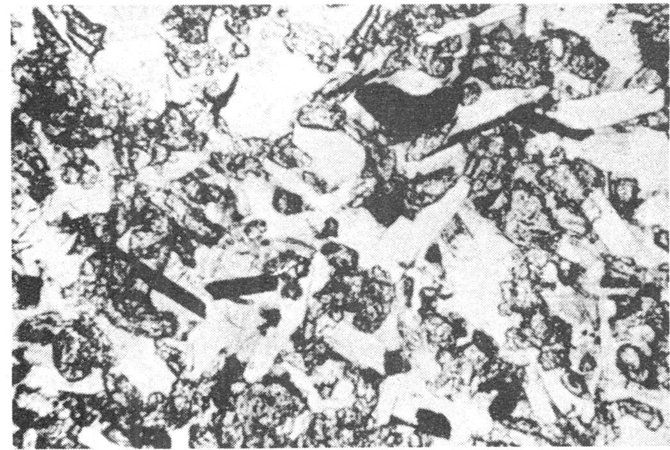

(f) Below 990° the rock is almost totally crystalline. Note the rounded grains of resorbed olivine.

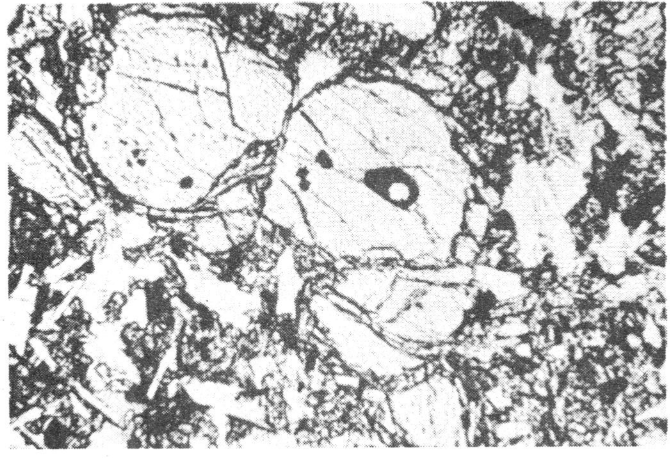

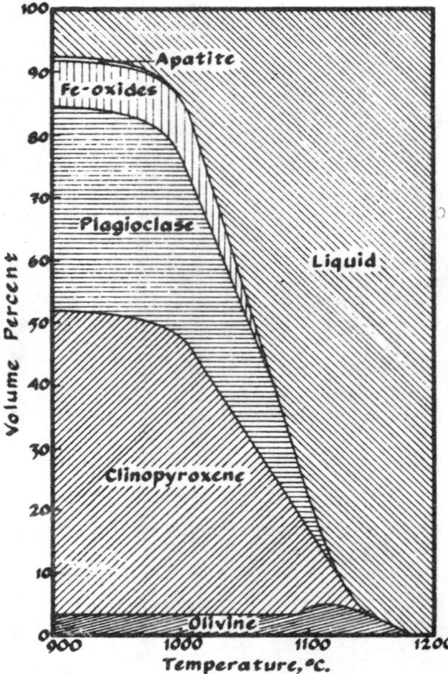

Figure 3–2 Proportions of crystals and liquid for a basalt such as that shown in Figure 3-1. Olivine was present as phenocrysts at the time of eruption and later was resorbed in the cooling magma. With falling temperature olivine was followed by clinopyroxene, plagioclase, magnetite, and ilmenite, and, finally, by apatite, and the proportion of liquid declined to less than 10 percent. The liquid indicated in the low-temperature range would be in the form of glass, as it is in the quenched samples recovered by drilling. If cooling were slower, the basalt would be entirely crystalline at all temperatures below about 1,000 degrees.

$$dS = dQ/T \tag{3-2}$$

With falling temperature and energy content, the structure of crystals becomes increasingly well-ordered. Fewer impurities and less solid solution can be accommodated, and, at a temperature of absolute zero, an ideal crystal would be pure, its atoms would be at rest and perfectly ordered, and its entropy would be zero.

Chemical potential can be defined as the amount by which the energy of a system is increased when a given infinitesimal amount of an element or compound is added in a way that does not alter the thermal or mechanical energies. The total chemical energy of a system is equal to the sum of the chemical energies of the components present, or

$$\text{Total chemical energy} = \mu_1 n_1 + \mu_2 n_2 + \cdots = \mu n \tag{3-3}$$

where n is usually expressed in moles or mole fractions.

Since all systems tend to seek their lowest energy level, the driving forces of magmatic processes are energy differences between one condition and another, and the change of energy is equal to the algebraic sum of the individual components.

$$dE = dQ + dW + dU \tag{3-4}$$

In a given reaction or change, the signs for individual types of energy may be positive or negative. Positive values indicate that energy has been gained by the system; negative values indicate energy that is given up to the surroundings. Thus, in a process involving heat energy, if dQ is negative, the result is a liberation of heat, and the process is said to be *exothermic*, whereas a change that brings an increase of heat energy to the system is *endothermic*.

There is no way of establishing an absolute measure of energy; only relative energy levels can be measured, but, for most practical purposes, this poses no problem. The change of energy, which is our main concern, can be determined by measuring the amount of heat a system absorbs or the work performed as the system goes from one state to another. These changes can usually be measured or calculated with enough precision to serve our purposes.

The general equation expressing the change of energy level for a change occurring at a given temperature in a system at constant pressure (the condition under which most geological processes take place) can be written

$$dE = dQ - PdV + \mu dn \qquad (3\text{–}5)$$

The negative sign of the second term results from the fact that when volume increases, work is expended by the system on its surroundings as it expands against the prevailing lithostatic pressure. Thus an increase of volume entails a decrease of mechanical energy.

The third term represents any chemical energy absorbed or lost. Most processes of petrologic interest involve only thermal and mechanical energy, and the concentrations of the chemical components are constant. If so, equation 3–5 reduces to

$$dE = dQ - PdV \qquad (3\text{–}6)$$

Enthalpy

In the processes of igneous petrology, the energy levels of systems of constant composition are most conveniently defined in terms of heat content and mechanical energy, PV. The term *enthalpy*, H, used for this purpose, is defined

$$H = E + PV \qquad (3\text{–}7)$$

Differentiating and combining with equation 3–6 gives

$$dH = dQ + VdP \qquad (3\text{–}8)$$

and for isobaric conditions (i.e. $dP = 0$),

$$dH = (dQ)_P \qquad (3\text{–}9)$$

which simply states that, for a process at constant pressure, the change of heat content or enthalpy is equal to the heat exchanged between the system and its surroundings.

This may seem like a devious way of stating the obvious, but dH is not just a measure of how much hotter or cooler a substance has become. Its magnitude is a function of the change of state, which entails more than just temperature, pressure, and volume. Consider, for example, the changes that take place as heat is added to ice at atmospheric pressure (Fig. 3–3). If the ice is initially at some temperature, T_1, below 0°C, the added heat will raise the temperature of the ice at a rate that is governed by the *heat capacity* at constant pressure, C_P. Since the

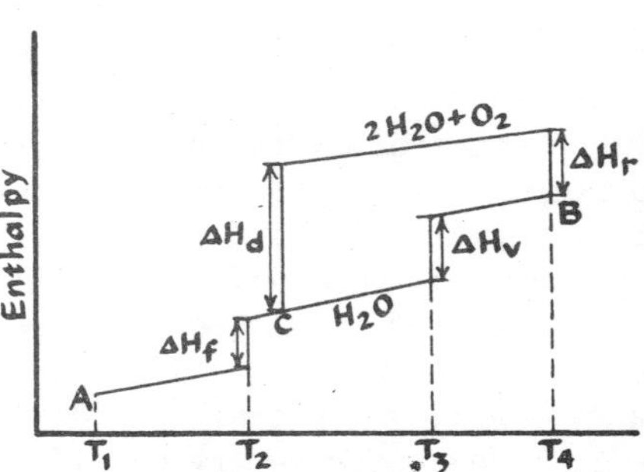

Figure 3–3 Schematic diagram showing the variation of the enthalpy of H_2O with temperature. (Not to scale.) The lower stepped lines starting at A and ending at B show the increase of enthalpy as ice is heated and converted first to liquid water at T_2 and then to steam at T_3. The upper lines trace the course from condition C if water is dissociated by electrical energy, ΔH_d, to hydrogen and oxygen which, when heated to T_4, reacts by combustion releasing thermal energy, ΔH_r, and drops to condition B.

change of enthalpy, ΔH, is equal to the amount of heat absorbed at constant pressure (equation 3–9), then

$$\Delta H = \Delta T C_P \qquad (3\text{–}10)$$

and the value of C_P determines the slope of the curve between T_1 and T_2.

On reaching T_2, the ice must change from the solid to liquid state before any further change of temperature can take place. The amount of heat required to do this, ΔH_F, is known as the *latent heat of fusion*. Hence, the enthalpy of the system increases at constant T and P, and, after the ice is melted, the next increment of heat absorbed, dQ, will again result in a rise in temperature at a rate governed by the heat capacity of the liquid. A similar step in enthalpy occurs at 100°C when the liquid passes to the gaseous state, and the heat of vaporization, ΔH_V, is added to effect this transition.

The value of enthalpy at any stage includes all the heat that has been added to bring the system to its present state, regardless of how that state was reached. For example, if liquid water at condition "C" were dissociated by means of an electrical current to equivalent amounts of hydrogen and oxygen at the same temperature, the combined enthalpies of the two gases would be greater than that of water (for a reason that we shall note shortly). Adding heat raises the temperature of the gases to T_4, as shown in the upper curve of Figure 3–3. If the two gases are now combined to form H_2O, they will liberate heat during combustion. If this process takes place under isothermal conditions (i.e., at constant temperature), the gases will arrive at the same state as was reached in the first example and have the same enthalpy, despite the fact that the way heat was exchanged was very different.

Enthalpy is usually expressed in calories per mole and, for the uncombined elements, is taken as zero at an arbitrary reference point—atmospheric pressure and room temperature (298° Kelvin), usually referred to as the *standard state*. The enthalpy of a compound is measured with reference to the same standard state but includes its *heat of formation*, ΔH_0, from the elements, a quantity that can be determined by measuring the amount of heat absorbed or given off when the compound is formed at the standard state. For example, when one mole of quartz is formed from silicon and oxygen, 205 calories are given off, so that $\Delta H_0 = -205$ cal/mole.

EQUILIBRIUM IN REVERSIBLE OR IRREVERSIBLE PROCESSES

The exchanges of energy during the changes of H_2O from one state to another require interaction with the surroundings of the system. For work to be expended, there must be a pressure difference across the boundaries of the system, for if there were not the system would be in mechanical equilibrium. Likewise, the system can only absorb heat from its surroundings if it is at a lower temperature. If there is no temperature difference, the system is in thermal equilibrium. In the same way, if the chemical potentials of all components in all phases are equal, the components have no tendency to react, and the system is in chemical equilibrium. When a system has no differential pressure, temperature, or chemical potential, it is stable and said to be in thermodynamic equilibrium with its surroundings.

The term "reversible" is used for a process or change resulting from an infinitesimal displacement of the conditions of equilibrium. The direction of the process can be reversed, so that it goes in one direction or the other with a very small change of conditions. Thus a reversible process can be visualized as the passage of a system through a series of equilibrium states. An example would be the change of the amount of vapor that accompanies a gain or loss of heat by a liquid-vapor combination at its boiling temperature; the process will go in either direction as heat is added or removed. This is in contrast to processes that are irreversible, such as flow of heat from a hot to a cold body or mixing of gases or liquids of differing compositions; these cannot reverse their direction any more than water can flow uphill.

Free energy

The step-like changes of enthalpy that accompany a reversible process at constant temperature (Fig. 3-3) stem from a change of energy at constant temperature, $T\Delta S$, that represents the increase or decrease of the degree of internal ordering of the substance. It is sometimes referred to as bound energy, because it is that part of the heat content that is not available to perform work. Because the change of volume involved in the phase change is a necessary consequence of that change, it cannot perform work on the surroundings without reducing or reversing the process. The same holds for any change of state; part of the energy change is absorbed in establishing the new level of internal order and becomes a specific property of each substance at a given condition.

In a reversible process of this kind, the heat gained or lost is

$$dQ = d(TS) = TdS + SdT \qquad (3\text{–}11)$$

and if, as in the example above, the process is isothermal, $dT = 0$, this reduces to

$$dQ = TdS \qquad (3\text{–}12)$$

And at constant pressure, from equation 3-9,

$$dH = dQ_P = TdS \qquad (3\text{–}13)$$

which is the basic equation for equilibrium of a reversible isothermal process at constant pressure.

For practical purposes, the energy relations that are of most interest are those that express the net amount of heat and work associated with a particular process. The term "free energy," which serves this function, is the difference between the combined heat and work that a process involves and that part of the energy that is in the form of "unavailable work" (TS). Free energy is usually expressed as *Gibbs Free Energy*, designated G and defined as

$$G = H - TS \tag{3–14}$$

This quantity is useful for determining the equilibrium conditions of a system. At equilibrium, $\Delta G = 0$, and for isothermal changes at constant pressure, the magnitude of ΔG is a measure of the divergence of a system from the equilibrium state.

Clapeyron's Equation

It is often important to be able to predict how changes of conditions will affect equilibrium at different depths in the earth. The Clapeyron equation is very useful in this respect, because it defines the relation between pressure and temperature at which two phases are in equilibrium.

If the system has a constant composition and is at equilibrium, $dQ = TdS$ (equation 3–12), and we can write equation 3–6 as

$$dE = TdS - PdV \tag{3–15}$$

By definition, $H = E + PV$, so that

$$dH = dE + PdV + VdP \tag{3–16}$$

Combining equations 3–15 and 3–16, we obtain

$$dH = TdS + VdP \tag{3–17}$$

By definition, equation 3–14, $G = H - TS$, and

$$dG = dH - (TdS + SdT) \tag{3–18}$$

Substituting the value for dH in equation 3–17, we obtain

$$dG = VdP - SdT \tag{3–19}$$

This equation holds for both of the phases that are in equilibrium, 1 and 2, so

$$dG_1 = V_1dP - S_1dT, \text{ and}$$

$$dG_2 = V_2dP - S_2dT.$$

Combining these two equations and making $V_2 - V_1 = \Delta V$ and $S_2 - S_1 = \Delta S$, and recalling that at equilibrium conditions, $\Delta G = 0$, we have

$$dP\Delta V = dT\Delta S \tag{3–20}$$

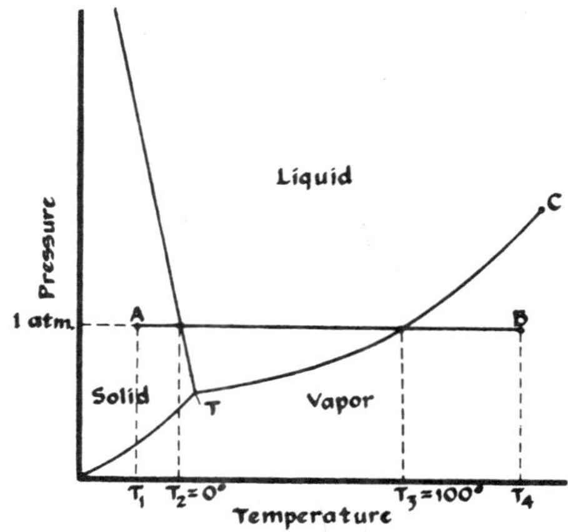

Figure 3–4 Schematic pressure-temperature phase diagram for H_2O. The scale has been distorted, and the various forms of ice have been omitted in the interest of clarity.

Since, from equation 3–13, $\Delta H = T\Delta S$, at equilibrium, we can write equation 3–20 as

$$\frac{dT}{dP} = \frac{T\Delta V}{\Delta H} \quad (3\text{–}21)$$

In the sections to follow, we see how these relations can be applied to a great variety of important geologic problems.

ONE-COMPONENT SYSTEMS

Figure 3–4 is a pressure-temperature (P-T) diagram showing the stability ranges of the three principal phases of H_2O: steam, water and ice. It can be thought of as a map showing the realms of pressure and temperature within which only a single phase is stable, and the boundaries between the three fields delineate the temperatures and pressures at which the two adjacent phases can coexist in equilibrium.

The changes we considered earlier can be traced along the path for atmospheric pressure, A–B, and show how, with increasing temperature, the system passes from one phase to another. These changes can be related to the free energies, G, of the three phases, which are shown schematically in Figure 3–5 as a function of temperature at constant pressure. Since $G = H - TS$, the slopes of these curves reflect the differing entropies of the three phases. Ice, having the lowest entropy, has the lowest slope, and vapor, with the highest entropy, has the steepest slope. At temperatures above T_3, the vapor phase has the lowest free energy and is therefore the stable phase. With falling temperature, first the liquid and then the solid has the lowest free energy and becomes the stable phase.

In real systems, phases do not always change spontaneously on crossing their boundaries but may persist for some distance into the adjacent field. At

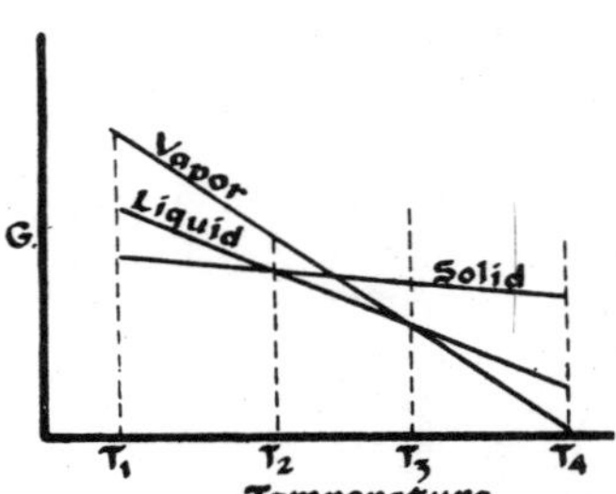

Figure 3–5 Free-energy versus temperature for the three phases of H_2O. The slopes are a function of the differing entropies of the solid, liquid, and vapor. It can be seen from equation 3–19 that at constant pressure the slopes of the curves, dG/dT, are equal to -S.

temperatures slightly above or below the intersections in Figure 3–5, the energy differences may be smaller than those required to form stable nuclei of the low-energy phase and another with a slightly higher free energy may persist as a metastable phase. This is why very pure water can be cooled several degrees below 0°C before freezing, and obsidian persists for thousands of years without crystallizing, even though it is far below the temperatures at which its minerals should nucleate and grow. Even in slowly cooled lavas, plagioclase may not begin to crystallize until undercooled by as much as 25°C. This is an important factor in crystallization of igneous rocks, especially rapidly cooled lavas and pyroclastic ejecta.

Figure 3–6 is a phase diagram for SiO_2. It resembles that of water, except for the absence of a vapor field that is so small for SiO_2 that it has been omitted. Most diagrams like Figure 3–6 have been constructed by conducting a series of experiments at different temperatures and pressures to determine the stable phase under given conditions. Proceeding one point at a time, the limits of the stability fields of the various phases are delineated.

Experimental construction of phase diagrams for natural minerals requires much time and care, mainly because of the large numbers of experiments that are needed and the difficulty of controlling conditions with the required precision, especially at very high temperatures and pressures. Because of the problems of nucleation mentioned earlier, it may be difficult to determine the exact

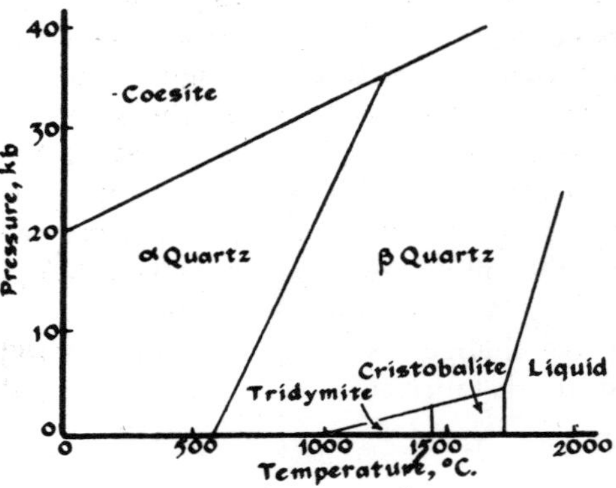

Figure 3–6 Part of the phase diagram for SiO_2. Several crystalline forms have been omitted.

positions of the phase boundaries. This uncertainty can be avoided by "seeding" the sample with small crystals and seeing whether they increase or decrease in size. Another technique is to "reverse" the phase changes, by testing transitions in both directions across phase boundaries. To determine a melting curve, for example, two starting materials, crystals and glass (or liquid), are held at the same temperature and pressure. If, at the end of the experiment, both take on the same form, there can be little doubt that the observed phase is the stable one.

A second method of constructing phase diagrams, though less laborious, has even more serious limitations. If the thermodynamic properties of the substance are well known, the positions and slopes of the phase boundaries can be determined by the Clapeyron equation (3–21). The diagram in Figure 3–4 could be constructed in this way. Ice, as we have seen, melts at 273°K with a 10 percent decrease of specific volume and a release of latent heat, ΔH, of about 79.7 cal g^{-1} (which, in units of mechanical energy, is equivalent to $79.7 \times 41.3 = 3292$ atm cm g^{-1}). The slope of the equilibrium curve is therefore

$$dT/dP = 273 \times (-.1)/\ 3292 = -.008^{\circ}\ \text{atm}^{-1}$$

(Ice is unlike most common substances in that its volume decreases on melting, and, for this reason, the melting curve has a negative slope.) Using this method, each of the phase boundaries can be drawn to complete the phase diagram, provided, of course, at least one point is known on each curve.

The main problem with this method of constructing phase diagrams lies in the difficulty of determining the thermodynamic properties, such as heats of reaction, with sufficient accuracy to define the field boundaries precisely. In most cases, the necessary data for silicate minerals are still inadequate, and it is easier to determine phase relations experimentally.

THE PRINCIPLE OF LE CHATELIER

If we examine the behavior of systems in which two or more phases coexist in equilibrium, we find a simple basic rule that can be very useful in predicting the response of a system to changes of temperature or pressure. Consider, for example, a system consisting of a liquid and vapor initially in equilibrium, to which heat is added at constant volume. Some of the liquid will be vaporized, absorbing heat until equilibrium conditions are restored at a higher temperature. So long as the liquid phase has not been entirely vaporized, the increased temperature and greater proportion of vapor cause an increase in pressure, and the effect of this is to raise the temperature at which the two phases remain in equilibrium. In other words, the effect of increasing temperature is absorbed by the system in such a way that equilibrium is restored at a new condition, in this case at an elevated pressure. In a similar fashion, if the pressure on the system is lowered, liquid will be vaporized to occupy the enlarged volume. Heat is absorbed, the temperature falls, and the system moves to a lower position on the liquid-vapor equilibrium curve.

These relations are expressed in a more general way by the *Principle of Le Chatelier*, which simply states that:

> Any external change that affects a system of two or more phases at equilibrium will cause a reaction to proceed in the direction of least resistance. By absorbing the change, the reaction tends to restore equilibrium by adjusting to the new condition.

In each of the examples just considered, the tendency of the two-phase system is to absorb and moderate the changes imposed on it. It acts much as a thermostat does, in that it stabilizes the system and prevents it from leaving the conditions defined by the two-phase equilibrium curve. This effect is often referred to as a *buffer*. For example, the climates of regions near the sea are more moderated than those of inland areas, because their temperatures are buffered by the nearby water. When conditions are altered by an influx of warm air, water evaporates, absorbs heat, and cools the air; an influx of cold air has the opposite result. Thus by Le Chatelier's principle, the system responds in a way that absorbs the change and buffers the system at equilibrium.

THE PHASE RULE

Another fundamental relationship seen in stability diagrams, such as Figure 3–4, is expressed by the Phase Rule of J. Willard Gibbs, which is usually written:

$$F = C - P + 2 \tag{3–22}$$

F is the number of degrees of freedom (sometimes called the "variance") of a system and is the number of independent intensive variables, normally temperature, pressure, or the concentration of a component. C is the minimum number of components by which the compositions of the phases can be expressed, and P is the number of phases that can coexist under equilibrium conditions.

The examples in Figures 3–4 and 3–6 have only a single component, H_2O or SiO_2, but they have several phases including liquid, vapor, and one or more crystalline polymorphs. In the diagram for the one-component system H_2O we see that a single phase—solid, liquid, or vapor—can exist within a two-dimensional field representing ranges of the two intensive variables, temperature and pressure. Within these areas T and P can vary independently. Thus, since

$$F = C - P + 2 = 1 - 1 + 2 = 2$$

the system has o degrees of freedom, nperature and pressure, and is said to be *divariant*.

Liquid and solid, liquid and gas, or solid and gas can coexist under the conditions defined along the boundaries of the individual stability fields, but on these boundaries pressure and temperature must vary sympathetically according to the slopes of the P–T curves if the two phases are to remain in equilibrium. Only one factor, temperature or pressure, can vary independently. Hence,

$$F = 1 - 2 + 2 = 1$$

and the system is *univariant*. The "triple point," where three phases coexist, has a unique temperature and pressure. Hence,

$$F = 1 - 3 + 2 = 0$$

and the system has no degrees of freedom. It is said to be *invariant*. Neither temperature nor pressure can vary without at least one phase becoming unstable.

In the chapters to follow we shall see examples in which the Phase Rule can be used to predict the behavior and stable mineral assemblages in geological systems, but first we must examine the effects of adding additional components to the simple one-component systems considered thus far.

TWO-COMPONENT SYSTEMS

Systems with two or more components in varying concentrations have much in common with simple aqueous solutions. A solution becomes saturated and precipitates NaCl when the chemical potential, μ, of the crystalline phase falls below that of the liquid, and, once saturated, the equilibrium is independent of the number or volume of crystals. So long as a single crystal is present, solid NaCl can be added or removed without upsetting the equilibrium. Changing the amount of NaCl in the liquid is a different matter. If the liquid is diluted, the chemical potential of dissolved NaCl is decreased, equilibrium is upset, and solid NaCl will dissolve to restore the equilibrium. This basic difference reflects the fact that the amount of crystalline material is an extensive property of the system, whereas the concentration or chemical potential of the liquid is an intensive property, and, as the phase rule indicates, only the latter affects the number of stable phases.

These relations can be better understood if we consider the relation between chemical potential and temperature. It can be shown that at constant pressure these two intensive properties are linked in a very simple way:

$$d\mu = -SdT \quad (3\text{–}23)$$

At the saturation temperature of a pure substance, A, the chemical potentials of the liquid and solid are equal, and the two phases are in equilibrium. If temperature falls below the equilibrium value, equation 3–23 shows that the chemical potentials of both phases increase (because dT is negative), but that of the solid increases less than that of the liquid, because its entropy, S, is smaller. Thus the solid, having the lower chemical potential, becomes the stable form. But the chemical potential of liquid A can also be lowered by diluting it with another component, B, and in this way the liquid could still be in equilibrium with the solid at a temperature below the melting temperature of pure A. This effect, known as "melting-point lowering," explains why the freezing temperature of water is lowered by an addition of NaCl or antifreeze.

The chemical potential of any component i at a given temperature in an ideal solution is

$$\mu_i = \mu_0 + RT \ln X_i \quad (3\text{–}24)$$

where:

μ_0 = the chemical potential at a standard reference state
R = the gas constant (1.9872 cal $mole^{-1}$ deg^{-1}), and
X_i = the mole fraction of i.

Most real solutions deviate from the ideal logarithmic relation, and a factor γ_i, known as the *activity coefficient*, takes this difference into account. (The quantity $\gamma_i X_i$ is known as the *activity*, a_i, of component i.) Thus, a more general form of equation 3–24 would be

$$\mu = \mu_0 + RT \ln \gamma X = \mu_0 + RT \ln a \qquad (3\text{–}25)$$

The relationship between the melting temperature of a component i and its concentration in the liquid can be obtained by integrating equation 3–23 from T_i to T, substituting the equivalent value, $\Delta H_i/T_i$, for ΔS (assumed to be constant in the range between T and T_i), and combining the result with equation 3–25 to obtain

$$\ln a_i = \ln \gamma X_i = \frac{\Delta H_i}{R}\left(\frac{1}{T_i} - \frac{1}{T}\right) \qquad (3\text{–}26)$$

where T_i is the melting temperature of pure i, and ΔH_i, the heat of fusion, is positive and assumed to be constant. This is the basic equation defining the temperature at which crystals of A are in equilibrium with a liquid having varying concentrations, X, of that component.

These relations are depicted in Figure 3–7. Each component, A and B, has its own melting or saturation curve, known as a *liquidus*, which defines the compositions and temperatures of liquids in equilibrium with the corresponding solids. The intersection of these curves at point E is referred to as a *eutectic*.

Theoretically the form of the liquidus curves can be calculated from equation 3–26, if all the thermodynamic functions are known, and, in many cases, the calculated curves correspond closely to those determined experimentally. For some systems, however, the fit is poor, especially in the middle compositional range. Much of this discrepancy can be attributed to the heat of mixing of intermediate liquids, which has not been taken into account in equation 3–26.

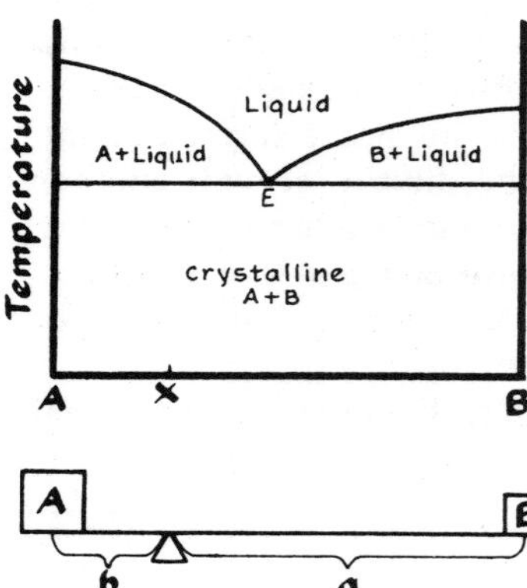

Figure 3–7 The principal fields and boundary curves for a simple, two-component system with a eutectic. The proportions of components or phases at any particular temperature can be calculated by the lever rule using the proportional lengths of constant-temperature lines parallel to the base. The composition X, consisting of A and B in the proportions of a and b, can be thought of in terms of a lever with its fulcrum at X.

Free-energy relations

The stability relations of a two-component system can also be depicted in terms of free energy, G, much as it was for a single component in Figure 3–5, but with addition of another intensive variable, concentration, the system cannot be plotted in a two-dimensional diagram as it was in the earlier example; a series of temperature sections is required (Fig. 3–8).

As we saw earlier, the free energy of crystals of fixed composition is determined by

$$G = H - TS \tag{3-14}$$

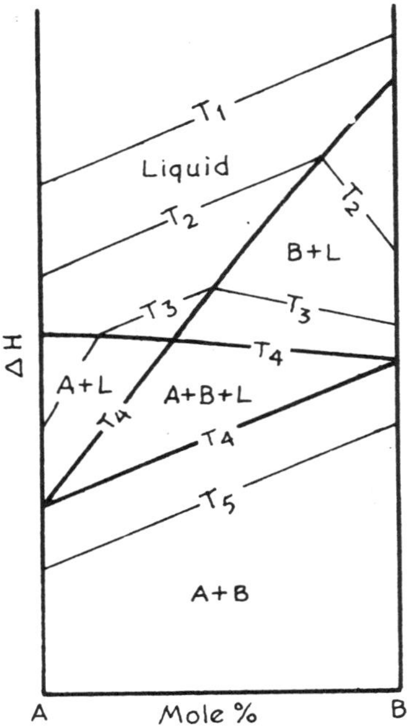

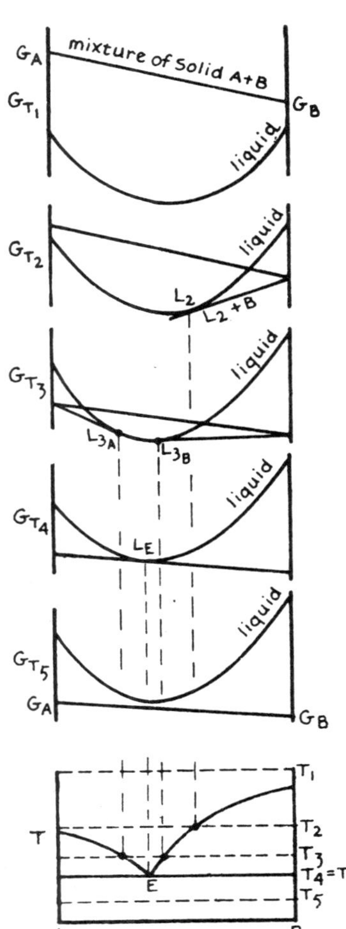

Figure 3–8 A G–X diagram (right) shows the relations between the free energies (G) of the liquid and solid phases at different temperatures. X is in mole proportions. (Adapted from S. A. Morse, 1980, *Basalts and Phase Diagrams*, p. 59.) The same system can be shown in an H–X diagram (above) in which the stability fields are defined in terms of enthalpy and composition, and temperature is shown by contours. The advantage of such a diagram is that the proportions of phases can be determined in terms of the extensive variable, enthalpy, which, for most geological conditions, is of more interest than temperature. Note that the temperature in the triangular area is constant at T_E, but the proportion of phases varies with composition and enthalpy. The diagram assumes that changes of entropy with temperature are proportionately small. (Adapted from H. S. Yoder, Jr. 1976. *Generation of Basaltic Magma*. Nat. Acad. Sci. 265 pp. and from W. Ussler and A. F. Glazner, 1992. *Jour. Volc. Geoth. Res.*)

and the free energy of any mechanical mixture of two crystalline phases, A and B, is a simple linear function of the free energies of the two phases. But this is not true of a solution. Mixture of two end-member components of the liquid results in a spectrum of intermediate liquids with chemical potentials that are a function of the proportions of their components. Unlike mechanical mixtures of solids, intermediate liquids must have higher entropies than their pure end-members, and, by equation 3–14, their free energies must be lower.

Consider the relations between the molar free-energy curves for the solid and liquid phases in the two component system shown schematically in the lower part of Figure 3–8a. Free energy has been plotted for the solid and liquid at five temperatures corresponding to T_1 through T_5 in the T–X diagram at the base of the figure.

At the highest temperature, T_1, the entire range of liquid compositions has a lower free energy than does any solid, and the liquid is the stable phase for all values of X. With falling temperature, the free energy of the solid rises less rapidly than that of the liquid, (owing to the higher entropy of the liquid, as illustrated in Figure 3–5), and, as it does so, the value for B falls below that of the liquid. Crystalline B is therefore stable, whereas A is not. The composition of the liquid in equilibrium with crystals of B at T_2 is the point of tangency of a line from solid B to the G–X curve for the liquid. All compositions between these two points form stable mixtures of crystals and liquid along the straight line between B and the point L_2. (The liquid cannot have any composition other than that of L_2, because any other lines representing B and coexisting liquids would intersect the liquid curve at two points with higher values of G.) For all compositions richer in A than L_2, the liquid has a lower free energy and is therefore the only stable phase.

At a lower temperature, T_3, A is now stable and coexists with a liquid defined by the tangent at L_{3A}, and two crystal-liquid assemblages are possible, one for compositions between A and L_{3A} and another between B and L_{3B}. Intermediate compositions are still all liquid. At T_4, the temperature of the eutectic E, the straight line between A and B is exactly tangent to the liquid curve at the composition of the eutectic, so that A, B, and the eutectic liquid coexist in equilibrium. At any lower temperature, such as T_5, the solid is stable for all compositions.

The two-component system (Fig. 3–8) can also be depicted in terms of heat content (enthalpy, H), just as the one-component system was in Figure 3–3. Because the two end-members have different thermal properties (C_P, S, and ΔH_F), the rates of temperature change and crystallization or melting for a given gain or loss of heat will depend on the rate of change of enthalpy and the proportions of the two components.

Crystallization, melting, and assimilation

Crystallization and melting in a simple two-component system with a eutectic can be illustrated by Figure 3–9. In tracing the following examples, it will be helpful to refer back to Figures 3–8a and b and observe how the behavior is expressed in terms of free energy and enthalpy.

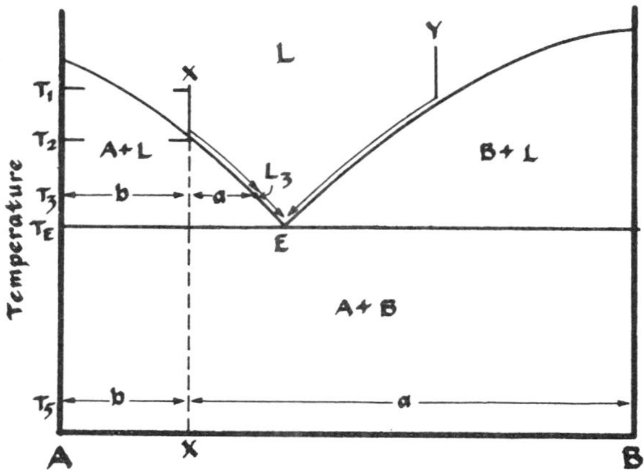

Figure 3–9 Crystallization and melting relations in a simple, two-component system with a eutectic. The proportions of phases at different temperatures can be measured by the lever rule (Fig. 3–7). For example, at T_3, the bulk composition, X, consists of crystals of A and liquid L_3 in the proportions of a to b. At T_4 the bulk composition consists entirely of crystals of A and B in the proportions a to b.

Any intermediate liquid, such as X, at an initial temperature T_1, will not begin to crystallize until it cools to T_2, at which point its chemical potential is equal to that of crystalline A, and it begins to precipitate that phase. With removal of heat, crystals of A are formed, and the liquid is residually enriched in B. The composition of the cooling liquid follows a course down the liquidus until it reaches the eutectic at E. At that point the liquid has been so enriched in B that it is saturated with both A and B, and, if more heat is removed, the liquid will crystallize those two minerals without changing temperature or composition until the last drop of liquid is gone. Only then will the temperature of the system decline again below T_E. A similar course would be followed for a liquid Y except that it would crystallize B first, and A would only appear at the eutectic.

In systems of this kind, the course of melting is simply the reverse of crystallization. If heat is added to a mixture of crystals of A and B with the proportions of X, the temperature rises until melting begins at T_E, and an initial liquid forms with eutectic composition E. Melting continues at constant temperature until the last crystal of B disappears, at which time crystalline A is still present. With further addition of heat, the temperature rises, more of A melts, and the liquid is enriched in A as it follows the path of the liquidus upward. When the last crystal of A disappears at T_2, the liquid has the composition of the original crystalline mixture, and any additional heat merely raises the temperature of the liquid.

The effect of contamination can be seen if we consider two simple cases. Suppose first that a very small crystal of B, already at temperature T_3, is added to a large volume of liquid L_3 that has evolved by cooling and crystallization of the original liquid X. Because the liquid is undersaturated with B, the crystal will dissolve. Note that this tends to shift the liquid toward B, but this is impossible as long as the liquid is in contact with crystals of A. If the process is isothermal, a small amount of A may dissolve and, by contributing that component to the liquid, maintain the original composition L_3. Solution of the crystalline phases is endothermic, however, and would tend to lower the temperature.

Suppose, now, that the added crystals were solid A, initially at a temperature lower than T_3. The crystal would be chemically stable, because the liquid is saturated with that phase, but it absorbs heat from the rest of the system and lowers its temperature. This causes more A to crystallize from the saturated liquid, which becomes poorer in A, the component that was added to it. The bulk composition, of course, must shift slightly toward A.

The effect of pressure is illustrated in Figure 3–10. The liquidus curves in the two-dimensional diagram become curved surfaces in a three-dimensional diagram for T, X, and P, and the point E becomes the line of intersection of the two liquidus surfaces. The effect of pressure may differ for the two components and cause the eutectic to migrate toward one or the other as it rises in temperature.

The Phase Rule can be applied to such a two-component system, but we now have a third intensive variable, X, the composition of the liquid, which adds another possible degree of freedom. For example, in Figure 3–10 the three-dimensional space above the two liquidus surfaces represents the conditions under which a single liquid phase can vary independently in temperature, pressure, and composition, so that

$$F = C - P + 2 = 2 - 1 + 2 = 3$$

On the liquidus surfaces where crystals coexist with a liquid, temperature, pressure, or composition can all vary, but fixing two of these determines the third. The assemblage has two degrees of freedom, and the liquidus surface is said to be divariant. At the intersection of the two surfaces, three phases, A, B, and liquid, coexist, but if any of the three variables T, P, or X, changes, the other two must also change in a proscribed way to remain in the linear axis of the trough. The system is therefore univariant. An invariant condition, which would be represented by a point, is possible if a fourth phase, such as a vapor, is in equilibrium with the liquid and crystalline A and B.

In the region below the eutectic temperature where only crystals of A and B are present, it would appear that there are three degrees of freedom, T, P, and X. But for two components and two phases the phase rule indicates that there

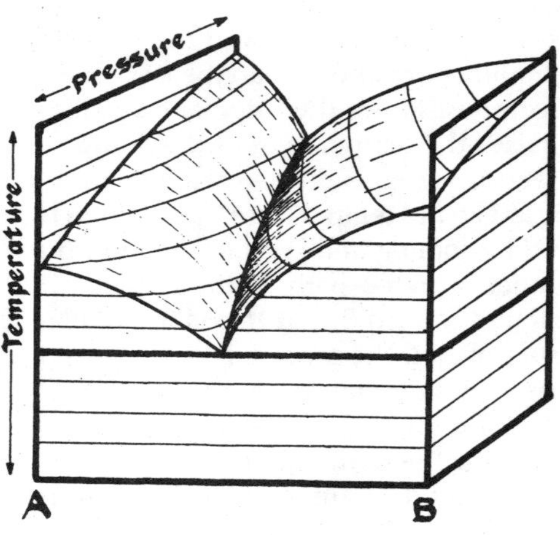

Figure 3–10 Perspective view of the three-dimensional form of a T–P–X diagram for a two-component system with a eutectic.

should be only two (F = 2 − 2 + 2 = 2). The explanation of this apparent anomaly lies in the fact that in this region there is no liquid, and X, the ratio of two crystalline phases, is not an intensive variable but merely an extensive one. With only two degrees of freedom, T and P, and two phases, A and B, the phase rule is still valid. Similar reasoning applies to the volumes representing A + liquid and B + liquid under the liquidus surfaces and above the temperature of the eutectic. Having three dimensions, these volumes appear to have three degrees of freedom, T, P, and X, so that, again, the phase rule seems to give 3 = 2 − 2 + 2. But no liquids can have a composition and temperature within the limits defining this space; it is occupied only by mixtures of crystals and liquids, and since a variation of the proportions of these phases is not an intensive variable, F is only 2 (T and P).

Systems with an intermediate compound

If two components have an intermediate crystalline form, the relations resemble those of two individual eutectic systems. For example, if two end-members, A and B, have an intermediate compound, AB, each adjacent pair can be treated as a binary system (Fig. 3–11).

If the melting temperature of one of the end-members is very high, its liquidus may override part of the liquidus of the intermediate compound. This condition is illustrated in Figure 3–12a. Note that, on heating, AB cannot melt directly to a liquid of its own composition, because its melting temperature is below the liquidus of A. Instead, it melts *incongruently* to a liquid, R, and crystals, A, neither of which has the same composition as the original material.

What happens on melting is this: as heat is added to crystals of AB, they reach the temperature T_R and begin to form a liquid, not of composition AB but of R (Fig. 3–12b). At the same time the crystals are converted to the form and composition of crystalline A. This process continues as more heat is added, and, when the last crystal of AB disappears, the assemblage, still at temperature T_R, consists of liquid of composition R and crystals of A. Then, as more heat is

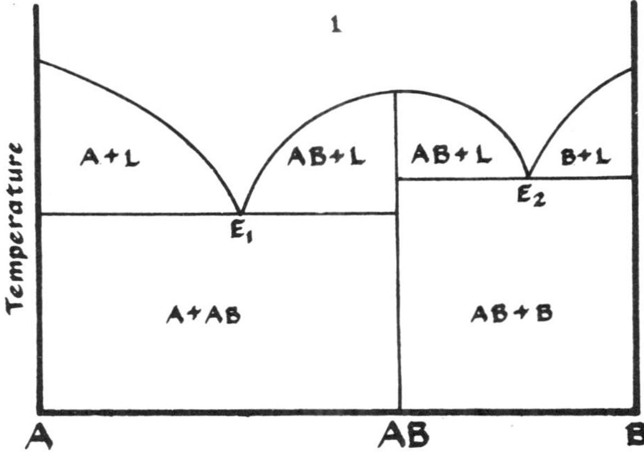

Figure 3–11 A two-component system with an intermediate compound, AB, that melts congruently to a liquid of its own composition.

added, the crystals of A begin to melt, the liquid becomes richer in A, and the temperature rises. At T_2, the last crystal of A disappears, and the liquid has the original composition of AB. The process on cooling is the reverse.

The most interesting effects in such a system are those of compositions between A and AB. A liquid X, for example, crystallizes A on cooling and is enriched in B as it does so. Although the low-temperature crystalline assemblage should consist of A and AB, the liquid that evolves during crystallization of A must eventually reach a composition R between AB and B before AB can start to form. If liquid R were to crystallize independently, it would first precipitate AB and finally AB + B. But if earlier-formed crystals of A are present, this would result in a violation of the phase rule. Although the system has three crystalline phases, the number of components is only two, because that is the minimum number necessary to define all compositions in the system. Hence the assemblage of three crystalline phases, A, AB, and B, is incompatible with a two-component system with two

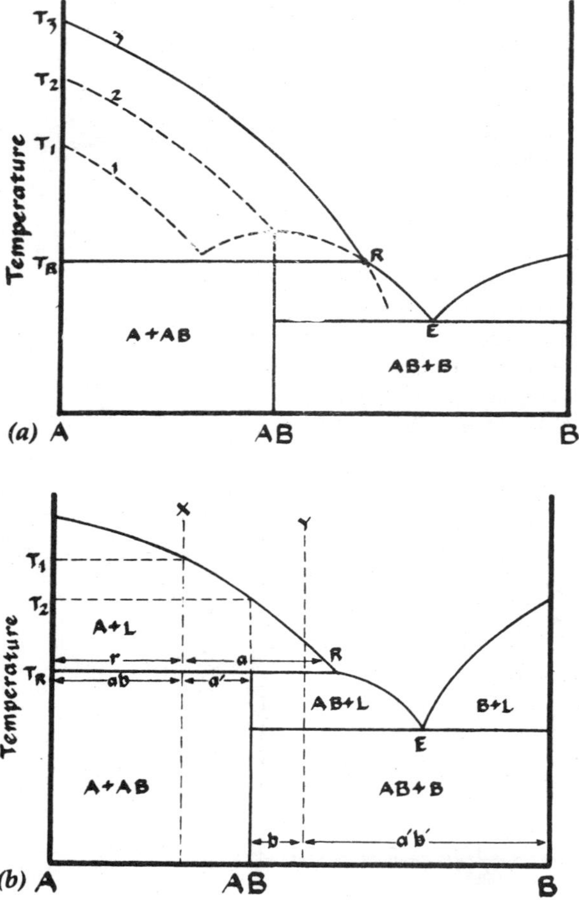

Figure 3–12 (a) Liquidus relations in a two-component system with an intermediate compound, AB, that melts incongruently. Note that as the liquidi of increasingly refractory forms of A rise in temperature from condition 1 to 3 their intersections with the liquidus of AB change from a eutectic to a reaction point, R. When AB rises in temperature under condition 3, the first liquid forms at R where the liquidus of A intersects that of AB. The temperature cannot rise above T_R as long as AB is still present, because the liquidus of AB passes below the liquidus of A, making AB unstable at higher temperatures. AB must dissolve at the same time that A crystallizes before the temperature can rise. The reverse holds for cooling and crystallization. A liquid with the composition of AB will first crystallize A and continue to do so until it intersects the liquidus of AB at R. At any lower temperature, the liquidus of A falls below that of AB, so that only the latter is stable, and earlier-formed crystals of A must dissolve as AB crystallizes. (b) Crystal liquid relations in a two-component system with an intermediate compound that melts incongruently. See text for discussion.

degrees of freedom, T and P, in the low-temperature region. In other words, A and B cannot coexist in equilibrium without forming AB.

The liquid R cannot continue to crystallize down to the eutectic E under equilibrium conditions so long as crystals of A are present. Instead, it reacts with some of the earlier-formed crystals, dissolving them while forming new crystals of AB. Even though the heat consumed in dissolving A is gained by crystallizing AB, and the temperature remains constant, heat must be removed from the system as a whole, because the amount of AB that crystallizes is more than equivalent to the amount of A that is dissolved. If it were not, the composition of the liquid would become richer in A than the composition of R, an obvious impossibility that is prevented by crystallization of additional AB.

The proportions of phases involved in this reaction can be determined by means of the lever rule. When the liquid first reaches R, it contains liquid and crystals in the proportions r and a respectively. As reaction proceeds, liquid is consumed in forming AB in an amount proportional to ab; a is reduced to a′, and r is converted to ab; and the final proportions of minerals are those of the starting composition X.

A liquid Y with a composition between AB and B but richer in AB than R would first crystallize A. But for such a composition, the final equilibrium assemblage of crystals of bulk composition Y must be made up of only AB and B in the proportions a′b′ and b respectively. Although crystals of A are formed initially, they are entirely consumed by reaction to form AB when the liquid reaches R. After they disappear, a quantity of liquid still remains and continues crystallizing AB until the eutectic is reached and B is formed.

If such a liquid were to crystallize under natural conditions, equilibrium might not be achieved, and reaction of the liquid with early-formed crystals might not go to completion. If, for example, the crystals of A form on the floor or walls of a magma chamber and are buried there as more crystals accumulate, the remaining liquid may cool without access to the earlier crystals. In this case, it will cool and pause at R only long enough to consume those crystals to which it is exposed before going on to precipitate AB down to the eutectic where it will crystallize B along with AB. The end result is an assemblage of three crystalline phases, one of which would not have crystallized under equilibrium conditions. More important, the course of evolution of the liquid was greatly extended.

Comparison of such a system with one without incongruent melting shows several important differences. In Figure 3–11, in which a eutectic lies between each pair of crystalline phases, the course of any liquid is fixed; it must reach its appropriate eutectic. The high melting temperature of AB forms a thermal barrier resembling a divide at a watershed, and, just as a drop of rain falling on the west side of the Continental Divide must ultimately reach the Pacific Ocean, a liquid only slightly richer in A than pure AB must reach the eutectic E_1, where A crystallizes. Two liquids that are initially very close in composition but on opposite sides of the thermal divide must diverge in composition as they crystallize. A similar relation holds for melting. An assemblage of crystals of AB containing even a trace amount of A will begin to melt at E_1 and form a liquid that is very different from E_2, the first liquid to form from an assemblage of AB with a small amount of B. This simple relation illustrates an important aspect of igneous differentiation, namely that liquids of very different compositions can result from crystallization or melting of very similar starting compositions if the system has two eutectics separated by a thermal divide.

This is not to say that a thermal divide is essential to the evolution of widely differentiated liquids. A similar difference can result from crystallization in systems in which an intermediate compound melts incongruently and does not constitute a thermal divide. In systems of this latter type (Fig. 3–12), we saw that, when equilibrium is not maintained and reaction is incomplete, liquids can evolve through much greater ranges of composition than they would with complete reaction, and the final assemblage may differ from that expected from equilibrium crystallization and reaction.

Systems with solid solution

Few igneous minerals are simple compounds; most are composed of two or more end-members that substitute for each other through a continuous range of compositions known as a solid-solution series. Plagioclase and olivine are important examples.

Because minerals of a solid-solution series are not simply mechanical mixtures of their end members, but, as their name implies, are more like liquid solutions in which the components are combined in an intermediate composition, their free energy varies in a non-linear way with composition. The entropy of intermediate compositions is greater, so that the free energy of intermediate compositions is less than that of the end-members (Fig. 3–13).

Crystallization of minerals of this kind differs from that of crystals of fixed composition. The higher-melting component in an intermediate liquid is below its pure melting temperature when crystallization begins, but the low-melting end-member is not. The higher-melting component is therefore favored by the solid phase, whereas the low-melting one tends to be concentrated in the liquid. For this reason two separate curves, a *liquidus* and a *solidus*, are required to define the compositions of crystals and liquids that coexist at a given temperature. The curves for this "solid-solution loop" can be calculated in a manner similar to that of the simple system with a binary eutectic, but the equations are more complex.

$$\ln \frac{x'}{x} = \frac{\Delta H_A}{R}\left(\frac{1}{T_A} - \frac{1}{T}\right) \tag{3–27a}$$

$$\ln \frac{1 - x'}{1 - x} = \frac{\Delta H_B}{R}\left(\frac{1}{T_B} - \frac{1}{T}\right) \tag{3–27b}$$

x′ and x are the molar fractions of the high-temperature end-member in the liquid and crystals respectively, and ΔH_A and ΔH_B are the heats of crystallization of the high- and low-temperature end-members respectively. T_A and T_B are the melting temperatures of the pure end-members.

Consider an intermediate liquid, such as X in Figure 3–14, cooling from an initial temperature above the liquidus. On reaching temperature T_2, it precipitates crystals of composition m which, because they differ from the liquid, cause the liquid to change composition as the temperature falls and more crystals grow from the liquid. At a lower temperature, T_3, the composition of both the liquid and the crystals in equilibrium with it have changed and are now richer in B. The earlier-formed crystals are poorer in B than the equilibrium composition and, if conditions favor equilibration, they will be changed to the new composition by reacting with the liquid. Under ideal conditions, this equilibration process keeps pace with cooling, so that at all stages the crystals have a uniform composition and, when the temperature reaches T_4, the last drop of liquid is consumed, and all the crystals have the composition of the original liquid, X.

Under conditions that prevent complete reaction, early-formed crystals do not equilibrate with the evolving liquid and are not made over to new composi-

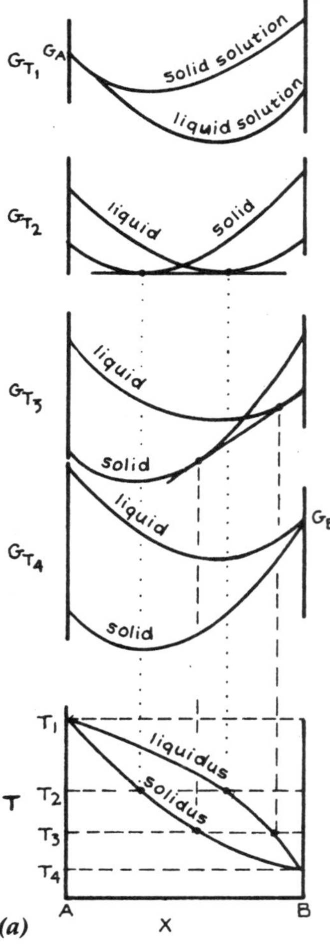

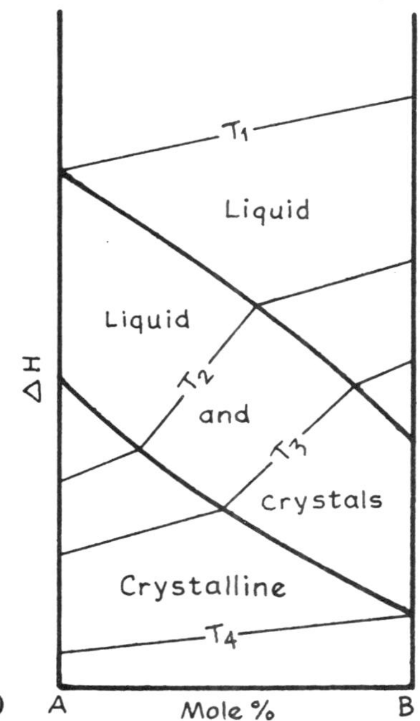

Figure 3-13 (a) G–X and crystal-liquid relations in a two-component system with a complete range of solid solution between the two end-members. (After S. A. Morse, 1980, *Basalts and Phase Diagrams*, 91.) (b) An H–X diagram for the same system shows temperature as a function of enthalpy and composition. Because the thermal properties of the end-members differ, the temperature contours are not horizontal, and the amount of cooling and crystallization or melting for a given input or loss of heat differs according to the proportions of the two components. (Adapted from H. S. Yoder, Jr. 1976. *Generation of Basaltic Magma*. Nat. Acad. Sci. 265 pp.)

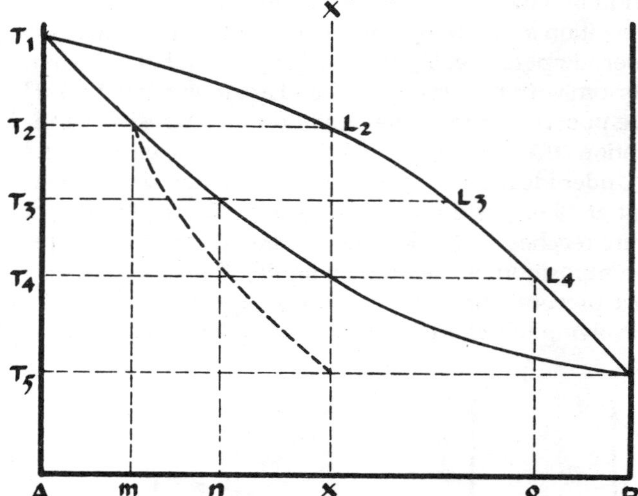

Figure 3–14 Crystallization and melting relations in a two-component system with a complete range of solid solution. See text for discussion.

tions. Less of the low-temperature form, B, is extracted from the liquid to re-equilibrate early crystals, and, instead, the residual liquid is more strongly enriched in B. When this happens, liquid still remains when the temperature reaches T_4, and crystallization may continue, with the final liquid reaching the composition of pure B. The resulting crystals are zoned from cores of composition m to rims of B, and their average composition follows the course shown by the curved broken line.

In nature, the course of crystallization is normally between these two extremes. Olivine tends to equilibrate well and has little zoning, because reaction requires only an exchange of Mg and Fe ions. Plagioclase, however, can only equilibrate by a paired exchange of Ca for Na and Al for Si. Both of these latter ions are strongly bound in large framework structures and diffuse so slowly that equilibration is possible only in very slowly cooled magmas. For this reason, zoning is much more common in plagioclase than in other solid-solution minerals.

For homogeneous, unzoned, solid-solution crystals, the course of melting with rising temperature is essentially the reverse of equilibrium crystallization, provided, of course, that equilibrium is maintained between the crystals and liquid. The first liquid formed from crystals of composition x in Figure 3–14 has composition L_4, and with rising temperature the crystals and liquid change composition along the solidus and liquidus curves. The last crystal, now made over to composition m, disappears when the liquid reaches composition L_2. With incomplete equilibration, however, the effect of melting is the opposite of that during crystallization; it reduces the range of temperature between the completely crystalline and liquid states. The crystals, if they fail to equilibrate, are richer in the low-melting component and disappear completely at a lower temperature than they would if they were able to adjust their composition to the rising temperature.

Zoning can have an important effect on both crystallization and melting. We have seen that crystallization without reaction produces zoned crystals and drives the residual liquid to compositions much richer in the low-temperature component, B, than one evolving under equilibrium conditions with complete reaction. In the same way, the first liquid produced by melting of zoned crystals will be richer in B and appear at a lower temperature than one resulting from melting of unzoned crystals of the same average composition.

The effects of contamination can be seen by considering an intermediate liquid, such as L_3. If crystals are added with a composition, such as m, which would be precipitated at an earlier stage of crystallization, they tend to react with the liquid, depleting it slightly in B in order to attain the equilibrium composition, *n*, for the liquid at T_3. This reaction tends to drive the liquid to the left of the liquidus composition, L_3, and causes it to precipitate additional crystals of *n*, in order to maintain the composition appropriate for that temperature. If, on the other hand, the added crystals have a composition, such as *o*, which would only be precipitated later in the course of cooling, those crystals are unstable in L_3 and tend to dissolve and make the liquid slightly richer in B. As a result, some of the earlier-formed crystals on *n* are dissolved, and the liquid maintains its composition appropriate for temperature T_3. Note that the first process is exothermic; it shifts the bulk composition slightly toward the high-temperature component A and reduces the range of crystallization on subsequent cooling. The second is endothermic; the added crystals shift the liquid toward the low-temperature end and tend to extend the range of possible liquids produced during cooling.

Systems with limited solid solution

In many minerals that form a solid-solution series, the crystal structure of the end-members may differ to the extent that the amount of substitution of one component in the other has a limited compositional range. This is the case, for example, in the monoclinic and orthorhombic pyroxenes and in the monoclinic and triclinic feldspars. This type of two-component system with limited solid solution has the form shown in Figure 3–15a. It has a temperature minimum at M between two solid-solution loops. The point M differs from the eutectic of a binary system without solid solution in that liquids reach such a composition only under conditions of strong fractionation, i.e., when crystals and liquid are separated and prevented from equilibrating. In a binary system without solid solution they must always reach the eutectic, but with solid solution they do so only under certain conditions, as when no reaction takes place between the liquid and early-formed crystals. In a similar way, the first liquid produced by melting has a composition corresponding to the temperature minimum only if the crystals have this exact composition in their outermost layers. Otherwise the first liquid is higher on the liquidus curve at a composition appropriate for that of the crystals.

Solid solution between two species of differing crystal structure decreases with falling temperature, so that a crystal that is homogeneous at high temperature may separate into two structurally and compositionally different forms. This

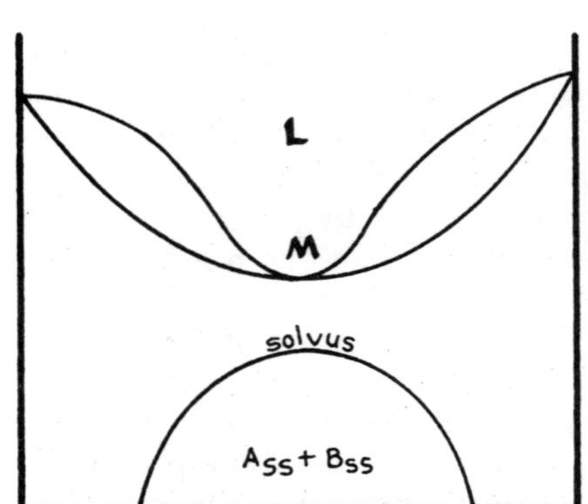

(a)

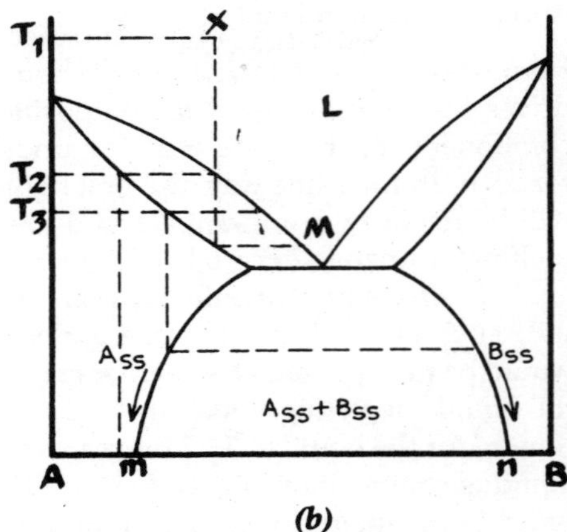

(b)

Figure 3–15 Two-component system with limited solid solution between the end members. In (a) the solvus defining the compositions of coexisting crystals is completely below both solidus curves, whereas in (b) it intersects them. Note the different forms of the temperature minimum in (a) and (b). This difference can be understood if the phase rule is used to test the conditions at the temperature minimum. In (a), where the minimum liquid coexists with only one crystalline phase, F = 2 − 2 + 2 = 2, and the minimum must be a divariant surface extending back in the third dimension, pressure. In (b), the liquid coexists with two crystalline phases, A_{ss} and B_{ss}, and F = 2 − 3 + 2 = 1, so that, in three dimensions, the minimum is a univariant line.

may take place well below the solidus, as in Figure 3–15a, or in the range of crystallization, as in Figure 3–15b. The boundary curve defining the limits of solid solution is known as a solvus and encloses a region in which the bulk composition can only be made up of two coexisting solid phases.

A liquid of composition X, cooling to temperature T_2, initially crystallizes the composition *m* which, if no reaction takes place, would cool without intersecting the solvus and have a homogeneous composition. As the remaining liquid migrates down the liquidus, it eventually precipitates crystals with compositions richer in B than *m*, and these, when they intersect the solvus on cooling, exsolve increasing amounts of phase B. In the case where the solidus curves do not intersect the solvus (Fig. 3–15a), crystal fractionation can drive the liquid to the temperature minimum at M, where a single phase of intermediate composition will crystallize and split into two forms, A_{SS} and B_{SS}, only when it cools to the solvus. In the case where the solidus is low enough to intersect the solvus (Fig. 3–15b), the two separate forms will crystallize simultaneously from a liquid at the eutectic, and on cooling each will exsolve the other as they become progressively purer with falling temperature. This behavior is an important feature of crystallization of pyroxenes and alkali feldspars.

Systems with Immiscibility

In some compositional ranges, the limits of complete mixing may extend above the liquidus into the liquid region. Two liquids may form physically distinct phases that resemble oil and water in that they will not mix to form intermediate compositions. This phenomemon, long thought to have only limited significance in geology, has recently been shown to extend to geologically reasonable compositions and conditions and is an important factor in the evolution of certain types of magmas.

The cause of immiscibility can be visualized in terms of the form of the free-energy relations of certain non-ideal liquids (Fig. 3–16a). Instead of having a form that is concave upward throughout the entire range of compositions, as it is in ideal liquids, the free-energy of a non-ideal liquid may be higher in the intermediate range of compositions than that of liquids somewhat richer in the end-member components. Thus the intermediate liquid will be less stable than two coexisting liquids and will spit into two conjugate compositions.

A possible binary relation is shown in Figure 3–16b. A liquid X cooling from a temperature such as T_1 begins to split when it reaches the two-liquid field at T_2, and with further cooling the two coexisting liquids diverge in composition. At temperature T_3, crystals of A begin to grow from liquid L_1, and the proportion of liquid L_1 diminishes while that of L_2 increases. Only when L_1 disappears completely can liquid L_2 crystallize A and continue its descent to lower temperatures.

Note that at T_3 the crystals of A formed from liquid L_1 are also in equilibrium with liquid L_2, because the liquids themselves are in equilibrium. (If two phases are in equilibrium, and one of the two is also in equilibrium with a third, so too is the other.) This relation provides a rigorous test for immiscibility: two magmas cannot have an immiscible relation if both are not in equilibrium with the same minerals.

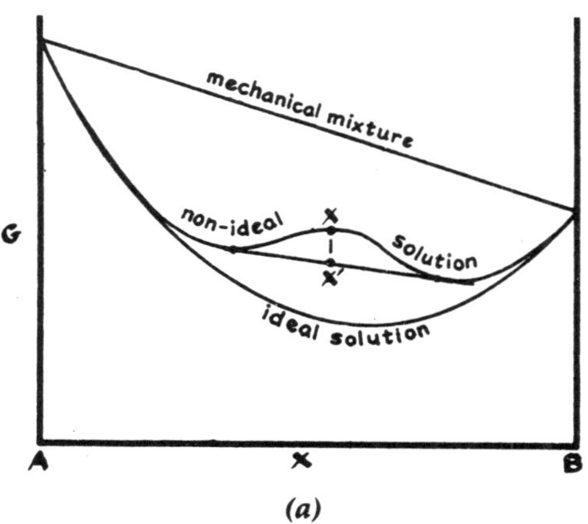

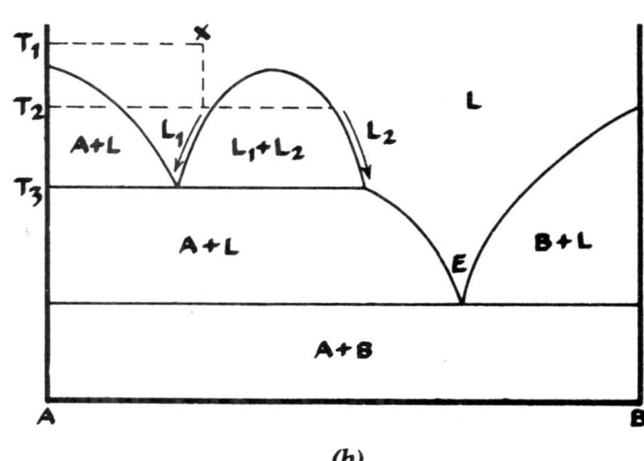

Figure 3–16 (a) G–X relations for a non-ideal liquid that is immiscible in its middle range of composition. Note that the free energy of a mixture, X′, of two liquids is lower than that of a single liquid X. (b) A possible phase diagram for a two-component system in which a field of immiscibility intersects the liquidus of one of the crystalline phases, A.

THREE-COMPONENT SYSTEMS

The basic principles we observed in two-component systems still hold when another component is added, but their graphical representation in phase diagrams becomes more restricted. Addition of another component requires that we sacrifice one of the variables when we plot the compositions on a two-dimensional diagram.

Geometrical relations

If the three components, A, B, and C, are plotted in a triangle, such as Figure 3–17a, the compositional range of the liquidus of each mineral, which was a curve in the binary system, now becomes a surface. Temperature can be shown by contours on the liquidus surface, so that the interior of the triangle resembles a topographic relief map on which the field boundaries correspond to stream courses down valleys (Fig. 3–17b).

Points such as E are commonly referred to as quadruple points, because they correspond to compositions where four phases—three crystalline and one liq-

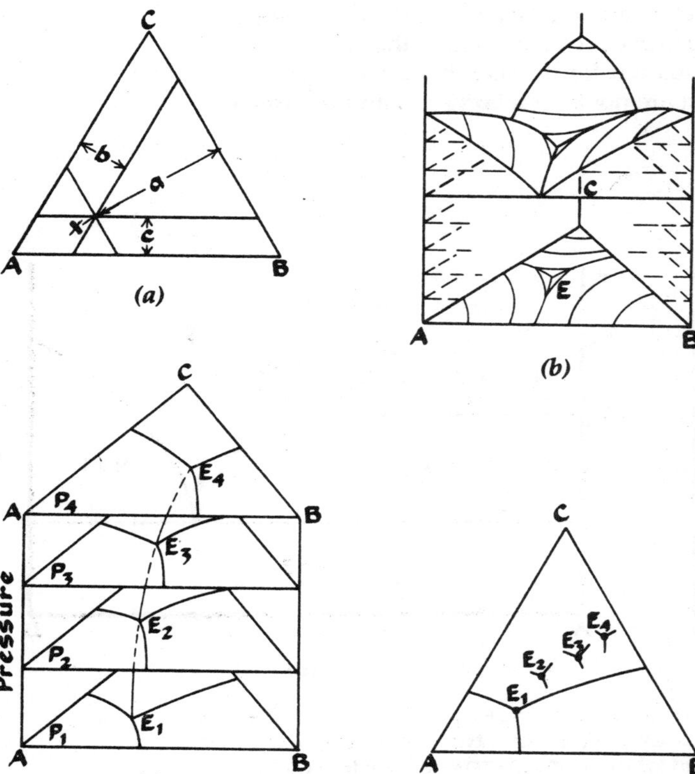

Figure 3–17 Geometrical relations for diagrams depicting three-component systems. In (a) a composition X has the proportions of A, B, and C shown by the lengths of the lines a, b, and c respectively. (b) shows the three-dimensional form of a prism, in which temperature is the vertical axis. The liquidus surfaces descend toward the interior of the triangle and can be contoured like the sides of valleys. The base of the figure shows these contours projected onto a two-dimensional surface. The effect of pressure can be shown in a series of diagrams, each for a different pressure, as in (c). If the boundaries of the fields are projected onto a single plane, their intersections at successive pressures can be shown as in (d).

uid—can coexist. (The vapor phase is usually ignored in "condensed systems.") We see from the phase rule that, with three components and four phases, there can be only one degree of freedom. But since all three variables, temperature, pressure, and composition, cannot be shown in a single two-dimensional diagram, it is necessary to illustrate this relation in a series of diagrams (Fig. 3–17c).

Systems with a eutectic

The simplest case is that in which a eutectic falls between the three components (Fig. 3–18a). A composition X in the primary field of A crystallizes that mineral when it reaches the liquidus temperature, and, as A is removed, the course of the liquid crosses the field away from A. It descends across temperature contours until it intersects the field boundary at d, at which point it begins to crystallize an additional mineral, B. As this phase is now removed along with A, the liquid takes a new direction down the thermal valley toward the ternary eutectic, E, where C joins the crystallizing phases. The curve followed by the crystallizing liquid is more properly called a *cotectic*, because it defines the course of liquids precipitating two phases together. Its shape is determined by the proportions of crystals A and B that are being separated at any particular temperature; if this proportion is constant, it is straight line; if not, it curves away from the phase being removed in greater quantities. Thus, the proportions of crystals being removed at any stage can be determined by projecting a tangent to the cotectic curve from the composition of the liquid, e, back to f, and by applying the lever rule to determine the proportions of crystallizing phases. In this example, the ratio of A to B is as fB is to fA. The composition of the total assemblage of crystals precipitated between X and e is obtained by projecting a straight line from the liquid e back through the original bulk composition X to the point g. The proportion of the remaining liquid to crystals at this stage will be as gx is to ex, and ex is

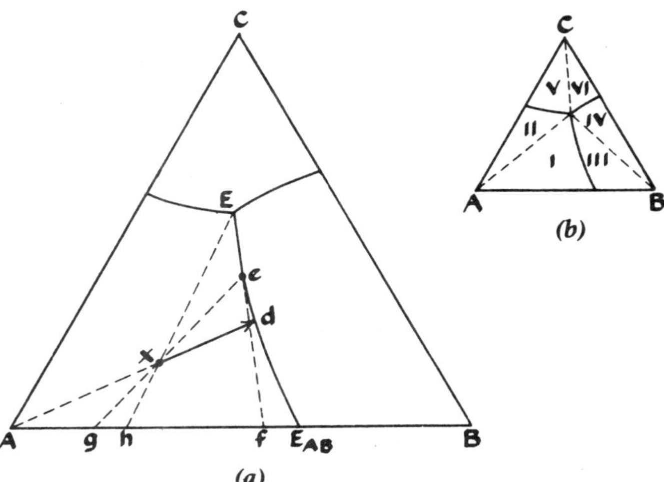

Figure 3–18 A typical three-component system with a eutectic is illustrated in (a). The course of crystallization of liquid X will be A, A + B, and A + B + C. A total of six different orders of crystallization can be defined for liquid compositions in the fields I through VI in (b).

composed of A and B in the proportions gB to gA. When the liquid reaches its final composition at the eutectic, E, and C begins to crystallize, the proportion of liquid will be hX and the crystals EX. As C is removed along with A and B, the bulk composition of the crystals moves from h toward X and will reach X at the instant the last drop of liquid disappears. The composition of the liquid, of course, does not change after reaching E.

By inspection, we can see various possible paths of crystallization for compositions within the triangle ABC. All compositions in the primary field of A (I and II of Fig. 3–18b) will crystallize that mineral first, but in field I the next mineral will be B, then C, while in II, C will appear before B.

In melting, the process is simply the reverse of the one we have just followed for crystallization, provided the liquid and crystals are not separated as melting advances. Under conditions of crystal-liquid segregation, however, a very different sequence of liquids is obtained. We saw that crystallization produces a continuous series of liquids from the initial composition X to d and finally to E, and, if no phases react with the liquid, the course would not be altered if crystals were completely removed as soon as they formed. This is not true of melting. A crystalline assemblage of composition X would begin to melt with an initial liquid E, but if that liquid is removed as quickly as it forms, an abrupt discontinuity will occur when the last crystal of C is consumed. The only crystals remaining are now A and B, and the temperature must rise until it reaches that of the eutectic between those two minerals before a new liquid of that composition is formed. If the same process continues, and the liquid is removed as soon as it forms, B will eventually disappear, and the next liquid will have the composition and melting temperature of pure A. This process is known as *fractional melting;* its significance will become apparent when we come to consider processes of magma generation in a later chapter.

Systems with an intermediate compound

Ternary systems with an intermediate compound that melts congruently (Fig. 3–19a) can be treated as two separate ternary systems separated by a thermal divide. They have many of the features of the corresponding binary systems. The join between C and AB divides the system into two parts, each with its end point at a eutectic, and compositions crystallizing on one side of that division have no way of crossing to the other.

As in the binary system, a mineral that melts incongruently may cause a liquid to crystallize a phase that is not an equilibrium component of the original composition at low temperatures. In Figure 3–19b, the mineral AB melts incongruently, so that instead of a eutectic within the triangle A–AB–C a reaction curve, or *peritectic*, rR, and a reaction point, R, fall within the triangle AB–B–C.

It is a simple matter to distinguish a reaction point from a eutectic, even if a diagram has no temperature contours. Note that in Figure 3–19a, temperatures always decline along the cotectic curves in the directions indicated by arrows away from the line joining the two phases that are crystallizing. In the same way, temperature must fall along the entire curve from R toward E, because the two

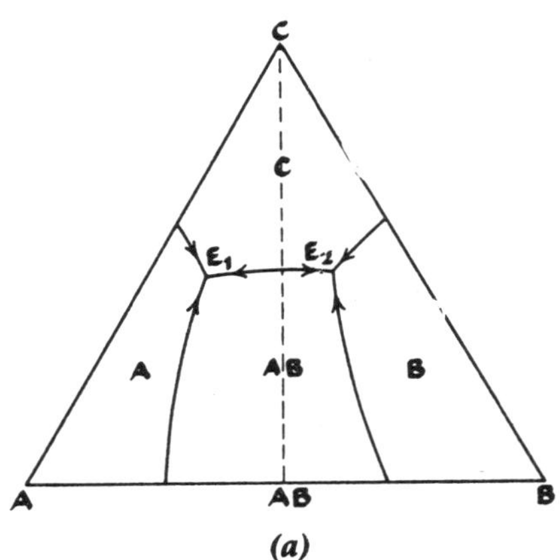

(a)

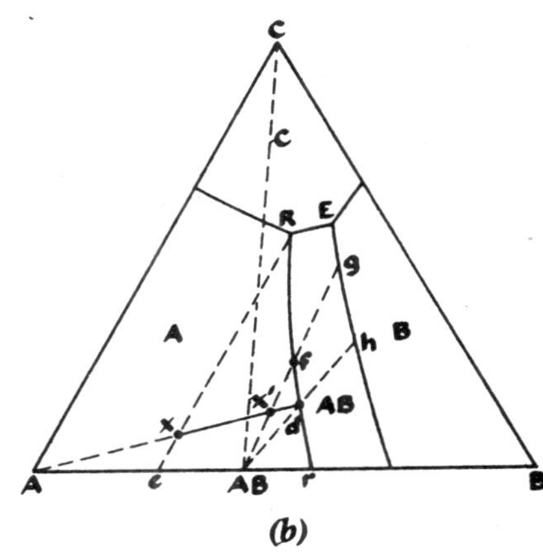

(b)

Figure 3–19 (a) A three-component system with an intermediate compound, AB, that melts congruently, has two eutectics, and can be treated as two independent, three-component systems. (b) A three-component system with an intermediate compound, AB, that melts incongruently can be recognized by the fact that the boundary between the fields of two crystalline phases (A and AB) does not fall within the triangle of which those phases are corners (A–AB–C) but outside it, in AB–B–C. Instead of two eutectics, as in (a), the system has one eutectic and a reaction point, R.

phases crystallizing on that curve, AB and C, are joined by a line that lies to the left of R and does not intersect the curve. If the line AB-C intersects the curve, as it does in Figure 3–19a, the temperature falls in both directions away from that intersection toward both E_1 and E_2.

Even though crystallization drives the course of a liquid X outside the subtriangle A–AB–C, the final crystalline product must consist of A, AB, and C if equilibrium prevails. Similarly, even though a liquid, such as X′, initially crystallizes A, the fact that it is not in the triangle having A as a corner indicates that the final equilibrium assemblage of crystals cannot include that mineral. The way this comes about will be clear if we trace the course of crystallization of these two liquids.

First consider liquid X. The first mineral to appear is A, and removal of A drives the composition of the liquid along the course XX′d. When the liquid reaches d, the proportion of liquid to crystalline A, by the lever rule, is AX to Xd. As it follows a course along the boundary with the field of AB toward R, the liquid precipitates AB, but its composition cannot stay on the boundary curve unless A is dissolved; removal of AB or any combination of AB and A would drive the liquid away from those compositions and off the curve. As in the binary system, crystals of A are dissolved at the same time that AB is being crystallized, and the vector that determines the course of the liquid has one component away from AB and another toward A, so that the resulting vector of the liquid composition coincides with a tangent to the curve at d. A boundary of this kind is known as a *reaction curve,* or *peritectic.*

As the liquid descends toward R the composition of the total crystalline assemblage, which is obtained by projecting from the liquid composition back through the total original composition X to an intersection with the join A–AB, migrates toward AB. When the liquid reaches R, C begins to crystallize, and the composition of the crystals leaves the join A–AB and follows a course along eX, until the last drop of liquid R is consumed and the crystal assemblage has a composition X.

If the original liquid composition were X′, the course of crystallization would be similar until the liquid reaches f. At that point the crystalline assemblage has reached AB, and A is entirely consumed. From that point on, the liquid can only crystallize AB and must leave the boundary curve and move across the field of AB until it intersects another field boundary at a point such as g. The liquid then crystallizes AB and B as it descends toward E. At E, C begins to crystallize, and the final crystalline assemblage is composed of AB, B, and C in the proportions of X′.

Both of these examples assume complete reaction and re-equilibration of early-formed A along the peritectic. If reaction is prevented, the liquids would not follow the peritectic but would immediately cross it at d and take a new course from d to h as they crystallize AB. On reaching h, B begins to crystallize, sending the liquids down to an end point at the eutectic E.

Systems with solid solution

A ternary system in which two of the components form a solid-solution series cannot have a ternary eutectic. Instead, a boundary curve divides the system into two fields, as shown in Figure 3–20. A liquid with an initial composition X is equivalent to a crystalline assemblage of C and an intermediate solid solution of AB, having the composition S_3. If crystallized under ideal conditions, the final product will have this mineral composition.

Because the composition of the solid-solution crystals in equilibrium with liquid X must be richer in the high-temperature component, B, than the liquid, the first crystals to form have a composition such as S_1. With falling temperature, the

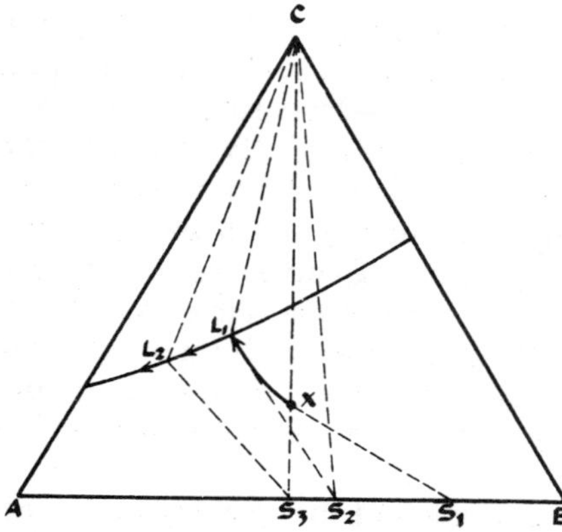

Figure 3–20 A three-component system in which two components, A and B, have a complete range of solid solution. See text for discussion.

liquid follows a curving course toward the field boundary, and at any instant the course of the liquid is directly away from the composition of AB that is currently being removed. Because the crystals of AB are steadily becoming richer in A and moving from S_1 toward S_3, the course of the liquid is concave away from A. When the liquid reaches the cotectic field boundary, C appears and crystallizes along with AB as the liquid moves toward the temperature minimum between A and C. The sides of the triangle L_1–C–S_2 join the three coexisting phases, and the bulk composition of the system must fall within its boundaries.

With complete reaction, early-formed crystals of AB, such as S_1, are made over to a composition in equilibrium with the changing liquid. At the instant the last drop of liquid, L_2, disappears, it will be precipitating C together with AB of composition S_3. The bulk composition falls on the join between C and S_3 and is composed of those components in the proportions S_3X and CX, respectively. Every liquid starting in the field AB has a unique path that cannot be determined from the ternary diagram alone. If there is no reaction between the liquid and early-formed crystals, A is removed at a slower rate, and the liquid has a straighter path across the field. With extreme fractionation, it can descend to the temperature minimum between A and C.

Systems with a field of immiscibility

The course of crystallization of a three-component system that includes a field of immiscibility (Fig. 3-21) is similar to that of the corresponding binary system. A liquid with an initial composition, X, first crystallizes A and moves away from that component until it intersects the two-liquid field. It then splits into two liquids, L_1 and L_2, the compositions of which follow the boundary of the two-liquid field. At any point the compositions of the coexisting liquids must, of course, fall on the same isotherm, and their proportions can be determined by the lever rule. As the system cools and crystallizes A, the composition of one of the liquids, L_2, returns to intersect a linear projection from the original composition, X, away from A and on the low, temperature side of the two-liquid field. At that stage all

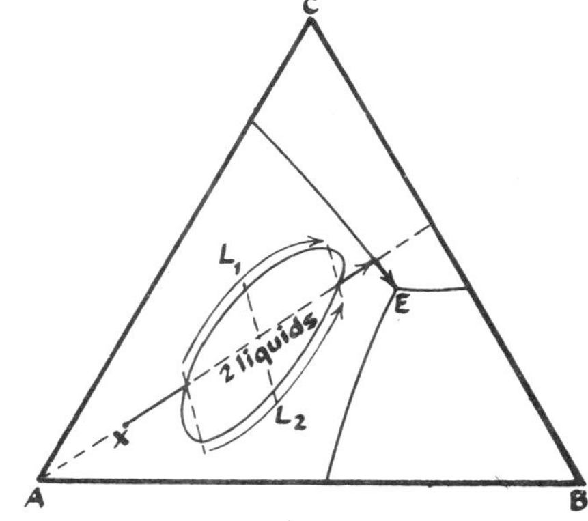

Figure 3–21 A three-component system with a field of liquid immiscibility intersecting the liquidus surface of one of the crystalline phases. A section through the triangle from the corner A and through X to the opposite side of the triangle would have the same form as the two-component system illustrated in Figure 3-16b.

of the liquid L_1 will have been converted to crystalline A and liquid L_2. Thereafter the course of crystallization is identical to a normal three-component system.

It is interesting to note that, unless the course of crystallization is interrupted and the identity of the two liquids is in some way preserved, the final products of crystallization will show no evidence of the system having passed through a two-liquid field.

SYSTEMS OF FOUR OR MORE COMPONENTS

Systems with more than three components follow the same principles as simpler systems, but they are more difficult to depict in diagrams. Although a quaternary system can be illustrated in three dimensions (Fig. 3-22), the course of a liquid cannot be traced precisely in the interior of the tetrahedron. For this reason, it is customary to project points within the interior of the three-dimensional volume to a plane, which may either be a face of the tetrahedron or an interior section. The plane can then be treated as a ternary system in which each of the three components is also accompanied by the fourth, with which the liquid is assumed to be saturated at all times.

For example, if a magma with an initial composition X in the system A–B–C–D is in the volume D–a–b–c–E, D is the first phase to crystallize, and the magma is saturated with that phase throughout its subsequent cooling history. One can therefore project the interior boundaries away from the corner D onto a plane, such as the base of the tetrahedron. The three-dimensional spaces are now the two-dimensional fields A + D, B + D, and C + D. Liquid X projects to point X′ and follows a course of crystallization: D, D + A, D + A + B, and finally D + A + B + C.

Projections of this kind can lead to serious errors. Note that the interior boundaries of the quaternary system projected from D do not coincide with

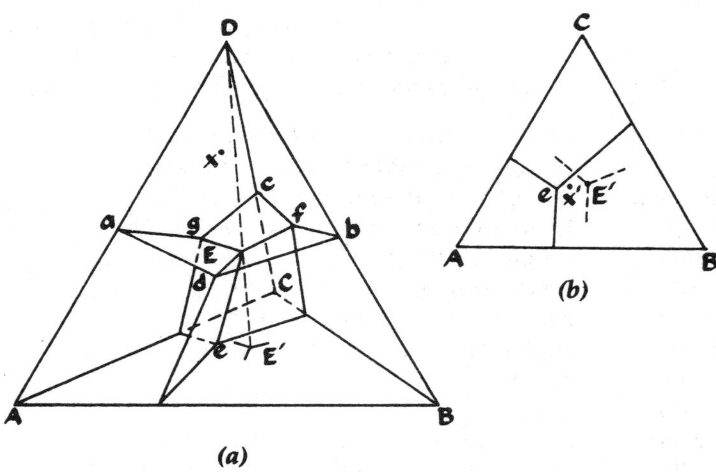

Figure 3–22 Four-component systems can be depicted by a three-dimensional tetrahedron having the components, A, B, C, and D, as corners. The base of the tetrahedron illustrated in (b) shows the three-component A–B–C with the four-component eutectic and field boundaries projected from D onto the same surface (dashed lines). Note that the composition X, which would appear to precipitate B first if the component D is ignored, would in fact be in the region in which A crystallizes first in the four-component system.

those of the ternary system A–B–C in which D is not present. This is a reflection of the fact that the behavior of a liquid saturated with D differs from that of one lacking that component. Consequently, the order of crystallization of A, B, and C from a liquid X may be different from what one would deduce by ignoring component D and plotting compositions in the three-component system. In the example shown in Figure 3–22b it appears that A would crystallize after B, whereas in fact it precedes B. In later sections we shall see examples of how this problem can lead to confusion when dealing with natural rocks.

SELECTED REFERENCES

Bowen, N. L. 1928. *The Evolution of Igneous Rocks*. Dover, 334 pp. A classic work in which Bowen first laid out the basic concepts by which igneous rock are interpreted in terms of crystal fractionation. This has been by all measure the most influential book in igneous petrology, and, though somewhat outdated, it still remains one of the most elegant treatments of crystal-liquid relations in natural silicates.

Cox, K. G., J. D. Bell, and R. J. Pankhurst 1979. *The Interpretation of Igneous Rocks*. George Allen & Unwin, 450 pp. A broad, introductory text dealing with igneous rocks in terms of phase relations, including numerous complex natural systems.

Darken, L. S., and R. W. Gurry. 1953. *Physical Chemistry of Metals*. McGraw-Hill, 535 pp. Although written for metallurgists, this well-written text has long been considered a standard reference for petrologists.

Morse, S. A. 1980. *Basalts and Phase Diagrams*. Springer-Verlag. 493 pp. A very thorough and clearly presented treatment of phase diagrams with examples of their use in the interpretation of differentiated basaltic magmas.

Wood, B. J., and D. G. Frazer. 1978. *Elementary Thermodynamics for Geologists*. Oxford University Press. 303 pp. An introductory text on the thermodynamics of geological systems.

Yoder, H. S., Jr., ed. 1979. *The Evolution of Igneous Rocks, Fiftieth Anniversary Perspectives*. Princeton University Press. 588 pp. An updating of Bowen's 1928 book. Chapters 3 through 7, in particular, deal with many of the principles discussed in this chapter.

4

IGNEOUS MINERALS AND THEIR TEXTURES

THE IGNEOUS ROCKS making up the vast bulk of the earth's crust consist of a remarkably small number of common minerals. About half a dozen phases accommodate the principal elements, O, Si, Al, Ca, Mg, Fe, Ti, Na, and K, and account for all but a percent or two of the entire range of volcanic and plutonic rocks. Most other igneous minerals occur only as accessories or in rare rocks of unusual composition. The purpose of this chapter is to outline the occurrences, phase relations, and textural features of these common minerals and relate them to the concepts set out in the preceding chapter.

COMMON IGNEOUS MINERALS

Silica minerals

Although silica is the most abundant oxide component of almost all igneous rocks and is an essential constituent of most rock-forming minerals, it seldom forms a separate phase in rocks having less than about 55 to 60 weight percent SiO_2. Of the various polymorphs—quartz, tridymite, cristobalite, coesite, and stishovite—quartz is by far the most common. It occurs as anhedral grains or in intergrowths with alkali feldspars in felsic sub-alkaline plutonic rocks and as euhedral to sub-rounded phenocrysts in siliceous volcanic rocks, especially ignimbrites. The high-temperature form, tridymite, is confined to volcanic and hypabyssal rocks. It almost always inverts to quartz on cooling, so that it has the optical properties of quartz even though it may retain the bladed morphology of tridymite. Cristobalite is found mainly in fractures and vesicles where it has been deposited hydrothermally, usually as a metastable phase. Coesite (monoclinic) and stishovite (tetragonal) are high-pressure forms of silica with densities of 2.93 and 4.35 g cm^{-3} respectively. They are formed only at very high pressures in the deep mantle or in rocks that have been subjected to intense shock by meteoritic impact or underground nuclear explosions. Coesite has been found as inclusions in diamonds brought to the surface from depths of 100 km or more.

Quickly cooled silicate liquids and glasses can contain large amounts of SiO_2 without nucleating and precipitating a silica mineral and, because of this, the amount of quartz in intermediate and felsic volcanic rocks is always less than that in chemically equivalent plutonic rocks. Silica has a high solubility in water-rich solutions, particularly at high temperatures and pressures. It is readily leached from volcanic glass by hydrothermal solutions or circulating meteoric water and may be redeposited in cavities as amorphous opal and chalcedony. It is also concentrated in water-rich fluids formed in the late stages of crystallization of plutonic rocks and is deposited as euhedral crystals, commonly of great size, when these fluids move into gas pockets and open fractures in and around intrusions.

Quartz and tridymite are virtually the only common igneous minerals that do not form solid-solution series. Their phase relations are, therefore, relatively simple. The stability relations of the polymorphs have already been shown in Figure 3–6; other systems in which silica minerals are possible phases are shown in several of the following sections.

Feldspars

Feldspars are by far the most abundant minerals in the earth's crust and are major components of almost all crystalline igneous rocks. Because of their range of solid solution and the diverse conditions under which they form in nature, they have many forms and compositions. Their basic properties are given in Table 4–1.

Table 4–1 Compositions and properties of the common feldspars

Feldspar	Formula	Crystal System	2V	Density
Albite	$NaAlSi_3O_8$	Triclinic	45° (−)	2.60
Anorthite	$CaAl_2Si_2O_8$	Triclinic	78° (+)	2.76
Orthoclase	$KAlSi_3O_8$	Monoclinic	69° − 72° (−)	2.59
Sanidine	$(K,Na)AlSi_3O_8$	Monoclinic	0° − 12° (−)	2.59
Anorthoclase	$(Na,K)AlSi_3O_8$	Triclinic	18° − 54° (−)	2.59

Plagioclase Compositions

	Pure	Typical Natural Plagioclases				Pure
	Albite	An 20	An 40	An 60	An 80	Anorthite
SiO_2	68.74	63.35	58.03	53.38	47.67	43.20
Al_2O_3	19.44	22.89	25.81	29.71	33.46	36.65
Fe_2O_3	—	0.09	0.68	0.19	tr.	—
CaO	—	4.09	8.01	11.86	16.23	20.16
Na_2O	11.82	8.90	6.47	4.44	2.19	—
K_2O	—	0.65	0.46	0.18	0.07	—

Alkali Feldspar Compositions

	Pure	Typical Natural Feldspars		
	Orthoclase	Orthoclase	Sanidine	Anorthoclase
SiO_2	64.76	64.28	64.03	64.33
Al_2O_3	18.32	19.40	19.92	20.94
Fe_2O_3	—	0.34	0.62	0.78
CaO	—	0.48	0.45	2.01
Na_2O	—	2.74	4.57	7.22
K_2O	16.72	11.80	10.05	4.71

Plagioclase is far more abundant than potassium feldspar, especially in volcanic rocks. Because the calcium and sodium contents (and hence the normative anorthite and albite) of most mafic and intermediate magmas exceed the potassium content (and normative orthoclase), plagioclase is normally the first and most abundant feldspar to precipitate. Most of the potassium in common volcanic rocks is incorporated as a minor element in plagioclase or is concentrated in interstitial glass. In the sub-alkaline series, it rarely forms a separate feldspar in any but the most felsic rocks, such as dacites and rhyolites, and in most of these the alkali feldspar is a high-temperature form in the intermediate compositional range of anorthoclase. In more alkaline series, however, sanidine, orthoclase, and anorthoclase may be important constituents of quite mafic rocks, especially in highly potassic series, such as the shoshonitic and lamprophyric rocks discussed in chapter eleven. Potassium feldspar is more common in plutonic rocks in which the conditions of protracted cooling and higher water contents favor better equilibration and crystallization of two separate feldspars. The high-temperature potassium feldspar, sanidine, is found only in very potassic volcanic rocks and in reheated xenoliths that originally contained orthoclase or microcline. The low-temperature form, microcline, is characteristic of plutonic rocks that have been extensively recrystallized under metamorphic conditions.

The end-members of the feldspar system (Fig. 4–1) differ in crystal structure and in their ranges of solid solution. The sodium and calcium feldspars (Ab and An) form a complete series of plagioclase compositions (Fig. 4–2) and crystallize in the manner of the solid-solution series discussed in chapter three. The sodic (Ab) and potassic (Or) feldspars have a limited range of solid solution that diminishes with falling temperature and increasing water pressure, and An and Or are separated by a wide compositional gap at all temperatures. The relations are further complicated by the fact that the potassium feldspar has high, intermediate, and low-temperature forms (sanidine, orthoclase, and microcline) and melts in-

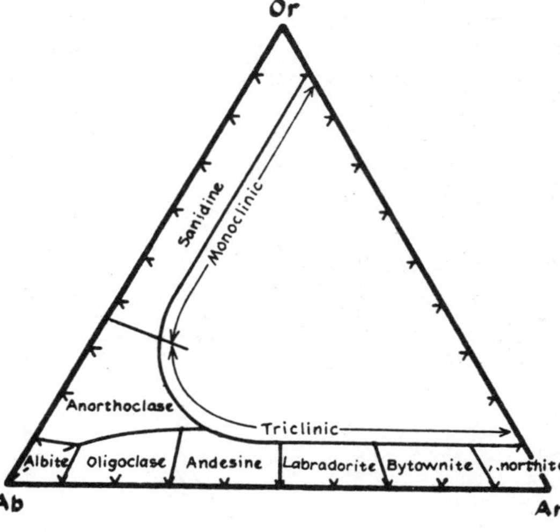

Figure 4–1 Volcanic feldspars are classified in terms of their molecular proportions of the three end-members, anorthite (An), albite (Ab), and potassium feldspar (Or). No feldspars fall in the intermediate range between plagioclase and alkali feldspars. The range of plutonic feldspars is shown in Figures 4–3 and 4–6.

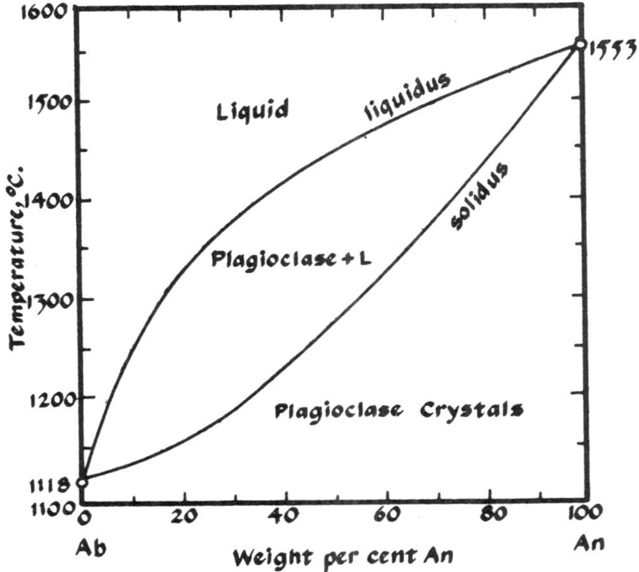

Figure 4–2 The plagioclase feldspars form a continuous solid-solution series between calcium-rich anorthite and sodium-rich albite.

congruently to form leucite ($KAlSi_2O_6$) and liquid. For simplicity, the potassium feldspar is labelled orthoclase on most phase diagrams, and its incongruent melting is ignored, because it disappears with addition of small amounts of other components and plays little or no role in crystallization of any but a small group of very potassic magmas.

Most mafic magmas have initial compositions on the plagioclase side of the cotectic curve that descends across the feldspar triangle (Fig. 4–3). With progres-

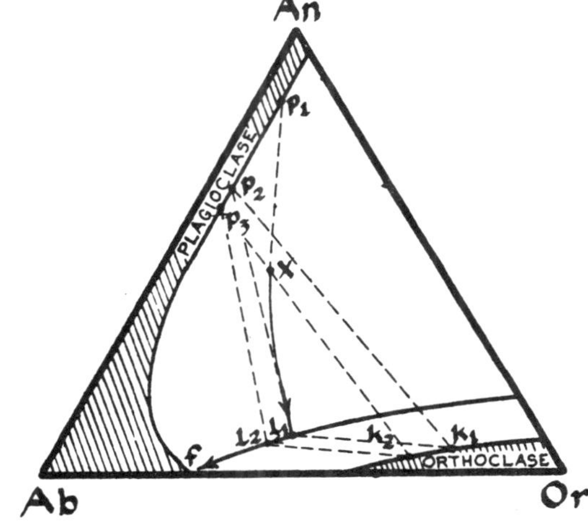

Figure 4–3 Crystallization in the feldspar system is governed by a cotectic separating the field of plagioclase from that of potassium feldspar. Typical tie-lines connecting compositions of coexisting feldspars and liquids are shown by broken lines. The course of crystallization of common liquids is discussed in the text.

sive crystallization such a liquid follows a curved path away from plagioclase that becomes more albitic with falling temperature. On reaching the cotectic, the liquid begins to crystallize an alkali feldspar the composition of which also changes as the liquid descends toward the temperature minimum on the Ab–Or join at f. At any point along its course the liquid is in equilibrium with two feldspars, as indicated in the diagram by the successive triangles, but the exact compositions of coexisting phases cannot be determined without more information than is given in Figure 4–3. With complete reaction, the last drop of liquid would disappear when the join between the two feldspars coexisting in equilibrium with the liquid overtakes the initial composition X. Normally, however, reaction is incomplete, and the liquid continues to descend toward f.

Because plagioclase requires large amounts of undercooling to nucleate and, once crystallized, is very slow to equilibrate by reaction, it characteristically has a wide range of compositions, even in individual crystals. Figure 4–4 illustrates a common form of oscillatory zoning that is especially characteristic of plagioclase.

In most respects, plagioclases in igneous rocks show relations broadly consistent with those of the simplified system of Figure 4–3; the anorthite content of early-crystallizing phenocrysts is greater than that of the groundmass and declines as cooling and crystallization advance. One cannot, however, make a direct quantitative correlation between the natural and simple systems. The temperatures of crystallization are lower in magmas, owing to the presence of other components in the liquid, and the forms of the liquidus and solidus curves differ when other phases are co-precipitated.

This difference between the simple two-component system and systems containing other components is illustrated by the effect of adding a single additional component, diopside, to the plagioclase system (Fig. 4–5). The liquidus and solidus temperatures of plagioclase are lowered by amounts that are a function of the proportion of diopside in the liquid, and, for that reason, the amount of plagioclase that crystallizes in a given temperature interval also changes. When plagioclase crystallizes alone (from X to L_1 and P_1 to P_2), the slopes of the liquidus and solidus are steepened as diopside is residually enriched in the liquid; they then flatten when the two phases crystallize simultaneously (from L_1 to L_2 and P_2 to P_3) and the proportion of diopside in the liquid diminishes. Note the large compositional change resulting from a small change of temperature when the liquid is on the cotectic, and compare this with the change over a similar interval in the simple system for albite-anorthite alone.

The alkali feldspars (Fig. 4–6) form a continuous solid-solution series at high temperatures, and if quickly cooled may preserve a homogeneous, intermediate composition. Thus, one or the other of the two high-temperature alkali feldspars, anorthoclase or sanidine, may be found in alkali-rich volcanic rocks, whereas slowly cooled plutonic rocks of similar chemical composition do not contain these high-temperature forms. Instead, they have two feldspars, orthoclase and albitic plagioclase, either as intergrown or distinctly separate crystals. The behavior of the alkali feldspars under these latter conditions is illustrated in Figure 4–6b; details of the textural relations and the effects of water pressure on the feldspars are discussed in chapter ten.

Figure 4-4 Oscillatory zoning in plagioclase feldspar. Repeated overgrowths of layers of different compositions resemble the annual growth rings in trees. Each sequence becomes more albitic outward, then reverts back to a more anorthitic composition to begin the next layer. In this specimen, narrow zones of sharp zoning at W, X, Y, and Z alternate with more weakly zoned layers. The area B is an inclusion of basaltic glass. Width of the view is about .25 mm. (Courtesy of A. T. Anderson.)

Feldspathoids

Highly alkaline rocks may have too little silica to form feldspar as the only alumino-silicate phase; if so, they may have one or more of the alkaline feldspathoids, nepheline or leucite, or a related mineral, such as analcite, sodalite, noselite, or zeolites. These minerals (Table 4–2) can be thought of as silica-deficient equivalents of feldspar, and, as such, cannot coexist in equilibrium with a silica mineral. Leucite is unstable at elevated pressures and is all but unknown in plutonic rocks, but it is an abundant constituent of leucite basanites, wyomingites, and a number of other types of uncommon potassic peralkaline rocks that are found in small but widespread occurrences, mainly in continental regions. Nepheline forms under a wider range of conditions, and is found in plutonic rocks ranging from mafic and ultramafic rocks to nepheline syenites. It is an equally important constituent of very sodic volcanic rocks ranging from basic basanites to felsic phonolites. Both of the feldpathoids tend to be unstable at low

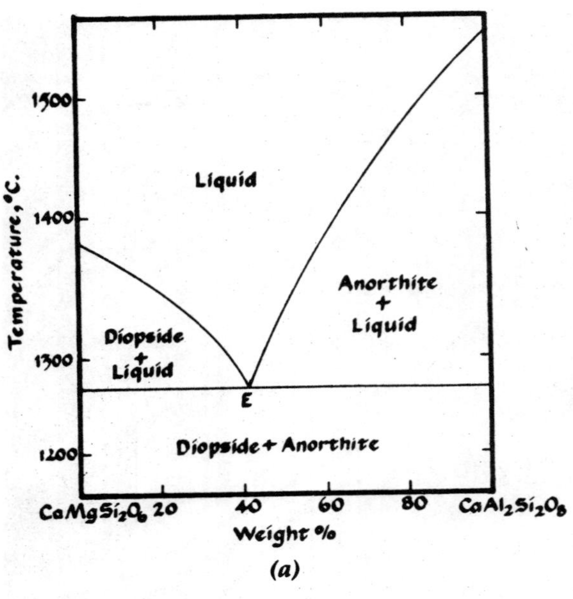

(a)

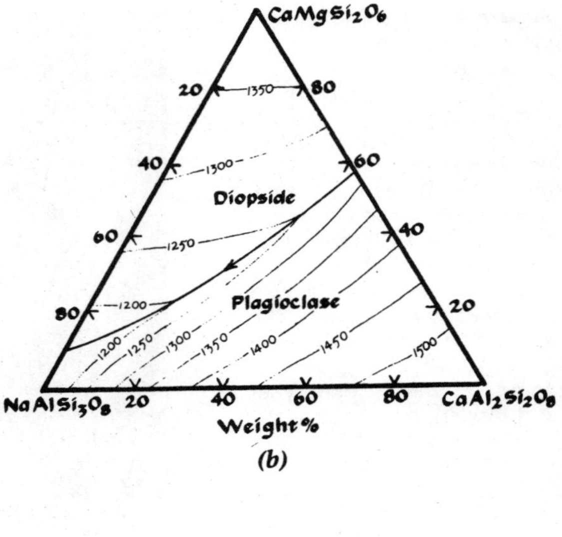

(b)

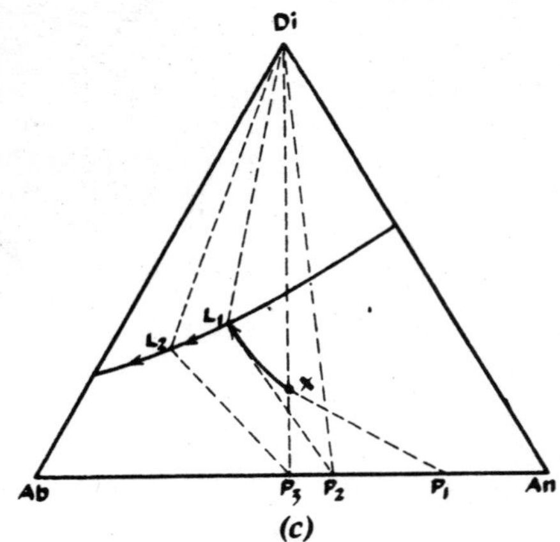

(c)

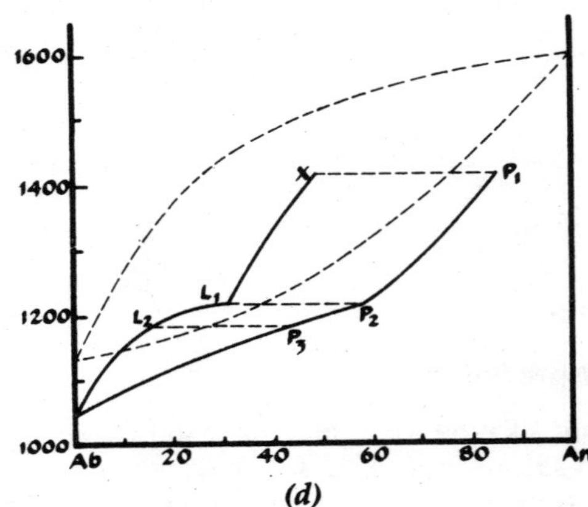

(d)

Figure 4–5 (a) The system diopside-anorthite is a simple two-component system with a binary eutectic. (Because small amounts of alumina enter diopside, the system is not strictly binary.) When albite is added to the system (b), crystallization follows the principles outlined in chapter three for a three-component in which two of the components form a solid-solution series. The temperatures of the liquidus and solidus curves for plagioclase (c) now vary according to the amount of the third component, Di, in the liquid. During the early course of plagioclase crystallization, a liquid X approaches the cotectic and becomes richer in Di. The liquidus and solidus of plagioclase are depressed to progressively lower temperatures, but when Di begins to crystallize, depleting that component in the liquid, the liquidus and solidus curves rise to temperatures approaching those of the pure two-component system. (After P.J. Wyllie, 1963, *Min. Soc. Am. Spec. Paper 1*, 204–212.)

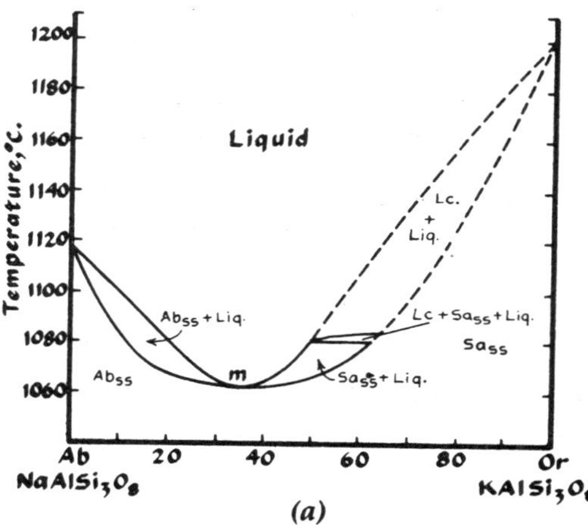

(a)

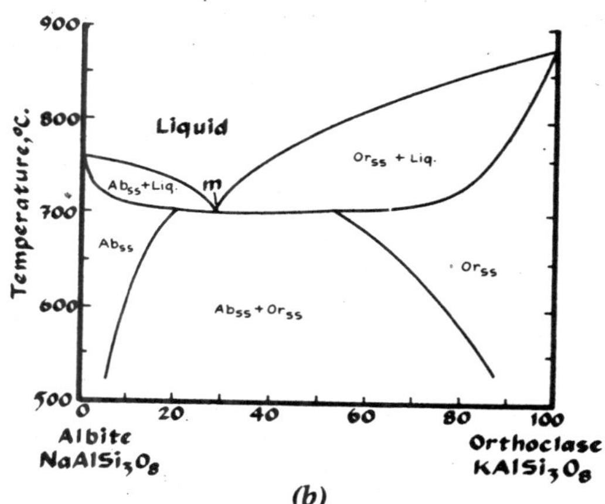

(b)

Figure 4–6 (a) The alkali feldspars form two solid-solution series descending to a minimum temperature at m. In volcanic or shallow intrusive magmas, homogeneous feldspars can form with compositions anywhere between pure albite and pure sanidine. The field of leucite (Lc) disappears in most natural liquids of subalkaline compositions. (After D. R. Waldbaum and J. B. Thompson, 1969, *Amer. Min.* 54:1249–1298.) (b) Elevated pressures of water depress the temperatures of both the liquidus and solidus curve, and, at 5 kilobars, they are low enough to intersect the solvus, so that two separate feldspars, one sodic and the other potassic, are separated by a field in which intermediate compositons are not stable. Crystallization of the alkali feldspars is dealt with in greater detail in chapter ten. (After S. A. Morse, 1970, *Jour. Petrology,* 11:221–251.)

temperatures. Leucite breaks down on cooling to an intergrowth of orthoclase and nepheline, and nepheline alters readily to analcite, sodalite and zeolites. The genetic relations of the feldspathoids are discussed in chapter eleven.

Pyroxenes

Pyroxenes are second only to feldspar in abundance in crustal rocks. They have several different compositional and structural forms (Fig. 4–7 and Table 4–3). Ca-rich pyroxenes are common constituents of almost all igneous rocks, but the Ca-poor pyroxenes can form only in subalkaline and certain types of ultramafic rocks. Pyroxenes with intermediate calcium contents, usually referred to as subcalcic augites, are found in many if not most volcanic rocks, especially as a component of the groundmass, but only rarely in plutonic rocks.

Both the Ca-poor and Ca-rich pyroxenes form solid-solution series between Mg and Fe end-members and have limited solid solution with each other. The Ca-rich series, diopside-hedenbergite, is a continuous solid-solution series similar to those of plagioclase or olivine. Very iron-rich calcium pyroxenes crystallize initially with the triclinic form of Fe-wollastonite (or ferrobustamite) and invert on cooling to the monoclinic structure of hedenbergite. Few magmas reach this degree of iron enrichment, however, and natural examples of the inversion are rare.

An aluminous (tschermakitic) component may enter both monoclinic and

Table 4–2 Compositions and properties of feldspathoids and analcite

Mineral	Formula	Crystal System	Optic Sign	Density
Nepheline	$Na_3K(AlSiO_4)_4$	Hexagonal	(−)	2.61
Leucite	$KAlSi_2O_6$	Pseudoisometric	isotropic	2.47
Sodalite	$Na_4Al_3Si_3O_{12}Cl$	Cubic	isotropic	2.30
Analcite	$NaAlSi_2O_6 \cdot H_2O$	Cubic	isotropic	2.27

Chemical Compositions

Pure Minerals	Nepheline	Leucite	Sodalite	Analcite
SiO_2	39.00	53.12	34.49	48.82
Al_2O_3	33.08	22.53	32.92	20.71
Na_2O	18.98	—	20.01	15.84
K_2O	8.94	24.35	—	—
H_2O	—	—	—	14.63
NaCl	—	—	12.58	—

Typical Natural Minerals	Nepheline	Leucite	Sodalite	Analcite
SiO_2	44.65	56.39	36.72	54.23
Al_2O_3	32.03	23.10	31.63	23.67
Fe_2O_3	0.59	—	0.55	—
CaO	0.71	0.27	0.28	—
Na_2O	17.25	2.17	24.02	13.81
K_2O	3.66	18.05	0.46	tr.
H_2O	0.96	—	0.28	8.67
Cl	—	—	5.56	—

orthorhombic pyroxenes, as $CaAl_2SiO_6$ and $(Mg,Fe)Al_2SiO_6$ respectively, but it is most important in Ca-rich monoclinic pyroxenes. The same is true of Ti and, to a lesser degree, Cr. The sodic, ferric-iron component, $NaFeSi_2O_6$ (called aegerine or acmite), is abundant in the clinopyroxenes in many peralkaline rocks, whereas jadeite ($NaAlSi_2O_6$) is an important constituent of the clinopyroxenes of mafic or ultramafic rocks formed at high pressures.

Two effects may cause alumina to enter pyroxene—the composition of the liquid and the pressure at which the mineral crystallizes. When pyroxene crystallizes from liquids of low silica contents, Al substitutes for Si in the tetrahedral site (with four-fold coordination) and results in an increase of the c dimension of the unit cell. This substitution of Al for Si is often coupled with substitution of Ti for Mg and Fe to maintain a charge balance. The Al that enters pyroxenes at high pressures does so in a different way. It is substituted simultaneously for both Si and Mg or Fe, and by entering the octahedral site in six-fold coordination it reduces the b and c crystallographic dimensions. It may also enter as the jadite molecule, $NaAlSi_2O_6$, in which case it leads to an even greater reduction of volume, as shown by the volumes of three end-member molecules:

Diopside	$CaMgSi_2O_6$	438.0 Å^3
Ca-tchermakite	$CaAl_2SiO_6$	421.7 Å^3
Jadeite	$NaAlSi_2O_6$	405.0 Å^3

Figure 4–7 (a) The principal pyroxenes are defined in terms of their molecular proportions in the pyroxene quadrilateral. No compositions fall within the shaded areas, and the iron end-member of the Ca-poor pyroxenes, ferrosilite, is not found in igneous rocks. (b) Sodic pyroxenes are classified in terms of the end members, jadeite, acmite, and the Ca-rich clinopyroxenes (diopside, hedenbergite, and Ca-tschermak molecule). (c) shows the trends of compositions of common igneous pyroxenes, and the numbered lines join typical coexisting Ca-rich and Ca-poor compositions in a series of differentiated rocks.

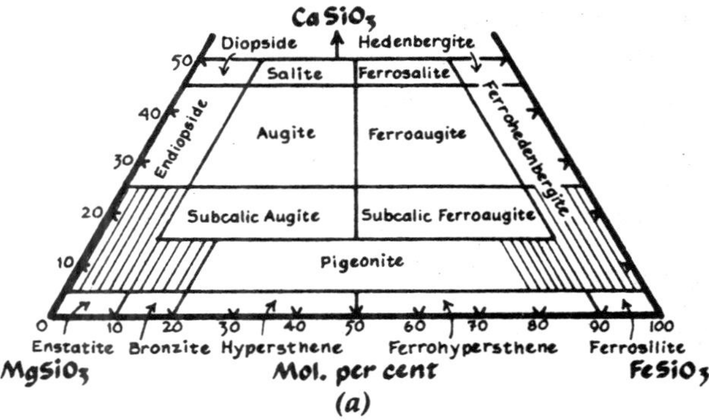

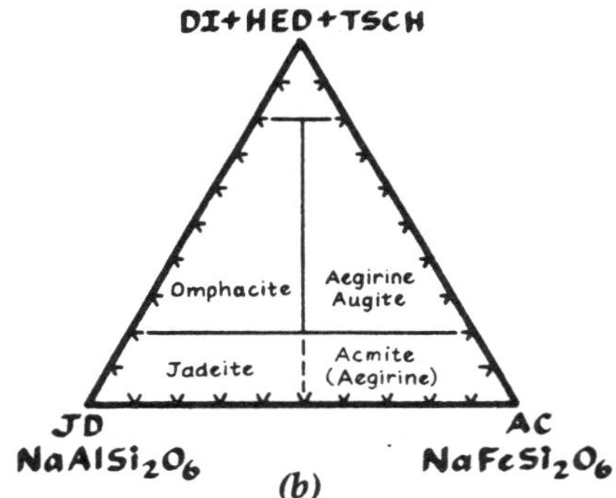

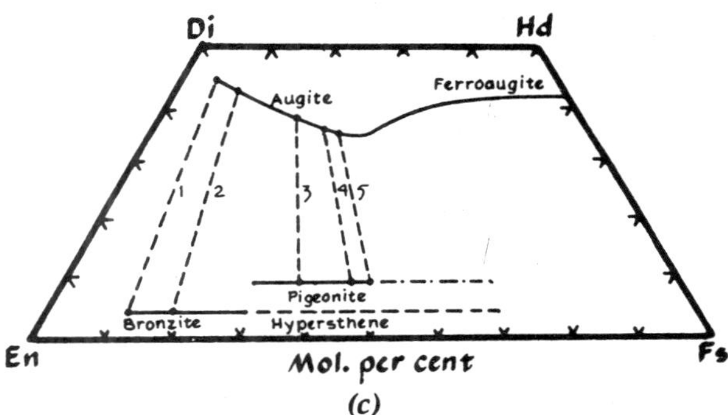

Thus, substitution of either of the two Al-bearing pyroxene components, since it reduces the volume of diopside, would be expected in pyroxenes formed at high pressures.

Crystallization of the Ca-poor pyroxenes (Fig. 4–8) resembles that of other solid-solution minerals but is complicated by the two polymorphic Ca-poor forms found in natural rocks—a high-temperature, monoclinic form, clino-

Figure 4–8 The Ca-poor pyroxenes crystallize as a solid-solution series, but the inversion curve separating the stability field of monoclinic pigeonite (cpx) from the orthorhombic form (opx) crosses the liquidus and solidus in the middle range of compositions. The iron end-member, ferrosilite, is replaced by fayalitic olivine and a silica mineral, such as quartz or tridymite. The diagram is greatly simplified.

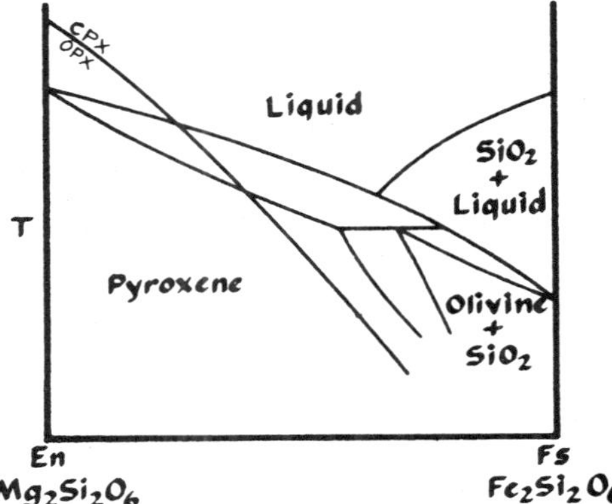

Table 4–3 Compositions and properties of pyroxenes

Mineral	Formula	Crystal System	Optic Sign	Density
Enstatite	$Mg_2Si_2O_6$	Orthorhombic	(+) 56°	3.21
Hypersthene	$(Mg,Fe)_2Si_2O_6$	Orthorhombic	(−) 52°–90°	3.40–3.80
Pigeonite	$(Mg,Fe,Ca)(Mg,Fe)Si_2O_6$	Monoclinic	(+) 0°–25°	3.30–3.46
Ferrosilite	$Fe_2Si_2O_6$	Orthorhombic	(+) 55°	3.96
Diopside	$CaMgSi_2O_6$	Monoclinic	(+) 59°	3.30
Augite	$Ca(Mg,Fe)Si_2O_6$	Monoclinic	(+) 25°–60°	3.23–3.52
Hedenbergite	$CaFeSi_2O_6$	Monoclinic	(+) 52°–62°	3.56
Jadeite	$NaAlSi_2O_6$	Monoclinic	(+) 67°–70°	3.42
Acmite (aegirine)	$NaFeSi_2O_6$	Monoclinic	(−) 60°–70°	3.58

Chemical Compositions

Pure End Members

	Enstatite	Ferrosilite	Diopside	Hedenbergite	Jadeite	Acmite
SiO_2	59.84	45.54	55.49	48.44	57.19	50.28
Al_2O_3	—	—	—	—	24.26	—
Fe_2O_3	—	—	—	—	—	33.41
FeO	—	54.46	—	28.96	—	—
MgO	40.16	—	18.62	—	—	—
CaO	—	—	25.89	22.60	—	—
Na_2O	—	—	—	—	18.55	16.31

Natural Minerals

	Augite	Ti-augite	Ferroaugite	Hypersthene	Pigeonite	Acmite
SiO_2	49.68	46.20	49.73	53.18	51.53	52.48
TiO_2	0.56	3.21	0.77	0.21	0.58	0.57
Al_2O_3	0.78	5.38	1.39	3.08	1.41	0.96
Fe_2O_3	3.29	3.22	1.50	0.25	0.12	31.74
FeO	18.15	5.41	19.20	18.05	23.17	0.93
MgO	16.19	12.90	9.40	23.26	16.10	0.15
CaO	9.90	23.16	17.75	2.09	7.05	0.28
Na_2O	0.65	0.47	0.24	—	0.26	12.05
K_2O	0.15	0.02	—	—	0.23	0.35

enstatite or pigeonite, and a low-temperature, orthorhombic form, enstatite or hypersthene. The temperature of inversion between these two forms declines with increasing iron content at a greater rate than the liquidus and solidus, so that the two sets of curves intersect in the intermediate compositional range.

A liquid of Mg-rich composition that initially crystallizes in the orthorhombic form becomes richer in iron as it cools; after crossing the inversion curve, it crystallizes initially in the monoclinic form, pigeonite, which on cooling tends to change to hypersthene, the stable orthorhombic form at low temperatures. In slowly cooled rocks, pigeonite almost always inverts to hypersthene, but most volcanic rocks cool too quickly for this inversion to take place, and pigeonite is preserved in a metastable state.

As one would expect from their differing crystalline structures, the range of solution between the monoclinic and orthorhombic forms is limited (Fig. 4–9); a broad solvus separates their coexisting sub-solidus compositions, and, on cool-

Figure 4-9 Limited solid solution between the Ca-rich and Ca-poor pyroxenes resembles the relations in the alkali feldspars, but the solvus intersects the solidus at all pressures, and relations are complicated by the initial crystallization of olivine from Ca-poor liquids. Fields of various forms of Ca-poor pyroxene are omitted.

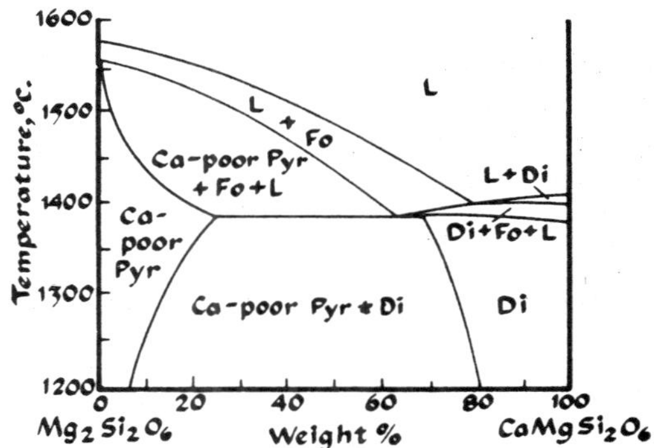

ing, each of the end-members tends to become purer as it exsolves the other. Exsolution of the two forms of pyroxenes has a distinctive crystallographic pattern (Fig. 4-10). When the stable form of the Ca-poor pyroxene is orthorhombic, the lamellae of exsolved pyroxene form along (100) planes of the host crystal; if the stable Ca-poor pyroxene is monoclinic, the lamellae form along (001) planes. These relations hold regardless of which pyroxenes is the host. If exsolution begins when the stable pyroxenes are both monoclinic and continues through an interval in which the Ca-poor pyroxene inverts to the orthorhombic structure, the orientation of lamellae will first be along (001) and then later on (001), and the final crystal will have two intersecting sets.

Enstatite melts incongruently to form olivine plus liquid in the manner explained in the discussion of binary systems with intermediate compounds in chapter three. For this reason, a liquid with the composition of enstatite does not crystallize that mineral directly. Instead, olivine crystallizes first and later reacts with the evolving liquid to form pyroxene. Figure 4-11a shows the liquidus fields within the pyroxene quadrilateral and illustrates the range of liquid compositions that initially crystallize olivine. Also shown are the fields of iron-wollastonite (or ferrobustamite), the high-temperature, triclinic form of hedenbergite, and pigeonite, the high-temperature, monoclinic form of Ca-poor pyroxene. Figure 4-11b shows typical tie-lines joining cotectic liquids with the different coexisting forms that crystallize at successive stages of evolution as the liquid descends to lower temperatures and higher iron contents.

Pigeonites normally have about 5 to 9 percent of the calcium component ($CaSiO_3$), in solid solution. This is more than that of the orthorhombic pyroxenes under the same conditions and reflects the greater range of solid solution between forms sharing a monoclinic structure. Owing to this difference, the inversion curve that was a simple line in the Ca-free system (Fig. 4-8) becomes a set of curves, one for each of the coexisting pyroxenes, that forms a curved wedge extending into the diagrams for more iron-rich pyroxenes (Fig. 4-11d and e).

The crystallization behavior through a range of pyroxene compositions is best illustrated by a series of hypothetical examples. The sketches of crystals shown in Figure 4-11 represent the three stages of differentiation in Figures 11c, d, and e. At an early stage (Fig. 4-11c), diopsidic augite crystals have small exso-

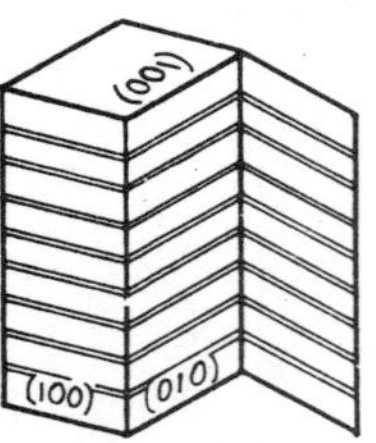

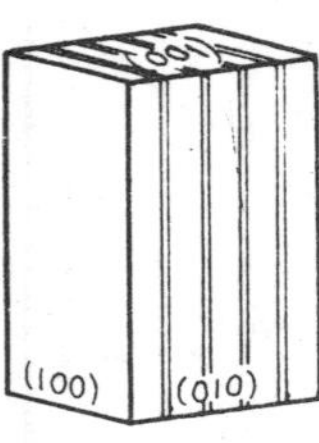

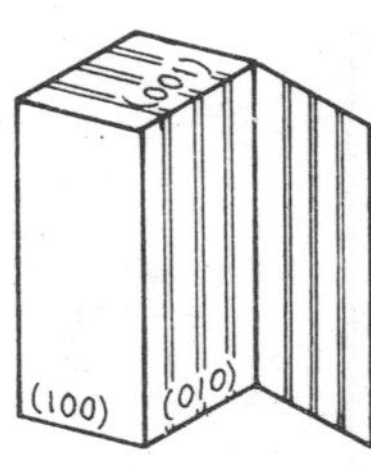

(a)

Figure 4–10 (a) Crystallographic relations of exsolution lamellae in pyroxenes. (b) Examples of exsolution in inverted pigeonite. The monoclinic crystals of pigeonite were twinned, as can be seen from the inclined exsolution along the original (001) planes of their host. In the crystal on the left, all exsolution occurred while the host was still monoclinic, but the crystal on the right continued to exsolve after the inversion, so that a second set of lamellae has formed parallel to the (100) plane of the orthorhombic host.

(b)

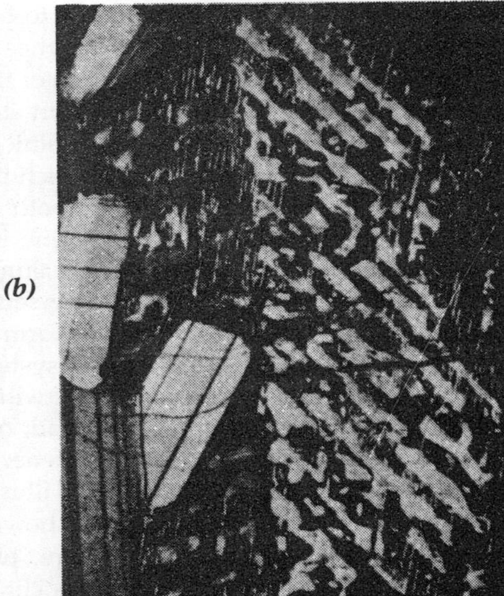

lution lamellae parallel to (100), while a coexisting enstatite has embayed cores of olivine and exsolved diopside along (100) in its outer rims. Several deductions could be made from these relations. It is clear that crystallization took place below the monoclinic-orthorhombic inversion temperature, because all exsolution is parallel to (100). Second, the initial liquid was probably on the Ca-poor side of the low-temperature trough, so that olivine crystallized first, reacted with the liquid to form enstatite, and was later joined by diopside. This we know from the embayed cores of olivine, which would be less likely to form if the liquid had first crystallized diopside and approached the trough from the Ca-rich side.

A later stage of crystallization is illustrated in Figure 4–11d. The liquid has now migrated down the thermal valley to a more Fe-rich composition. Each

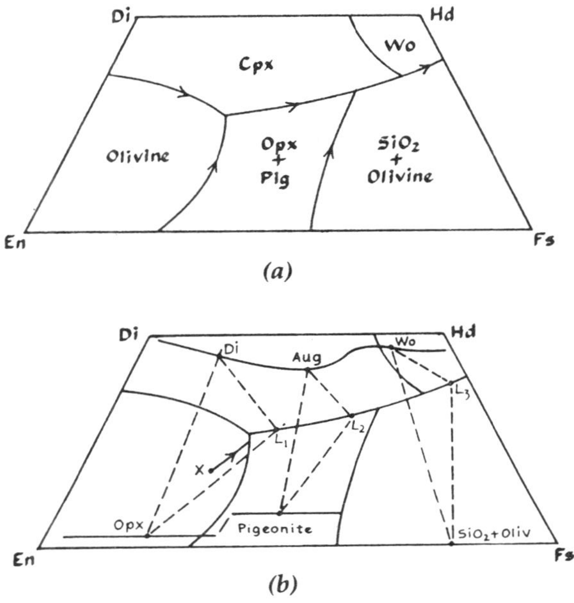

Figure 4–11 (a) The liquidus surface of the pyroxene system has several phases other than pyroxene. Olivine is the first phase to crystallize from liquids with compositions close to enstatite, and a silica mineral crystallizes from liquids close to ferrosilite. The first phase to crystallize from a liquid of hedenbergitic composition has the structure of wollastonite (or ferrobustamite), and inverts on cooling to a pyroxene structure. (b) shows the positions of the three sections illustrated schematically in (c), (d), and (e). Triangles connect coexisting pyroxenes to liquids descending along the cotectic shown in (a). The initial liquid, X, would precipitate olivine until it reaches a boundary with pyroxene. (c) Liquid L_1 precipitates a diopsidic Ca-rich pyroxene, which on cooling exsolves the Ca-poor form. Because the inversion temperature is above the solidus of the Ca-poor pyroxene (Fig. 4–8), the latter crystallizes initially in the orthorhombic form. Note that even though the bulk composition is in the field of primary crystallization of olivine, liquid L_1 is not, so that the liquidus phases are both pyroxenes. (d) Liquid L_2 precipitates augite together with pigeonite, because the inversion curve for pigeonite to hypersthene (Fig. 4–8) now lies below the solidus. Both pyroxenes exsolve their counterpart, but on cooling a subsolidus inversion takes place, so that only the orthorhombic Ca-poor pyroxene, hypersthene, is stable at lower temperatures. (e) Liquid L_3 has migrated to a more Ca-rich composition, and only a single pyroxene crystallizes, initially with the structure of Fe-wollastonite (or ferrobustamite), which, on cooling, inverts to hedenbergite. Fayalitic olivine and a silica mineral are in equilibrium with the Ca-rich pyroxene.

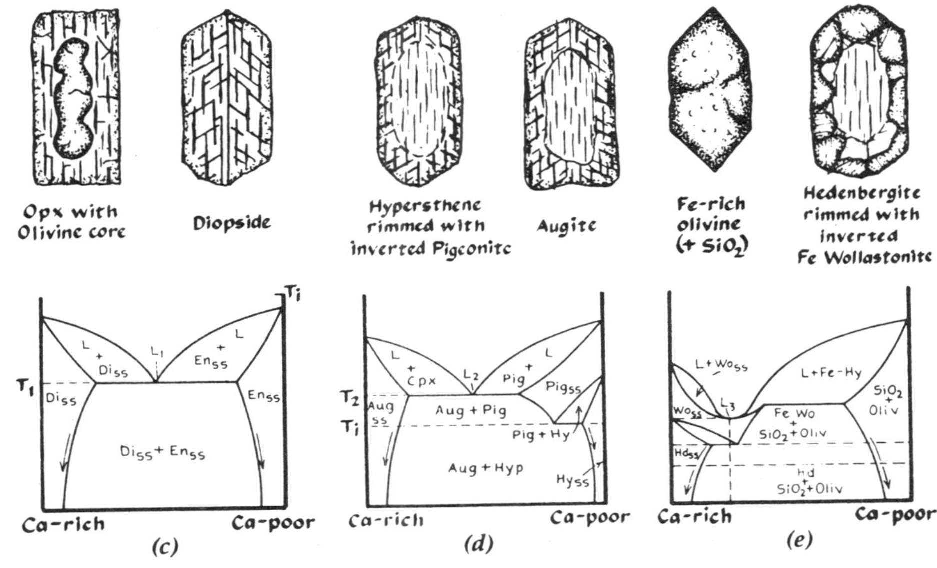

pyroxene has two sets of lamellae, one parallel to (100) and the other along (001). This relation shows that crystallization began above the inversion temperature where both forms were originally monoclinic, but after cooling and exsolving one set of lamellae on (001), the pigeonitic pyroxene was replaced by hypersthene and subsequent exsolution was on (100).

The late stages of iron enrichment are illustrated in Figure 4–11e. The magma precipitates only a single pyroxene, ferroaugite, containing two sets of exsolution lamellae, and an iron-rich olivine and quartz crystallize in place of the Ca-poor pyroxene. On approaching the Hd corner of the quadrilateral, the thermal trough has migrated toward the Di-Hd join until it has "fallen off" the solvus, and from that point on only a single pyroxene can precipitate directly from the liquid.

Olivine

In subalkaline rocks, olivine is confined almost entirely to compositions more mafic than andesite or diorite. Though normally absent from the groundmass, it may be an abundant phenocryst, especially in basalts. When it is, it commonly shows evidence of reaction with the groundmass. Iron-rich olivine is a stable phase in highly evolved felsic volcanic and hypabyssal rocks, such as rhyolites, granophyres, and ferrogabbros, but it is rare in felsic plutonic rocks.

In alkaline rocks olivine can occur either as phenocrysts or as part of the groundmass, regardless of the degree of differentiation. Indeed, stable groundmass olivine is a useful petrographic criterion by which the alkaline rocks can be distinguished from sub-alkaline types (chapter seven).

Olivine forms a solid-solution series between forsterite and fayalite (Table 4–4 and Fig. 4–12) similar to that of plagioclase, but because it has a simpler structure and equilibrates more readily, olivine is less likely to be zoned. It also differs from plagioclase in the reaction that occurs between Mg-rich crystals and liquids to form pyroxene (Fig. 4–13). The reaction relations will be recognized as an ex-

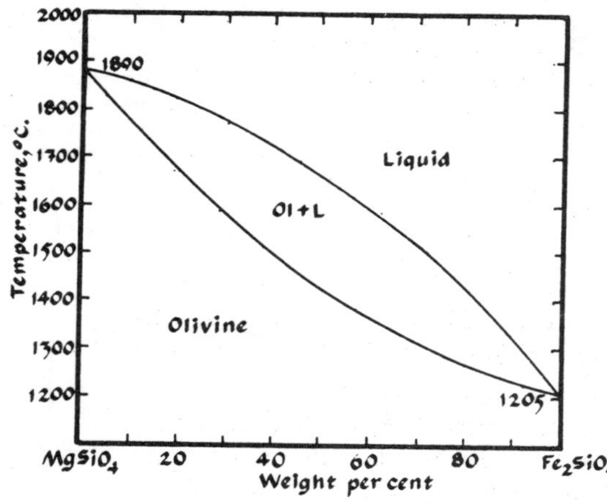

Figure 4–12 The common igneous olivines form a continuous range of solid solution between magnesium and iron end-members, forsterite and fayalite. Their crystallization and melting relations are similar to those of plagioclase. Effects of oxidation or reduction are ignored, and all iron is assumed to be in the ferrous state. (After N. L. Bowen and J. F. Schairer, 1935, *Amer. Jour. Sci.*, 29:151–217.)

Table 4-4 Compositions and properties of olivines

Mineral	Formula	Optic Sign	Density
Forsterite	Mg_2SiO_4	(+) 82°	3.22
Fayalite	Fe_2SiO_4	(−) 46°	4.39
Monticellite	$Ca(Mg,Fe)SiO_4$	(−) 72°–82°	3.08–3.27

Chemical Compositions of Pure and Natural Olivines

	Pure Forsterite	Fo 96	Fo 86	Fo 47	Fo 3	Pure Fayalite	Monticellite (in Periodotite)
SiO_2	42.71	41.07	39.87	34.04	30.15	29.49	36.67
TiO_2	—	0.05	0.03	0.43	0.20	—	0.13
Al_2O_3	—	0.56	—	0.91	0.07	—	0.75
Fe_2O_3	—	0.65	0.86	1.46	0.43	—	0.10
FeO	—	3.78	13.20	40.37	65.02	70.51	7.57
MnO	—	0.23	0.22	0.68	1.01	—	0.17
MgO	57.29	54.06	45.38	20.32	1.05	—	21.11
CaO	—	—	0.25	0.81	2.18	—	32.56

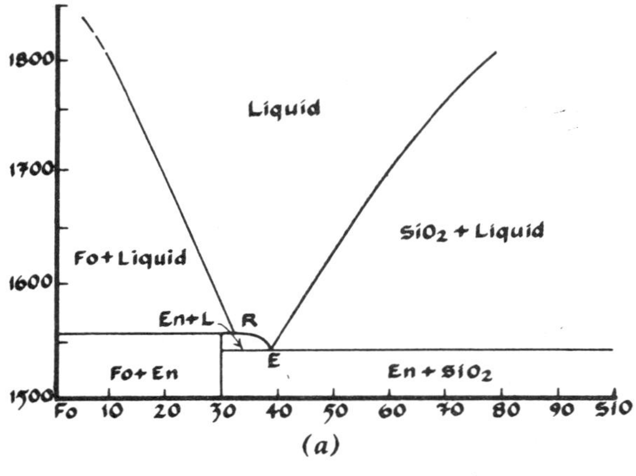

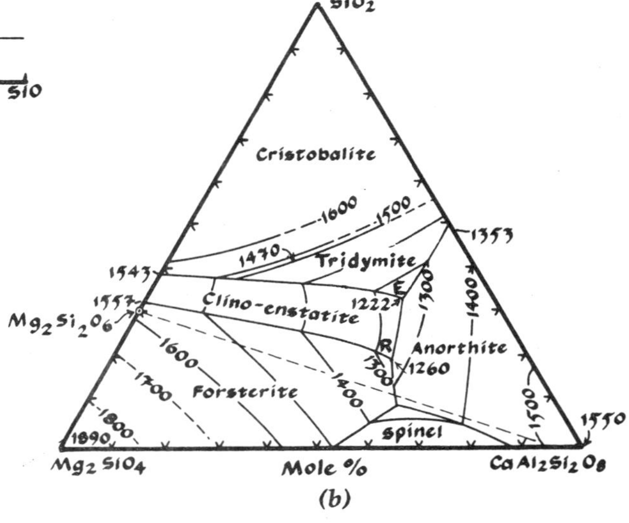

Figure 4-13 (a) The system forsterite-silica is an important example of a binary system with an intermediate compound, enstatite, that melts incongruently. (After N. L. Bowen and O. Andersen, 1914, *Amer. Jour. Sci.*, 37:487–500.) (b) When anorthite is added to the forsterite-silica system, the intermediate compound, En, occupies a field extending into the interior of the three-component system. The boundary between the pyroxene and olivine field is a peritectic descending to an invariant reaction point, R. (After O. Andersen, 1915, *Amer. Jour. Sci.*, 39:407–454.)

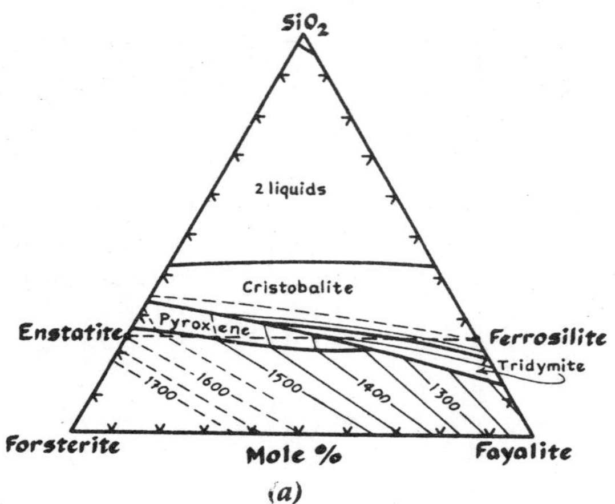

(a)

Figure 4–14 Crystallization of iron-bearing olivines is illustrated by the system forsterite-fayalite-silica. Depending on the composition of the starting liquid and the degree of fractionation, several courses of crystallization are possible. The most important of these are discussed in the text.

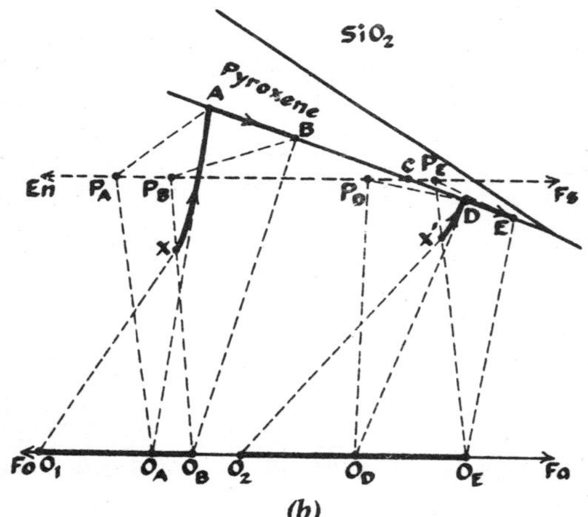

(b)

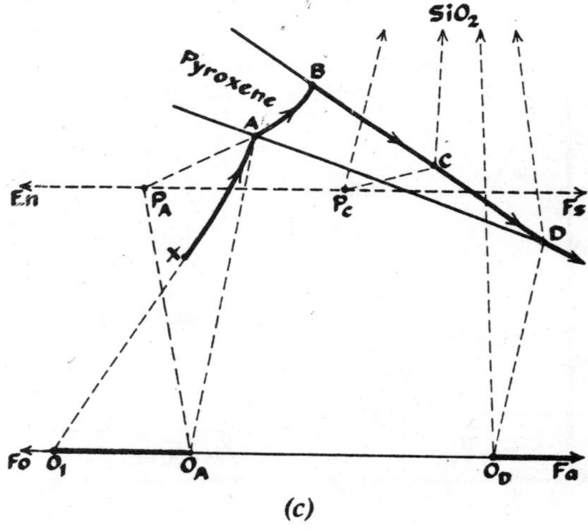

(c)

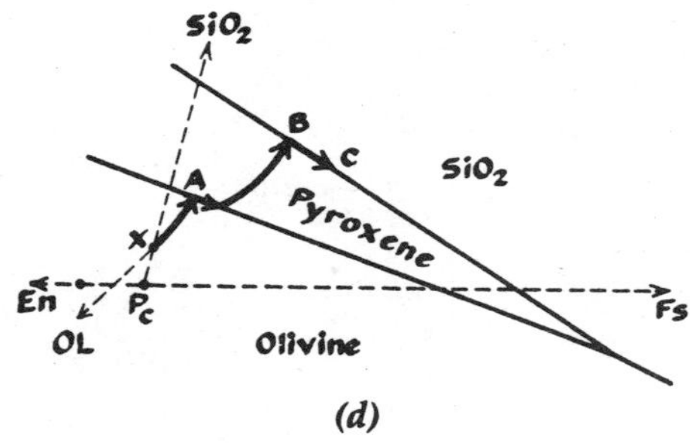

(d)

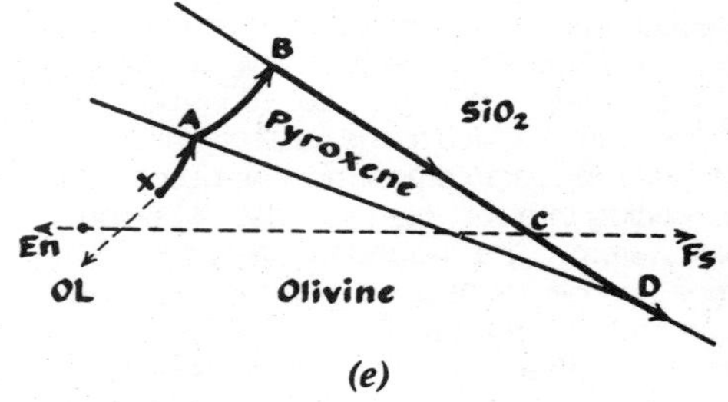

(e)

ample of a system with an intermediate compound, in this case enstatite, that melts incongruently. Crystallization and melting follow the principles outlined for such systems in chapter three (Figs. 3–12 and 3–19b).

These reaction relations do not extend to the full range of olivine compositions; with greater iron contents the crystallization behavior changes in several ways, depending on the degree of enrichment and oxidation state of the iron. Crystallization of olivine from reduced Fe-bearing liquids is illustrated by the system forsterite-fayalite-silica (Fig. 4–14). Several possible courses are shown in expanded schematic diagrams of the central part of the system.

Consider first liquids with compositions in the field between the olivine and pyroxene joins, Fo-Fa and En-Fs. With complete reaction and equilibration, such liquids crystallize to assemblages of olivine and pyroxene with the same bulk composition as the starting liquid, but, depending on their initial composition, they may do this in different ways. The liquid X in the left part of Fig. 4–14b first crystallizes olivine of composition O_1 and follows a curved course across the olivine field as the composition of the crystals becomes more fayalitic. On reaching the peritectic boundary of pyroxene at A, the olivine has a composition O_A (indicated by a tangent from the liquid at A). Pyroxene of a composition such as P_A then begins to crystallize, and at the same time the liquid reacts with early-formed olivine and converts part of it to pyroxene. The composition of both the pyroxene and remaining olivine become more iron-rich. When the liquid reaches a composition such as B at which the compositions of the pyroxene and olivine have reached P_B and O_B respectively, a line joining these phases passes through the bulk composition X. At that point the last liquid crystallizes, and the crystalline assemblage consists of X-P_B parts olivine and X-O_B parts pyroxene.

A liquid X′ in the right-hand part of the same diagram is somewhat richer in iron. It follows a similar course of crystallization, but, when the olivine-pyroxene boundary crosses below the En-Fs join, it becomes a cotectic. The reaction relation disappears, and olivine and pyroxene crystallize together. The reason for this change can be seen by examining the effects of crystallization or reaction on the composition of the liquid. The early pyroxene P_D lies below the boundary, and, if reaction did not take place, it would cause the liquid to leave the boundary, but when the pyroxene composition crosses point C to a composition, such as P_E, this relation changes, and reaction is no longer required to keep the liquid on the boundary.

Without reaction the course of both of these liquids, X and X′, will be extended to more iron-rich compositions (Fig. 4–14c). The liquid X, for example, would again follow a curved path across the olivine field, but on reaching the pyroxene boundary it would not follow it. Instead, it would embark on a curved path across the pyroxene field, crystallizing increasingly more iron-rich pyroxene, until it reaches the boundary of the silica field. It then descends along the pyroxene-silica cotectic, crystallizing a silica mineral, first together with pyroxene and then with olivine. (Note that during this sequence the silica content of the liquid first increases and then decreases as crystallization proceeds.)

Liquids with compositions above the En-Fs join, such as X in Fig. 4–14d initially precipitate olivine, but with complete reaction they should crystallize to a final assemblage consisting only of pyroxene and SiO_2. The liquid, after crossing part of the olivine field, reaches the peritectic pyroxene boundary and follows it as pyroxene crystallizes and olivine reacts with the liquid. The small amount of olivine is soon consumed, however, and the liquid must leave the peritectic, cross the pyroxene field, and reach the cotectic boundary with SiO_2. It then crystallizes pyroxene together with quartz or tridymite until the composition of the pyroxene reaches P_C, at which point the last drop of liquid has crystallized. Without reaction (Fig. 4–14e) the course is similar to that outlined in Figure 4–14c.

The iron-rich pyroxene, ferrosilite (Fs), is unstable at low pressures and has never been found in igneous rocks. The stability field of pyroxene gradually narrows with increasing proportions of iron and gives way to a cotectic boundary between silica and iron-rich olivine. Thus, a liquid increasingly enriched in iron eventually ceases to crystallize Ca-poor pyroxene and instead precipitates a second generation of olivine together with a silica mineral. This relation explains why olivine can crystallize, not only from basic magmas, but also from rhyolites and granophyres in equilibrium with quartz or tridymite.

Iron-titanium oxides

Iron and titanium oxide minerals are minor but almost ubiquitous components of almost all volcanic and plutonic rocks. They may occur as primary phases or as products of alteration of other minerals, such as olivine, amphibole, and biotite. Ten percent or so of the total iron content of most natural magmas is in the ferric state, Fe^{+3}, and does not enter appreciably into the crystal structures of common iron-bearing silicates. Instead, it combines with ferrous iron to form magnetite (Fe_3O_4). TiO_2, though a minor component of most igneous rocks, may exceed 3 or 4 weight percent in some basalts and gabbros, particularly those of alkaline composition. At concentrations below about 1 weight percent or so, most of this titanium is taken up in solid solution in titaniferous magnetite, but at greater concentrations it forms a separate phase, ilmenite.

The principal oxide phases and their compositional ranges are shown in Figure 4–15. Magnetites may contain up to 80 percent of the isostructural titanium component, ulvospinel (Fe_2TiO_4), as well as small amounts of magnesium- and aluminum-rich spinel. Magnesium-rich spinels are referred to as magnesioferrites or, more loosely still, spinel. In a similar fashion, ilmenite can contain up to 15 percent or so of hematite (Fe_2O_3).

The amount of solid solution of the titanium component in magnetite and of hematite in ilmenite is a function of temperature and oxidation state (Fig. 4–16a). Provided they have not exsolved and recrystallized their respective components at lower temperatures, the compositions of these minerals record the temperature and partial pressure of oxygen at which the magma crystallized, and they are widely used as a measure of these parameters. Re-equilibration at lower temperatures is rapid, however, and temperatures estimated in this way must be interpreted with caution.

With increasing degrees of oxidation, the ratio of ferric to ferrous iron increases, and larger proportions of the iron in magmas enter magnetite, and less

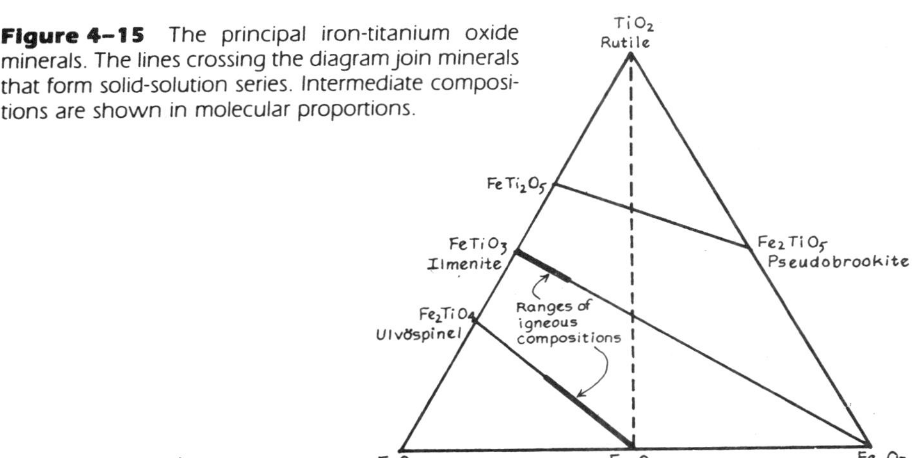

Figure 4–15 The principal iron-titanium oxide minerals. The lines crossing the diagram join minerals that form solid-solution series. Intermediate compositions are shown in molecular proportions.

goes into the ferrous iron-bearing silicates, such as olivine and pyroxene. The effect is well-illustrated by the system olivine-silica at two different oxidation states (Fig. 4–17). The reduced system without ferric iron (Fig. 4–17a) is the same as that shown earlier as Figure 4–14; in the oxidized system, fayalite is replaced by magnetite and silica:

$$\underset{\text{fayalite}}{3Fe_2SiO_4} + \underset{\text{oxygen}}{O_2} \longrightarrow \underset{\text{magnetite}}{2Fe_3O_4} + \underset{\text{silica}}{3SiO_2} \qquad (4\text{–}1)$$

Note that the large field of magnetite cuts off the fields of both olivine and pyroxene and restricts the range of differentiated liquids to much lower levels of iron enrichment. In natural magmas, the oxidation state is normally between these two extremes.

A reaction such as equation 4–1 has an equilibrium constant that is a function of the activities of the various reactants and products. Being a gas, the activity of oxygen is referred to as its *fugacity*, which is simply the partial pressure of the gas multiplied by an activity coefficient that corrects for the deviation of its properties from those of a perfect gas. Its function is basically the same as that of chemical potential discusssed in the preceding chapter.

A number of reactions involving oxidation of iron, such as the one described in equation 4–1, have equilibrium constants that place them within the realm of oxidation conditions in natural magmas. They provide a convenient reference to which the oxidation state of an iron-bearing system can be related. They are referred to as *buffer reactions*, because, so long as all the components of the reaction are present, the oxygen fugacity is constrained to a well-defined curve that varies in a fixed way with temperature (Fig. 4–16b). In the case of the FMQ reaction of equation 4–1, for example, an increase in the partial pressure of oxygen in the system drives the reaction toward the right; fayalite goes to magnetite and quartz

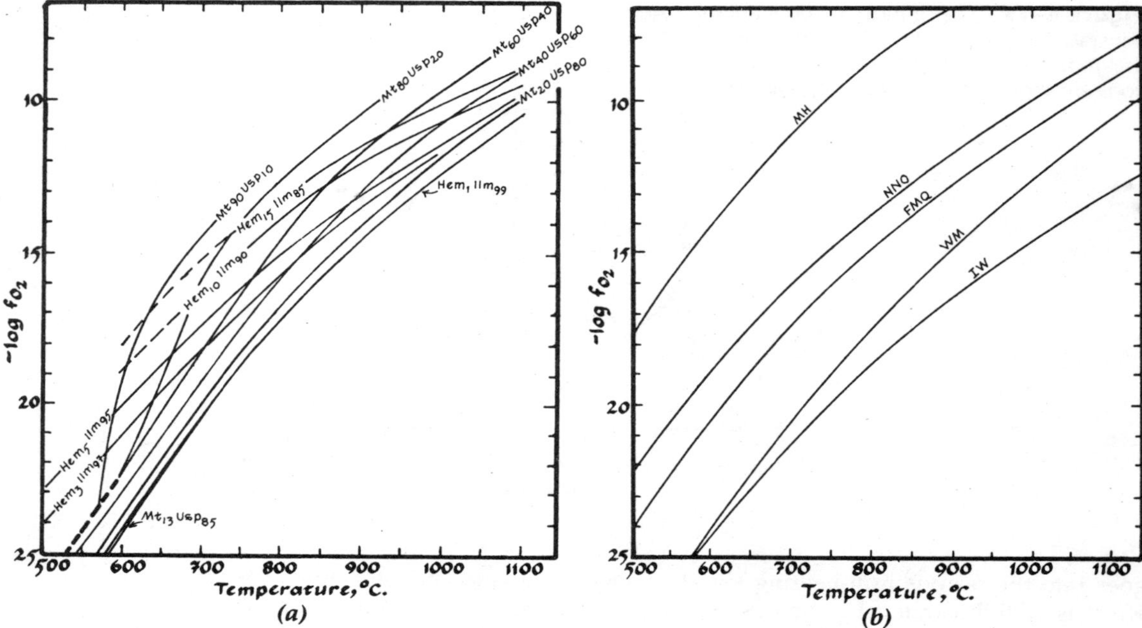

Figure 4–16 (a) The compositions of coexisting magnetites and ilmenites are a function of temperature and the partial pressure or fugacity of oxygen (fO_2 in atmospheres). The intersecting curves for the compositions of the two minerals form a grid from which it is possible to estimate the temperature and oxygen fugacity at which a pair of coexisting oxide minerals last equilibrated. (After A. F. Buddington and D. H. Lindsley, 1964, *Jour. Petrology*, 5:310–357.) (b) Certain oxidation-reduction reactions, often referred to as "buffers," are taken as standard references for the relationship between temperature and oxygen. Those shown here are the most common in the range of magmatic conditions on the Earth or Moon. Abreviations stand for: MH, magnetite-hematite; NNO, nickel-nickel oxide; FMQ, fayalite-quartz-magnetite; WM, wustite-magnetite; and IW, metallic iron-wustite.

with an absorption of oxygen. A decrease operates in the opposite direction with a liberation of oxygen. Thus, by the Principle of Le Chatelier, the effect of the change is absorbed or "buffered." From the form of the curve in Figure 4–16b, it should be possible to deduce whether the reaction (4–1) is endothermic or exothermic.

Amphiboles and micas

The hydrous minerals amphibole and mica (Tables 4–5 and 4–6) occur in almost all felsic plutonic rocks and in many mafic alkaline rocks as well. They are also found in many dacites and rhyolites, but because they are unstable at high temperatures and atmospheric pressure, they are less common in volcanic than in plutonic rocks of equivalent composition.

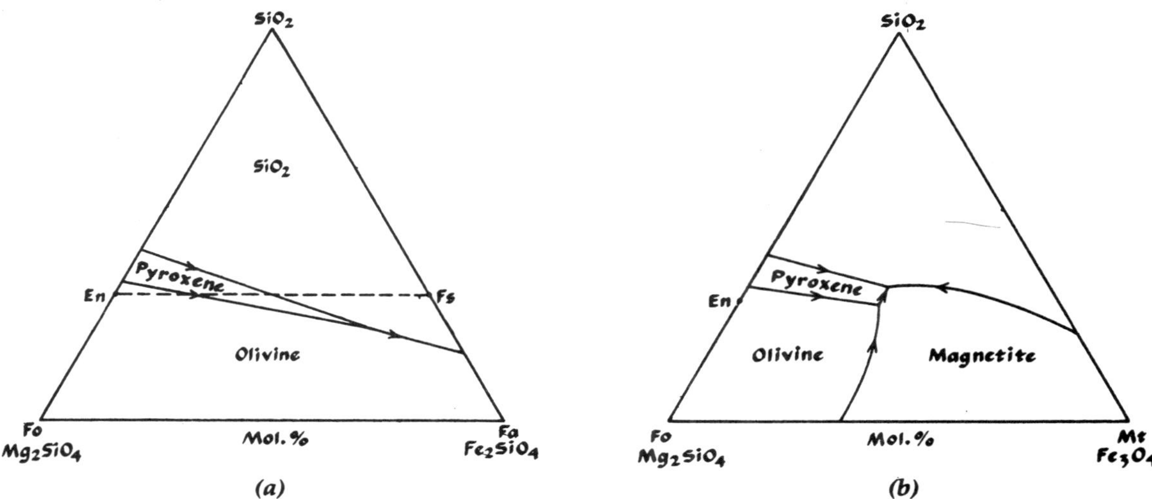

Figure 4-17 The effect of oxidation of iron is seen by comparing the system forsterite-fayalite-silica at two oxidation states, one (a) in which all iron is in the ferrous state (as in Fig. 4–14a) and another (b) at atmospheric conditions where much of the iron is in the ferric state, and magnetite replaces fayalite as a liquidus phase.

The common hornblendes of subalkaline volcanic rocks and most diorites and tonalites are members of the pargasite-hastingsite series. In volcanic rocks they may be the deep reddish-brown form, oxyhornblende. The Ca-poor amphibole, cummingtonite, is common in rhyolites and dacites and may coexist in equilibrium with common hornblende. In more alkaline rocks, such as trachytes, phonolites, and equivalent sub-volcanic rocks, the sodic amphibole, riebeckite, is more characteristic. The Al-poor amphiboles are, as a rule, most common in felsic rocks. Many alkaline gabbros contain the titaniferous amphibole, kaersutite, but barkevikite and arfvedsonite are more characteristic of alkaline plutonic rocks containing less Ti.

Owing to their wide compositional range, the effect of fractionation of amphiboles on the composition of a differentiating magma can be predicted only if the composition of the specific amphibole is known. Crystallization of some amphiboles tends to enrich the remaining liquid in silica, while others may have the opposite effect. The composition of the pargasite in Table 4-5, for example, is equivalent to an assemblage of normative minerals including nearly 12 percent nepheline, whereas the cummingtonite in the same table has the equivalent of about 7 percent quartz. Because of this same effect, the first liquids produced by partial melting of rocks containing pargasitic amphiboles are more silica-rich than a melt produced from a rock of the same chemical composition but with no stable hydrous mineral.

The micas of volcanic rocks tend to be magnesian biotites; muscovite is found mainly in pegmatites and plutonic rocks formed at moderately high pressures. Phlogopitic mica is especially characteristic of ultramafic and highly potas-

Table 4–5 Compositions and properties of common igneous amphiboles. Owning to the great variation of optical properties, only the general chemical features of amphiboles are given here. For more details on the identification of individual minerals, reference should be made to standard mineralogical tables. Most analyses given here are taken from: Deer, W. A., Howie, R. A., and Zussman, J., 1963, *Rock Forming Minerals*, Vol. Two.

Minerals	Formula	Color	Density
Oxy-hornblende	$Ca_2(Na,K)_{.5-1}(Mg,Fe^{+2})_{3-4}(Fe^{+3},Al)_{2-1}Si_6Al_2O_{22}(O,OH,F)_2$	dark brown	3.2–3.3
Hornblende	$(Ca,Na,K)_{2-3}(Mg,Fe^{+2},Fe^{+3},Al)_5(Si_6(Si,Al)_2O_{22})(OH,F)_2$	green or brown	3.0–3.4
Pargasite	$Na,Ca_2Mg_4(Al,Fe^{+3})(Si_6Al_2O_{22})(OH,F)_2$	pale brown	3.05
Cummingtonite	$(Mg,Fe^{+2})_7(Si_8O_{22})(OH)_2$	pale green	3.36
Ferrohatingsite	$NaCa_2Fe_4^{+2}(Al,Fe^{+3})(Si_6Al_2O_{22})(OH,F)_2$	dark green	3.50
Kaersutite	$Ca_2(Na,K)(Mg,Fe^{+2},Fe^{+3})_4Ti(Si_6Al_2O_{22})(O,OH,F)_2$	dark red-brown	3.2–3.3
Barkervikite	$Ca_2(Na,K)(Fe^{+2},Mg,Fe^{+3},Mn)_5Si_{6.5}Al_{1.5}O_{22}(OH,F)_2$	dark brown	3.35–3.44
Riebeckite	$Na_2Fe_3^{+2}Fe_2^{+3}(Si_8O_{22})(OH,F)_2$	dark blue	3.0–3.4
Arfvedsonite	$Na_{2.5}Ca_{.5}(Fe^{+2},Mg,Fe^{+3}Al)_5Si_{7.5}O_{0.5}O_{22}(OH,F)_2$	green	3.50

Typical Chemical Compositions of Natural Amphiboles

	Horblende (gabbro)	Hornblende (tonalite)	Pargasite (periodotite)	Cummingtonite (diorite)	Ferrohastingsite (granite)	Kaersutite (alkali gabbro)	Riebeckite (granite)
SiO_2	48.71	44.99	43.61	50.78	39.56	40.67	51.01
TiO_2	0.32	1.46	1.15	0.40	1.46	6.22	0.96
Al_2O_3	9.48	11.21	15.06	1.77	12.18	10.45	0.80
Fe_2O_3	2.33	3.33	1.59	1.88	4.10	3.86	16.41
FeO	9.12	13.17	5.14	29.64	23.18	7.56	17.62
MnO	0.23	0.31	0.08	0.14	0.09	0.15	0.48
MgO	14.43	10.41	16.53	11.83	4.43	11.54	0.22
CaO	11.93	12.11	11.80	1.33	9.98	15.55	0.19
Na_2O	1.16	0.97	2.78	0.00	1.81	1.83	7.89
K_2O	0.15	0.76	0.11	0.00	1.38	1.14	1.80
H_2O	1.83	1.52	1.74	2.01	1.26	1.28	0.91
F	0.23	—	—	—	1.20	—	1.70

Table 4–6 Compositions and properties of igneous micas

Mineral	Formula	Color	Density
Muscovite	$K_2Al_4Si_6Al_2O_{20}(OH,F)_4$	colorless	2.8–2.9
Phlogopite	$K_2(Mg,Fe)_6Si_6Al_2O_{20}(OH,F)_4$	pale brown	2.8–2.9
Biotite	$K_2(Mg,Fe^{+2})_{6-4}(Fe^{+3},Al,Ti)_{0-2}Si_{6-5}Al_{2-3}O_{20}(OH,F)_{4-2}$	dark brown	2.7–3.3

Chemical Compositions

	Muscovite	Phlogopite	Biotite	Ti-Biotite
SiO_2	46.77	40.16	36.67	36.52
TiO_2	0.21	0.45	3.39	8.77
Al_2O_3	34.75	12.65	17.10	13.29
Fe_2O_3	0.71	5.52	4.58	0.58
FeO	0.77	4.39	16.36	15.91
MnO	—	0.03	0.04	0.20
MgO	0.92	22.68	9.20	11.28
CaO	0.13	0.24	0.38	0.68
Na_2O	0.47	—	0.2	0.73
K_2O	10.61	9.62	9.17	9.00
H_2O	4.48	3.00	1.98	3.02
F	0.16	—	1.37	—

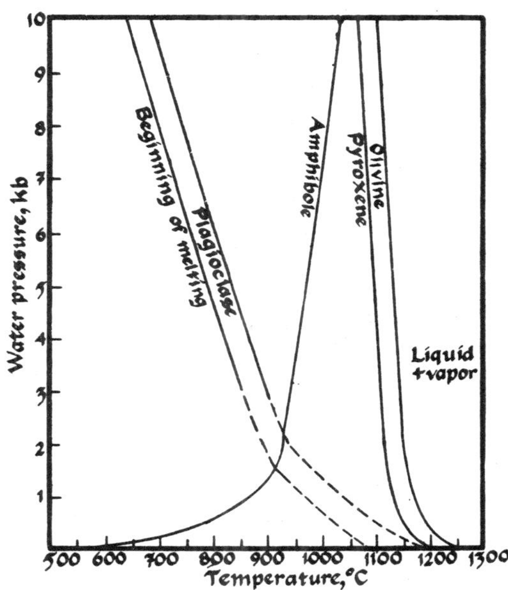

Figure 4–18 Crystallization of amphibole is illustrated by the liquidus relations of a basaltic magma as a function of water pressure. Note that with increasing water pressure, the stability of amphibole increases to higher temperatures, while the anhydrous minerals crystallize or melt at lower temperatures than they do under dry conditions. (After H. S. Yoder and C. E. Tilley, 1962, *Jour. Petrology* 3:342–532.)

sic alkaline rocks. The typical micas of alkali gabbros are a deep red titaniferous variety.

Micas, like the pargasitic amphiboles, are silica-poor minerals. The composition of biotite, for example, is equivalent to the anhydrous assemblage olivine + leucite + kaliophilite (the strongly silica-deficient equivalent of orthoclase—$KAlSiO_4$). Hence fractionation of mica tends to enrich the remaining liquid in silica, whereas melting or assimilation of the same mineral has the opposite effect.

Because water is an essential component of their crystal structures, the temperatures at which amphiboles and micas are stable increase with an increasing vapor pressure of water. A typical example is the curve for crystallization of hornblende from basaltic liquids (Fig. 4–18). Note the contrast between the negative slopes for the upper stability limits of anhydrous minerals and the positive slope for that of hornblende at increasing water pressure. This difference illustrates the contrasting role played by water in crystallization of the anhydrous and hydrous minerals.

The reason for this difference can be understood in terms of the familiar Clapeyron equation,

$$\frac{dT}{dP} = \frac{T\Delta V}{\Delta H} \tag{3-21}$$

and the volume changes on melting (or reaction) in the presence of a separate water-vapor phase. As we have seen, an anhydrous mineral in the presence of water vapor melts with a decrease of volume at constant pressure, because the water dissolves in the melt with a large negative ΔV. But when a hydrous phase breaks down to an anhydrous assemblage plus water vapor, the volume change is positive, because the water has a much greater molar volume as a gas than it has in solution. All dehydration reactions must require an input of heat, for we know by experience that one heats a substance to drive out its water, and the ΔH of a dehydration reaction must be positive, just as it is in melting an anhydrous phase. It can be seen, therefore, that, if P in the Clapeyron equation is pressure of water vapor, the slope dT/dP for an anhydrous phase will be negative (because ΔV is negative), while that of a hydrous mineral will be positive for the opposite reason.

Owing to this general principle, it can be taken as a rule that if water does not enter the crystalline structure it acts as an unsaturated constituent of the liquid and lowers the melting temperature, as would any other added component. If it is an essential component of a crystalline phase, however, the increased pressure of water acts to stabilize the mineral and increases the temperature range in which it can coexist with liquids.

The stability relations of biotites are affected not only by water pressure but by the oxidation state as well. With increasing partial pressure (or fugacity) of oxygen, the temperature at which the iron-rich micas break down decreases. The effect is illustrated by the reaction

$$\underset{\text{biotite}}{3K(Mg,Fe)_3AlSi_3O_{10}(OH)_2} + \underset{\text{silica}}{3SiO_2} + \underset{\text{oxygen}}{2O_2} \rightleftarrows \underset{\text{olivine}}{3Mg_2SiO_4} + \underset{\text{magnetite}}{Fe_3O_4} + \underset{\text{sanidine}}{3KAlSi_3O_8} + \underset{\text{water}}{3H_2O}$$

The same equation shows that the activity of silica must also affect the stability of biotite, so that the mineral would be stable at higher temperatures in silica-poor magmas. This is in accord with the more common occurrence of biotite in alkali gabbros than in more silica-rich rocks.

CRYSTALLIZATION OF IGNEOUS MINERALS

The great compositional and textural variety of igneous rocks attests to the diverse conditions under which magmas cool and crystallize. The nucleation and growth of minerals and the efficiency with which they equilibrate with the cooling liquid are strongly dependent on the cooling rate of the body and a host of physical and chemical properties of the system.

Nucleation and growth of crystals

Most magmas reach their final level of eruption or intrusion charged with phenocrysts that began to grow at some lower level or in transit upward. The origins of these suspended crystals are poorly understood; some may be fragments of the source rocks or of the walls lining the conduit, but most are probably precipitated from the rising liquid as a consequence of changing conditions, such as falling temperature and pressure and loss of volatiles from the magma.

We noted in the preceding chapter that cooling liquids seldom begin to precipitate crystals at the exact temperature at which they become saturated with a particular mineral. Unless crystals are already present to serve as nucleii for further growth, a certain degree of supersaturation is required before stable nuclei can form.

In a liquid containing small nuclei, the smallest crystals, since they have a proportionately large number of atoms with unbalanced charges, have a high surface energy and low stability. In a saturated liquid containing these small ephemeral crystals, a balance is reached between the number of new crystals forming and the number going back into solution. A larger crystal has a distinct advantage in such a liquid. Because the number of its unbalanced surface atoms is small compared to the number in the interior, the structure is more stable. Hence, a single liquid cannot be in perfect equilibrium with both large and small crystals; large crystals are able to grow, while smaller ones are unstable and dissolve.

With falling temperature and increasing oversaturation, the probability and frequency of formation of ephemeral lattice structures increases, and the rate of accretion of small nuclei exceeds the rate at which they break down and return to the liquid. Thus the probability increases that an individual nucleus will exceed the critical size necessary for its survival. The minimum radius of a stable crystal nucleus is a function of its surface energy, molar volume, degree of undercooling, and the entropy difference of the liquid and crystalline phases. It is usually in the range of 10^{-5} to 10^{-6} cm, well beyond the resolving power of a petrographic microscope.

Because the rate at which nuclei of a critical size are formed is a function of the properties of individual minerals, it will not ordinarily be the same for two or more phases that are precipitating simultaneously from the same liquid. A given amount of undercooling and supersaturation produces differing rates of nucleation and growth for each species being precipitated (Fig. 4–19.) A mineral forming many stable nuclei grows simultaneously from numerous growth centers while another mineral with only a few stable nuclei must grow on a smaller number of individual crystals. Thus, the once-popular notion that the largest crystals in a rock were the first to grow is not necessarily valid.

At the earliest stages, when crystals have dimensions of the order of a few microns or when the degree of supersaturation is small, the rate of crystal growth is governed by growth dislocations or steps on the crystal surface where the lower surface energy favors an addition of molecular or ionic units. With increasing size or degree of supersaturation, growth proceeds on multiple surfaces of each crystal. Under these conditions it is the number and surface energy of growth sites that controls the growth rate. Because the relative levels of surface energy of crystal faces vary with differing conditions of crystallization, it is not uncommon for certain minerals, such as plagioclase or pyroxene, to grow with a distinctive form under conditions that favor elongation along a particular axis, while under other conditions the mineral will assume a very different shape.

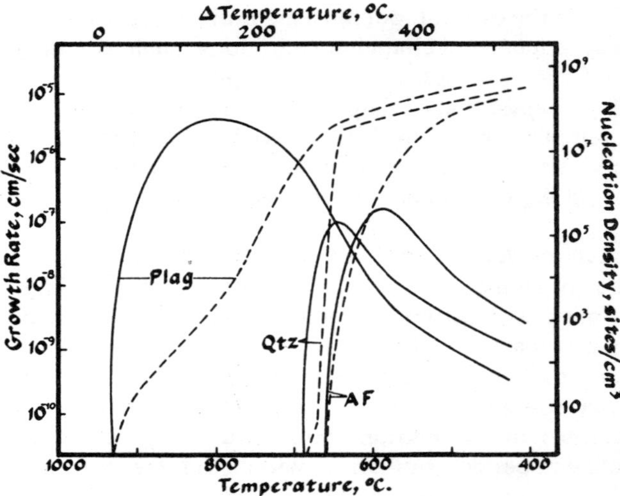

Figure 4–19 Rates of nucleation (broken lines) and growth (solid lines) of quartz, plagioclase, and alkali feldspar (AF) from a granodioritic liquid with 6.5 wt percent H_2O as functions of the amount of undercooling, ΔT. The numbers of nuclei tend to decrease if they remain at constant temperature after an initial burst of nucleation, because the smallest crystals are resorbed and disappear as larger crystals grow at their expense. (After S. E. Swanson, 1977, *Amer. Min.*, 62:966–978.)

The growth rate, R_g, of crystals with dimensions greater than a few microns is controlled in part by the rates of reactions taking place at the crystal surface and in part by the rate of diffusion of the slowest component through the adjacent liquid. The first of these effects is poorly understood and difficult to evaluate. The second is governed by a relation such as:

$$R_g = K(D/t)^{1/2} \tag{4–2}$$

where K is a factor that includes the free-energy difference due to undercooling, surface energy, and the ionic volume of crystallizing components. D is diffusivity, and t is time. For a given cooling rate the crystals that will reach the largest size are those formed from components with the highest diffusion coefficient and largest ionic volume.

Diffusion, as we saw in chapter two, is governed by Fick's first law, which can be written

$$\frac{dn}{dt} = DA\frac{dc}{dx} \tag{4–3}$$

where n is the number of atoms passing through a cross-sectional area A in unit time t, D is the diffusion coefficient in cm^2sec^{-1}, C is concentration in atoms per cm^3, and x is distance.

The diffusion rates governing the movement of ions in complex silicate melts are probably in the range of 10^{-8} to 10^{-10} cm^2 sec^{-1}, but they vary widely with temperature and viscosity, and they are strongly dependent on the size and charge of the ion. Small, monovalent ions diffuse much faster than large ions with higher valences, and complex ions formed by extensively linked silicon, aluminum, and oxygen atoms have a much lower mobility than separate cations.

Diffusion is an important factor in crystal growth only when a crystal is static with respect to its surrounding liquid; relative motion of the liquid and crystal can reduce the limiting effect of diffusion by bringing fresh liquid to the crystal surface. This is why stirring causes sugar to dissolve more quickly in a cup of coffee. Crystals that sink or float or that grow on a surface adjacent to a flow of saturated liquid have an advantage over those growing in stagnant magma.

The process of crystal growth does not necessarily stop at the liquidus, or even at the solidus. The temperatures of large plutonic bodies remain for thousands of years in a range equivalent to those at which high-grade metamorphic rocks acquire their distinctive textures and mineralogical assemblages, and the same reactions that lead to metamorphic recrystallization under these conditions must also prevail in large intrusions.

So long as temperatures remain within two or three hundred degrees of the solidus, the trend toward equilibrium continues to cause a readjustment of the compositions, sizes, and shapes of crystals and may even form new phases. This process is known as *Ostwald ripening.* Large crystals grow at the expense of smaller ones, while minerals with limited ranges of solid solution steadily approach end-member compositions by exsolving their secondary components. This is particularly true of the iron oxides, magnetite and ilmenite, and other solid-solution series, such as alkali feldspars and pyroxenes, which show extensive exsolution in slowly cooled rocks.

Theoretically, a very slowly cooled assemblage of crystals would eventually recrystallize to a rock with only a single large crystal of each phase, because this would be the lowest energy state. Under natural conditions, however, diffusion is so slow and the differences of surface energy of crystals so small that, once they reach half-a-centimeter or so in size, this process comes to an end.

Large grain-sizes are commonly attributed to slow cooling, but the rate of crystallization is by no means the only factor contributing to coarse crystals. Rocks with exceptionally large crystals, broadly referred to as *pegmatites,* owe their coarse-grained textures to crystallization in the presence of a fluid phase, usually one rich in water. The fluid facilitates the transfer of components to the growing crystals, either by flowing over them or by providing a medium in which diffusion is greatly accelerated over what is normally in volatile-poor silicate melts. Other components, such as fluorine or chlorine, may have a similar effect.

TEXTURES OF IGNEOUS ROCKS

Many of the factors governing the nucleation and growth of crystals described in the preceding section are reflected in the textures of volcanic and plutonic rocks. The principal effects fall into several general categories.

a. *High rates of cooling and supersaturation* (Fig. 4–20) tend to cause rapid growth of slender crystals that are greatly elongated in one crystallographic direction. The crystals may radiate from a common center or form curved and branching clusters of tiny microlites. Because the edges and corners of crystals can draw on larger volumes of adjacent liquid than can planar faces, they grow more rapidly and produce crystals with hollow cores and "swallow-tail" longitudinal sections.
b. *Differing rates of nucleation and growth* (Fig. 4–21) can cause one mineral to

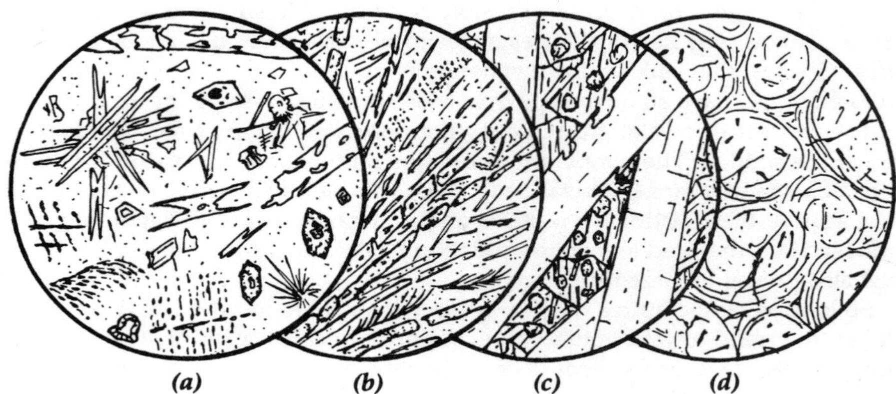

Figure 4–20 Textures produced by rapid cooling and high supersaturation. (a) Crystals in rapidly quenched basaltic lavas are commonly very elongated and may have hollow cores. Small microlites form curved and branching clusters. (b) *Spinifex* textures in ultramafic lavas are characterized by long, slender needles of olivine or pyroxene. In this case, elongation may result from the very low viscosity and high diffusivity of the liquid. (c) Similar textures are produced by elongated plagioclase or olivine crystals in gabbros, which may have had high water contents that facilitated diffusion. The texture illustrated here is that of the "perpendicular feldspar rock" of the Skaergaard intrusion, but similar textures are found in some olivine-rich gabbros, such as the *harrisitic* rocks of Rhum, Scotland. (d) Quenched siliceous liquids rarely nucleate large crystals but may have small microlites. The *perlitic* texture common to many rhyolites erupted in a wet environment probably forms as a result of hydration, expansion, and cracking of glass after it cooled.

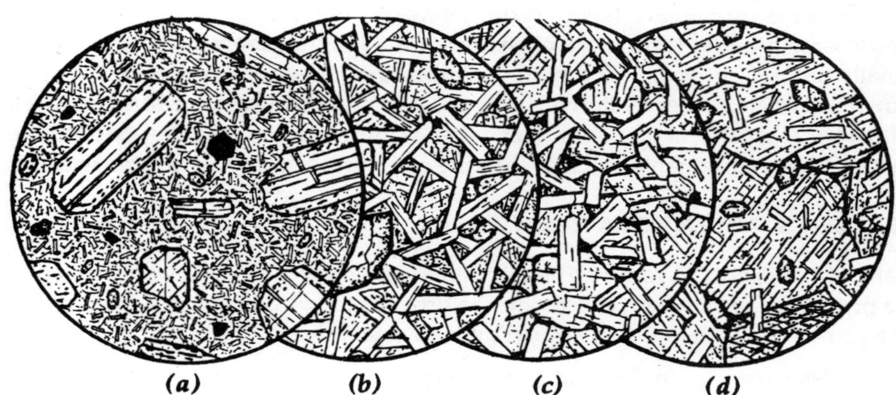

Figure 4–21 Textures illustrating differing rates of nucleation and growth. (a) Phenocrysts formed during an early period of crystallization, usually prior to eruption, give rocks a *porphyritic* texture. (b) If the principal groundmass minerals grow from many nuclei and at similar rates, the mafic minerals tend to occupy the spaces between plagioclase laths and give the rock an *intergranular* texture. (c) If pyroxene grows from a smaller number of nuclei and partly encloses the plagioclase crystals, as it does in many dolerites, the texture is said to be *ophitic*. (d) *Poikilitic* textures represent an extreme case in which large crystals grow through extensive parts of the rock and completely enclose smaller grains.

form large numbers of small crystals while another forms larger crystals growing on a smaller number of nuclei. If one of the minerals crystallizes earlier or faster than the others, it may form large *phenocrysts*, that give the rock a *porphyritic* texture. But, if most crystals nucleate and grow at the same rates, they tend to develop *intergranular* textures, in which grains of pyroxene, olivine, and oxide minerals lie between laths of plagioclase. If, as often happens in slowly cooled basalts, pyroxene forms few nucleii but larger individual grains, it may partly encase the laths of plagioclase and form what is referred to as *ophitic* textures. In extreme cases one of the minerals may grow from a small number of nuclei and completely enclose many other crystals of smaller size to form what is called *poikilitic* texture.

c. *The amount of residual glass* (Fig. 4–22) may vary between wide extremes. If small pools of glass occupy the interstices between crystals, the texture is said to be *intersertal*, but if the glass is continuous through the groundmass it produces a *hyalophitic* texture, in which glass partly surrounds individual crystals. *Hyalopilitic* textures are common in siliceous lavas, such as dacites and trachytes. They are distinguished by a glassy matrix crowded with many small crystals. But this term would not be applied to a rock with only glass in its groundmass; instead, a rock with large phenocrysts suspended in a matrix that is wholly glassy, or very nearly so, is said to be *vitrophyric*.

d. *Flow structures* in highly viscous magmas that were moving at the time they solidified may align the crystals in wavy or planar layers (Fig. 4–23).

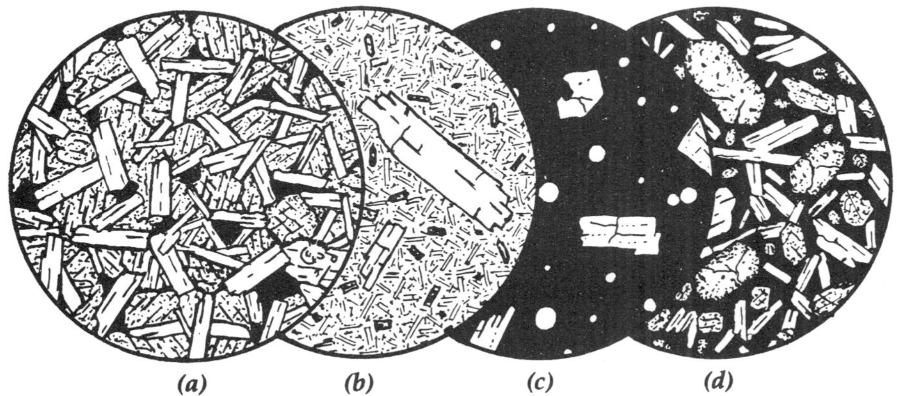

(a) (b) (c) (d)

Figure 4–22 Textures resulting from differing proportions of residual glass (a) *Intersertal* textures are common in basaltic lavas in which small pools of glass remain between crystals of plagioclase, pyroxene, and olivine. (b) The groundmasses of many andesites and dacites are composed of clear glass, with many randomly oriented small crystals. Such textures are called *hyalopilitic*. (c) *Vitrophyric* textures in which large phenocrysts are scattered through a glassy groundmass are common in pyroclastic rocks. In this example, the glass has small gas cavities, which make the rock *vesicular*. With larger proportions of crystals, vitrophyric rocks grade into those with *hyaloophitic* textures (d), in which glass partly or completely encloses the crystals.

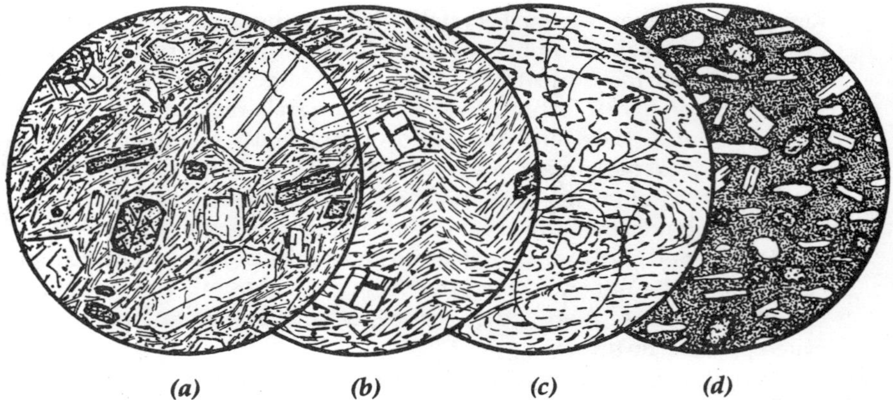

Figure 4–23 Flow structures in viscous lavas. (a) Many andesites and dacites have *pilotaxitic* textures in which the groundmass consists of crudely aligned small crystals that swirl around larger phenocrysts. (b) In *trachytic* rocks the alignment of small crystals is stronger, and they give the entire rock a felted appearance. (c) *Flow-banding* in rhyolite results from concentration of tiny crystals or vesicles along planes of shear and deformation. (d) The vesicles of basaltic lavas may be stretched if the lava is too viscous for them to maintain a normal spherical shape.

Many andesitic and dacitic lavas have a *pilotaxitic* groundmass crowded with small, crudely aligned crystals. The alignment of feldspars may be so pronounced that they give the rock a felted appearance that characterizes *trachytic* textures. If the rock has much glass, however, flow-banding may develop along planes of shear, and, if vesicles have formed, they tend to be stretched parallel to the direction of flow.

e. *The relative development of crystal faces and mutual interference of grains* (Fig. 4–24) results in a variety of textures ranging between those that are *panidiomorphic* and have a large proportion of euhedral grains, through *hypidiomorphic* rocks, in which some minerals form well-developed crystals while others do not, to *allotriomorphic* textures in which few if any of the crystals have euhedral outlines. Rocks with textures that have adjusted during prolonged, slow, cooling tend to develop nearly equidimensional anhedral grains with boundaries that intersect at angles approaching 120 degrees. Such rocks contain few minerals that preserve their crystal faces, but some phases, particularly apatite, zircon, sphene, and other accessory minerals, have well-developed forms, just as they do in metamorphic rocks. A particular feature of intergrowths developed from rapid eutectic crystallization is *granophyric* or *myrmekitic* texture, in which one mineral forms wormy or cuneiform blebs within another.

f. *The degree of crystal-liquid fractionation* (Fig. 4–25) during slow crystallization has an important influence on the modal proportions, compositions, and textural relations of individual minerals. These effects are best seen in *cumulate* rocks formed from crystals that *accumulate* near the cooling margins of a crystallizing magma. The original definition of these rocks

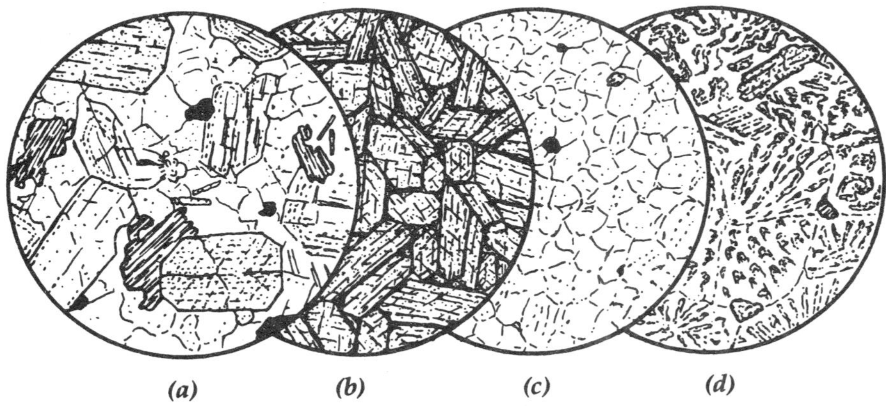

Figure 4–24 Textures resulting from differences of crystal form. (a) Most granitic rocks have *hypidiomorphic granular* textures in which some crystals have euheral forms, some have poorly developed faces, and others have no crystal form at all. (b) If most of the crystals are euhedral, the rock is said to be *panidiomorphic*, but (c) if crystal faces are rare the texture is *allotriomorphic*, as it is, for example, in many aplites. (d) Rapid eutectic crystallization of siliceous liquids produces *granophyric* textures characterized by intergrowths of quartz and alkali feldspars. The patterns of intergrowth are crudely controlled by crystallographic features of the host crystal, and, if this produces a coarse texture with strong alignment of the enclosed crystals, the texture is said to be *graphic*.

assumed that they resulted from gravitational segregation, but similar textural relations are observed in rocks that appear to have crystallized in place.

The main types of cumulates are distinguished by the amount of growth of early-formed crystals, or *primary precipitates*, prior to the appearance of later crystals that grew from the *interstitial* or "trapped" *liquid*. If minerals nucleate and grow from the trapped liquid, the rock is said to be an *orthocumulate*. But if the

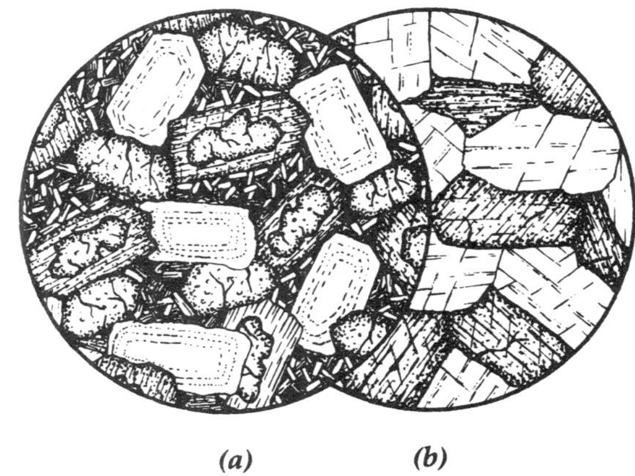

Figure 4–25 The effects of separation or re-equilibration of the inter-crystalline liquid between early-crystallizing minerals as they grow can be thought of in terms of two hypothetical extremes. With no separation (a), the liquid between the liquidus minerals is "trapped" and, as it cools and evolves, precipitates minerals with compositions different from the initial ones. The resulting rock is referred to as an *orthocumulate*. If, as in (b), continued exchange between the interstitial liquid and a much larger reservoir of magma makes it possible for the primary precipitates to continue to grow without changing composition, components excluded from these crystals are expelled and are not precipitated by later crystallization as they would have been if trapped. The final assemblage consists of only the primary precipitates, unchanged from their liquidus compositions, and is known as an *adcumulate*.

first-formed crystals continue to grow with a constant composition through efficient equilibration with the main reservoir of liquid, the residual components are effectively excluded and the final assemblage, known as an *adcumulate*, contains few if any crystals precipitated from a trapped liquid. In this latter case, in which diffusion keeps up with crystallization and the concentration gradient between the interstitial liquid and the main reservoir of magma is weak, the interstitial liquid may never nucleate new phases. The result is a rock consisting of unzoned crystals of one or more minerals. Intermediate cases may result from a combination of adcumulus enlargement, zoning of early crystals, and nucleation and growth of later ones through the interstices; this type of crystallization produces *mesocumulates* that may differ widely in the proportions and grain sizes of their crystals.

Many cumulate rocks, especially those of gabbroic and syenitic compositions, have pronounced layering, normally parallel to the floor and walls of the intrusion. The layering may result from differences of the proportions of dark and light minerals or from differences of grain size. Various kinds of layering have been attributed to different proposed mechanisms, but the origins of most layering are still poorly understood. Examples are discussed in chapter six.

Tabular or prismatic minerals having a preferred orientation may give a rock *igneous lamination* (Fig 4–26a). The orientation is usually parallel to the cooling surface of the floor, wall, or roof, but under certain conditions of cooling and strong supersaturation, crystals may grow with a marked elongation perpendicular to the solidification front. The name *crescumulate* has been coined for textures of this kind (Fig. 4–26b). Long, slender crystals of olivine, plagioclase, or pyroxene may grow like blades of grass on the floor or walls of the intrusion. Crescumulate textures are most common in mafic plutonic rocks,but they have also been found in the margins of granitic plutons.

Growth of slender crystals normal to the cooling surface has been attributed to a phenomenon known as *constitutional supercooling*. If the rate of cooling is rapid compared to that of diffusion, a condition can result in which liquid in a

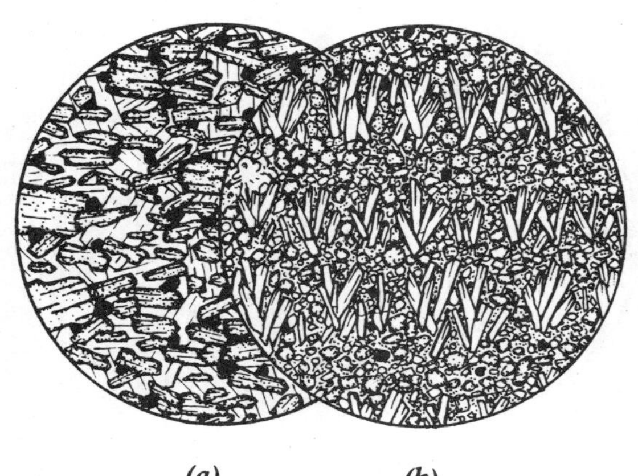

Figure 4-26 (a) *Igneous lamination* in a gabbro of the Stillwater Complex, Montana, is the result of pyroxene having a preferred orientation in a plane of layering. Elongated crystals may have a linear orientation within the same plane. (b) Crystals may also have a preferred orientation perpendicular to the plane of the layering. In this case, the elongated, sub-parallel crystals of plagioclase give the rock a *crescumulate* texture. Layers of crystals oriented in this way are referred to as "Willow Lake type layering."

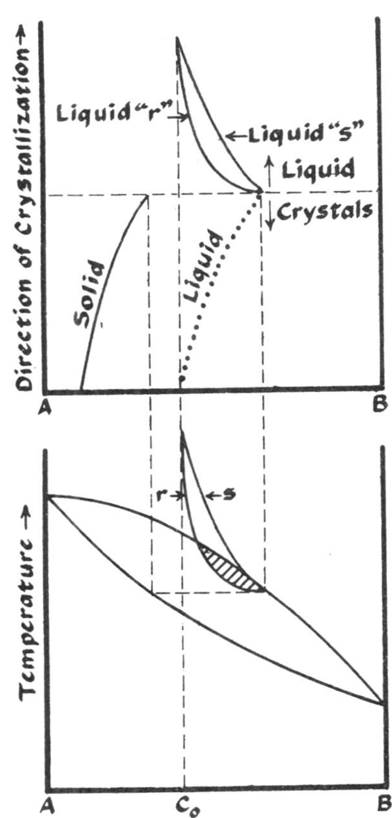

Figure 4–27 If a front of crystallization advances into a liquid with an initial composition C_o, and crystals are richer in the high-temperature component A than the coexisting liquid, the components will have a distribution similar to that shown schematically in the upper diagram. The liquid immediately adjacent to the crystals is enriched in B relative to the solid and the main magma reservoir, and a compositional gradient extends away from the crystals into the hotter liquid above. If the front advances rapidly, the gradient is steep, as in curve "r," but with slower crystallization diffusion reduces the gradient to a more gentle form like "s." In the lower diagram, the temperature in the liquid is shown in relation to liquidus and solidus curves. Under conditions of rapid advance, the compositional gradient may be steep enough to cause the concentration of B to fall below the saturation level defined by the liquidus curve, and an unstable zone of supersaturation (shown by diagonal ruling) can cause the liquid to be "constitutionally supercooled." Any crystal that extends into this zone provides a site for rapid growth in the direction normal to the main crystal-liquid boundary. With slower crystallization (curve "S"), the concentration of B does not fall below the saturation level, and crystal growth is restricted to a narrow zone parallel to the front.

zone adjacent to the crystals becomes supersaturated, because the profile of temperature and composition falls below the liquidus curve. The mechanism is explained more fully in the legend of Figure 4–27.

A WORD OF CAUTION

One final point before going on. In dealing with these mineral assemblages and textures, it is well to remember that what we see or measure in an igneous rock is the final product of a long and complex process of cooling and crystallization under conditions that can only be guessed by indirect means. No magma has ever been observed while crystallizing under conditions of slow cooling and equilibration. Laboratory experiments are too brief, and even the deep lava lakes described earlier crystallize far too rapidly to provide a true analog of processes taking place in the crust or mantle. One cannot always be certain, therefore, which of the textural features of plutonic rocks can be attributed to crystallization from a magmatic liquid and which reflect the later cooling history of an essentially solid rock. Recent work on plutonic intrusions has revealed that many rocks that were once interpreted as unaltered products of magmatic crystallization have, in fact, recrystallized and no longer retain their original compositions or textures.

SELECTED REFERENCES

Cashman, K. V., 1990, Textural constraints on the kinetics of crystallization of igneous rocks. *Modern Methods of Igneous Petrology: Understanding Magmatic Processes*. J. Nicholls and J. K. Russell, ed., *Rev. in Mineral.* 24:259–314. An excellent review of the origins and interpretations of igneous textures with many well-documented examples.

Hargraves, R. B., ed. 1980. *Physics of Magmatic Processes*. Princeton University Press. 585 pp. Contains especially useful chapters on the theory and experimental studies of crystal growth.

MacKenzie, W.S., C. H. Donaldson, and C. Guilford. 1982. *Atlas of Igneous Rocks and Their Textures*. Halstead Press. 148 pp. A magnificently illustrated reference on the textures and mineral assemblages of igneous rocks. Although it is purely descriptive and offers no interpretations of textural relations or paragenetic associations, the book is very useful for identifying the petrographic features of all the common types of volcanic and plutonic rocks.

Williams, H., F. J. Turner, and C. M. Gilbert. 1982. *Petrography: An Introduction to the Study of Rocks in Thin Sections*, 2d ed., W. H. Freeman & Co. 626 pp. A standard reference to the mineralogical and textural features of igneous, as well as metamorphic and sedimentary rocks. The classification system is outdated, but the hand-drawn illustrations of hundreds of igneous rocks are still of great value.

5

MAGMATIC DIFFERENTIATION: MECHANISMS AND EFFECTS

DIFFERENTIATION IS DEFINED as any process by which magmas evolve and become more diversified. Most types of differentiation have two essential parts, one chemical and the other physical. The first establishes a compositional difference in one or more phases, usually in response to changing physical conditions, and the second preserves these differences by segregating or fractionating the phases so they can form distinctive rocks. The *trends* of magmatic differentiation are determined by crystal-liquid relations, such as those portrayed in phase diagrams, but the *degree* to which these trends develop is governed by the effectiveness of the physical mechanism of fractionation. The term *fractionation* is applied to any process by which different phases are mechanically separated. It is not synonymous with *differentiation*. Fractionation is a mechanism; differentiation is its effect.

MECHANISMS OF DIFFERENTIATION

It will be recalled that, by definition, a phase has specific physical properties by which it can be mechanically separated. All processes of mechanical segregation depend on contrasts of these physical properties—density, viscosity, diffusivity, or geometric form—and derive their driving force from the thermal or gravitational energy of the system. They can be divided into several types according to the nature of the phases being fractionated.

Crystal-liquid fractionation

The compositions of igneous minerals are much simpler than those of the natural liquids in which they form; they consist of a relatively small number of essential constituents, most of which have proportionately greater concentrations in the crystal than in the liquid. Because of these differences, elements that have a high concentration in a crystal are depleted from the liquid in which it grows, while those that are excluded become concentrated in the diminishing volume of residual liquid. If crystals and liquid are separated before the magma solidifies completely, the remaining liquid can continue to crystallize to form a rock with a chemical composition quite different from that of the original liquid. This, in essence, is the basic principle of crystal fractionation: separation of crystals from a magma depletes those components having greater concentrations in the crystals than the liquid and enriches the remaining elements that are left in the reduced volume of liquid.

Consider again the Hawaiian lava lake mentioned earlier and the compositional changes that developed in the liquid as it crystallized (Fig. 5–1). As crystals grew in its cooling margins, they extracted certain components of the magma while leaving others to accumulate in the remaining liquid, and in this way the liquid immediately adjacent to the crystals took on a composition different from that of the hotter, still-liquid interior. These differences resulted in compositional gradients in the liquid, and elements removed by the crystals diffused down these gradients to feed continued growth, while rejected ones diffused in the opposite direction. The slower the diffusion of these components and the more rapid the growth of the crystal, the greater will be the compositional contrast between the liquid next to the crystal faces and that at some greater distance. At the same time, rapid crystallization usually inhibits efficient fractionation, so that, even though the liquid changes composition, it is not effectively segregated, and differentiation is restricted to the interstitial liquid.

This is what is happening in the lava lake. As in most small bodies of magma emplaced at shallow levels of the crust, crystallization is so rapid and diffusion so slow that compositional differences are confined chiefly to the late liquid in inter-

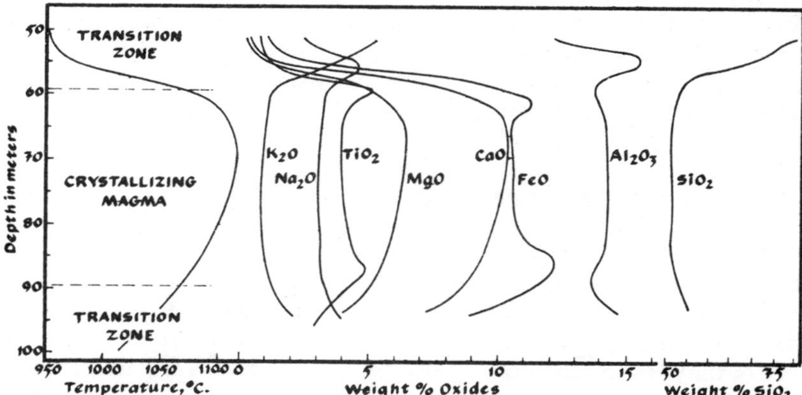

Figure 5–1 As the basaltic magma in the lava lake of Kilauea Iki solidified, the concentrations of the various components changed in response to progressive crystallization. The plot above shows the variations of several of these components in liquids (quenched to glass) in samples recovered by drilling into the crystallizing basalt. Note that some components are depleted from the liquid while others are enriched. The rates of enrichment or depletion depend on the compositions and proportions of crystallizing minerals. If the differentiated liquids were removed and allowed to crystallize elsewhere, they would form a series of rocks of different compositions. Without this second step of segregation, the process of differentiation is incomplete. (Data from W. C. Luth, Sandia Corporation, personal communication.)

stices between early-formed crystals (Fig. 5–2). The composition of the rocks as a whole, at least on the scale of a hand specimen, is the same as the original basaltic lava. Were the interstitial liquid removed to crystallize as a separate rock, the process of differentiation would be complete. If not, the crystals become zoned, the remaining liquid is enriched, first in iron and titanium then in silica, and, when certain components become highly concentrated, new minerals may form. Magnetite and apatite, for example, crystallize when the remaining liquid becomes strongly enriched in iron and phosphorus. If the liquid were separated (or fractionated) at this stage, it could crystallize to form a rock very different from its parent.

Crystallization can produce large-scale compositional differences only under conditions of efficient crystal-liquid fractionation; diffusion alone is too slow to

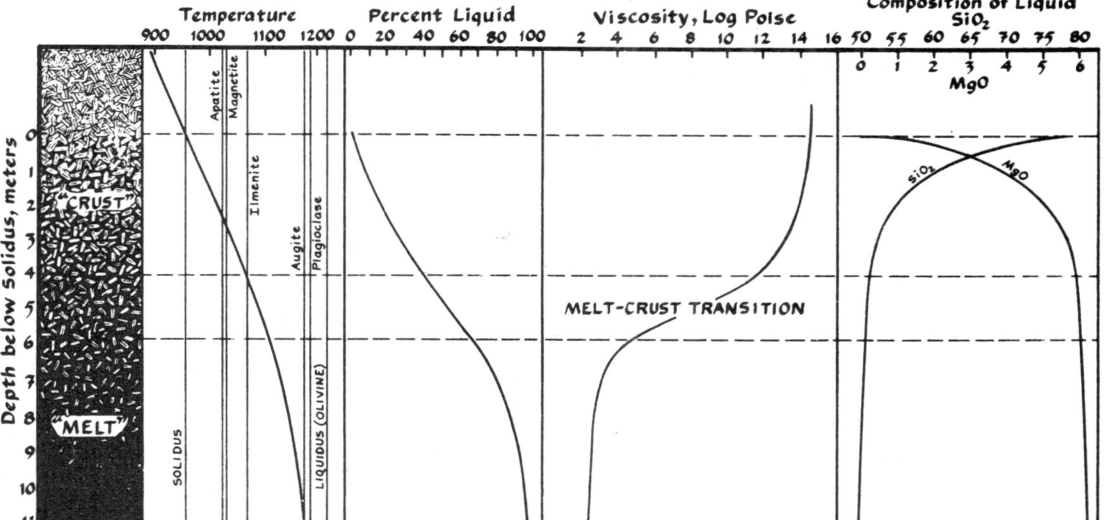

Figure 5–2 Looking more closely at crystallization under a roof, a zone of solidification can be distinguished between the solid crust and liquid interior. The curves above are a schematic synthesis of the relations in three Hawaiian lava lakes. As crystallization advances, the viscosity of the magma increases sharply in a transition interval bounded by the two horizontal broken lines, and, with less than about 40 percent liquid, takes on the properties of solid rock. Note the slow initial rate of change of the composition of the liquid fraction. Most of the increase of SiO_2 and decrease of MgO, for example, occurs in the last 10 to 20 percent of crystallization. At this stage the differentiated liquid is too far from the front of nucleation for diffusion to be an effective mode of mass transfer between interstitial liquid and the main reservoir below. As a result, the trapped liquid crystallizes in place, and the bulk composition of the final rock remains close to that of the original magma. Small crystals nucleating at the base of the section settle more slowly than the front of increasing viscosity advances and are caught in the solidifying crust before they can escape. (Based on a summary of the crystallization behavior of three Hawaiian lava lakes by T. L. Wright, D. L. Peck, and H. R. Shaw, 1976, *Amer. Geoph. Union Geophysical Monograph 19*, 375–392, and analytical data obtained from Kilauea Iki by W. C. Luth, pers. comm. Viscosities are from measurements by T. Murase.)

do this unless the phases are mechanically segregated. If crystals sink, float, or are otherwise separated from the liquid as they grow, they come in contact with fresh, undepleted liquid from which they can extract the elements essential to their growth. In this way they may remove these components from a much larger mass of magma than would be possible by diffusion alone. The same effect can result from flow of liquid over static crystals growing on the walls of a magma chamber or volcanic conduit. Regardless of which is moving, crystals or liquid, the efficiency of fractionation is greatly enhanced by any relative motion of the two phases.

Consider, for example, a trace element such as chromium, which, in basaltic magmas, seldom has a concentration greater than about 100 parts per million. This metal is mined from large gabbroic intrusions in which layers of almost pure chromite have thicknesses of several tens of centimeters. This amount of chromium would have to be extracted from a volume of liquid at least ten thousand times greater than that of the layer in which it now resides. It could not have done this by any known process of diffusion. Because the diffusivity of heat (about 4×10^{-3} cm^2 sec^{-1}) is several orders of magnitude greater than chemical diffusivity (10^{-6} to 10^{-8} cm^2 sec^{-1}), the time required to concentrate chromium by chemical diffusion alone would be far greater than the time required for the intrusion to cool and crystallize. It seems clear, therefore, that crystals can only concentrate a component to such a remarkable degree by moving through a large volume of magma or, alternatively, by a similarly large amount of magma flowing over the zone of crystallization. In either case, the crystallizing phase must be exposed to enough undepleted liquid to extract the element in the relatively short time that crystals grow.

Any mechanism that involves relative motion of crystals and liquid is strongly dependent on the viscosity of the magma and the relative densities of the phases. The reason for this will be evident if we consider the case of crystals nucleating and growing under the roof of a cooling intrusion. Settling rates, U, of these crystals are governed by the simplified form of Stokes' Law from equation 2-6.

$$U = \frac{2\ \Delta\rho g r^2}{9\eta} \qquad (5\text{-}1)$$

in which $\Delta\rho$ is the density difference between the liquid and crystals, r is the radius of the crystal, and η is the viscosity of the liquid. The initial velocities of crystals must be very slow, owing to their small sizes, but as they continue to grow their velocities increase with the square of the radius. At the same time, cooling results in an increase in the viscosity of the liquid and in the volumetric proportion of crystals it contains. Depending on their rates of sinking relative to the rate of advance of the front of solidification and increasing viscosity, some crystals may escape, whereas others may be trapped in the zone of cooling. The crystals most likely to be segregated by gravity are those having a large density contrast with the liquid and a large size at an early stage of cooling.

Filter pressing

Even if the liquid between growing crystals evolves without equilibrating effectively with the main reservoir of magma, it may be separated before crystallization is complete simply by squeezing it out, much as water is squeezed from a sponge. This mechanism is often referred to as filter pressing. A buoyant liquid in a mush of loosely packed crystals under differential stresses may migrate toward zones of lower pressure, just as compaction drives water from a thickening pile of accumulating sediments. Processes of this kind have been observed in the Hawaiian lava lakes, where plumes of volatile-rich residual liquid become buoyant with respect to the rest of the crystal mush and rise through it to form diapiric pipes of siliceous pegmatites. A similar process could occur during partial fusion of the mantle or lower crust when melting reaches a stage at which rocks lose most of their strength, and the overlying load forces the liquid into channel-ways leading toward the surface.

Flow segregation

Segregation can also occur when magmas containing suspended crystals flow along the walls of a dike or a convecting pluton. As we noted in chapter two, the velocity gradient of a viscous fluid is steepest at its margins and declines to a nearly uniform velocity near the center. The shearing produced by a gradient of this kind results in a weak force, usually referred to as *dispersive shear pressure,* that tends to drive crystals out of the zone of maximum shear next to the walls and into the interior of the flow (Fig. 5–3). The result is to redistribute suspended crystals in such a way that their concentration is inversely related to the gradient of velocity. Effects of this kind of crystal-liquid segregation can be seen in porphyritic dikes and, less commonly, in the basal zones of sills and lava flows.

Before this mechanism was recognized, dikes with concentrations of large crystals in their centers were thought to be formed by slower cooling and crystallization of the liquid in the interior of the dike, but, if this were the case, the bulk composition of the porphyritic interior would be the same as that of the fine-grained margins, and this is rarely the case. The distribution of crystals could also be the result of an intrusion of a compositionally graded magma. If the first liquid to enter a fissure and solidify against its walls comes from the upper crystal-free part of a deeper reservoir, then the crystal-rich interior could be a later part of the intrusion coming from a lower level of the same reservoir. Examples will be seen in the next chapter showing that some dikes and sills have in fact inherited inhomogeneities from a magma that was compositionally graded at the time of intrusion. Their origins can be distinguished from those due to flow segregation, because the composition of the groundmass of the crystal-rich rocks differs from that of the crystal-free margins.

FRACTIONATION BY MELTING

Partial melting

The processes of melting are in many ways the reverse of solidification; the compositions of liquids vary as melting advances, much as they do with crystalliza-

Figure 5–3 The concentration of solid particles toward the interior of a body of flowing magma, as shown by this dike in East Greenland, is due to the effect of dispersive shear forces explained in the text.

tion. If melt is extracted at an early stage of melting, it will be richer in low-temperature components, whereas more advanced melting produces liquids with larger proportions of the more refractory components. Thus a series of liquids can be produced that resembles the compositions of liquids evolving by crystal fractionation, but their order of appearance in the magmatic sequence would, of course, be reversed.

Despite these broad similarities, details of the two processes may differ in several important ways. We shall see in a later section that the relative concentrations of certain trace elements in liquids produced by melting may differ from those evolved by crystal fractionation. Moreover, the compositions and proportions of liquids may differ, depending on how melting takes place. If the source rock contains strongly zoned crystals and minerals that melt at very different temperatures, then the contributions of the individual phases to the liquid at any stage of melting will be very different from those of minerals of more homogeneous compositions. The difference is analogous to that between crystallization of a solid-solution series with or without complete reaction and equilibration (Fig. 5–4a).

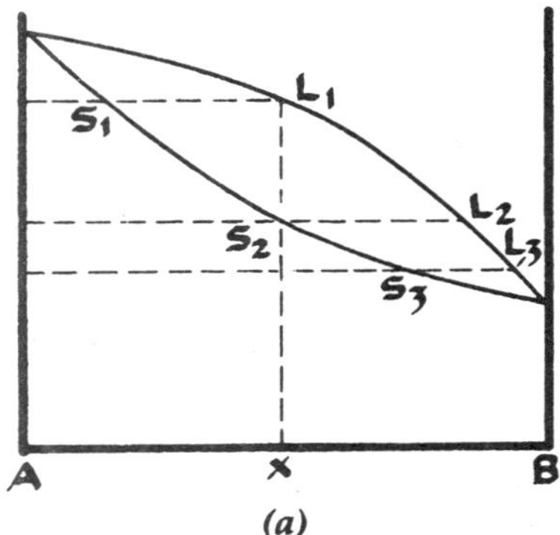

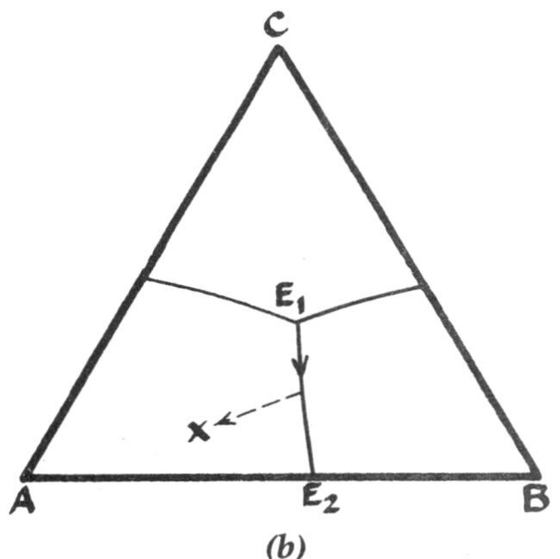

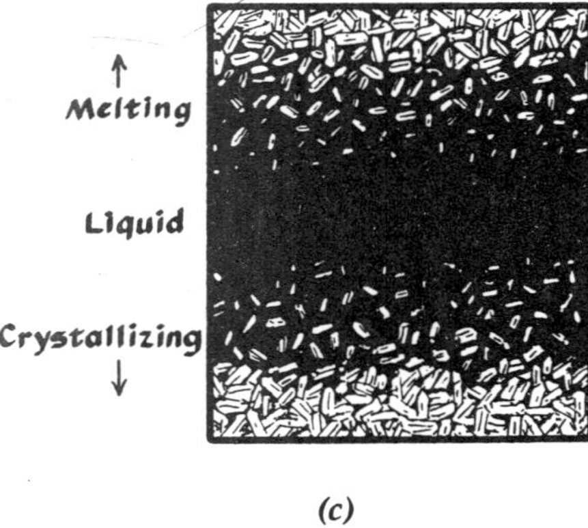

Figure 5-4 Compositions of liquids produced by partial melting. (a) If a rock of composition X is formed by equilibrium crystallization, all crystals would have composition S_2, and the first liquid to be produced by melting would be L_2. But if the rock contained crystals zoned from S_1 to S_3, the first melt would have the composition L_3. (b) Melting of a rock of composition X would begin at eutectic E_1, and, assuming the liquid is not removed, the composition would leave the eutectic when C is consumed and follow the cotectic until B is completely melted. Thereafter the liquid crosses the field of A until it reaches the starting composition, X. If the liquid is removed as rapidly as it forms, it will start at E_1, but the next composition to form after C disappears will be at E_2. After B is consumed the next liquid will have the composition of pure A.

Fractional melting

The compositions of liquids produced by partial melting will also differ according to the frequency with which the liquid is removed. Note that in a multicomponent system, such as the one shown schematically in Figure 5-4b, the first liquid has the composition of the eutectic, and, if melting advances without removal of the liquid, the composition leaves the eutectic when one of the crystalline phases is exhausted, and subsequent liquids will evolve, first up the cotectic, then, when the next phase disappears, into the field of the last remaining crystalline phase. But if the liquid is withdrawn as rapidly as it is formed, the course of melting is very different. The first liquid is still that of the eutectic composition, but, when the first crystalline phase is exhausted, the remaining crystals constitute a system of only two solid phases, and the next liquid will be that of the binary eutectic. No intermediate compositions will be produced; instead a large step in both composition and temperature will result. Again, if the liquid is removed as melting proceeds at the binary eutectic, melting will stop temporarily when the next crystalline phase is exhausted and will not resume until the temperature reaches the melting temperature of the last remaining crystalline component. Thus, fractional melting, as this latter process is called, would be expected to yield discontinuous rather than smoothly changing compositions and would have steps of time and temperature separating successive stages of melting.

Zone melting

A process known to metallurgists as *zone refining* is used as an industrial process to purify certain types of alloys. A bar of impure metal is passed through a heating element so that a fraction of the metal is melted, and, as the bar slowly moves, this zone of melt passes from one end to the other carrying with it elements that are preferentially concentrated in the liquid. With repeated passes, these elements are swept to one end of the bar. One can visualize how a similar mechanism could lead to compositional changes in magmas. Suppose that a lens-like zone of melt is rising through the mantle in such a way that crystallization at its base is accompanied by melting of its roof (Fig. 5–4c). This could happen if volatile components were more concentrated at the top or even if the magma has a nearly constant composition provided the pressure difference between its roof and floor were enough to make the liquidus temperature at the base of the column a degree or so higher than that at the top. Either situation could lead to a thermal balance between crystallization and melting. Heat liberated by crystallization at the floor can be transferred by convection to the top of the melt zone where it would provide the heat necessary to melt the roof. In this way, the heat of crystallization would be balanced by the heat of fusion, and a zone of melting would pass upward with little net loss of heat. As it does so, elements that are preferentially concentrated in the low-melting fraction would tend to become progressively enriched in the pocket of rising melt.

The concentration of a component in the liquid, C_L, is governed by the equation:

$$\frac{C_L}{C_O} = \frac{1}{K} - \left(\frac{1}{K} - 1\right)e^{-Kn} \qquad (5\text{–}2)$$

in which C_O is the initial bulk concentration, K the bulk distribution coefficient (i.e., the ratio of the concentration in the solid to that in the liquid), and n the ratio of the mass of solid processed to the mass of liquid. Note that as n becomes large, C_L/C_O approaches a constant value of 1/K. This is a limiting value at which the concentration of the component ceases to increase, because the amount entering the liquid from melting at the top is the same as that removed by the crystals at the base.

In natural conditions, the amount of liquid in the remelted zone will increase as the zone advances and collects incompatible components, such as H_2O, which have the effect of lowering the melting temperature and increasing the proportion of liquid. This tends to increase the effectiveness of the process, because the liquid does not become saturated as quickly as it would be at constant volume.

The efficiency of this process as a mechanism of differentiation is strongly dependent on the relative rates of diffusion and motion of the zone of liquid. Unless the zone of melting moves very slowly, or unless the process is repeated many times, the degree of segregation and differentiation is likely to be small. The process would be most effective at depths where the temperatures of rocks are already high and little heat is needed to raise the rocks to their melting temperature.

LIQUID-LIQUID FRACTIONATION

Most differentiation in magmatic intrusions takes place in a narrow zone, or *boundary layer*, at or near the margins where the magma interacts thermally and chemically with its surroundings. Because the liquids in this zone are characterized by gradients of temperature, crystallinity, and composition, their mechanical instability is conducive to several possible processes of differentiation.

Boundary layer fractionation

A potentially important mechanism is one in which a layer adjacent to the wall of an intrusion becomes lighter or heavier than the main mass of the magmatic body and is segregated by gravity under the roof or on the floor. Such a process could result when crystallization, melting, or absorption of volatiles at the wall changes the composition of the adjacent liquid and causes its density to differ from that of the interior. The simplest case is that in which the boundary layer absorbs water from its surroundings, so that the density of the liquid is lowered by an amount that exceeds the effect of falling temperature and thermal contraction. A buoyant, water-rich layer may then rise along the wall and collect under the roof. The same effect could result from any other compositional effect, such as crystallization or melting, that changes the relative concentration of heavy components and causes the boundary layer to be gravitationally segregated from the original magma in the interior (Fig. 5-5).

A process of this kind may contribute to differentiation of shallow intrusions of magma in which dense components tend to be preferentially concentrated in the crystalline phases, thus making the residual liquid lighter. Andesitic magma, for example, is less dense than basalt, even though its temperature is lower, and rhyolitic magma, because it is poor in iron and other dense components, is lightest of all. Crystallization against the wall of such an intrusion could produce a thin layer of compositionally different liquid that may flow along the contact to collect at the top of the intrusion and eventually produce a compositionally zoned column of magma.

Immiscibility

Three types of magmatic systems are known to have compositional ranges in which two immiscible liquids may separate under geologically reasonable conditions. Sulfide liquids may separate from mafic silicate magmas, even at low concentrations of sulfur; highly alkaline magmas rich in CO_2 can split into two

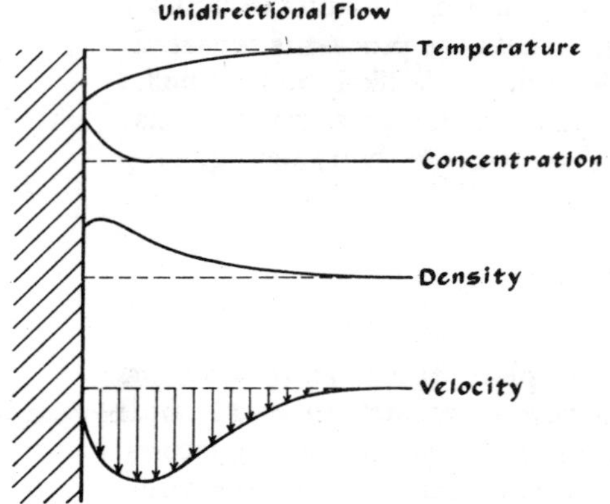

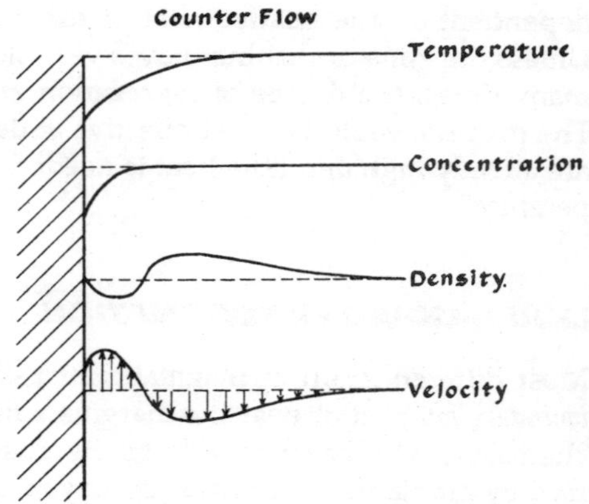

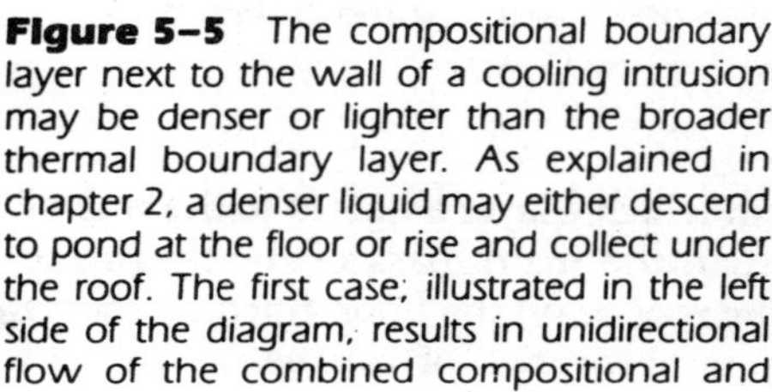

Figure 5–5 The compositional boundary layer next to the wall of a cooling intrusion may be denser or lighter than the broader thermal boundary layer. As explained in chapter 2, a denser liquid may either descend to pond at the floor or rise and collect under the roof. The first case, illustrated in the left side of the diagram, results in unidirectional flow of the combined compositional and thermal layers, whereas the second case may lead to counterflow with an ascending compositional layer and a descending thermal one. The diagram greatly simplifies natural conditions in which the "wall" is actually a zone of increasing crystallinity. Much of the compositional boundary layer probably moves through this porous zone.

immiscible fractions, one rich in alkalies and silica and another rich in CO_3; and very iron-rich tholeiitic magmas may form two separate liquids, a felsic one rich in SiO_2 and a mafic one rich in iron. We shall encounter examples of each of these in later chapters.

The densities of two coexisting immiscible liquids may be sufficiently different for them to separate gravitationally, just as oil does when it rises and floats on water. Sulfide liquids, rich in iron and other heavy metals, may collect as small droplets and settle through basic magmas to collect on the floor. When they do, they collect the chalcophile metals, such as iron, copper, nickel, and cobalt, and the platinum group for which they have a strong affinity, and form rich concentrations of these elements in economic ore deposits.

The felsic liquids of tholeiitic systems have much lower densities than the iron-rich basic magmas from which they separate and must have a strong tendency to rise and collect in the upper levels of a magmatic reservoir. Much depends, however, on the stage of crystallization at which immiscibility develops. Often the magma has crystallized to a viscous mush of entangled crystals, so that the felsic liquid, when it finally forms, does not separate as a continuous mass but remains as small, dispersed droplets locked in the interstices between early-crystallizing minerals.

Immiscibility may be an attractive explanation for closely associated liquids of contrasting compositions, but it is not the only one. Contamination, mixing, and a variety of crystallization phenomena can produce textural features suggestive of immiscible globules of one liquid in another. On closer scrutiny, many of these clot-like inhomogeneities have been found to have compatible and completely miscible compositions. A simple but rigorous test can be applied to these associations. Because two immiscible liquids are in equilibrium with each other, the crystals in one liquid must also be in equilibrium with the other liquid. Therefore, if the two proposed liquid compositions have precipitated different crystalline phases, they could not have been an immiscible pair and probably have another origin.

This rule does not apply to elements that are not essential constitutents of the crystallizing minerals. Certain minor or trace elements that are partitioned in different concentrations between two coexisting liquids can be very diagnostic. In the case of tholeiitic magmas, for example, most of the elements concentrated in felsic immiscible liquids are the same that are residually enriched by normal crystal fractionation. One notable exception is phosphorus. During normal crystallization, this element accumulates in felsic liquids and increases in abundance until apatite begins to crystallize. It is also concentrated in the first liquids produced by partial melting. In immiscible systems, however, it is strongly partitioned into the iron-rich, silica-poor liquid and is relatively depleted from the coexisting felsic member. In this way, the distribution of phosphorus provides a useful way of distinguishing immiscible siliceous liquids from those evolved by crystal fractionation or partial melting.

The Soret effect

At least passing mention should be made of another process of liquid fractionation that could be important in magmas subjected to very strong temperature gradients. Owing to the differing effects of temperature on the chemical potential of the various components of magmas, a weak difference of free energy causes some elements to be more concentrated at the hot end of a temperature gradient, while others tend to migrate toward low temperatures. Recent experiments indicate that the components moving toward high temperatures include SiO_2, Al_2O_3, Na_2O, and K_2O, whereas those drawn toward the low-temperature end of the gradient would be FeO, MgO, TiO_2, and CaO (Fig. 5–6). Thus the distribution is

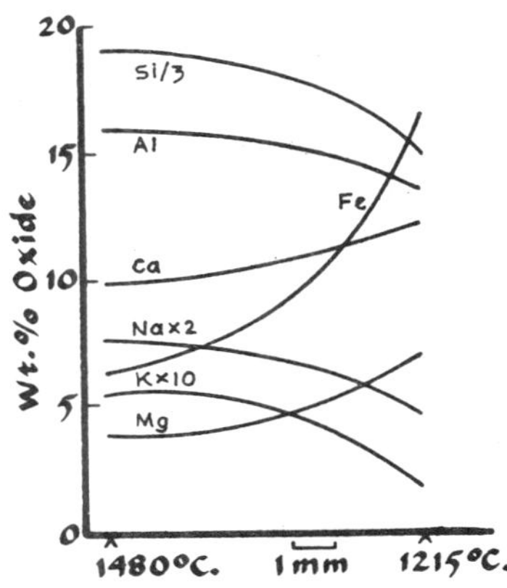

Figure 5–6 The distribution of the components of a basaltic liquid changes in response to a strong thermal gradient in the manner shown in this experimental example. Note that the elements enriched at the hot end of the sample (SiO_2, Al_2O_3, and alkalies) are the same that are concentrated in low-temperature liquids that evolve by crystal fractionation. The sample was held in the temperature gradient at 10 kilobars pressure for 137 hours. (After D. Walker and S. E DeLong, 1982, *Contr. Mineral. Petrol.*, 79:231–240.)

the opposite of what would be expected in gradients produced by crystallization and melting. Although no clear evidence has yet been found to show that this effect is strong enough to be important on a large scale, the unusual distribution of elements it entails may account for a number of anomalous effects that are difficult to explain by more conventional mechanisms.

ASSIMILATION

When one considers the great variety of crustal rocks and the large compositional differences between these rocks and the magmas rising through them, it would seem that assimilation would be a common phenomenon capable of producing a wide range of igneous compositions. Evidence that crustal material is caught up in magmas is easy to find. Many igneous rocks contain *xenoliths* and *xenocrysts* (rocks and crystals of foreign origin) that come from fragments of the crust in various stages of assimilation. In order to understand how these contaminants affect the compositions of magmas, we must first examine the basic principles underlying the process of assimilation.

Consider first a simple hypothetical system, such as the one illustrated in Figure 5-7. Suppose that a magma of composition L is precipitating crystals of A and is suddenly contaminated with a rock consisting of crystalline B. Obviously the liquid cannot be in equilibrium with both crystalline phases at the temperature T_1. This is apparent from the phase diagram, which shows that liquid L is not saturated with crystals of B at any temperature above the eutectic. But we can also see from the phase rule that a system with two components (A and B), and three phases (liquid, A, and B), should have only one degree of freedom,

$$F = C - P + 2 = 2 - 3 + 2 = 1$$

whereas the liquidus surface of the diagram (if we include the third dimension, pressure) has two. This tells us that one of the phases is unstable.

So long as the liquid is not yet saturated with B, it will react with the added crystals and dissolve them. The heat required to do this can be derived from crystallization of A, and the total effect will be to lower the temperature of the

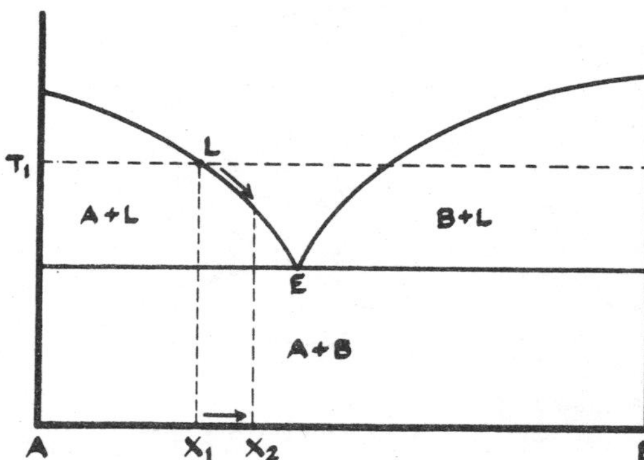

Figure 5-7 If a liquid L at temperature T_1 is saturated with crystals of A, and crystals of B are added, the added crystals will dissolve, because the liquid is not saturated with that phase. The heat required to dissolve the added B is gained by cooling and crystallization of more A, and the liquid evolves down its normal line of descent, as it would had no crystals of B been added. The bulk composition is shifted toward B, however, and the end result is increased proportions of B in the rock.

magma without leaving the liquidus of A. If the amount of B that is added is small enough to be absorbed without completely crystallizing the liquid, the eventual result will be a liquid, somewhat more evolved but with a composition no different from what it would have reached in due course had assimilation never taken place. The bulk composition will be shifted in the direction of B by an amount proportional to the added component and can be calculated by the lever rule.

A slightly different situation is illustrated in Figure 5-8. Suppose that a liquid, L_1, is crystallizing an intermediate compound, AB, and with falling temperature approaches eutectic E_1. If it is contaminated with a small amount of crystalline B, the liquid, since it is not saturated with B, will react with the added crystals and gain the heat to do so by crystallizing additional AB. The crystals of B combine with A from the liquid to precipitate more AB, the only phase with which the liquid is saturated. Note that the effect is to drive the composition of the liquid farther from AB, so that, with falling temperature, it becomes more *unlike* the composition of the added component, B. Of course, if the amount of added crystalline B is large enough to make the bulk composition richer in B than AB, and, if the temperature remains nearly constant, all of L_1 would be consumed in the reaction, and another liquid, L_2, would form in equilibrium with the crystals of AB.

Although the heat required to dissolve the added crystals normally comes from crystallization of a thermally equivalent amount of the mineral with which the liquid is already saturated, the amounts of crystalline material dissolved and crystallized will not normally be the same, unless their heats of fusion and crys-

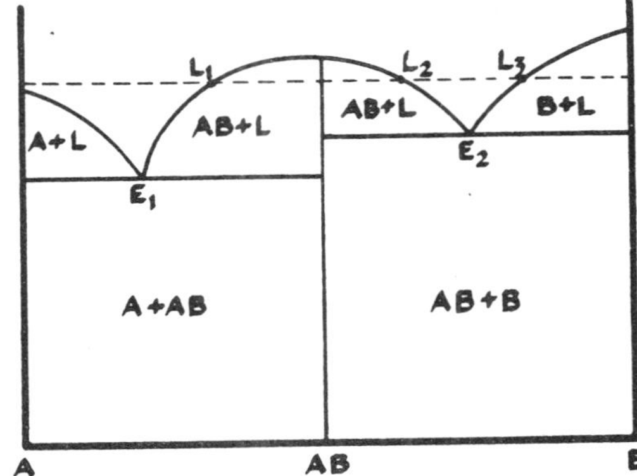

Figure 5-8 In some systems, such as the schematic one shown here, addition of a contaminating phase may cause the liquid to be depleted in the components that have been added. If liquid L_1 is precipitating AB, and crystals of B are added, the latter will react with the liquid-removing component A to form additional AB. At the same time the heat absorbed by the added crystals cools the liquid and causes it to evolve further down its line of descent, becoming poorer in B, the component that was added. Under conditions of disequilibrium, a liquid of composition L_3 may form around the crystals of B, while the liquid adjacent to nearby crystals of AB would have the composition L_2, and the liquid between these two crystalline phases could range between L_2 and L_3. Elsewhere in the same magma, the liquid in equilibrium with AB would still have the composition L_1.

tallization are exactly equivalent. For geological conditions in which temperature varies with the intensive variable, enthalpy, the thermal balance and proportions of phases are best shown by an enthalpy-composition (H-X) diagram, such as Figures 3–8b or 3–13b, rather than T-X diagrams like Figures 5–7 and 5–8.

The important point to note here is that one cannot assume that the major-element composition of an evolving magma will reflect the effect of an added component in any simple way. Its composition may actually become more depleted in the same components that were assimilated. So long as the liquid is in equilibrium with crystals it remains tied to the liquidus surface and does not diverge from the line of descent it would have followed had contamination never taken place.

This limitation applies only to equilibrium conditions, and, if the magma is poorly mixed, local variations may develop in the liquid. In the case just discussed, for example, a liquid of composition L_3 may form adjacent to the added crystals of B and produce a range of liquid compositions grading toward another liquid, L_2, adjacent to the earlier crystals of AB. Thus the local compositions of the liquid may differ from that of the main mass at some greater distance from the contaminant, and, if the assemblage crystallizes before these disequilibrium assemblages disappear, the result will be a series of compositions (Fig. 5–9).

Figure 5–9 A block of felsic gneiss in gabbro is surrounded by a coarse-grained zone of reaction. The minerals around the block are the same as those in the host rock, but their proportions are different and they are coarser, probably because of the effect of water released from the xenolith.

The effects of different contaminants on the end products of a differentiated magma can best be seen by examining what happens to a simple solid-solution series under two conditions, one in which an added crystal has a composition that could have been produced earlier in the history of the liquid and another in which the phase would only crystallize from a more evolved liquid. Consider an example (Fig. 5–10) in which a cooling liquid, L_1, is currently precipitating crystals of S_1. If a small crystal of S_2 is added, we see that its composition is one that would have been precipitated at a higher temperature, T_1, at an earlier stage of crystallization. To equilibrate with the present liquid, it cannot dissolve (because the liquid is already saturated with this composition), but must react and add to its composition the low-temperature component, B, in order to attain a composition in equilibrium with the liquid at the temperature T_2. In doing so, it draws B from the liquid and tends to make the liquid poorer in that component. In order to maintain the composition L_1, the liquid must precipitate more S_1 and give up an equivalent amount of heat. The bulk composition of the system, originally at X_1, is shifted slightly toward A, so that the end result must be a smaller proportion of the low-temperature component, B, in the final product of crystallization. Hence, if the crystals continue to equilibrate as the temperature falls, the range of crystallization is reduced accordingly.

Addition of a crystal of composition S_3, richer in B than those in equilibrium with L_1, will have the opposite effect. It will be dissolved, and the heat of solution will be gained from crystallization of an additional amount of S_1. The added crystal shifts the bulk composition toward the low-temperature end of the series. The result will be that crystallization will produce a larger proportion of B-rich crystals, and the final temperature of equilibrium crystallization is lower. The amounts of crystalline material that dissolve and crystallize are determined by their relative heats of fusion and crystallization. Figure 5–11 illustrates some of the textural relations that can result.

From these relations, we can draw the general conclusion that assimilation of

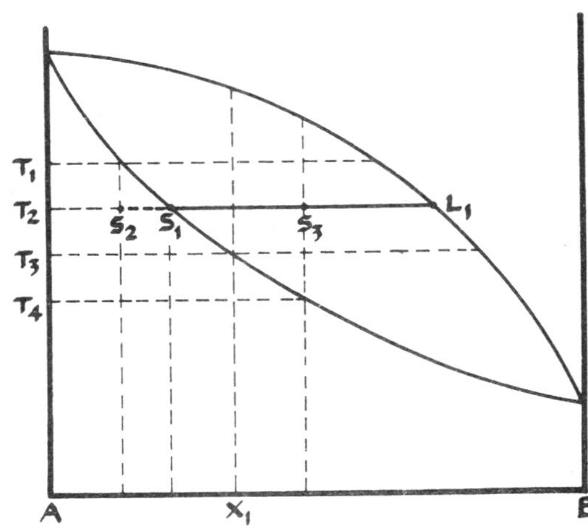

Figure 5–10 Assimilation of crystals, such as S_2, that would be in equilibrium with an earlier liquid of a solid-solution series tend to shift the bulk composition in the direction of the high-temperature component, A, and reduce the range of differentiated liquids that would evolve on cooling. Addition of crystals, such as S_3, that would only appear later, has the opposite effect.

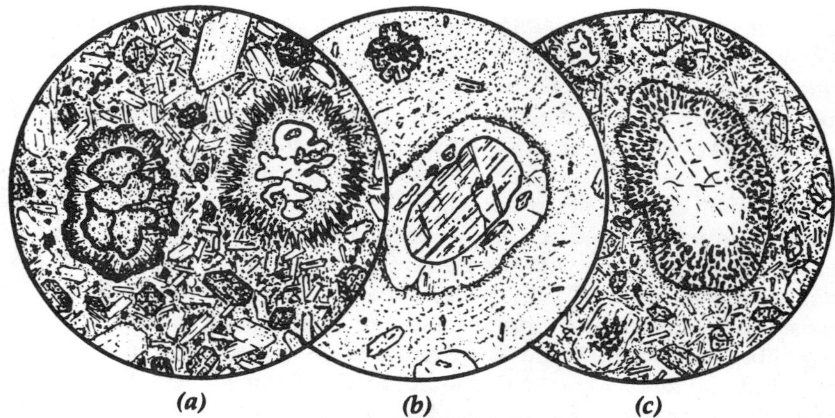

Figure 5–11 Textures of contaminated volcanic rocks. (a) Xenocrysts of quartz are jacketed by pyroxene, and nearby crystals of olivine have reaction rims of the same mineral. Specimen is from a basaltic lava erupted through granitic basement rocks in southeastern Guatemala. (b) Rounded and resorbed xenocrysts of plagioclase have reacted with a rhyolitic liquid and precipitated a rim of potassium feldspar. A small grain of olivine is rimmed with pyroxene. Specimen is from a group of mixed rhyolitic and basaltic lavas near Gardiner River, Yellowstone National Park. (c) An alkali basalt from the vicinity of Gharian, Libya, contains xenocrysts of potassium feldspar and quartz derived from granitic rocks through which the magma rose. The feldspar is rimmed with a vermicular zone of glass.

material that would have crystallized at an earlier high-temperature stage of crystallization tends to reduce the proportion of differentiated products, whereas addition of crystals with which the liquid has not yet become saturated will have the opposite effect; it will extend the range of evolution of the liquid and produce a larger proportion of low-temperature end-members. In terms of natural conditions, this means that a mafic magma that assimilates felsic crustal rocks will tend to differentiate with larger proportions of more evolved products than would the same magma if it had assimilated more mafic material or nothing at all. In both cases, however, the course of the liquid, in terms of its major-element composition and mineral phases, will tend to follow the same line of descent that would be possible without assimilation; only the proportions of the products are changed.

Mixing of magmas

Just as they assimilate rocks, magmas can also assimilate other liquids by mixing with them. Mixing is in some respects the opposite of fractionation. The latter process entails separation of an originally homogeneous magma to form rocks or liquids of differing compositions, whereas mixing combines two initially different liquids to produce a less differentiated product. It has been well-documented in contrasting magmas mixed during eruption from the same or closely connected vents (Fig. 5–12).

Figure 5–12 A mixture of basalt and rhyolite in a bomb ejected from a cinder cone on the flank of Newberry Volcano, Oregon. The mixing must have taken place during rapid eruption from two magmatic bodies in close proximity at a shallow depth beneath the volcano.

Mixing is most efficient when magmas of similar physical properties are turbulently intermingled. The density differences of strongly contrasting liquids inhibit mixing and, instead, cause them to become gravitationally stratified with dense liquids remaining near the floor and lighter ones rising to collect under the roof. Any new magma must seek a level at which it is gravitationally stable, and, unless convection causes wholesale overturn and mixing, the new and old magmas may have very little interaction. Because chemical diffusion is so slow, thorough mixing requires strong, turbulent stirring, in order that different liquids may be mechanically associated on an intimate scale. Two mechanisms have been proposed as possible ways that this might come about.

If hot, dense, mafic magma lies beneath a cooler, lighter one and begins to crystallize and differentiate (Fig. 5–13), the resulting compositional change may lower its density until it is lighter than the overlying liquid and is able to rise and mix with it turbulently. Such a process has been proposed, for example, for mixing of a primitive tholeiitic magma that is initially rich in magnesium and iron and becomes lighter by precipitating olivine. This could lower the density of the magma enough to cause it to rise and mix turbulently with an overlying liquid. A variety of textural features of inhomogeneous lavas, such as crystals out of equilibrium with their groundmass or with other crystals in the same rock, point to some such process of mechanical mixing, but the physical plausibility of the process is still a matter of debate.

A second and perhaps more general process may be associated with crystallization on the walls of certain types of shallow intrusions (Fig. 5–5). If, as we noted earlier, crystallization produces a differentiated liquid that is less dense than the original magma from which it is derived, a buoyant boundary layer may rise along the walls of the intrusion and accumulate under the roof. If the flow of this rising layer is turbulent, it may entrain magma of the interior and, by mixing with the undifferentiated liquid, produce a range of intermediate compositions. This second mechanism, unlike the preceding one, does not involve mixing of

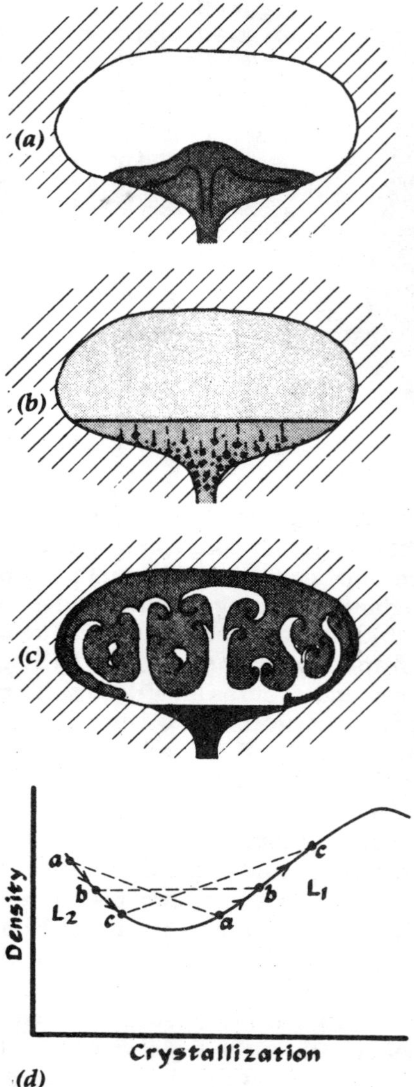

Figure 5–13 Owing to the density minimum in the basic range of tholeiitic magmas (Fig. 2–12), it is possible that a new injection of hot basic magma, L_2, could be denser than a slightly more evolved magma, L_1, that had already begun to differentiate in a shallow chamber. On intrusion, the denser new magma would pond at the base of the reservoir (a), but on cooling and crystallizing the new magma could fractionate olivine and become lighter, while the original magma could fractionate olivine and plagioclase and evolve toward a more iron-rich and denser composition (b). If this process continues, the density relations might be reversed (c), in which case the two liquids could overturn and, if mixed turbulently, the resulting magma could have an intermediate composition and density. The schematic diagram (d) at the bottom shows the density relations with tie-lines connecting the two magmas at each of the stages above. (Based on a model by R. S. J. Sparks, P. Meyer, and H. Sigurdson, 1980, *Earth & Planet. Sci. Ltrs.*, *46*:419–430.)

two independently derived magmas, but rather back-mixing of a derivative liquid with its parent.

The effect of mixing of magmas, if it leads to homogenization of two liquids, is to produce intermediate compositions and temperatures that will be determined by the proportions, compositions, and heat contents of the two original liquids. A series of mixed liquids will have a linear variation of their components between two end-members of the series. The range of intermediate compositions may not be unlimited, however, if either of the liquids contains abundant phenocrysts. Referring again to Figure 5–8, we see that an intermediate liquid cannot result from mixing of a liquid of composition L_2 with another, L_3, that contains crystals of B, unless the crystals are dissolved. If the mass of crystals is large compared to the mass of L_2, the second liquid may be consumed by reaction with the crystals. Even if the two liquids are both crystallizing the same mineral but are separated by a thermal divide, as L_1 and L_2 would be, they cannot combine to form an intermediate composition but would crystallize the mineral with which they are saturated until one or the other of the two liquids were consumed. In either of these cases, if the mixed magmas cool before equilibration is complete, a variety of compositional and textural features can result.

LIQUID-VAPOR FRACTIONATION

The differences between the physical properties of gases and silicate liquids are much greater than those between solids and liquids. This, together with the great mobility of volatile components, can make fractionation in a separate vapor phase a potentially effective way of transferring components. A number of processes involving gases have been proposed, but much less is known about them than about the more conventional mechanisms discussed in the preceding sections.

Absorption from wall-rocks

Most of the water in shallow magmas is probably absorbed from crustal rocks when intrusions quickly heat the rocks through which they rise. With a sudden increase of temperature, the water in pores and fractures is vaporized and may even be superheated if it is heated faster than it can diffuse away from the contact zone. The greatly increased vapor pressures drive the water into the margins of the intrusion. Under these conditions of elevated temperature and pressure, water vapor can dissolve large amounts of silica, alkalies, and other components of wall-rock minerals; it carries these components with it when it enters the magma.

The effect is to decrease the density and viscosity of the contaminated magma at the margins of the intrusion. As a result, a thin, buoyant boundary layer may rise along the wall to accumulate at the top of the column. With time, this can produce a zone that is much richer, not just in water but in silica and other components derived from the wall rocks.

Gaseous transfer

Owing to the differing effects of pressure and temperature on the chemical potential of each individual component of a magma, these components cannot be uniformly distributed in any magmatic body that differs in temperature or pressure from one level to another. To attain a uniform chemical potential, large light ions with weak bonding energies tend to diffuse toward zones of low pressure and temperature near the top of a column of magma. In general, however, rates of diffusion are too slow for important compositional differences to develop by diffu-

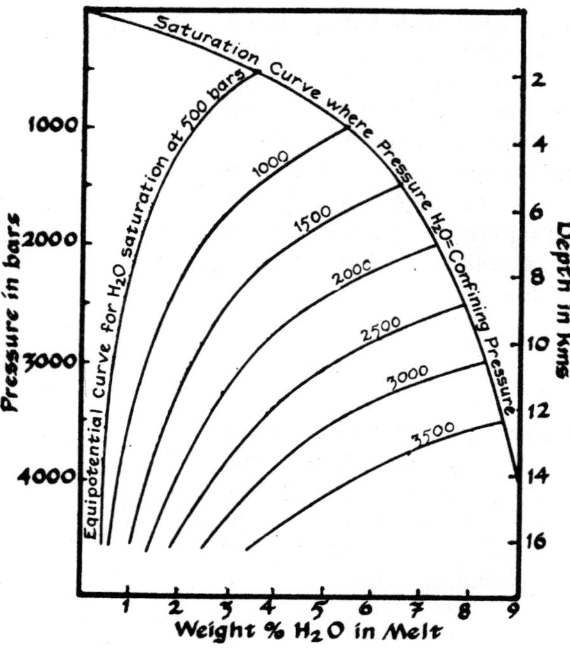

Figure 5–14 The solubility of water in felsic magmas increases with increasing water pressure, but at constant water pressure, increasing load pressure on the magma decreases the solubility in the manner illustrated by the equipotential curves for different water pressures. Because water pressure increases more slowly with depth than load pressure in the magma, a vertical column of magma will tend to have a greater concentration of water at the top. (After G. C. Kennedy, 1955, *Geol. Soc. Amer. Spec. Paper 62*, 489–504.)

sion over distances of more than a meter or so. Heat diffuses so much faster than chemical components that a magma is more likely to crystallize before diffusion of volatile components can have large compositional effects. Some other mechanism of transport is required, such as segregation of a separate vapor phase that rises through the column of magma, not by diffusion but as a buoyant gas.

Figure 5–14 illustrates the equilibrium distribution of water in an isothermal column of magma of large vertical dimension. It shows how the concentration of a component, such as water, will tend to vary with depth. The solubility of water in a silicate melt is a direct function of the pressure of water; i.e., as the pressure of water vapor increases, more water is driven into the melt and absorbed. But the solubility of water also varies inversely with the total pressure on the melt. When the latter exceeds the partial pressure of water, it tends to "squeeze" the water out of solution. If the load pressure and pressure of water on the melt vary independently, the former normally increases more rapidly with depth. The density of magma is much greater than that of water, and with increasing depth the pressure on the magma must increase more rapidly than would the pressure on a column of water of the same dimensions. For this reason, the ratio of water pressure to load pressure, and hence the water content, must decrease with depth. The result is an equilibrium distribution having the form shown by the lines of equal chemical potential in Figure 5–14.

It can be seen from these relations that a column of magma of initially uniform water content could be oversaturated at depth and undersaturated at its top. It could therefore nucleate bubbles at some lower level, and these bubbles could rise and be resorbed in upper levels of the column. Any components having a higher solubility in the gas than in the liquid would tend to be carried in the bubbles and transferred upward.

The importance of this effect, as well as that of absorption from wall-rocks, is seen in explosive volcanic eruptions in which the opening phases erupt magma that is richer in volatiles than later stages coming from deeper levels. Certain components, such as silica and alkalies, are concentrated along with volatiles at the top of the column, and their degree of enrichment is often a function of the length of repose between eruptions.

Volatiles in late, interstitial liquids

During shallow crystallization, water and most other volatiles are excluded from the principal crystalline phases and tend to be concentrated in the remaining liquid. As crystallization advances and dissolved volatile components are concentrated in progressively smaller amounts of liquid, their concentrations will eventually reach saturation levels, so that a separate gas phase can evolve. This phenomenon is often referred to as "retrograde boiling," because the vapor phase evolves with cooling rather than with heating.

A separate gas phase is less likely to develop at deep levels where hydrous minerals are stable. Amphibole or mica, because they take in water, can absorb much of the effect of the increased concentration of that component in the liquid. We shall examine some of these relations in greater detail in chapter 10.

COMBINED MECHANISMS OF DIFFERENTIATION

In nature, many of the processes of differentiation we have been considering can take place concurrently; rarely do magmas evolve by one mechanism alone during the full course of generation, intrusion, and cooling of a body of magma. The initial composition resulting from melting at a source in the mantle will be modified by cooling, decompression, and reaction with the rocks through which the liquid rises. Once emplaced in a crustal reservoir, it may assimilate wall rocks as it cools and crystallizes, and at periodic intervals part of the magma may be erupted and replaced by a new influx of fresh, undifferentiated magma. The individual contributions of all these different processes may be combined and superimposed on each other to produce magmas of complex, hybrid origins.

Although it is difficult to distinguish the individual effects of these different processes in a complex magma, one can calculate the effects of some of the simpler combinations by use of certain diagnostic trace elements and geochemical ratios. References to two commonly used models (O'Hara and Mathews 1981, and DePaolo 1981) are given at the end of this chapter, and examples of their applications will be found in later chapters. These techniques provide ways to relate the members of a series of magmas in terms of combinations of as many as three or four different processes.

With so many possible mechanisms to draw on, one can usually calculate some combination that could account for the compositional relations of various groups of rocks, including some that are in fact unrelated. Because they are so often ambiguous, these calculations seldom inspire confidence as precise solutions to petrogenetic problems. Nevertheless, they may be more realistic than simplistic models that ignore the true complexity inherent in magmatic systems.

COMPOSITIONAL EFFECTS OF DIFFERENTIATION

The compositional changes of differentiating liquids, regardless of how they are produced, depend primarily on the manner in which individual components are partitioned between crystals and liquid during crystallization or melting. An element that is preferentially concentrated in fractionated crystals will be depleted in the remaining liquid, whereas one that is alien to the crystallizing phases will be enriched, because it is concentrated in a diminishing amount of liquid. Thus the degree of enrichment or depletion depends on the compositions and amounts of the phases being subtracted or added.

In a multi-saturated magma, i.e., one that is precipitating more than a single crystalline phase, the entire crystalline assemblage must be considered in order to determine whether an individual component is enriched or depleted. One cannot assume, for example, that because a particular element, such as aluminum, has a lower concentration in the liquid than in a fractionated mineral like plagioclase, that the element will necessarily be depleted by removal of that mineral. The concentration of the element in the liquid may decline if plagioclase is the only mineral being fractionated, but, if another mineral with little or no aluminum, such as olivine, is also being removed, the liquid may actually be enriched in that component. Thus, depending on the proportions of the crystallizing minerals, individual components can be either enriched or depleted. The effect can best be seen in variation diagrams representing the changing concentration of components in crystallizing liquids.

Variation diagrams

It is often helpful to depict the changing abundances or ratios of elements graphically by plotting components against each other or against some measure of differentiation. A common technique is to plot selected components against another component, such as silica, that varies with differentiation. Such a plot, usually called a "Harker diagram" after Alfred Harker, the petrologist who first used it more than eighty years ago, is useful for sub-alkaline igneous series that increase markedly in SiO_2. In other suites, the variation of SiO_2 may be quite irregular; in some it actually declines with progressive differentiation, and in such cases other indices must be used.

Figure 5–15 is an example of a two-component Harker diagram. Assume a magma having an initial SiO_2 content of 50 percent and an Al_2O_3 content of 15 weight percent, as indicated by the point M_1. Crystallization of olivine with 45 percent SiO_2 and essentially no Al_2O_3 (point O) causes both the SiO_2 and Al_2O_3 contents of the residual liquid to increase along a trend indicated by a vector from M_1 directly away from O. The distance the liquid composition is displaced along

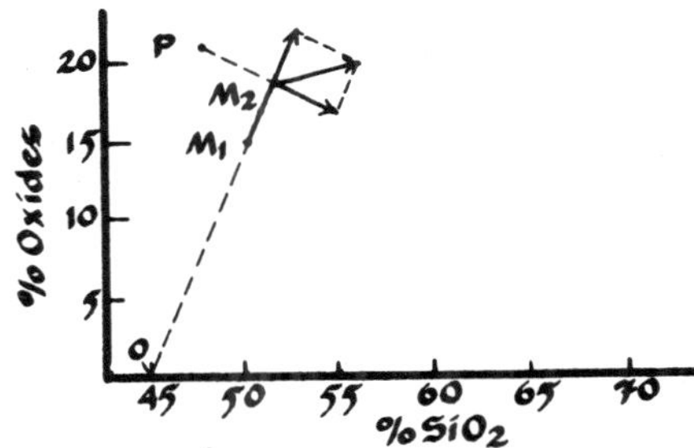

Figure 5–15 The effects of fractionating minerals from a crystallizing magma can be illustrated by a variation diagram showing the changes of concentrations of the oxide components with increasing silica content. See text for explanation.

this "control line" is a function of the fraction of the original liquid that crystallizes. Suppose, next, that plagioclase of composition P begins to crystallize when the liquid reaches point M_2. With removal of this new mineral, the course of the liquid must change and follow a new path that is the resultant of two vectors, one away from olivine and the other away from plagioclase. Depending on the proportions of the two crystallizing phases, Al_2O_3 may increase or decrease in the subsequent evolution of the liquid.

In multicomponent systems in which the compositions and proportions of fractionating phases are constantly changing, variations of individual components follow curves rather than straight lines. The slopes of curves change whenever a new phase begins to crystallize or another is no longer precipitated. In Figure 5-16A, for example, the change of slope for TiO_2 marks the beginning of crystallization of ilmenite, and the change of $FeO + Fe_2O_3$ corresponds to the appearance of magnetite. This pattern of curved lines differs from that produced

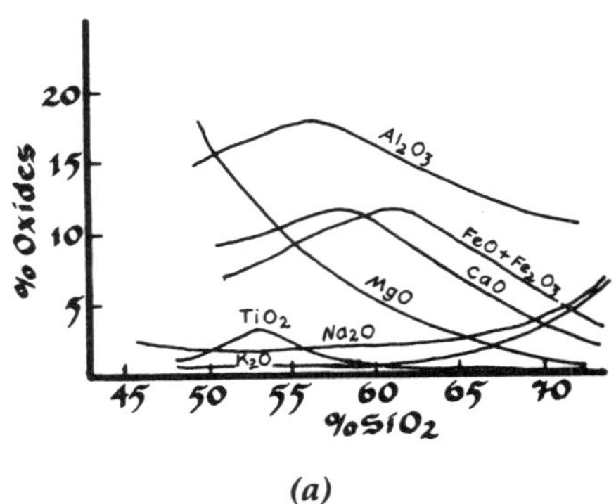

(a)

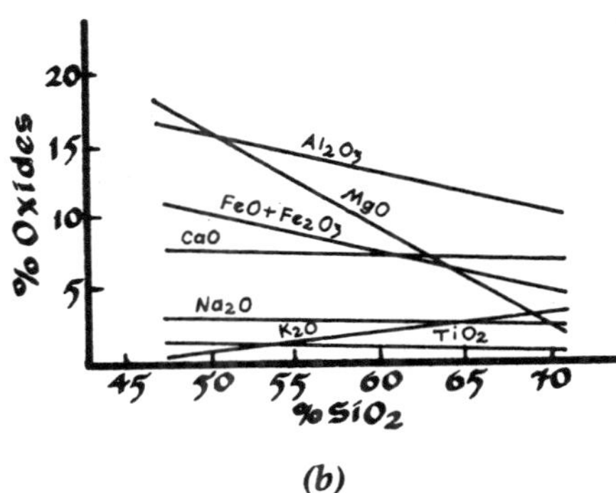

(b)

Figure 5–16 The variations of individual components of a differentiating magma will plot as curved lines on a Harker diagram (a), because the compositions and proportions of the crystallizing phases change as cooling progresses. Inflections mark the appearance or disappearance of a phase that affects the abundance of that component. (b) shows the type of straight-line variation that would result from mechanical mixing of two end-members, one basaltic and one granitic.

by mixing two liquids (Fig. 5–16B). In the latter case, the abundances of the components are simple linear functions of the proportions of two end-members.

One can use diagrams of this kind to calculate the composition and proportions of material that must be subtracted or added to produce one composition from another. Suppose, for example, that two magmas, M_1 and M_2 in Figure 5–17, are lavas erupted from a single volcano. Assuming that the magma with the smaller SiO_2 content is the most primitive and could be the parent of the other, then M_2 could be produced either by fractionation of a crystalline assemblage having less SiO_2 than M_1 or by addition and assimilation of material, such as crustal rocks, with a composition richer in SiO_2 than M_2. If we ignore physical-chemical constraints and consider only the mass balance of components, an infinite number of possible combinations could be calculated to relate the two liquids by all combinations of these two effects; the only limitation on the proportions of added or subtracted material is that no component can have a concentration less than zero.

If straight lines are drawn through the components of M_1 and M_2, the abundances of these components in all possible fractionated or assimilated assemblages must lie somewhere along these lines. The composition of a particular fractionated or assimilated material is indicated by the intersection of these lines with a vertical line at the appropriate value of SiO_2. The SiO_2 value at which the first component reaches zero is a limiting composition. For example, K_2O goes to zero at R, and MgO goes to zero at A, and the corresponding values of SiO_2 at these points represent the limiting values for material that could have been removed or added to produce the observed change from M_1 to M_2. By applying the lever rule we can say that the minimum amount of crystalline material that could be removed from a given unit of M_1 would be proportional to M_1-M_2, and the remaining liquid would be in the proportion R-M_1. Similarly, the proportion of the minimum amount of added material to original liquid would be $(M_1\text{-}M_2)/(M_2\text{-}A)$.

Calculations based on this principle have long been used to test various schemes of differentiation. Having determined the oxide proportions of the components in this way, it is a simple matter to calculate the normative composition of the fractionated or added material in order to determine whether the calculated compositions are mineralogically reasonable. Modern computers can perform such calculations quickly and in much more sophisticated ways. It is possible, for example, to calculate the effect of simultaneously fractionating two or more minerals while adding assimilated material in various proportions and then compare the results with the observed compositions of a series of differentiated rocks. Examples of the use of these calculations in interpreting differentiated series will be seen in later chapters.

This technique provides a means of testing the relations of two or more liquid compositions through crystal fractionation, assimilation, or mixing. It is especially valuable when large amounts of analytical and petrographic data are available for both liquids and crystals, because constraints on the mathematical solutions become increasingly rigorous as the compositions of phases are defined in terms of larger numbers of components. It must be borne in mind, how-

Figure 5–17 The compositions of the minimum amounts of material that would have to be removed from (R) or added to (A), a magma of composition M_1, to produce a second magma, M_2, can be determined graphically by drawing straight lines through the individual components of the two magmas and projecting them to lower and higher silica contents until one of the components intersects the baseline where its abundance goes to zero. The concentrations of the other components can then be read directly from the intersection of the straight lines with a vertical axis at the silica content of R or A. The proportion of A that must be added to M_1 to produce M_2 is M_1M_2, and the proportion of M_1 to which it is added is M_2A. In a similar way, the proportion of composition R that must be removed is M_1M_2, and the amount of remaining liquid M_2 is proportional to RM_1.

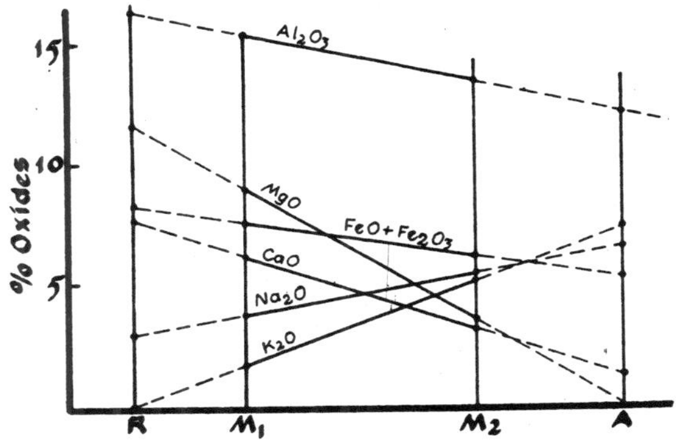

ever, that these calculations ignore the principles of phase equilibria and may yield results that are mathematically sound but petrologically absurd. The fact that mass-balance relations are consistent with a particular scheme of differentiation does not mean that other mechanisms could not have produced the same results.

Plots of chemical data on variation diagrams may be used to test whether a group of rocks is genetically related, the rationale being that if the data fall on smooth curves they are likely to be cogenetic. As in the calculations just mentioned, this technique does not prove that rocks are cogenetic; it only shows that their compositions are not inconsistent with such a relationship.

Thus, smooth curves on variation diagrams are a test but not a proof of fractionation in closed systems. They can even be misleading, especially when multiple combinations of components are plotted. As a general rule, the more closely the sum of the variables being plotted approaches unity, the stronger will be their negative correlation. If, for example, a number of components, such as A, B, C, D, and E, totals 100 percent, there may be significance in a smooth correlation between A and B, especially if it is a positive one, but there is none whatever between A+B and C+D+E, because any plot of these combinations will yield a straight line with a negative slope. For this reason, variation diagrams in which components are plotted against a "differentiation index" that includes SiO_2 and other components that together constitute a large proportion of the total almost always yield good linear trends with negative slopes.

It would seem that trace elements would be immune to such influences, because their abundances contribute little to the sum of the components, but they too can be misleading. Here one is dealing with elements that may vary in absolute abundance by factors of a hundred or more from one specimen to another, depending on the distribution of the phases in which the elements occur in the rock. Figure 5–18 shows how the total variation of a group of trace elements from one sample to the next may be so great that it overshadows the relative variations of individual elements. For this reason one may find an apparent positive correlation between the absolute concentrations of two elements that in fact have a negative correlation of their relative concentrations. Here the effect is the reverse of what it is in major elements; a negative correlation is more likely to be meaningful than a positive one. The problem is best avoided by carefully examining the mineralogical content of samples and taking care not to use trace-element analyses of rocks containing an accessory phase rich in those elements.

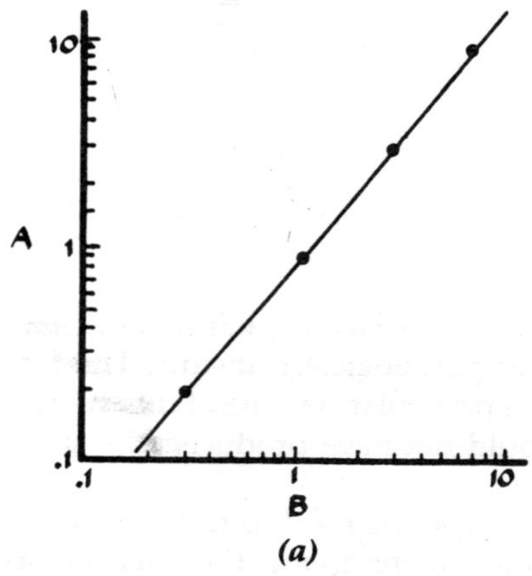

(a)

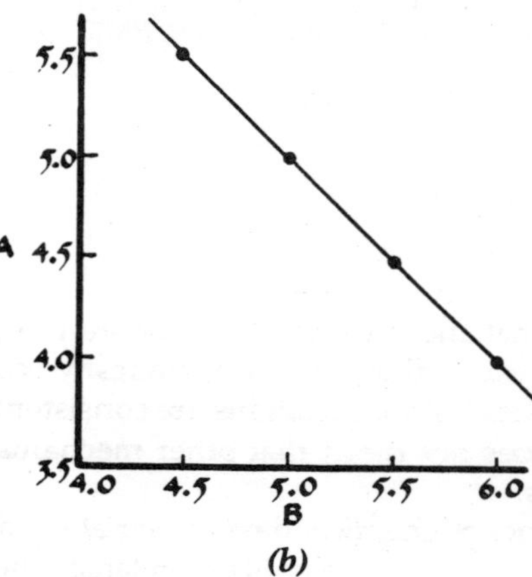

(b)

Figure 5–18 Suppose that two trace elements, A and B, are strongly excluded from all major rock-forming minerals but can form an accessory phase that may be present in minute amounts in a wide range of rocks. Suppose also that A and B enter the accessory phase as a solid-solution series, so that they have an inverse relation, i.e., as A goes up, B goes down. Assume that in four random rocks the contents of A and B in the accessory mineral are as follows:

	A	B	B/A
Rock 1	4.0	6.0	.667
Rock 2	4.5	5.5	.818
Rock 3	5.0	5.0	1.000
Rock 4	5.5	4.5	1.222

If the rocks contain small but differing amounts of the accessory phase, their contents of A and B could be:

	Wt. % of phase	A in rock	B in rock
Rock 1	.0005	.2 ppm	0.3 ppm
Rock 2	.0020	.9 ppm	1.1 ppm
Rock 3	.0060	3.0 ppm	3.0 ppm
Rock 4	.0160	8.8 ppm	7.2 ppm

If the contents of A and B in the rocks are plotted on a log scale they show an excellent positive correlation (a). But if the contents of A and B in the accessory mineral are plotted on a linear scale, they have a negative correlation, as in (b), reflecting the solid-solution substitution of one for the other. Because of the high concentrations of the elements in the accessory phase, a small, random variation of the abundance of that mineral has a greater effect than that of the variation in the mineral alone, and the latter relation is swamped by what may seem to be a genetic relationship of the rocks but in fact could be a meaningless, random fluctuation.

Another solution is to avoid plotting absolute abundances and to use, instead, ratios of cation abundances. These "Molecular Proportion Ratio" (MPR) or "Pearce Element Ratio" diagrams (Fig. 5–19) surmount the closure problem of major-element Harker diagrams by dividing the abundances of two elements or groups of elements by a third that does not enter the principal minerals in important amounts and is therefore neither added to nor subtracted from the system. In this way the ratios of components removed in a mineral of fixed composition remain constant and plot as straight lines. Such a diagram may be useful for identifying the minerals responsible for the variation of a series of cogenetic liquids, because the slope of a curve defined by a series of differentiated magmas is an undistorted measure of the bulk ratio of minerals lost or gained. For complex systems with multicomponent minerals, the diagram is less useful than computer-aided calculations, such as those illustrated in later chapters.

The ideal type of variation diagram, if such a thing exists, is one that corresponds to known crystal-liquid relations and depicts compositional changes in terms of the petrologic processes that produce them. When the proportions of mineral components, either modal or normative, are plotted on an experimentally determined phase diagram, they should fall in the fields of primary crystallization of those minerals that occur as phenocrysts in the rocks. Their distribution should define a trend that is a line of liquid descent resulting from fractionation of the minerals that are crystallizing at a particular stage of differentiation. Figure 5–20 illustrates the use of such a diagram. While they can be in-

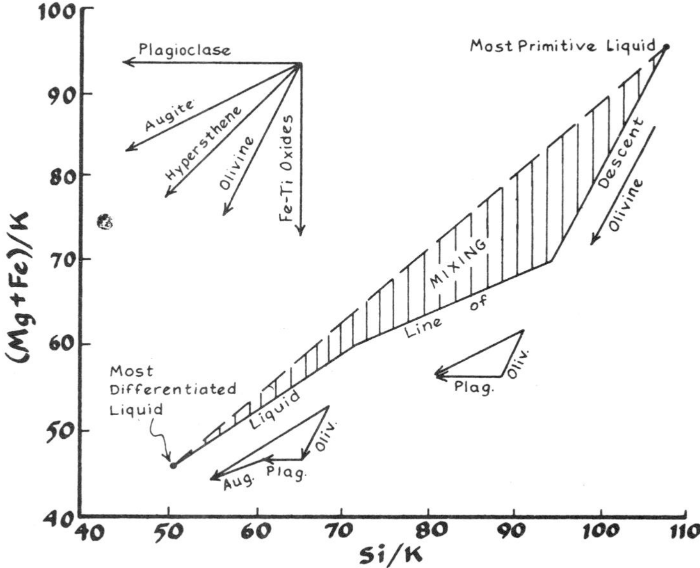

Figure 5–19 When the compositions of series of lavas, such as those illustrated in Fig. 5–16a, are plotted in terms of their ratios of (Mg + Fe)/K vs. Si/K, they define a line with segments of differing slopes determined by the ratios of these components in the fractionated minerals. As shown in the inset, the effects of removing the minerals olivine, augite, plagioclase, and Fe-oxides are indicated by lines with slopes corresponding to their proportions of (Mg + Fe) to Si; i. e., 0/1 for plagioclase, 1/2 for augite, 1/1 for hypersthene, 2/1 for olivine, and 1/0 for Fe-Ti oxides. The upper segment of the trend of compositions corresponds to the slope for olivine, whereas the lower parts reflect the addition of, first, plagioclase and then augite to the crystallizing assemblage. Note that, unlike SiO_2 in Figure 5–16a, Si/K declines in proportion to the rate of removal of Si from the liquid. The ruled area indicates the range of possible compositions that could result from mixing of any combination of liquids along the liquid line of descent. A composition could fall outside this field if crystals from one liquid were added to another.

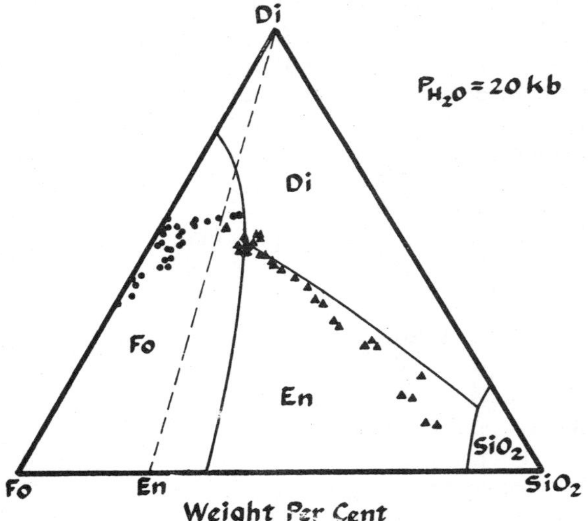

Figure 5–20 When the compositions of the rocks of the Oregon Cascade volcanoes are expressed in terms of the normative components, diopside, olivine, hypersthene, and quartz, and plotted on the phase diagram for the system Di-Fo-SiO_2, they correspond to the course liquids would take if basalt (shown by dots) fractionates olivine (Fo) and augite (Di), and more differentiated rocks (Δ) fractionate two pyroxenes, augite and hypersthene (En), and follow the cotectic toward SiO_2 as they evolve to dacite, rhyodacite, and finally rhyolite near the eutectic close to the SiO_2 corner. (Based on the system Fo-Di-SiO_2 at 20 kilobars determined by I. Kushiro, 1969, *Amer. Jour. Sci.*, 267–A:269–294.)

structive, most diagrams of this sort are highly simplified and, because some of the components must be ignored, the plotted points are in effect projected into the plane of the diagram from all the other components, and the trends they define can be misleading. We noted this effect in chapter three when we considered the problems raised by projections in multicomponent phase diagrams. We will see it again in some of the chapters to come.

Many types of variation diagrams have been devised to depict particular features of related rocks and minerals. Depending on the relationship being explored, any combination of components can be plotted in the way that best demonstrates a specific petrologic feature. These diagrams, if properly used, are well-suited for visual presentations of data but are by no means a substitute for numerical calculations.

TRACE ELEMENTS AND DIFFERENTIATION

The main questions that confront us in petrology are genetic ones—how magmas are generated and evolved in their particular tectonic settings. By now, the student will have perceived that the major-element compositions of rocks give us few unambiguous answers to questions of this kind. In all the processes considered thus far, we have seen that major-element compositions of liquids are controlled by the phase relations at the last conditions of equilibration and are insensitive to how the liquid arrived at that state. Trace elements provide ways of surmounting these limitations.

As noted in chapter three, the individual components of a differentiating magma are concentrated either in the crystals or in the residual liquid, depending on their relative free energies in the two phases. Plagioclase crystals are richer in the high-temperature end-member, anorthite, than the liquid from which they grow; crystals of olivine and pyroxene are preferentially enriched in Mg relative to Fe, because their high-melting components have a smaller free energy and hence a greater stability in the solid than do the corresponding low-melting end-members of the solid-solution series.

To an even greater degree, certain trace elements are preferentially concentrated in either crystals or in a coexisting liquid. Ni, for example, is strongly partitioned into olivine, because it has the same charge (+2) and nearly the same atomic radius (0.69 Å) as Mg (0.66 Å). But its concentration does not follow the same rules that govern elements that are essential constituents of the crystalline structure. The concentrations of Mg and Fe in olivine crystallized from basaltic magmas have a narrow range that is fixed by the Mg/Fe ratio that crystals must have to be in equilibrium with such a liquid. So long as the intensive parameters remain nearly the same, changing the absolute amounts of Mg and Fe in the liquid changes the amount of olivine precipitated but has little effect on its composition. The same is not true of a trace element. The concentration of Ni in olivine will be greater than it is in the liquid by a nearly constant factor; if the amount of Ni in the liquid is doubled, so too is the amount in the crystals. As a result olivines with the same Mg/Fe ratios can differ in their Ni contents by large factors, depending on the Ni content of the liquid in which they grew.

The reason for this difference lies in the inherent behavior of very dilute components in liquids. According to Henry's Law, the activity coefficient of such a component has a nearly constant value, and the chemical potential of the component in a particular phase varies directly with its concentration. It follows, therefore, that the concentration, C_S, in the solid will have a constant ratio, K_d, to the concentration in the liquid, C_L.

$$K_d = \frac{C_S}{C_L} \tag{5-3}$$

The value K_d is known as the *distribution coefficient* for a particular element in a given mineral, and, depending on whether it is greater or less than 1.0, the element is preferentially concentrated in the mineral or liquid. Ni has a distribution coefficient for olivine in equilibrium with most basaltic liquids of about 10. So long as equilibrium prevails, Ni will be ten times as plentiful in the crystals as in the liquid.

Typical distribution coefficients for a number of important trace elements are given in Appendix G. These values are only approximate and vary with composition from one magma to another and also with temperature. Moreover, the equilibrium distribution coefficient may differ from the effective one that governs partitioning during rapid crystallization or melting, because the degree of equilibration between crystals and liquid is strongly affected by the rate of diffusion through the liquid.

Trace elements such as Ni that have large distribution coefficients in favor of a particular mineral ($K_d \gg 1$) are strongly depleted from a liquid when that mineral crystallizes. This effect is reduced, of course, if other minerals that exclude the element are crystallizing, for their effect is to increase the concentration of the element in a reduced amount of liquid. Knowing the distribution coefficients of a trace element in the minerals that have been fractionated from an evolving magma, one can calculate the net effect on the abundances of that element that would result from removal of specific amounts and proportions of those minerals.

Elements that are strongly partitioned into only a single mineral may provide a sensitive measure of the amount of that mineral that has crystallized. Conversely, a trace element with a small distribution coefficient ($K_d \ll 1$) is preferentially concentrated in a liquid and reflects the proportion of liquid at a given stage of crystallization or melting, because its concentration varies inversely with the amount of liquid diluting its abundance.

These relations can be seen more clearly by considering the equations governing the distribution of trace elements and how they determine concentrations of elements with different distribution coefficients. (Space does not permit the derivation of these equations but the interested student can find this information in the works of Shaw (1970) and Greenland (1970) listed in the references at the end of this chapter.)

Partial melting

We noted in an earlier section that partial melting of a multicomponent rock can take place in a number of ways depending on how the melt collects and re-equilibrates with residual minerals before being separated. In fractional melting, the liquid is removed as rapidly as it forms; in batch melting, it is collected and reaches a certain amount before being separated.

Consider first the case of batch melting in which the liquid remains in contact with the residual crystals, equilibrates with them as melting proceeds, and is removed only after a certain amount of melt has collected. In this process, the ratio of the concentration of a trace element in the liquid, C_L, to that in the total original assemblage, C_O, is

$$\frac{C_L}{C_O} = \frac{1}{D + F(1 - P)} \tag{5-4}$$

where F is the fraction of melt, and D is the bulk distribution coefficient for all the solid phases combined. The latter term is simply the effective distribution between a number of different minerals and a liquid with which they are in equilibrium. It is determined by

$$D = X_\alpha K_\alpha + X_\beta K_\beta + \cdots . \tag{5-5}$$

where X_α and X_β are the initial weight fractions of phases α, β, etc., and K_α and K_β are the corresponding solid-liquid distribution coefficients. The term P represents the combined contributions of the various phases to the melt and is given by

$$P = P_\alpha K_\alpha + P_\beta K_\beta + \cdots . \tag{5-6}$$

where P_α and P_β and so on are the fractions of liquid contributed by each individual mineral. If the minerals contribute to the melt in the same proportions as their abundances, P would be the same as D.

Figure 5–21 shows how elements with various distribution coefficients will be concentrated in a liquid (relative to the original solid) as melting proceeds for the case where P = D. In the extreme case of an element that is perfectly excluded (D = O), the ratio C_L/C_O from equation 5–4 becomes a simple inverse function of F:

$$\frac{C_L}{C_O} \approx \frac{1}{F} \tag{5–7}$$

In other words, the amount of melting that produced a given magma can be estimated directly if one knows the concentration of a strongly excluded element in both the source rock and in the melt derived from it.

On the other hand, if the amount of melting, F, is small, equation 5-4 reduces to

$$\frac{C_L}{C_O} \approx \frac{1}{D} \tag{5–8}$$

Thus, the concentration in a source rock from which a small amount of melt has been derived can be estimated from the concentration in the melt and D, even though the source rock is conjectural. The larger the value of D, the greater is the extent of melting, F, for which this relation applies. For example, if D = 10, then

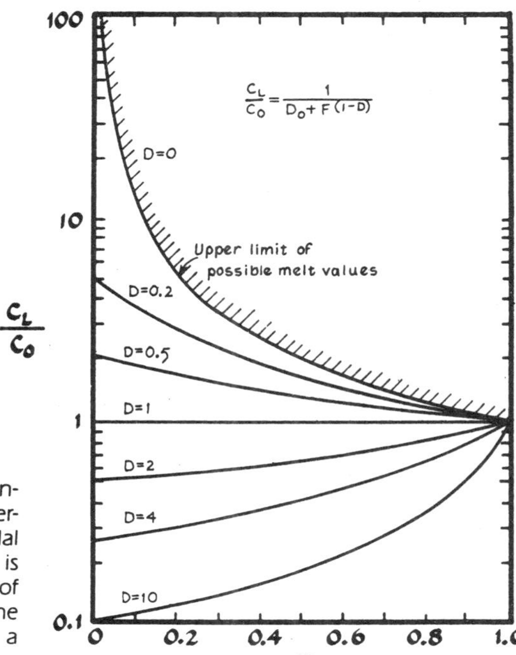

Figure 5–21 Variations of relative concentrations of trace elements with different distribution coefficients during "modal melting" according to equation 5–4. P is assumed to equal D, and the fraction of melt, F, is assumed to equilibrate with the remaining crystals until it is removed as a "batch."

C_L/C_O has a value of about 0.1 until nearly 30 percent is melted. These relations will be altered, of course, as soon as the first mineral phase disappears during melting. As soon as an individual mineral is exhausted, it no longer has an effect on the trace-element content of the liquid, and both D and P change accordingly.

In practice, the most valuable trace elements for interpreting the history of a particular liquid will be those with a wide range of distribution coefficients for the minerals in the source rock. According to equation 5-4, an element with a very low value of D for the assemblage as a whole provides an estimate of the extent of melting. But an element that has a large value of K_d for one specific mineral phase and a small value for all others in the rock provides a way of estimating the amount of that particular mineral in the crystalline residue. This can be seen if D is taken to be approximately $X_\alpha K_\alpha$, in which case equation 5-8 reduces to

$$X_\alpha \approx \frac{C_O}{C_L K_\alpha} \tag{5-9}$$

By this means, it is possible to estimate the contribution of an individual mineral to the partial melt.

Take, for example, the ratio of potassium to rubidium, which is often used to determine the importance of amphibole in an ultramafic source rock. Olivine and pyroxene contain very little of either of these elements, so their contributions to the bulk distribution coefficient are negligible. Almost all the K and Rb must therefore reside in the amphibole, which has a distribution coefficient of about 1.0 for K and about 0.3 for Rb. Because amphibole has a larger distribution coefficient for K than for Rb, melting of an assemblage including this mineral results in a decrease in the ratio of K to Rb in the liquid over what it was in the original rock. Other factors being equal, a magma produced by partial melting of an amphibole-bearing source rock would have a smaller ratio of K to Rb than would one derived under conditions where that mineral was not stable. This effect is quite different from what would be expected if K and Rb were essential major-element constituents of amphibole. Most amphiboles have large ratios of K to Rb, and melting would produce an equivalent ratio in the melt. As melting progresses, the absolute abundances of these elements in the liquid would approach that in the original rock, but their ratio would remain constant. Thus, the resulting trend in a series of liquids produced by partial melting is not one of constant K/Rb, as it would be if these elements were essential components of amphibole, but one of changing K/Rb, because they are trace components.

The effects are somewhat different in a process of fractional melting, in which the melt is continuously removed as it is formed. If the minerals melt in the same proportions as they occur in the solid, the distribution of a trace element between liquid and solid is governed by

$$\frac{C_L}{C_O} = \frac{1}{D}(1 - F)^{[(1/D)-1]} \tag{5-10}$$

Trace-element concentrations are sensitive to the disappearance of a minor phase from the assemblage being melted, especially if that phase is one that is very rich in a particular trace element. So long as that phase is present, it contributes the element to the melt, but, once exhausted, the abundance of that element in subsequent liquids drops to a much lower value. This sudden drop would not be detected in protracted batch melting, because the liquid would still contain an amount of the element contributed during earlier stages of melting before the mineral disappeared.

Fractional crystallization

As in partial melting, trace-element partitioning during crystallization depends to a large extent on the proportions of liquid and crystals that equilibrate during the time the two phases are in close association. Conditions can range between two extremes, one in which crystals remain in the liquid and re-equilibrate continuously as the liquid slowly crystallizes, and another in which crystals become separated as rapidly as they form and cannot re-equilibrate. The first case is essentially the reverse of equilibrium melting, but the second is closer to the condition likely to prevail in nature.

Crystallization in which crystals are segregated from the liquid and do not re-equilibrate as crystallization advances is often referred to as *Rayleigh fractionation*, and partitioning of trace elements under this condition is governed by the equation

$$\frac{C_L}{C_O} = F'^{(D-1)} \tag{5-11}$$

where F' is the fraction of liquid remaining. The bulk distribution coefficient, D, is given by

$$D = X_\alpha K_\alpha + X_\beta K_\beta + \cdots . \tag{5-12}$$

where K_α, K_β, etc., are the distribution coefficients, and X_α, X_β, etc., the weight fractions of individual crystallizing phases, α, β, etc.

Note that, just as in the case of partial melting, when D approaches zero,

$$\frac{C_L}{C_O} \approx \frac{1}{F'} \tag{5-13}$$

so that the concentration of an element strongly excluded from all growing crystals is a simple inverse function of the amount of crystallization. It follows that the parameter $(1 - C_O/C_L)$ for an excluded trace element is a good index of differentiation, since it represents the fraction of a parental magma that has crystallized to produce a derivative magma.

The effect of fractional crystallization on elements with different distribution coefficients is shown in Figure 5-22. The curve for D = O delineates the upper limit of concentration of a totally excluded element in a fractionated liquid as a function of the amount of crystallization. Comparison with the behavior of another element having a large value for D, such as the curve for D = 10, shows how rapidly an element that is strongly partitioned into the crystallizing minerals will be depleted from the liquid as crystallization advances.

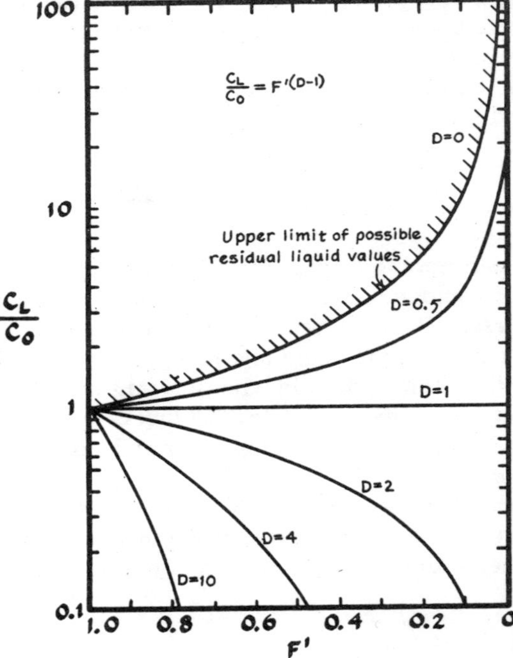

Figure 5–22 Variations of relative concentrations of trace elements with different distribution coefficients during crystallization, according to the Rayleigh-type model of equation 5–10. The fraction of liquid remaining, F', equilibrates only with the surface of the coexisting crystals and not with the total solid.

Comparing Figures 5-21 and 5-22, we see the contrasting effects of partial melting and crystal fractionation and the differences between the amounts of depletion and enrichment that are possible in the two types of systems. For elements with large distribution coefficients, liquids produced by fractional crystallization are more strongly depleted than those produced by partial melting at comparable proportions of crystals and liquid. Conversely, in the middle range of crystal-liquid proportions, elements with distribution coefficients less than 1.0 are more concentrated in a liquid that has evolved by fractional crystallization than in one produced by partial melting. A small amount of melting produces liquids with large initial concentrations of strongly excluded elements, and, with further melting, that element is simply diluted by the growing mass of liquid. In crystal fractionation, however, the concentration of a strongly excluded element increases slowly so long as the amount of remaining liquid is large but rises at an increasing rate as the amount of liquid diminishes. When the fraction of liquid is large, the amount of crystallization required to change its composition is also large.

As an example of how these two processes might affect the compositions of a series of magmas produced by different stages of melting and crystallization, consider the hypothetical case in which melting proceeds in such a way that batches of liquid are extracted periodically and then evolve by crystal fractionation. From the behavior of included and excluded elements just outlined, we can see that the result would be a series of curves with a form somewhat like that shown in Figure 5–23. As in the preceding diagrams, these relations are highly idealized, and in magmas the patterns are seldom this simple.

Behavior of specific trace elements

Trace elements can be divided into several broad groups according to their behavior in magmatic systems. The first includes large cations with low valences (+1 or +2), such as Rb, Ba, Sr, and Cs. These large-ion lithophile (LIL) elements have distribution coefficients of less than 1.0 for most minerals; that is, they tend to be enriched in the first products of partial melting or in the residual liquids of crystal fractionation. The effect, however, differs according to the specific minerals involved. Sr, for example, is excluded from most common minerals except plagioclase, and Ba is similarly excluded from most minerals except K-feldspar. Thus the ratio of Ba to Sr tends to increase with crystallization of plagioclase, but may decrease when orthoclase begins to crystallize. In a similar way, Rb is excluded from most minerals but is included in micas, and would be a sensitive indicator of fractionation of that phase. Another example would be K and Rb, which, as we noted earlier, are sensitive to crystallization or melting of amphibole.

The group of large cations with high charges, sometimes referred to as high-field-strength elements, are more uniformly excluded. They include Zr, Hf, Ta, Nb, Th, and U, all of which tend to be rejected by the common igneous minerals and strongly concentrated in residual liquids. They may, however, be concentrated in accessory minerals, such as zircon, apatite, or sphene, especially in highly differentiated rocks, such as granites. For this reason they are useful indicators of the degree of crystal fractionation so long as the liquid is not saturated

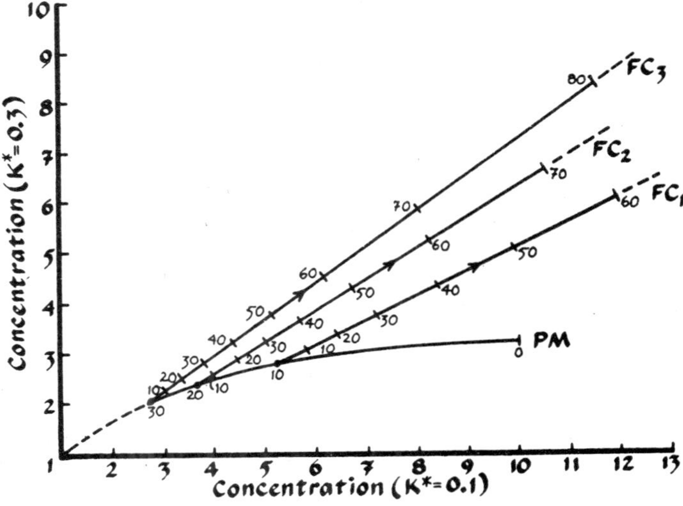

Figure 5–23 The differing effects of partial melting and crystal fractionation are illustrated by a comparison of the variations of two excluded trace elements, one with a distribution coefficient of 0.1 and the other 0.3. The first liquid produced by melting will have the concentrations represented by the point 0 on the line PM, and the elements will become more dilute (at differing rates) as the amount of liquid increases to larger percentages indicated by numbers along the line. A liquid extracted after 10 percent melting and crystallized without reaction will follow the course of FC_1, and melts separated at more advance stages will follow similar trends, such as FC_2 and FC_3. The amount of crystallization is indicated on each of these lines and shows the accelerating rate of enrichment in later stages of crystallization. (B. H. Baker, pers. comm.)

with one of these minerals. These same elements are also important components of sialic continental rocks and may be enriched in magmas that are strongly contaminated by crustal material. A batch of magma produced by melting of a source rock having a particular ratio of two such elements will preserve that ratio through its subsequent differentiation if neither of the elements is extracted more than the other. Hence, the ratios of high-field-strength elements may indicate a cogenetic relation for rocks having similar ratios and distinguish them from other rocks derived from batches of magma or source rocks with different ratios.

These highly excluded elements tend to be concentrated along grain boundaries between crystals, unless there is an accessory mineral into which they enter, as Zr does in zircon or Cu in sulfides. As we noted earlier (Fig. 5–18), the concentration of trace elements in the bulk rock may be very sensitive to the abundance of a minor phase of this kind, and may differ so much from one specimen to another that bulk-rock analyses are difficult to interpret.

A third group is made up mainly of transition elements, such as Ni, Co, Cr, and Sc. These elements tend to be included in the mafic minerals, but to different degrees depending on their size. Ni, as we saw, is strongly included in olivine but less so in pyroxene. Cr and Sc, on the other hand, enter olivine only in small amounts but are strongly included in pyroxenes. The ratio of Ni to Cr or Sc, for example, can provide a way of distinguishing the effects of crystallizing olivine and augite. Again, the concentration of these elements in crystalline rocks may be very sensitive to the presence of a minor phase in which they are strongly concentrated. Sulfide minerals have distribution coefficients measured in thousands for certain metals, such as platinum, that enter readily into their structure, and a small variation in the abundance of such a mineral will result in huge differences in the bulk rocks.

Finally, special mention must be made of a group of elements that has proved particularly useful in petrogenetic interpretations, namely the group of elements with atomic numbers between 57 (lanthanum) and 71 (lutetium). These rare-earth elements (REE) have very similar geochemical properties. Under geological conditions, their valence is +3, except for Eu and Ce, which may be +2, +3, or +4, depending on oxidizing conditions. Their atomic radii are large, so they enter only minerals with sites that can take large atoms. For this reason their distribution coefficient is very small for minerals like olivine but is larger for others, such as hornblende and apatite, and differs for individual elements according to their atomic radii, which increase with their atomic number. Because the degree to which they enter minerals varies according to their ionic radius and the nature of the sites available, the concentrations of individual elements in a given mineral will differ by large factors.

Owing to the analytical difficulties of determining some of these elements, only six or seven are commonly used, but these are enough to establish the pattern for most rocks and minerals. In order to smooth out the effect of their differing natural abundances, their concentrations are usually normalized by dividing their abundances by those in a reference standard, usually chondritic meteorites. When these normalized abundances are plotted on a logarithmic scale against their ionic radius, they form curves with distinctive forms and slopes reflecting the relative enrichment of the light or heavy REE in a particular phase (Fig. 5–24).

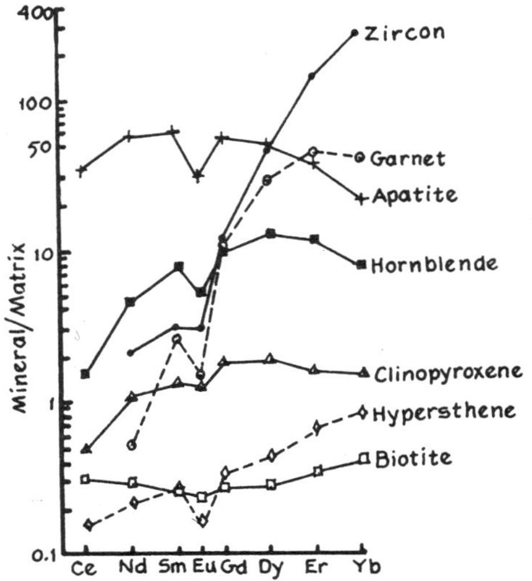

Figure 5–24 The ratios of concentrations of the rare-earth elements in common minerals to their coexisting groundmass composition (which is taken as the liquid from which they formed) is shown in the diagram on the left. The REE on the horizontal axis are plotted according to increasing atomic radii. The corresponding patterns for feldspars are shown in the diagram on the right. (After G. N. Hanson, 1978, *Earth Plan. Sci Ltrs., 38*: 26–43.)

A similar technique is used to compare the abundances of diagnostic elements by means of normalized multicomponent diagrams, often referred to as "spider diagrams" (Fig. 5–25). Selected elements are normalized by dividing their abundances in the sample by those in a suitable reference, such as chondritic meteorites, average mantle, mid-ocean ridge basalt, or any other composition to which it is convenient to relate the sample. (A set of commonly used values is provided in Appendix G.) The elements are listed at equal intervals on the X axis, preferably in the order shown here, and the normalized values are plotted on the vertical axis, using either a linear or logarithmic scale. Irregularities of the resulting curves often reflect the distinctive signature of a particular fractionated mineral or mechanism of differentiation. As will be seen from examples in later chapters, the diagrams are most useful for graphic comparisons of related rocks.

KINETIC EFFECTS

Many common textural features of igneous rocks, such as zoning and compositional differences between phenocrysts and groundmass minerals, show that equilibrium is seldom achieved in magmas crystallizing under natural conditions. The rates of equilibration between crystals and liquid are severely limited by the rate of diffusion between the interior and surface of crystals and between

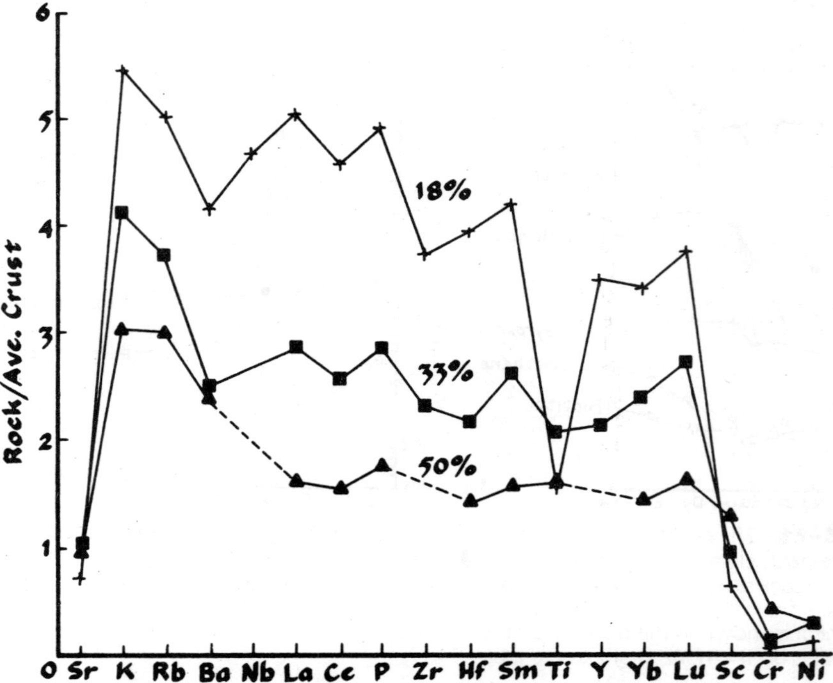

Figure 5–25 Normalized multi-element (spider) diagrams are constructed by dividing the abundances of selected elements in a given sample by their abundances in a reference standard, such as those given in Appendix G. The resulting pattern of enrichment or depletion often reveals how the composition of the sample has been affected by crystal fractionation, contamination, or hydrothermal alteration. In this example, three successive liquids segregated from a thick, ponded flow of Columbia River basalt have been normalized to the average composition of the upper and lower crusts. Numbers on each curve indicate the fraction of liquid remaining at the time of segregation. Note that Ti is first enriched and then depleted when Fe-Ti oxides crystallize. Sc, Cr, and Ni are depleted in all liquids, owing to crystallization of augite and olivine. (After Eric Sonnenthal, 1990, PhD Thesis, Univ. of Oregon.)

crystal faces and the main reservoir of liquid some distance away (Fig. 5–26). If the rate of crystal growth is rapid, diffusion is unable to supply included elements or remove excluded ones fast enough for crystals to maintain the compositions they would have if they were growing in a well-stirred liquid. Instead, a boundary layer develops in which the liquid is locally depleted or enriched, and the liquid that the crystals "see" differs in composition from that of the larger reservoir some distance away.

The effect of these kinetic limitations is that the concentrations of excluded elements in a growing crystal tend to be more and those of included elements less than they would be under conditions of perfect equilibrium. With increasing rates of crystal growth or slower diffusion, the effective distribution coefficient, i.e., the ratio of the concentration in the crystal to the concentration in the main mass of liquid far from the crystal, approaches a value of 1.0 for both included

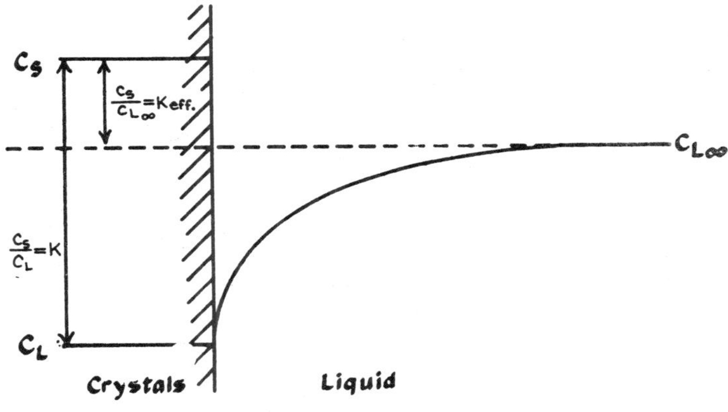

Figure 5–26 Advancing crystallization produces compositional gradients in the layer adjacent to the growing crystals, with depletion of elements that are preferentially included in the solid phases. As a result, the liquid next to the crystals is impoverished in these elements relative to the concentration at a greater distance in the interior of the static liquid. The concentration of an element in the crystals is still determined by the distribution coefficient, K, but, because the concentration in the liquid at the crystal face is lower, so too is the concentration in the growing crystals, and the effective distribution is correspondingly lower. The greater the rate of crystallization or the slower the rate of diffusion, the larger this effect will be and the closer the effective distribution comes to a value of 1.0.

and excluded elements. The result is that magmas crystallizing rapidly remain undifferentiated, and the composition of the final crystalline assemblage is essentially the same as that of the starting liquid.

Even with relatively slow cooling, kinetic effects may cause the concentrations of trace elements to differ from what they would be in a perfectly equilibrated system. The form these effects may take in a multicomponent liquid is illustrated by a hypothetical three-component system in Figure 5–27. With perfect equilibration, if the temperature of a liquid X drops to that of the temperature contour shown by the curved line, crystals of C begin to grow, and the course of the liquid composition X would be directly away from C in the direction of the

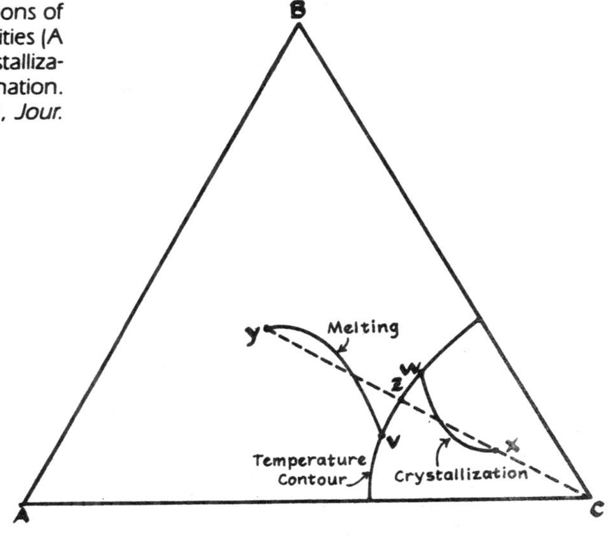

Figure 5–27 A hypothetical illustration of the variations of concentration of two components with differing diffusivities (A diffusing more rapidly than B) during melting and crystallization in a three-component system. See text for explanation. (After Y. Oishi, A. R. Cooper, and W. D. Kingery, 1965, *Jour. Amer. Ceramic Soc.*, *48*:88–95.)

broken line C–Y. When the liquid reaches point Z, it is just saturated at the prevailing temperature, and the crystal ceases to grow. If we consider the role diffusion could play, we see that the actual course of the liquid may be somewhat different. As the growing crystals remove component C from the adjacent boundary layer, the components A and B are residually enriched (Fig. 5–28a). As C diffuses down the compositional gradient to feed the growing crystals, A and B must diffuse in the opposite direction. If A has a greater diffusivity than B, its concentration gradient will be less steep, and the ratio of A to B will vary with distance away from the crystals. As a result the course of the liquid during crystallization will deviate from a straight line and follow a curved path such as that shown by the line X–W in Figure 5–27.

A similar but opposite effect would accompany melting. If a crystal of C were added to a liquid of composition Y, and the temperature remains as before, the crystal would melt and, under conditions of perfect equilibration, the course of the liquid would be a straight line toward C. But if the liquid is not stirred, and the components diffuse through the boundary layer at different rates, the effect would be to produce differing diffusion gradients of A and B toward the crystal-liquid interface (Fig. 5–28b), and the course of the liquid would follow a curved path, such as Y–V in Figure 5–27.

The diffusivities of trace elements in silicate liquids vary inversely with their ionic radius and the square of their charge. It is not known whether these elements take the form of uncombined ions in silicate melts, but if they do their diffusivities will be very different. Because cations may range in charge from +1 in the case of alkalies, such as lithium, cesium, and rubidium, to as much as +6 in certain LIL elements, such as uranium, molybdenum, and tungsten, the diffusivities of elements may differ by orders of magnitude, and the degrees to which they are fractionated may differ accordingly. Even though an element may have a very large or very small distribution coefficient, if it also has a low diffusivity its effective distribution coefficient may be closer to 1.0, and fractionation will be less effective than would be anticipated from its equilibrium distribution coefficient alone.

The effective distribution coefficient is related to the equilibrium value, K, and the ratio of the rate of linear crystal growth to diffusivity, R/D, according to the equation

$$K_{eff} = \frac{1}{2}\left\{1 + \text{erf}\left[\frac{\sqrt{(R/D)X}}{2}\right] + (2K - 1) \times \exp\left[-K(1 - K)\left(\frac{R}{D}\right)X\right] \text{erfc}\left[\frac{(2K - 1)}{2}\sqrt{\left(\frac{R}{D}\right)X}\right]\right\} \tag{5-14}$$

in which X is the linear dimension of the solid. This rather formidable-looking equation can be solved quite easily by use of the table of error functions in Appendix C. In doing so one finds that, for excluded elements for which K is small (less than about 0.3), the effective distribution coefficient will be within about 20 percent of the equilibrium value so long as the value RX/D is less than about 0.2. For rates of growth less than about a tenth of a millimeter per year, diffusivities of

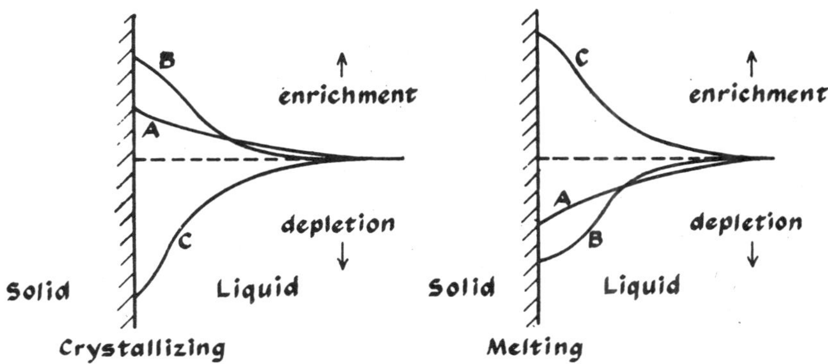

Figure 5–28 Schematic traces of compositional gradients for crystallization and melting in the three-component system in Figure 5–27.

10^{-8} cm^2 sec^{-1} or more, and crystal sizes of less than 5 cm, the effective distribution coefficient does not differ greatly from the equilibrium value, but for elements with large values of K the problem is more serious and can result in an effective value that is only 30 percent or so of the equilibrium one. Thus excluded trace elements can be modeled with reasonable accuracy, especially in slowly cooled magmas, but included elements of low diffusivities may deviate widely in their partitioning from the patterns predicted by equilibrium models.

In summary, then, we see that the effect of diffusion can be to change the effective distribution coefficents, especially for included elements. In systems in which individual components have differing diffusivities, the variations of concentration during crystallization or melting may result in paths of evolution of the differentiated liquid that are functions, not just of their distribution coefficients, but of their rates of crystallization and diffusivities as well.

In the next chapter we examine a number of well-studied examples of differentiated magmas and see how these effects are reflected in the compositions of igneous rocks.

SELECTED REFERENCES

Arth, J. G. 1976. Behavior of trace elements during magmatic processes—a summary of theoretical models and their applications. *Jour. Research, U. S. Geol. Surv.* 4:41–47. A very concise and well-written explanation of the basic relations in trace-element fractionation.

DePaolo, D. J. 1981. Trace element and isotopic effects of combined wallrock assimilation and fractional crystallization. *Earth Planet Sci Ltrs.* 53:189–202. A theoretical model for calculating the effects of simultaneous assimilation and crystal fractionation.

Greenland, L. P. 1970. An equation for trace element distribution during magmatic crystallization. *Amer. Mineral.* 55:455–465. A basic treatment of the equations for fractionation of trace elements during crystal fractionation.

Hart, S. R., and C. J. Allegre. 1980. Trace-element constraints on magma genesis, Chap. 4. *Physics of Magmatic Processes.*

R. B. Hargraves, ed. 121–160. An excellent summary of the principles of trace-element fractionation with somewhat more detail than the reference by Arth listed above.

Helz, R. T. 1987. Differentiation behavior of Kilauea Iki lava lake, Kilauea Volcano, Hawaii: An overview of past and current work. *Magmatic Processes: Physicochemical Principles*. B. Mysen, ed. The Geochemical Society. 241–258. A summary of studies of the most important of the Hawaiian lava lakes. Contains much data on the effects and mechanisms of differentiation.

Hoffmann, A. W. 1980. Diffusion in natural silicate melts: a critical review, Chap 9. *Physics of Magmatic Processes*. R. B. Hargraves, ed. 385–418. A summary of both the theory and experimental data bearing on diffusion in silicate melts.

O'Hara, M. J., and Mathews, R. E. 1981. Geochemical evolution in an advancing, periodically replenished, periodically tapped, continuously fractionated magma chamber. *Jour. Geol. Soc. London, 138*: 237–277. A theoretical analysis of the evolution of a magma chamber from which magma is periodically withdrawn and replenished. The basic principles are laid out in chapter seven.

Shaw, D. M. 1970. Trace element fractionation during anatexis. *Geochim. Cosmochim. Acta*. 34:237–243. A basic treatment of the equations for fractionation of trace elements during partial melting.

Watson, E. B. 1990. Chemical diffusion in magmas: an overview of experimental and geochemical applications. in *Physical Chemistry of Magmas*. L. Perchuk and I. Kushiro, ed. Springer-Verlag, Berlin. A comprehensive review of the role of diffusion in petrologic processes.

6

MAGMATIC DIFFERENTIATION: BASIC INTRUSIONS

HAVING CONSIDERED the basic principles of crystallization and differentiation, we can now turn to geological examples in which these processes have operated under natural conditions. The most instructive examples of this kind are found in large intrusions that have cooled slowly at moderate depths and have later been exhumed by uplift and erosion. Although these bodies represent only the shallowest kinds of differentiation and must differ in many ways from what would be seen at greater depths in the lower crust or mantle, they are the only ones accessible to our view, and, as such, they provide the best direct evidence we have.

Two broad groups of bodies can be distinguished: basic intrusions, mainly of gabbroic or doleritic rocks, and granitic plutons of more felsic composition. Here we consider only the former and leave granitic intrusions until a later chapter dealing with more evolved types of magmas.

Petrologists have long been fascinated by large basic intrusions, especially those that offer clues to the ways in which magmas evolve. Vastly more has been written about the structural, mineralogical, and geochemical characteristics of these bodies than about the ways in which they crystallized and differentiated. The reason for this imbalance is simply that it is far easier to describe rocks than to explain physical processes that can only be inferred from indirect evidence, never observed. The petrologist attempting to understand these cold, dissected intrusions without ever having observed a large body of slowly crystallizing magma is in much the same position as a paleontologist trying to interpret fossil remains without ever having seen the living organism. Despite these limitations, however, much has been learned, especially in the last ten years or so, and our understanding advances rapidly.

DOLERITIC SILLS

Although they differ widely in detail, basic intrusions fall into two distinct groups that differ conspicuously in their dimensions, rates of solidification, and textures and compositions of their rocks. As we noted in chapter two, *hypabyssal*

Figure 6–1 One of a large number of Mesozoic sills forming a belt extending from Australia to South Africa is exposed in steep, glaciated cliffs in the Taylor Glacier region of Antarctica.

bodies are distinguished from *plutonic* intrusions mainly by their smaller size and shallower depth of emplacement (Fig. 6–1). The former are more common than are plutonic bodies of equivalent mafic compositions, whereas the reverse is true of felsic intrusions; felsic plutons are more common than are sills and dikes of similar composition. The mafic rocks of basic dikes and sills are usually referred to as *dolerites* or *diabases*, because their grain sizes are intermediate between those of basalt and gabbro. The felsic differentiates are normally *granophyres*, consisting chiefly of fine intergrowths of quartz and alkali feldspar. Unlike the coarse, hypidiomorphic, granular textures so typical of large, slowly cooled bodies, dolerites are typically sub-ophitic (Fig. 4–22c), with a range of grain sizes from one mineral to another. They include a relatively restricted range of compositions and lithologies. Most commonly, their trends of differentiation resemble those of the Hawaiian lava lakes mentioned in earlier chapters.

Although many varieties of doleritic sills have been described, most have broadly similar characteristics that can be illustrated with a few examples, such as the well-studied Palisades Sill of New Jersey. This intrusion is part of a large group of Triassic sills, dikes, and subaqueous lava flows that were emplaced in a subsiding basin during an episode of continental rifting. Exposed for 80 km along the western bank of the Hudson River, it reaches thicknesses of more than 300 m.

Because of a 10 or 20 m thick olivine-rich zone near its base (Fig. 6–2a), the sill was often cited in the early literature as an example of magmatic differentiation by crystal settling. The compositional variations are far from spectacular, however. In part, they are the result of initial differences in three or four succes-

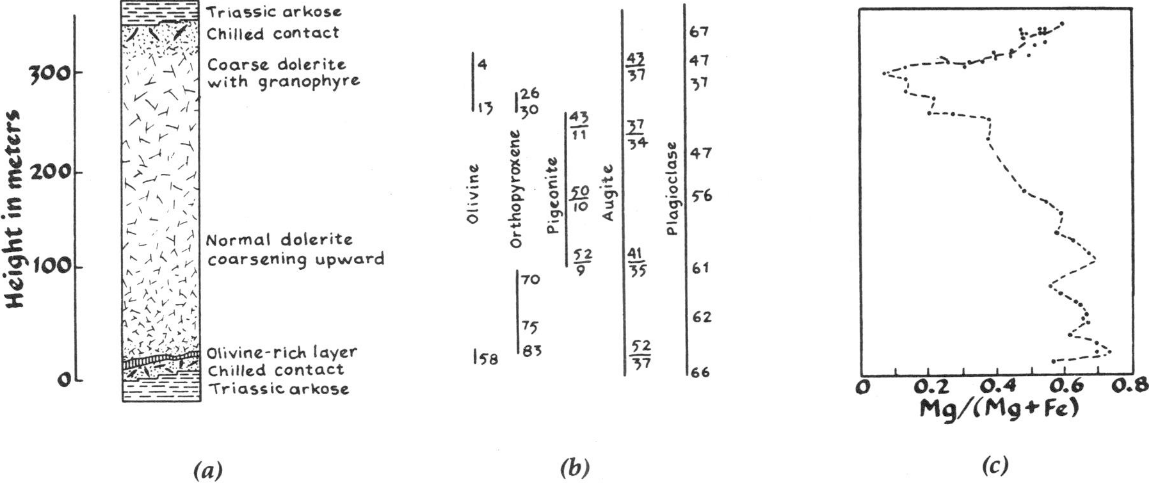

(a) (b) (c)

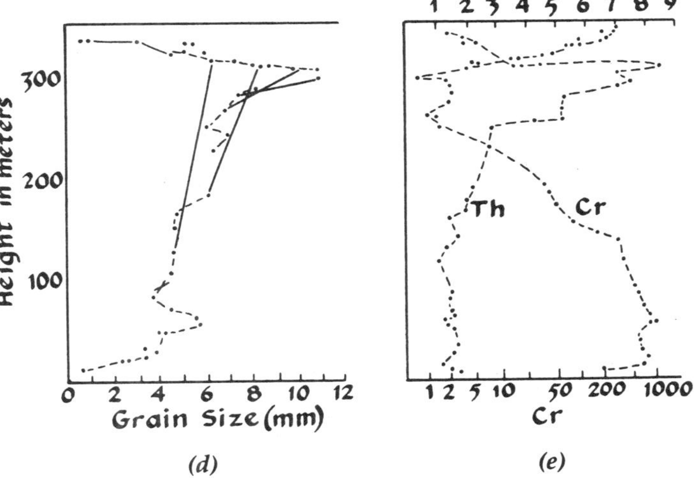

(d) (e)

Figure 6–2 (a) A schematic section through the Palisades Sill of New Jersey and New York. (b) Mineral compositions vary systematically, with height as mafic minerals become more iron-rich and plagioclase more sodic. The section from the floor up to about 300 m has a compressed, inverted counterpart in the rocks that crystallized from the roof downward. (c) The ratio of Mg to Mg + Fe is a good measure of differentiation. Its value declines from the floor up and from the roof down to reach a minimum at the 300 m level. Several reversals mark places where new batches of less-differentiated magma were injected and reset the composition of the remaining liquid. (d) The sizes of mineral grains increase toward the 300 m level where the last liquid crystallized. Lines join corresponding stages in the mineralogic sequence shown in (b) and illustrate the somewhat coarser texture of the roof rocks at any given stage. (e) Concentrations of chromium and thorium illustrate the variations of included and excluded trace elements. Note that the scale for Cr is logarithmic and that Cr is depleted more rapidly than Th is enriched. (Adapted from K. R. Walker, 1969, *Geol. Soc. Amer. Spec. Pap. 111* and D. N. Shirley, 1987, *Jour. Petrol.* 28:835–865.)

sive pulses of intruded magma. Although compositional breaks marking these separate injections are difficult to detect in outcrops, they are evident in chemical variations, such as the ratio Mg/(Mg + Fe), which is a good measure of the degree of differentiation of basic magmas. When plotted against height in the Palisades Sill, this ratio decreases inward from both the base and roof to a minimum about 300 m above the base (Fig. 6-2c). In detail, however, the trend has small but distinct reversals that are thought to result from new injections that set the magma back to a slightly more primitive composition.

The vertical section illustrated in Figure 6-2 is probably typical of most of the sill. Above the chilled base and the conspicuous olivine-rich layer a few meters higher, the dolerite becomes coarser and more felsic up to the 300 m level where granophyre accounts for more than 50 percent of the rock. It was in this "sandwich horizon" that the last crystallizing liquid was sandwiched between the dolerite accumulating simultaneously on the floor and under the roof. The sequence of minerals in the roof rocks is a compressed mirror image of the one on the floor. It is also coarser and has suffered more hydrothermal alteration.

Most of the range of differentiation is characterized by a steady enrichment of iron (Fig. 6-3); only in the very late stages does this trend reverse when silica and alkalies are greatly enriched in the granophyres. The silica content, which averages about 54.6 percent for the sill as a whole, exceeds 62 percent in the most differentiated rocks. Plagioclase increases, both in modal abundance and anorthite content, from An_{66} in the chilled base to An_{37} at the 300 m level, while pyroxenes, including both Ca-rich and Ca-poor varieties, become increasingly iron-rich. After the initial segregation of olivine phenocrysts, which were probably in the magma at the time it was intruded, olivine ceased to crystallize. The rare grains found in the main body of the sill are rounded and rimmed with pyroxene as a result of reaction with the liquid. In the late stages of differentia-

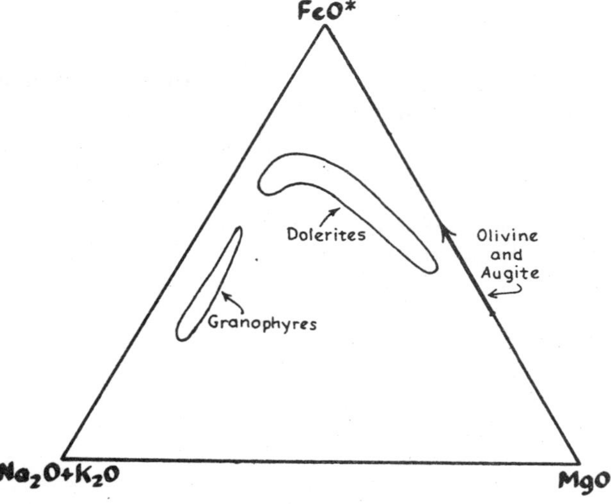

Figure 6-3 AMF ($Na_2O + K_2O$, MgO, FeO) diagram showing compositional variations of the Palisades Sill and Red Hill dolerites. The original compositions of the magmas were rich in MgO and became relatively more iron-rich in the main stages of differentiation. At later stages, however, alkalies increased at a greater rate as crystallization of magnetite removed iron. At that point the trend turned sharply toward the composition of granophyres near the lower left side of the triangle. (After K. R. Walker, 1969, *Geol. Soc. Amer. Spec. Paper 111* and I. McDougall, 1962, *Bull. Geol. Soc. Amer.* 73:279–316.)

tion, however, the magma became rich enough in iron to precipitate fayalitic olivine, which, as we saw in chapter four (Fig. 4–14), is stable in the presence of quartz.

Mechanisms of differentiation

Owing to its shallow depth and rapid rate of cooling, the sill crystallized in much the same way as the Hawaiian lava lakes. Despite its apparent simplicity, however, the manner in which it differentiated is far from obvious.

Crystal settling seems not to have played a major role. The rate of advance of the front of crystallization under the roof was so much faster than the settling velocities of crystals that nucleated and grew there that few crystals escaped entrapment in the growing crust. Clusters of crystals may have been able to break loose from the mush under the roof and, owing to their greater aggregate size, settle to the floor, but the importance of this process is difficult to assess. The preservation of sharp discontinuities marking the boundaries of different pulses of magma is difficult to reconcile with vertical movements of large amounts of material.

A more important effect was probably the segregation of interstitial liquid from between the growing crystals. As the mush on the floor thickened, it was compacted under its own weight, expelling at least part of the liquid from the space between crystals. This process may have been enhanced by the density inversion that took place after the interstitial liquid passed its maximum enrichment of iron and titanium and became increasingly enriched in silica and volatile components. These changes caused a decrease of density that enabled the evolved buoyant liquid to rise through the permeable network of crystals and reenter the main overlying mass of magma.

This upward migration of late-stage liquids resulted in a redistribution, not only of silica and volatiles, but of most trace elements as well (Fig. 6–2e). For example, the concentration of thorium, which is effectively excluded from all minerals of the dolerite, reaches a maximum at the sandwich horizon where the growing crust of the roof and floor converged, while Cr, which enters readily into magnetite and pyroxene, is progressively depleted until it reaches a minimum concentration at the same 300 m level.

If the crystals nucleated and grew *in situ*, why is the sequence on the floor so much thicker than the one that formed under the roof? Comparisons of the mineral assemblages and compositions indicate that, from a very early stage until the last liquid crystallized, solidification advanced about seven times faster on the floor than under the roof. This large difference is difficult to reconcile with the way the sill cooled. Heat lost through the floor could not have been greater than that lost through the roof. If anything, it was probably less, because a vigorously convecting hydrothermal system in the overlying sediments would have enhanced cooling of the roof. Why, then, did a thicker mass of crystals accumulate on the floor than under the roof?

One possibility is that the redistribution of components in the rising interstitial liquid changed the composition of the magma and lowered the temperature at which it crystallized. As we have seen in chapter three, the addition of a new component to a crystallizing liquid tends to decrease its liquidus temperature. This effect is especially pronounced for late-stage residual components, particularly water. Thus, the accumulation of differentiated components in the upper part of the magma could have caused it to lag behind the front of crystallization on the floor. In any case, there can be little question that much of the differentiation, especially of the granophyric component, can be attributed to the rise of buoyant, volatile-rich liquids that separated from the crystal mush on the floor.

A spectacular example of this is seen in the Red Hill intrusion, one of a large group of doleritic sills in Tasmania. Differentiation followed a trend very similar to that of the Palisades Sill. In places, however, the Red Hill intrusion has much larger accumulations of granophyre (Fig. 6-4). The normal thickness of the sill is about 400 meters, but the roof was uplifted locally by as much as 300 meters to form a cupola where disproportionately large amounts of granophyre collected. The upfaulted roof seems to have provided a structural trap into which late-crystallizing liquid migrated from a broad lateral extent.

Alkaline dolerites

Basic sills of more alkaline composition have many of the features of tholeiitic dolerites, but instead of quartz-rich granophyres they differentiate to felsic rocks devoid of quartz and rich in alkali feldspar and silica-poor minerals, such as analcite and, more rarely, nepheline. A particularly well-studied example is the Prospect intrusion near Sidney, Australia. Part of the same large group of Mesozoic sills as the Tasmanian dolerites, the Prospect body is exposed in quarries where extensive sections reveal complex lithologic variations, both vertically and along strike (Fig. 6-5).

The magma must have been very inhomogeneous with large concentrations of olivine crystals in the last pulse of intruded liquid. No other explanation can be found for the very olivine-rich compositions in the middle of the sill, precisely where one would expect to find the most differentiated rocks. Although some olivine settled and accumulated near the floor, olivine-rich rocks are also found at almost all levels, especially near irregularities and elevated parts of the roof where crystals seem to have been concentrated by flow segregation at the time of emplacement.

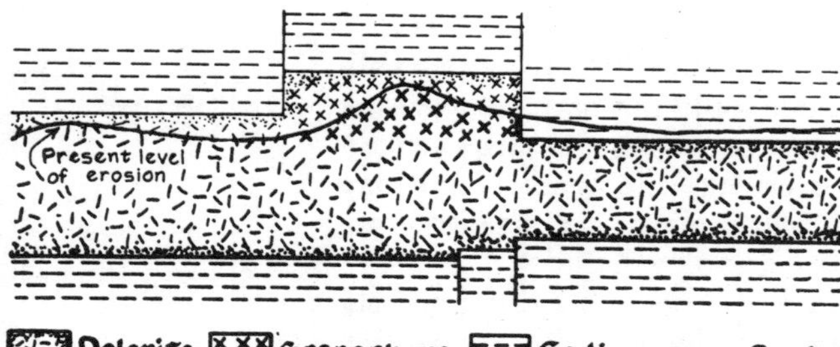

Figure 6-4 A schematic section through the Red Hill Sill of Tasmania. The maximum thickness is about 700 m where granophyre has accumulated under an up-faulted block of the roof. (After I. McDougall, 1962, *Bull. Geol. Soc. Amer.* 73:279–316.)

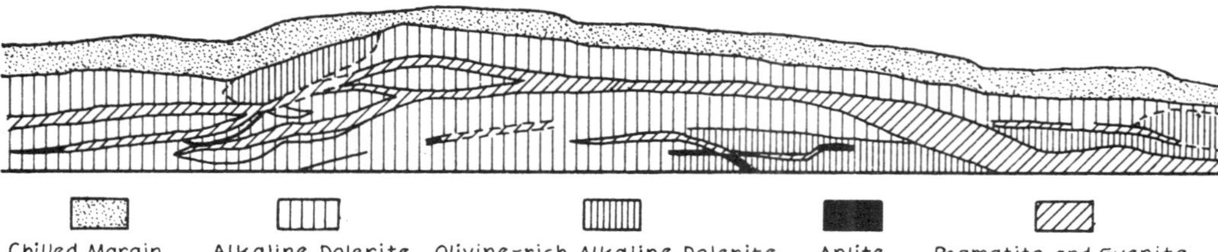

Figure 6-5 Part of the Prospect intrusion near Sidney, Australia. Note the irregular form of the lithologic variations, some of which are crudely conformable to the shape of the roof. (After H. G. Wilshire, 1967, *Jour. Petr.* 8:97–163.)

The rocks and minerals have a broad range of composition. The most differentiated rocks are in long, thin lenses of very coarse-grained syenite that cross the sill at odd angles. They are thought to have formed when late-stage liquids, rich in alkalies and volatiles, moved into fractures, cutting the viscous, partly crystalline magma. In places, this caused extensive replacement of plagioclase by alkali feldspars to form syenites rich in anorthoclase, oligoclase, and analcite. Veinlets of compositionally similar but finer-grained rocks, called *aplites* because of their felsic composition and granular texture, appear to have been filter-pressed into dilational fractures that cut the sill at various angles.

With the effects of all these processes of differentiation—crystal settling, flow segregation, volatile transfer, and filter pressing—superimposed on each other, the result has been a complex vertical and horizontal distribution of the chemical components and lithologic units of the intrusion (Fig. 6-6).

FORM AND MODE OF EMPLACEMENT OF LAYERED INTRUSIONS

Basic intrusions that reach thicknesses of more than four or five hundred meters tend to be notably more coarse-grained than thinner dikes and sills, and almost all have some form of layering. The critical thickness that separates basic intru-

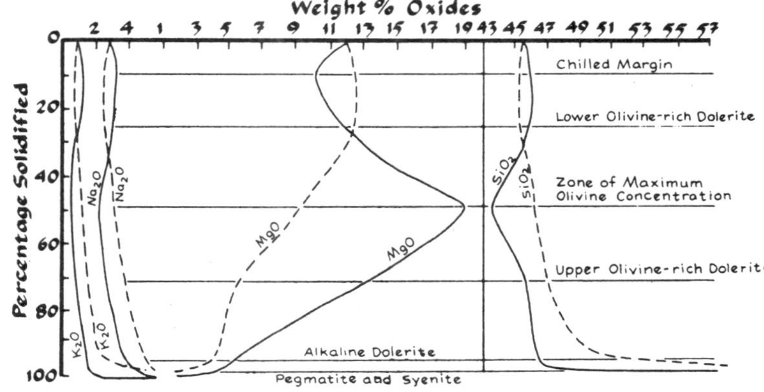

Figure 6-6 Variations of key components of successive liquids (dashed lines) and rock compositions (solid lines) with progressive solidification of the Prospect intrusion. Note that the rates of enrichment or depletion of components in the liquid tend to vary according to the relative concentration in the mineral assemblage of the rocks, but not always in a systematic way. (After H. G. Wilshire, 1967, *Jour. Petr.* 8:97–163.)

sions into two distinct groups, one nearly structureless and the other layered, must be in some way related to the ways in which magmatic bodies of differing dimensions crystallize while losing heat to their surroundings. It seems that above some critical size the mechanisms of crystal-liquid fractionation are much more effective. Whatever the reason, however, most large, basic intrusions have undergone more extensive differentiation and contain more rocks of extreme compositions.

The largest layered intrusions measure tens or hundreds of kilometers across and several kilometers in thickness. Most of the largest bodies are of Precambrian age; younger intrusions are, on average, much smaller. Unlike granitic plutons, which tend to be tall and steep-sided, basic intrusions are generally flatter. Many early decriptions referred to the latter as *lopoliths*, which are defined as large, basin-shaped bodies with thicknesses less than 5 to 10 percent of their diameters, but only a few, such as the Sudbury intrusion of Canada, are depressed in their centers. Instead, they tend to be funnel-shaped or trough-like with a narrow feeder-dike. Though intrusions are only rarely eroded in ways that expose their roots, at least two, the Muskox intrusion of Canada and the Great Dyke of Zimbabwe, have feeder-dikes that extend for tens or hundreds of kilometers. They seem to have been intruded passively into zones of tension and dilation, and, as in the case of sills, the magma probably rose and spread laterally at a level determined by its density relative to that of the surrounding rock.

Most shallow intrusions have a narrow, fine-grained margin resulting from chilling of the magma against cold wall-rocks. This quenched selvage may preserve the initial composition of the undifferentiated magma, but in most cases its composition has been altered by reaction with the walls or by transfer of components across the steep thermal and compositional gradients at the contact.

The calculated cooling times of large masses of magma range from a few tens to hundreds of thousands of years. These estimates are uncertain, however, because they are very sensitive to how much heat is assumed to have been carried away in meteoric water circulating through the surrounding rocks. The heat of the intrusion tends to set up a convective hydrothermal system that can greatly enhance the transfer of heat.

It may be significant that nearly all well-layered basic intrusions are of tholeiitic composition. Apart from a few ultramafic and syenitic intrusions that seem to be in categories of their own, the original magmas of almost all known bodies with well-developed layering were hypersthene-normative gabbros that differentiated with a pronounced trend of iron enrichment. Why layering is absent or only weakly developed in other types of magmas is unclear; the reason must lie in some physical attribute of the magmas. Suffice it to say that if layering were better understood petrologists would be able to say what this special property might be, but at the moment the origin of layering is one of the most puzzling and controversial phenomena in igneous rocks.

Layering and zoning

Three main types of layering have been recognized. Most conspicuous is *modal layering* in which the proportions of minerals differ over vertical distances ranging from a centimeter or so to a few meters (Fig. 6–7a and b). Layers of this kind may have a uniform spacing, in which case they are said to be "rhythmic" (Fig. 6–7c), but many are far from regular and are more properly referred to as "intermittent." The modal differences may be either sharp or gradational, and, in extreme cases, alternating layers may be nearly monomineralic (Fig. 6–7b). Differences of grain size can also define layers (Fig. 6–7d). In some instances, the sizes are graded, as they are in many kinds of sediments, but more commonly they are not.

The term *phase layering* is used to denote intervals defined by the presence or absence of a particular mineral in the crystallization sequence. Thus, a distinctive mineral can serve to delineate units of a differentiated intrusion, just as diagnostic fossils are used to identify sedimentary horizons in a stratigraphic sequence.

Finally, the compositions of minerals, such as plagioclase, olivine, and pyroxene, change in systematic ways during progressive differentiation. When recorded in a continuous series of rocks, these changes are usually referred to as *cryptic layering*, because they produce no marked contrast in the appearance of rocks in outcrops. They are, however, a basic feature of the compositional variations of all rocks produced by the evolution of a differentiating magma.

The origins of modal layering

Most early studies of igneous differentiation assumed that gravitational settling and various mechanisms of sedimentation were responsible for modal layering. It is now recognized, however, that layering may have a number of different origins.

Certain intrusions of peridotite have well-developed layering with many of the characteristics of sedimentary deposits. The best example, by far, is the intrusion of Duke Island, Alaska. Figures 6–7d and 6–8a illustrate some of the features, such as size sorting and cross-bedding, that closely resemble alluvial deposits of coarse sand and gravel. The crystals were probably laid down by swift currents of fluid magma sweeping across the floor of the intrusion.

Intrusions of gabbroic composition also show evidence of magmatic currents, but the graded layers (Fig. 6–8b) bear only a superficial resemblance to beds laid down by density currents during rapid sedimentation. Minerals of higher density may be concentrated at the base, but their grain sizes are not systematically greater than those deposited at higher levels in the same layer. It will be recalled from the preceding chapter (equation 5–1) that because settling rates vary with the square of the radius of the particle, they are much more sensitive to size than to density contrast. Large grains should settle faster and be concentrated near the base, but this is seldom seen. Moreover, graded layering is not confined to the floor; it can be found in rocks that crystallized under the roof or on near-vertical walls. Dark minerals tend to be concentrated in the outer, cooler part, regardless of how these layers are oriented with respect to gravity. The density relations of the crystals and liquid pose an added problem. Magnetite, olivine, and pyroxene, which must have been denser than the liquid from which they grew, accumulated under the roof, while plagioclase, which was probably lighter than the iron-rich magma, is an abundant constituent of layered rocks on

(a)

Figure 6-7 Types of modal layering. (a) Layering in the Skaergaard intrusion results from differing proportions of plagioclase, magnetite, pyroxene, and olivine, which vary in spacing and proportions from one layer to the next. (b) Nearly pure chromite forms layers within very plagioclase-rich rocks of the Bushveld intrusion. Both rocks are nearly monomineralic. (c) Fine-scale alternations of plagioclase and pyroxene in the Stillwater Complex form a regular pattern on a scale of inches. (d) Differing sizes and proportions of olivine and pyroxene emphasize the layering and cross-bedding of peridotites in the Duke Island intrusion of southeastern Alaska.

(b)

(c)

→

Figure 6–8 Two types of graded layers. One (a) from the Duke Island ultramafic intrusion has large crystals concentrated at the base as would be expected from gravitational settling, whereas the other (b) from the Skaergaard intrusion is mainly the result of larger concentrations of dark minerals near the base.

(d)

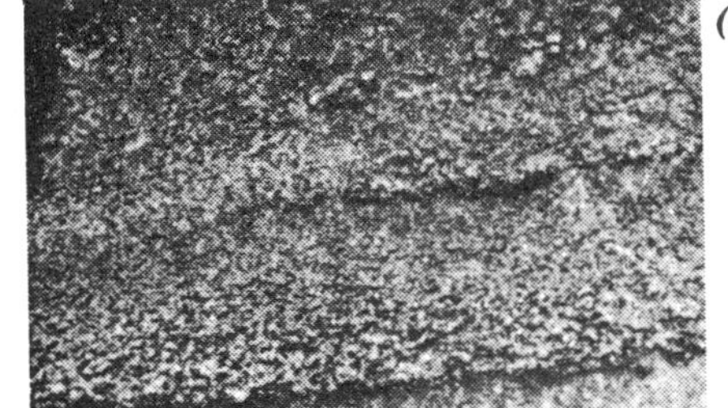

(a)

(b)

the floor. It is clear that some mechanism other than gravitational segregation must be capable of producing layering of these types.

A number of alternative origins have been proposed; most involve some form of *in situ* crystallization and compositional stratification. This must certainly be true of rocks with crescumulate textures, in which slender crystals have grown perpendicular to the plane of layering (Fig. 6–9). The unusual, elongated form of crystals in rocks of this kind results from nucleation and rapid growth in the manner explained in chapter four (Fig. 4–27). Under some conditions, a process of this kind may be repetitive and produce a succession of layers, just as it does in oscillatory zoning of plagioclase (Fig. 6–10).

Another mechanism governed by compositional gradients and diffusion has been proposed to explain regular rhythmic layering of the kind illustrated in Figure 6–7c. We saw in chapter four that, owing to their greater surface area, large crystals have an advantage over smaller ones whenever crystals with a range of sizes are in contact with the same liquid (Fig. 6–11). During very slow cooling, an aging process results in large crystals growing at the expense of small ones. Because of small differences in surface energy, a homogeneous interstitial fluid cannot be in perfect equilibrium with both small and large crystals; it may be slightly undersaturated with respect to the small crystals, which will tend to dissolve, and oversaturated with respect to larger ones, which will tend to grow. As a result, compositional gradients are set up between the liquids adjacent to crystals of differing sizes. Whether the initial differences in grain size result from

Figure 6–9 Crescumulate layers of pyroxene and plagioclase near the base of the Skaergaard intrusion. Slender crystals of plagioclase and pyroxene that have grown perpendicular to the floor of the intrusion are an example of rapid growth from an undercooled liquid, as explained in Figure 4–27.

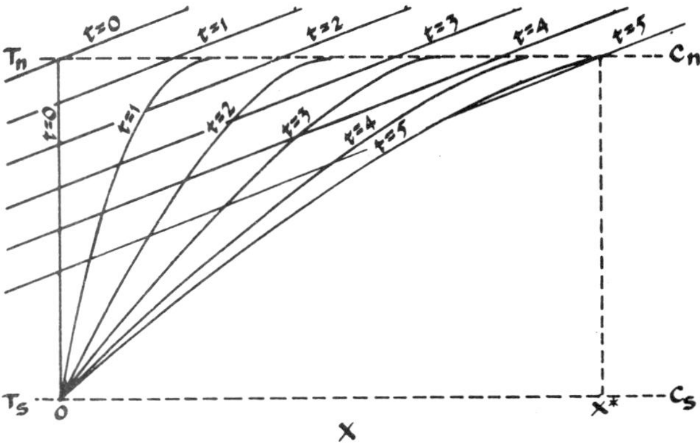

Figure 6–10 Oscillatory crystallization may result from differing rates or diffusion of heat and chemical components through the liquid adjacent to a front of nucleation and crystal growth. Nucleation requires a combination of temperature, T_N, and concentration, C_N (both on the vertical axis). The liquid is supersaturated at time t = 0 when crystals begin to grow at X = 0. Instantly, the concentration drops to the saturation level, C_S, and a concentration gradient (curved lines) is set up. This diffusion-controlled gradient retreats rapidly at first but gradually becomes slower until at time t = 5 the temperature gradient (straight lines) overtakes it. A new layer forms at X* where the combination of concentration and temperature is again appropriate for nucleation.

irregularities of crystallization or from inhomogeneities of some other origin, they may lead to small-scale cyclical variations in the sizes and distribution of crystals. It is doubtful, however, whether they can be responsible for large-scale layering, because the rates of diffusion are too slow to be effective over distances greater than a few centimeters.

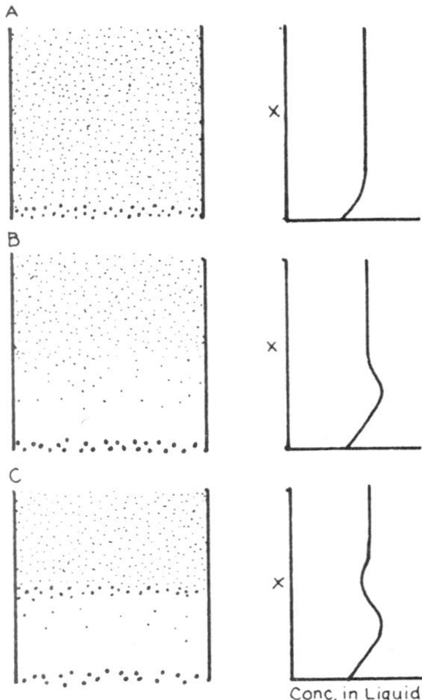

Figure 6–11 Layering can also develop at a late stage of cooling and recrystallization. Any initial condition that gives the crystals at one level an advantage over others and causes them to grow larger will produce a compositional gradient through the intercrystalline liquid. Owing to their lower surface energy, large crystals grow and extract components from the adjacent liquid, while crystals of smaller size dissolve and cause a local enrichment of the liquid. This sets up a compositional gradient allowing components to be transferred from the dissolving crystals to those that are growing. As this process advances, the differences of crystal sizes and liquid compositions become greater, and, with time, the small crystals may be completely dissolved. The process can be repetitive, because the dissolving crystals are also at a disadvantage with respect to other crystals at a higher level, and the latter will begin to grow and generate a new layer. (After Alan Boudreau, 1982 Master's Thesis, University of Oregon.)

THE BUSHVELD COMPLEX

Any discussion of layered intrusions must begin with the Precambrian Bushveld Complex of South Africa. Not only is it the largest intrusion known, but, in many ways, it is one of the most remarkable bodies of igneous rock on Earth. Apart from its geological interest, it has great economic importance as a rich repository of platinum, chromium, vanadium, and other valuable metals. Thanks to extensive mapping, undergound mining, and exploratory drilling, a wealth of data is available on the intrusion, but, owing to its enormous size and complexity, much still remains to be learned.

The intrusion was emplaced as a nearly flat tabular mass of gabbroic magma that spread laterally from at least two separate feeders beneath a thin cover of sediments and volcanic rocks. The present area of outcrop (Fig. 6–12) measures about 270 km north-south by 450 km east-west, and its original thickness must have exceeded eight kilometers. The time required to crystallize this huge mass is thought to have been on the order of 200,000 years.

Much of the roof of the intrusion is made up of metamorphosed and partly fused sediments and felsic volcanic rocks of the Rooiberg Series. The latter are only slightly older than the intrusion and may have been related to the same magmatic episode. The central part of the Bushveld is occupied by a composite granitic pluton emplaced 50 to 100 million years after the gabbroic magma had crystallized.

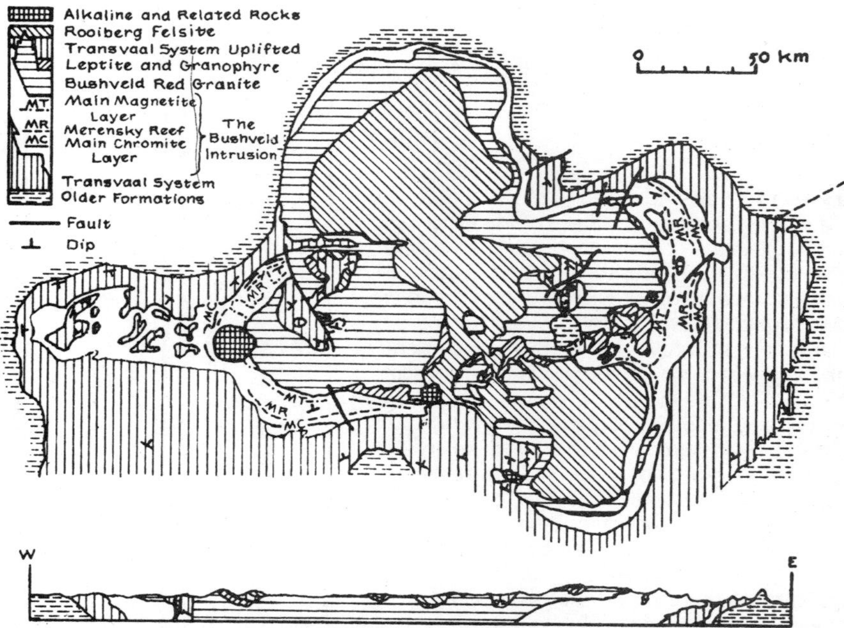

Figure 6–12 Simplified map and cross section of the Bushveld intrusion of South Africa. (Based mainly on a compilation by J. Willemse.)

The igneous rocks of the complex resemble a thick section of stratified sediments. They are well-layered, and individual horizons have remarkable continuity over vast distances. The best known unit, the Merensky Reef, is a complex assemblage of orthopyroxene, olivine, chromite, and sulfides, from which much of the world's platinum is mined. Though only one to five meters thick, it has been traced for distances of more than 300 km.

The gabbroic and ultramafic rocks making up the Layered Series have been divided stratigraphically (Fig. 6–13) on the basis of distinctive mineral assemblages that crystallized with progressive cooling and differentiation. The Lower Zone is divided into two parts by the Main Chromite Seam, below which olivine is an essential component of the rocks and above which it was not precipitated.

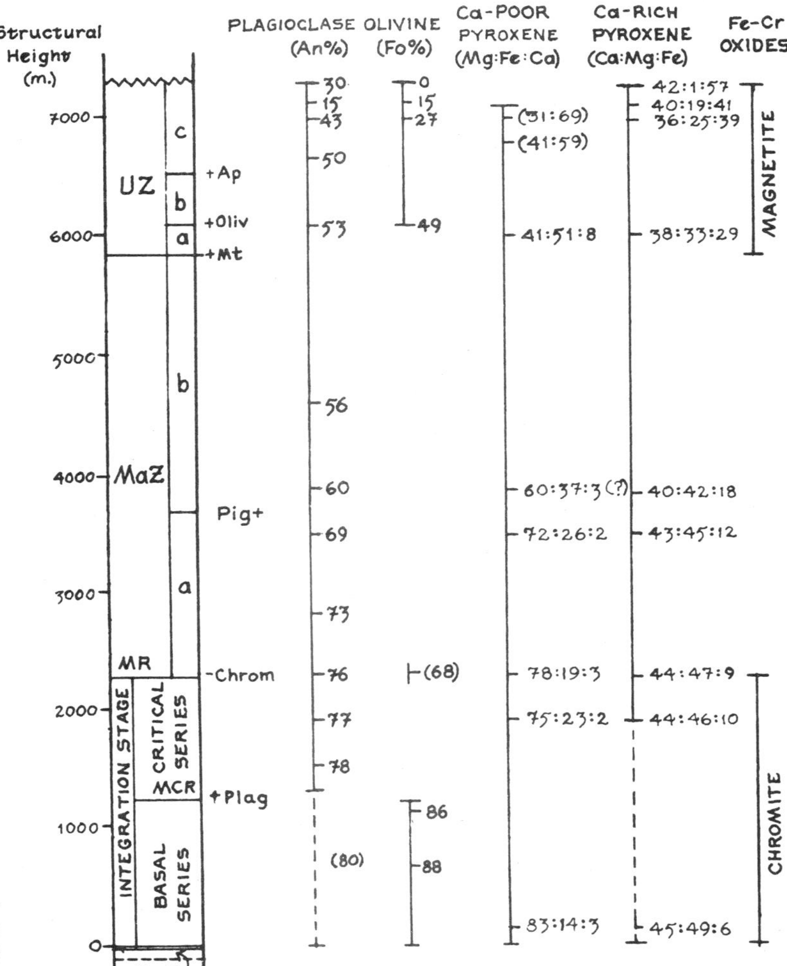

Figure 6–13 Stratigraphic section of the Bushveld intrusion. (After L. R. Wager and G. M. Brown, 1967, *Layered Igneous Rocks*, Oliver & Boyd.)

The platinum-bearing Merensky Reef occupies a similar stratigraphic position close to the level where chromite ceased to crystallize at the base of the Main Zone. The top of the Main Zone is marked by the first appearance of magnetite as a primary phase, and the Upper Zone is subdivided at the level where olivine reappears and again at the first crystallization of apatite as a primary phase.

Superimposed on these major divisions is a cryptic zoning resulting from the compositional changes of individual minerals precipitated from the magma as its composition steadily evolved. The earliest pyroxenes and olivines are magnesium-rich but become more iron-rich upward, until, in the most extreme differentiates, they approach the pure iron end-members, hedenbergite and fayalite. The first plagioclase has the composition of bytownite (about An_{80}) and becomes more albitic until it reaches calcic oligoclase (An_{30}) in the uppermost horizons. As the differentiating magma was steadily enriched in ferric iron, phosphorus, potassium, and silica, it eventually became saturated with these components and precipitated them as magnetite, apatite, potassium feldspar, and quartz.

It is difficult to conceive of a body of molten magma with the enormous dimensions of the Bushveld Complex solidifying with such regularity that crystal assemblages maintained nearly uniform compositions over great distances, but for the most part this was the case. Apart from minor differences between the western and eastern parts of the intrusion, certain of the units consist of layer upon layer of crystals, varying little in composition from one part of the intrusion to another. Many of these rocks are essentially monomineralic and have monotonously homogeneous compositions.

The lower parts of the intrusion contain a complex series of orthopyroxenites, gabbros, and anorthosites, as well as a number of economically important horizons rich in chromite. Some of these units are repeated in cyclical sequences in which the modal variations and cryptic zoning of minerals are repeated in regular sawtooth patterns. The base of each cycle is marked by an abrupt step to a more olivine-rich assemblage, often with interlayered chromite in its lower level, followed by greater proportions of orthopyroxene that first become more magnesian and then progressively more iron-rich upward. The cyclic units as a whole become more iron-rich upward and at the same time become progressively thinner until they eventually disappear near the base of the Main Zone.

The origin of these units is still a matter of dispute. It was long assumed that they resulted from sudden introductions of new magma that mixed with the earlier magma and then evolved as separate units. More recently, petrologists have begun to question the plausibility of this explanation, because, as they point out, it requires an unrealistic regularity of the spacing of new injections of magma, each with the precise volume and degree of differentiation needed to produce the orderly repetition of mineralogical assemblages. Among the alternative explanations that have been suggested are periodic changes of water pressure or oxygen fugacity, possibly as a result of volcanic eruptions, or periodic convective overturn that brought fresh magma to the floor. Whatever their origin, patterns of this kind are by no means confined to the Bushveld rocks. They are common in almost all large basic intrusions.

THE MUSKOX INTRUSION

Most of the basal horizons that crystallized during the earliest stages of cooling of the Bushveld magma are buried deep below the present level of erosion. If they could be seen, they might resemble the root zones of more deeply eroded bodies, such as the Muskox intrusion in northern Canada. This long, trough-shaped body has an exposed length of 120 km, and geophysical surveys indicate that it has at least that much additional length beneath its roof rocks. It has been tilted slightly toward its upper end, so that the exposed section is equivalent to an original vertical dimension of over 6 km (Fig. 6–14). A thin feeder-dike of olivine-rich gabbro can be seen passing upward into a prism-shaped body of more differentiated rocks.

The main part of the intrusion is made up of numerous cyclical sequences that follow a regular order of crystallization before reverting to a more primitive composition. The cyclic units consist, from their base upward, of dunite, olivine clinopyroxenite, and olivine gabbro, so that the order of appearance of crystallizing minerals was first olivine, then clinopyroxene, followed by plagioclase. Orthopyroxene appears late in the lower units, but, higher in the section, it enters at an earlier stage of the cycle of crystallization. The nearly monomineralic character of the dunites testifies to efficient segregation of olivine crystals with only small amounts of interstitial pyroxene or plagioclase. Overlying layers of olivine clinopyroxenite become increasingly rich in clinopyroxene upward, then end abruptly with the appearance of plagioclase. From that level upward the gabbroic rocks become proportionately richer in plagioclase.

The cyclical series may have resulted from new injections of fresh magma that reset the bulk composition and gave rise to repeated sequences of crystallization. The effects of these influxes are clearly shown by the nickel content of the rocks, which have a remarkably regular sawtooth pattern (Fig. 6–15). The order of crystallization of minerals was slightly different in later cycles, possibly because the new liquid differed in composition from the earlier one or, more likely, the magma became contaminated with greater amounts of siliceous roof rocks.

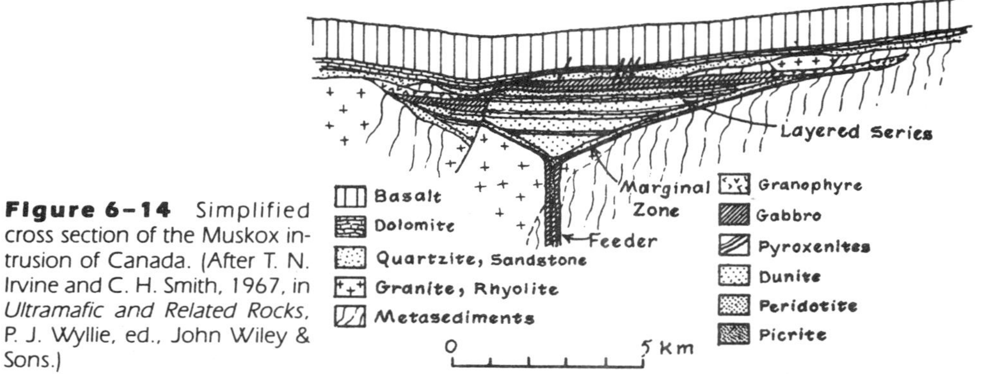

Figure 6–14 Simplified cross section of the Muskox intrusion of Canada. (After T. N. Irvine and C. H. Smith, 1967, in *Ultramafic and Related Rocks*, P. J. Wyllie, ed., John Wiley & Sons.)

Olivine appeared first, but orthopyroxene preceded clinopyroxene and plagioclase, and the corresponding rocks are dunite, orthopyroxenite, websterite (orthopyroxene and clinopyroxene), and gabbro.

The earlier sequence of crystallization corresponds well to one predicted by experimentally determined phase relations. Figure 6–16a shows the modal compositions of the early series of dunites, clinopyroxenites, and olivine gabbros; Figure 6–16b shows how crystallization in the system olivine-clinopyroxene-silica could have produced each of the observed rocks from an evolving liquid as it first crossed the olivine field, then descended along the pyroxene boundary until it reached the plagioclase field.

The gabbroic section of the intrusion is capped by a thick layer of granophyre immediately under the roof. The volume of the siliceous liquid from which these rocks crystallized was too great to be a simple product of differentiation of the main magma. Instead it must have come from melting of sediments in the roof where, owing to its low density, it remained as a segregated body in the uppermost levels of the chamber.

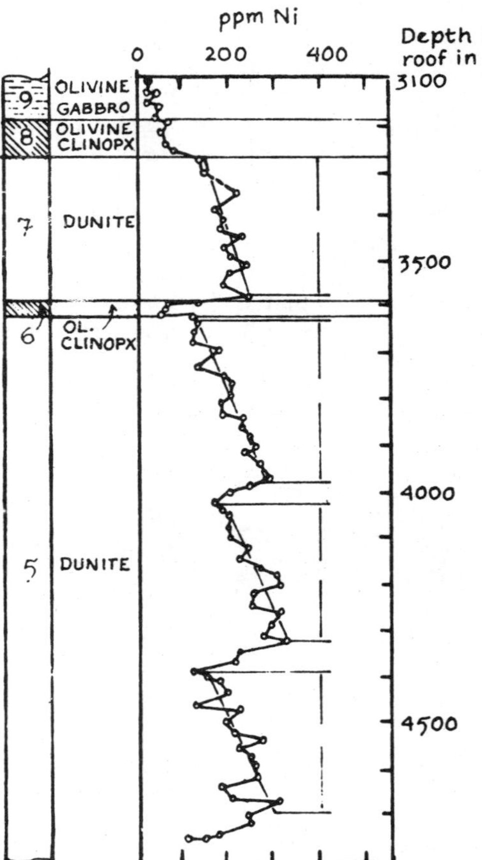

Figure 6–15 Cyclical variations of nickel in the Muskox intrusion. These sawtooth patterns result from new injections of fresh, undifferentiated magma that replenish the concentration of nickel in the magma. Strongly included elements of this kind are useful for detecting a new influx of more primitive magma, because their concentrations are rapidly depleted in the early stages of differentiation and are therefore more sensitive to a fresh liquid that resets their abundances. (After T. N. Irvine, 1969, *Geol. Soc. South Africa, Spec. Publ. 1*, 441–476.)

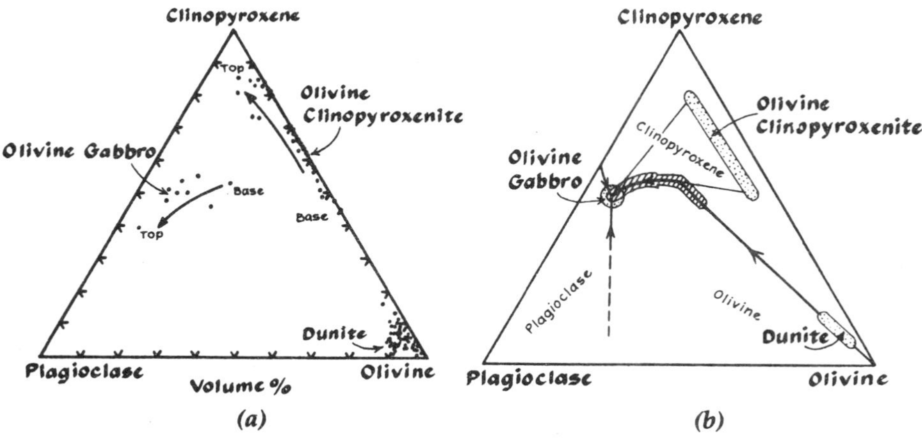

Figure 6–16 Modal compositions of rocks of the Muskox intrusion (a) and their relations to the course of crystallization of liquids in the system clinopyroxene-plagioclase-olivine (b.) (After T. N. Irvine, 1969, *Geol. Soc. South Africa, Spec. Publ. 1*, 441–476.)

THE STILLWATER COMPLEX

The Stillwater Complex of southwestern Montana (Fig. 6–17) was probably comparable to the Bushveld intrusion in its original thickness but somewhat smaller in lateral extent. It is difficult to be sure, because the rocks have been tilted, eroded, and partly buried by sediments. The base and slightly more than five kilometers of the lower section are exposed in a thirty-kilometer-long strip. Like the Bushveld intrusion, the Stillwater rocks can be divided into major stratigraphic units on the basis of distinctive minerals that appeared at successive horizons as the magma differentiated (Fig. 6–18). Much of the section is poorly exposed, but detailed stratigraphic data are available from drill holes and mining. The intrusion has been mined for chromite, which forms rich layers similar to those of the Bushveld, and has at least one platinum-bearing horizon having much in common with the celebrated Merensky Reef but a somewhat lower grade.

The Ultramafic Zone

The principal minerals, in order of appearance, are olivine, chromite, orthopyroxene, plagioclase, and augite. The ultramafic series laid down prior to crystallization of primary plagioclase contains at least fifteen cyclic units not unlike those of the Bushveld complex. From base to top, a typical cycle (Fig. 6–19) consists of dunite, commonly with a chromite horizon near its top, followed by poikilitic harzburgite (olivine plus orthopyroxene), granular harzburgite, and, finally, orthopyroxenites. Plagioclase and clinopyroxene are sporadic interstitial phases, and a few cycles lack orthopyroxene. The way in which these units evolved individually and as a whole is illustrated schematically in Figure 6–20.

The poikilitic harzburgites consist of grains of partly resorbed olivine sur-

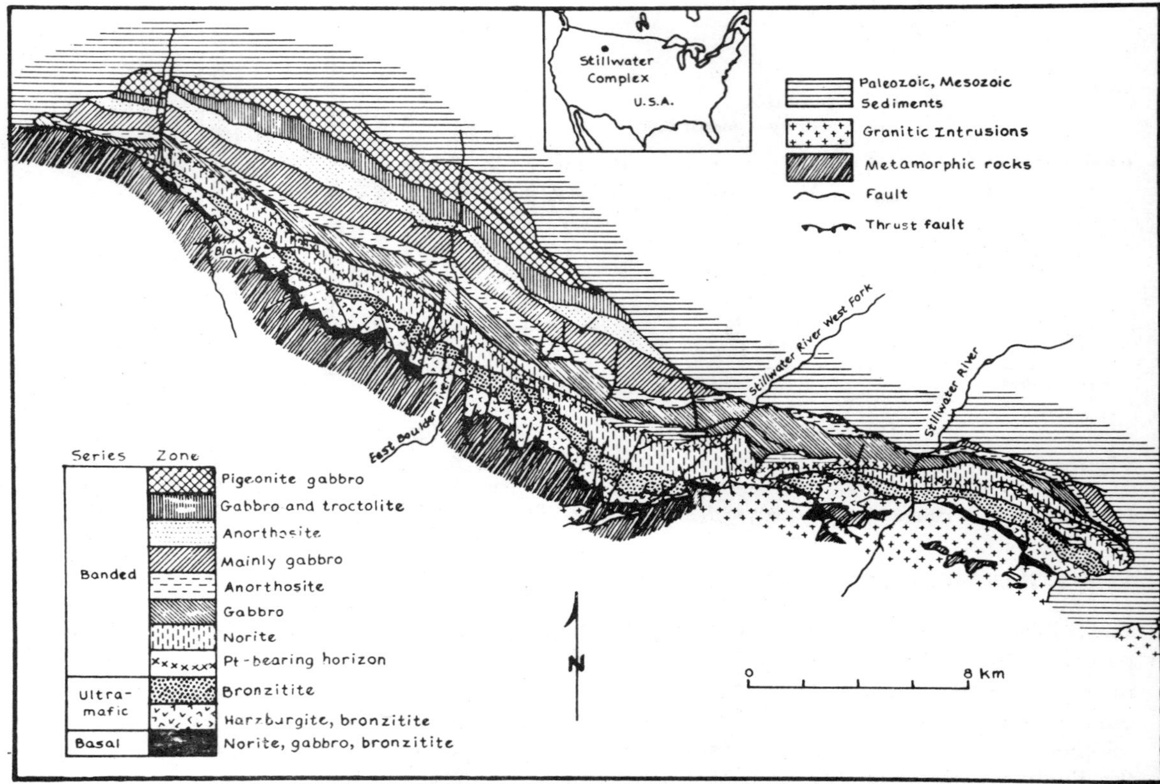

Figure 6–17 *Simplified geological map of the Stillwater intrusion of Montana.*

rounded by larger crystals of orthopyroxene that appear to have grown by reaction of the liquid with earlier olivine. This textural relation is in contrast to that of the granular harzburgites slightly higher in the succession where olivine and orthopyroxene appear to have grown simultaneously from the same liquid. The resorption of olivine in the poikilitic harzburgite is an excellent illustration of the reaction relation between olivine and orthopyroxene. After first crystallizing olivine, the composition of the cooling liquid reached a peritectic, and part of the olivine was resorbed while orthopyroxene crystallized around it. The granular harzburgites, on the other hand, show no sign of this reaction; their textures indicate that olivine and orthopyroxene crystallized together without reaction.

The changing pattern of crystallization in these rocks seems to have resulted from independent crystallization and differentiation of individual magmas, each derived from the main reservoir but evolving as a more or less isolated system (Fig. 6–20b). As noted in chapter four (Fig. 4–14), the reaction relation along the peritectic boundary between olivine and pyroxene changes to a cotectic as the liquid becomes richer in the fayalitic component. (At elevated pressures this change takes place at somewhat lower degrees of iron enrichment.) Thus, the change from reaction in the poikilitic harzburgites to co-precipitation in their

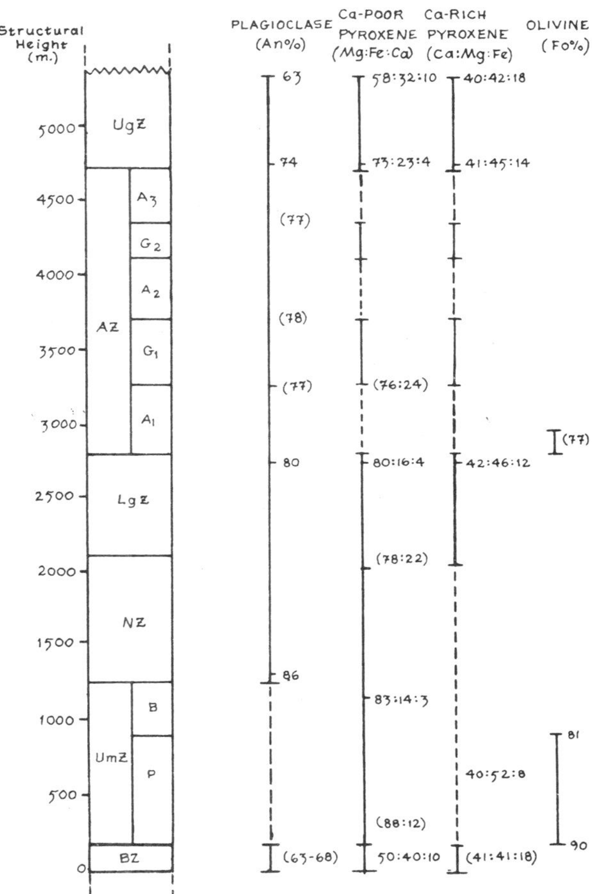

Figure 6–18 Stratigraphic section of the Stillwater intrusion. The Border Zone (BZ) is a group of hornfelsic contact rocks. The Ultramafic Zone (UmZ) consists of peridotite (P) and bronzitite (B) members. The appearance of large crystals of plagioclase marks the base of the Norite Zone (NZ), and, in a similar way, the incoming of augite marks the base of the Lower Gabbro Zone (LgZ). The Anorthosite Zone (AZ) consists of alternating zones of anorthosite (A) and gabbro (G). This is overlain by the Upper Gabbro Zone (UgZ) in which the Ca-poor pyroxene is inverted pigeonite. (After L. R. Wager and G. M. Brown, 1967, *Layered Igneous Rocks*, 303.)

granular equivalents could reflect the enrichment of iron in successive liquids evolving down the olivine-pyroxene boundary. Higher in the cycle, the remaining liquid left this boundary and crossed the pyroxene field, crystallizing only pyroxene to form monomineralic orthopyroxenites.

While this sequence of crystallization seems to be in accord with many textural relations and the general sequence of rocks, it may not be the sole explanation. Detailed studies of the rocks have revealed many irregularities in their compositions and apparent order of crystallization, and future work may reveal a more complex history of crystallization and differentiation.

Gabbros and anorthosites

The appearance of abundant plagioclase at a structural height of 1,300 meters marks the base of the Norite Zone, in which plagioclase and orthopyroxene are the sole primary precipitates. (By definition, it will be recalled, norite is a gabbro

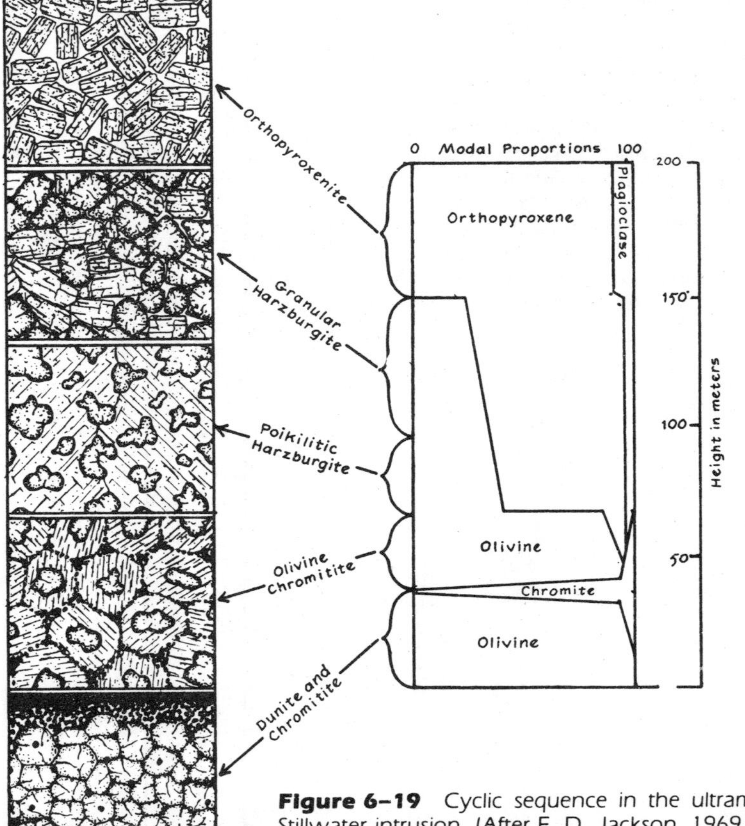

Figure 6–19 Cyclic sequence in the ultramafic zone of the Stillwater intrusion. (After E. D. Jackson, 1969, *Geol. Soc. South Africa, Spec. Publ. 1*, 391–424.)

in which the dominant mafic phase is hypersthene.) With appearance of augite, about 900 meters higher, hypersthene becomes subordinate, and the Norite Zone gives way to the overlying Lower Gabbro Zone. Quartz, magnetite, and ilmenite are also present in the lower gabbros, but only as minor interstitial phases. A remarkable feature of this part of the intrusions is the fine "inch-scale" layering (Fig. 6–7c) in which pyroxene alternates with plagioclase in thin, regularly-spaced layers through sections of several tens of meters.

Plagioclase is increasingly abundant in the upper part of the intrusion. The Anorthosite Zone contains three major units, each about 400 to 500 meters thick, consisting of more than 90 percent plagioclase. For some unknown reason, olivine (Fo_{77}) made a brief reappearance in the lower-most anorthosite even though quartz is a common interstitial mineral elsewhere in the same section. The thick, nearly monomineralic layers of anorthosite are equally difficult to explain. At the time they formed, the magma had been precipitating pyroxene and should have been saturated with that phase as well, but even though the magma should have

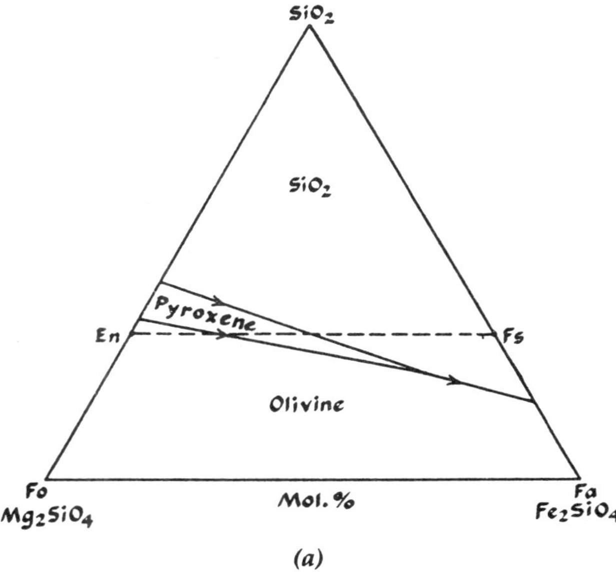

(a)

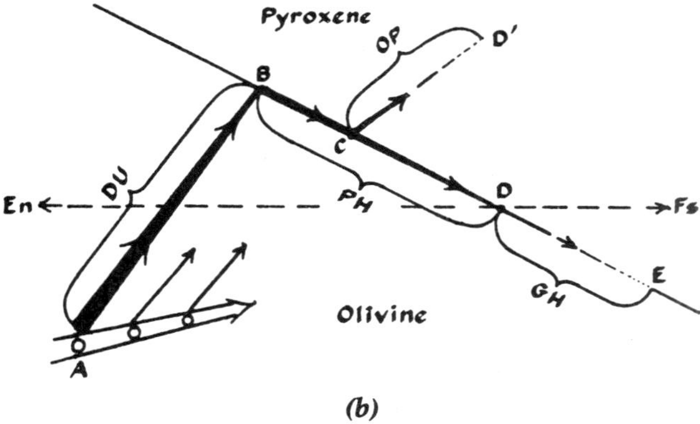

(b)

Figure 6-20 (a) The system forsterite-fayalite-silica and (b) an expanded and exaggerated part of the same system showing the evolution of liquids in cyclic sequences in the ultramafic zone of the Stillwater intrusion. DU is dunite, PH poikilitic harzburgite, GH granular harzburgite, and OP orthopyroxenite. The main course of the magma is indicated by the lower open arrow, and the course of a separate unit that differentiated independently is shown by a heavy line of diminishing width. Depending on the degree of reaction, the liquid may at some stage leave the boundary between olivine and pyroxene and embark on a new course (CD') across the field of pyroxene.

precipitated the two minerals together, it obviously did not. To make matters worse, the plagioclase was probably lighter than the liquid from which it precipitated, and there is no apparent reason why it should accumulate on the floor.

One can visualize changes of conditions that might move the composition of the liquid into the plagioclase fields, but to precipitate hundred of meters of plagioclase in this way would require changing the composition of an enormous mass of magma. Moreover, the process would have to be repeated by three identical events. A variety of explanations have been contrived. Most involve new injections of magma with the appropriate composition and density to allow it to remain on the bottom and crystallize abundant plagioclase. If the crystals were lighter than the new dense liquid but heavier than an overlying lighter one, they might have accumulated as mats beneath the interface between the two magmas. Implausible as this explanation may sound, it is the best we have.

The uppermost gabbros of the exposed section contain hypersthene, which, because it contains inclined exsolution lamellae of augite, must have inverted from pigeonite. At this level, the magma was moderately enriched in iron, silica, alkalies, and other residual components, but the amount of differentiation shown by the compositions of the minerals is relatively small compared to that of the upper parts of the Bushveld Complex. We cannot say how the rest of the Stillwater intrusion differentiated, because only about 40 percent of the total thickness of the original intrusion is exposed; the rest lies hidden beneath the cover of younger rocks north of the present exposures.

THE SKAERGAARD INTRUSION

The Skaergaard intrusion of East Greenland (Fig. 6–21) is probably the single most intensively studied body of igneous rocks in the world. Soon after it was first described by L. R. Wager and W. D. Deer in the 1930s, it became a prime example of igneous differentiation, and in ensuing years the principles deduced from its study have had an unparalleled influence on many basic concepts of igneous differentiation. For these reasons, it is worth discussing in more detail than the other intrusions dealt with so far.

Form and structure

The intrusion was emplaced during the Eocene magmatic episode associated with the opening of the North Atlantic Ocean and is closely related, both in time and space, to voluminous fissure eruptions of flood basalts. The magma rose through Precambrian gneisses and amphibolites to enter the base of a thick pile of basaltic lavas. It may even have breached the surface in a volcanic vent or caldera. Later uplift, tilting, and erosion have revealed a vertical section of the intrusion measuring about 3,200 meters, most of which is now exposed in fresh glaciated outcrops.

Although the body was originally thought to have been a steep-sided pipe, geophysical surveys have shown that it narrows sharply into one or two slender feeders at a shallow depth, and, though smaller, it differs little in form from other gabbroic intrusions (Fig. 6–22). The magma seems to have been emplaced in a single surge, displacing a block of the gneissic basement upward and flaring into an asymmetrical wedge near the gneiss-basalt contact. Its chilled margin (Fig. 6–23) forms a dense, relatively fine-grained selvage, about a meter in width between the wall rocks and coarse-grained gabbro of the interior.

If the quickly cooled rocks of the chilled margin were indeed a quenched selvage of the original magma, they would provide a valuable record of the initial composition from which the differentiated rocks evolved. Unfortunately, most of the chilled margin seems to have been altered from its original composition. Although they appear fresh and contain unaltered minerals, many of the rocks of

Figure 6–21 Simplified map of the Skaergaard intrusion of East Greenland. Units of the Layered Series are Lower Zone (LZ) a, b, and c; Middle Zone (MZ); and Upper Zone (UZ) a, b, and c. The Marginal Border Series (MBS) and Upper Border Series (UBS) merge in the southern part of the map and are not shown separately. The cross section below is drawn along the line A–B normal to the southward dip of the intrusion.

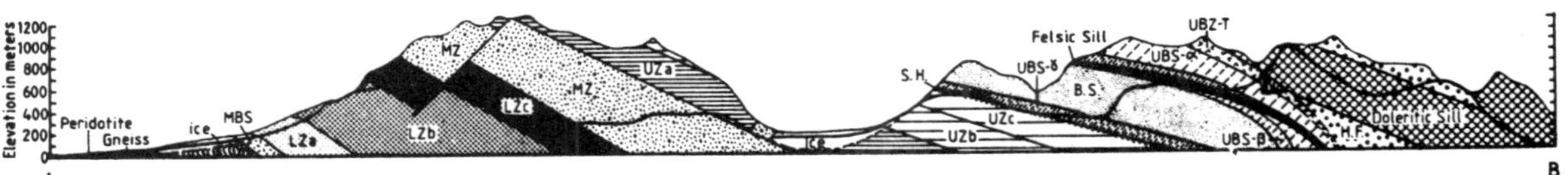

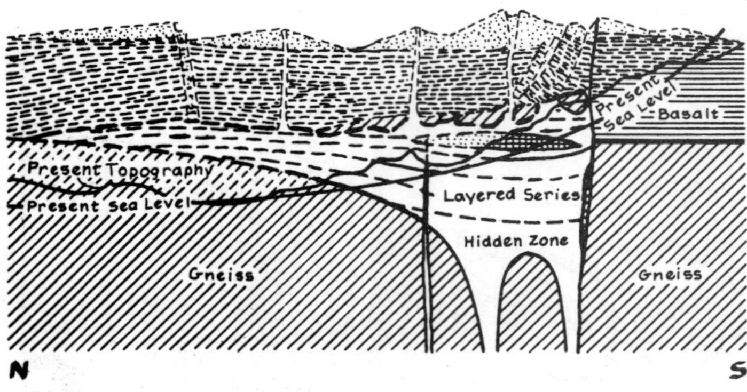

Figure 6–22 (a) Schematic north-south section through the Skaergaard intrusion showing its inferred original form before tilting and erosion. The line of present sea level indicates the amount of flexure toward the south. The cross-hatched pattern indicates a later intrusion known as the Basistoppen Sheet. The structure and topography above the present surface is inferred from the estimated original depth of the intrusion and its relationship to contemporaneous volcanic rocks. The root zone is constructed from geophysical data. (b) Simplified east-west section through the Skaergaard intrusion at its present level of exposure. View is toward the south looking down dip.

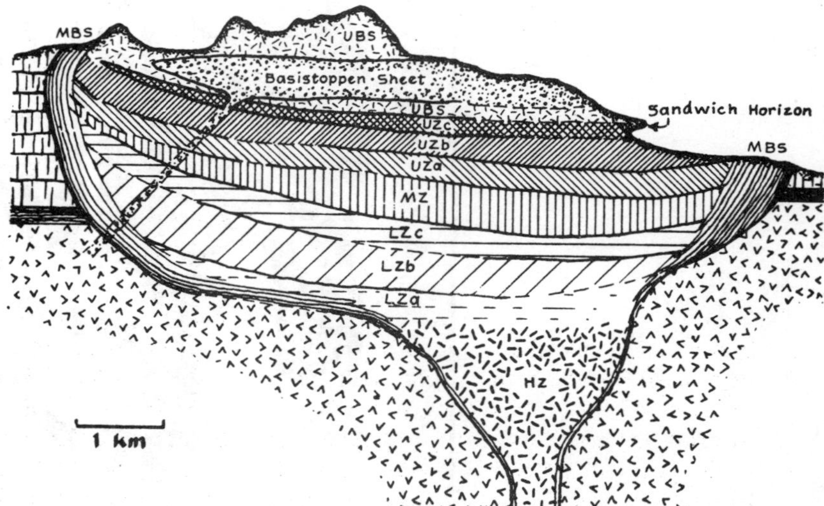

the chilled margin are contaminated with fragments of gneiss in various stages of assimilation. Moreover, during the tens of thousand years it took to cool, an extensive exchange took place between the margins of the intrusion and its walls. As a result, the composition of the chilled margin varies widely from place to place and, except for one or two localities where it seems to have changed little, it provides only a crude record of the original undifferentiated liquid.

Structural and stratigraphic divisions

The intrusion has been divided into three major units (Fig. 6–24), the Layered Series that crystallized from the floor upward, the Upper Border Series that crystallized from the roof down, and the Marginal Border Series that crystallized

Figure 6-23 The Skaergaard magma was chilled against felsic gneiss (lower right) and overlying sediments and basaltic lavas (above) to form a fine-grained selvage a meter or so in width and grading laterally into coarser-grained gabbro toward the left.

against the walls. As the Layered Series and Upper Border Series converged, they met at the "Sandwich Horizon" where the last and most strongly differentiated magma crystallized. Each of the major units is subdivided on the basis of its phase layering, and, although their mineral sequences differ in minor ways, the Layered Series, Upper Border Series, and Marginal Border Series all show similar trends of differentiation.

The 2,500-meter section of the Layered Series is divided into a lower, middle, and upper zone, and the lower and upper zones are further divided into three subdivisions. The sequences and compositions of the principal minerals are shown in Figure 6–24. The divisions of the two Border Series are similar to those of the Layered Series but more compressed. The order, of course, is inverted in the Upper Border Series, because the rocks crystallized from the roof down, and the Marginal Border Series is zoned inward from the wall.

Calcium-rich pyroxene is an interstitial or poikilitic mineral in the lowermost unit, Lower Zone A, but became a primary liquidus phase at the base of Lower Zone B. The textural basis of this distinction is illustrated in Figure 6–25. The base of Lower Zone C is marked by the first appearance of iron-oxides. Olivine, which was a primary precipitate in the earliest rocks, continued to crystallize up to the base of Middle Zone, at which level it disappeared only to reappear in the rocks of Upper Zone. Apatite is an abundant primary phase above the base of

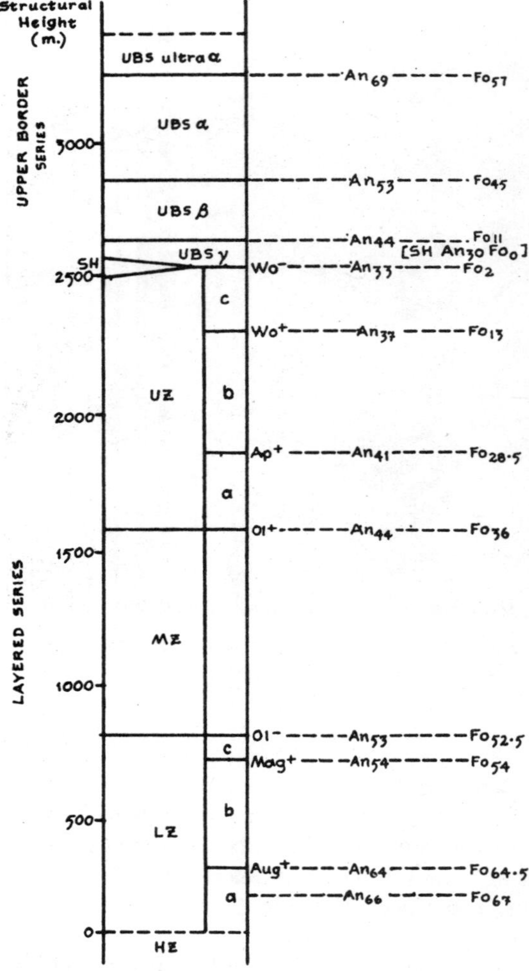

Figure 6–24 Stratigraphic column of the Skaergaard intrusion.

Upper Zone B; the base of Upper Zone C is defined by pyroxene that crystallized initially with a structure of wollastonite (or ferrobustamite) and on cooling inverted to hedenbergite.

Granophyres

The intrusion contains numerous bodies of granophyre that account for only a very small fraction of the total volume but occupy an important place in the series of differentiated compositions. They can be grouped into three types. The largest and most common are those forming dikes and sills (Fig. 6–26). Because they intrude and cross-cut the other rocks, they are referred to as "transgressive granophyres." Their trace elements and isotopic composition show that they are

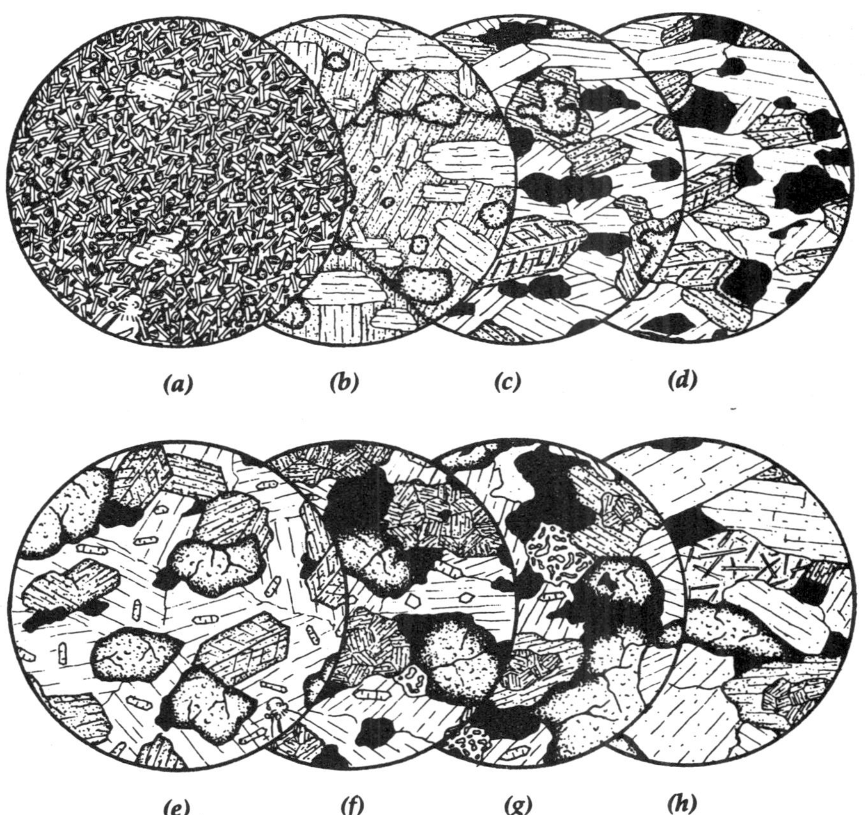

Figure 6–25 Petrographic features of the principal rocks of the Layered Series of the Skaergaard intrusion. (a) Rocks of the chilled margin have crystallized to granular "hornfelsic" rocks containing scattered xenocrysts of reversely zoned and partly resorbed plagioclase. (b) Lower Zone A consists of plagioclase and olivine encased in poikilitic crystals of clinopyroxene. (c) In Lower Zone C clinopyroxene forms separate crystals, some with exsolution lamellae of inverted pigeonite. Magnetite is an abundant primary phase, and, in this particular example, olivine is partly resorbed and encased in pyroxene. (d) Rocks of Middle Zone contain no primary olivine but reaction has produced thin rims of that mineral between pyroxene and magnetite. (e) Olivine returns as a primary mineral in Upper Zone; in Upper Zone B it is joined by apatite. (f) Upper Zone C is distinguished by the mosaic structure of hedenbergite that has inverted from an original wollastonite structure. Granophyric quartz and alkali feldspar fill interstices between the other minerals. (g) The Sandwich Horizon contains the same minerals as Upper Zone C, but granophyric quartz and alkali feldspar are more abundant. Zircon, sphene, and sulfides are accessory minerals. (h) The rocks of the Upper Border Series, represented here by an example from UBSγ, are somewhat more plagioclase-rich than equivalent units of the Layered Series. Some contain elongated crystals of quartz that originally crystallized as tridymite and on cooling inverted to quartz. (Diameter of fields 3 mm.)

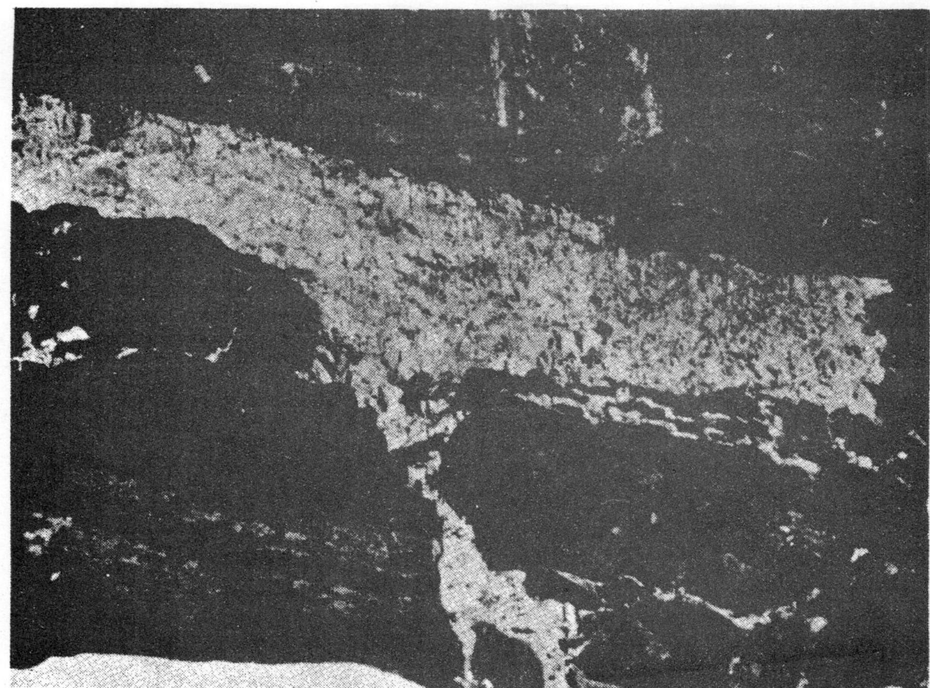

Figure 6–26 A granophyric sill in the upper levels of the Skaergaard intrusion is the result of partial melting and mobilization of felsic metamorphic rock underlying the intrusion. The part shown here is about four meters thick.

genetically related to the gneissic country rocks and must have been derived from them by partial melting.

Some of the smaller dikes in the upper part of the Layered Series have a much wider range of compositions, even within a single dike, and, unlike the transgressive granophyres intruded from greater depths, they are visibly rooted in the ferrogabbro. They appear to have resulted from some form of filter pressing and segregation of late liquids into pipes and dilational fractures in the partly crystallized gabbroic mush and as such can be interpreted as true differentiates of the Skaergaard magma.

A third group has been called "melanogranophyres" because of the large, irregular clots of ferromagnesian minerals that give them a somewhat more mafic bulk composition. They form pod-like bodies up to a meter or two across in Upper Zones B and C (Fig. 6–27). This group of granophyres is also thought to have differentiated from the iron-rich gabbroic magma, but they seem to have separated as immiscible liquids at an advanced stage of differentiation. A granophyric liquid, rich in silica and alkalies, has been shown experimentally to be immiscible with the more iron-rich and silica-poor liquid from which their gabbroic host rocks crystallized (Fig. 6–28).

Figure 6–27 Irregular pods of granophyre separated as immiscible liquids during crystallization of Upper Zones B and C. The host gabbro must have been crystallized to the extent that it was viscous enough to prevent the buoyant granophyres from rising to a higher level. The pod shown here is about a meter across.

Compositional variations

The mineralogical changes in the Skaergaard rocks resemble those of other intrusions discussed earlier, but their compositions vary in more regular ways. No evidence has been found for repeated injections of fresh magma, and no important cyclical variations have been identified. The exposed section also lacks an ultramafic zone of the kind laid down in the early stages of differentiation of the Bushveld and Stillwater magmas. (Blocks of peridotite found in parts of the Marginal Border Group were once thought to come from a deeper, unexposed, ultramafic zone but are now known to be xenoliths from an adjacent body of older and apparently unrelated rocks.)

The trends of cryptic layering are smooth and unbroken. Olivine and clinopyroxene became increasingly iron-rich upward until, in the last liquid to crystallize, they reached the compositions of the pure end-members, fayalite and hedenbergite (Fig. 6–29). Calcium-poor pyroxene is much less abundant in the Skaergaard rocks than it is in the other intrusions we have considered. It may not have been a primary phase, because it typically forms reaction rims on earlier crystals of olivine or augite. It ceased to crystallize, except by exsolution from Ca-

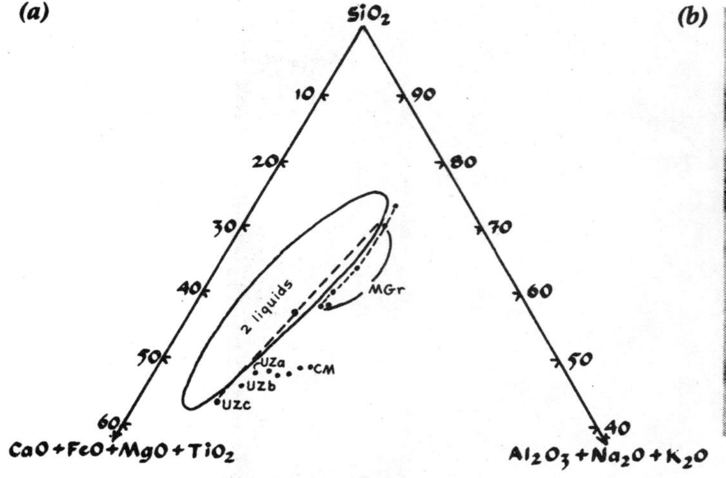

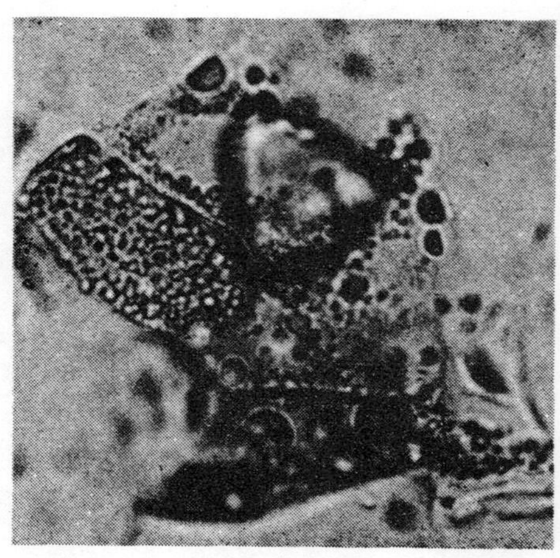

Figure 6–28 (a) The compositional relations of immiscible liquids are illustrated in a diagram plotting SiO_2 vs. Na_2O + K_2O + Al_2O_3 and CaO + FeO + MgO + TiO_2. The course of the main gabbroic magma is shown evolving from the chilled margin (CM) through successive stages until it reaches the boundary of a two-liquid field, then separates into two fractions, one rich in iron and the other in silica. The general form of the field of two liquids shown here was first outlined by Edwin Roedder. (1951, *Amer. Min.* 36:282–286.) (b) The immiscible relations of granopohyric and ferrogabboic liquids in the Skaergaard intrusion was verified experimentally by holding an intimate mixture of the two compositions (indicated by the dot in the two-liquid field of (a)) at their liquidus temperature and allowing them to separate into two discrete liquids, shown here as blebs of glass of differing refractive indices. Width of the view is about 0.5 mm.

rich pyroxene, soon after olivine reappeared at the base of the Upper Zone. It never crystallized directly as an orthopyroxene, but only as monoclinic pigeonite that inverted to hypersthene or cooling. Examples of pyroxene exsolution that reflect the changes of structural form are shown in Figure 4–10b. In contrast to the ferromagnesian minerals, which evolved to an extreme degree of iron enrichment, the change in plagioclase is limited to a smaller range; it advances from An_{66} at the base to An_{30} at the top of the Layered Series. It also differs in composition from one side of the Layered Series to the other (Fig. 6-29).

Differentiation produced marked changes in the bulk chemical compositions of both the Layered Series and Border Groups. Most obvious is the steady increase in iron content and corresponding decline in MgO (Fig. 6–30), which become especially pronounced in the Upper Zone of the Layered Series. The variations of trace elements are similar. Nickel, which is strongly included in olivine, and Cr, which is partitioned into magnetite and pyroxene, are rapidly depleted; whereas incompatible elements, such as Rb and Zr, which are excluded from all the important minerals of the intrusion, are strongly enriched.

The compositions given for the layered and border series in Figure 6–30 represent averages of several hundred analyses. This is the only way that representative values can be obtained, owing to the wide variations from one sample to

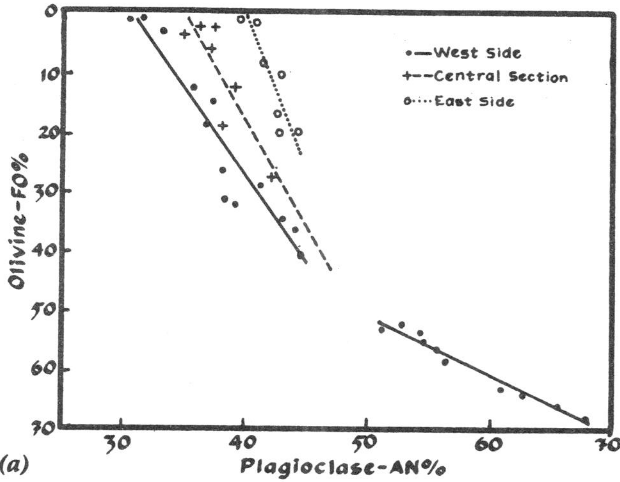

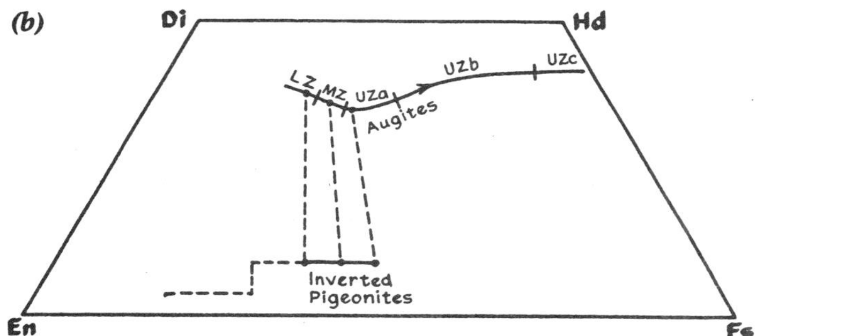

Figure 6–29 (a) Variations of plagioclase and olivine compositions with height in the center and margins of the Layered Series. (b) Compositional variations of pyroxenes in the Layered Series. Tie-lines connect coexisting Ca-rich and Ca-poor pyroxenes.

another, even within a given lithologic unit. Abundances of included elements are very sensitive to the modal proportions of minerals in which they are concentrated, while excluded elements vary according to the amount of trapped liquid the rock had and the degree to which it equilibrated with the main reservoir.

With the possible exception of the Sandwich Horizon and parts of the chilled margin, none of the rocks of the Layered Series and Border Series corresponds to the composition of a magma; the rocks differ widely from the liquid from which they formed. This is true of all differentiated intrusions, but especially of very large ones in which the process of crystal-liquid fractionation was very efficient. The assemblages of accumulated crystals differ in bulk composition, not only from their parental liquid, but also from one layered horizon to another. Moreover, recrystallization and re-equilibration during very slow cooling probably modified the original compositions and proportions of the mineral assemblages.

Unless the rocks of a large intrusion retained substantial amounts of residual liquid trapped between their primary mineral phases, the compositional evolution of the magma from which the minerals crystallized can only be inferred by indirect means. The composition of the differentiating magma of the Skaergaard

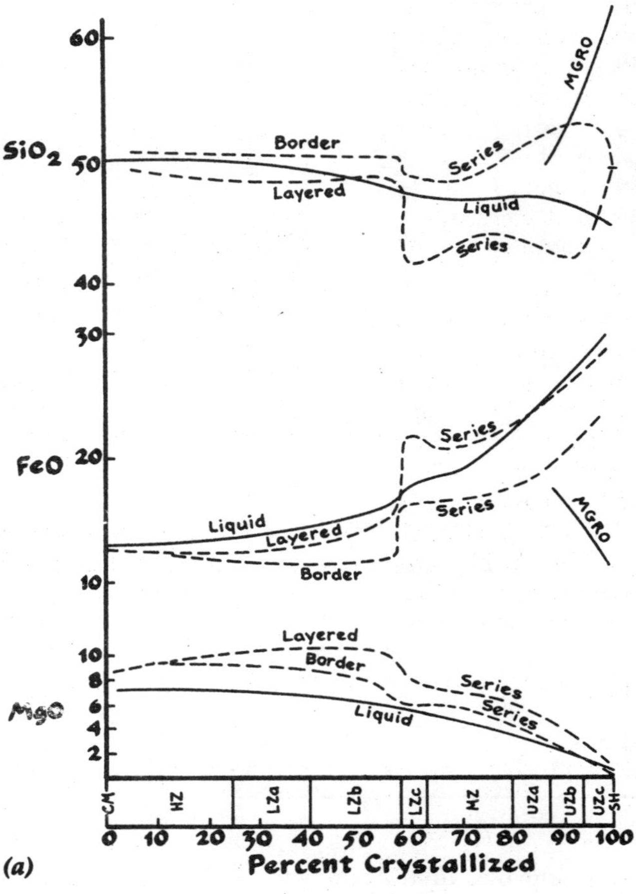

(a)

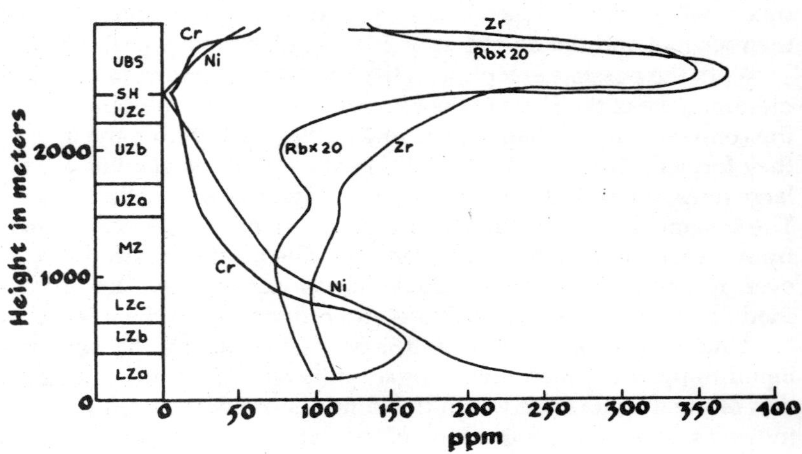

(b)

Figure 6–30 Variations of some key major elements of the Skaergaard rocks and magma. Liquid compositions are shown by solid lines, rocks of the Layered and Border Series by broken lines. The variations of included elements are illustrated by Cr and Ni and the excluded elements by Zr and Rb. The compositions of melanogranophyres (MGRO) in Upper Zones b and c are shown separately.

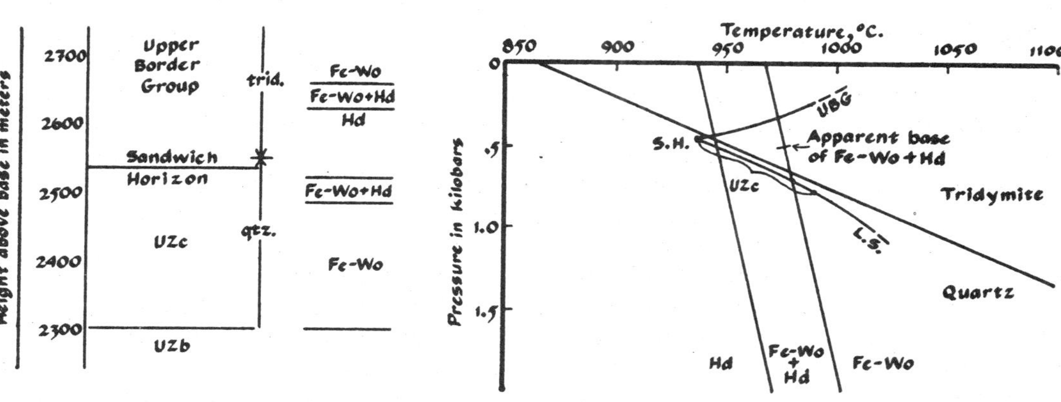

Figure 6-31 Temperature and pressure relations in the vicinity of the Sandwich Horizon (a) are defined by the stability relations of the polymorphic forms of SiO_2 and $CaFeSi_2O_6$ (b).

intrusion is not as difficult to estimate as that of larger intrusions like the Bushveld Complex, because, being smaller and shallower, it crystallized with less efficient fractionation of crystals and liquid, and the rocks still contain traces of the liquids from which they crystallized. Moreover, having cooled more quickly, they had less tendency to re-equilibrate at sub-solidus temperatures. These differences make it possible to obtain better estimates of the composition of the magma and the conditions under which it crystallized.

Estimated temperatures and pressures

Several methods have been devised to deduce from the mineral assemblages of rocks the temperatures and pressures at which they crystallized. The most reliable estimates for the Skaergaard intrusion are those for levels close to the Sandwich Horizon (Fig. 6-31).

Upper Zone C, as we noted earlier, is characterized by an unusual, iron-rich clinopyroxene that first crystallized with the structure of Fe-wollastonite (or ferrobustamite) and, after a short interval of cooling, inverted to hedenbergite. A similar polymorphic change from tridymite to quartz occurred in the Upper Border Group just above the Sandwich Horizon. Some of the quartz in these rocks has a distinctive, needle-like morphology inherited from its original tridymite structure, whereas the quartz in rocks below that level is more equidimensional, because it crystallized directly as that mineral and has not inverted from another form.

The experimentally determined conditions of temperature and pressure for the inversion to hedenbergite are plotted in Figure 6-31b. The pressure dependence of the tridymite-quartz inversion has not been determined experimentally but can be calculated by means of the Clapeyron equation. At atmospheric pressure, tridymite inverts to quartz at 867°C (or 1,140°K), giving off about 7.43 calories per gram. At that temperature, the density of quartz is 2.536, whereas that of tridymite is 2.189. The mechanical equivalent of heat is 42.7 kg cm cal^{-1}, and 1 kilobar is equal to 1,020 kg cm^{-2}. Using these values, we obtain

$$\frac{dT}{dP} = \frac{T\Delta V}{\Delta H} = \frac{1140(1/2.189 - 1/2.536)}{7.43 \times 42.7}$$
$$= 0.23°/\text{kg cm}^{-2} \text{ or } 229°/\text{kilobar} \quad (6\text{–}1)$$

for the rate at which the temperature for the inversion increases with pressure. When plotted on Figure 6–31b, the inversion curve for the polymorphs of SiO_2 has a high-angle intersection with those for hedenbergite and Fe-wollastonite and provides an excellent grid of temperature and pressure to which we can relate the mineral assemblage of Figure 6–31a.

The rocks of the Sandwich Horizon contain quartz and late rims of hedenbergite that crystallized originally in those forms, but, in rocks only a short distance above that level, these minerals originally crystallized as tridymite and Fe-wollastonite. Rocks just below the Sandwich Horizon are similar to those above it, but the quartz shows no evidence of having first crystallized as tridymite. The curves in Figure 6–31b show how the temperatures and pressures of the Layered Series and Upper Border Group would correspond to these assemblages. Note that the rocks of the Sandwich Horizon are narrowly confined to a liquidus temperature of about 940°C and a pressure close to 500 bars, the only conditions under which SiO_2 and pyroxene could have crystallized initially as quartz and hedenbergite.

If we assume a density of about 2.8 g cm^{-3} for the overlying rocks, this pressure for the Sandwich Horizon corresponds to a depth of 500 × 1020 / 2.8 = 182,000 cm, or about 2 km. Deducting the visible thickness of about 1,000 meters for the overlying Upper Border Series, the depth of the roof of the intrusion could not have been much greater than one kilometer and might well have been even less.

Again, using the thickness and density of the rocks, we can calculate the pressure at the level in Upper Zone C at which the pyroxenes entered the field of Fe-Wo + Hd, and we find that it falls at the level indicated in Figure 6–31b, well inside the field of tridymite. But we know that the silica mineral in these rocks was always quartz. How can this apparent anomaly be explained? One possibility is that the pyroxenes at that level are not pure $CaFeSi_2O_6$ but contain enough of the Mg component to alter the position of the inversion curve to lower temperatures where quartz could crystallize together with both Fe-wollastonite and hedenbergite. But such an effect could scarely be this great in rocks with such small amounts of MgO. A more plausible explanation is that the rocks crystallized, not at a single temperature, but through a range of forty or fifty degrees between their liquidus and solidus. By this reasoning the quartz would have crystallized later at a lower temperature than the pyroxene. This inference is supported by the textural relations of the minerals in the rocks of this zone (Fig. 6–26f), which show quartz to have been a late-crystallizing interstitial phase.

Other methods of estimating the temperatures and pressures of crystallization of the Skaergaard rocks are based on the experimentally determined conditions governing the equilibrium between coexisting iron-bearing minerals. We saw in chapter four, for example, that the compositions of coexisting iron-titanium oxides are governed by the temperatures and oxygen fugacities at which they last equilibrated. If magnetite and ilmenite are both present in the same rock and have not changed composition since they crystallized together from a liquid, then we can use the relations shown in Figure 4–16 to estimate these conditions. Temperatures obtained in this way for the Skaergaard oxide minerals are well below those at which the gabbros would have totally crystallized under any reasonable conditions. The explanation for this obvious inconsistency must be that the minerals re-equilibrated at lower temperatures during slow sub-solidus cooling.

Similar methods have been devised that use experimentally determined equilibrium constants for reactions such as:

$$\underset{\text{magnetite}}{2Fe_3O_4} + \underset{\text{quartz}}{3SiO_2} \rightleftarrows \underset{\text{fayalite}}{6Fe_2SiO_4} + \underset{\text{oxygen}}{O_2} \qquad (6\text{–}2)$$

and

$$\underset{\text{forsterite}}{Mg_2SiO_4} + \underset{\text{ferrosilite}}{Fe_2Si_2O_6} \rightleftarrows \underset{\text{fayalite}}{Fe_2SiO_4} + \underset{\text{enstatite}}{Mg_2Si_2O_6} \qquad (6\text{–}3)$$

The distribution of iron and magnesium between coexisting olivine and pyroxene, or of iron, silica, and oxygen between the liquid and crystals, is a function of the intensive parameters temperature, pressure, and oxygen fugacity. If the reactions are allowed to reach equilibrium under a range of controlled temperatures and oxygen fugacities, the iron and magnesium contents of coexisting phases can be measured and, in this way, a relation between composition and the conditions of crystallization can be established. The technique is subject to uncertainties stemming mainly from the sensitivity of the reactions to small differences of conditions and to the possible effects of other components of the natural system. It is encouraging that the estimates of temperature and oxygen fugacity obtained in this way (Fig. 6–32) are in fairly close agreement with values obtained by independent, experimental studies of the stability relations in the natural rocks. As more and better thermodynamic data are obtained for natural silicate systems, the precision of calculations of this kind will surely increase, and petrologists may eventually be able to determine the conditions under which igneous rocks have formed from their mineralogical and petrographic relations.

Reconstructing a liquid line of descent

We noted earlier that the more efficient the processes of crystal-liquid fractionation, the more difficult it is to define the line of descent of liquids from which a series of plutonic rocks has formed. This is because accumulated crystals contain few traces of the components that were partitioned into a liquid that has long since been removed by fractionation. This dilemma accounts for the fact that, despite a wealth of mineralogical data on large intrusions, it is still impossible to trace the compositional evolution of the magmas from which they crystallized.

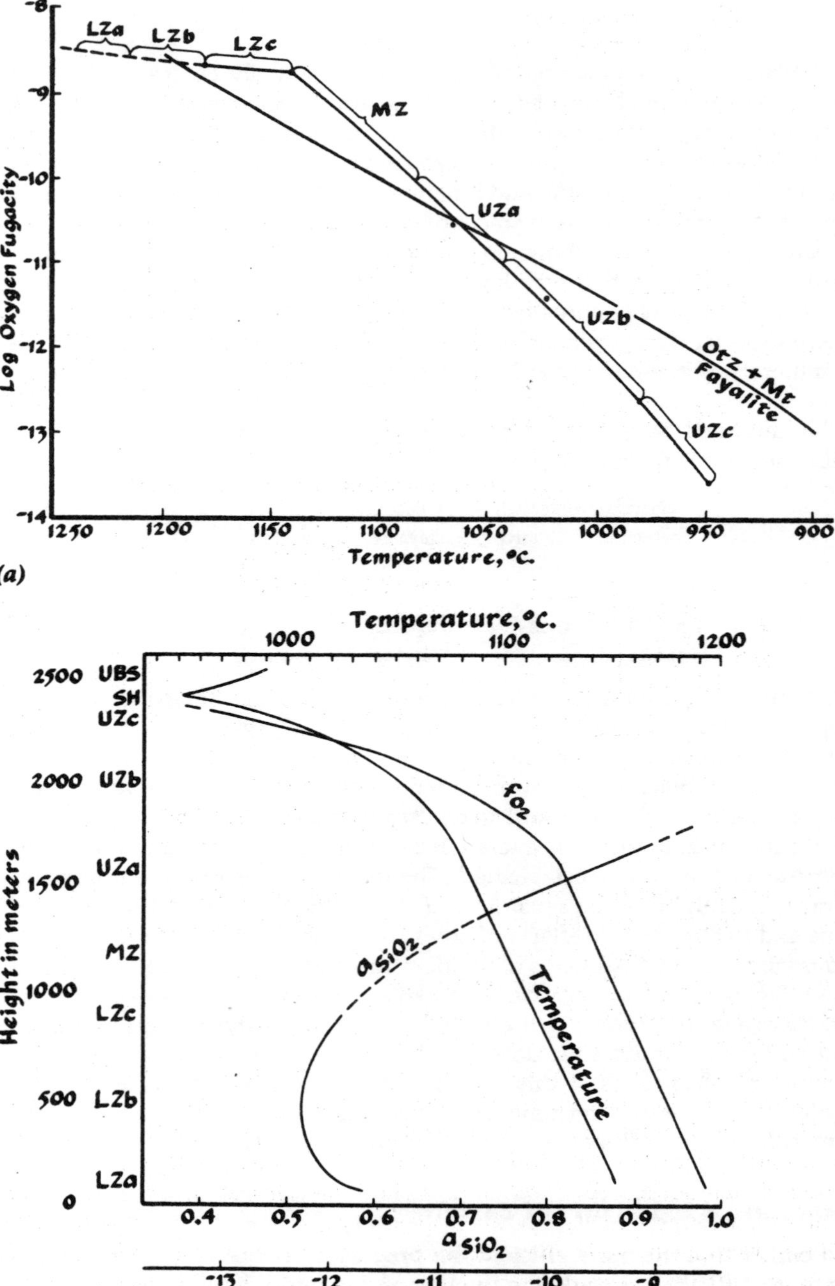

Figure 6-32 Temperature, oxygen fugacity, and silica activity of the Skaergaard magmas calculated from the compositions of coexisiting mineral phases and experimentally determined reaction constants. (After R. J. Williams, 1971, *Amer. Jour. Sci.* 270:334–360; S. A. Morse, 1980, *Amer. Jour. Sci.* 279:1060–1069; and S. A. Morse, D. H. Lindsley, and R. J. Williams, 1980, *Amer. Jour. Sci.* 280-A:159–170.)

The Skaergaard intrusion is the only large body for which this has been attempted, and, even in that case, none of the various devices that have been used turns out to be entirely satisfactory. Even the main trend of differentiation still remains a subject of debate.

The simplest way to estimate the composition of the liquid at successive stages of differentiation is one used in the early studies by L. R. Wager and his co-workers. If one assumes that the chilled margin preserves the original composition of the magma and represents the bulk composition of the body as a whole, a simple mass balance can be used to determine the composition of the liquid at various stages of solidification. This is done by subtracting, in the manner discussed in the preceding chapter, the amount of material removed by crystallization to obtain the composition of the liquid remaining at that stage. The procedure is repeated with each successive unit until a last stage is reached in which the remaining liquid should have the composition of the Sandwich Horizon. Such an approach has several limitations. First, the composition of the chilled margin may not be a reliable record of the original bulk composition. Second, the calculation is no better than the estimate of the average composition and volume of each rock unit. Although it is possible to measure their stratigraphic thicknesses, it is much more difficult to estimate the original horizontal extent of the units, and any calculation based on their volumes is subject to large errors. And third, all calculations based only on mass-balances ignore crystal-liquid equilibria and are without petrological constraints.

A more direct approach can be taken if the rocks preserve some fraction of crystallized trapped liquid that can be restored and analysed. Suppose, for example, one finds that a specimen from a given unit contains a certain amount of an element that is not included in the minerals formed as primary precipitates. The abundance of that component should be proportional to the amount of liquid trapped between primary-crystallizing minerals. Phosphorus in rocks below UZb would be an example of such a component. If the rock contains 0.2 percent P_2O_5, and the magma at that stage contained 2.0 percent, then 10 percent of the rock would be the product of crystallization of trapped liquid. One could reheat such a rock in the laboratory (Fig. 6–33) and restore it to conditions under which it has that proportion of melt, then quench the sample and analyse the resulting glass. If the intensive paramenters, such as temperature, pressure, and oxygen fugacity, can be accurately estimated, either experimentally or by the methods outlined in the preceding section, the conditions of the experiment can be made more realistic. A series of liquid compositions determined in this way can be used, together with the compositions of the rocks that should have crystallized from them, to carry out another mass-balance calculation in the reverse direction, which in turn yields the relative volumes of rock in each unit and enables one to estimate the original form of the intrusion.

Unfortunately this method, too, has its limitations. As seen in the preceding chapter, kinetic effects have an important influence on the proportions of components in the liquid around growing crystals. This would not be serious if the crystals simply sank to the floor and did not subsequently change composition, but if any amount of static crystallization took place, and equilibration was de-

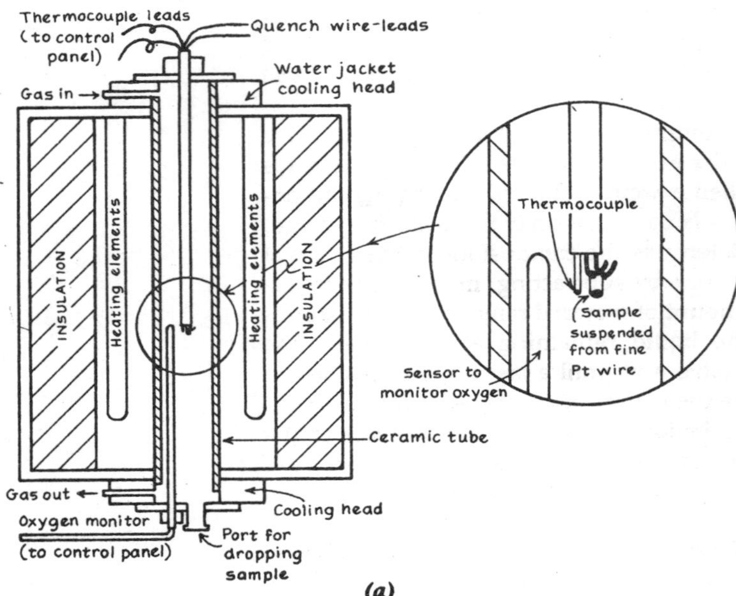

(a)

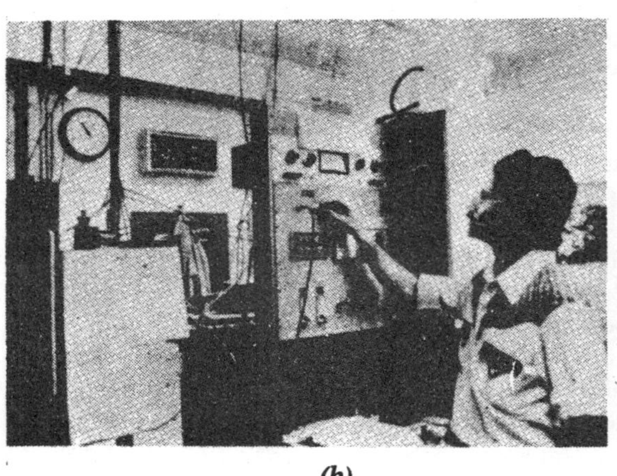

(b)

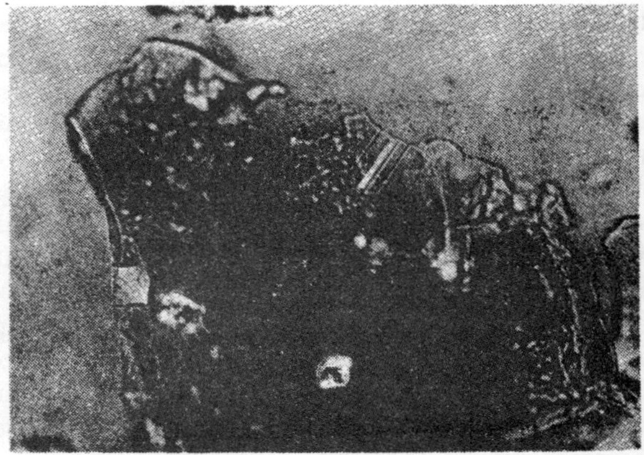

(c)

Figure 6–33 The liquid composition that would crystallize the observed minerals of the Layered Series at the conditions shown in Figure 6–31 can be tested experimentally using a controlled-atmosphere furnace of the kind illustrated here. A sample of each composition is held at its appropriate temperature for periods of five hours or more to reach equilibrium. The oxidation state of the sample is controlled by passing a mixture of carbon dioxide and carbon monoxide through the furnace and around the sample. At the end of the run, electric current is passed through the fine platinum wire suspending the sample. When the wire is fused, the sample drops from the furnace and is quenched in water. In this way, the liquid is converted to glass, and phases that were in equilibrium with the liquid can be identified under the microscope. (c) is a photomicrograph of a typical quenched charge with small crystals of plagioclase and pyroxene in glass.

pendent on diffusion, the composition of the trapped liquid could have been quite different from that of the main reservoir. Another difficulty arises if the interstitial liquid migrated through the crystal mush, as it appears to have risen through the Palisades Sill, discussed earlier. Not only would this alter the composition of the "trapped liquid," but metasomatic reactions could have changed the original mineral assemblage and bulk composition of the rock.

The ultimate solution to this problem will come when we know enough about crystal-liquid relations to specify the composition of a liquid that would be in equilibrium with a given assemblage of crystals at specified conditions. This would make it possible to trace the composition of an evolving magma directly from the minerals it crystallized. Unfortunately our knowledge is still not complete enough to do this for a multicomponent system as complex as the Skaergaard magma, but it is possible to deal with some of the individual components, at least in a preliminary way. Silica is one such component for which this can be done with reasonable confidence, because it plays a key role in determining the stability of one of the main minerals of the intrusion, olivine.

The hiatus of olivine crystallization at Middle Zone was seen in chapter four (Fig. 4–14) to reflect the relative rates of change of the concentrations (or, more properly, activities) of silica, magnesium, and iron in an evolving liquid according to the reactions:

$$\underset{\text{enstatite}}{MgSiO_3} = \underset{\text{forsterite}}{MgSi_{1/2}O_2} + \underset{\text{silica}}{1/2\ SiO_2} \tag{6–4a}$$

and

$$\underset{\text{ferrosilite}}{FeSiO_3} = \underset{\text{fayalite}}{Fe_{1/2}SiO_2} + \underset{\text{silica}}{1/2\ SiO_2} \tag{6–4b}$$

As with any chemical reaction, an expression can be written for the equilibrium constant, K, which is defined as the ratio of the activities of the products to those of the reactants. Knowing this value allows us to predict how the reaction will proceed under different conditions. Thus, the equilibrium constant for reaction 6–4a becomes

$$K = \frac{a_{forsterite}\,(a_{silica})^{1/2}}{a_{enstatite}} \tag{6–5a}$$

or, taking the log of both sides, rearranging, and eliminating fractions:

$$\ln a_{silica} = 2 \ln a_{enstatite} - 2 \ln a_{forsterite} + 2 \ln K \tag{6–5b}$$

Thus, the activity of silica in the magma can be calculated if we can evaluate K and place reliable values on the terms for the activities of pyroxene and olivine.

K can be calculated from the free energy change of the reaction:

$$K = e^{-\Delta G/RT} \tag{6–6a}$$

where R is the gas constant and ΔG the difference between the Gibbs free energies of the products and reactants. Using the definition of free energy in chapter three, equation 6–6a can be written in terms of its individual components

$$\ln K = \frac{-\Delta H + \Delta S - P\Delta V}{RT} \tag{6–6b}$$

where pressure, P, is assumed to be constant, and ΔV is the change of molar volume of the phases.

In principle, K can be calculated from the experimentally determined thermodynamic properties of the individual minerals, but, unfortunately, we are dealing with small differences between very large numbers that are not precise enough to yield a reliable value for K. Added precision can be gained, however, by examining the reaction experimentally and comparing the results with a natural system, such as the Hawaiian lava lakes, where the conditions can be closely observed and measured. A general empirical formula, determined in this way,

$$\ln K = -679/T + 0.258 - 0.0212(P - 1)/T \tag{6–7}$$

gives K in terms of temperature and pressure.

It will be recalled (equation 3–25, chapter three) that the activity of a component is equal to the product of its concentration, X, and an activity coefficient, γ, which takes into account the deviation from ideal behavior. The term X is expressed as the mole fraction of the component in the phase. From experimental studies we know that the value of γ is normally very close to 1.0 for olivine and Ca-poor pyroxene at magmatic temperatures. Thus, knowing the compositions of the olivine and coexisting Ca-poor pyroxene, it is a simple matter to calculate the activity of silica as a function of temperature and pressure by using the empirical equation for K (equation 6–7), its definition (equations 6–5a,b), and the estimated temperatures and pressures we determined earlier.

The curve for the activity of SiO_2 in Figure 6–32b has been produced in this way. Note that the calculated value is slightly greater in the very lowest part of the layered series than in the immediately overlying rocks of Lower Zone B. This may reflect contamination of the basal gabbros by the silica-rich gneiss upon which they rest, or it may simply indicate that, because these rocks cooled more quickly, they retained more silica-rich interstitial liquid. Apart from this anomaly, the activity increases steadily upward. The highest zone in which Ca-poor pyroxene can be found, Upper Zone A, approaches a silica activity of 1.0, at which point the magma would be saturated with quartz. These relations are consistent with the observation that quartz is a common, late-crystallizing, interstitial mineral in the rocks of upper zones A and B and may well have been a liquidus phase in Upper Zone C and the Sandwich Horizon.

Physical processes of crystallization and differentiation

Much of the process of crystallization and differentiation is governed by the way in which an intrusion gives up heat to its surroundings. In the Skaergaard case, hydrothermal alteration of the roof and upper walls indicates that copious amounts of water circulated through the highly permeable fractured and jointed lavas in the roof and upper walls (Fig. 6–34). As we noted in chapter two, a convecting hydrothermal system of this kind can increase the rate of cooling if the circulating groundwater penetrates close to the crystallizing margins and reduces the width of the zone of conductive heat transfer.

The magnitude of the hydrothermal system is well shown by its effect on the isotopic composition of the rocks. The two isotopes of oxygen, ^{18}O and ^{16}O, have very different proportions in rocks and meteoric water. Igneous rocks have a characteristic ratio inherited from the mantle, whereas the oxygen of meteoric water has an isotopic character governed by processes in the atmosphere and hydrosphere. As hot water flows through the rocks, oxygen is exchanged, and

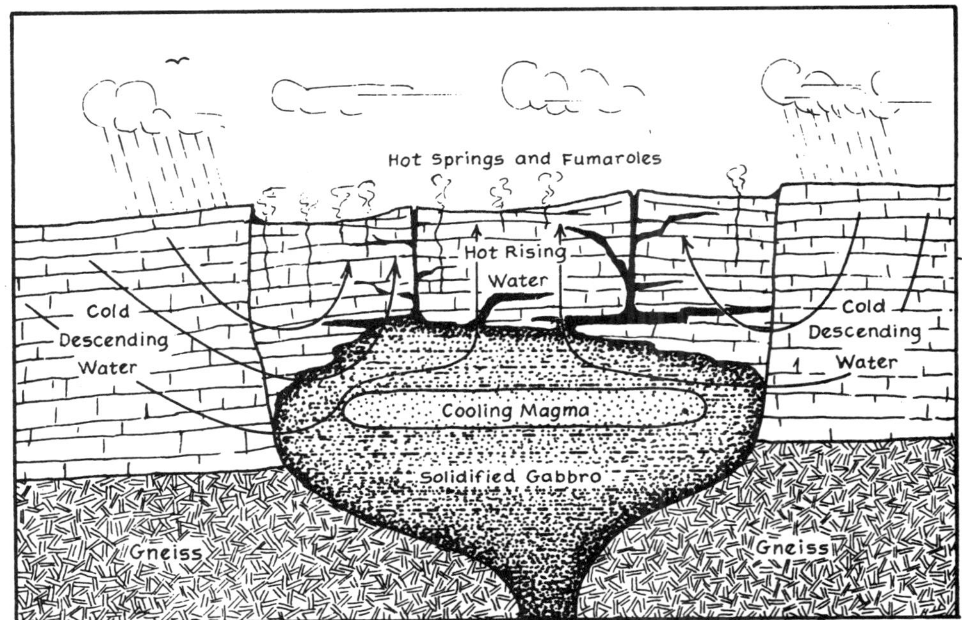

Figure 6–34 The Skaergaard intrusion set up a large hydrothermal system in which meteoric water heated by the cooling gabbro convected through the permeable basaltic rocks of the roof and upper walls. (After H. P. Taylor and R. W. Forester, 1979, *Jour. Petr.* 20:355–419).

the ratio of isotopes is altered by amounts that are functions of the temperature and quantity of circulating water. The result is a pattern of altered rocks in which the ratio of ^{18}O to ^{16}O records the effects of the hydrothermal system during cooling of the intrusion (Fig. 6–35a).

An ingeneous mathematical model has been devised to analyse the flow pattern of meteoric water and its effect on the rate of cooling of the intrusion. Knowing from experimental measurements the rates at which oxygen is exchanged between water and the major minerals at different temperatures, it is possible to calculate the amount and temperature of the water that moved through the rocks. Knowing from field relations the permeability of the rocks and the probable form of the groundwater system, one can set up a computer model to determine the flow lines and estimate how they affected the magma and the rocks surrounding it. Results of this calculation are shown in Figure 6–35b.

Estimates of the rates and geometry of heat loss arrived at in this way can be used to determine how the magma may have crystallized. This can be done mathematically using computer techniques similar to those used to analyse the hydrothermal system, or the system can be modeled in the laboratory by simple low-temperature analogs (Fig. 6–36). Mathematical modeling, if well conceived and executed, gives more quantitative results than a laboratory analog. The latter, while more graphic, cannot be a precise replica of a large intrusion; the problem

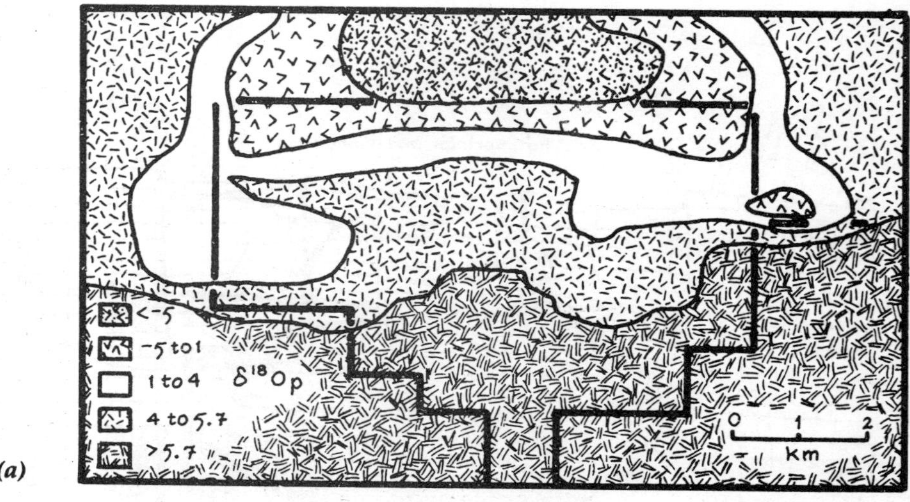

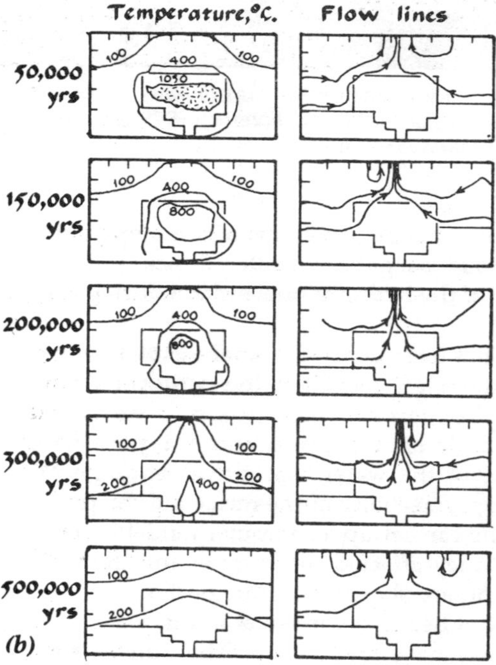

Figure 6–35 Convecting meteoric water exchanged oxygen with the rocks and reset their isotopic ratios by amounts that were functions of the temperature and amount of water that flowed through the rock. The result is the pattern of zoning shown in the schematic diagram (a) used to model the system. The calculated flow-lines and temperature contours of the hydrothermal system (b) provide a way of estimating the cooling history of the intrusion. The speckled pattern indicates magma; all else is solid rock. (After D. Norton and H. P. Taylor, 1979, *Jour Petr.* 20:421–486.)

of scaling the physical paramenters to appropriate dimensions is an insurmountable one. A good model need not be an exact analog of nature, however. By judiciously adjusting the properties of the liquid to the size and shape of its container, one can match certain key parameters affecting the fluid dynamic behavior of the model to that of the natural body and thereby produce a regime that is

(a)

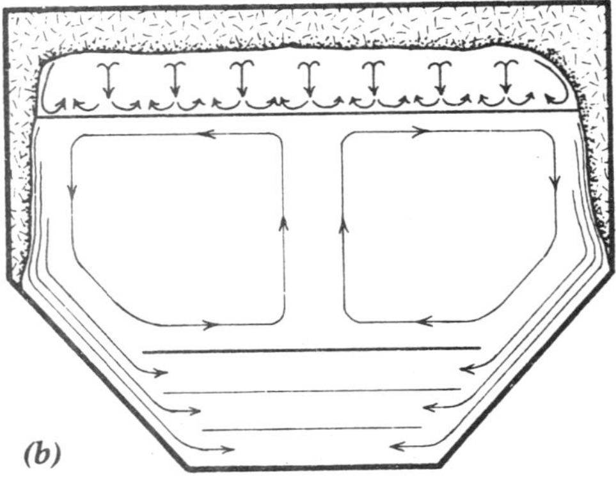

(b)

Figure 6–36 Cooling and crystallization of the Skaergaard magma has been modeled in the laboratory using dilute aqueous solutions of salts, such as sodium carbonate, in a tank with the form of an idealized cross-section of the intrusion (a). By varying the properties of the solution and the ways in which it cools and crystallizes, it is possible to study the nature of convective flow and compositonal stratification. The results of one such experiment (b) illustrate a possible form of convection in the major zones. Because the upper part of the intrusion was contaminated with felsic gneiss, its density was reduced to the extent that it convected and crystallized more or less independently to form the Upper Border Series. Meanwhile, the main magma cooled and crystallized against the walls to produce the Marginal Border Series. A heavy compositional boundary layer descended to pond on the floor where it formed the rocks of the Layered Series.

at least qualitatively similar. The model can then be of great value, especially if it generates unexpected insights that can be tested by means of observable geological relations.

While details are still uncertain, the general form of convection suggested by such studies is one with two separate and largely independent cells, one represented by the Layered Series and the other by the Upper Border Series. Owing to the large amount of felsic gneiss that must have floated to the top shortly after the magma was emplaced, a contaminated magma of low density ponded under the roof and crystallized with relatively little subsequent interaction with the main mass of magma below. When the latter cooled and crystallized against the steep walls, it precipitated the rocks of the Marginal Border Series and developed a compositional boundary layer that was depleted of the components of the crystallizing phases and enriched in iron, titanium, and other residual components. This, together with the thermal contraction due to cooling, led to an increase of density and a descending flow of differentiated liquid that ponded and crystallized on the floor to form the Layered Series.

This interpretation offers no obvious mechanism of differentiation other than the crystal-liquid fractionation accompanying crystallization on the wall. This alone was probably inadequate to achieve the extreme compositions found in the rest of the intrusion. It is possible, though the evidence is still sparse, that much of the differentiation resulted from segregation and upward migration of interstitial liquid, as a result of compaction of crystals on the floor, somewhat in the manner deduced for the Palisades Sill. This interpretation is supported by the distribution of excluded elements noted earlier (Fig. 6–30). The declining concentrations of these elements in Lower Zone, followed by a reversal near Middle Zone and a subsequent increase up to the Sandwich Horizon, is consistent with an increased segregation and upward migration of interstitial liquid as the thickness and amount of compaction of the crystal mush increased upward.

The difficulty of defining the precise mechanisms by which the Skaergaard magma differentiated stems not from any lack of field or analytical data, but from an inadequate understanding of how magmas cool and crystallize. In particular, we have only a vague understanding of the physical nature of the zone of crystallization where most of the critical processes of differentiation take place. The boundary we refer to when discussing the margins of a solidifying body of magma is easy to draw as a line on a schematic diagram but much more difficult to define in precise physical terms. What does such a line represent? Is it a sharp interface between a solid crystalline "wall" and a liquid interior, a broad gradational zone of declining temperature and increasing crystallinity, or a dynamic boundary separating a convecting magma from a static zone of greater viscosity? Because the proportions of crystals are governed simultaneously by changing gradients of temperature, composition, and velocity, it is no simple task to determine how all these interdependent factors interact. The problem would be easier to solve if one could define the spatial distribution of temperature and chemical components in terms of basic kinetic processes, such as heat and mass transfer and rates of nucleation and growth of crystals. Unfortunately, petrologists are still unable to write a complete set of integrated equations for cooling and solidification of magmas, and until this can be done, it will be impossible to deal with crystallization and differentiation in a rigorous way.

SELECTED REFERENCES

Jackson, E. D. 1961. Primary textures and mineral associations in the Ultramafic Zone of the Stillwater Complex, Montana. *U. S. Geol. Surv. Prof. Paper 358*. 106 p. A classic work on chromite-bearing ultramafic rocks with a number of important insights into their origins.

Jour. Petr. 1979. Vol. 20, 3 and 1989. Vol. 30, 2. These two issues contain collections of papers dealing with the most recent research on the Skaergaard and Kiglapait intrusions, as well as many references to other papers dealing with modern concepts of basic intrusions.

Parsons, I., ed. 1987. *Origins of Igneous Layering*. NATO ASI Series C, Vol. 196. 666 pp. A compilation of papers representing recent research on basic intrusions with special emphasis on the origins of layering.

Shirley, D. N. 1987. Differentiation and compaction in the Palisades Sill, New Jersey. *Jour. Petr.* 28:835–866. The most important recent work on differentiation of doleritic sills.

Visser, D. J. L., and G. Von Gruenewaldt, eds. Symposium on the Bushveld Igneous Complex and other layered intrusions. *Geol. Soc. South Africa Spec. Publ. No. 1.* 763 p. Contains many comprehensive summaries of studies of large, layered intrusions.

Wager, R. L., and G. M. Brown. 1967. *Layered Igneous Rocks*. Oliver and Boyd. 588 pp. Though somewhat out-of-date, this is still the best summary of layered intrusions.

7

BASALTS AND MAGMA SERIES

THE CONCEPT THAT CERTAIN GROUPS of igneous rocks have common genetic lineages stemming from different parents was first proposed by J. P. Iddings in 1892. Recognizing that their chemical nature is more important than their mineral assemblages, Iddings proposed that all igneous rocks fell into one of two "consanguinous" series, one alkaline and the other sub-alkaline. This basic division is still recognized today, even though several subsidiary series have been defined within the two major branches.

All but a few igneous rocks fit into one of a small number of types of sequential series, each having its own particular mineralogical and compositional trends; hardly any stand in isolation from other rocks. A set of rocks that are perceived to be linked through a process of differentiation, however obscure or tenuous, is said to be co-magmatic and is referred to as a series. Groups of rocks may be closely associated in the field or may even form an eruptive sequence from the same volcano without necessarily having a common magmatic origin. An assemblage of this latter type is usually called a suite to indicate that it has a spatial association whether or not the rocks have any direct genetic coherence. Thus, a suite of rocks from a given igneous center may include rocks from various sources and more than one series, whereas lavas of many different volcanoes may be assigned to the same series, if they share the same compositional trends.

The principal magmatic series recognized today were first established through geological studies of the natural associations of rocks in the field, and they were defined mainly on the basis of their mode of occurrence and mineralogical characteristics. Experimental studies later showed that the trends predicted by phase relations correspond quite well to those established from field and petrographic evidence.

It may seem odd that most of these series are based on petrographically diverse volcanic rocks rather than on plutonic rocks in which the assemblages of minerals are closer to equilibrium and less dependent on the vagaries of rapid crystallization. The reason effusive rocks are emphasized is that their trends and ranges of differentiation are more easily related to liquid lines of descent. There can be no doubt that their composition, at least of the groundmass, corresponds to a liquid and that phenocrysts were mineral phases contained in that liquid before it was erupted. In this way, an eruptive sequence can provide a way of tracing the trend of evolution of liquids and their coexisting minerals. Plutonic rocks with longer histories of crystallization and re-equilibration are more difficult to interpret in this way.

Basalts and other mafic rocks having high liquidus temperatures are normally thought to be the original magmas from which more evolved rocks are derived. For this reason, they are assigned a special place as parental magmas, even though they may not be the most voluminous or even the most distinctive members of their particular series. Most parental magmas are thought of as primary in the sense that they are direct products of melting and have not evolved from an earlier liquid. They need not be basaltic, so long as they are not derived from another magma. The process of producing a magma by total or partial melting is known as *anatexis*, and magmas produced in this way are said to be anatectic. The term is used most often to imply melting of crustal rocks, but its definition does not limit it to that sense.

The principal types of magma series and their relations to large-scale tectonic features were mentioned briefly in the opening chapter. Here we examine in more detail the distinguishing features and origins of two of those series, the tholeiitic and alkaline rocks.

CHEMICAL AND PETROGRAPHIC CHARACTERISTICS

Alkaline and sub-alkaline (tholeiitic) basalts

Before proceeding, we should review the differences between alkaline and sub-alkaline rocks and elaborate on the distinguishing criteria given in chapter 2. We shall focus on the main tholeiitic branch of the sub-alkaline group, deferring the other major divisions to separate chapters of their own.

The *Basalt Tetrahedron* (Fig. 7-1) illustrates the petrologic basis of the distinction between basic alkaline and tholeiitic magmas. Its components—diopside, olivine, hypersthene, nepheline, plagioclase, and quartz—correspond to the principal normative minerals used to characterize basalts. The tetrahedron is divided into three volumes by two interior planes, one a "plane of silica saturation" that separates compositions with normative quartz from those with normative olivine and hypersthene, and another, a "critical plane of silica undersaturation," separating the latter from compositions with normative nepheline. Thus the three volumes correspond to the principal types of basalt—quartz tholeiites, olivine tholeiites, and alkaline basalts.

The division between critically undersaturated basalts (i.e., alkaline basalts with normative nepheline) and olivine tholeiites (with normative olivine and hypersthene) is more important than that between saturated and oversaturated tholeiites. The reason for this can be seen from the simple system plagioclase-olivine-silica (Fig. 7-2) that corresponds to the base of the tholeiitic side of the tetrahedron. The broken line crossing the interior indicates the trace of the plane of silica saturation in Figure 7-1. Note that, owing to the incongruent melting of hypersthene (which corresponds to enstatite in Figure 4-13), the boundary be-

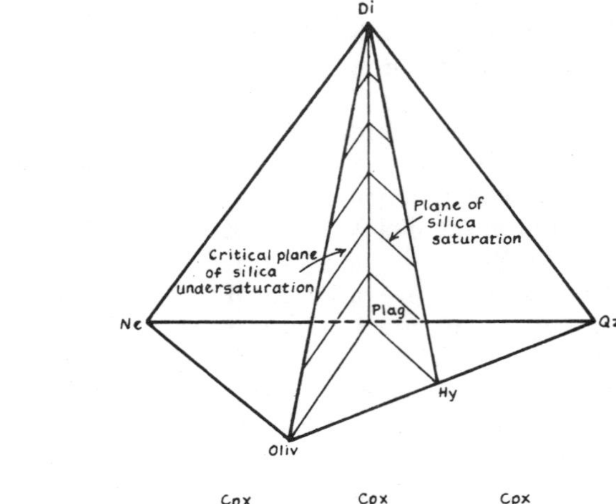

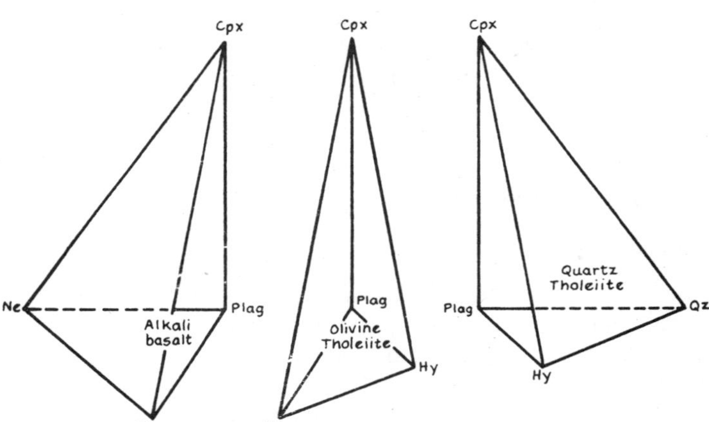

Figure 7–1 The basalt tetrahedron is divided into three volumes corresponding to alkaline basalt with normative Ne (or basanite with modal Ne), olivine tholeiites with normative Hy and Ol, and quartz tholeiites with normative Hy and Q. The first two are separated by the "critical plane of silica undersaturation" between alkaline rocks with normative Ne and tholeiitic rocks with normative Hy. Olivine tholeiites are separated from quartz tholeiites by the "plane of silica saturation."

tween the fields of olivine and hypersthene is a peritectic, and any liquid with both normative olivine and hypersthene, i.e., any composition to the left of the broken line, evolves by crystal fractionation to the same end point, E, as one with normative quartz (to the right of the line). Thus, both olivine tholeiites and quartz tholeiites evolve toward greater degrees of silica enrichment. This course of evolution is in contrast to compositions with normative nepheline, which evolve toward more silica-deficient compositions.

The triangle forming the back face of the principal tetrahedron (Fig. 7–1) corresponds to the system Di-Ne-SiO_2 (Fig. 7–3a), in which albite represents plagioclase, and the intersection of the planes of silica saturation with that face corresponds to the diopside-albite join. Albite is an intermediate compound between nepheline and SiO_2 and melts congruently to a liquid of its own composition, so the three-component system must have a thermal divide separating it into two sub-systems, Di-Ab-SiO_2 and Di-Ab-Ne, each with an end point at a eutectic.

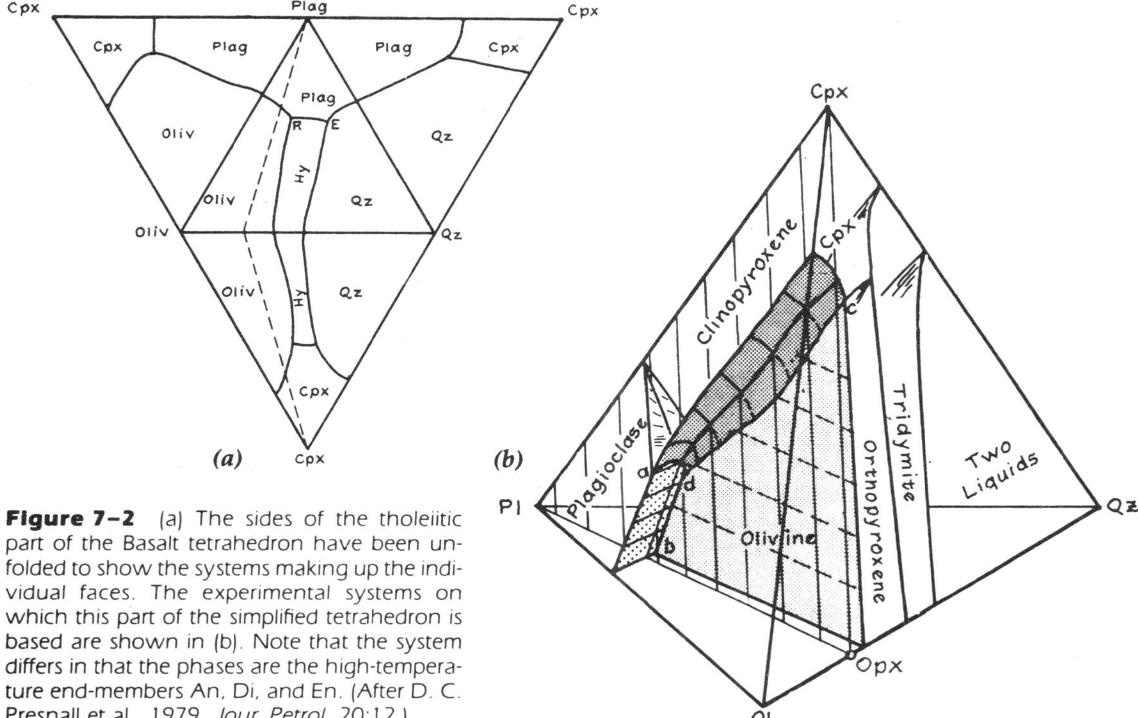

Figure 7–2 (a) The sides of the tholeiitic part of the Basalt tetrahedron have been unfolded to show the systems making up the individual faces. The experimental systems on which this part of the simplified tetrahedron is based are shown in (b). Note that the system differs in that the phases are the high-temperature end-members An, Di, and En. (After D. C. Presnall et al., 1979, *Jour. Petrol.* 20:12.)

This system can be visualized as a simplified analog for the different courses of evolution of alkaline and sub-alkaline magmas. If the points X and X′ are thought of as two parental liquids, the first alkaline and the second sub-alkaline, we see that, even though their initial compositions are very close and the minerals they crystallize are the same throughout most of their course of differentiation, they lie on opposite sides of a thermal divide and are destined to evolve with increasingly different degrees of silica saturation until one crystallizes nepheline and the other a silica mineral, such as quartz. A thermal divide persists through all the systems governing crystallization of nepheline-normative and hypersthene-normative liquids (Fig. 7–3) and becomes especially marked in the later stages of differentiation. It is seen most clearly in the system nepheline-kalsilite-silica (Fig. 7–4), often referred to as "Petrogeny's residual system" because it is an analog for the trends of felsic liquids evolving toward rhyolite or phonolite. Note that the join between albite and orthoclase divides the diagram into two parts, one in which liquids become increasing enriched in silica and another in which they become impoverished in that component.

The divergent trends of these synthetic systems correspond closely to those of many alkaline and sub-alkaline series in which felsic differentiates have compositions close to the eutectics and thermal minima. This is not to say, however,

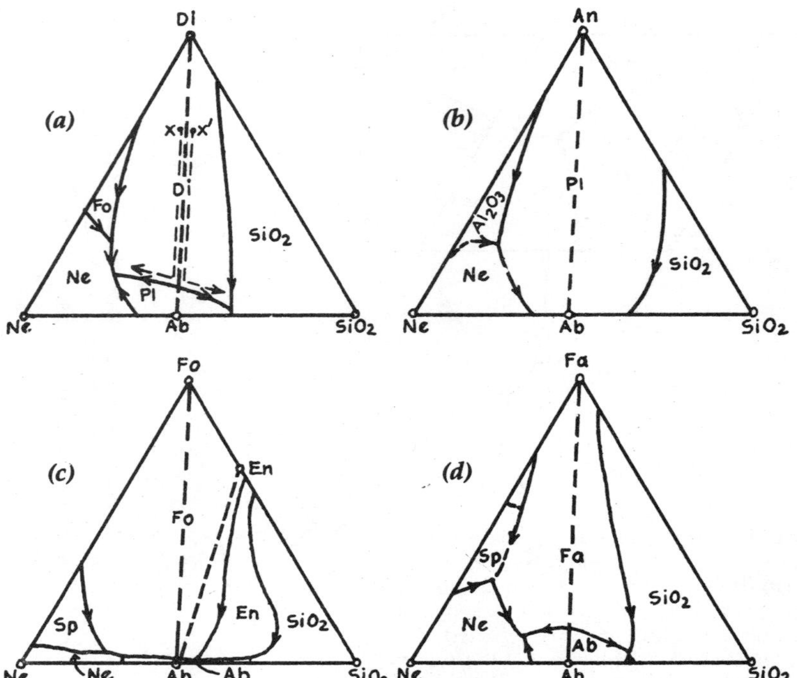

Figure 7–3 Four basic ternary systems have a thermal divide separating fields in which liquids evolve to different end-points. (From work of J. F. Schairer, H. S. Yoder, Jr., and N. L. Bowen compiled by S. A. Morse, 1980, *Basalts and Phase Diagrams*, Springer-Verlag, p. 249.)

that all magmatic series follow one or the other of these two lines of descent. We shall see shortly that some oceanic series follow an intermediate trend toward trachytes with neither strong enrichment nor depletion of silica. The factors governing these seemingly anomalous but geologically important groups of rocks will be discussed in a later chapter.

Chemical characteristics

When dealing with the multicomponent compositions of real magmas, the character of a magma series can usually be defined by the abundances or ratios of certain diagnostic elements. The tholeiitic and alkaline rocks of Hawaii, for example, can be distinguished by their ratios of Na_2O + K_2O to SiO_2 (Fig. 7–5a). The dividing line is entirely empirical, however, and cannot be applied directly to other suites of rocks. Its position, which corresponds to the critical plane of silica undersaturation in the basalt tetrahedron, is affected by the relative abundance of mafic and felsic minerals and is not an infallible criteria for all rocks. A sounder approach is to compare the proportions of the key normative minerals by means of a diagram that also includes the mafic normative minerals (Fig.

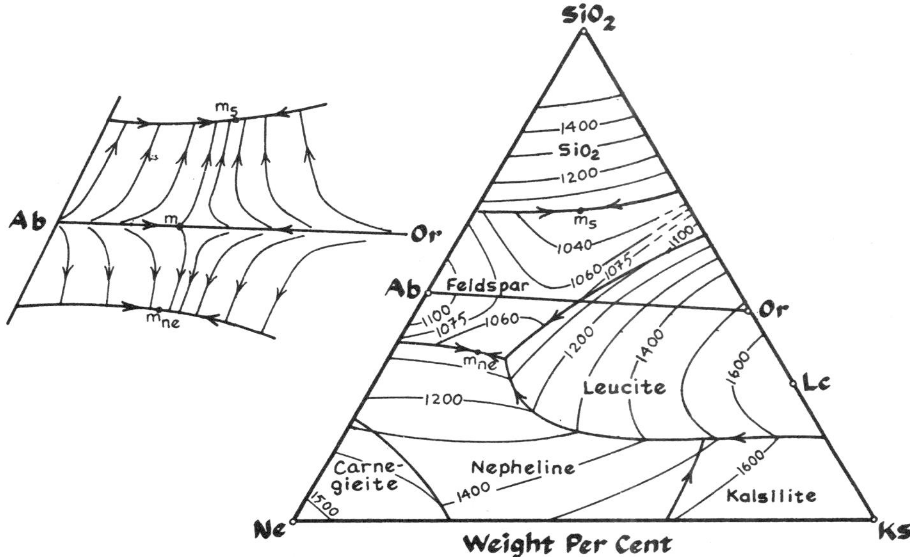

Figure 7–4 The system nepheline ($NaAlSiO_4$)-kalsilite ($KAlSiO_4$)-silica (SiO_2) illustrates the evolution of felsic differentiates toward compositions enriched or depleted in silica. The insert on the left shows paths of cooling liquids in the low-temperature region of the albite-orthoclase join. Orthoclase melts incongruently to leucite and liquid but only at low pressures. (After J. F. Schairer, 1950, *Jour. Geol.* 58:512–517. Diagram at left is adapted from a similar figure by S. A. Morse, 1980, *Basalts and Phase Diagrams*, Fig. 15.11.)

7–5b). Depending on the form of the diagram, however, even a three-component diagram can distort the proportional distribution of samples in the three fields.

A common source of difficulty is the oxidation state of iron, which can have a pronounced effect on the amount of normative Ne or Hy in basalts and can even affect their trends of differentiation. In calculating the norm for an oxidized rock, more iron is assigned to magnetite (as opposed to FeO-bearing silicates), leaving more silica to be assigned to other minerals. In this way, oxidation of iron may reduce and even eliminate normative nepheline that would otherwise be present. If oxidation results from surface weathering, it can be allowed for by recalculating the analysis with a more appropriate ratio of FeO to Fe_2O_3. If the oxidation state is inherent in the magma, however, it may have greater petrologic significance, for the effect seen in calculating normative components reflects the silica enrichment in real magmas when equivalent minerals, such as magnetite, are fractionated at early stages of differentiation.

Although a common feature of alkaline basalts is an abundance of MgO and TiO_2, these components, like alkalies and silica, must also be considered in the context of the total composition of the rock. A *picrite* (basalt with abundant olivine phenocrysts) may have a very high magnesium content, even though the rock as a whole has normative hypersthene. The same relation holds for TiO_2; the early stages of differentiation of tholeiitic basalts may result in strong enrich-

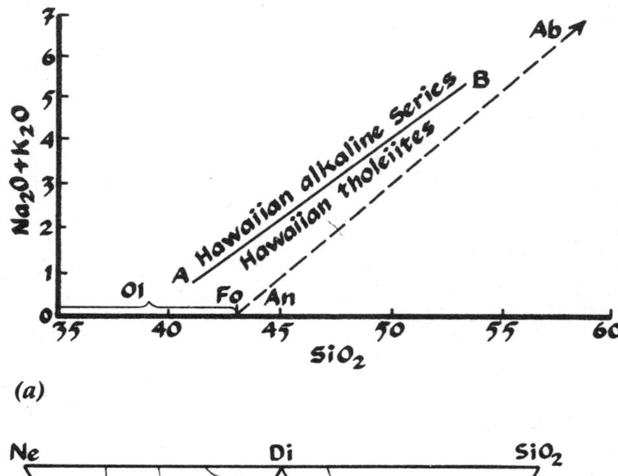

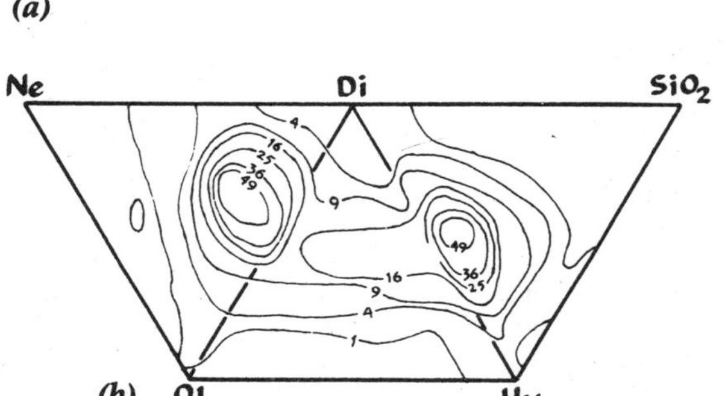

Figure 7–5 (a) When plotted on a diagram for alkalies vs. silica, the tholeiitic and alkaline rocks of Hawaii are separated by an empirical boundary parallel to the alkali-silica variation of the plagioclase feldspars. Note that in a rock without mafic minerals the plagioclase line would separate compositions with normative nepheline (above) from sub-alkaline compositions (below). Thus, the division for Hawaii, or any other province, will have the same slope, but owing to the presence of other minerals, such as olivine, which contain silica but no alkalies, the line has a different origin on the silica axis. Depending on the proportions of feldspar and mafic minerals, the boundary will differ for each rock series. (b) When the normative components of basalts are plotted in a diagram corresponding to the base of the basalt tetrahedron, they fall in the corresponding fields of alkaline basalts, olivine tholeiites, and quartz tholeiites. When large numbers of samples from many tectonic settings are plotted in this way, they tend to define two fields of maximum populations. Note, however, that the geometry of the diagram differs from that of the tetrahedron in that the relative length of the olivine-hypersthene base is increased. The two concentrations, one for alkali basalts and the other for quartz tholeiites, at opposite ends of the contoured field are exaggerated by this distortion.

ment of titanium, which normally increases along with iron in ferro-basalts. The result is a rock with much normative ilmenite but none of the other essential features of alkaline rocks.

The most important compositional factor governing the mineral assemblages and evolutionary trends of basalts is the concentration or, more properly, the activity of silica in relation to that of other components, such as alkalies. Some of the characteristics normally associated with the activity of silica are illustrated by the idealized compositions given in Table 7-1.

Petrographic characteristics

Petrographic criteria can often be just as useful as chemical analyses in characterizing basalts (Table 7-1). Rocks containing a modal feldspathoid, such as nepheline or leucite, are obviously alkaline, but, unfortunately, these *basanites,* as alkaline basalts with modal feldspathoids are called, are less common than alkaline basalts that lack these diagnostic minerals. The latter are often called *basanitoids* and in most cases are poorer in alkalies and richer in silica than basalts with modal nepheline. Whether they have a modal feldspathoid or not, most alkaline rocks contain a late-crystallizing alkali feldspar, normally anorthoclase, which can be recognized from its low refractive index and small negative optic angle.

With few exceptions, nepheline-normative basalts have olivine in their

Table 7–1 Characteristics of alkaline and tholeiitic basalts.

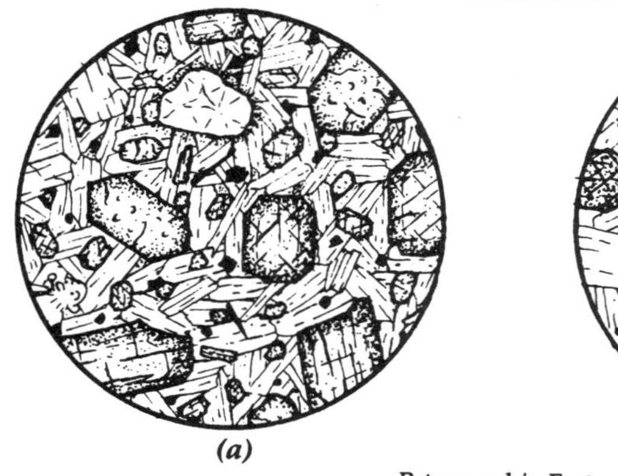

(a)

(b)

Petrographic Features

Alkaline Basalt	*Tholeiitic Basalt*
Stable groundmass olivine	Hypersthene or pigeonite
Nepheline or leucite (in basanites)	Interstitial quartz
Reddish titaniferous pyroxene	Phenocrysts of olivine resorbed and rimmed with pyroxene, none in groundmass
Interstitial alkali feldspar	
Plagioclase with sodic rims	
Vesicles lined with analcite or zeolite	Vesicles line with a slicia mineral

Note: Though common in their respective types of basalts, it is rare to find all of these features in a single rock.

Chemical Features

	Normative Ne	*Normative* Hy
SiO_2	46–48	48–52
TiO_2	2–3	1–2
Al_2O_3	14–16	14–16
FeO^*	4–7	5–7
MgO	5–8	4–6
CaO	8–10	7–10
Na_2	2–3	1.5–2.5
K_2O	0.3–1.5	0.1–1

groundmass; tholeiitic basalts do not. The latter may contain phenocrysts of olivine, but if they do the olivine tends to be rounded and shows evidence of reaction with the groundmass. A Ca-poor pyroxene, either hypersthene or pigeonite, is, of course, highly diagnostic of tholeiites. The titaniferous pyroxenes that are so characteristic of alkaline basalts can be recognized by their reddish brown or purplish tinge; they are rarely seen in sub-alkaline rocks, even when the latter have bulk compositions rich in titanium. The amount of titanium in the pyroxene structure is a function, not only of the titanium content of the rock, but also of silica content. If the activity of silica in the magma is low, greater amounts of aluminum (+3) enter the tetrahedral site of pyroxenes in place of silica (+4), and the resulting charge deficiency causes a paired substitution of titanium for cations of lower valence. For this reason, titaniferous pyroxenes are a sensitive sign of low silica activity in the melt from which they have crystallized.

EXAMPLES OF THOLEIITIC AND ALKALINE SERIES

Two oceanic examples will suffice to illustrate the salient features of the two series. The differentiated rocks of the Galapagos Islands and Tahiti are ideal for this purpose, because both have volcanic and plutonic counterparts of the full range of differentiates, and they are in a setting where the absence of continental crust makes their genetic evolution by crystal fractionation unambiguous.

The Galapagos tholeiitic series

The active volcanoes of the Galapagos Islands are products of a hotspot in the eastern equatorial Pacific. The differentiated lavas are concentrated in the center of the archipelago immediately downstream from the core of the hotspot, and the plutonic rocks are found as xenoliths among the pyroclastic ejecta erupted from cinder cones in the same region.

The most basic analysed sample of the series is an olivine tholeiite with 6.85 percent MgO. This is somewhat less than a value of 8 percent that is considered a minimum MgO content for primary melts of the mantle and indicates that even these basalts have already differentiated before erupting. This illustrates an important point: the most basic basalts that can be sampled at the surface may not be the true parental magma of the series; the primary mantle-derived magma may never be erupted in its original form, possibly because it is too dense to rise through lighter crustal rocks or because it cools and differentiates while rising through the colder crust.

The series of differentiated volcanic rocks, consisting of *ferro-basalts, icelandites, dacites*, and *sodic rhyolites*, is matched by a parallel suite of coarse-grained *olivine gabbros, ferrogabbros, diorites*, and *quartz syenites*. Typical compositions are given in Table 7–2, and the more notable petrographic features are illustrated in Fig. 7–6.

The differentiated series follows a typical tholeiitic trend (Fig. 7–7a). In the early and middle stages, MgO declines steadily, while iron first increases to a maximum in ferro-basalts, then declines in icelandites, dacites, and rhyolites. Later stages are dominated by an increase of silica and alkalies. At the same time, plagioclase changes from labradorite to oligoclase, olivines and pyroxenes become richer in iron, and hypersthene gives way to pigeonite. Amphibole and biotite are common in the middle and late members of the plutonic series.

As Figure 7–7b illustrates, these changes can be related to fractionation of the minerals seen in plutonic xenoliths or as phenocrysts in the lavas. The mass-balance comparisons used to test these relations are based on the principles described in chapter five, but, for ease of calculation, are carried out by a computer. They compare the observed composition of each member of the differentiated series with the calculated composition that would result from removal of a speci-

Table 7–2 Compositions of representative lavas of the differentiated tholeiitic series of the Galapagos Islands. Analyses are recalulated to 100 percent water-free with a uniform ratio of Fe_2O_3 to FeO* of 0.15. (Original data from M. Lindstrom, PhD thesis, Univ. of Oregon, with corrections and additions.)

	1.	2.	3.	4.	5.	6.	7.
SiO_2	48.73	49.72	49.21	52.02	54.82	64.71	71.61
TiO_2	2.52	2.81	3.55	2.92	2.43	0.93	0.38
Al_2O_3	15.08	14.56	13.47	14.17	14.62	15.35	13.39
Fe_2O_3	1.87	1.96	2.18	1.91	1.72	0.87	0.59
FeO	10.64	11.13	12.36	10.79	9.71	4.96	3.35
MnO	0.16	0.17	0.20	0.13	0.14	0.09	0.12
MgO	6.85	5.53	5.18	4.43	3.38	1.57	0.21
CaO	10.49	9.90	9.42	8.13	7.06	3.71	1.51
Na_2O	2.96	3.17	3.26	3.76	4.07	5.35	5.65
K_2O	0.43	0.69	0.76	1.15	1.39	2.17	3.10
P_2O_5	0.27	0.36	0.41	0.59	0.66	0.28	0.09
				Molecular Norms			
Ap	0.58	0.77	0.89	1.26	1.40	0.59	0.19
Il	3.54	3.98	5.07	4.14	3.44	1.29	0.53
Mt	1.97	2.09	2.34	2.03	1.83	0.91	0.61
Or	2.59	4.13	4.59	6.93	8.36	12.83	18.32
Ab	26.86	28.99	29.96	34.39	37.11	47.96	50.78
An	26.87	23.88	20.39	18.71	17.81	11.44	2.01
Di	19.17	18.96	19.80	14.72	10.70	4.11	3.92
Hy	8.86	13.32	13.63	16.82	14.98	8.21	3.06
Ol	9.54	3.88	3.33	—	—	—	—
Q	—	—	—	1.00	4.35	12.66	20.59
				Trace Elements			
Ba	80	130	147	160	185	320	441
Zr	157	223	262	344	445	617	673
Rb	6	12	11	21	25	43	62
Sr	320	310	290	296	287	194	74
Cr	60	46	25	15	14	8	4
Ni	93	39	29	13	7	3	—
La	12	17.1	19	25.9	31	41	52
Sm	5.1	6.9	9	10.1	11.9	11.7	17
Lu	0.43	0.61	0.65	0.77	0.9	1	1.6

1. Olivine tholeiite
2. Tholeiite
3. Ferrobasalt
4. Basic icelandite
5. Icelandite
6. Dacite
7. Rhyolite

fied set of minerals from their parental liquid. Taking each step of differentiation in turn, successive compositions can be related in this way to a diminishing volume of remaining liquid.

Having determined the proportions of crystallizing phases and remaining liquid consistent with the major-element variations, the relations can be further

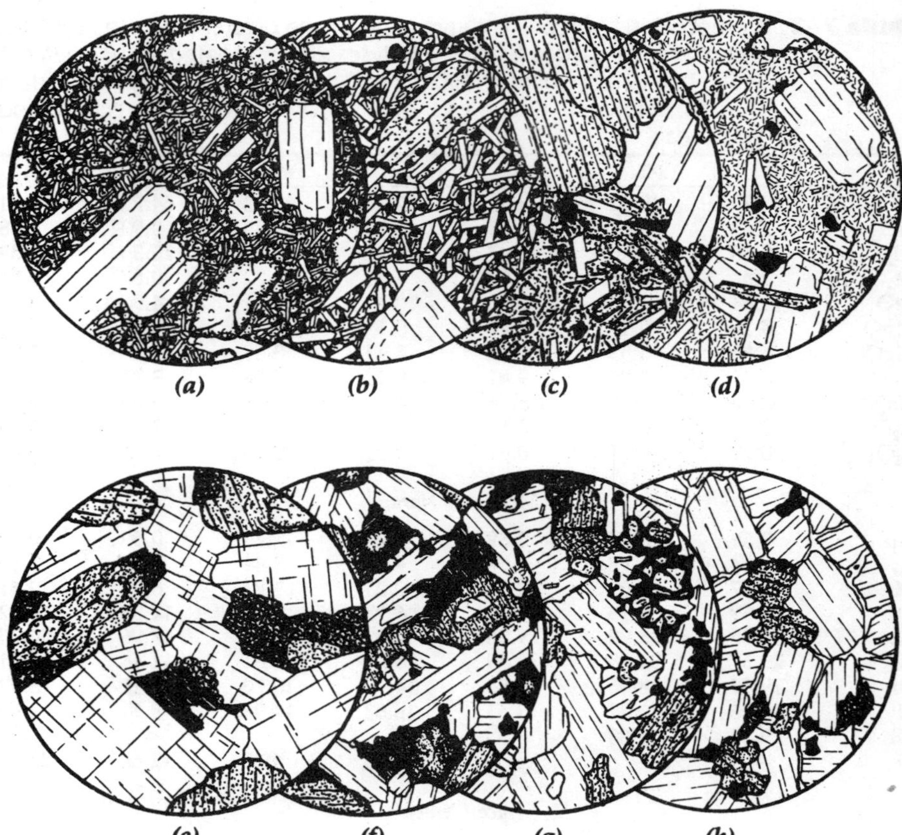

Figure 7–6 Petrographic features of tholeiitic lavas and plutonic rocks of the Galapagos Islands. (a) is a typical tholeiitic basalt with rounded phenocrysts of olivine, (b) is a ferro-basalt with abundant groundmass magnetite, (c) is an icelandite with large phenocrysts of ferro-augite and labradorite, and (d) is a siliceous dacite with hedenbergitic pyroxene and vesicles rimmed with cristobalite. Equivalent plutonic rocks are (e) olivine gabbro, (f) ferro-gabbro with magnetite rimmed with biotite, (g) hornblende-bearing leucodiorite, and (h) quartz-syenite with potassic oligoclase, apatite, and sphene.

tested by use of a number of trace elements that are sensitive measures of crystal fractionation. Taking appropriate distribution coefficients and the equations in chapter five, the predicted effect of fractionation is compared with the observed trends in successive liquids. A sample calculation is shown in Table 7–3, and calculated and observed trends for two key elements are shown for the entire series in Figure 7–7c. The effects of differentiation are well-illustrated by plotting the excluded trace elements on a normalized-element diagram (Fig. 7–7d) in which the concentrations in the differentiated lavas have been normalized to those in the most basic parent from Table 7–2.

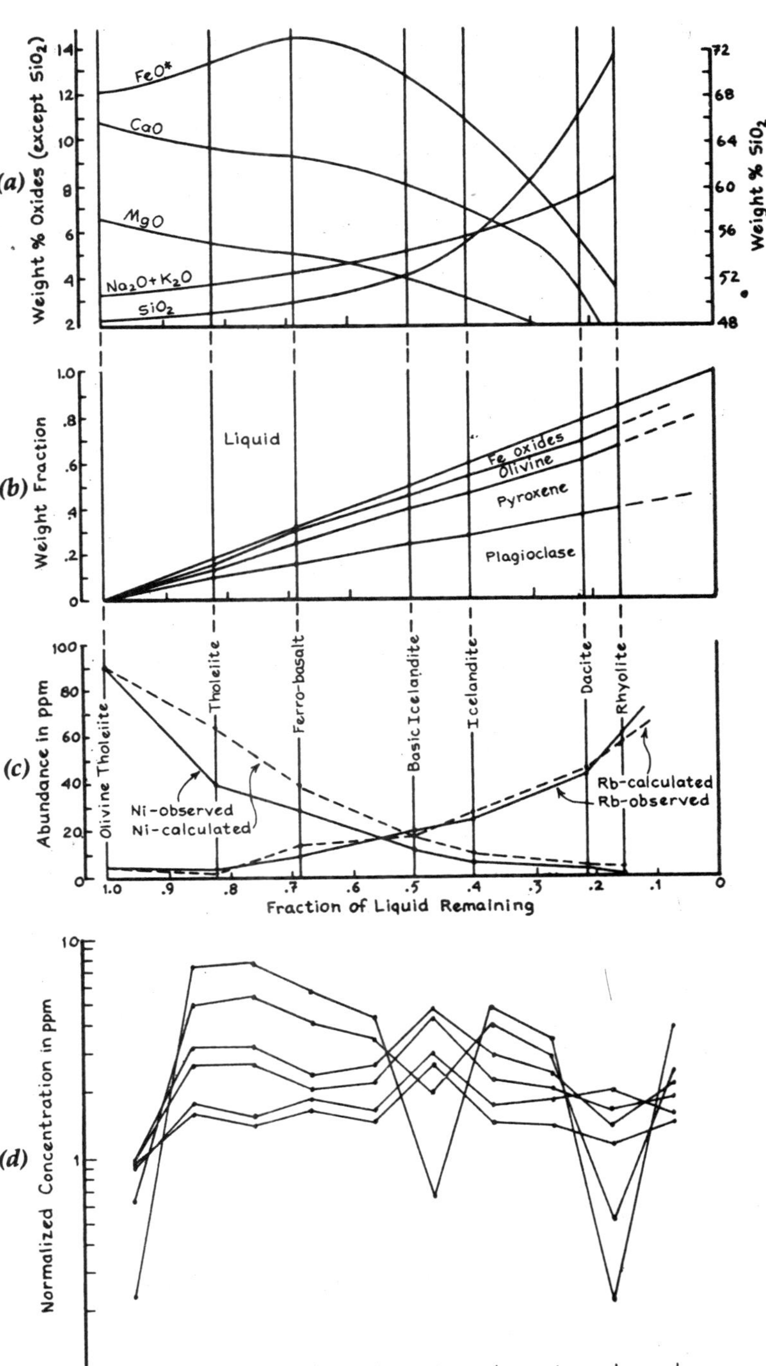

Figure 7–7 (a) The trend of differentiation of tholeiitic Galapagos lavas shows a strong enrichment of iron and titania in the early stages followed by a decline of those components as silica and alkalies are more strongly enriched. Variations are plotted against the fraction of remaining liquid (F) calculated by the method described in the text. (b) The proportions of minerals that are fractionated at each stage of differentiation have been calculated in the manner illustrated in Table 7-3. In (c) the concentrations of trace elements predicted by these calculations (broken lines) are compared with those observed in the rocks (solid lines). See text for explanation. (d) is a normalized-element diagram showing the increase of excluded trace elements relative to their abundances in the most primitive liquid. Note that although most of the elements are enriched with differentiation, Sr remains almost constant until a late stage, when it is depleted. Ti first increases, then decreases, when Fe-Ti oxides start to crystallize; P does the same when apatite is removed.

Table 7–3 A sample of a mass-balance calculation for differentiation of a Galapagos olivine tholeiite (OLIV-TH) to a more evolved tholeiite (TH) by fractionation of plagioclase (AN75), augite (AUG), olivine (FO85), and an iron-oxide (MT-ILM), which occur as phenocrysts in the parent. Compositions of the components are listed under INPUT DATA, and the calculated composition of the derivative liquid is compared to the observed composition under SOLUTION. Weight proportions of the minerals subtracted and the remaining liquid are listed under PROPORTIONS OF PHASES. A measure of the quality of the calculation is given by the SUM OF SQUARES OF RESIDUALS, which is a total of the squared differences (DIFF) between the true analysis of the daughter and calculated best-fit composition. By squaring the difference, the effect of the positive and negative signs of these differences is removed. Depending on the reliability of the input data, a value of less than 1.0 is considered satisfactory.

INPUT DATA

	OLIV-TH	AN75	AUG	FO85	MT-ILM	THOL
SIO2	48.73	48.82	51.30	40.01	0.00	49.72
TIO2	2.52	0.00	0.00	0.00	15.80	2.81
AL2O3	15.08	32.21	0.00	0.00	0.00	14.56
FE2O3	1.87	0.00	0.00	0.00	36.84	1.96
FEO	10.64	0.00	6.10	14.35	47.36	11.13
MNO	0.16	0.00	0.00	0.00	0.00	0.17
MGO	6.85	0.00	21.10	45.64	0.00	5.53
CAO	10.49	15.19	21.10	0.00	0.00	9.90
NA2O	2.96	2.80	0.00	0.00	0.00	3.17
K2O	.43	0.00	0.00	0.00	0.00	.69
P2O5	.27	0.00	0.00	0.00	0.00	.36

PARENT – FRACTIONATED MINERALS = DAUGHTER

SOLUTION

	PROPORTIONS OF PHASES	% FRACTIONATED MINERALS
OLIV-TH	1.000	--
FO85	-0.032	18.601
AUG	-0.037	21.048
AN75	-0.092	53.151
MT-ILM	-0.013	7.201
THOL	0.826	--

	DAUGHTER ANALYSIS	DAUGHTER CALC	DIFF
SIO2	49.72	49.63	-.09
TIO2	2.81	2.81	.00
AL2O3	14.56	14.62	.06
FE2O3	1.96	1.71	-.25
FEO	11.13	11.33	.20
MNO	0.17	0.19	.02
MGO	5.53	5.55	.02
CAO	9.90	10.04	.14
NA2O	3.17	3.27	.10
K2O	.69	.53	-.16
P2O5	.36	.32	-.04

SUM OF SQUARES OF RESIDUALS = 0.172

TRACE ELEMENTS:

	BULK D	PARENT	DAU OBS	DAU CALC
CR	1.62	60	46	53
NI	2.96	93	39	64
BA	0.05	80	130	98
RB	0.11	6	12	7
SR	1.14	320	310	310

The Tahitian alkaline series

Perhaps the most remarkable suite of oceanic alkaline rocks is that of Tahiti in the Society Islands of the central equatorial Pacific. Two large, steep-sided volcanoes, long inactive and deeply incised by erosion (Fig. 7-8), have been cut by near-vertical canyons that expose their plutonic cores.

The most common lavas are *alkaline basalts, basanites,* and *ankaramites* (basalts in which both olivine and augite are especially abundant), but a wide range of more differentiated lavas can be found among the products of later eruptions. Two diverging trends can be distinguished (Fig. 7-9). One is a good example of the type of intermediate series mentioned earlier. It consists mainly of marginally alkaline *hawaiites* and *mugearites* and culminates in *trachyte* and its plutonic equivalent, *syenite*. Some members contain small amounts of normative nepheline, others normative hypersthene. The second series is more strongly undersaturated and includes a variety of feldspathoidal lavas and plutonic rocks (Table 7-4 and Fig. 7-10) that have differentiated to *nepheline syenites* and *phonolites* (a fine-grained felsic rock similar to trachyte but with modal nepheline).

Strongly alkaline rocks, including those of Tahiti, have been given an inordinate number of special names in keeping with their great mineralogical and petrographic diversity. These names are useful when describing the series in detail, but for our present purposes it will suffice to mention some of the typical minerals that characterize rocks of this kind without dwelling on the nomenclature the mineral assemblages define. Most of the pyroxenes are rich in titanium, which gives them a deep, reddish brown color. Some are strongly zoned with green sodic rims. The dark brown amphibole, kaersutite, is also titaniferous, as is the biotite, which is particularly abundant in the more felsic members of the plutonic suite. The alumina-silicates include, in addition to sodic plagioclase, nepheline, analcite, and brilliant blue hauyne.

Unlike the Galapagos series, the Tahitian alkaline rocks are difficult to explain in terms of their observed mineral assemblages. Although both the trachy-

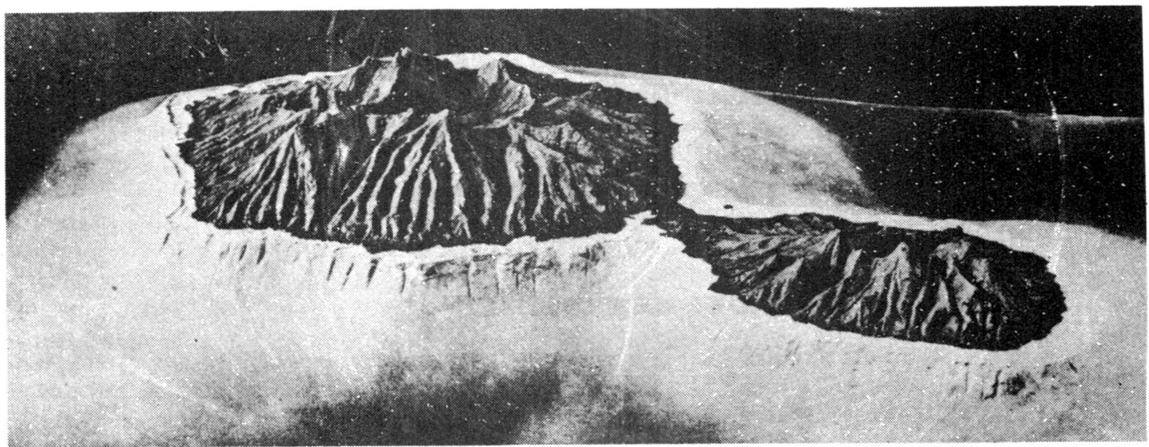

Figure 7-8 Topographic model showing the twin volcanoes of the island of Tahiti.

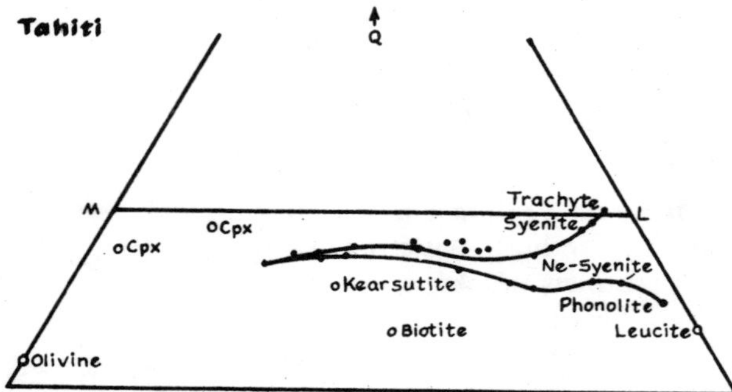

Figure 7–9 Von Wolff diagram for the rocks of Tahiti showing compositions in terms of their normative components. On the left side are the mafic components, pyroxene, olivine, and iron oxides, with "M" at the composition of pyroxene, and the more silica-deficient minerals below. Similarly, the leucocratic minerals, feldspar and feldspathoids, are plotted on the right side with feldspars at "L" and leucite and nepheline below. The degree of silica saturation is plotted as the distance from the apex "Q," so that rocks with normative quartz are above the line LM and those with normative Ne and Lc below. Note the two trends diverging from a common basaltic composition toward more felsic liquids with differing degrees of undersaturation of silica. One series terminates at trachyte and syenite, the other at phonolite and nepheline syenite. Minerals that appear as phenocrysts are clinopyroxene (Cpx), kearsutitic amphibole, olivine, and biotite.

tic and phonolitic series seem to stem from similar parental compositions, each has followed a separate course of differentiation. The von Wolff diagram in Figure 7–9 illustrates this divergence by emphasizing the amount of silica enrichment relative to the proportions of mafic ("M") and leucocratic components ("L"). A fractionation scheme of the kind described for the Galapagos tholeiites cannot account for either series by fractionation of the minerals seen in the plutonic rocks, namely olivine, pyroxene, feldspar, and amphibole. The problem is particularly acute for the phonolitic series, because none of the minerals that crystallized from the basic magmas contain enough silica to drive the composition toward strongly silica-deficient felsic liquids.

The most probable explanation for this apparent inconsistency is that the magmas differentiated at greater depths where the mineral assemblages differed from those that crystallized near the surface. The high-pressure assemblage of minerals may have had a somewhat greater silica content, causing that component to be relatively depleted in the evolving liquids. The role of pressure will be considered in more detail shortly; the important point to note here is that the minerals seen in the rocks at the surface are not necessarily the ones responsible for differentiation. Magmas can differentiate under a variety of conditions, and even in a single volcano differentiation may proceed independently at more than one level.

THE ORIGINS OF MAGMA SERIES

Modern theories for the origins of the various types of magmatic series have evolved as a result of many years of research, much of it stimulated by intense debates. Although distinctive types of magmas were recognized as early as the 1880s, the causes of their differences were not given serious consideration until the first decades of this century, when the Scottish Geological Survey turned its

Table 7–4 Major-element compositions of some typical members of the phonolitic suite of Tahiti.

	Volcanic Rocks				Plutonic Rocks			
	1.	2.	3.	4.	5.	6.	7.	8.
SiO_2	43.26	44.13	42.53	55.81	43.79	43.17	46.18	53.23
TiO_2	3.40	4.02	4.78	0.26	2.57	4.92	2.30	1.10
Al_2O_3	9.69	15.36	16.61	22.00	9.43	14.71	19.32	20.54
Fe_2O_3	3.66	3.08	3.80	1.68	3.47	4.53	4.11	2.86
FeO	8.97	9.09	7.84	0.89	8.80	7.94	4.41	1.81
MnO	0.16	0.14	0.13	0.06	0.14	0.15	0.13	0.07
MgO	12.64	6.37	5.56	0.21	15.72	5.39	3.13	0.77
CaO	12.10	10.61	10.03	0.93	12.46	10.64	8.47	3.26
Na_2O	1.59	2.56	3.85	9.26	1.59	3.43	4.71	7.09
K_2O	1.18	1.77	1.96	5.45	0.72	1.84	2.83	5.40
H_2O+	1.79	1.50	1.27	2.17	1.25	1.13	3.49	3.45
H_2O-	0.67	0.63	0.45	0.46	0.03	0.22	0.07	0.39
P_2O_5	0.61	0.55	0.90	0.02	0.26	1.71	0.89	0.13
Total	99.72	99.81	99.71	99.20	100.09	99.78	100.04	100.10
Molecular Norms								
Ap	1.32	1.20	1.94	0.04	0.54	3.71	1.92	0.27
Il	4.89	5.82	6.85	0.35	3.58	7.10	3.30	1.54
Mt	3.95	3.35	4.09	1.49	3.63	4.90	4.43	1.92
Hm	—	—	—	0.15	—	—	—	0.73
Or	7.20	10.87	11.91	31.54	4.26	11.26	17.22	32.08
Ab	10.83	17.50	14.25	33.95	6.63	22.10	22.39	27.66
An	16.35	26.21	22.90	2.33	16.48	20.01	23.93	8.33
Di	33.23	19.83	17.78	1.32	34.93	18.46	10.69	4.50
Ol	19.88	11.39	7.52	—	25.35	6.59	3.41	—
Ne	2.35	3.84	12.78	28.50	4.59	5.87	12.70	21.81

1. Ankaramite
2. Alkaline basalt
3. Basanite
4. Phonolite
5. Olivine-rich alkali gabbro
6. Biotite-rich alkali gabbro
7. Kaersuite essexite
8. Nepheline syenite

attention to the Inner Hebrides and the Eocene volcanic centers on the small islands of Skye, Rhum, Eigg, Muck, and Mull (Fig. 7–11). Together with the peninsula of Ardnamurchan, these "monosyllabic appendages of western Scotland" comprise a remarkable assemblage of differentiated volcanic and subvolcanic rocks eroded to levels exposing the inner structures of what were once large volcanic complexes.

Geologists working with the rocks of these centers, particularly on Mull, recognized two principal genetic lineages, a "Plateau Magma Series" and a "Main Magma Series." The former is represented by a voluminous sequence of flood basalts and lesser amounts of differentiated rocks discharged mainly from fissures related to rifting that accompanied opening of the North Atlantic Ocean. It was the first magma erupted, and it reappeared repeatedly at intervals throughout much of the subsequent igneous history of the province. The Main Magma

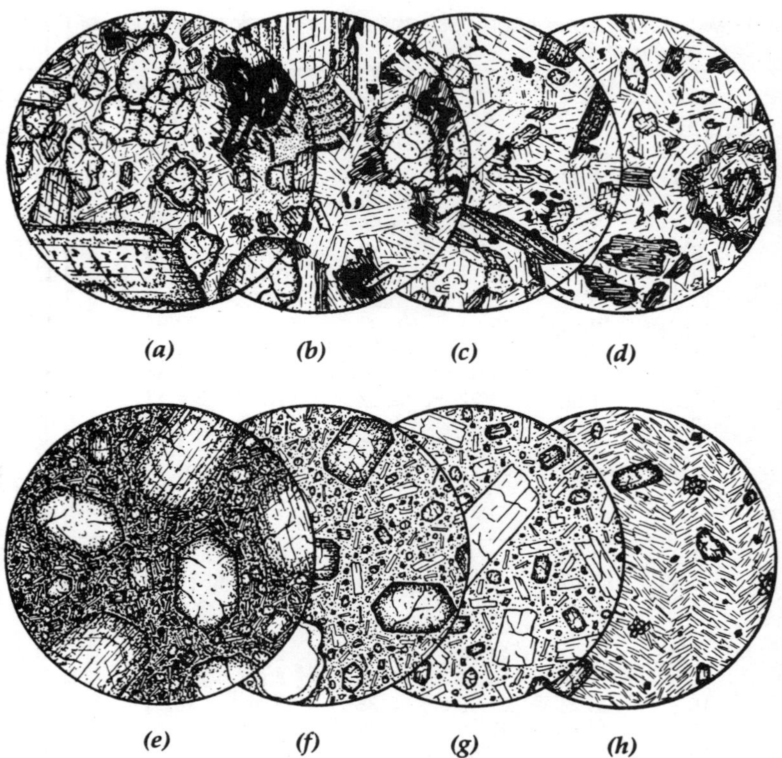

Figure 7-10 Petrographic features of the alkaline plutonic (a-d) and volcanic rocks (e-h) of Tahiti. (a) is an olivine gabbro with zoned Ti-augite and titaniferous magnetite rimmed with bioite. A more evolved gabbro (b) has alkali feldspar between the earlier-crystallizing plagioclase crystals. Apatite is an abundant accessory mineral. A nepheline-bearing, two-feldspar monzonite (c) contains a Ti-rich amphibole, kaersutite. (d) is a nepheline syenite containing reddish biotite, green Na-augite, sphene, and clots of magnetite, augite, and biotite. The most mafic lavas are ankaramites (e) with abundant phenocrysts of olivine and augite. They grade into intermediate compositions (f and g) with increasing amounts of alkali feldspar, analcite, and feldspathoidal minerals, such as hauyne. The most differentiated lavas are phonolites (h) composed of alkali feldspar, nepheline, sphene, and lesser amounts of amphibole and magnetite in a glassy trachytic groundmass.

Series, which formed large, central-vent volcanoes, evolved during a later stage and though volumetrically subordinate had a greater proportion and range of differentiated rocks. The basic magma of the Plateau Series has all the chemical and petrographic attributes of alkaline basalts. It differs from the tholeiitic basalts of the Main Magma Series in being poorer in SiO_2 and richer in MgO, TiO_2, alkalies, and olivine.

Each of these basalts has its own series of differentiates. The alkaline basalts of the Plateau Series are associated, both in space and time, with small volumes of mildly alkaline hawaiites, mugearites, benmoreites, and trachytes, not unlike Hawaiian rocks of the same names. In a similar way, the tholeiitic basalt of the

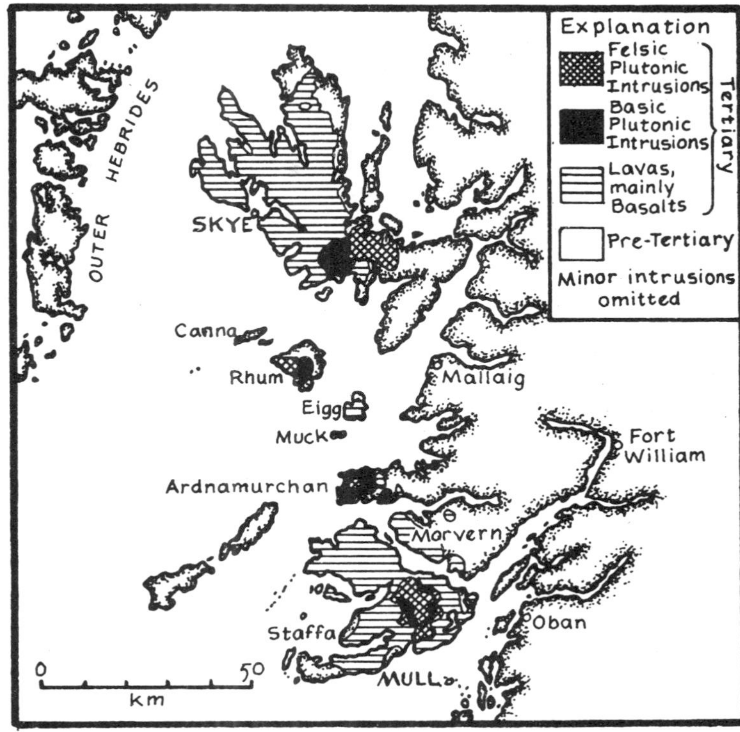

Figure 7–11 The principal igneous centers of western Scotland.

Main Magma Series was the forerunner and presumed parent of a series of progressively more differentiated rocks that culminated in granites and rhyolites. The local names originally assigned to the intermediate rocks correspond closely to what are now called ferro-basalts and icelandites.

It is instructive to consider the reasoning that led different geologists to arrive at directly opposing interpretations of the relations between these two series. The original workers who studied the field and petrographic relations concluded that the voluminous alkaline basalt of the Plateau Series was a primary mantle-derived magma and that the tholeiitic basalt of the Main Magma Series was the product of contamination of the original magma with continental crust. This inference seemed logical, because siliceous granitic and metamorphic rocks visibly underlie the volcanic centers and are found as inclusions in the lavas. Because olivine-rich alkaline basalts are widespread on oceanic islands as well as continents, they were deemed the best candidates for a primary, worldwide, basaltic magma derived directly from an olivine-rich mantle. Tholeiites, it was thought, were confined to continental settings, where basaltic magma rose through thick sialic crust. It seemed reasonable, therefore, to attribute them to contamination of alkaline basaltic magma with siliceous metamorphic and granitic material.

An American petrologist, N. L. Bowen, demonstrated the weakness of this interpretation. He showed by a simple calculation that the composition of any material that must be added to the alkaline basalts to produce tholeiites is quite unlike that of any plausible continental rock. He pointed out that the compositional variations on Harker diagrams are consistent with crystal fractionation of the kind predicted by laboratory experiments, and he outlined a sequence of crystallization by which he thought the tholeiites could have evolved from the alkaline basalts.

Bowen's work had a logic and rigor that gave it great intellectual appeal. His explanation of the Scottish magmas, however, was not without its own problems. Indeed, the geologists who originally studied the rocks had already considered and rejected the possibility that parental magmas of the two series were related by crystal fractionation. They reached this conclusion mainly from petrographic evidence that was in clear conflict with Bowen's explanation. Look again at the two basalts shown in Table 7-1 and note that the last interstitial liquid to crystallize from the alkaline magmas was not a silica-rich differentiate, as Bowen said it should be if olivine crystallized in abundance and without reaction. Instead, alkali feldspar and silica-poor minerals, such as analcite or natrolite, occur as late-crystallizing phases in the interstices between earlier crystals of plagioclase, pyroxene, and olivine. But where the alkaline basalt contains interstitial minerals enriched in alkalies and depleted in silica, the tholeiite contains quartz. In other words, each rock contained within its groundmass a late differentiate with the essential mark of its derivative rock series—one enriched in silica, the other poor in silica and rich in alkalies. Neither Bowen nor the Scottish geologists knew at that time that a thermal divide separates the liquid lines of descent of the two contrasting magmas, but, if they had, this simple observation, based solely on petrographic evidence, could have provided the clue needed to explain the basic relationships between the two magma series.

It was impossible to reconcile the difficulties inherent in any mechanism, whether it be contamination, crystal fractionation, or any of the various ingenious schemes invoked to make one basalt from another, so long as the Plateau Magma was thought to be the only primary mantle-derived magma and, hence, the parent of all others. In Scotland, it was logical to assume this to be so. The Plateau Lavas had almost all the attributes of a primary magma—it was the earliest, most frequently recurring, most voluminous, and most basic rock in the province—but it was not necessarily the only primitive undifferentiated basalt, and the belief that it was proved to be the basic fallacy underlying the entire controversy.

Debate continued for a decade or more, until the hypothesis of crustal contamination was dealt a fatal blow by the simple observation that tholeiites are not confined to continents. Alfred Lacroix was the first to point out, in 1928, that sub-alkaline (tholeiitic) basalts are also found in the oceans, notably in Hawaii where they make up the main mass of huge shield volcanoes, such as Mauna Loa and Kilauea. Other workers reached similar conclusions, and as samples from the deep ocean floor became available in increasing numbers, it was soon apparent that tholeiites are by far the most common basalt in the oceanic basins. Since continental crust is absent from the deep oceans, it is obviously impossible for tholeiites to be products of assimilation of silica-rich granitic and metamorphic rocks by a primary alkaline basalt.

It did not follow, however, that Bowen's scheme offered a better solution. The Hawaiian volcanoes discharge enormous volumes of tholeiitic basalt throughout the main shield-building period, and alkaline basalts appear only in small volumes in the late stages of declining growth. Thus, the order of appearance and relative volumes are the reverse of those in Scotland, and if one uses the accepted criteria for a parental magma and holds to the concept of a single primordial basalt, a tholeiite must be the primary magma of Hawaii and alkaline basalts the products of its differentiation!

With the problem now reversed, several schemes were devised to explain these inferred relations. One of the most durable of these was a process of assimilation of limestone and "de-silication" proposed by R. A. Daly as early as 1910. Daly was an unusually perceptive geologist with wide experience in the field. He documented many field occurrences of strongly alkaline rocks closely associated with limestones, and he described how reaction with carbonate xenoliths caused lime to combine with silica and other components of the magma to precipitate Ca-rich pyroxene and plagioclase, leaving a de-silicated liquid. These effects have been described in terms of simple chemical reactions, such as

$$\underset{\text{calcite}}{CaCO_3} + \underset{\text{hypersthene}}{3(Mg,Fe)SiO_3} \rightarrow \underset{\text{augite}}{Ca(Mg,Fe)Si_2O_6} + \underset{\text{olivine}}{(Mg,Fe)_2SiO_4} + \underset{\text{gas}}{CO_2\uparrow}$$

and

$$\underset{\text{calcite}}{CaCO_3} + \underset{\text{plagioclase}}{2(Ca,Na)(Al,Si)_2Si_2O_8} + \underset{\text{melt}}{Al_2O_3} \rightarrow \underset{\text{anorthite}}{2CaAl_2Si_2O_8} + \underset{\text{nepheline}}{NaAlSiO_4} + \underset{\text{gas}}{CO_2\uparrow}$$

The first equation expresses the way in which addition of lime might convert a hypersthene-normative magma to an olivine-normative one, and the second shows how the melt could become nepheline-normative. If the assimilated material also contained aluminous clay, Al_2O_3 would not be depleted from the melt. The limestone would also act as a flux to reduce the viscosity of the magma and facilitate crystal settling and differentiation. At the same time, CO_2 released in the same process would account for the explosive nature of many alkaline magmas. It seemed quite reasonable to postulate coral reefs buried within the internal structure of oceanic volcanoes where they could be assimilated in a shallow reservoir. A lively debate raged over the merits of this scheme until it was finally put to rest by clear geochemical evidence. If alkaline basalts are richer than tholeiites in certain elements, such as Ni, TiO_2, and alkalies, how could they be produced by assimilation of rocks that are nearly devoid of these components?

Clearly, the solution to the problem is not to be found in processes operating at shallow depths; one must look to levels of the mantle where the magmas originate.

MANTLE ORIGINS OF BASALTS

Having seen that the concept of a single primary basaltic magma from which all others can be derived through shallow differentiation fails to explain the diversity of igneous series, we are left to conclude that the mantle is capable of yielding more than one type of primitive magma. The question, then, is not how all magmas can stem from a common parent but rather how basalts of differing compositions can be derived from the mantle.

Before addressing this question, we should examine more critically the assumption that the parental basaltic magmas to which magma series have been related are the most basic (or "primitive") visible member of that series and that this parental magma is a primary, mantle-derived liquid. At first glance, it seems inconceivable that basalts could themselves be derivative liquids. They erupt at high temperatures, often in very large volumes of nearly uniform compositions. On closer examination, however, certain characteristics of common basalts are difficult to reconcile with direct derivation through melting of the mantle.

We noted in chapter 2, for example, that most basalts erupt at temperatures on or close to their liquidus, and all their essential minerals begin to crystallize within a narrow interval of temperature. We speak of such basalts as being "multiply saturated." The basalt of the Hawaiian lava lake, to which we have referred so often, is an example. Though its temperature of eruption, about 1,200 °C, is close to the maximum ever recorded, the magma already contained phenocrysts of olivine. Moreover, the other major minerals, pyroxene and plagioclase, began to crystallize after only ten to twenty degrees of cooling. Neither of these observations is consistent with what would be expected if basaltic magmas rise directly from their source in the mantle.

Consider first the fact that the temperature of eruption is close to or slightly below the liquidus. We can say at the outset (from the principle of LeChatelier) that melting, because it entails an increase of volume, must occur at higher temperatures at depth than at atmospheric pressure. The amount by which the melting temperature increases with pressure can be estimated from the Clapeyron equation. If we assume that a basalt with a liquidus temperature of 1,200 °C at the surface has a volumetric increase, ΔV, on melting of .03 cm^3 and a heat of fusion, ΔH_f, of 100 cal g^{-1}, and the mechanical equivalent of heat is 41.84 bar cm^3 cal^{-1}, then

$$\frac{dT}{dP} = \frac{T\Delta V}{\Delta H_f} = \frac{1473 \times 0.03}{100 \times 41.84} = 0.01° \text{ bar}^{-1} \text{ or } \sim 3° \text{ km}^{-1} \qquad (7\text{-}1)$$

Thus, the liquidus temperature of the basalt at a depth of fifty kilometers would be about 150° above the value at surface conditions. A basalt at a temperature of 1,200° would be largely, if not totally, crystalline at that depth. It is clear, therefore, that a magma of this kind must originally have been hotter and lost heat en route to the surface.

Cooling could result from two effects. A magma loses heat to the rocks through which it rises, and it cools as a result of its expansion with relief of pressure. Just as a compressed gas cools when it expands, so too does a liquid. The amount of this adiabatic cooling (i.e., cooling at constant heat content) resulting from relief of pressure on a rising magma can be estimated from the relation

$$\frac{dT}{dP} = \frac{T\alpha}{\rho C_P} \tag{7-2a}$$

where α is the coefficient of thermal expansion (about 3×10^{-5} deg^{-1}), and C_P is heat capacity (about 0.3 cal g^{-1} deg^{-1}). Thus, for mantle temperatures and densities, the effect of adiabatic cooling would be:

$$\frac{(1200 + 273) \times 3 \times 10^{-5}}{2.7 \times 0.3 \times 41.84} = 0.001° \text{ bar}^{-1} \tag{7-2b}$$

or between 0.2 and 0.3 degrees per kilometer of rise. This value is only a tenth or so of the melting-temperature gradient estimated from the Clapeyron equation and is negligible compared to the difference between the temperature of eruption and that of melting. Hence, the fact that basalts erupt with little if any superheat and at temperatures well below those at which they formed cannot be attributed to relief of pressure. It must mean that rising basaltic liquids lose heat to their surroundings. They expend part of the heat by melting crystals that they initially had in suspension or are exposed to in the walls of a conduit.

Consider next the observation that many basaltic liquids are close to being multiply saturated; that is to say they begin to crystallize their three principal minerals—olivine, pyroxene, and plagioclase—over a narrow range of temperature. A liquid close to equilibrium with all of these minerals at low pressures (Fig. 7–12a) is not likely to be in equilibrium with the same minerals at high pressure, nor can it have the same composition (Fig. 7–12b). The effect of pressure on the liquidus temperatures must differ from one mineral to another. Each mineral has different thermodynamic properties, and the rate of increase of its liquidus temperature with pressure, dT/dP, must also differ. Thus, liquid compositions that crystallize a given set of minerals simultaneously at the surface cannot have been multiply saturated and in equilibium with those same minerals at some greater pressure. By the same reasoning, any liquid produced by melting must have been saturated simultaneously with the crystalline phases of its source rock at the conditions of melting, and a basalt that preserves its primary composition inherited from saturation with the residual phases of its source at high pressures would precipitate these minerals over a wide span of temperature at the surface (Fig. 7–12c).

The fact that many basalts contain phenocrysts of olivine does not necessarily mean these same basalts would be in equilibrium with an olivine-rich mantle at high pressures. Experimental studies of natural basalts at high pressures indicate that most are not. Because olivine is among the most abundant phases of the mantle, even at advanced stages of melting, it follows that basaltic liquids that are not saturated with olivine at high pressures must have evolved in composition from a more primitive, mantle-derived melt.

Most rising magmas must react thermally and chemically with the cooler rocks through which they rise, and in so doing change composition, either by precipitating one or more minerals or by melting or reacting with their wall-

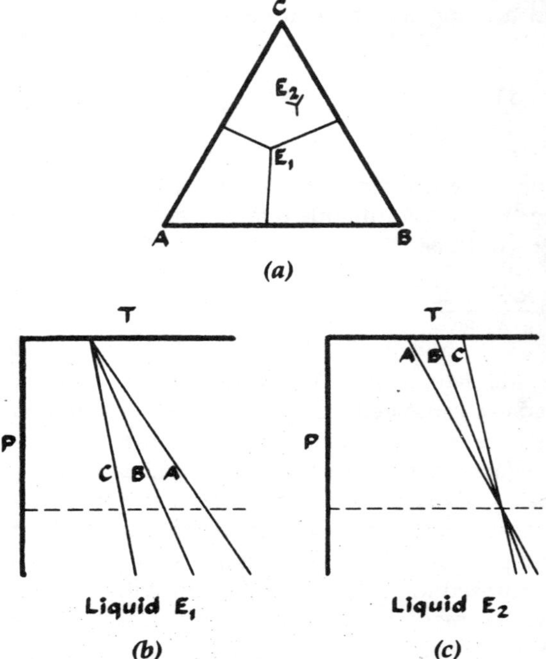

Figure 7–12 Schematic illustration of the stability relations of minerals in basaltic liquids at two different pressures. A liquid in equilibrium with three minerals, A, B, and C, at the surface would have the composition of the low-pressure invariant point E_1 (a). When projected to high pressures, as shown in (b), the stability curves of the individual minerals diverge and are no longer in equilibrium with the same liquid at the same pressure and temperature. Conversely, a liquid, E_2, in equilibrium with the same minerals at high pressure (c) will not be in equilibrium at a single temperature with the same minerals at the surface.

rocks. The net effect, then, is for magmatic liquids to approach temperatures and compositions at the surface that correspond to equilibrium conditions at low pressures. One implication of this conclusion is that few aphyric lavas can be original, mantle-derived liquids. Before this simple fact was recognized, petrologists searching for the elusive "primary magma" shunned porphyritic rocks, because they feared that the phenocrysts could have accumulated from other liquids and that the bulk composition of such a rock would not correspond to that of a liquid. It is realized now that porphyritic lavas, such as picritic basalts containing many phenocrysts of olivine, may be closer in composition to original, mantle-derived liquids than are aphyric lavas that must have evolved from another composition.

If the mantle produced only one primary magma, and re-equilibration of that magma were always perfect, all basalts would arrive at the surface with identical major-element compositions and would retain little decipherable evidence of their origin in the mantle. The fact that all basalts are not reduced to a single composition shows that, although they may re-equilibrate, they do so to differing degrees and may follow somewhat different lines of evolution depending on their initial composition and mode of ascent. We cannot see through these later effects without knowing more about how magmas are generated at unseen depths of the mantle.

MECHANISMS OF MAGMA GENERATION

At the outset, we should note that it is unlikely that melting of the mantle is simply a spontaneous result of an accumulation of heat produced by decay of its radioactive elements. Mantle concentrations of U, Th, and K are so small (Table 1-2) that, even if all their heat were to contribute to melting, times of the order of ten million years would be required to yield just one weight percent of melt. Moreover, these elements are so effectively partitioned into the first fraction of melt that separation of this liquid would leave the mantle so depleted of heat-producing elements that it would lose its capacity to generate further magma. The earth has many regions where magmatism has continued for many tens or hundreds of millions of years.

The largest and most readily available source of energy for melting is the heat in the rocks themselves. The problem of magma generation is primarily one of finding mechanisms that draw on the stored heat of large masses of rock to produce relatively small amounts of melt. A number of mechanical and thermal schemes have been proposed to explain how this might be accomplished.

Consider a temperature profile in the lithosphere and a convecting asthenosphere, such as the one shown schematically in Figure 7-13. Several changes could lead to melting under these conditions: (a) an influx of heat and increase of temperature at constant pressure and composition, (b) a decrease of pressure at constant heat content and composition, and (c) a change of composition at constant heat content and pressure. Certain physical limits can be placed on each of these.

(a) Assume, first, that an influx of heat from some unspecified deeper source enters the horizon where rocks are already close to their solidus temperature. A critical thermal property of silicates, noted in chapter two, is their large heat of fusion, ΔH_f (about 65 to 100 cal g^{-1}), relative to specific heat, C_P (about 0.2 to 0.3 cal g^{-1} deg^{-1}). Each calorie of added heat produces about 0.01 gram of melt. On the other hand, the same amount of heat can raise the temperature of a gram of rock (while still below its melting temperature) by more than three degrees. Because melting absorbs such large amounts of heat, it tends to hold the temperature within the melting range. But only a relatively small amount of heat is needed to raise a rock to its melting temperature. Thus, any added heat quickly raises the temperature profile in rocks below their solidus, but once melting begins temperatures rise much more slowly. In this way, melting has the effect of stabilizing temperature gradients and smoothing the effect of any heat flux.

(b) Suppose that, instead of an influx of heat, the rocks are raised to a level of lower pressure, possibly as a result of convective upwelling of the mantle. A rock that was already close to the temperature at which it would begin to melt would now be in a realm where it should be partly liquid. Even though no heat is added, crystals will begin to melt by drawing on the stored heat of the rocks.

As we saw from equation 7-2, adiabatic expansion results in cooling of about 1°C per kilobar or roughly a third of a degree per kilometer. But the reduction of pressure lowers the solidus temperature much more, about 10° per kilobar; so for one kilobar the amount of heat available for melting would be (10 − 1) deg. ×

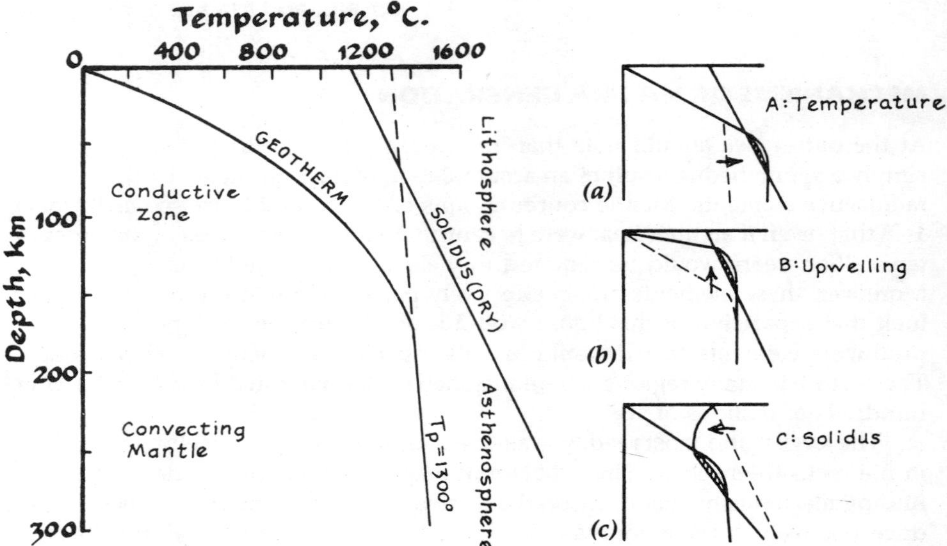

Figure 7-13 The configuration shown on the left represents a possible relationship between a conductive thermal gradient in the lithosphere and an adiabatic gradient in a convecting asthenosphere having a potential temperature of 1300°C. These two gradients are separated by a thermal boundary layer near the boundary between the lithosphere and asthenosphere. The solidus temperature for the mantle is shown for dry conditions. The small diagrams on the right illustrate the effects of (a) raising temperature by an influx of heat, (b) lowering pressure by upwelling of the asthenosphere, and (c) lowering the solidus curve by introducing another component, such as a volatile. Note that in all three cases, the temperature of the cross-hatched zone of melting is less than it would be if there had been no melting. (Adapted from D. P. McKenzie and M. J. Bickle, 1988, *Jour. Petrol.* 29:625–679 and D. M. Latin, J. E. Dixon, J. G. Fitton, and N. White, 1990, *Geol. Soc. Spec. Publ.* 55:207–227).

0.3 cal g^{-1} deg^{-1} = 2.7 calories per gram, or enough to melt 2 or 3 percent of a rock with a heat of fusion of 100 cal g^{-1}.

This effect tends to hold the temperature of the rising mantle close to its melting curve. Just as the amount of adiabatic cooling of rising air is moderated by the heat liberated when moisture condenses, the temperature of upwelling mantle is strongly buffered by melting or any other endothermic, pressure-induced phase change.

Note, however, that if the temperature of the mantle is close to the adiabatic gradient and below the melting curve, upwelling results in no excess of temperature or enthalpy, because, by definition, the adiabatic gradient is one of constant heat content. Thus mantle rising from any depth along this gradient will have the same temperature when it reaches a given level, provided, of course, that no melting or phase changes occur en route. One can speak of the adiabatic mantle as having a *potential temperature*, which is defined as the temperature at which the adiabatic gradient would intersect the surface. This term provides a useful way of visualizing the behavior of upwelling mantle that is on an adiabatic gradient and below the solidus curve where melting begins.

(c) The third melting mechanism requires neither an influx of heat nor a change of pressure but an addition of components, such as H_2O or alkalies, that lower the melting temperature. This fluxing action might result from an introduction of volatiles, either from a source at greater depth or from breakdown of a volatile-bearing mineral in the rock itself.

Although the combined volatile contents of H_2O and CO_2 in basalts are probably less than 1 weight percent, even these small amounts could have a large effect on melting. Liquidus temperatures of basalt are lowered as much as 100°C by only 0.1 percent water, and other volatiles, as well as alkalies, have comparable effects.

Several mechanisms have been proposed by which mechanical energy could generate heat and cause melting. One, of course, is meteorite impact. This was certainly important in the early history of the earth and moon.

A more important mechanism today is one based on the effect of stress on the physical properties of rocks at high temperatures. If mechanical energy is converted to heat in a zone of deformation, the result could be a "positive feedback" effect that leads to melting. Part of the heat generated by shear is normally dissipated by conduction into the surrounding colder rocks, leaving the highest temperatures centered near the locus of maximum deformation. The elevated temperature in that region reduces the viscosity and strength of the sheared rocks by amounts that are proportional to the rise in temperature. This causes further deformation to be channeled into a progressively narrower zone where the rocks are hottest and hence weaker. The concentration of shear in a narrower zone also localizes the heat production and further reduces the strength of the rocks. Under conditions of constant stress, the result would be to concentrate the deformation and heat in a narrow zone that would eventually begin to melt. Under conditions of constant strain, however, the opposite is true; the decrease of viscosity results in less energy being consumed by viscous dissipation for a given strain rate, and the system approaches a steady state. Deformation in nature is probably somewhere between these two limiting conditions.

Favored depths of melting

Certain levels of the mantle are more likely to melt than others. One example was seen in Figure 7–13 where the change of slope of the thermal gradient creates a zone that is convex toward the melting curve; a similar effect can result from the effect of pressure on the form of the solidus. Because the slope of the solidus curve varies with the nature of the phases in the stable assemblage at different pressures, the melting curve for the mantle cannot be a simple straight line. Instead it will change slope, particularly where the aluminous phase changes, first from plagioclase to spinel and then to garnet (Fig. 7–14). The resulting curve will have one or more cusps where these changes occur. If a cusp is convex toward lower temperature, a rising thermal gradient will first intersect the solidus at that level, and melt will be produced there in greater proportion than elsewhere. Similar relations are thought to hold where the geothermal gradient changes abruptly near the base of the lithosphere (Fig. 7–13.) We shall see later that these conditions may have an important effect on the depths of melting and compositions of oceanic basalts.

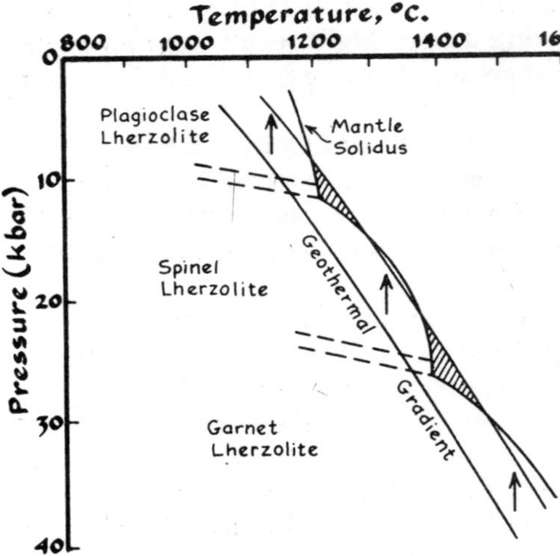

Figure 7-14 Melting at a cusp in the mantle solidus. Note that the change of slope resulting from a transition from one aluminous phase to another causes the solidus to be convex toward the thermal gradient. The levels at which this occurs would be favored places for melting, either by rising temperature, falling pressure, or lowering of the solidus. (Adapted from E. Takahashi and I. Kushiro, 1983, *Amer. Min.* 68:859–879.)

Mobilization of mantle-derived liquids

Under the high pressures at depths where melting occurs, extraction of even small amounts of liquid may be very efficient. Melting of a mantle peridotite normally begins around unstable hydrous minerals or at grain boundaries where incompatible components tend to be concentrated. Junctions where three or more minerals are in close proximity are especially favored, because the melting temperature is lower where more phases are in close contact.

The form of pockets of melt depends in large measure on the degree to which the liquid wets the surfaces of crystals. If the "wetability" is strong, the liquid penetrates grain boundaries, and pools of melt at triple junctions have the form of prisms or tetrahedra with concave sides and dihedral angles of less than about 60 degrees (Fig. 7–15). The liquid in isolated pockets moves very slowly, if at all, but when these pockets become interconnected and form a continuous, interconnected network it can begin to move under any driving force, such as buoyancy or stress, that provides a pressure differential. The amount of melt necessary for this to happen is probably very small, certainly less than 10 percent and possibly as little as 1 percent. More melt is required for pyroxene-rich peridotites than for more easily deformed olivine-rich rocks, such as dunite.

As it moves, the liquid tends to collect in fewer but larger channels where the resistance to flow is least. The moving melt generates heat by viscous dissipation and tends to enlarge channelways where the flow is greatest. Thinner, more tortuous routes are abandoned in favor of a smaller number of larger channels, and with time a dendritic system could form much like the roots of a tree.

Rising to shallower depths, the liquid eventually reaches the transition from plastic to brittle deformation where, instead of seeping slowly upward through intergranular channels, it rises through fractures that it propagates as it advances. Owing to the difference in density between the liquid and solid

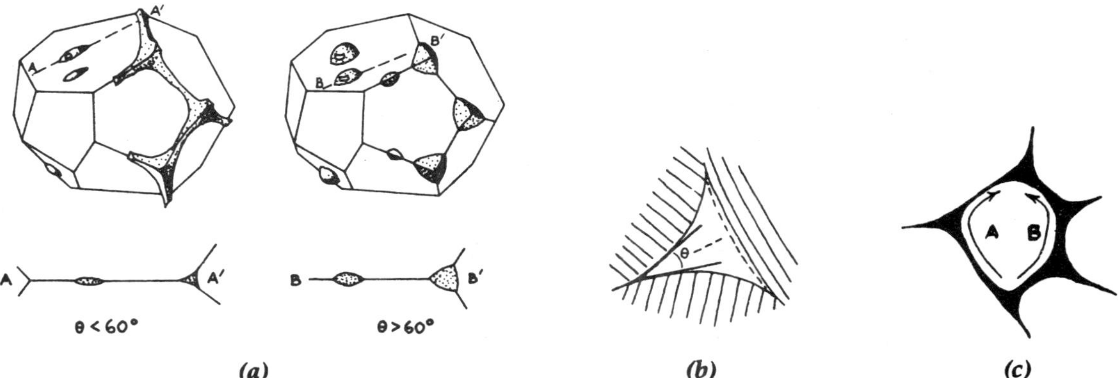

Figure 7-15 (a) Melting begins at the junctions of a combination of mineral grains that corresponds to the lowest-temperature melt. The form the melt takes depends on the amount of melting and the degree to which the liquid wets the surface. Pools of melt tend to have concave sides with dihedral angles, θ, less than 60° if they wet the crystals (left) but convex sides (right) if they do not. (b) The dihedral angle also varies with the crystallographic orientation of minerals that melt more readily in one direction than another. (c) The permeability of the rock is governed mainly by the narrowest channels, which are usually between the flat surfaces of crystals. As liquid migrates through these spaces it tends to follow a progressively smaller number of preferred channels. The liquid following course A, for example, will be slower than that along course B, if it must follow a thinner or more tortuous channel. The flow tends to widen the preferred channels even more by thermal erosion. In addition to the heat brought from greater depths, the moving liquid generates heat by viscous dissipation, and the channel with the greatest rate of flow will also have the greatest heat. With time, course A will be abandoned, and course B will be enlarged. (Part (a) after E. B. Watson and J. M. Brenan, 1987, *Earth Planet. Sci. Ltrs.* 85:497–515.)

columns, the liquid exerts a stress on its walls that is proportional to the density difference and vertical dimension of the channel. Depending on the temperature and state of regional stress in the rocks, this change from plastic to brittle conditions is probably in the vicinity of twenty-five to thirty kilometers.

Entering this new regime, the liquid can flow more rapidly. Chemical equilibration with the walls is less efficient under these conditions than thermal equilibration, owing, of course, to the large difference between the rates of chemical and thermal diffusion. Thermal erosion can still enlarge the channel. Because the large surface area of a fracture allows a liquid under pressure to exert a large total force on the rock, a planar shape is mechanically the most efficient form for opening a channel. But it is not the most efficient form once the liquid is flowing. A pipe-like channel, since it has less surface area, offers less resistance to viscous flow and reduces the loss of heat by conduction to the wall rocks. Hence, with time thermal erosion tends to make planar channels more cylindrical.

Magmas may not necessarily rise through the mantle as crystal-free liquids; under some conditions, they may be mushes with large proportions of crystals. As we noted in chapter 2, the viscosity of crystal-liquid assemblages declines sharply when the fraction of melt exceeds 40 or 50 percent. A marked transition occurs when crystals are no longer in grain-to-grain contact, and most of the stress is borne by the liquid. At that stage, a crystal-rich melt can deform more easily and flow as a viscous entity. If mantle rocks reach this degree of melting, they could rise as crystal-rich diapirs, provided, of course, they are less dense than the surrounding mantle. Much evidence suggests that this happens under subduction-related volcanic belts (chapter nine).

Although melting is normally thought of as producing a light, buoyant liquid and a refractory residue of increased density, this may not always be the case for melting of the deep mantle; more likely, both the basaltic liquid and residual products of melting are less dense than the original rock. The reason for this lies in the density relations of the liquid and crystals. The two most important components contributing to the high density of the mantle are the aluminous phases, garnet and spinel, and the iron-rich components of olivine and pyroxene. During melting, both of these tend to enter the liquid fraction. Garnet and spinel contribute proportionately large amounts to the liquid, and melting depletes them more rapidly than it does other minerals of lower density. Moreover, since all silicate liquids are more iron-rich than the ferromagnesian crystals with which they are is in equilibrium, melting must lower the iron contents of residual crystals. Hence, the result could be a marked decrease in the density of the refractory residue, making it lighter than the original undepleted mantle. If so, both the liquid and residual solid would be less dense than the original unmelted rock.

MINERALOGICAL COMPOSITION OF SOURCE ROCKS IN THE MANTLE

We saw in the opening chapter that the large-scale geochemical balance of the earth places broad limits on the possible compositions of the core, mantle, and crust (Table 1–1). Moreover, the mantle must include enough of the essential components of basalts to yield mechanically separable quantities of liquid, and the degree of melting required to do this must be compatible with the physical properties of the mantle measured by geophysical means.

Geochemical and geophysical evidence indicates that the most important minerals of the mantle must be olivine and pyroxene, and, if so, these minerals contain Si, Mg, Ca, and Fe in amounts that are more than adequate to satisfy the requirements of basaltic melts. Accounting for the other essential components of basalt—Al, Na, K, and a host of minor and trace elements—is more difficult. Some may be in accessory phases; others may be secondary components or impurities of the more abundant minerals.

Al_2O_3

At low pressures, almost all the alumina in mafic igneous rocks is contained in plagioclase. As already noted (in chapter four), at high pressures this component enters clinopyroxene as the Ca-tschermak's molecule (CaTs–$CaAl_2SiO_6$) and jadeite (Jd–$NaAlSi_2O_6$) and, to a lesser extent, it enters Ca-poor pyroxenes as the Mg-tschermak molecule (MgTs–$MgAl_2SiO_6$). Experiments show that the amount of alumina contained in pyroxenes increases with both pressure and temperature; it reaches a maximum of about 4.5 percent for mantle assemblages at pressures of about twenty kilobars and at temperatures approaching those of basaltic melts. Beyond that limit, any additional alumina must enter a separate phase, such as spinel or garnet, and, because these latter minerals are denser than pyroxene, they become increasingly important at higher pressures.

The experimentally determined stability ranges of the principal aluminous phases are shown in Figure 7-16. The boundaries are only approximate, because they are affected by the bulk composition of the rock. For example, rocks rich in alumina may contain both plagioclase and spinel together over a range of pressures and temperatures. This is especially true of compositions rich in normative albite, which tends to extend the stability range of plagioclase to higher pressures.

At pressures greater than about fifteen kilobars, garnet may be a stable aluminous phase, at least at temperatures below the melting range of basaltic liquids. At temperatures approaching the solidus, where melting begins, the thermally expanded crystal lattice of pyroxene can accommodate more alumina, and the stability of garnet is reduced. For this reason it is difficult to say from phase relations alone whether or not garnet is a stable phase in equilibrium with basaltic melts in the mantle; one must also know the bulk composition of the rocks and the position of the melting curve with respect to the stability fields of garnet and aluminous pyroxene.

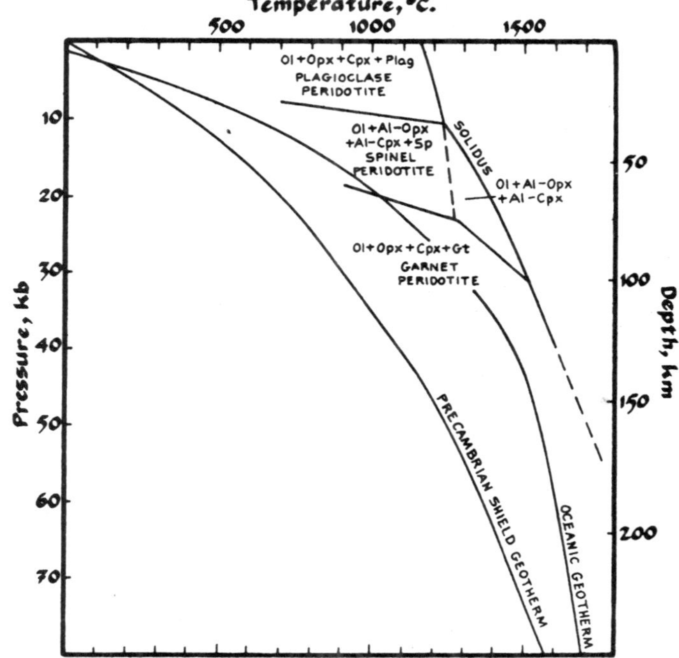

Figure 7-16 Stability ranges of the essential phases of the mantle. (Adapted from D. H. Green, 1970, *Trans. Leicester Lit. Phil. Soc.* 64:28–54 and E. Takahashi and I. Kushiro, 1983, *Amer. Min.* 68:859–879.)

The succession of reactions for the changes from one aluminous phase to another can be written in terms of plagioclase and olivine in the following simplified sequence:

$$\underset{\text{An}}{2CaAl_2Si_2O_8} + \underset{\text{Fo}}{2Mg_2SiO_4} \rightarrow \underset{\text{Di}}{CaMgSiO_2O_6} \cdot \underset{\text{CaTs}}{nCaAl_2SiO_6} + \underset{\text{En}}{2Mg_2Si_2O_6}$$

$$\cdot\ \underset{\text{MgTs}}{mMgAl_2SiO_6} + \underset{\text{spinel}}{MgAl_2O_4}$$

and for the albitic component:

$$\underset{\text{Ab}}{NaAlSi_3O_8} + \underset{\text{Fo}}{Mg_2SiO_4} \rightarrow \underset{\text{Jd}}{NaAlSi_2O_6} + \underset{\text{En}}{Mg_2Si_2O_6}$$

At higher pressures, the products of the first reaction above go to:

$$\underset{\text{An}}{CaAl_2Si_2O_8} + \underset{\text{Fo}}{Mg_2SiO_4} \rightarrow \underset{\text{garnet}}{CaMg_2Al_2Si_3O_{12}}$$

Because the proportion of olivine to plagioclase in the mantle is much greater than that of the reactants in these equations, olivine is an additional mineral among the products of both reactions.

Alkalies

The jadeite molecule of pyroxene is the main Na-bearing constituent of ultramafic rocks at mantle pressures. Ca-rich pyroxene accepts increasing amounts of jadeite in solid solution at high pressures and depths of more than a few tens of kilometers. With appropriate degrees of melting, it could supply the sodium essential to melts of basaltic composition. Minor amounts of sodium may also be contained in amphibole but only under shallow mantle conditions, because that mineral is unstable at depths of more than a hundred kilometers or so.

Potassium is a different matter; it does not enter pyroxene, olivine, spinel, or garnet in appreciable amounts, and the amounts found in basaltic liquids can be contained only in a separate mineral, such as the magnesian mica, phlogopite, or the potassium feldspar, sanidine. The former is common in peridotites, especially in continental settings; the latter is a theoretical possibility but is very rare in rocks from the mantle. Phlogopite is of special interest for other reasons; first, it contains a potentially important radioactive heat source, potassium, and, second, one of its essential constituents is water.

Volatiles

Of the various possible volatile components of the mantle, H_2O is probably the most important. Even though it is not likely to account for more than a fraction of a percent by weight, it plays an important role in magmas, because, as we shall see shortly, even small amounts can greatly reduce melting temperatures and affect the stability relations of major minerals. Pargasite, a magnesium-rich amphibole, is a common hydrous mineral, particularly in ultramafic xenoliths found in continental volcanoes, but it is stable only at relatively shallow depths, certainly less than 100 kilometers. Phlogopite is probably the most important hydrous mineral that is stable at very high pressures.

Carbon dioxide is another important volatile component of the mantle, especially at depths greater than 70 km. It is contained in calcite, dolomite, and other carbonates that are found as minor but widespread constituents of ultramafic xenoliths of deep origin. Small inclusions of dolomite found in diamonds show that it must be stable at high pressures in the mantle.

ULTRAMAFIC INCLUSIONS

The most direct evidence of the mineral composition of the mantle comes from ultramafic rocks brought to the surface as xenoliths in basaltic magmas. Not all volcanoes yield these exotic inclusions, but a few produce a wealth of coarse-grained "nodules" having great varieties of textures and modal assemblages. A spectacular example is the lava discharged in late 1800 and early 1801 from the Hawaiian volcano Hualalai (Fig. 7–17). Cobble-size fragments of gabbro, dunite, and peridotite are scattered throughout the lava in such numbers that, in places,

Figure 7–17 An alkali olivine basalt erupted from the Hawaiian volcano Hualalai in 1801 and 1802 contains large numbers of mafic and ultramafic xenoliths. Where the fluid lava drained from between the inclusions, it left banks of cobble-size nodules with a thin coating of black glass. (Photo courtesy of D. C. Presnall.)

they settled out of the fluid lava to accumulate in banks several meters thick. Despite the great numbers of these inclusions, it is difficult to find two specimens with the same modal proportions and textures.

Inclusions are especially plentiful in explosive volcanic vents, such as diamond pipes, and in tuff rings or maars formed by magma blasting craters in water-saturated sediments. It is not clear why inclusions should be so much more common in these particular settings. Perhaps the rapid rise and sudden cooling of explosively erupted magma enables them to reach the surface in relatively unaltered form. Where the same magmas erupt more quietly as lava flows, inclusions are less common and tend to show more evidence of re-equilibration to low-pressure conditions.

Most inclusions in oceanic lavas fall into one of four groups (Fig. 7–18):

I. Gabbroic rocks, typically *eucrites*, containing calcic plagioclase (bytownite or anorthite), augite, and olivine.

II. Dunites and wehrlites composed of differing proportions of forsteritic olivine and diopsidic pyroxene. Most contain accessory spinel, plagioclase, or both.

III. Lherzolites and harzburgites containing, in addition to minerals of group II, a magnesian orthopyroxene, usually enstatite. The aluminous phase is spinel.

IV. Garnet peridotites and eclogites consisting of differing proportions of Ca-rich and Ca-poor pyroxene, olivine, and pyrope-rich garnet.

Gabbroic inclusions of Group I are most common; dunites and wehrlites of Group II are slightly less so. In oceanic settings the enstatite-bearing assemblages of Group III are much less common, and the last group of garnet-bearing rocks is known only from a single occurrence at Salt Lake Crater on the island of Oahu, Hawaii. On the continents, however, nodules of Groups III and IV are more widespread.

Garnetiferous inclusions from continental occurrences have been divided into two petrographic types (Figs. 7–18e and f), one with a granular texture and another showing evidence of intense shearing. The latter must result from large-scale plastic flow of the mantle. The name *eclogite* is given to rocks consisting of pyrope-rich garnet and sodium-rich pyroxene (Fig. 7-18g). Orthopyroxene and olivine, if present, are only minor components. The bulk chemical compositions of this type of eclogite are close to that of basalt, of which it is the high-pressure equivalent.

Depths of origin

This remarkable array of exotic rocks must represent a sampling of the levels traversed by rising magmas. The evidence contained in the inclusions, if one can decipher it, provides invaluable clues to the nature of the mantle and the sources from which basalts are derived.

Using the experimentally determined stability relations described in the preceding section (and summarized in Figure 7–16), one can relate the mineralogical

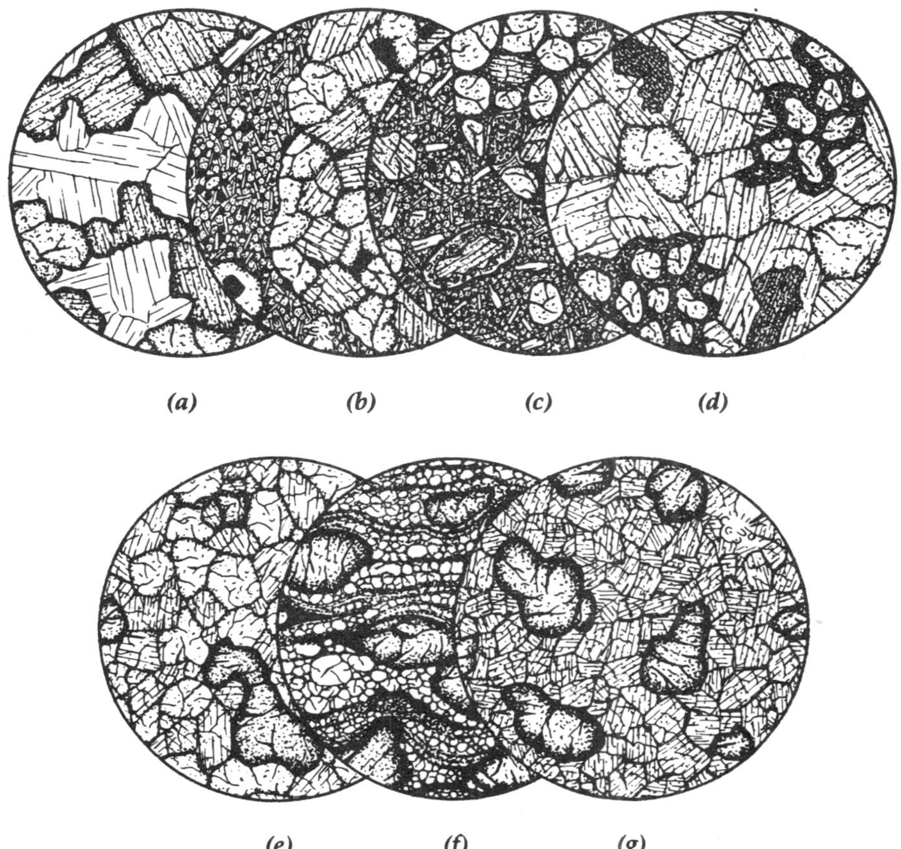

(a) *(b)* *(c)* *(d)*

(e) *(f)* *(g)*

Figure 7–18 Principal types of mafic and ultramafic inclusions found in volcanic rocks. (a) Eucritic gabbro from a tholeiitic volcano in the Galapagos Islands consisting of calcic plagioclase, augite, and olivine. (b) Spinel wehrlite from Hualalai volcano, Hawaii. (c) Spinel lherzolite from a strongly alkaline basanite on Kerguelen Island, south Indian Ocean. Enstatite from the nodule is scattered through the lava. Where it has reacted with the liquid, it is rimmed by a fine-grained aureole made up of the same minerals, olivine and augite, that were crystallizing from the liquid. Enstatite in the outer parts of the nodule also shows evidence of reaction. (d) Garnet peridotite from Kakanui, New Zealand. Dark brown glass surrounds the partly melted garnet and fills interstices between other minerals. Some crystals of pyroxene contain patches of brown amphibole. (e) A granular garnet lherzolite from a South African diamond pipe consists of nearly equidimensional grains of pyroxene, olivine, and garnet with grain boundaries meeting at angles of approximately 120 degrees. This textural configuration is the most stable one for minerals coexisting at high temperatures and pressures. (f) Similar mineral assemblages may be highly sheared, giving the rock a crushed and highly irregular texture. (g) A garnet pyroxenite or "eclogite" from Salt Lake Crater, Oahu, Hawaii.

assemblages to the pressures and temperatures at which they last equilibrated. Spinel, we have seen, replaces plagioclase as the stable aluminous phase at intermediate depths, whereas garnet is stable at greater depths. Thus, the sequence of assemblages in Groups I through IV must be one of increasing pressure.

By calibrating the compositions of associated minerals experimentally, quantitative values can be assigned to the temperatures and pressures recorded by the mineral compositions of mantle xenoliths. For example, the compositions of Ca-rich and Ca-poor pyroxenes coexisting with plagioclase, spinel, or garnet are functions of temperature and pressure. Their contents of calcium and aluminum vary in such a way that the abundances of these two components form a grid on a P-T diagram (Fig. 7–19). Thus, by determining the compositions of pyroxenes in a particular peridotite, one can estimate the temperature and depth at which they last equilibrated.

Figure 7–20 summarizes the estimated temperatures and pressures for two suites of peridotite nodules, an oceanic one from Hawaii and a continental one, mainly from South African diamond pipes. For comparison, estimated geothermal gradients for oceanic and old continental regions are shown, along with two solidus curves corresponding to the beginning of melting of basaltic compositions. The overlap of these various curves shows that the nodules and their host magmas must be closely related and that the latter could be produced by melting at depths of less than 200 km.

The temperatures and pressures recorded by inclusions indicate that magmas are formed in the oceanic mantle at somewhat higher temperatures or lower pressures than those formed under continents. This conclusion is in accord with

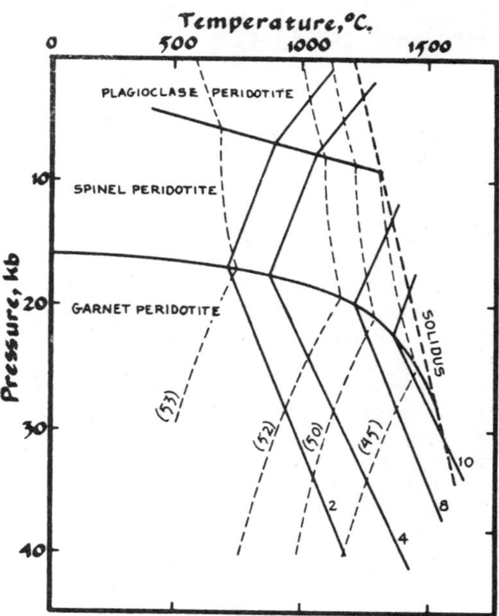

Figure 7–19 T-P-X relations of pyroxenes in equilibrium with olivine and plagioclase, spinel, or garnet. Broken lines are contours of Ca contents (numbers in parentheses), and solid lines are contours of Al contents, (numbers without parentheses). (Adapted from compilation by Carmichael et al., 1974, *Igneous Petrology*, Fig. 12–11.)

Figure 7–20 Ranges of temperature and pressure estimates for ultramafic inclusions from Hawaii (vertical ruling) and continental diamond pipes (horizontal ruling). A range of estimated temperature gradients is indicated by diagonal ruling between the oceanic and continental geotherms. Two curves for the melting of ultramafic mantle rocks are shown, one for dry conditions and another in the presence of 0.2 percent water. The general concordance of temperatures and pressures estimated from pyroxene in ultramafic nodules with the range of probable temperature gradients and melting curves indicates that basaltic liquids can be produced by melting in the upper levels of the mantle if small amounts of water are present.

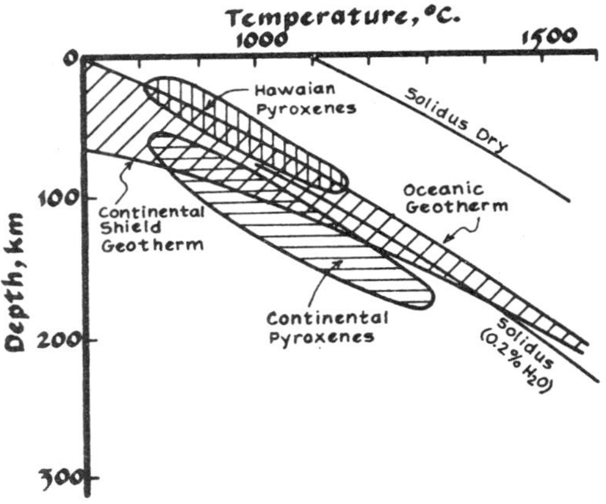

geophysical evidence that indicates a steeper geothermal gradient under the oceans, and it helps explain the differences in suites of ultramafic inclusions found in continental and oceanic volcanoes.

Although many ultramafic inclusions found in continental volcanic rocks resemble those of their oceanic counterparts, the proportions of various types differ in the two settings. As we noted, enstatite-bearing peridotites are much more common in continental suites, and garnetiferous inclusions, which are all but unknown in the oceans, are found in many continental localities. In contrast, peridotites consisting mainly of olivine and aluminous pyroxenes, which are so plentiful in oceanic suites, are less commmon in continental settings. These differences may be related to the differing geothermal gradients of the two types of regions. Referring again to Figure 7–16, note that the steeper oceanic geotherm crosses the stability fields at higher temperatures, where pyroxenes are more aluminous and garnet is less likely to be a stable phase. The lower thermal gradient under the continents, on the other hand, favors garnet-bearing assemblages over a wider pressure range.

Relations of ultramafic inclusions to basaltic magmas

It was obvious even to early investigators that inclusions contain valuable evidence of the deep origins of magmas, but the complex associations and great diversity of these rocks were difficult to fit into any simple genetic scheme. At least three possible origins can be imagined. Some inclusions might be interpreted as fragments of the original mantle from which magmas are derived by partial melting; others are so impoverished in alumina, alkalies, and other essential components of basalt that they could be the depleted refractory residue left after segregation of a partial melt. Still others have textures, compositions, and even layering that give them the appearance of rocks formed by crystal accumulation from cooling magma.

A Japanese petrologist, Hisashi Kuno, was the first to draw attention to a systematic relationship between Hawaiian inclusions and the types of basalt in which they are found. He noted that tholeiitic basalts contain only gabbroic inclusions of Group I, whereas mildly alkaline basalts contain gabbro, dunite, and wehrlite of both Groups I and II. Enstatite-bearing inclusions of Group III are found along with Groups I and II in basalts of more alkaline composition, and inclusions in the strongly silica-deficient basanites on the island of Oahu include, in addition to all other types, garnet-bearing assemblages of Group IV. Thus, the more alkaline and undersaturated the basalt, the greater the range of inclusions it is likely to contain.

Kuno reasoned that if successively more alkaline magmas come from increasing depths in the mantle, each may bring up fragments of the shallower horizons through which it rises. If gabbroic inclusions are the only type found in tholeiitic basalts, then tholeiites have the shallowest source. More alkaline magmas from greater depths bring with them not only rocks from their own source but those of higher levels as well.

This simple interpretation explained why the sequence of increasingly alkaline basalts and their associated inclusions is also one of progressively greater mineralogical contrasts and disequilibrium. Gabbroic inclusions differ only slightly from their tholeiitic host; both contain plagioclase, olivine, and pyroxene, all of which are stable at the surface. This is in contrast to ultramafic rocks in alkaline lavas, which are much poorer in silica and alumina than their hosts and commonly contain spinels that tend to break down or react with other minerals at low pressures. The enstatite in lherzolites and harzburgites of group III is unstable in silica-deficient magmas, and as we would anticipate from what we know about systems like forsterite-silica, it reacts with the alkaline liquid that has brought it to the surface.

Kuno and his co-worker, Ikuo Kushiro, saw in this relationship evidence that the observed minerals have a pressure-dependent stability relationship to their coexisting liquids. They predicted that experiments would show that enstatite is stable in silica-poor liquids at high pressures, and, in due course, when experimental equipment was developed to explore the effects of high pressures (Fig. 7–21), their prediction was fulfilled. This astute deduction, which proved to be a key element in explaining the compositional differences of basalts, was arrived at by a simple projection of the melting temperatures of olivine and enstatite from atmospheric conditions to high pressure.

Although the melting temperature of forsterite is far above that of enstatite at atmospheric pressure (1,890° versus 1,557°C), pressure has a greater effect on enstatite than on forsterite. The reason for this difference is that the change of volume of enstatite on melting, ΔV, is larger, and its heat of fusion, ΔH_f, is less. Substituting appropriate values in the Clapeyron equation, the effect of pressure on the melting temperature, dT/dP, was found to be about 26° per kilobar for enstatite, compared to only 5° for olivine. Hence, with increased pressure the stability field of enstatite expands rapidly at the expense of olivine, and the incongruent melting of enstatite disappears at pressures of more than a few kilobars (Fig. 7–22).

An effect, such as increased pressure, that reduces or eliminates the incongruent melting of enstatite would account for the lower silica contents of liquids

Figure 7–21 Using modern experimental techniques, petrologists can reproduce temperatures and pressures equivalent to those at depths as great as 150 km in the earth's mantle. The apparatus illustrated here is one developed at the Geophysical Laboratory, Washington, D.C., by J. L. England (foreground) and F. R. Boyd (rear). (Courtesy of H. S. Yoder, Jr., Director of the Geophysical Laboratory, Carnegie Institution of Washington.)

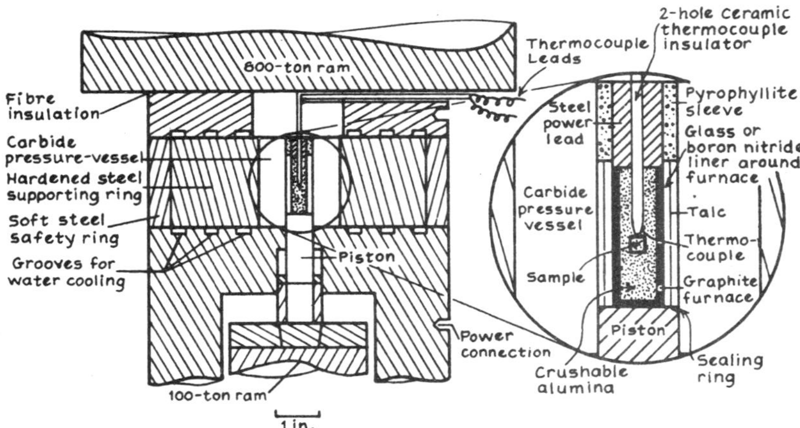

generated at greater depths. At the same time, it would explain why enstatite can be stable in an alkaline magma at mantle depths but react with the same liquid at the surface.

MELTING AT HIGH PRESSURES

The effects of pressure are well-illustrated by the system forsterite-nepheline-silica (Fig. 7-23a) that corresponds to the base of the basalt tetrahedron in Figures 7-1 and 7-3c. The invariant point where melting begins is shown at atmospheric pressure and at ten, twenty, and thirty kilobars. Note the steady

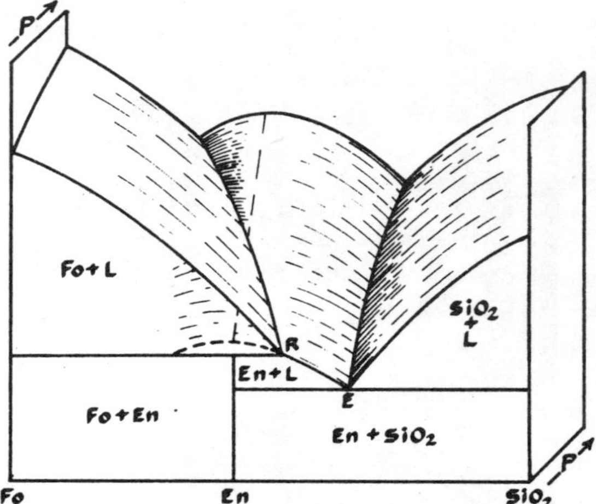

Figure 7–22 Schematic illustration of the effects of pressure on the system forsterite-silica. Note that pressure elevates the liquidus curves of enstatite more than that of forsterite, causing the stability field of forsterite to become smaller as that of enstatite is enlarged. At the same time, the reaction point, R, retreats to lower silica contents until it passes the composition of enstatite and becomes a eutectic. Melting of any asemblage of olivine and enstatite at high pressures will result in a liquid of lower silica content than one produced at low pressures.

migration toward liquids of increasingly more silica-deficient compositions. Similar effects are seen in several other systems.

The relevance of these synthetic systems to natural rocks is illustrated by the results of experiments in which samples of mantle peridotite have been melted at

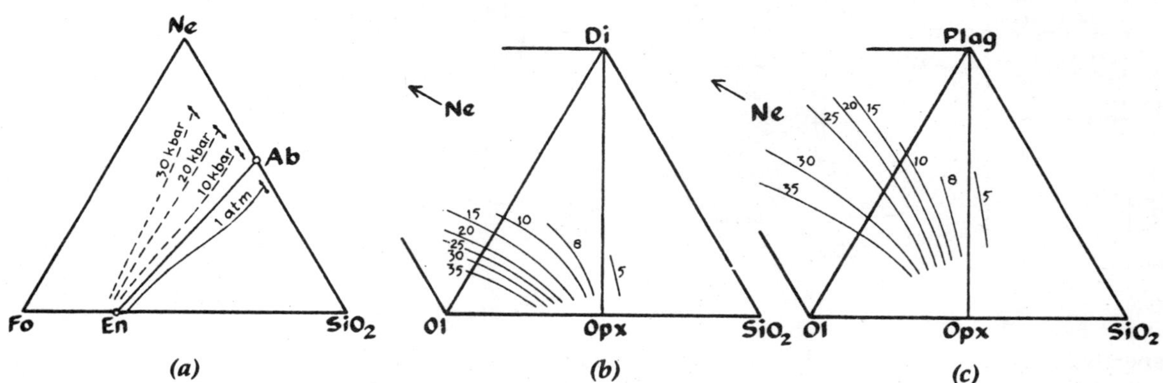

Figure 7–23 (a) Part of the system forsterite-nepheline-silica (Fig. 7–3c) at pressures of one atmosphere, and ten, twenty, and thirty kilobars. Only the invariant points and olivine-pyroxene cotectics are shown. Note the migration of the invariant point toward lower silica contents with increasing pressures. The effects of pressure and degree of melting on the compositions of liquids in equilibrium with a mantle peridotite are shown in terms of the normative components olivine-[illegible]x-quartz and olivine-plagioclase-quartz in (b) and (c) respectively. The light numbered lines define the range of liquids produced by different degrees of melting at constant pressure. (Sources: (a) F. Schairer and H. S. Yoder, Jr., 1961, *Carnegie Inst. Washington Yrbk.* *60*, 141–144 and I. Kushiro, 1968, *J. Geoph. Res.* 73:619–634; (b) and (c) E. Takahashi and I. Kushiro, 1983, *Amer. Min.* 68:859–879.)

high pressures. The compositions of melts produced at different pressures and degrees of melting are shown in Figures 7–23b and c. Note that the diagrams correspond to the front face and base of the tetrahedron in Figure 7–2. Again, the chief effect of pressure on liquid compositions is a decrease in silica content, but increased melting has the opposite effect.

These melting relations are more easily visualized by comparing the compositions of the liquid and residual assemblage produced by melting a mantle peridotite (Table 7–5). If we assume that the liquid produced by melting a garnet lherzolite is a picritic basalt, it is a simple matter to calculate, by means of a simple mass balance (Fig. 5–18), the bulk composition of the refractory minerals that would be left after the maximum amount of melt has been removed. The effects are most clearly seen if the compositions of the liquid and residue are expressed in terms of the same set of minerals as the original peridotite. (A procedure by which a chemical composition can be recast into any convenient set of minerals is outlined in Appendix A.) Note first that the minerals of the peridotite have not been consumed in the same proportions as they had in the original

Table 7–5 Comparisons of a basaltic magma, postulated to be the parental magma for Kilauea Volcano, and a garnet lherzolite that could be a possible source rock for such a basalt. Also given is the calculated composition of the residue left on extraction of the liquid.

	Basalt	Peridotite	Residue
	Major Elements—Wt %		
SiO_2	46.70	44.50	44.44
TiO_2	1.85	1.30	1.29
Al_2O_3	9.17	2.80	2.64
FeO*	11.90	10.30	10.26
MgO	20.00	37.90	37.90
CaO	7.86	3.30	3.18
Na_2O	1.54	0.40	0.37
K_2O	0.40	0.01	0.00
	Trace Elements—ppm		
Ni	855	2300	2337
Cr	1400	3000	3041
Ba	195	5	<0.01
U	0.7	0.02	<0.01
Th	0.3	0.08	<0.01
	Normative and Modal Minerals		
Olivine	5.1	50.6	54.0
Opx	31.9	20.5	18.0
Cpx	32.4	14.3	20.2
Garnet	25.6	14.4	6.5
Phlogopite	3.2	0.2	0.0
Rutile	1.8	0.0	1.3
Density	2.81	3.47	3.46

peridotite. Instead, garnet, clinopyroxene, and phlogopite have been preferentially incorporated into the liquid, whereas olivine and enstatite are residually enriched in the residue. Second, the maximum proportion of such a liquid that can be obtained is limited by the K_2O content of the peridotite; it cannot exceed 2.5 percent, the value at which all phlogopite is exhausted, without the amount of K_2O in the liquid falling below its observed concentration. And third, because this amount of liquid is proportionately small, its removal has a correspondingly small effect on the more abundant major-element components of the remaining peridotite.

We should note that the result obtained in this way was entirely dependent on the initial assumptions that melting takes place in a closed system and that the phlogopite content of peridotite determines the proportion of melt. We have no assurance that the modal proportions we assumed are applicable to a mantle in which mobile components can be collected from a larger volume than that of the rock being melted. If, for example, additional K_2O were introduced metasomatically, the volume of the source rock required would be proportionately less. As in so many calculations of the kind, the solutions show possible relations but provide no proof that a particular peridotite was the parent of a specific magma, because the mass-balance calculation ignores the phase relations of real rocks.

High-pressure crystal-liquid relations

Phase relations become increasingly complex as the components of natural rocks are added to simple synthetic systems. Each additional factor increases the number of degrees of freedom and adds to the difficulty of portraying melting relations in two-dimensional diagrams. The CMAS system, illustrated in Figure 7–24, was devised in an attempt to surmount this problem. It groups components that behave similarly in basaltic systems and plots them as in a four-component tetrahedron for which the nominal end-members are CaO, MgO, Al_2O_3, and SiO_2. These end-members are calculated according to the following combinations:

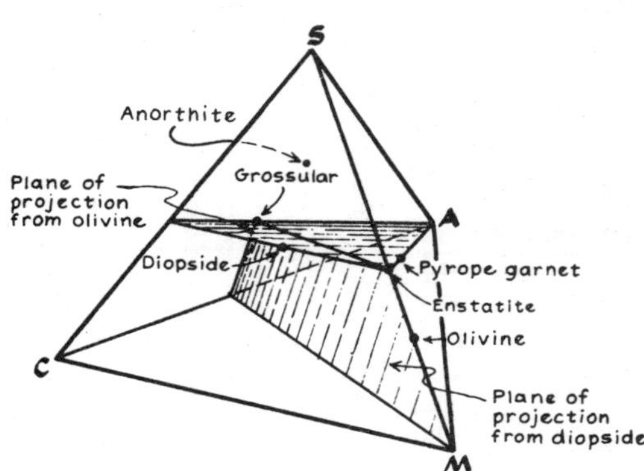

Figure 7–24 The CMAS tetrahedron. Compositions of important minerals are shown at their appropriate locations on or within the tetrahedron. The composition of anorthite falls on the rear face above the plane of the olivine projection.

$$C = (\text{mol. prop. CaO} - 3.33P_2O_5 + 2Na_2O + 2K_2O) \times 56.08$$
$$M = (\text{mol. prop. FeO} + \text{MnO} + \text{NiO} + \text{MgO} - TiO_2) \times 40.31$$
$$A = (\text{mol. prop. } Al_2O_3 + Cr_2O_3 + Fe_2O_3 + Na_2O + K_2O + TiO_2) \times 101.96$$
$$S = (\text{mol. prop. } SiO_2 - 2Na_2O - 2K_2O) \times 60.09$$

This rather elaborate arrangement has the advantage that all the major components of natural rocks and all the important mineral phases—olivine, Ca-rich and Ca-poor pyroxenes, plagioclase, spinel and garnet—can be plotted conveniently in terms of the composite end-members.

This system can be simplified even more. At pressures where olivine is present at all stages of melting, liquids can be assumed to be olivine-saturated, and their compositions within the CMAS volume can be projected from olivine to a plane defined by the other phases, pyroxene and garnet or spinel. In this way, melting behavior can be viewed in a simple, two-dimensional diagram, such as the one shown in Figure 7–25. The form of the diagram varies with pressure as the fields of individual minerals expand or contract, but for present purposes we need only examine a single section corresponding to a pressure at which garnet is the stable aluminous phase.

The first liquid produced by melting of the four-phase assemblage, diopside, enstatite, olivine, and garnet, will have the composition of point B. (Although B is actually the piercing point of a univariant line passing through the plane, it can be thought of as a eutectic in the projection of Figure 7–25.) With rising temperature, one of the residual crystalline phases will eventually be consumed, and the liquid would leave point B to follow a path that is governed by the original bulk composition. The course of such liquids can be predicted by comparing the melting relations in Figure 7–25 with those that would produce the residual mineral phases of natural mantle rocks.

In progressive melting of a composition, such as X, the liquid would leave B when garnet is exhausted, follow the cotectic to Y until diopside is exhausted, and then cross the olivine field. Looking again at the mantle xenoliths described earlier, we can arranged the ultramafic members of the suite in order of decreasing numbers of mineral components:

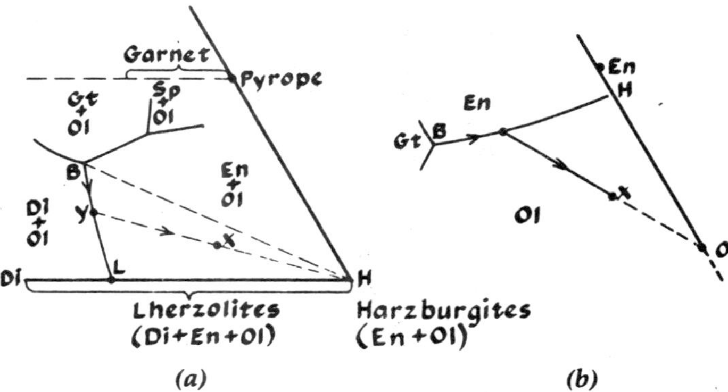

Figure 7–25 (a) Olivine-saturated liquidus field boundaries of diopside, enstatite, garnet, and spinel at thirty kilobars are projected from olivine onto the upper plane shown in Figure 7–24. At this pressure, the point B is just inside the CMAS tetrahedron. At pressures less than twenty-seven kilobars it lies slightly outside the CAS face of Figure 7–24. (b) A similar projection from diopside shows the field boundaries of garnet, enstatite, and olivine.

Olivine + Opx + Cpx + Spinel or Garnet + Phlogopite
↓
Olivine + Opx + Cpx
↓
Olivine + Opx
↓
Olivine

This sequence corresponds to the residual mineral assemblages that would be in equilibrium with successive liquids at each stage of melting of a composition such as X. Lherzolites (with olivine and two pyroxenes but no aluminous mineral) correspond to the area on the front face of the tetrahedron and to the line between Di and En + Ol along the lower edge of the plane of the projection. Harzburgites (olivine + opx) fall along the front edge of the tetrahedron and at point H in the projection, while pure dunite would be below that point at the composition of olivine.

The order of progressive depletion outlined here may not be the only one; some petrologists argue on the basis of the abundances of certain trace elements in basalts that clinopyroxene may disappear before the aluminous phase. Note that if the point X in Figure 7–25 is slightly richer in garnet, Di would disappear first, and the liquids would follow a different path. In either case, the order of depletion of mineral phases on melting affords a way of tracing the course of liquids in the CMAS system. First to disappear are the accessory phases. These are followed by either garnet or diopside and then by enstatite; olivine would be the last and most refractory mineral.

The amount of melt that can be produced before the composition of the liquid leaves point B depends on the amount of the least abundant major phase in the rock. For most estimated mantle compositions, something on the order of 25 to 30 percent liquid would be produced at the eutectic-like point B. After one phase is exhausted, however, the liquid must leave composition B and rise in temperature. It can do this in two ways.

If the liquid accumulates at the site of melting, its composition eventually leaves point B and follows a course up the cotectic BL to Y. At this point the last crystal of clinopyroxene has melted, and the liquid Y and crystals of enstatite and olivine have the proportions of XH parts liquid and XY parts crystals. As temperature continues to rise, the liquid composition leaves Y and moves toward H. When orthopyroxene finally disappears, the liquid leaves the plane of the projection and moves toward X, finally reaching that point when the last crystal of olivine disappears.

In this type of equilibrium or *batch* melting, no separation of liquid and crystals occurs as melting advances. The course is very different if liquid is extracted soon after as it forms. In that case, when the first phase is exhausted at B, the only phases left are crystals of diopside, enstatite, and olivine. No new liquid can be produced from these minerals until the temperature reaches that of the invariant point L, the composition of the first liquid produced by melting the remaining crystals. Similarly, when diopside disappears, no further liquid is produced until the temperature reaches the eutectic between enstatite and olivine at H.

With orthopyroxene exhausted, no additional liquid would appear until the temperature reaches the melting point of pure olivine. Thus the effect of this type of fractional melting would be to produce a discontinuous series of melts separated in time and with large steps in composition and temperature.

The fact that melts with the extreme compositions that would result from advanced degrees of fractional melting are seldom, if ever, observed among the products of basaltic volcanoes would suggest that fractional melting is less common in the mantle that batch melting. And yet, experimental studies indicate that at these pressures only a percent or two of liquid can be produced before it is squeezed from its crystalline residue. Moreover, we have seen that ultramafic nodules seem to indicate that melting continues until only one or two residual minerals remain. A possible explanation for this apparent inconsistency would be that the liquids are, in fact, extracted as soon as a small amount accumulates, but that they rise to collect in a larger mass produced by different degrees of melting throughout a thick vertical section of the mantle.

PRIMARY MELTS OF THE MANTLE

We noted earlier that few common basaltic magmas are primary magmas; most have probably evolved to some degree from the original compositions of mantle melts. This is not to say, however, that primary magmas never reach the surface. One example was given in Table 7-5, and others will be seen when we examine magmas of different tectonic origins.

What criteria can be used to test whether these are reasonable candidates for primary magmas? Such a liquid must, of course, have a higher liquidus temperature than the products of its differentiation, and it must be richer in those components that would be removed in the processes of differentiation. It must also have a composition that would be in equilibrium with the minerals of the mantle at high pressures. Such a liquid may not necessarily reach the surface in proportionately large volumes. Very dense, mafic magmas would erupt only under unusual circumstances; in most cases, they would intrude beneath lighter rocks of the lithosphere, and only the lighter differentiates that evolve from them would reach the surface.

If, as seems likely, olivine is a principal phase of the mantle, any postulated primary magma must be saturated with that mineral at high pressures. Because the field of olivine is reduced by increased pressure, liquids that precipitate that mineral at near-surface condition must have MgO contents great enough (normally in excess of 10 weight percent) for the liquid to be saturated with olivine at high pressures as well.

Second, the ratio of FeO to MgO in the liquid must be one that would be in equilibrium with an olivine having a composition appropriate for residual mantle peridotites, which is normally between Fo 90 and Fo 94. The equilibrium distribution coefficient, K_D, for Fe and Mg between olivine and liquid,

$$K_D = \frac{(Fe/Mg)_{olivine}}{(Fe/Mg)_{liquid}} = 0.3 \pm 0.03 \qquad (7\text{-}3)$$

is nearly constant for a wide range of temperature and pressure. Using this equation and appropriate values for the distribution coefficient, one finds that liquids in equilibrium with mantle olivines should have weight ratios of FeO to MgO between about 0.4 and 0.7. Thus, primary basaltic melts with typical FeO contents of about 10 or 12 percent should have at least 14.3 to 30 weight percent MgO. The liquidus temperatures of basalts are very sensitive to their magnesium-iron ratio (Fig. 7–26), and that of a liquid with the ratios indicated by these relations would be at least 1,400° C, far above temperatures measured in any historic eruption.

Because most proposed primary magmas are rich in forsteritic olivine, they satisfy these criteria, provided, of course, the olivine is not accumulated from other liquids. The best candidate for a primary liquid would therefore be an olivine-rich rock that can be shown to have crystallized from a liquid of its own composition. Certain ultramafic lavas that meet this criterion, namely *komatiites*, have petrographic textures (Table 7–6) typical of quenched aphyric liquids and could have had the requisite temperatures of primary melts of the mantle. Though very rare among the products of Cenozoic volcanoes, lavas of this kind were common during the Archean, when the temperature gradient of the earth seems to have been steeper, and magmas with such high temperatures were able to reach the surface. Komatiitic compositions approach those postulated for the mantle as a whole (Table 1–1) and could result only from very advanced degrees of melting. Their textures, which have been given the name *spinifex*, are characterized by highly acicular blades, mainly of olivine but also of pyroxene, resembling crystals in rapidly quenched lavas (Fig. 4–19a).

Because the high degrees of melting required for such extreme compositions are unlikely to have prevailed in post-Archean time, primary melts of the mantle today would probably be porphyritic lavas intermediate in composition between komatiites and common basalts. Picrites and ankaramites both have the requisite MgO contents and compositions that qualify them as primary melts of the mantle.

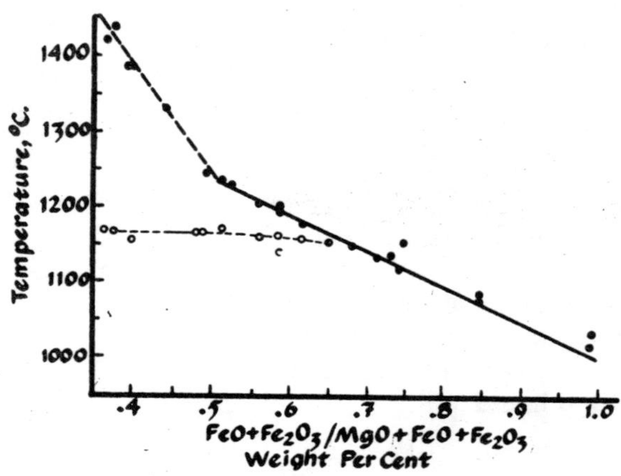

Figure 7–26 Liquidus temperatures of tholeiitic basalts determined experimentally at atmospheric pressure. The sloping line through solid dots defines the beginning of crystallization when olivine is the first mineral to appear on the liquidus in the upper part of the curve. The break in slope corresponds to the composition at which the liquid has crossed the field of olivine and meets a cotectic boundary with plagioclase or pyroxene. The broken horizontal line through open circles indicates the temperatures at which all major minerals begin to precipitate together. Note that this temperature varies little with the magnesium-iron ratio until it reaches relatively iron-rich compositions. (From H. S. Yoder, Jr., 1976, *Generation of Basaltic Magmas*. Nat. Acad. Sci., 265 pp.)

Table 7–6 Compositions and petrographic features of komatiites. (From Compilation by R. W. Nesbitt and Shen-Su Sun, 1976, *Earth Planet. Sci. Ltrs.* 431:433–453.) The appearance of spinifex textures in outcrop and under the microscope are shown in the two drawings.

Typical Chemical Compositions

	1.	2.	3.
SiO_2	45.9	44.4	45.2
TiO_2	0.4	0.3	0.2
Al_2O_3	8.4	5.4	3.7
FeO*	10.9	11.3	11.0
MnO	0.2	0.2	0.2
MgO	23.5	31.7	32.2
CaO	8.7	4.9	5
Na_2O	0.8	0.3	0.4
K_2O	0.2	0.0	0.2
Ni (ppm)	1049	1930	1931
Cr "	3250	3100	3190
Ba "	13	4	11

Molecular Norms

	1.	2.	3.
Il	0.5	0.4	0.3
Or	1.1	0.0	1.1
Ab	7.0	2.6	3.4
An	18.1	12.7	7.3
Di	18.8	8.3	14.1
Hy	9.0	17.7	14.7
Ol	45.4	58.4	59.2

1 Munro Township, Canada
ʹ. Yilgarn Block, Australia
3. Barberton Mts., S. Africa

* Total iron as FeO

Depths and degrees of melting

The trace elements of basalts and their postulated source rocks can be used to estimate the conditions under which a particular magma was produced in the mantle. As we saw in chapter five, the ways in which certain diagnostic components are partitioned between crystals and liquids can be a sensitive index of the degree of melting and the mineral assemblage from which the liquid was derived.

Because the minerals of the mantle have very different distribution coefficients for various trace elements, the abundances of these elements in a liquid produced by melting of a given source rock will depend on the compositions, proportions, and amount of melting of its constituent minerals. Thus a genetic relation for a given basalt and set of mantle minerals can be tested by comparing the observed abundances of trace elements in the basalt with those predicted for differing degrees of melting of the modal assemblage of its postulated source. The rare-earth elements (REE) are particularly useful in this regard. As we noted in chapter five, all of the REE tend to be strongly concentrated in the liquid phase, but the light and heavy REE are partitioned to differing degrees between various minerals and a coexisting liquid. Garnet, for example, normally contains proportionately greater concentrations of the heavy REE, so that liquids produced by small amounts of melting of a garnet-bearing assemblage would have proportions of REE mirroring that of garnet. Orthopyroxene has the same effect but to a less pronounced degree.

Figures 7–27a and b show two sets of curves calculated for different degrees of melting of two source rocks, one with garnet and one without. Note the stronger relative enrichment of light REE in liquids derived from the garnetiferous assemblage and the manner in which the pattern becomes flatter with more advanced degrees of melting. This change results from the fact that garnet, being less abundant than pyroxene and olivine, is soon depleted, and as it melts it contributes more heavy REE to the liquid until, at advanced stages of melting, the pattern approaches that of the original rock.

Figure 7–27c illustrates three commonly observed REE patterns found in oceanic basalts. Normal mid-ocean ridge basalts (N-MORB) tend to have flat or light-depleted patterns, whereas many alkali basalts from intra-plate hotspot centers, such as Hawaii, are relatively depleted of their heavy REE. This difference is consistent with the interpretation, based on other lines of evidence, that intra-plate basaltic magmas are derived from deep horizons where garnet is stable; basalts at mid-oceanic ridges, where melting is shallower, tap levels where garnet is not a stable constituent of the mantle. But this interpretation is not unambiguous unless the degree of melting is also taken into account. Other things being equal, a similar pattern could result from more advanced melting at high pressures, for, as Figure 7–27b shows, the light-enriched pattern produced by small degrees of melting of garnetiferous rocks disappears as more liquid is produced and garnet is exhausted from the residual assemblage.

Plagioclase has a similar effect on the light rare-earth elements (Fig. 7–28). It takes in slightly more of the light REE than does spinel, so that the liquid produced by melting within the stability range of plagioclase is more light-depleted

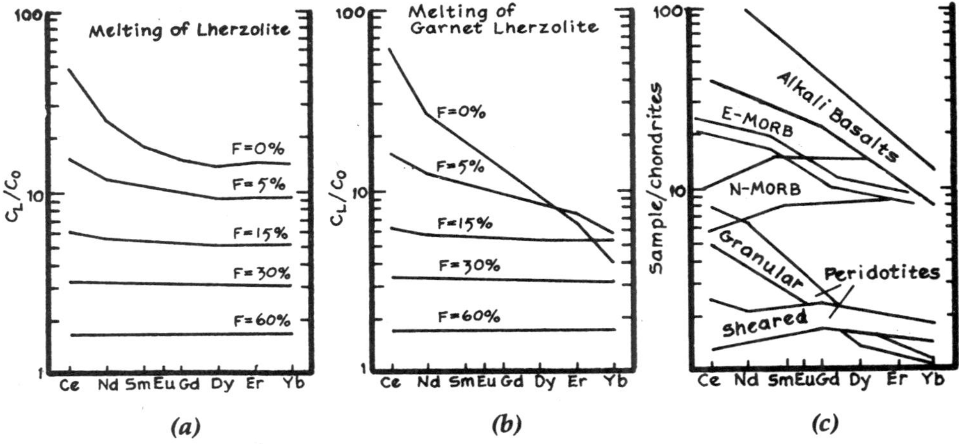

Figure 7–27 Calculated REE distribution patterns for melts derived by batch melting of two lherzolites, one (a) without garnet and another (b) with 5 percent garnet. Note the stronger depletion of heavy REE in small fractions of melt from the garnetiferous lherzolite and the similarity of melts evolved beyond 5 percent melting. Patterns in natural basalts (c) from some intra-plate volcanoes are strongly depleted in heavy REE as one might expect from small amounts of melting of a garnet-bearing source rock, whereas most basalts from mid-ocean ridges (N-MORB) have flatter slopes that could result from melting at shallow levels where garnet is not stable or, alternatively, by advanced degrees of melting. An enriched type of mid-ocean ridge basalt (E-MORB) has a steeper pattern, suggesting a deeper origin where garnet is stable. Abundances of REE in all three diagrams are plotted on logarithmic scales; those of (a) and (b) are normalized to the abundances in the original peridotite, while those in (c) are normalized to the abundances in chondritic meteorites. The differences between abundances in chondritic meteorites and sheared mantle peridotites are not large. (a) and (b) after G. N. Hanson, 1978, *Ann. Rev. Earth Planet. Sci.* 8:371–406.

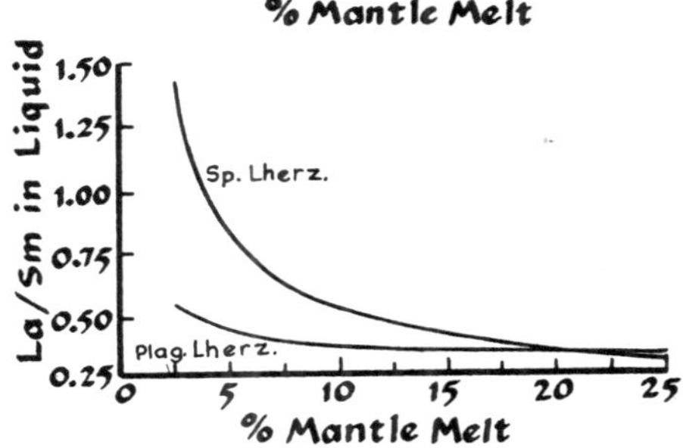

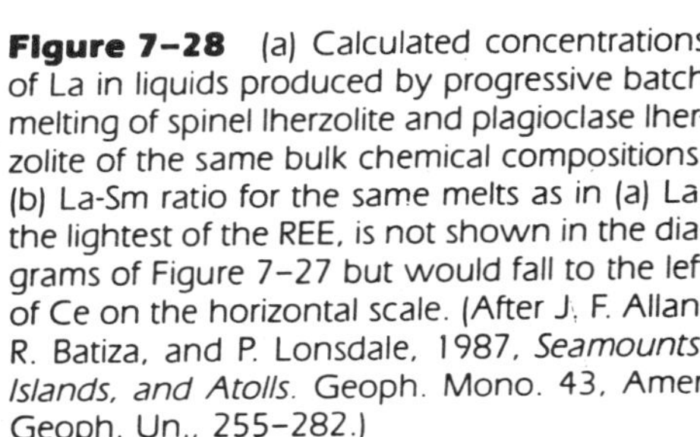
Figure 7–28 (a) Calculated concentrations of La in liquids produced by progressive batch melting of spinel lherzolite and plagioclase lherzolite of the same bulk chemical compositions. (b) La-Sm ratio for the same melts as in (a) La, the lightest of the REE, is not shown in the diagrams of Figure 7–27 but would fall to the left of Ce on the horizontal scale. (After J. F. Allan, R. Batiza, and P. Lonsdale, 1987, *Seamounts, Islands, and Atolls*. Geoph. Mono. 43, Amer. Geoph. Un., 255–282.)

than one derived from a spinel-bearing rock. This difference may explain the contrast between the two types of MORB shown in Figure 7-27c. Again, this difference disappears as melting advances.

As we saw in chapter 5, the degree of melting can be estimated from the abundances of those trace elements that are strongly partitioned into liquids. To determine the distribution of trace elements between a source rock, such as the peridotite of Table 7-5, and a liquid produced by equilibrium melting (the picrite in the same table), we can use the equation for equilibrium melting from chapter five:

$$\frac{C_L}{C_0} = \frac{1}{D + F(1 - D)} \tag{5-3}$$

in which

C_L = the concentration in the liquid,
C_O = the concentration in the original solid,
D = the bulk distribution coefficient, and
F = the fraction of melting.

And for values of D close to zero,

$$\frac{C_0}{C_L} \rightarrow F$$

Thus, certain elements, such as U, Th, or Ba, that have very small distribution coefficients for all the major minerals of peridotites, can be used to estimate F. For example, the concentrations of Ba in Table 7-5 give

$$F = \frac{5}{195} = 0.026$$

or about 3 percent, a value in agreement with that calculated from the mass-balance of major elements.

Included elements, such as Ni and Cr, are less useful in this regard, because their abundances are relatively insensitive to small degrees of melting. Moreover, it is difficult to estimate their bulk distribution coefficients, because the modal proportions of peridotites vary so widely that a single specimen that yields a realistic solution to equation 5-3 would be quite fortuitous.

SELECTED REFERENCES

Basaltic Volcanism Study Project. 1981. *Basaltic Volcanism on the Terrestrial Planets*. Pergamon Press, 1,286 pp. A giant volume covering all aspects of basaltic rocks on the earth, moon, and inner planets.

Hess, H. H., and A. Poldervaart. 1967. *Basalts: The Poldervaart Treatise on Rocks of Basaltic Composition*. Interscience, 2 Vol. A collection of papers dealing with all aspects of basalts. Though somewhat outdated, still an excellent reference.

Morse, S. A. 1980. *Basalts and Phase Diagrams*. Springer-Verlag, 493 pp. A comprehensive treatment of differentiation of basaltic magmas with emphasis on phase equilibria.

Richey, J. E. 1961. *Scotland: The Tertiary Volcanic Districts.* 3rd ed., British Geological Survey and Museum, 120 pp. A condensed summary of the geology of the classical igneous centers of western Scotland.

Wyllie, P. J. 1979. *Petrogenesis and physics of the earth.* in *The Evolution of Igneous Rocks: Fiftieth Year Perspectives.* H. S. Yoder, Jr., ed. Princeton Univ. Press, 483–520. A review of geophysical and petrologic evidence relative to the nature of the mantle and the origin of basalts.

Yoder, H. S., Jr. 1976. *Generation of Basaltic Magma.* Nat. Acad. Sci., 265 pp. A comprehensive survey of the state of research into the origins of basalts with emphasis on phase equilibria and physical mechanisms of magma generation. After more than fifteen years, this still remains one of the best general treatments of the subject.

8

OCEANIC AND FLOOD BASALTS

IF VOLUMETRIC PROPORTIONS are any measure of the petrologic significance of any group of rocks, the basalts of the ocean floor are by far the most important on Earth, for they cover about 70 percent of the surface and are produced at greater rates today than any other igneous rock.

The first evidence that basalt is an important constituent of the seafloor was obtained on the voyage of HMS Challenger, between 1872 and 1876, when Murray and Renard obtained the first samples of deep-sea sediments and noted that they contained large amounts of fresh volcanic glass. Solid basaltic rocks were not recovered until 1905 when Wiseman succeeded in dragging a dredge along the floor of the Indian Ocean by means of a long steel cable. Since then, great numbers of samples have been obtained in this way. Starting in the early 1960s, new drilling techniques made it possible to obtain cores to depths of several hundred meters below the seafloor, and geophysical methods now provide detailed information on the bottom topography and subsurface structure.

A composite section of the ocean floor has been pieced together by matching this information against observations in regions where oceanic lithosphere has been exposed on land. Beneath a thin cover of sediments (layer one) the oceanic crust consists of about two kilometers of basaltic pillow lavas. In the Atlantic, many basalts seem to be interlayered with peridotite, but in the Pacific Ocean only basaltic lavas have so far been found. The lavas become denser downward and grade into increasing numbers of basaltic dikes, many of which were feeders of lava flows. Near the base of this zone of lavas and sheeted dikes, which together make up layer two, the dikes pass into coarse gabbro. Much of this part of the section has been extensively altered by low-grade metamorphism caused by a hydrothermal system that circulated large amounts of hot seawater through layers one and two.

The uppermost gabbros are unlayered and have small, irregular pods and dikes of diorite and leucocratic differentiates; the rest of the gabbro is strongly layered and cut by ultramafic dikes. This group of rocks, which makes up layer three, has a total thickness of four to five kilometers. It rests on peridotites of the mantle.

Oceanic basalts can be divided into two basic types, mid-ocean-ridge basalts

(MORB) and ocean-island basalts (OIB). The first is volumetrically more important; it comprises all basalts originating at spreading axes. Relatively flat-lying lavas far from ridges are often referred to as "abyssal tholeiites" or "ocean-floor basalts," particularly if their origin is uncertain. Although most lavas on the ocean floor are tholeiitic basalts, and nearly all were probably erupted near a ridge, lavas of other compositions have been found, and not all have been discharged from sources at divergent plate boundaries. The term MORB is best confined to rocks that demonstrably originated at a ridge. The second group (OIB) includes basalts erupted from intra-plate volcanoes, whether they formed islands or not. Although they are much more varied than MORB, they are compositionally distinct. Most, but by no means all, are thought to have been erupted from hotspots. We shall look first at the products of spreading ridges and later turn our attention to those of intra-plate volcanic centers.

MID-OCEAN-RIDGE BASALTS

By far the greatest proportion of igneous rocks on Earth originate at oceanic spreading axes. The 65,000 kilometer-long system of oceanic ridges is a major tectonic feature extending around the earth and passing through the interior of each ocean basin, in most cases near its geometric center. With an average height of about 2.5 km and width of about 2,000 km, the total volume of the ridges is more than a hundred million cubic kilometers. The crests of ridges are characterized by many shallow earthquakes, high heat flow, and strong hydrothermal activity that is probably responsible for much of the heat transfer. Farther from the ridge, cooling is thought to be mainly by conduction through the lithosphere, because the seafloor subsides at a regular rate that is proportional to the square root of time (Equation 2–13), at least out to crustal ages of eighty million years or so.

The oldest oceanic rocks, which reach Jurassic ages along the western margins of the Pacific Ocean, are almost indistinguishable in chemical and mineralogic character from the most youthful lavas at mid-oceanic ridges. We can infer, therefore, that basalts of this kind have been produced with little or no change in composition for at least 140 million years. Estimates of the total production of basaltic magma range from ten to twenty km^3 per year, depending on the assumed thickness of layer two. Less than half the total amount of magma has erupted as lava; the greater part is intruded as doleritic dikes and gabbro beneath the axis of the ridge.

The average rate of formation of oceanic crust is probably close to 10,000 m^3 per kilometer per year, but varies greatly from one ridge to another, according to the spreading rate. Even on an individual ridge segment, spreading rates vary widely with time, so that only the averages over periods of centuries or more can be correlated with plate motions. Spreading results in a combination of fissures and normal faults. Ridges with half-spreading rates slower than three cm per year have prominent axial grabens up to a kilometer or two in depth and bounded by multiple, inward-dipping, normal faults. Faster-spreading ridges lack these features. Volcanism is largely restricted to the innermost axis of the rift, where it is fed by a narrow zone of dikes. The magma does not rise uniformly into the axial magma chambers but is fed from centralized plumes or pipes spaced a few tens of kilometers apart along the axis of the ridge. From there it is injected for many kilometers laterally along the axial rift to feed dikes and fissures (Fig. 8–1).

The compositions of basalts erupted within the axial zones of ridges show no measurable difference with time and little if any with the rate of spreading. Those of fast-spreading ridges seem to be somewhat more varied, possibly because conditions are more favorable for shallow differentiation. This is consistent with the smaller rates of heat-flow measured on slow-spreading ridges. The residual peridotites associated with fast-spreading ridges are said to be mainly harzburgites, and those under less active ridges lherzolites. Such a difference would indicate a direct correlation between spreading rates and the degree of melting.

The nature of the source of magma is still a matter of debate. Seismic profiles of slow-spreading ridges, such as those of the Atlantic and Indian oceans, have failed to detect any sizable body that could be interpreted as a magma chamber, but recent work on the East Pacific Rise has revealed prisms of material with low seismic velocities that can only be explained as magma. Even there, however, the structural relation of the magmatic system to the structure and dynamics of the ridge are difficult to interpret in terms of examples on land, where the oceanic crust can be observed directly.

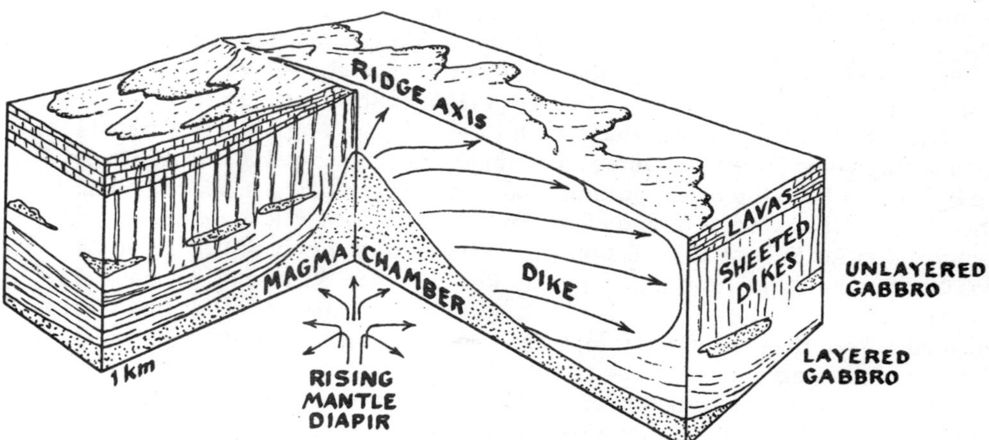

Figure 8–1 Schematic section through a ridge axis above a mantle diapir. The magma chamber is larger than normal where it is directly over the upwelling mantle. Adjacent parts of the ridge are fed by lateral injections. As the magma solidifies, the accreted crust moves outward, making room for new magma. Note that both the direction and velocity of the mantle differ from those of the lithosphere. The motion of the former is radial from the diapir, while the latter is outward from the ridge axis. (After A. Nicolas, 1989, *Ophiolites and Dynamics of Oceanic Lithosphere*. Kluwer Acad. Publ., 367 pp.)

Iceland

One of the few places where an active spreading axis can be studied at close range is in Iceland, where the Mid-Atlantic Ridge emerges and crosses the island (Fig. 8–2). The record of volcanism, which extends well back into Tertiary time, shows an intensity of activity at least ten times greater than that of the main Mid-Atlantic Ridge. This large difference is taken as evidence that a hotspot coincides with the spreading axis in this region. The fact that the rate of spreading is not measureably greater in this region than it is on adjacent parts of the ridge beyond the effect of the hotspot demonstrates that rates of spreading are largely independent of the rate of magmatism.

The presently active rift zone emerges from the sea on the Reykjanes Peninsula and is offset along a series of disconnected segments toward south-central Iceland, where it joins a second rift zone that has been the focus of most recent activity. It then follows a nearly straight course toward the Arctic Ocean. Tensional fractures and fissure eruptions have resulted in a dilation of about 30 me-

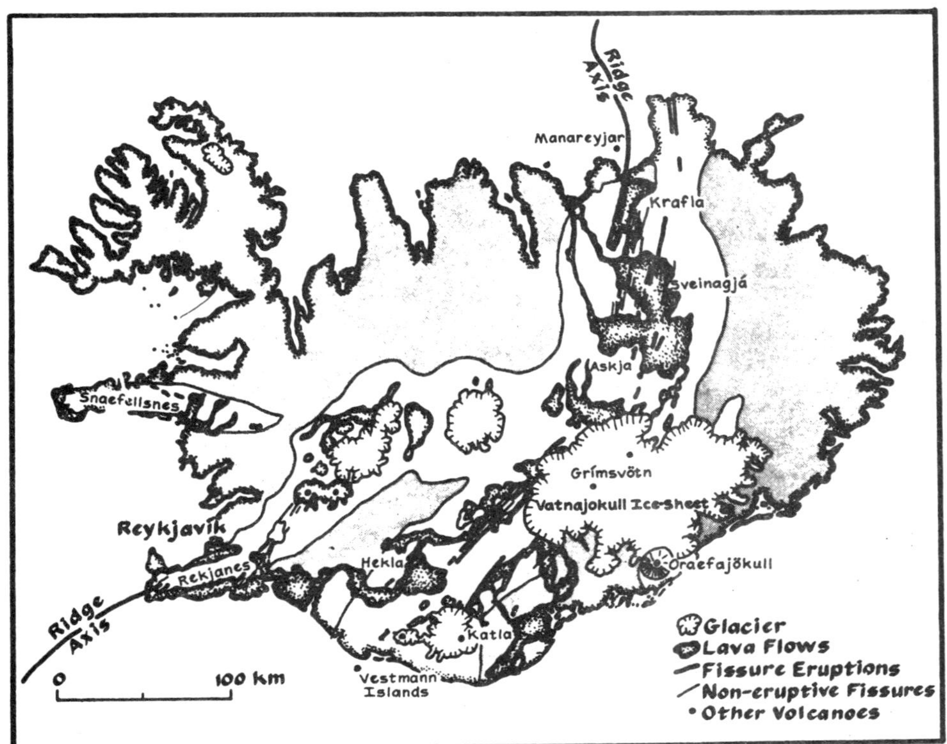

Figure 8–2 The island of Iceland stands astride the Mid-Atlantic Ridge, which emerges along the Reykjanes Peninsula and is offset eastward before running into the Arctic Ocean. Tertiary rocks are shaded, whereas younger rocks are left blank, except for certain individual lava flows of particular interest.

ters during the last 3,000 to 5,000 years, but the rate is far from uniform on a short-time scale. At present the rate of spreading is sporadic, even though the average for the past decade or so has been unusually rapid.

The most recent volcanism in northern Iceland has been associated with active faulting within the rift zone. Sudden extensional displacements of as much as several centimeters accompany intrusion of very shallow dikes, which appear to be injected in a horizontal direction from a source centered in one part of the active rift. Not all dikes erupt at the surface; many intrude the rift zone with no surface manifestations other than dilation of the crust. The shallow depth of magma in these zones was dramatically demonstrated in 1977 when basaltic scoria rose and erupted through a 1,136-meter-deep geothermal well a short distance from an active fault.

The greatest recorded outpouring of lava of historic time was the 1782 eruption of Laki volcano, which discharged more than twelve cubic kilometers of basalt over an area of 565 square kilometers. Magma poured from a twenty-five-kilometer-long fissure at a rate of 5,000 cubic meters per second. Where the fissure passed under a broad ice sheet, great floods of melt-water were released, causing wide devastation near the southern coast.

Many sub-glacial eruptions of this kind must have flooded Iceland during the Pleistocene. When basalt erupts under ice or water, it is quenched to a type of clear glass called *sideromelane* (or *tachylite* if it is the more slowly cooled opaque variety). The glass quickly absorbs water and changes to a yellowish-brown, amorphous material called *palagonite*. Great blankets of palagonite cover much of the island; it is also a major component of layer one of the ocean floor near large seamounts.

Most lavas of the central zone of recent fissure eruptions are olivine-poor tholeiitic basalts similar to rocks dredged from the Mid-Atlantic Ridge. In the recent past, however, eruptions west and east of the main rift zone have produced lavas that tend to be increasingly alkaline with distance from the main axis. A few large volcanic complexes of Tertiary age are scattered over a broad region, mainly east of the central rift. Most of these centers are tholeiitic, and they have some of the most extensively differentiated series on the island. They form a series of ferro-basalts, icelandites, and rhyolites that, like the differentiates of MORB, are characterized by an initial strong enrichment of iron and titanium followed by more marked increases of silica and alkalies.

Extensive sheets of rhyolite are interlayered with Tertiary flood basalts on the flanks of the rift, and smaller volumes of rhyolitic pumice and obsidian are closely associated with basalt in large mature volcanic complexes, such as Hekla and Askja. A few small bodies of sodic granophyre, locally referred to as "granite," are probably subvolcanic intrusions. The total volume of these felsic rocks, variously estimated at 3 to 9 percent of the Cenozoic section, is much greater in Iceland than on other oceanic islands, and their abundance led early geologists to speculate that Iceland might be a small continental fragment covered by a thin veneer of basalt. Geophysical and petrologic evidence now rules out any possibility of sialic crust under the island. The siliceous differentiates have little or no potassium feldspar and differ from typical continental rhyolites and granites in their trace-element abundances and isotopic ratios.

Ophiolites

Much of what is inferred about the structure of the oceanic crust and mantle under spreading axes is based on studies of a remarkable group of rocks known as ophiolites. Originally defined as an assemblage of mafic and ultramafic lavas and hypabyssal rocks associated with greywackes and cherts in geosynclines, the term has more recently been applied to a somewhat different structural and lithologic association of rocks thought to be typical of oceanic crust. Many ophiolites that were previously considered part of the roots of Alpine-type orogenic belts are now interpreted as originating at oceanic spreading axes, and their occurrence in mountain belts is the result of tectonic emplacement of oceanic lithosphere into highly deformed thrust sheets and fold belts. Geologists are far from unanimous in this new interpretation, however. It is probably an oversimplification to think that all ophiolites originate at oceanic ridges.

Ophiolitic complexes have been described from such diverse regions as Cyprus, New Guinea, Newfoundland, and the Coast Range of California and Oregon, but by far the most thoroughly studied and instructive example is in the mountains of southeastern Oman on the Arabian Peninsula. The body is thought to have been formed at a Cretaceous ridge crest, near what is now the mouth of the Persian Gulf, and thrust westward over much older rocks of the Arabian Shield (Fig. 8–3).

A composite section through the complex, shown in Figure 8–4, is probably typical of much of the oceanic lithosphere. The section rests on a series of late Paleozoic and Mesozoic sedimentary rocks over which the ophiolitic complex was thrust. The peridotite at the base of the ophiolite is interpreted as depleted mantle underlying what was originally the magmatic reservoir along a ridge crest. It is composed of highly deformed harzburgite with many concordant and cross-cutting dikes and irregular pods of dunite, wehrlite, and gabbro. The base of the overlying section is also deformed but less so than the mantle rocks. It passes upward into layered gabbro and wehrlite and then into unlayered gabbro with small, irregular bodies of more differentiated rocks. In most places the gabbros intrude the overlying dikes and pillow basalts, but a few dikes rise through the gabbro from sources at unseen depths. The contact relations suggest that the

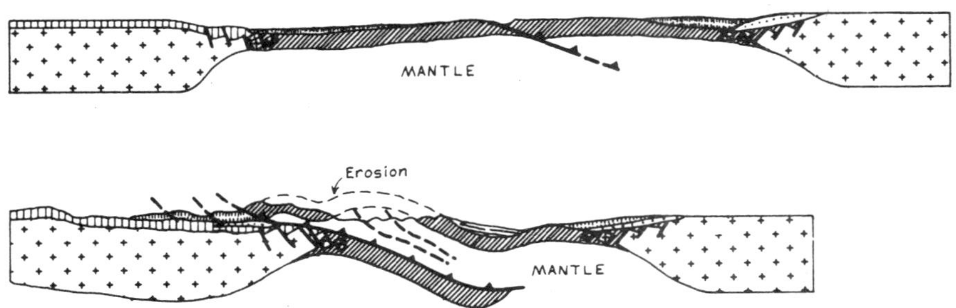

Figure 8–3 The Samail ophiolite of Oman was emplaced by thrusting of the oceanic crust over the Arabian Shield during a period of compression following opening of the Gulf of Oman. (After R. C. Coleman, 1981, *Jour. Geoph. Res.* 86:2497–2508.)

dikes and lava flows making up layer two were derived from the underlying reservoir in layer three at a time when the top of the latter was still largely liquid; only a few tapped lower levels after the roof began to thicken. Small pods of plagioclase-rich sodic granophyres, usually referred to as *plagiogranites,* are found in the uppermost levels of the gabbroic section. They must have crystallized during later stages of cooling, after injections of dikes had become less frequent.

The amount of differentiation shown in cryptic layering is very small until a late stage when dioritic and granophyric liquids were filter-pressed from the last crystal mush and intruded upward (Fig. 8–5). This restricted variation in the gabbros is thought to result from frequent injections of new magma that continued to replenish the reservoir and hinder differentiation except in those parts that had receded far enough from the axis to crystallize without further mixing.

Several models have been proposed to explain the gabbros in terms of dynamic systems of modern oceanic ridges. Two that are based on the Oman ophiolites are shown in Figure 8–6. The first (Fig. 8–6a) postulates a broad body of frequently replenished magma that crystallized mainly on the floor. The layering is attributed to new pulses of magma and density currents of suspended crystals sweeping down a floor that deepens toward the central feeder. The layers steepen and die out as the amount of magma diminishes at the outer margins.

An alternative interpretation (Fig. 8–6b) assumes a much smaller body of magma confined to a narrow axial region. The layering is initiated by the repeated pulses of magma entering this zone and forms mainly on the steep walls and roof. It is accentuated by deformation resulting from the differing velocities

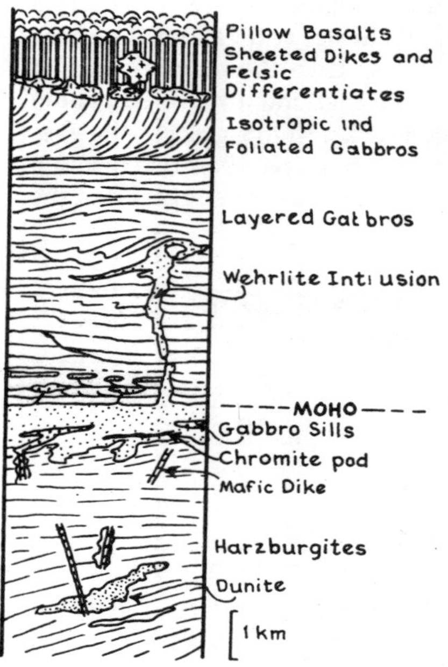

Figure 8–4 A composite section of oceanic crust based on the Oman ophiolite. (After R. C. Coleman, 1981, *Jour. Geoph. Res.* 86:2497–2508 with modifications based on A. Nicolas, 1989, *Ophiolites and Dynamics of Oceanic Lithosphere.* Kluwer Acad. Publ., 367 pp.)

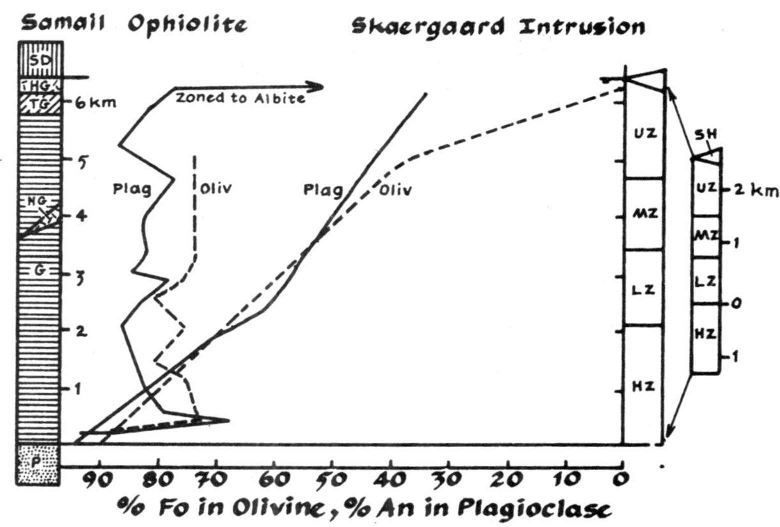

Figure 8–5 When compared with the compositional trends of an intrusion, such as the Skaergaard, which crystallized from a single injection of magma, the gabbroic rocks of the Samail ophiolite show only minor irregular variations reflecting periodic replenishment of the magma and resetting of its composition. Only at the very top, where light differentiates accumulated, do the rocks show strong changes in the composition of their plagioclase. The vertical scale for the Skaergaard Intrusion on the right has been expanded to make it equal to that of the Samail ophiolite on the left. (After J. S. Pallister and C. A. Hopson, 1981, *Jour. Geoph. Res.* 86:2593–2644.)

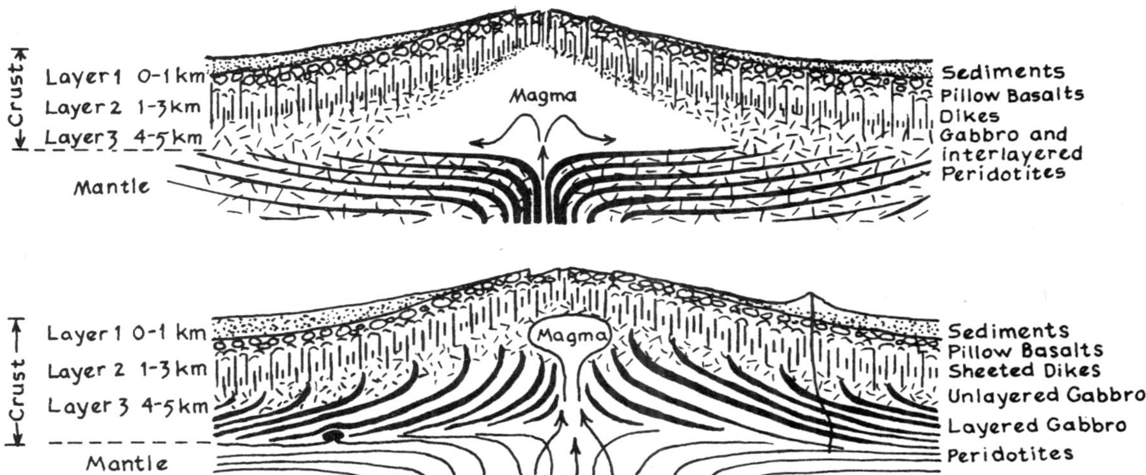

Figure 8–6 Two models for the dynamic evolution of a frequently replenished magma chamber along an oceanic spreading axis. In (a), a relatively broad body of magma deposits layers of crystals on its floor as the walls retreat and the magma is replenished by periodic additions. (Adapted from J. S. Pallister and C. A. Hopson, 1981, *Jour. Geoph. Res.* 86:2593–2644.) The body of magma in (b) is smaller and much narrower. The layering of the gabbro (heavy curves) is the result of crystallization along a steep wall. It is accentuated while being rotated and drawn out by the more rapid flow of the underlying peridotite (fine lines). The direction of flow of the latter is not entirely parallel to the direction of spreading; it tends to diverge in all directions from the central, pipe-like feeders spaced at intervals along the axis. Small amounts of magma spread along the top of the peridotite, and wehrlite dikes intrude up into the layered gabbro. (Adapted from A. Nicolas, 1989, *Ophiolites and Dynamics of Oceanic Lithosphere*. Kluwer Acad. Publ. and D. R. Toomey *et al*., 1990, *Nature*, 347:639–645.)

and directions of motion of the mantle and the more slowly moving crust. This shear causes the layers to be stretched and rotated to more gentle inclinations as they move away from the axis. In the first model, the upper dunites and peridotites are formed when olivine and pyroxene settle to the floor of the chamber. In the second, these ultramafic rocks are mainly intrusive or metasomatic, few if any being of cumulate origin. Neither model totally satisfies all the geophysical and petrologic evidence.

Since the magma must have come from a source in the mantle directly under the ridge, it is logical to interpret the thick, depleted harzburgitic peridotites beneath the gabbros as the residue left after this liquid was extracted and intruded upward. If so, there is an apparent anomaly, because the magma of the gabbro and basalts precipitated olivine and Ca-rich pyroxene long before orthopyroxene. The latter is rare as an early-crystallizing mineral in mid-ocean ridge basalts. A magma derived from a harburgitic source rock consisting chiefly of olivine and orthopyroxene would have been saturated with orthopyroxene and, on cooling, would have precipitated that mineral rather than the Ca-rich pyroxene found in the gabbro. The probable explanation is that the basaltic liquids were formed at greater depths where, as we saw in the previous chapter, the stability of Ca-poor pyroxene is increased relative to olivine. If so, the harzburgites must have risen to shallower depths as part of the upwelling mantle below the axis of the ridge.

Compositions of mid-ocean ridge basalts

The compositions given in Table 8–1 illustrate some of the distinguishing features of N-type, or "Normal," MORB. These rocks are olivine-normative tholeiites with small amounts of K_2O (normally less than about 0.2 percent) and TiO_2 (less than 1.0 percent). They are so common in dredge hauls from the deep ocean floor that they were once thought to pervade the entire oceanic crust, but more thorough sampling has shown the lavas to be far from uniform. In certain parts of the ridge system, particularly in the vicinity of hotspots, the basalts are somewhat richer in potassium, titanium, and many lithophile elements, even though they do not seem to be more differentiated; these are usually referred to as "enriched," or E-type, MORB (Fig. 8–7). Neither of these two general varieties is a fixed type; both include a range of compositions, and they grade into "transitional basalts" that are intermediate between the two. But within each group the variations are coherent in the sense that the rocks form continuous series and seem to be co-genetic.

Part of the compositional variation of MORB is certainly due to differing proportions of phenocrysts, but because it is difficult to be sure that these crystalline phases have not been gained or lost from the original parent liquid, the bulk compositions of the basalts may not represent true liquids. Even among crystal-free basaltic glasses, which, because of the strong quenching effect of seawater, make up a large fraction of ocean floor basalts, a substantial range of compositions shows that the liquid fractions of MORB do in fact differ from one sample to the next, even at a single locality.

The compositional effects of differentiation on the major elements of a typical MORB series are illustrated in Figure 8–8. These trends are very similar to

Table 8–1 Chemical characteristics of mid-ocean ridge basalts (MORB), ocean-island basalts (OIB), and ocean plateau basalts (OPB). FeO* is total iron as FeO. Norms are calculated assuming a uniform ratio of Fe_2O_3 to FeO* of 0.15. Data are taken mainly from the references listed at the end of this chapter. Where incomplete, they have been supplemented by illustrative estimates from other sources, including W. M. White and A. W. Hoffmann, 1982, *Nature* 296:821–825 and unpublished work.

	1.	2.	3.	4.	5.	6.
SiO_2	50.53	49.98	49.28	47.73	43.05	49.60
TiO_2	1.56	1.99	2.61	3.30	2.83	1.08
Al_2O_3	15.27	15.11	12.56	15.53	10.19	14.20
FeO*	10.46	11.04	11.20	10.67	12.34	10.74
MnO	—	—	0.17	0.14	0.19	0.20
MgO	7.47	6.87	9.74	8.37	16.43	8.02
CaO	11.49	11.25	10.80	8.71	10.23	12.44
Na_2O	2.62	2.81	2.10	2.89	2.08	2.01
K_2O	0.18	0.47	0.48	1.70	1.21	0.06
P_2O_5	0.13	0.32	0.27	0.66	0.48	0.10
			Molecular Norms			
Ap	0.27	0.68	0.57	1.39	0.99	0.21
Il	2.19	2.80	3.69	4.61	3.91	1.54
Mt	1.65	1.75	1.78	1.67	1.67	1.52
Or	1.07	2.80	2.88	10.08	7.08	0.36
Ab	23.70	25.46	19.13	26.05	4.37	18.45
An	29.59	27.48	23.77	24.48	14.76	30.20
Di	21.58	21.39	23.04	11.66	25.94	25.77
Hy	18.05	13.13	22.17	2.33	—	20.30
Ol	1.89	4.52	2.97	17.74	32.80	1.65
Ne	—	—	—	—	8.48	—
			Trace Elements (ppm)			
Ba	6	57	125	760	449	2
Zr	74	73	141	255	216	52
Rb	1	5	8	62	35	1
Sr	90	155	368	792	719	88
Cr	960	960	630	—	655	342
Ni	249	487	200	—	467	125
La	2.5	6.3	14.6	41.2	36.0	2.7
Sm	2.6	2.6	5.6	8.1	—	2.3
Lu	0.5	0.4	0.3	0.3	—	0.4
$^{87}Sr/^{86}Sr$	.7028	.7036	.7035	.7053	.7043	.7037

1. Typical N-type MORB. (Average basaltic glass from the Atlantic, Pacific, and Indian ocean spreading axes. Trace elements are taken from Table f, Appendix G.)
2. Typical E-type MORB. (Average basalt from the vicinity of the Galapagos hotspot on the Galapagos spreading axis. Trace elements are taken from Table f, Appendix G.)
3. Olivine tholeiite, 1921 eruption of Kilauea.
4. Potassic tholeiite, Gough Island, South Atlantic Ocean.
5. Nodule-bearing basanite, Tahiti, Pacific Ocean.
6. Ocean plateau basalt, Nauru Basin.

Figure 8–7 Trace-element abundances of "normal" and "enriched" mid-ocean ridge basalts normalized to the composition of primitive mantle. Note that the differences are greatest for elements that are most strongly depleted in N-MORB and decrease with increasing compatibility in the mantle. This is consistent with the more depleted nature of normal MORB. (After D. A. Wood, 1979, *Geology* 7:499–503.)

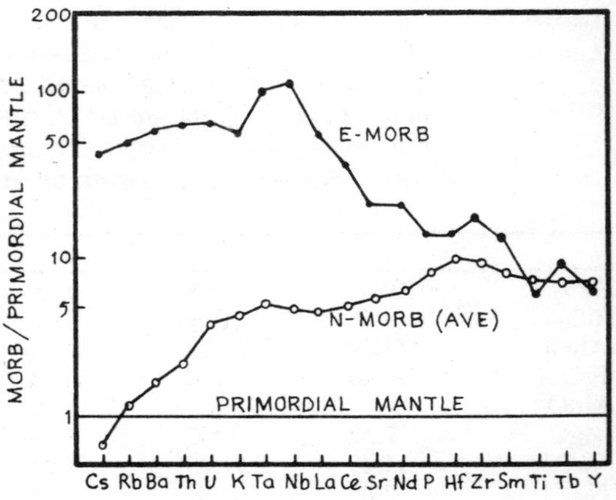

those of the Galapagos tholeiitic series described in the preceding chapter (Fig. 7–7); they are consistent with fractionation of the observed phenocrysts—olivine, plagioclase, and augite—which, taken as a whole, cause depletion of MgO and residual enrichment of TiO_2, alkalies, P_2O_5, and other excluded elements. Note that FeO* first increases and then declines and that SiO_2 increases only slightly until well over half of the original liquid has crystallized. This differentiation must take place at a shallow depth below the ridge in intervals between injections of new magma. As much as 50 percent of the initial magma would have to crystallize to account for the amount of variation in individual suites, so the period of repose between magmatic episodes must be correspondingly prolonged.

ocean ridge basalt should first crystallize olivine, then plagioclase, and finally augite. The most common phenocryst, however, is plagioclase. Olivine and augite tend to be less abundant if not totally lacking, possibly because these heavier minerals settle out while plagioclase, which is less dense than the liquid, remains in suspension or floats to the top of the shallow reservoir.

The olivine crystals in a single basalt can have a wide range of sizes and compositions. Large phenocrysts are as forsteritic as Fo_{90}, while smaller crystals in the groundmass may reach Fo_{65}. Obviously all the olivine could not have been in equilibrium with the same liquid. The phenocrysts tend to be partly resorbed by reaction with the liquid, while the small crystals are not. Similar relations can be found in both the plagioclase and pyroxene.

The most reasonable explanation advanced for the range of mineral compositions and the lack of equilibrium between the phenocrysts and groundmass is that the basalts are mixtures of two magmas, an initial one that was cooling, crystallizing, and differentiating in a shallow reservoir, and a later, less-differentiated magma carrying phenocrysts. Injection of the more primitive magma into the shallow reservoir could have triggered eruptions before the magmas were thoroughly equilibrated.

This same mechanism probably explains why basalts of the same MgO con-

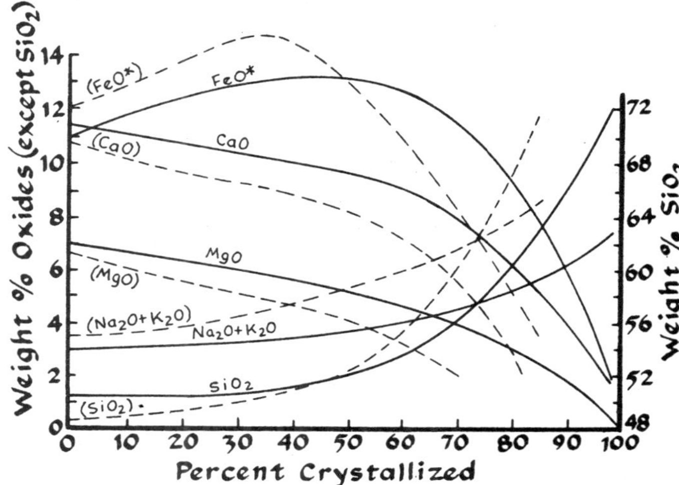

Figure 8–8 Compositional trends of MORB differentiates from the Clipperton Fracture Zone (solid lines) plotted in terms of the calculated fraction of liquid crystallized. Note the close similarity to the tholeiitic differentiation trends of the Galapagos rocks in Figure 7–7(a), which are shown here as dashed lines. (After G. Thompson, W. B. Bryan, and S. E. Humphis, 1989, in *Magmatism in the Ocean Basins*, A. D. Saunders and M. J. Norry, ed., 181–200.)

tent can have very different trace-element abundances. If the reservoir under a ridge is periodically recharged with new magma, so that the mass discharged to the surface is continually replaced by a new influx, the reservoir would maintain an almost constant volume with the losses to crystallization and discharges of lavas being balanced by equal amounts of new magma. Each renewal would partly reset the earlier magma back to a more primitive composition. Differentiation under these conditions would differ from that of a closed reservoir with only a single injection of magma. Excluded trace elements would accumulate and included elements be depleted, while the major elements would remain almost constant. The process eventually would approach a steady state in which the concentrations are functions not only of the bulk distribution coefficients but also of the mass fractions that are crystallized and erupted during each cycle of replenishment.

The concentration of an element in such a reservoir can be calculated from the equations:

$$C_D = C_{N-1}(1 - X)^{D-1}$$

$$M_N = M_{N-1}(1 - X - Y) + Z$$

$$C_M = C_D(M_N - X - Y) + (C_O \times Z)/M_N$$

where:

C_O = concentration of the element in the primary undifferentiated magma,
C_D = concentration after differentiation,
C_M = concentration after mixing,
C_{N-1} = concentration at the beginning of the current cycle (C_O for the first cycle),
D = bulk distribution coefficient,

X = mass fraction crystallized per cycle,
Y = mass fraction discharged per cycle,
Z = mass fraction replenished (Z = X + Y for a reservoir of constant volume),
M_N = total mass after the Nth cycle.

The nature of this process is illustrated in Figure 8-9. Crystal fractionation of an initial magma of composition C_O depletes the concentration of an included element ($D > 1.0$), while an excluded element is residually enriched. The trend follows the curved course defined by the normal equation 5-11 for Rayleigh fractionation. When the process is interrupted by discharge of part of the differentiate, C_D, and an influx of primitive magma, C_O, the composition is set back toward the original composition at point C_M, determined by the proportion of old and new liquids. This mixture then proceeds to differentiate along a new curved path, and the process continues. With time, the compositions approach a steady state in which the concentrations, C_{SS}, are:

$$C_{SS} = C_O \frac{(X + Y)(1 - X)^{D-1}}{1 - (1 - X - Y)(1 - X)^{D-1}}$$

Primary MORB compositions

Athough much of the variation in basalts erupted at the ridge crest can be related to differentiation at a shallow level, at least part of it must be inherited from differing depths and degrees of melting. It is seldom easy to distinguish between these effects, and opinions differ widely as to their relative importance.

Certain general relationships are helpful in identifying the effects of differen-

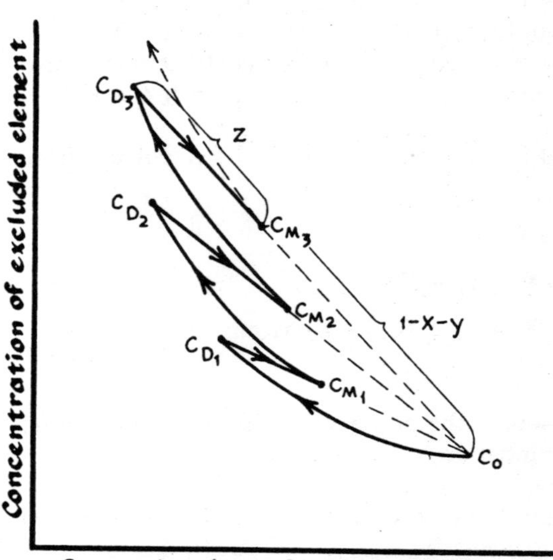

Figure 8-9 Variations of included and excluded trace elements in a differentiating magma chamber that undergoes periodic discharge and replenishment. See text for explanation. (Adapted from M. J. O'Hara, 1977, *Nature* 266:503–507.)

tiation and the degree and depth of melting. For example, the MgO content of basalts is very sensitive to differentiation, and any sample with less than 9.5 to 10 percent of that component would not be a good candidate for a primary melt of the mantle. If only basalts with large MgO contents are considered, the ratio of CaO to Al_2O_3 should increase with the depth of origin, owing to the more aluminous compositions of residual pyroxenes at elevated pressures (Fig. 7–19). At the same time, excluded components like Na_2O or K_2O should decline with progressive melting, all other things being equal. We noted earlier that the REE can be used to distinguish parental mineral assemblages and hence the depth at which a melt last equilibrated.

It is important to bear in mind, however, that basalts are not derived from a single depth; more likely, they are aggregates coming from a vertical section of unknown thickness and differing degrees of melting. Moreover, their compositions are modified by re-equilibration with shallower mantle as they rise. This is what makes interpretations so difficult.

Another difficulty is that of interpreting experimental studies at elevated pressure and relating the results to real magmas. It would seem that a simple way to resolve many questions would be to put a suitable peridotite in a high-pressure furnace, melt it to various degrees, and analyze the liquids. This has been done, but with less than total success. Experiments under these conditions are vulnerable to a host of technical problems. It is often difficult to maintain the composition of a sample during the period of days needed to reach equilibrium. In early work, it was found that platinum, which is one of the few materials that can be used as a container at high temperatures, absorbs large amounts of iron from the sample. More recent experiments have surmounted this problem by using graphite capsules, which do not react with the sample; others use hollow single crystals of olivine with a composition in equilibrium with the liquid. Even then, however, problems arise. For example, it is difficult to lower the temperature of the sample at the end of a run quickly enough to quench it and avoid recrystallization of the small amounts of intergranular melt. Very few experiments have succeeded in producing analyzable amounts of glass with a uniform composition in equilibrium with all the crystals of the peridotite.

A variety of ingenious techniques have been devised to avoid these difficulties. One is to prepare a glass that has a composition as close as possible to that of the expected result and to sandwich it between two much larger pieces of peridotite. The amount of basaltic glass is greater than that produced by partial melting, but because it is thin and in close contact with a relatively large amount of peridotite equilibrium is more easily achieved. Unfortunately, the resulting composition is found to vary with the modal proportions of the peridotite and the starting composition of the basaltic glass.

Yet another method is to determine the minerals that crystallize from basaltic liquids over a range of temperatures and pressures. By doing this with basalts of a number of compositions one can determine the liquidus fields of the principal minerals at successive pressures and construct a series of phase diagrams, such as the one shown in Figure 8–10.

This diagram is a section through a modified CMAS tetrahedron of the kind

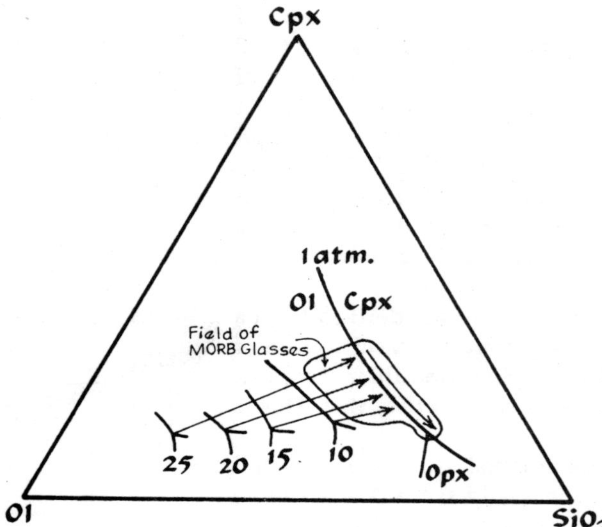

Figure 8–10 When the compositions of N-MORB glasses with more than 9 percent MgO are plotted on an olivine-cpx-silica plane within the CMAS tetrahedron, most fall between the olivine-cpx cotectics for one atmosphere and ten kilobars. Those with less than 9 percent MgO are closer to the low-pressure cotectic, as one would expect if they have differentiated in a shallow reservoir. Liquids produced by small amounts of melting at high pressures would crystallize olivine as they rise, owing to the expansion of the olivine field with declining pressure. Their compositions will follow a course away from olivine in the direction indicated by arrows. If they then collect and differentiate in a shallow reservoir, they will move quickly to the low-pressure cotectic with Ca-rich pyroxene and follow it toward the pseudo-invariant point. Plagioclase also crystallizes but is not shown in this projection. After D. Elthon, 1989, in *Magmatism in the Ocean Basins*, A. D. Saunders and M. J. Norry, eds. Geol. Soc. Spec. Publ. No. 42:125–136.)

described in the preceding chapter. Compositions are projected from plagioclase, so that only the fields of mafic minerals, olivine and Ca-rich or Ca-poor pyroxene, are shown. A liquid that is simultaneously saturated with all the essential phases—olivine, two pyroxenes, and either plagioclase, spinel, or garnet—would have the composition of the pseudo-invariant point and would correspond to the first melt of a peridotite having those same minerals. (The name "pseudo-invariant point" is used for the eutectic-like junction of the three cotectic curves, because its position varies in another dimension. It is really the point where a univariant line penetrates the plane of the diagram.)

When the range of primitive mid-ocean ridge basalts is plotted on the same diagram, it is found to fall mainly between the olivine-CPX cotectics for one atmosphere and ten kilobars. The compositions at the upper end of this field are more iron-rich and silica-poor than those closer to the invariant point. Because the iron contents of tholeiitic basalts at constant pressure normally vary sympathetically with silica, regardless of whether the variation is due to differentiation or partial melting, the opposed variation of these components in basalts that plot in this region is more logically attributed to some factor other than low-pressure differentiation or partial melting. Their spatial relation to the migration of the phase boundaries shows that their differences are the result of melting at a range of higher pressures.

Note that liquids produced by small degrees of melting at a high pressure are poorer in silica than those of shallower origin. Because the field of olivine expands with falling pressure (Fig. 7–22), they would crystallize olivine as they rise to shallower levels, and their liquids would follow a course away from the olivine corner, as indicated by the four arrows. If many separate liquids from a range of depths collect and cool at shallow levels where the pressure is less than ten kilobars or so, they would lie on or close to the olivine-CPX cotectic at that pressure. Subsequent differentiation would carry the liquids along the cotectic toward increased silica contents, as indicated by the arrow toward the low-pressure invariant point. This combination of melting at a range of depths, followed by fractionation of olivine during rise to shallower depths, and, finally, differentiation at pressures of about ten kilobars or less seems to explain much of the observed variation of mid-ocean ridge basalts. For example, it explains the apparent anomaly noted in ophiolites of basalts leaving an OPX-rich mantle residue but not having that mineral on the liquidus at low pressures.

Collection and differentiation of magma beneath spreading ridges

The enormous masses of nearly uniform basalt added to the oceanic lithosphere at spreading axes over long periods of time require a steadily renewed mantle from which the magmas are derived. At the same time, the divergent plate motion that accompanies magmatism indicates that this supply of fresh material is achieved by large-scale convection centered under the ridge. It follows, therefore, that magma generation under ridge axes probably results from relief of pressure on the upwelling limb of this system (Fig. 8–11).

The proportion of mantle required to feed the ridge systems must be some forty or fifty times larger than that of the crust derived from it. As explained in the preceding chapter, the amount of melt that can be obtained from a mantle source is severely limited by the scarcity of elements that are strongly partitioned into the liquid. Even depleted MORB, which has very small concentrations of incompatible elements, can scarcely be the product of more than a few percent melting. Thus the large volumes of magma produced at ridges must be collected from a column of huge dimensions. If so, it is remarkable that magmatism is largely confined to narrow axes, many less than a kilometer in width.

Much smaller amounts of magma with most of the characteristics of MORB are erupted sporadically on the flanks of the East Pacific Rise out to distances of about fifty kilometers, indicating that melt can be derived from a zone of at least that width. The flank lavas, however, are more varied and less differentiated than those from the axis, probably because the latter collect and differentiate in a narrow reservoir closer to the axis. The narrow dimensions of the reservoir indicated by this contrast between differentiated basalts at the crest and undifferentiated basalts on the flanks is consistent with the slender magma body of the second model in Figure 8–6.

The sharp focusing of magmatism close to the axis could be due to the anisotropy of highly deformed mantle that funnels the melt from a broad region into more central channels. Owing to the strong flexuring that must take place as the rising mantle turns sharply and diverges, the orientation of fractures and joints will be at increasing angles to the flow lines, much as it is in crevassed ice near

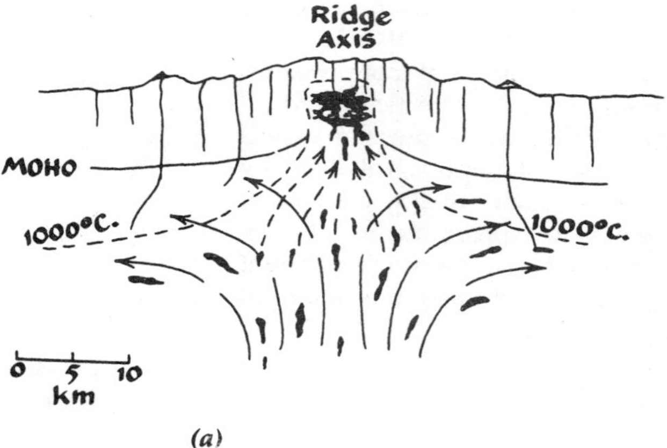

(a)

Figure 8–11 (a) Schematic cross section of an active spreading ridge. Most of the magma produced by passive pressure-relief in the rising mantle is channeled by the anisotropic structure of the deformed rock into a narrow zone under the ridge axis. Because liquids resulting from differing degrees of melting are collected into a single reservoir, the geochemical signature of the aggregated melt is derived from a large vertical and horizontal regime of melting. After differentiating in a shallow chamber part of the magma solidifies and is added to layer three, and another part is intruded or erupted from a narrow fissure zone. Small batches of magma segregated from the diverging limbs of the flowing mantle fail to join the main supply system and are erupted on the outer flanks with relatively little differentiation and a wider range of compositions. (b) shows the temperature paths of rising asthenosphere undergoing adiabatic decompression and intersecting the melting interval of dry peridotite. Paths are shown for mantle with four different potential temperatures. Curves between the solidus and liquidus indicate amounts of melting. (c) shows the total thickness of melt generated by rising mantle of different potential temperatures. (b and c are taken from D. P. McKenzie and M. J. Bickle, 1988, *Jour. Petrol.* 29:625–679.)

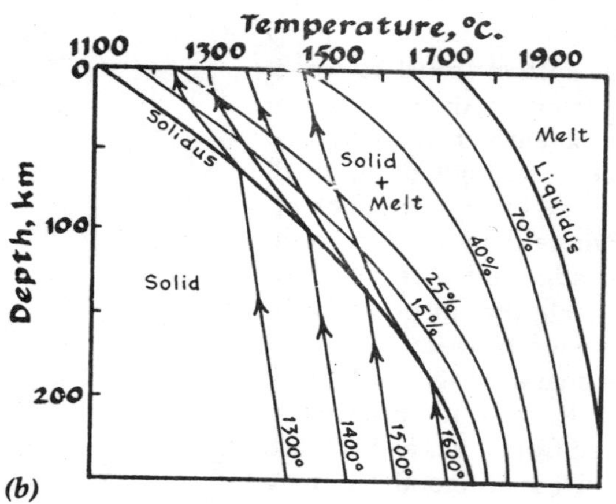

(b)

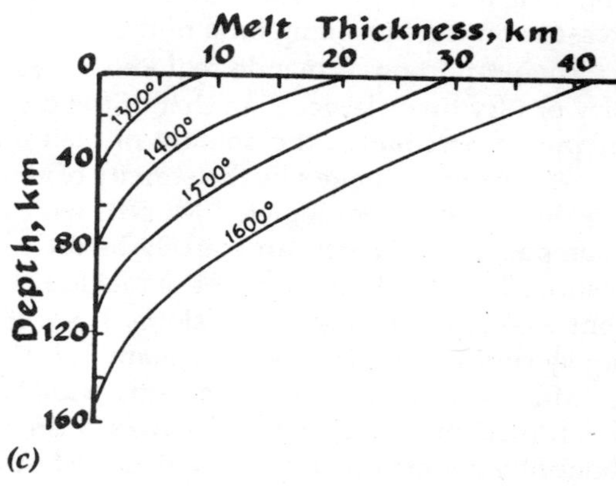

(c)

the margins of a curving glacier. Melt is effectively extracted in this highly anisotropic stress regime and follows converging flow lines upward and inward.

In this same zone, deformation of the mantle changes from plastic flow to brittle fracture. Hence, the tendency of melts to equilibrate declines abruptly when melts cease to rise slowly by intergranular flow and enter discrete channels where they move more rapidly over a smaller surface area of crystals. When this happens, chemical re-equilibration declines sharply. Thermal equilibration is probably less affected, because the rate of diffusion of heat is much more rapid than chemical diffusion.

INTRA-PLATE VOLCANISM

The magmatism of hotspots and other eruptive centers in interior regions of the oceanic plates is second in importance only to that of spreading ridges. The global rate of production from these sources, though it differs widely from one region to the next, is of the order of 1.5 km^3 per year.

The most conspicuous expression of this volcanism is seen in long chains of volcanic islands in the central and northern parts of the Pacific Ocean. These islands are only a small fraction of the thousands of large and small seamounts scattered in seemingly random fashion on the seafloor. Not all of these volcanoes are products of hotspots. Many form lines that are randomly oriented relative to the direction of plate motion and remain active for long periods of time. Some that are grouped in elongated clusters or chains have ages and eruptive episodes unrelated to their position with respect to the direction of plate motion. This group has received much less attention than the well-defined chains that are more clearly related to hotspots, and much less can be said about them, except that their compositions differ widely from one volcano to another with no discernable temporal or spatial order.

Compositions of ocean island basalts

The basalts of intra-plate volcanoes, collectively referred to as ocean-island basalts (OIB), differ from those of oceanic ridges, mainly in being richer in incompatible elements, such as K, Rb, Ba, Zr, and the REE (Table 8–1). They also tend to have more radiogenic isotopic ratios, most notably Sr and Nd (Fig. 8–12). Beyond these general differences, however, they have such a wide range of compositions that they are difficult to categorize. In the final chapter we will see that some of these variations reflect regional mantle differences on a global scale.

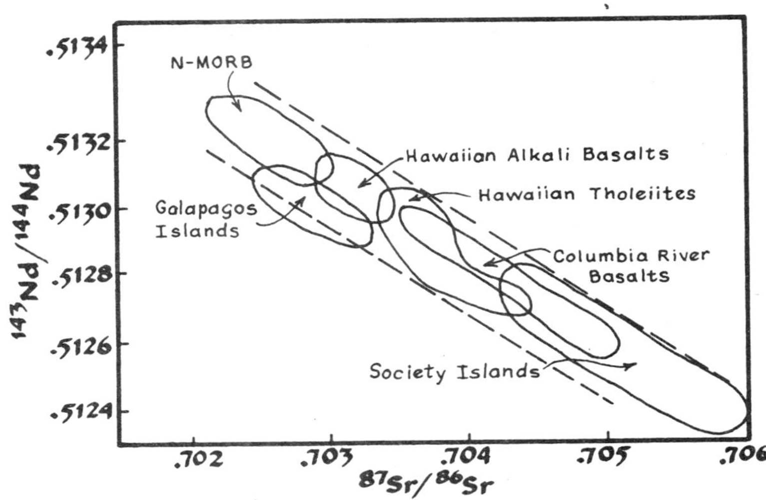

Figure 8–12 The isotopes of Nd and Sr show distinct ranges for basalts of different tectonic settings. Basalts of the mid-ocean ridges have the greatest Nd and smallest Sr ratios, while those of intra-plate volcanoes and flood basalts are more varied and from less-depleted mantle. Although each region and tectonic setting has its own characteristic ratios, most fall within the "mantle array" outlined by dashed lines.

Although each hotspot has its own distinctive basalts and differentiated series, a crude relation has been found between the lavas of individual islands and their distance from a spreading ridge. Although many islands have both tholeiitic and alkaline basalts, those close to spreading axes tend to be predominantly tholeiitic, especially their differentiated suites. On islands more distant from an axis alkaline rocks tend to be more abundant and more strongly differentiated. All islands with true rhyolites, such as Iceland, Easter Island, and the Galapagos, stand close to spreading axes; all islands with strongly alkaline differentiated lavas, such as Cook Island and Tahiti in the Pacific and Trindade and Fernando Po in the Atlantic, are far from spreading axes.

Since it is impossible to consider all the varieties within this very diverse group, a few of the most instructive examples must suffice.

Hawaii

One of the most active and better known hotspot-related systems is that of the Hawaiian-Emperor Seamount Chain (Fig. 8–13). It was the first in which a clear relation was found between the ages of individual islands or seamounts and

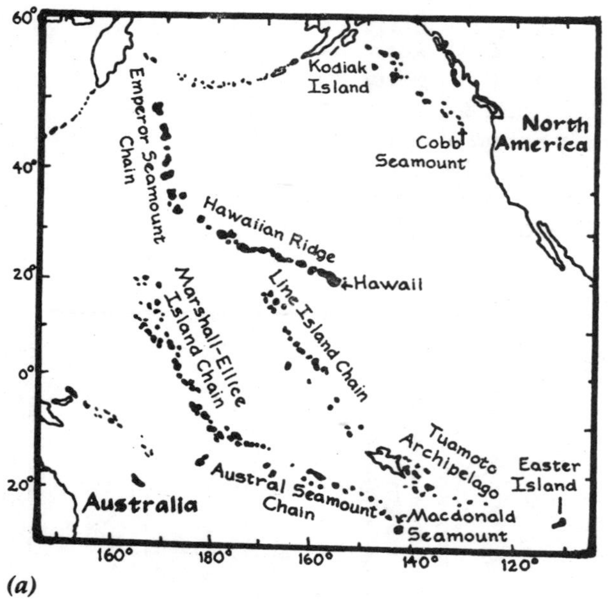

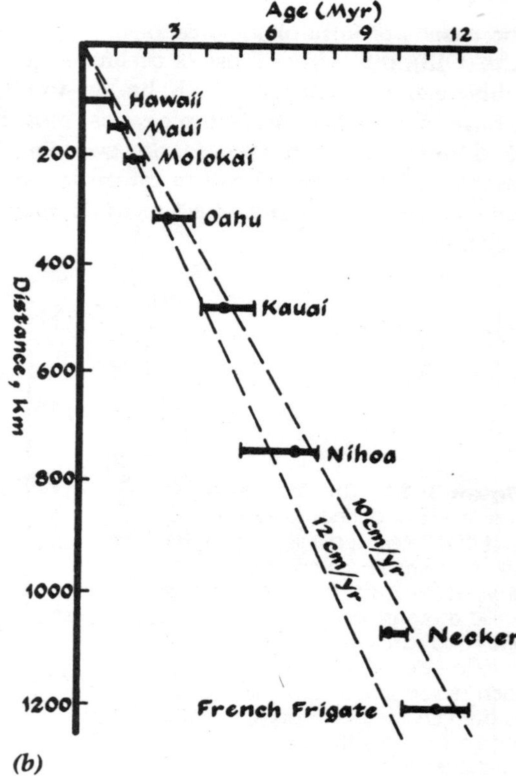

Figure 8–13 (a) Chains of volcanic islands and seamounts in the central Pacific. (b) Relationship beween ages of the volcanoes of the Hawaiian Emperor seamount chain and distance from the hotspot near the island of Hawaii. (Adapted from G. B. Dalrymple, E. A. Silver, and E. D. Jackson, 1973, Amer. Sci. 61:294–308.)

their distance from the hotspot. The chain has evolved as the oceanic lithosphere passes over a persistent source of magma in the underlying mantle. Each volcano grows for a few hundred thousand years, then drifts downstream at a rate of ten to twelve cm per year until, on separating from its source, it becomes extinct.

The development of these huge volcanoes can be divided into several stages (Fig. 8–14), each characterized by a distinctive type of activity and group of lavas. The birth and earliest growth of a volcano at the leading edge of the chain is shown in the small seamount, Loihi, just south of the island of Hawaii. During the brief period it has been active, the volcano has erupted distinctly alkaline basalts, but tholeiites have also been found among its lavas, and with time it is expected that the latter will become dominant.

The lavas making up the main mass of mature volcanoes like Mauna Loa or Mauna Kea are almost entirely tholeiitic. They were discharged in rapid succession, first as submarine pillow basalts and later as sub-aerial pahoehoe lavas,

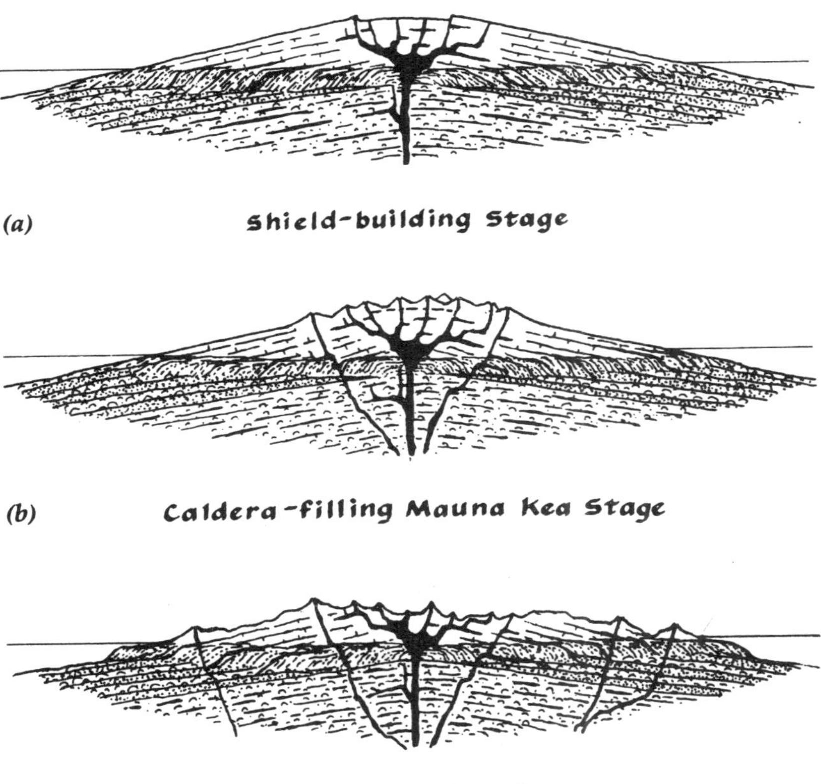

Figure 8–14 Stages of evolution of the Hawaiian volcanoes. The initial shield-building stage (a) is followed by a stage (b) in which the caldera is filled and small vents break out in the summit region. Later, after an interval of erosion, a final stage (c) is characterized by small eruptions of very alkaline magmas, mainly on the lower slopes.

until they attained volumes of as much as 40,000 cubic kilometers. Measured from their base five kilometers below sea level, their heights approach that of Everest, and their huge mass is many times greater than even the largest land volcanoes (Fig. 8–15).

In the later part of this shield-building stage, a shallow caldera develops by passive subsidence of a circular or eliptical part of the summit. Nearly all lavas of this stage are erupted within the caldera or from one or more rift zones radiating down the flanks. Kilauea, currently the most active of the Hawaiian volcanoes, is in this stage of evolution. Activity inside its caldera was long characterized by persistent lakes of convecting lava that, until 1924, occupied a deep pit on the floor of the caldera. More recently, however, summit eruptions have migrated southward from the caldera and have alternated with fissure eruptions on the East Rift Zone.

Eruptions from the summit and flanks tap a complex, shallow reservoir that swells and contracts with each episode of activity. Most large eruptions are preceded by inflation of the summit region, but eruptions lower on the flanks deflate the reservoir and usually bring activity to an end until a new batch of magma rises from the mantle and begins a new cycle. Most basalts erupted from rifts on the lower slopes are richer in olivine phenocrysts than those of the summit. Some have so much olivine that they are more properly called picrites. Apart from their conspicuous difference in olivine content, however, the character of basalts coming from the two levels during a sequence of eruptions is essentially the same. In fact, most of the compositional variations of lavas of this stage can be accounted for simply by subtraction or addition of this single mineral. The differences must be the result of gravity segregation during the period of years or decades that an individual batch of magma resides in the high-level reservoir.

Seismic studies and the geometry of inflation of the summit region indicate that magma is stored in a steep, narrow complex of dikes and sills in the upper half of the volcano. Other oceanic volcanoes have shallow plutonic rocks that form broader, more coherent bodies. A bore hole on the lower flanks of the large shield volcano, Piton de la Fournaise on the island of Reunion, encountered olivine gabbros and peridotites starting only a kilometer below the surface and extending to depths of at least another two kilometers. Similar rocks are exposed in the older, deeply eroded volcano Piton des Neiges on the same island. We have noted other occurrences of shallow plutonic rocks on Tahiti and in parts of the Galapagos. All these examples point to sizable magmatic reservoirs at high levels of the volcanic edifice.

In later stages, as activity declines in intensity, Hawaiian lavas tend to become increasingly olivine-rich before eventually giving way to alkaline compositions. At the same time, eruptions from scattered vents near the summit begin to fill and obliterate the caldera. Haleakala on the island of Maui is now in this "caldera-filling" stage, and Mauna Kea on the island of Hawaii has evolved to a stage in which its caldera is filled and is no longer discernable. With the change from tholeiitic to alkaline basalts, *ankaramites* (very mafic basalts containing abundant, large phenocrysts of olivine and augite) become common and later give way to several types of differentiated lavas that resemble basalts petrographically

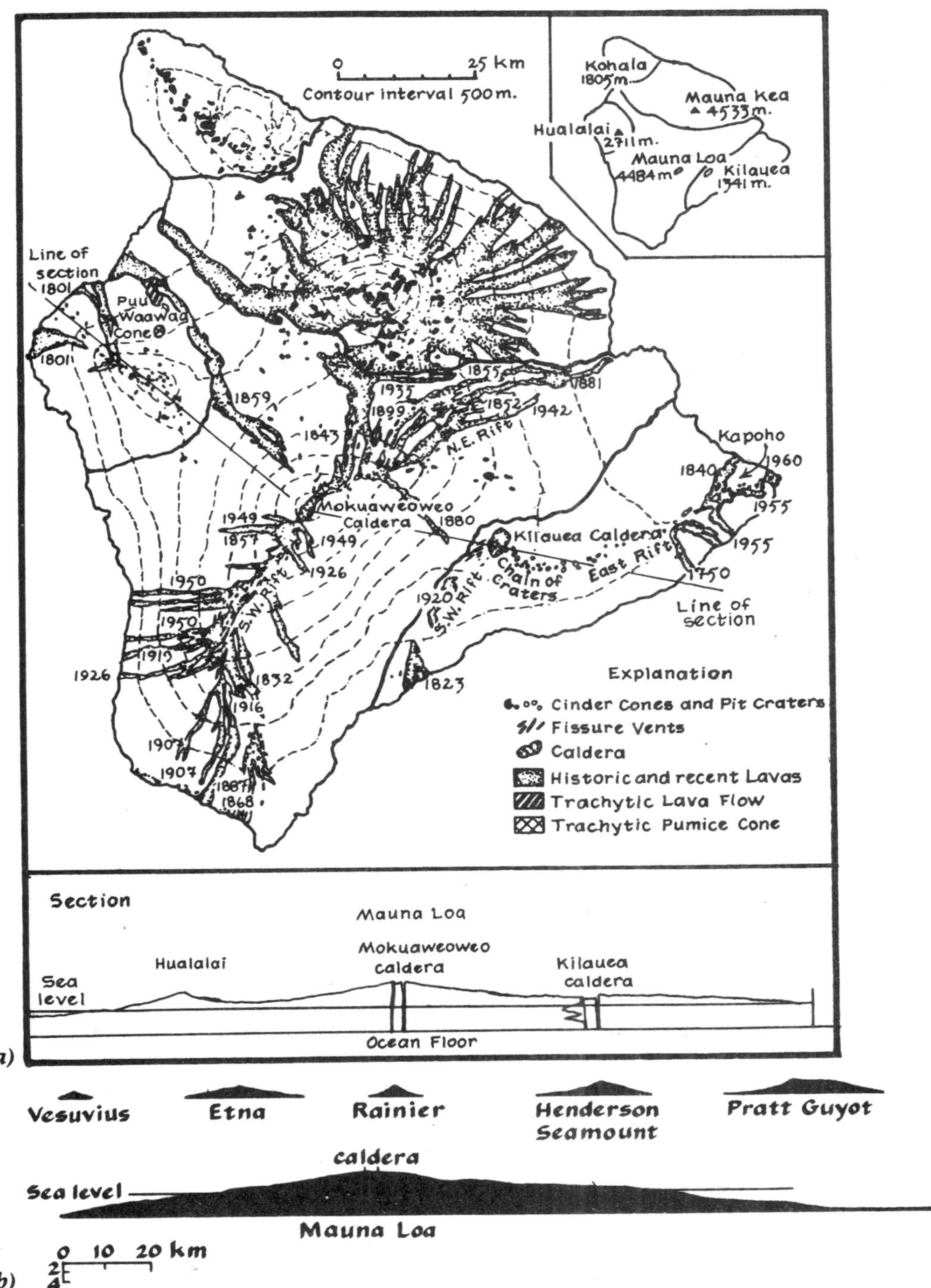

Figure 8–15 (a) Simplified map of the island of Hawaii showing the principal volcanoes and their radial rift zones. (b) Profiles through Mauna Loa and other oceanic and continental volcanoes showing their great difference in size.

but have a more sodic plagioclase. Those with modal or normative andesine are called *hawaiites,* and those with oligoclase, *mugearites*. In rare instances, more felsic rocks, such as *benmoreites* and *trachytes,* form stubby lava flows and small viscous domes. The overall trend (Fig. 8–16a) of these differentiates straddles the division between nepheline-normative and hypersthene-normative compositions.

With declining activity, the Hawaiian volcanoes enter a long period of repose and erosion, but after an interval of a million years or so, some revive briefly to erupt small amounts of highly alkaline magma. The rocks around Honolulu belong to this late, "post-erosional" alkaline series; they include nepheline basanites rich in melilite $(Na,Ca)_2(Mg,Al)(Si,Al)_2O_7$, a mineral found only in very silica-deficient mafic rocks. These late-stage eruptions come from scattered vents on the lower flanks, often close to the shoreline where they form palagonitic tuff cones, such as the well-known landmark Diamond Head.

Some of the ultramafic inclusions brought up in the late-stage alkaline magmas of Hawaii have textures and well-developed layering similar to that of large, layered intrusions, but their mineral assemblages, some of which include garnet, could only have formed at depths below fifty or sixty kilometers, well within the mantle. It may well be that the highly alkaline differentiates of oceanic islands

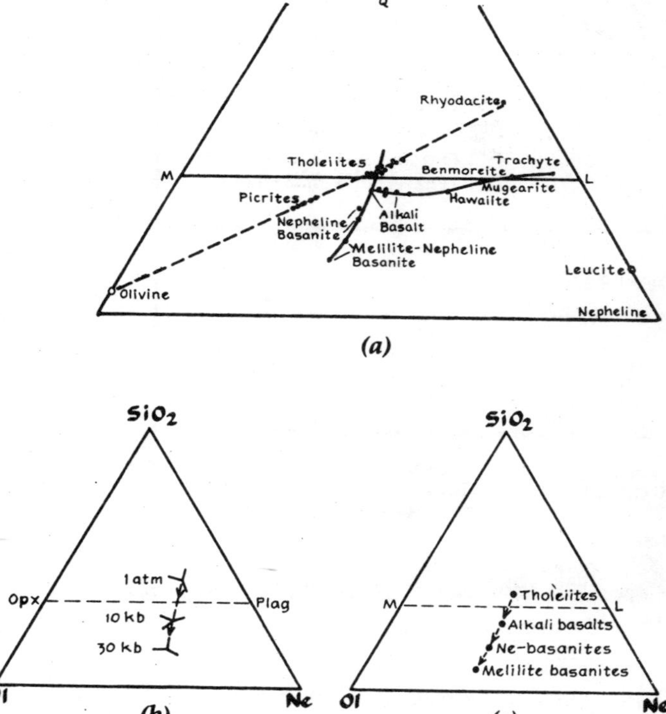

Figure 8–16 (a) Von Wolff diagram for the rocks of Hawaii. Note the trend of tholeiitic compositions directly away from olivine (along the dashed "control line") and the course of differentiation from alkaline basalts to trachyte close to the line of silica saturation, ML. The change of compositions of basalts during evolution of the islands is shown by the steep solid line from tholeiites to melilite-nepheline basanites. The construction of the diagram is explained in Figure 7–9. (Adapted from G. A. Macdonald, 1968, *Geol. Soc. Amer. Mem.* 116:477–522.) (b) The system olivine-nepheline-silica projected from anorthite is a close analog to the diagram in (a), even though it does not include as many components. When the Hawaiian basalts in (a) are plotted in the same way (c), they define a trend close to that of the invariant point in the synthetic system.

evolve at these depths rather than in the high-level reservoirs within the volcano itself. It will be recalled from the preceding chapter that differentiation of the alkaline series of Tahiti could not be explained as the result of fractionation of the minerals found in plutonic rocks within the upper levels of the volcano but was quite consistent with crystallization of garnet and an aluminous sodic pyroxene.

With the exception of the varied products of the small volcano Loihi at the leading edge of the chain, the overall trend of the Hawaiian basalts is toward increasingly more alkaline compositions. This is shown most clearly by comparing their normative components on a von Wolff diagram (Fig. 8–16a) of the kind used to trace the Tahitian series (Fig. 7–9). The diagram is analogous to the system olivine-plagioclase-silica (Fig. 8–16b and c). The migration of the invariant point toward more silica-deficient compositions with increasing pressure parallels that of the Hawaiian basalts and indicates that the source of the Hawaiian lavas becomes deeper with time and distance from the hotspot. This is also consistent with the mineral assemblages of mafic and ultramafic inclusions, which, as we saw in the preceding chapter, indicate deeper origins for the more alkaline basalts.

The Galapagos Islands

The volcanoes of the Galapagos Islands are of special interest because of their extraordinary zoning and relationship to a nearby spreading ridge. The islands rise from a shallow submarine platform at the west end of the Carnegie Ridge and on the southern flank of the Galapagos Spreading Center (Fig. 8–17).

The character of volcanism in the Galapagos Islands differs from the simple pattern of Hawaii and other intra-plate chains, in that the volcanoes have a broader distribution and a greater range of compositions and eruptive behavior. Most historic eruptions have been concentrated in the large, youthful shield volcanoes close to the hotspot. The islands are generally older toward the east, but several have had renewed activity after drifting as far as 250 km to the east. These young lavas are almost indistinguishable from those erupted closer to the hotspot.

While the lavas follow no regular sequence as the islands become older and drift away from the hotspot, they have a remarkable spatial zoning that seems to have persisted for at least five million years (Fig. 8–18). With increasing distance outward from the central axis, basalts become richer in olivine, alkalies, MgO, and radiogenic Sr. All the differentiated rocks are confined to a narrow belt down the center of the archipelago. The origin of this zoning is suggested by Figure 8–18c, in which the minimum Mg numbers for individual eruptive centers have been contoured for the system as a whole. The low values near the center reflect the differentiated character of the ferro-basalts, icelandites, and rhyolites described in the preceding chapter. Higher values near the margins correspond to lavas of basaltic composition, but only part of their variation can be attributed to differentiation; near the edges of the platform, the increase of MgO coincides with a change from tholeiitic to more alkaline compositions, suggesting that it is due less to differentiation than to differing depths or degrees of partial melting.

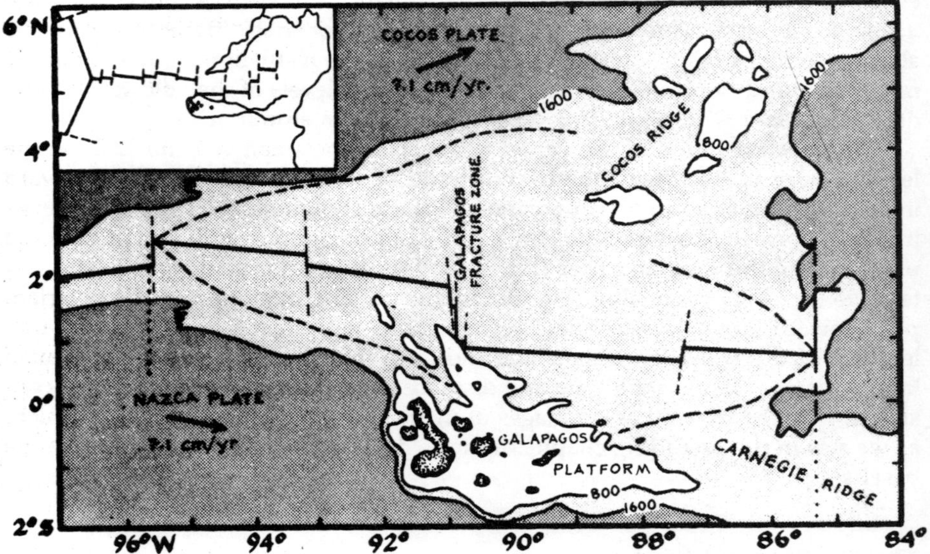

Figure 8–17 The Galapagos Islands stand on a broad platform south of the Galapagos Spreading Axis in the eastern equatorial Pacific. The Carnegie and Cocos ridges extend from the Galapagos hotspot in the directions of spreading indicated by arrows on the Nazca and Cocos plates on opposite sides of the spreading axis.

Support for this interpretation is found in the trace-element patterns of the lavas (Fig. 8–19). If the abundances of two incompatible elements, such as Zr and Th, are plotted against one another, they define linear trends of constant ratio for lavas that are related by crystal fractionation under conditions where both elements are equally excluded. Because the distribution coefficients for the crystallizing minerals are both very small, the two elements are concentrated to the same relative degree as the fraction of remaining liquid declines. Hence, slightly different initial Zr-Th ratios of the parental magmas are preserved and magnified throughout the differentiated series. Note that the trend for these same elements in the lavas of Floreana Island on the southern edge of the platform differs from those of more central islands in being non-linear and having a much greater enrichment of Th than of Zr. Using the equations of trace-element distributions for crystal fractionation and partial melting in chapter five (equations 5–4 and 5–11), the observed distribution can be compared with that predicted for crystallization or melting of a mineral assemblage that includes different possible mantle minerals, namely spinel and plagioclase. Because the distribution coefficient of Zr for spinel is slightly larger than for plagioclase, the closest fit to the observed pattern of relatively slow Zr enrichment is obtained using that mineral. The calculated curve for partial melting reproduces the observed variation much more closely than the one for crystal fractionation. One can conclude, therefore, that the variations near the margins of the hotspot are due mainly to differing amounts of melting at a level below the plagioclase-spinel transition. This is consistent with the more alkaline character of the rocks in the same region.

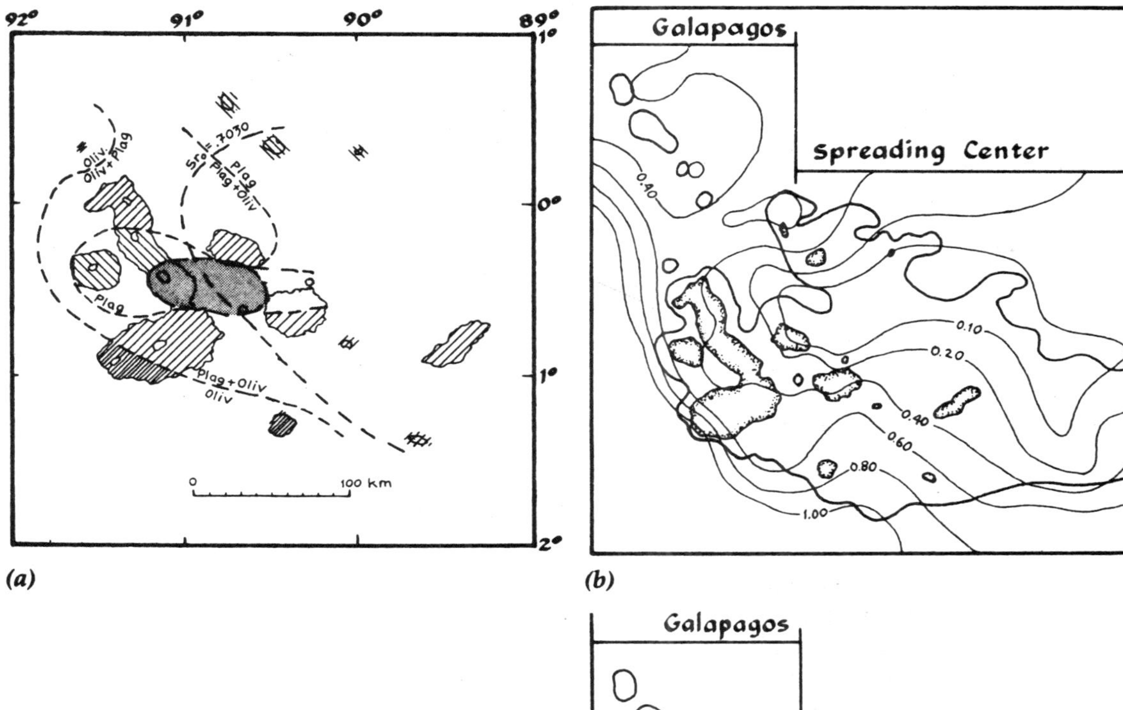

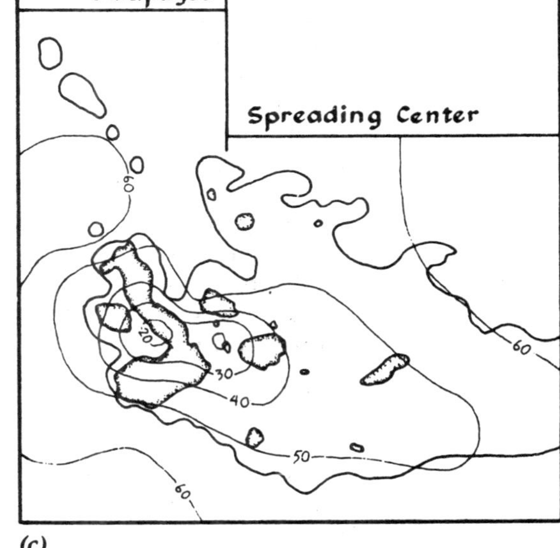

Figure 8–18 Compositional zoning of the Galapagos. (a) The most important phenocrysts of basalts are plagioclase in the central part of the archipelago, but olivine becomes more important toward the margins at the same time that the basalts become more alkaline. Differentiated lavas and plutonic xenoliths are found in the central zone with dark shading. (b) The K_2O contents of basalts (at a uniform value of 8 percent MgO) increase outward from the central axis. Basalts of the central islands closely resemble those of mid-ocean ridges, whereas those toward the outer margins are more like basalts of intra-plate settings. The edge of the Galapagos Platform is shown by a heavy line corresponding to the 1,000 fathom contour. (c) When the minimum MG numbers (MgO/MgO + FeO*) for individual eruptive centers are contoured for the archipelago as a whole they reflect the strong differentiation just downstream from the hotspot and the gradational change to more primitive compositions at the margins.

Origins of intra-plate magmas

While there is general agreement that the magmas of mid-ocean ridges are products of pressure-relief melting in the upwelling asthenosphere, interpretations of intra-plate magmas are much less unanimous. Deciphering the origins of these magmas is currently one of the most challenging problems of modern petrology.

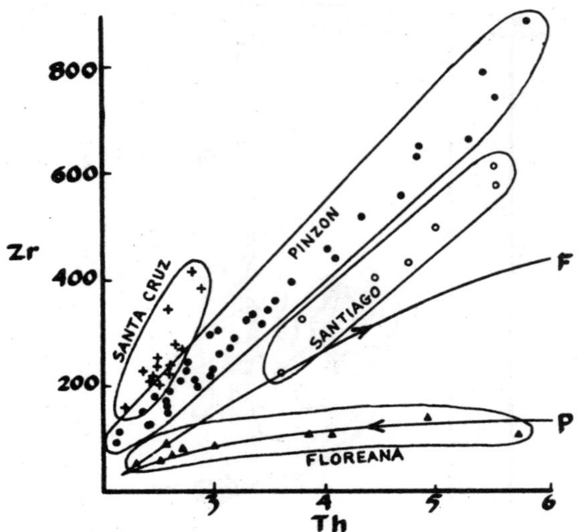

Figure 8–19 Variations of Zr and Th in the lavas of four islands of the Galapagos Archipelago. Curves labeled F and P are calculated variations of Zr and Th for crystal fractionation and partial melting respectively. The arrows indicate the directions of increasing differentiation and melting. See text for explanation. (After C. S. Bow, 1979, PhD Thesis, Univ. of Oregon.)

Most agree that hotspots are fed by some kind of mantle plumes rising from great depths, but the source and mechanism of melting is in dispute.

Although hotspots are, by definition, conventionally considered to be thermal anomalies, even this basic premise has been questioned. Recent studies suggest that melting is due, not to an anomalous heat source, but to an influx of volatile components that induce flux melting by lowering the solidus temperature of the source rocks. A study of the basalts and associated peridotites of the Azores hotspot, for example, has revealed that, despite the greater degrees of melting required to account for the volumes and compositions of the lavas, the mineral assemblages indicate that temperatures were no greater than those that produce normal MORB and may well have been substantially lower.

Whatever the melting mechanism responsible for these magmas, their distinctive character indicates that they have a source quite different from that of normal MORB. This is best seen from the isotopic ratios of certain elements that provide a way of seeing through the effects of shallow differentiation. As we noted in the opening chapter, the distinctive isotopic ratios that characterize basalts coming from different mantle reservoirs are not materially altered by most processes of partial melting or differentiation; they can be changed only by long term radioactive decay or by interaction with other material with an isotopically different character. Thus, the isotopic ratio of a magma preserves the imprint of its source, even after the absolute abundances of the elements have been changed. The basic principles of isotopic geochemistry are explained in Appendix D, and the theory of the isotopic evolution of the earth was outlined in chapter 1. Here we need only note that basalts of different tectonic settings tend to have distinctive ratios of certain radiogenic isotopes, such as Sr and Nd, and that these ratios are inherited from their sources in the mantle.

The characteristic Sr and Nd ratios of basalts in different tectonic settings are illustrated in Figure 8–12. Note that the two ratios have a remarkable negative correlation. Mid-ocean ridge basalts fall at the upper end of this "mantle array," and oceanic islands tend to be spread along lower parts of the trend with the measured values for particular islands or groups of volcanoes forming clusters, each with its own isotopic character. The variation along this trend results mainly from differences in the abundances of the parent radioactive elements, Rb and Sm, from which the daughter products, ^{87}Sr and ^{144}Nd, are derived, so that ratios falling along the lower-right part of the array come from sources that were relatively richer in these elements. The differences between the basalts of mid-ocean ridges and those of intra-plate hotspots, like the Galapagos, Hawaiian, or Society islands, suggest that the former come from more depleted and well-mixed mantle, whereas hotspots tap sources that are both less depleted and less homogeneous.

Intra-plate basalts, unlike MORB, have isotopic ratios that vary on several scales with time, age, and location. On a very local scale, small seamounts differ from one another over short distances, and even the lavas of a single volcano may differ from one flow to the next. Large volcanoes are more uniform. Unlike the small, scattered volcanoes that seem to be formed by small, discrete batches of magma drawn from a limited source in an inhomogeneous mantle, the magmas that produce large volcanoes are the integrated products of larger systems in which local inhomogeneities are absorbed and averaged out in a greater volume. This is not to say, however, that large volcanoes are totally uniform. Even the giant Hawaiian volcanoes have minor geochemical variations, particularly as they drift away from a hotspot and pass through successive stages of activity.

Clues to the origins of hotspots can be found in the way they interact with spreading ridges. The thermal regimes of hotspots and spreading ridges seem to provide favorable paths for one another. Certain hotspots seem to have controlled the positions of ridges, and, because the former remain fixed, they restrict the freedom of ridges to move. The hotspot under Iceland, for example, appears to have determined the location of rifting when the Mid-Atlantic Ridge was formed in the Eocene and has remained under the ridge axis ever since. The Galapagos hotspot remained directly under the Galapagos Spreading Center for at least 20 million years and separated from it only after the rest of the ridge had migrated farther than the plume could be deflected. Wherever they are close to one another, spreading ridges and hotspots interact both geochemically and tectonically, even when they are separated by several hundred kilometers. The basalts erupted from ridges on or near hotspots are more voluminous and are a distinctive "enriched" type of MORB.

The Galapagos hotspot is an excellent example. While it was centered under the spreading ridge, the augmented production of that part of the spreading axis produced the Carnegie and Cocos ridges as the Nazca and Cocos plates separated toward the southeast and northeast respectively. Even after migrating north, the ridge has continued to produce greater volumes of basalt in the section immediately adjacent to the hotspot. The elevation of that part of the ridge is higher than normal (Fig. 8–20), and its basalts are richer in K_2O, light REE, and most incompatible elements. They also have larger $^{87}Sr/^{86}Sr$ ratios. Similar rela-

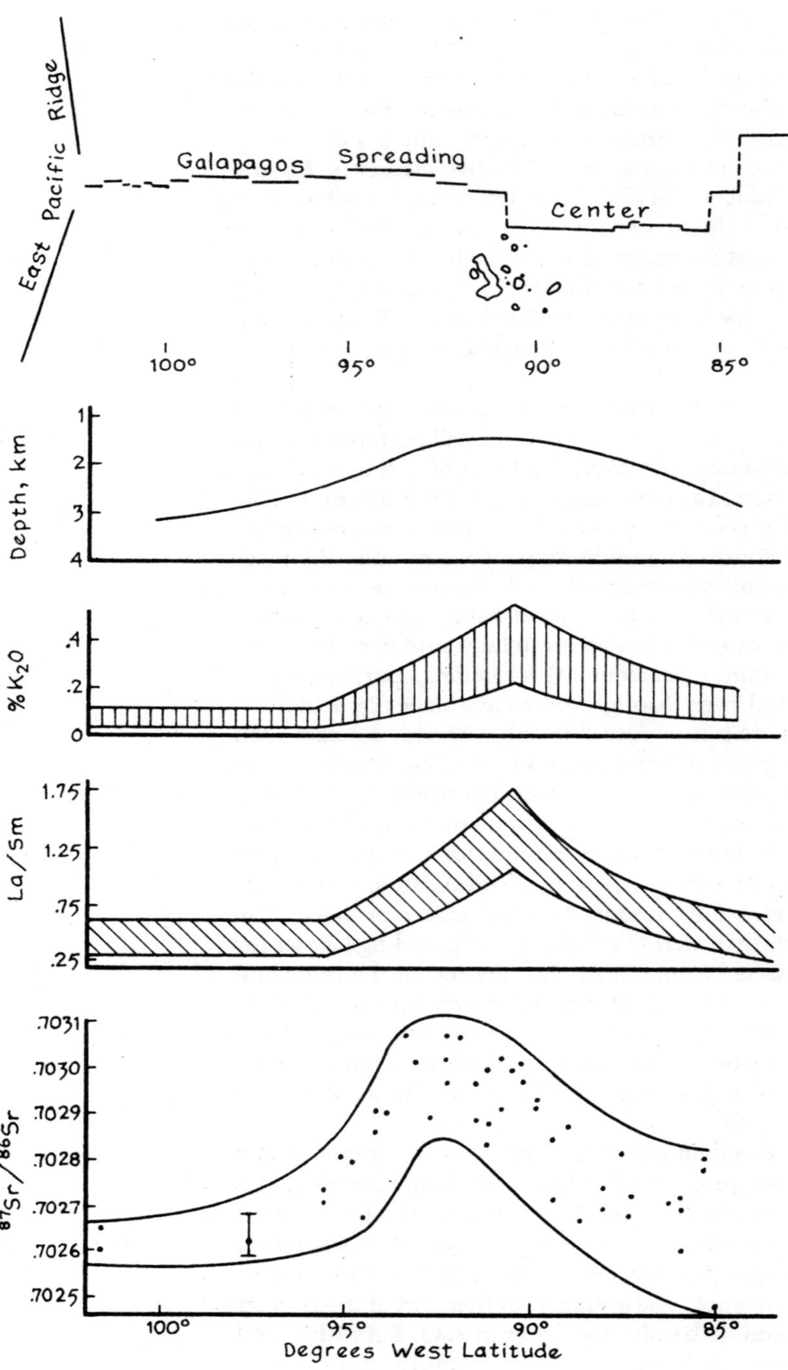

Figure 8–20 Variations of depth, K_2O, La/Sm, and $^{87}Sr/^{86}Sr$ along the axis of the Galapagos spreading center show the effect of the Galapagos hotspot, which occupied that part of the spreading ridge until five million years ago. (After S. P. Verma and J-G. Schilling, 1982, *Jour. Geoph. Res.* 87:10,838–10,856, and S. P. Verma, J-G. Schilling, and D. G. Waggoner, 1983, *Nature* 306:654–657.)

tions are found in the Atlantic, most notably south of Iceland and near the hotspots underlying the Azores, Jan Mayen, and Tristan da Cunha, where marked geochemical gradients extend along the adjacent ridges. These differences are attributed to different proportions of magma derived from enriched and depleted sources in the mantle.

The compositions of enriched MORB at ridge-centered hotspots are much less varied than those of basalts erupted from hotspots much farther from spreading axes (Table 8–1). Their isotopic ratios have a smaller range, and they have more uniform major and trace-element compositions. These relations indicate that hotspot magmas have at least two main components, one with a relatively constant composition represented by enriched MORB and a second derived from a source that varies widely in composition on a regional scale. The first component could be the result of small degrees of melting of the asthenosphere, but it is unlikely to be the same mantle source responsible for the basalts of normal ridges, because, as we have seen, the two types of MORB have basic differences in their trace-element and isotopic characteristics. An additional component could come from the lithospheric mantle. Plumes rising from deeper sources may partially melt the basal part of the lithosphere, either by an influx of heat or by volatile fluxing. When entrained in the plume, the resulting melt would contribute a geochemical factor that would vary with the amount of melting and local composition of the lithosphere.

As we noted earlier, the magmas of the Galapagos hotspot have compositional variations complementary to those of the adjacent ridge. Basalts erupted near the center are MORB-like (Fig. 8–18b), while those toward the margins are more like normal ocean-island basalts. This reversed relation has been explained as the result of melting and entrainment of the youthful lithosphere by a plume having an original composition more like that of basalts erupted on the outermost peripheral islands. Because the lithosphere is so close to the ridge, it has had little time to evolve compositionally and still retains a composition close to that of MORB.

Not all the variation in hotspots can be due to melting of the lithospheric mantle; some must reflect inhomogeneities in the source region. Some petrologists attribute them to subducted lithosphere that has accumulated at some level of the mantle, possibly at the core-mantle boundary or in the transition zone between the upper and lower mantles (Fig. 1–8). Others call upon streaks or pods of enriched mantle within the asthenosphere. We shall return to consider these possibilities in the final chapter when we take an overview of the earth as a whole.

FLOOD AND PLATEAU BASALTS

Somewhat akin to mid-ocean ridge basalts are the great flood basalts that from time to time overwhelm vast areas of the continents and seafloor (Fig. 8–21, Table 8–2). Both are discharged in great volume from fissures rather than central-vent volcanoes. Wherever feeder systems of flood basalts have been exposed by ero-

Figure 8–21 View of the basaltic flood lavas of the Columbia River plateau of Washington and Oregon in the northwestern United States.

sion, they are seen to be mazes of dikes, typically of great number, extent, and complexity (Fig. 8–22).

No other form of basaltic volcanism even approaches the scale of these outpourings. The most familiar example in America is the group of basalts forming the Columbia River Plateau of Oregon and Washington. Hundreds of lava flows, some with volumes exceeding 2,000 km^3, covered about 163,000 km^2 and had a total volume of about 174,300 km^3. Yet the Columbia River basalts rank only tenth in size among the flood basalts of the world. The Mesozoic Karoo basalts

Table 8–2 Notable features of some of the more important flood-basalt provinces. Types of basalt are listed according to their normative classifications and their estimated relative volumetric proportions. The original dimensions of pre-Tertiary provinces are very conjectural. The Brito-Arctic Province encompasses parts of Eastern Greenland, Ireland, Scotland, and the Faeroe Islands.

Province	Age	Original Dimensions, km^2	Types of Basalt		
			Qtz Thol	Oliv Thol.	Alk. Bas.
Lake Superior	Precambrian	125,000	42	51	7
Siberia	Permo-Triassic	2,500,000	28	69	3
Karoo, S. Africa	Jurassic	2,000,000	57	37	6
Paraná, Brazil	Cretaceous	2,000,000	72	28	0
Ontang-Java	Cretaceous	1,500,000	20	80	0
Brito-Arctic	Eocene	200,000	5	50	45
Deccan, India	Eocene	500,000	55	35	10
Columbia River	Mid-Miocene	163,000	30	70	—

Figure 8–22 Dikes exposed in cliffs along the eastern coast of Greenland fed basaltic flood lavas along a rift formed at the time of the opening of the North Atlantic. As Greenland separated from northern Europe, the activity became focused in what is now the Mid-Atlantic Ridge.

are roughly twelve times larger, both in areal extent and volume. While mid-ocean ridges produce greater total volumes of basalt, this is only because their activity is more prolonged. Eruptions of flood basalt are restricted to shorter intervals of time. By far the greatest volume of basalt in the Columbia River group was erupted within a period of only two or three million years during the mid-Miocene (Fig. 8–23). Individual eruptions were separated by periods of repose lasting thousands of years, but, once initiated, their rates of discharge were colossal, in some cases of the order of tens or hundreds of cubic kilometers per day.

The total section of Columbia River Basalts reaches a thickness of about ten kilometers near their center, and yet the surface onto which the lavas flowed seems never to have been high or to have developed much relief. As basalts poured out on the surface, the underlying rocks subsided to form a basin with almost the same size and extent as the lavas that filled it. It would seem that the zone from which magmas were withdrawn had about the same extent and thickness as the pile of lava filling the basin; the process was simply one of transferring mass from the mantle or lower crust to the surface. If so, the source of a large part of the magma must have been within the lithospheric mantle, not in the convecting asthenosphere.

The great sill complexes mentioned in chapter 6 are also manifestations of the same type of magmatism, but the basins with which they are associated were

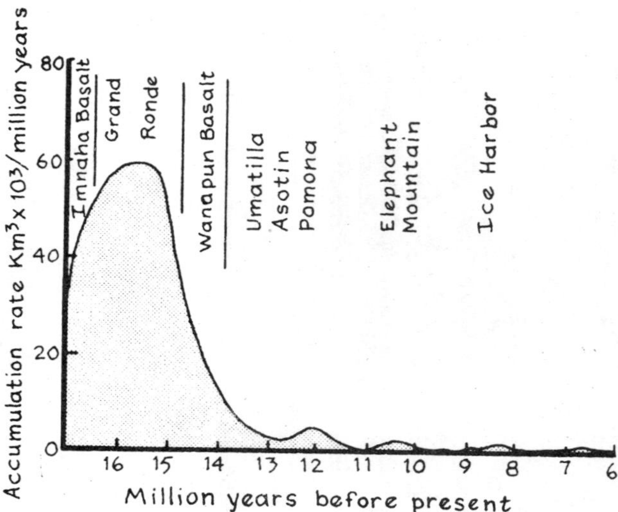

Figure 8–23 Volumes of Columbia River basalt erupted as a function of time. (After P. R. Hooper, 1988, in *Continental Flood Basalts*, J. D. Macdougall, ed., 1–33.)

filled with sediments. Because of their greater densities basaltic magmas are unable to rise through the light sediments and instead intrude laterally along planes of equal gravitational potential.

The term "plateau basalts" is often applied to extensive lavas that were not the products of voluminous fissure eruptions but of many scattered sources, each of which produced relatively small individual flows. Where these flows merge and overlap they form seemingly continuous sheets of great lateral extent, but their volumes are generally smaller than those of true flood basalts. Despite these differences, however, plateau and flood basalts may have much in common, both in tectonic setting and composition, and one may simply be a weaker counterpart of the other.

Oceanic plateau basalts of Cretaceous age cover a large region of the southwestern Pacific Ocean between New Guinea and the Marshall Islands. The largest group forms the Ontong-Java Plateau, covering an area of a million and a half square kilometers with a relief of about three kilometers above the normal depth of the seafloor. Though normally referred to as plateau basalts, their vent systems cannot be seen, so it is quite possible that they are actually flood basalts discharged from a large intra-plate fissure system. Erupted from sources near but slightly west of the Cretaceous spreading axis, they resemble mid-ocean ridge tholeiites, but their incompatible elements are somewhat less depleted (Table 8-1).

Large fissure eruptions of basalts are found in a variety of tectonic settings. Some were associated with continental rifting and opening of oceanic basins. The basalts along the east coast of Greenland, for example, correspond to similar flood lavas in northern Ireland and Scotland and date from the opening of the North Atlantic in Eocene time. Others, such as those of the Lake Superior region and Siberia, seem to have been associated with rifting that was less extensive or

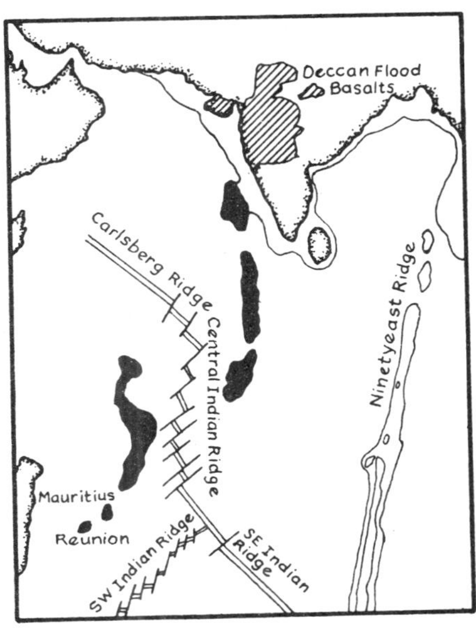

Figure 8–24 The Deccan flood basalts of India are the earliest products of a hotspot that was initiated at the end of the Mesozoic and beginning of the Cenozoic eras. As the Indian Plate drifted northward over the stationary hotspot, a ridge and chain of seamounts was created along the ocean floor. The hotspot is presently under the active volcano Piton de la Fournaise on the island of Reunion. (Adapted from R. A. Duncan, J. Backman, and L. Peterson, 1989, *Jour. Volc. Geoth. Res.* 36:193–198.)

aborted at an early stage. The origin of the Columbia River basalts is less clear. They were erupted behind an active belt of subduction-related volcanism that was at its peak intensity, but some consider this a coincidence, favoring instead an origin related to the beginning of the hotspot now under Yellowstone.

There is little doubt that several important flood basalts marked the initial volcanic expression of a new hotspot. The Deccan Plateau of India is perhaps the best example (Fig. 8–24). At the beginning of the Cenozoic Era, basalts flooded much of what is now the western coast of India. As the Indian and African plates moved northward, the hotspot formed a ridge and chain of submarine volcanoes that extends southward into the Indian Ocean. The present site of the hotspot is under the active volcano Piton de la Fournaise on the island of Reunion.

When activity on the Deccan Plateau ceased, it never returned, even long after moving far from the hotspot. The same is true of the Columbia Plateau and most, if not all, other sites of great basaltic eruptions. Having expended this much magma and thermal energy, the mantle seems unable to produce new magma from the same source region.

Compositions

Flood basalts differ widely in composition from one region to another and even within an individual province. While most are tholeiitic, some are alkaline, and others include both. Many plateau basalts, especially in the western United States, are a distinct, high-alumina variety (Table 8–3) characterized by Al_2O_3 contents in excess of 16.5 percent. Though most are hypersthene-normative, a few have small amounts of normative nepheline.

Table 8–3 Compositions of flood and plateau basalts of the continents, earth, and the moon. FeO* is total iron as FeO. All norms except 5 and 6 are calculated assuming a uniform ratio of Fe_2O_3 to FeO of 0.15.

	1.	2.	3.	4.	5.	6.
SiO_2	46.87	49.60	48.35	48.48	42.16	45.03
TiO_2	1.64	1.08	1.57	0.76	9.43	2.90
Al_2O_3	9.31	14.20	15.49	18.15	9.89	8.59
FeO*	12.17	10.74	10.98	9.11	19.11	21.03
MnO	0.17	0.20	0.17	0.18	0.28	0.28
MgO	15.91	8.02	7.03	9.23	5.67	11.55
CaO	9.06	12.44	9.92	11.23	12.15	9.42
Na_2O	1.32	2.01	2.76	2.36	0.45	0.23
K_2O	0.56	0.06	0.51	0.23	0.11	0.06
P_2O_5	0.20	0.10	0.24	0.05	0.04	—
Molecular Norns						
Ap	0.43	0.21	0.52	0.10	0.09	—
Il	2.32	1.54	2.26	1.05	14.23	4.23
Mt	2.14	1.52	1.96	1.42	—	—
Or	3.36	0.36	3.12	1.35	0.70	0.37
Ab	12.04	18.45	25.63	21.03	4.38	2.16
An	18.12	30.20	29.34	37.96	26.70	23.31
Di	20.99	25.77	15.95	13.60	30.67	20.55
Hy	21.56	20.30	13.66	7.91	19.95	36.87
Ol	19.05	1.65	7.58	15.57	—	12.50
Q	—	—	—	—	3.27	—
Trace Elements (ppm)						
Ba	272	2	280	62	88	69
Zr	129	52	108	39	334	107
Rb	23	1	6	4.7	0.9	1.1
Sr	445	88	274	205	194	96
Cr	848	342	188	259	1230	3780
Ni	675	125	77	175	<2	52
La	13.4	2.7	7.4	3.1	11.3	6.1
Sm	5.3	2.3	3.5	1.9	14.4	4.5
Lu	0.2	0.4	0.4	0.36	1.0	0.6
$^{86}Sr/^{87}Sr$	.7056	.7037	.7037	.7033	.6991	.6991

1. Picritic Karoo basalt (R. M. Ellam and C. K. Cox, *Earth Planet. Sci. Ltrs.* 92:207–218 and 105:330–342.)
2. Typical ocean plateau basalt, Nauru Basin (P. A. Floyd, 1989, *Magmatism in the Ocean Basins*, A. D. Saunders and M. J. Norry, eds. 215–230.)
3. Columbia River Basalt, Picture Gorge type.
4. Pliocene high-Al basalt, central Oregon (David Draper, pers. comm.)
5. High-Ti lunar basalt, Apollo 11.
6. Low-Ti lunar basalt, Apollo 12.

With few exceptions, all these varieties of flood and plateau basalts are less "primitive" than the basalts of oceanic spreading axes. Their MgO contents are normally less than eight weight percent, and many are less than five. The chief exceptions are picrites that are found among the earliest lavas of several major provinces.

The differentiated character of such large masses of magma has presented a long-standing dilemma. Despite their great volume, the lavas were surprisingly homogeneous when erupted, and sequences of many flows maintain almost constant compositions, even though many centuries elapsed between eruptions. And yet these same flows differentiated, much in the way the ponded lavas of Hawaii have, in the periods of a few decades it took them to cool and crystallize. Eternal petrologic fame awaits the student who finds the explanation for this paradox.

The most conspicuous variations in the Columbia River basalts are between major groups of lavas erupted at different times and from different dike swarms. But, taking the entire series as a whole, no consistent evolutionary trend is seen in the sequence of compositional changes or relative volumes with time. The different compositions are difficult to relate to each other by any simple scheme of crystal fractionation or mixing. A notable example is the suite of rhyolites erupted intermittently during the outpouring of Deccan basalts. These felsic magmas have no direct genetic relation to the basalts; most likely, they resulted from melting of the continental crust.

While it is difficult to imagine masses of basaltic magma of such dimensions being products of fractionation of even larger bodies, their compositions are difficult to reconcile with any other explanation. The size of the magma body required to produce batches of well-mixed magmas with volumes measured in hundreds or thousands of cubic kilometers would be comparable to that of the Bushveld Intrusion. The fact that most of the basalts, including even the most differentiated, are aphyric indicates that if the magmas evolved by crystal fractionation, the crystals must have accumulated along the cooling margins without settling through the interior. Unusually high seismic velocities found in the crust just below some flood basalt provinces indicate that dense layers of crystals did indeed accumulate on the roofs or floors of large, shallow reservoirs.

The most likely candidates for primary magmas that could be parental to the differentiated basalts are picrites found among the earliest lavas of several provinces, particularly the Karoo and North Atlantic. The resemblance of these picrites to the magmas of certain hot spots is consistent with the notion that the two are simply different expressions of the same basic phenomenon. The similarities are quite strong despite the greater interaction of the flood basalt with the continental crust or lithospheric mantle.

Large concentrations of incompatible elements are typical of flood basalts, especially the earliest, most primitive lavas. In some provinces, most notably the Karoo, the most magnesian lavas are those with the greatest concentrations of incompatible elements! The explanation offered for this apparent anomaly is that the incompatible elements were more readily scavenged from the lithosphere by the early, exceptionally hot, picritic magmas and that subsequent cooler magmas passing through rocks that had already been depleted were less affected.

LUNAR FLOOD BASALTS

Though found in an entirely different environment, the basalts of the moon offer a number of instructive contrasts to those of the earth. The surface of the moon, it will be recalled, is divided into two distinct types of topography, the highlands, consisting of plagioclase-rich anothosites, and the mare, flat lowlands and basins filled with flood basalts. Although the basalts cover about 17 percent of the surface, they are so thin that they account for less than one percent of the total mass of the moon. Their viscosity was very low, even lower than that of terrestrial flood basalts (Fig. 2-10), and many flows spread for distances of hundreds or even thousands of kilometers on nearly flat surfaces.

The greatest volumes were erupted between about 4.0 and 3.15 billion years ago, with very minor activity continuing a few hundred million years longer before all volcanism came to an end. The period during which most lavas were discharged followed formation of the lunar highlands and came shortly after bombardment by meteorites reached its peak intensity. The distribution of volcanism is extraordinarily asymmetrical, being confined largely to the earth-facing side of the moon. The far side has an equivalent density of impact craters, but they are not filled with lava. The explanation for the scarcity of lavas on the far

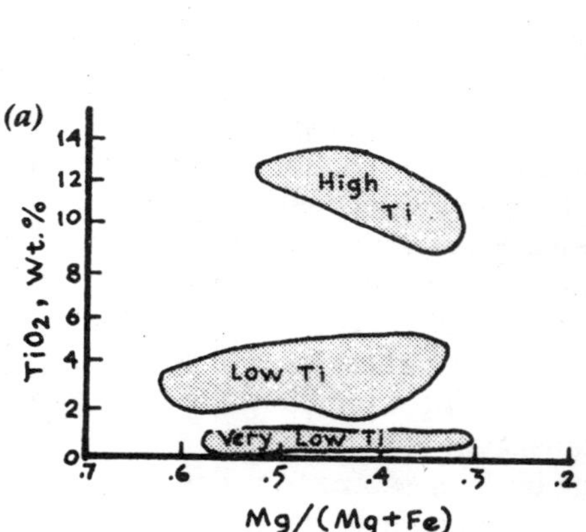

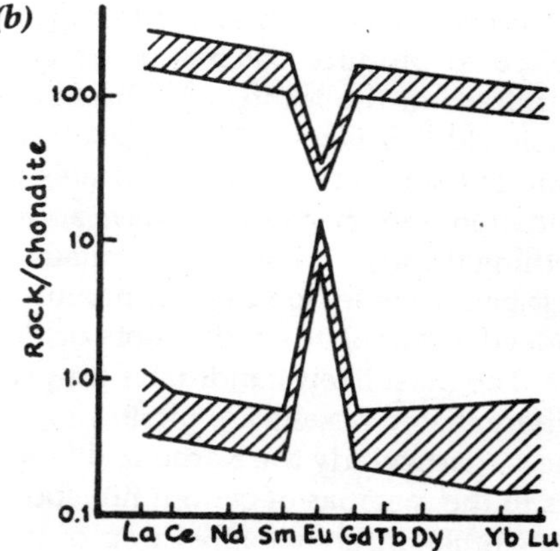

Figure 8-25 (a) Lunar basalts can be separated into three distinct groups on the basis of their TiO_2 contents. Note that their Mg ratios overlap, showing that they cannot be related to each other by any normal mechanism of differentiation. (b) The rare-earth concentrations in lunar anorthosites (below) have a reciprocal relation to those of basalts (above). Note the marked spike for Eu, which is preferentially concentrated in plagioclase, and its mirror image in basalts that result from fractionation of the plagioclase-rich anorthosites. (Adapted from compilations by S. R. Taylor, 1982, *Planetary Science: A Lunar Perspective*, Lunar Planet. Inst., 481 pp.)

side is based on the distribution of mass in the moon. Owing to the gravitational attraction of the earth, the center of mass is not at the geometric center but slightly closer to the earth, and the radius of the far side from the center of mass is greater. It is thought that magmas generated at depths of a few hundred kilometers were able to reach the surface on the near side, but on the far side they intruded the lighter rocks at some level not far beneath the surface.

The most conspicuous compositional feature that sets most lunar basalts apart from their terrestrial counterparts is their greater concentrations of titania, which in some samples reach 16 weight percent. This is particularly true of the earliest basalts; with time, TiO_2 shows a general decrease to values more like those of basalts on Earth. The decline was not a smooth one, however. The compositions of basalts fall into three groups, each with a distinctive TiO_2 content (Fig. 8–25a; Table 8-3). Owing to the more reducing conditions of the moon, ferric iron is absent, and a few rocks even contain small amounts of metallic iron. Water is also absent, and Na_2O, K_2O, and other components of feldspar are much less abundant than they are in terrestrial basalts.

The basaltic lavas are in some ways complementary to the anorthositic rocks of the highlands (Fig. 8–25b). The latter appear to be formed by a plagioclase-rich fraction that, being lighter, accumulated at the surface while a more mafic residue accumulated at a depth of 200 to 400 kilometers. The mechanisms by which the basalts evolved are still debated. The models currently entertained differ mainly in the timing and relative importance assigned to crystal fractionation, partial melting, and assimilation.

SELECTED REFERENCES

Basaltic Volcanism Study Project. 1981. *Basaltic Volcanism of the Terrestrial Planets*. Pergamon Press, 1,286 pp. This large compilation of data on basalts includes extensive sections on oceanic rocks.

Batiza, R. 1989. Seamounts and seamount chains of the Eastern Pacific. *The Geology of North America. Vol. N. The Eastern Pacific and Hawaii*. Geol. Soc. Amer., 289–306. An excellent summary of the structure, morphology, and tectonic relations of seamounts near the East Pacific Rise.

Coleman, R. G., C. A. Hopson, J. S. Pallister, and others. 1981. Oman Ophiolite, special issue of *Jour. Geoph. Res.* Vol. 86, No. B4. A collection of very stimulating papers dealing with a well-exposed and remarkably complete ophilitic complex.

Macdonald, G. A. 1968. Composition and origin of Hawaiian lavas. *Geol. Soc. Amer. Mem. 116*, 477–522. An excellent summary of the evolution of Hawaiian lavas and their relation to the stages of development of the volcanoes.

Macdougall, J. D., ed. 1988. *Continental Flood Basalts*. Kluwer Acad. Publ., 341 pp. A collection of outstanding papers on the major Phanerozoic flood basalts and their origins.

Nicolas, A. 1989. *Ophiolites and Dynamics of Oceanic Lithosphere*. Kluwer Acad. Publ., 367 pp. A detailed account of ophiolites with special emphasis on Oman. The treatment of dynamic processes is especially thorough.

Riedel, S. P., and P. R. Hooper, eds. 1989. *Volcanism and Tectonism in the Columbia River Flood-Basalt Province*. Geol. Soc. Amer. Spec. Paper 239, 386 pp. By far the most complete and up-to-date compilation of data on the Columbia River basalts.

Saunders, A. D., and M. J. Norry, eds. 1989. *Magmatism in the Ocean Basins.* Geol. Soc. Spec. Publ. 42, 398 pp. A collection of recent papers on the structure and petrology of oceanic igneous rocks.

Taylor, S. R. 1982. *Planetary Science: A Lunar Perspective.* Lunar and Planetary Inst., 481 pp. An excellent, comprehensive summary of the results of two decades of lunar studies.

Zindler, A., and S. Hart. 1986. Chemical geodynamics. *Ann. Rev. Earth Planet. Sci.* 14:493–571. A very extensive discussion of the origins of oceanic basalts with emphasis mainly on isotopic geochemistry.

9

OROGENIC VOLCANIC ROCKS

THE ROCKS CONSIDERED THUS FAR have been mainly those of simple geological settings where the composition and structure of the crust are less important than conditions in the mantle. The settings of convergent plate boundaries are more complex, and unambiguous interpretations are even more elusive than they are for oceanic rocks. In considering these orogenic rocks, we shall first examine their characteristic geologic settings and compositional features, then attempt to find how the two may be linked.

TECTONIC AND STRUCTURAL SETTINGS

Modern orogenic rocks occupy a distinctive place in global tectonics (Fig. 1–6). With few exceptions, they erupt only in island arcs or along active continental margins, mainly around the Pacific Ocean where oceanic lithosphere is subducted and descends to the mantle beneath volcanic chains. Although the descending lithosphere is in all cases oceanic, the overlying plate on which volcanism is focused may be either oceanic or continental. Where it is oceanic, the volcanoes tend to form arcuate chains of islands; where continental, they are elevated above sea level to form linear volcanic ranges close to the leading edge of the continent.

In most of these settings, a deep oceanic trench marks the surface expression of subduction and parallels the volcanic chain at a distance of about 150 to 250 kilometers (Fig. 9–1). At depth, the subducted slab is delineated by earthquakes concentrated in a dipping plane, known as a *Benioff zone*, that descends at angles of forty-five degrees or so beneath the volcanic axis to depths of up to 700 kilometers. Almost without exception, every region of plate convergence that has active volcanoes today also has earthquakes at depths of more than 100 kilometers. The reverse is equally true: no major region of deep seismicity, with the possible exception of parts of the Himalayan chain, is devoid of active andesitic volcanoes.

The most distinctive lavas erupted in these settings belong to a calc-alkaline series of which andesite is the most typical, though not necessarily the most

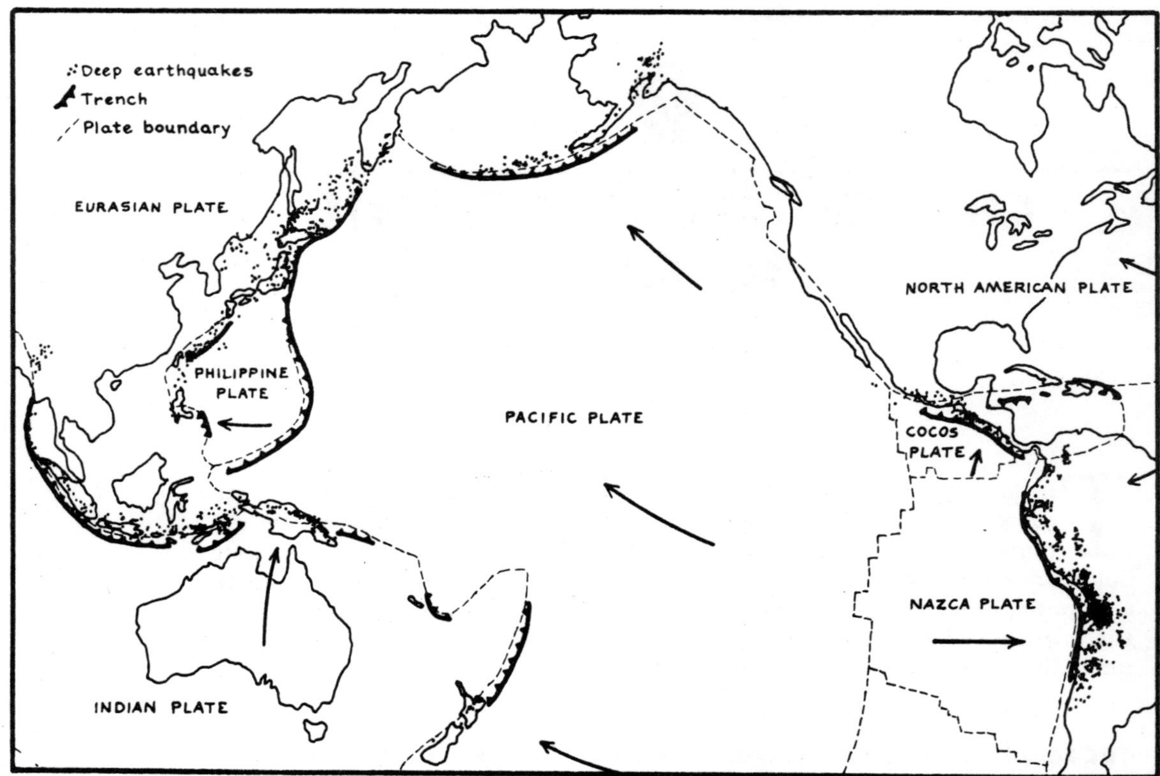

Figure 9–1 The principal setting of orogenic volcanism today is around the margins of the Pacific Ocean, where oceanic lithosphere spreading outward from the East Pacific Rise converges on the surrounding plates and plunges into the mantle. The nearly continuous line of trenches marking the convergent plate boundaries corresponds to an "andesite line," separating the chains of andesitic volcanoes from the interior of the oceanic basin where no calc-alkaline andesites are found. The distribution of volcanoes in island arcs and continental margins corresponds very well to the distribution of Benioff zones where earthquakes extend to depths as great as 700 km directly beneath the active volcanic belts.

abundant member. An "andesite line" drawn around the margins of the Pacific Ocean separates andesitic volcanoes from an interior region of the oceans in which orogenic rocks are totally absent. This is not to say that all rocks of these systems are calc-alkaline; many, especially those produced in the early stages of development of island arcs, have tholeiitic affinities. In some systems, individual volcanoes evolve from tholeiitic to more calc-alkaline compositions with time, and in a few modern chains, such as those of Central America and Japan, tholeiitic and calc-alkaline volcanoes stand side-by-side in the same chain. Nor are all andesites restricted to the margins of convergent plates above subduction zones; some are found in the interiors of continents far from the oceans. Nevertheless, calc-alkaline andesites are so characteristic of island arcs and active continental margins that their origin must be in some way related to the process of subduction.

The principal volcanoes of these systems form imposing chains along a "volcanic front" (Fig. 9-2). Few if any volcanoes are found on the trench side of this line, but in the opposite direction smaller cones, many of alkaline compositions, may be scattered over wide regions behind the volcanic arc. A low ridge of uplifted rocks may form an outer "non-volcanic arc" or coast range between the trench and volcanic front. Even where this structural block has no surface expression, geophysical profiles show that it lies below a cover of youthful shelf sediments. A second uplifted block is found closer to the volcanic axis of continental margins but is less conspicuous in island arcs.

Many volcanic chains of active continental margins are close to a shallow, graben-like depression. The volcanoes may be situated within the depression, along its margins, or even outside it, but depressions of this kind seem to develop only in volcanic belts with closely spaced active volcanoes producing large volumes of lava and tephra. Where these volcanic products have accumulated in the depression, only a subdued topographic expression marks the much greater structural relief of the basement.

An interior or marginal sea behind the main volcanic arc is characteristic of most island arcs, both in purely oceanic settings, as in the Marianas Arc, and where fragments of continental crust appear to have drifted seaward, as in New Zealand and Japan. Although few volcanoes rise from these marginal seas, the youthful ages of lavas on the seafloor testify to the volcanism associated with their formation. The igneous activity and types of rocks found in these *back-arc basins* resemble in many ways those of oceanic spreading axes and may have a similar origin.

Subduction and zones of earthquakes are not invariably accompanied by volcanism. This is seen most clearly in the Andes (Fig. 9-3). Although the Peru-Chile trench is continuous offshore and is everywhere associated with a dipping Benioff zone, volcanoes are active only in three segments where the angle of descent is steep and a wedge of asthenosphere lies between the Benioff zone and overlying lithosphere. Where the inclination of the zone of earthquakes is shallow and remains in the lithosphere to distances farther behind the axis of the Andes, volcanoes are scarce or totally absent. This relation indicates that the source of magma must lie in a wedge of asthenosphere between the Benioff zone and lithosphere, and only in that region are thermal and structural conditions appropriate for generation and rise of magmas.

ERUPTIVE BEHAVIOR

One of the most characteristic marks of andesitic volcanism is its high proportion of explosive eruptions. Unlike the shield volcanoes of oceanic islands, the large andesitic cones of the circum-Pacific system consist chiefly of pyroclastic ejecta with only subordinate amounts of lava. Not all of this eruptive material is pre-

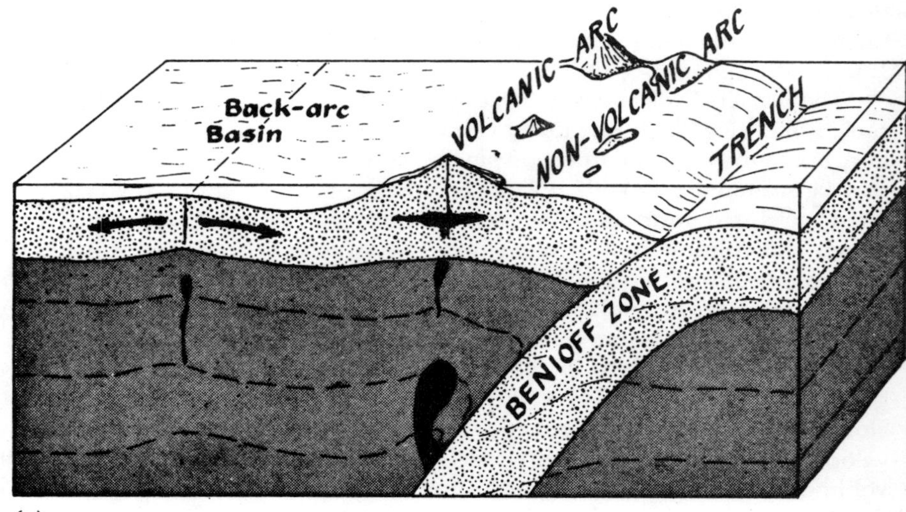

(a)

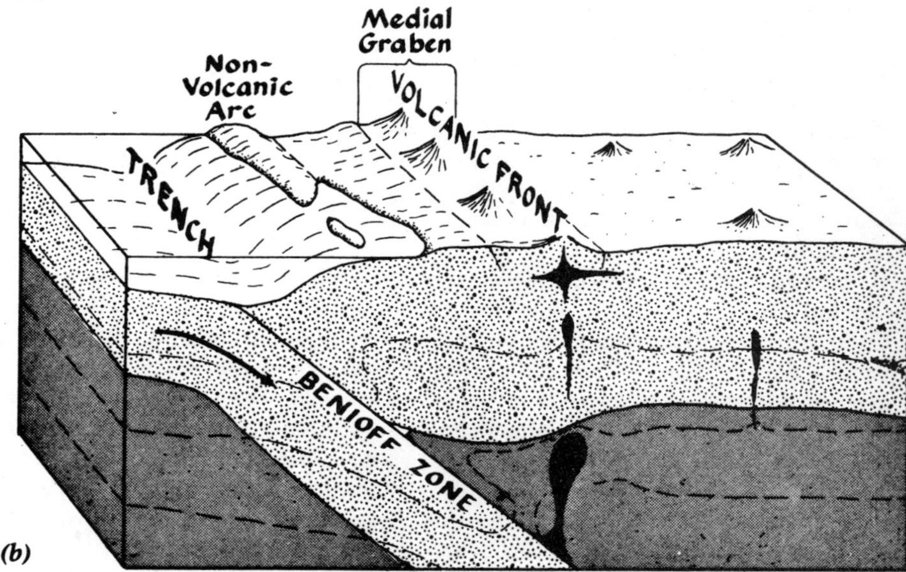

(b)

Figure 9–2 The volcanic chains of island arcs (a) and continental margins (b) share many essential elements. A trench, which in some places may be filled with sediments, marks the surface expression of subduction. Immediately inward and parallel to the trench a non-volcanic arc or coast range consists of uplifted and often highly deformed older sedimentary and igneous rocks. A second, less conspicuous, structural uplift rises to the main volcanic front on continental margins, and the volcanic front may stand within or along the margins of a medial graben. These features, though less apparent, are also present in some island arcs. In both settings, volcanoes may be distributed behind the volcanic front, but they are smaller and fewer in number. Most island arcs have a back-arc basin that seems to result from spreading behind the main volcanic arc.

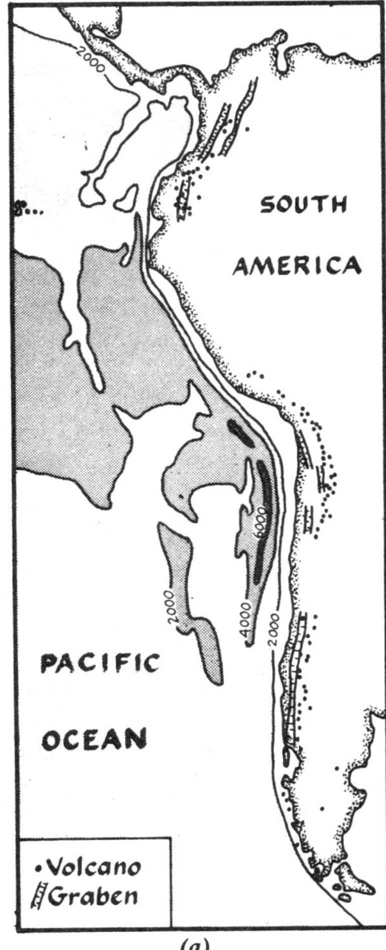

(a)

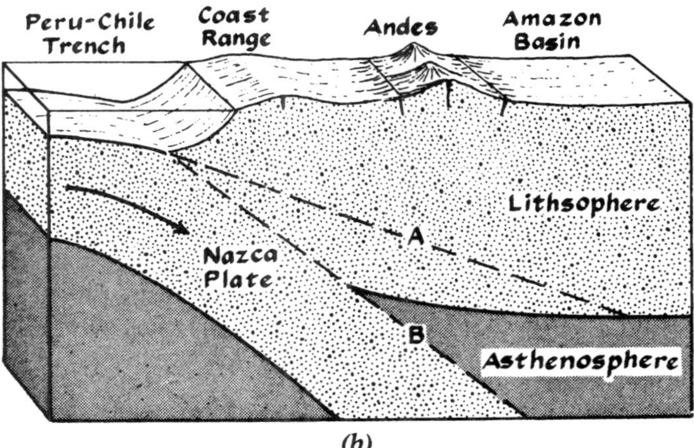

(b)

Figure 9–3 Even though the Peru-Chile Trench extends along almost the entire length of South America (a), volcanism is confined to three segments in which the dip of the Benioff zone (b) is steep enough to descend below the base of the lithosphere, so that a wedge of asthenosphere lies directly below the main axis of the Andes. Where the plane of the Benioff zone has a shallow dip, such as A, volcanism is absent; where it is steeper, as shown by B, a wedge of asthenosphere lies between the descending slab and lithosphere, and active volcanism is seen along the volcanic front. Medial grabens follow the volcanic axis and are absent from those parts of the chain without large active volcanoes.

served in the cones. Some of the most voluminous discharges from explosive eruptions, particularly those of the "Plinian" type, are spread over vast regions and tend to be carried away by erosion, leaving little evidence in the stratigraphic record. Deep-sea sediments preserve a record of this activity in the form of ash layers carried out to sea by wind or ocean currents. But these generalities apply only to large, mature volcanoes. In many places, particularly in the basal units on which the large volcanoes stand, basaltic lavas have issued from fissures or small cones, and although topographically less imposing than the majestic andesitic cones, these mafic lavas can account for large proportions of the total volume.

Orogenic volcanoes differ so widely in composition and eruptive behavior that it is difficult to identify any single pattern they have in common. Even within a single volcanic chain, adjacent volcanoes may develop in different ways. Most large andesitic volcanoes have probably grown from one or more cinder cones, commonly on dilational fissures, which, with time, became centralized in a symmetrical cone over a central complex of vents. Most produce large proportions of clastic material, including explosive air-fall tuffs, pyroclastic flows, and fragmental debris flows, or *lahars*. In their later stages, activity tends to become even more varied. Some mature volcanoes produce viscous domes of siliceous lava, others great eruptions of pumice triggering collapse of calderas. Still others have swarms of small cones of basalt or basaltic andesite around their base, while dacitic or rhyolitic domes or tephra are erupted on the upper flanks or summit. Perhaps the single most distinctive compositional feature of calc-alkaline volcanism is this close association in space and time of magmas of very different degrees of differentiation.

Growth is often rapid, especially in the early stages of cone building. Some volcanoes have grown to heights of 500 or 600 meters in periods of only a few centuries (Fig. 9–4). Basalt is common in youthful cones, andesite in more mature volcanoes, but this generalization has too many exceptions to have much petrologic meaning. Volcanoes of island arcs tend to have proportionately large volumes of andesitic basalt that, together with lesser amounts of andesite and dacite, form a continuous, differentiated series in which volumes decline with increasing silica content. On continental margins, the average silica contents of the rocks tend to be somewhat greater. The volcanoes of the Andes, for example, produce proportionately large amounts of andesite, dacite, and rhyolite, but little if any basalt. As a general rule, volcanoes on thick continental crust have larger proportions of silica-rich magmas than those on thin crust of more mafic composition.

The products of many continental volcanoes are distinctly bimodal, with large proportions of basic and siliceous rocks but few of intermediate compositions. This discontinuity is often referred to as a *Daly Gap* after the geologist R. A.

Figure 9–4 The volcano Izalco in El Salvador is an example of the rapid growth of andesitic cones. Since it first erupted in 1770, it has reached a height of about 500 meters. Eruptions of ash and lava were very frequent during its first century but have gradually declined. As can be seen in the foreground, much of the lava has accumulated around the base, while most of the volume of the cone is made up of pyroclastic material.

Daly, who drew attention to its importance. The bimodality may be expressed in a group of volcanoes, each producing a narrow range of compositions, either basic or siliceous, or it may characterize the products of a single volcanic center that erupts magmas of contrasting composition from one or more closely associated vents. The most extreme examples of bimodal assemblages are found in block-faulted continental regions where contrasting lavas erupt in seemingly random order from separate but nearby vents. Basalt-rhyolite complexes of this kind are found in most volcanic provinces, not only at the margins of continents but in the interiors of continents as well. An example from southeastern Guatemala is illustrated in Figure 9–5.

OROGENIC VOLCANIC ROCKS

Despite the importance of andesite in many provinces, especially those with thick continental crust, basalt is the most primitive composition of orogenic magma series and, as such, must be the parental magma from which andesites are differentiated. This is no less true of continental margins than of island arcs. The once-popular notion that andesites are primary magmas derived directly from melting of subducted oceanic crust would greatly simplify the problem of explaining their origin, but this interpretation is untenable in the light of what is

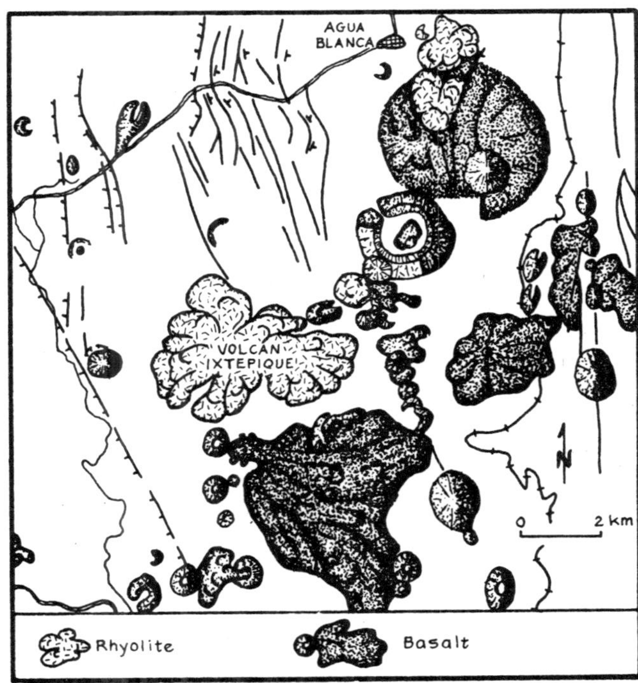

Figure 9–5 The Obrajuelo Complex of southeastern Guatemala is an example of the close association of basalt and rhyolite in a calc-aikaline province. Basaltic cinder cones and lava flows, many aligned along prominent fracture systems, are intermingled with pumice cones and viscous flows of obsidian.

now known about the rocks. Andesite is a derivative magma, and its parent is basalt.

Calc-alkaline rocks are often thought to be the most characteristic series of convergent plate boundaries, but, as we have already noted, tholeiitic rocks are no less important, especially in island arcs and in the early volcanoes of continental margins. Basalts of the tholeiitic and calc-alkaline series have broadly similar major-element compositions. Both types resemble the mid-ocean ridge basalts discussed in chapter 8 but have less olivine and are relatively depleted in Ni and MgO. One of the most distinctive differences is their TiO_2 contents, which normally do not exceed 1.3 percent.

Differences between the two series are most pronounced in their intermediate members. Calc-alkaline rocks lack the strong enrichment of iron so characteristic of ferro-basalts and icelandites but instead contain greater amounts of alumina and normative plagioclase. On average, their ratios of K_2O to Na_2O are greater (Table 9–1). Few intermediate calc-alkaline rocks contain more than 10 percent total iron oxide, but almost all have more than 16 percent alumina. These differences are shown most clearly when the proportions of iron oxides are plotted against alkalies or silica (Fig. 9–6). As a consequence of their greater iron enrichment, many intermediate members of the tholeiitic series have pigeonite rather than hypersthene in their groundmass, and few contain hornblende or biotite. They are less porphyritic, and as a group they tend to have larger proportions of basalt and basaltic andesite and proportionately fewer rocks of more siliceous compositions.

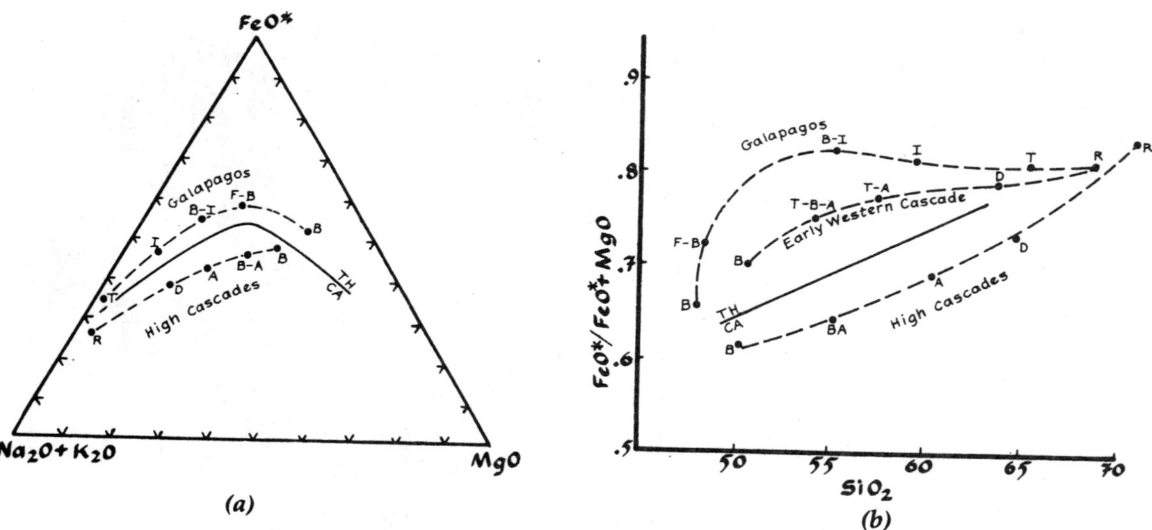

Figure 9–6 The tholeiitic and calc-alkaline orogenic series can be distinguished by their differing proportions of iron, alkalies, and silica. The AMF diagram (a) is a plot of Na_2O + K_2O vs. MgO and FeO* (total iron as FeO). (b) is a Harker diagram showing the rate of iron enrichment relative to silica. In both diagrams the solid line is an empirical division between tholeiitic and calc-alkaline trends.

Table 9–1 Typical compositions of the tholeiitic and calc-alkaline rocks of the Cascade Range of central Oregon. Tholeiitic rocks are of Oligocene age and come from the Western Cascades, whereas the calc-alkaline compositions are from the Quaternary High Cascades.

Tholeiitic Series

	Basalt	Basaltic Andesite	Tholeiitic Andesite	Dacite	Rhyolite
SiO_2	52.7	55.9	58.9	65.4	70.1
TiO_2	1.3	1.5	2.2	1.1	0.5
Al_2O_3	16.8	16.1	15.5	14.6	15.1
FeO*	10.4	9.1	7.9	5.8	3.3
MnO	0.3	0.2	0.2	0.2	0.2
MgO	5.2	3.3	2.7	1.8	0.8
CaO	10.1	9.5	6.7	4.8	2.7
Na_2O	2.7	3.6	4.1	4.5	5.6
K_2O	0.3	0.5	1.1	1.2	1.6
P_2O_5	0.2	0.3	0.4	0.1	0.1
Ba	101	158	240	225	635
Zr	100	168	175	240	262
Rb	10	11	21	30	88
Sr	275	365	220	150	190
Co	47	34	28	24	<5
Cr	65	40	31	24	<5
Ni	27	22	5	1	—

Calc-Alkaline Series

	Basalt	Basaltic Andesite	Andesite	Dacite	Rhyolite
SiO_2	51.7	55.9	60.4	65.6	73.0
TiO_2	1.2	1.0	0.9	0.7	0.3
Al_2O_3	17.5	18.1	17.5	16.4	14.2
FeO*	9.5	7.7	6.4	4.7	2.4
MnO	0.2	0.1	0.1	0.1	0.1
MgO	6.2	4.6	2.8	1.7	0.5
CaO	9.0	7.6	6.2	4.4	1.7
Na_2O	3.7	3.9	4.3	4.6	4.6
K_2O	0.8	0.9	1.2	1.6	3.1
P_2O_5	0.3	0.2	0.2	0.2	0.1
Ba	377	469	614	660	780
Zr	82	140	152	166	189
Rb	17	31	35	48	77
Sr	585	618	719	429	226
Co	36	26	20	7	—
Cr	194	118	42	11	6
Ni	92	48	20	9	2

Calc-alkaline rocks, being richer in alumina, normally contain large amounts of plagioclase, particularly as phenocrysts. Most have porphyritic textures (Fig. 9-7) with conspicuous disequilibrium between phases. Plagioclase phenocrysts can have normal, reversed, or oscillatory zoning, and the compositions and types of zoning may differ from one crystal to another, even in a single thin sec-

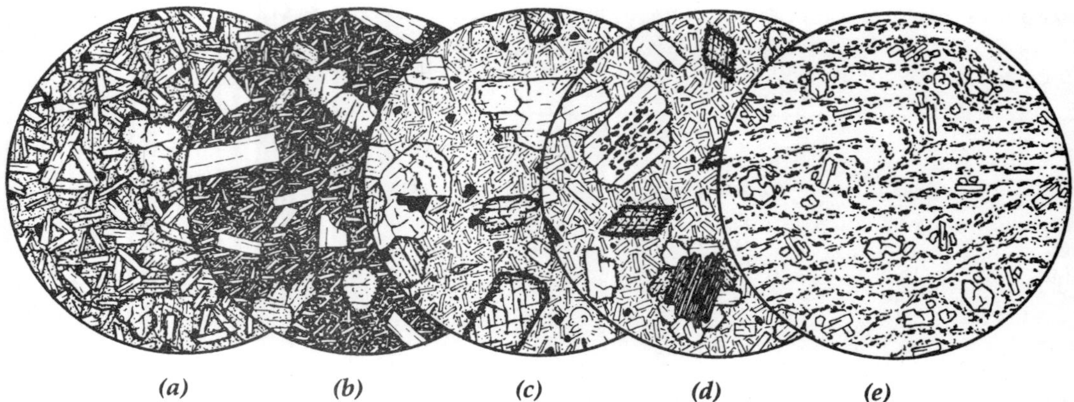

(a) (b) (c) (d) (e)

Figure 9–7 Typical petrographic features of calc-alkaline rocks. (a) is a high-alumina basalt from the High Lava Plain of Central Oregon. It consists of abundant laths of plagioclase and rounded phenocrysts of olivine, in a subophitic groundmass. Angular spaces between the plagioclase crystals give the rock a distinctive *diktytaxitic* texture. (b) is a basaltic andesite from Parícutin Volcano in Mexico. Phenocrysts of labradorite and resorbed olivine are set in a matrix of finer plagioclase, augite, and opaque glass. (c), an andesite from the summit of Mt. Jefferson in the central Oregon Cascades, shows the abundant phenocrysts and aggregated *glomerocrysts* of augite, hypersthene, and strongly zoned plagioclase that typify calc-alkaline andesites. (d) A dacite from the active dome of Mt. St. Helens, Washington, consists of *seriate* plagioclase zoned from calcic labradorite to medium oligoclase. Smaller phenocrysts of hypersthene, augite, and oxyhornblende are set in a hyalopilitic groundmass containing microlites of plagioclase, pyroxene, magnetite, and colorless glass. (e) A rhyolitic lava from the Platoro Caldera in the San Juan Mts. of Colorado has sanidine, oligoclase, and resorbed quartz in a flow-banded glassy matrix.

tion. Most phenocrysts are more anorthitic than either the plagioclase of the groundmass or the normative plagioclase of the rock as a whole. It is not uncommon, especially among the rocks of island arcs, to find phenocrysts of bytownite or anorthite in rocks in which the normative plagioclase is sodic labradorite or even andesine.

Sub-calcic augite is almost ubiquitous in all calc-alkaline rocks; hypersthene is also common, especially in andesites, dacites, and rhyolites. Olivine phenocrysts, deeply embayed and encased in pyroxene, may occur in rocks having as much as 60 percent SiO_2, and it is not unusual to find as many as four or five mafic silicate minerals—olivine, augite, hypersthene, hornblende, and biotite—in the same rock. These complex assemblages are especially common in andesites and dacites of viscous domes, plugs, and dikes. The hydrous minerals hornblende and biotite are unstable at surface conditions and may be rimmed with or totally altered to iron oxides, pyroxenes, and other anhydrous phases. For reasons not entirely clear, hydrous mafic minerals, as well as disequilibrium assemblages in general, tend to be more common in high, mature volcanoes built on thick continental crust.

Many of these disequilibrium relations can be attributed to the sluggish equilibration of high-viscosity magmas at relatively low temperatures. Other factors, such as contamination with older rocks or other magmas, may be equally important. Whatever the reason, it is remarkable that, despite their great textural and mineralogical diversity, the chemical compositions of these rocks can be monotonously uniform. The fact that variations in the proportions and compositions of minerals are only weakly reflected in the bulk composition of the rocks suggests that if mixing or contamination takes place, it does not result in wide deviations of the major-element concentrations.

Equally distinctive is the tendency for calc-alkaline suites to have linear variations between their mafic and felsic end members, so that, on almost all variation diagrams, their components plot close to straight lines. Some calc-alkaline suites show minor non-linear variations, especially in elements such as Mg, Ni, and Cr, in the most mafic members of the series, but these are uncommon and, in most instances, only weakly developed.

The ratios of CaO to Na_2O + K_2O are notably greater in the calc-alkaline rocks of island arcs than in those of continental margins, whereas the rocks of volcanoes in the interiors of continents tend to be relatively richer in alkalies, especially K_2O. Rocks of this latter type are often assigned to a separate potassic or "shoshonitic" series (Fig. 9–8).

EXAMPLES OF OROGENIC VOLCANIC PROVINCES

Calc-alkaline volcanic systems differ widely in structural settings, intensity o' activity, and evolutionary history, but they have so much in common that a few well-studied examples can illustrate most of the distinguishing elements of the group as a whole. We shall look first at the Cascade province of western North

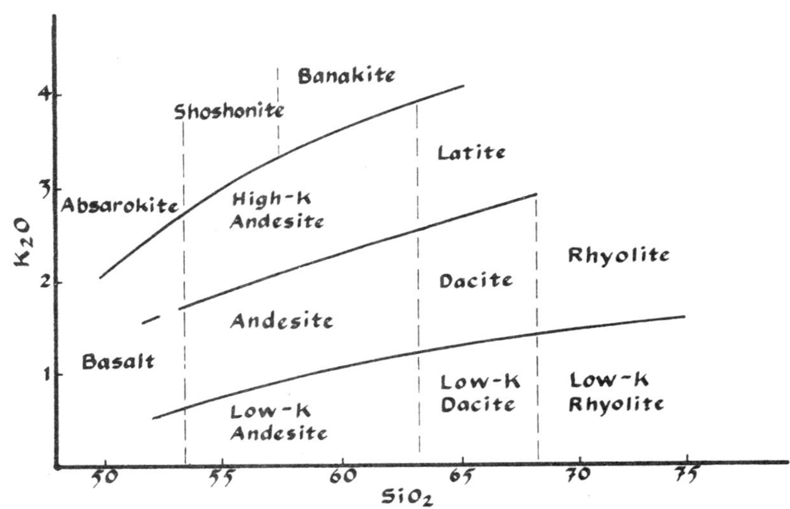

Figure 9–8 Calc-alkaline rocks can be further divided into subseries, depending on their potassium contents. Low-potassium rocks are more common in island arcs, whereas high-potassium, or "shoshonitic," rocks are found almost exclusively in the interior regions of continents.

America, a familiar example of a continental margin system, then at the Aleutian Islands, a well-developed island arc extending from the Alaskan Peninsula across the northern Pacific.

The Cascade Range

The Cascade Range comprises a line of large, composite, andesitic volcanoes extending a thousand kilometers along the margin of the North American continent from northern California to southern British Columbia (Fig. 9–9). Although the modern system has neither a trench nor a Benioff zone, it has most of the basic elements of a zone of plate convergence (Fig. 9–10). In addition, a well-preserved sequence of older rocks affords a rare perspective of the development of such a system through time.

Perhaps the single most important lesson to be learned from the record of earlier volcanism is that the linear chain of large, andesitic volcanoes we instinctively associate with subduction today has only seldom been a recognizable feature of the convergent plate boundary. Before the High Cascade Range developed a million years or so ago, volcanism was scattered, both in space and time, and although subduction continued at about the same rate, long periods passed in which volcanism was weak, if not totally absent.

The present chain of volcanoes is the most recent of several igneous belts that have followed the Pacific margin since the close of the Paleozoic era. The earliest activity that can be identified as clearly orogenic broke out toward the end of the Mesozoic era. Plutonic and weakly metamorphosed sedimentary and volcanic rocks of this age are exposed in a great sigmoidal belt extending from British Columbia in a southeasterly direction across Washington into northeastern Oregon and in isolated windows in central Oregon to connect with the major axis of the Sierra Nevada system in northwestern California. This belt may once have resembled the modern volcanic belt in its structure and lithologic relations, but erosion and an extensive cover of younger rocks limit any detailed reconstructions of the system as a whole.

Intense igneous activity marked the opening stages of the Cenozoic era in what is now the Coast Range of Oregon and Washington, but most if not all of the rocks in that region seem to be oceanic in character. Not until the end of the Early Eocene, following a strong tectonic event, did true calc-alkaline rocks appear, and by the end of the Eocene a swarm of small volcanoes formed a zone about 150 kilometers wide extending from British Columbia through Washington and into central Oregon. Volcanism increased in intensity and spread westward and southward until, by the early Oligocene, it covered a broad zone across most of western Oregon and Washington. Some lavas erupted along the western margin of this zone were tholeiitic, but those farther inland were distinctly calc-alkaline. With time, differentiated rocks became more important as basaltic lavas gave way to larger proportions of siliceous pyroclastic tephra discharged from several large, low-rimmed calderas in what is now central Oregon. Evidence of large composite volcanoes is hard to find, but in the more deeply eroded northern part of the system, Eocene stocks and plutons up to ten kilometers or so in diameter probably represent the roots of important volcanic centers.

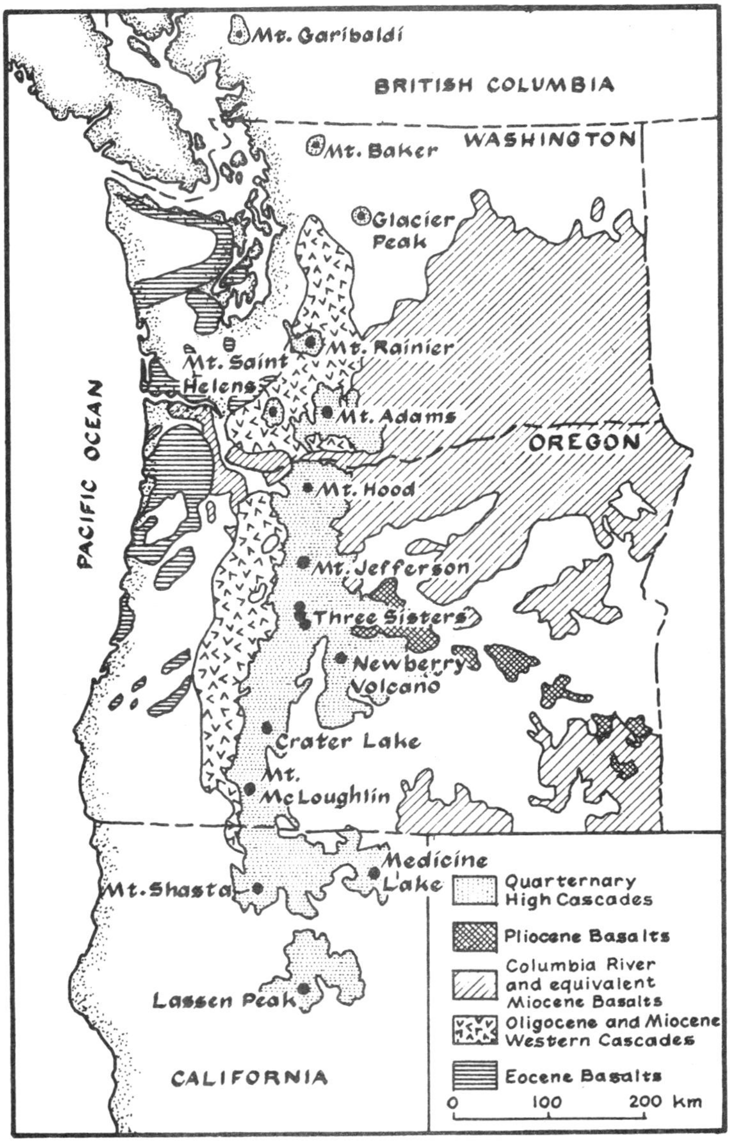

Figure 9–9 The Cascade Range extending along much of the northwestern coast of North America is a well-studied example of a chain of large andesitic volcanoes built on an active continental margin. Pre-Cenozoic metamorphic and plutonic rocks crop out along a broad arc extending southeastward from the northern part of Washington to eastern Oregon, then in scattered exposures to the southwestern corner of Oregon and adjacent parts of California. These continental crustal rocks have not been found in the central part of the chain; instead, the crust in that region consists mainly of basic volcanic rocks.

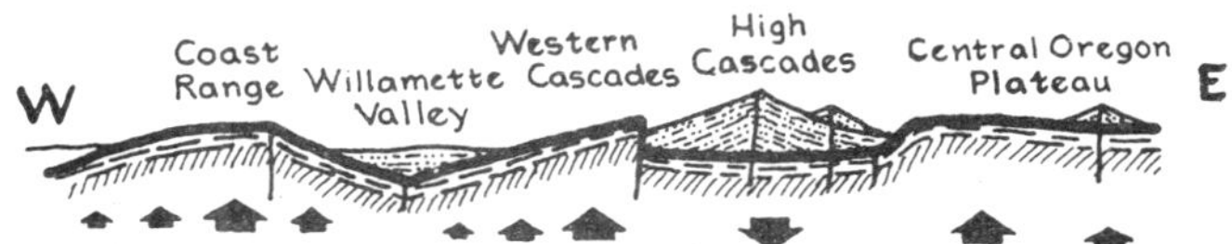

Figure 9–10 Schematic east-west section through western Oregon showing the principal structural elements of the Cascades and Coast Range.

Following an early Miocene episode of faulting, uplift, and erosion, volcanism again broke out in the middle Miocene. Though brief, this episode was extraordinarily intense; by any measure, it was the most important igneous event of the Cenozoic era, not only in the Cascades but throughout much of the circum-Pacific. Most mid-Miocene volcanic centers were located along a line trending slightly east of north and close to or slightly west of the present chain. Other large andesitic centers have been recognized in east-central Oregon, far behind the main axis, and most of the great outpourings of basaltic flood lavas of the Columbia Plateau were discharged during this same period. Apart from the Columbia River basalts, which have no apparent relation to the orogenic system of the Cascades, the products of these mid-Miocene volcanoes are strongly calc-alkaline with large proportions of andesite. Today, the principal centers are marked by stocks, mainly of quartz diorite, and by broad aureoles of hydrothermal alteration and mineralization. The volcanoes seem to have been the first to have the form and alignment we associate with andesitic belts today. Although they must have resembled the large, composite volcanoes of the modern High Cascades, they were restricted to a shorter and broader segment, mainly in central and northern Oregon.

Again, igneous activity was terminated by faulting, gentle folding, and broad tilting. Two minor episodes of widely scattered volcanism followed, one about nine to ten million years ago and another a few million years before the modern High Cascades became active. Most of the growth of the large Quaternary cones has taken place during a remarkably brief period. The fact that very few of their lavas have reversed magnetic polarities, even in the lowest levels of deeply glaciated cones, indicates that by far the greatest volumes must have been discharged since the present period of normal magnetic polarity began about 670,000 years ago.

Block faulting of the Central Cascade Range resulted in uplift and westward tilting of the Western Cascades, while subsidence of the basement below the active volcanoes began to form a steadily deepening axial graben. The graben is not topographically conspicuous, because it has been partly filled by the products of Quaternary volcanoes that rise within it. It is most pronounced in the central Cascades where volcanism has been strongest; it dies out toward the north and south where individual volcanoes are more widely spaced and the total volume of Quaternary volcanic rocks is small.

Andesite is the dominant rock of all the major volcanoes of the High Cascades. Taking the total volume of post-Pliocene rocks as a whole, however, andesitic cones account for a subordinate fraction of the total mass of erupted magma. The proportion of andesite is large only in those parts of the chain where the total volume of Quaternary rocks is small, namely in Washington and California (Fig. 9–11).

The rocks of the High Cascades have all the petrographic and chemical characteristics of calc-alkaline rocks of modern continental margins (Table 9–1). Apart from the most basic basalts and the most siliceous rhyolitic obsidians, almost all the rocks are strongly porphyritic and rich in plagioclase. Olivine is not uncommon as phenocrysts in basaltic andesites and andesites, but it is normally cor-

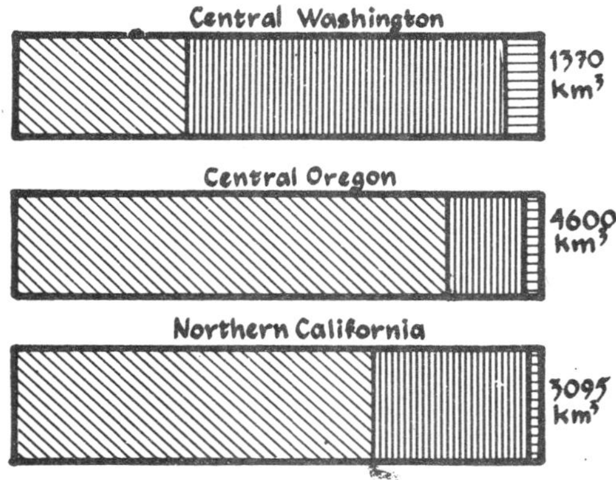

Figure 9–11 Relative volumes of basalt (diagonal ruling), andesite (vertical ruling), and rhyolite and dacite (horizontal ruling) in three sections of the Cascade Range.

roded and rimmed with pyroxene. Titaniferous magnetite, though abundant in the groundmass, is rarely an important phenocryst. Most andesites contain two pyroxenes, augite and hypersthene, which vary little in composition, even in rocks of very different silica contents. Hornblende is rare in andesites of the High Cascades. Well-preserved crystals are restricted almost solely to dacites and rhyolites, and, even in these, hornblende tends to break down under surface conditions to oxidized clots of anhydrous minerals.

Plagioclase, normally in the range of sodic labradorite to calcic andesine, is by far the most conspicuous phenocryst throughout the full range of rocks. The pattern of zoning tends to be increasingly more complex as the rocks become more differentiated. In many andesites and dacites, it even differs from grain to grain in the same rock. The composition of groundmass plagioclase is somewhat more sensitive to the alkali and silica contents of the rocks but is rarely more sodic than oligoclase.

Some large volcanoes, such as Mount Rainier and Mount Baker, are of a "coherent" type consisting mainly of monotonously similar andesite. Others, such as Mount Mazama (the volcano containing the caldera of Crater Lake) and the Three Sisters (Fig. 9–12), are strongly "divergent" in the sense that a main cone of andesite or dacite has evolved in later eruptions to contrasting basaltic and rhyolitic or rhyodacitic magmas. Most of the volcanoes of this latter type are in parts of the chain built on thick continental crust, but they are by no means confined to such settings. Newberry volcano in Oregon and the complex of vents in and around the flooded caldera of Medicine Lake, California, are extreme examples in which andesites are distinctly subordinate, and the basaltic and rhyolitic rocks form a strongly bimodal assemblage.

The Aleutian Arc

No single island arc has all the structural and petrologic elements of convergent plate boundaries in which both the subducted and overriding lithospheric plates

(a)

(b)

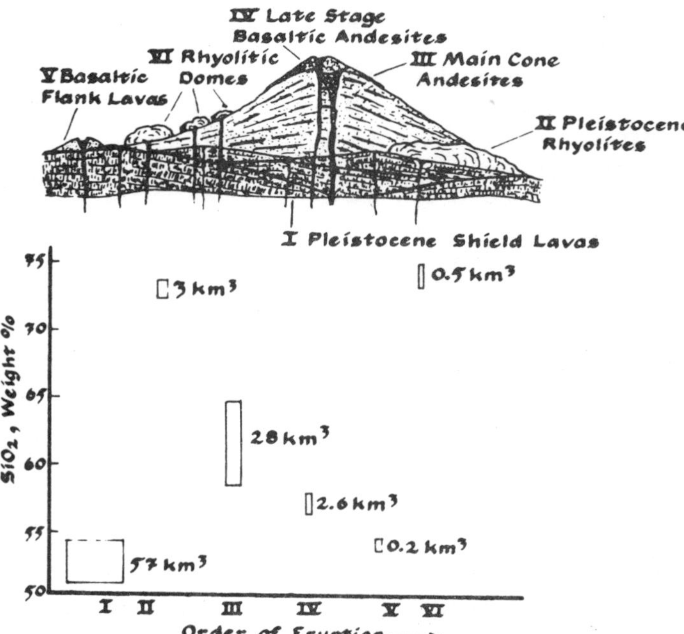

Figure 9–12 (a) The volcano South Sister in the central Oregon Cascades exemplifies large, composite cones of the "divergent" type in which late eruptions of basaltic lavas and rhyolite have broken out on the flanks of a cone consisting mainly of andesite and dacite. The viscous flow of obsidian in the foreground is slightly younger than the basaltic cone immediately in front of it, but the reverse relations are also found. An extensive series of nearly flat-lying basaltic lavas underlies the entire region. (b) illustrates the evolution of the volcano. Volumes of rocks in each stage are shown by the relative areas of the rectangles in the lower diagram. The midpoint on the vertical dimension of each rectangle is placed at the mean value of SiO_2 for the rocks of that stage, and the vertical height of the edge indicates one standard deviation for the silica value.

have an oceanic character. The volcanic arc of the Aleutian Islands (Fig. 9–13) probably serves as well as any, for it combines nearly all the essential features of such a system and has been studied in enough detail to define its magmatic history and structure. In addition, it has the advantage of being an extension of the volcanic chain of the Alaskan Peninsula and, as such, is a good example of an igneous belt that crosses from one type of crust to another.

The arc stretches some 2,500 km from the continental mainland of Alaska into the Bering Sea where it approaches the arc of Kamchatka and the Kurile Islands. Thus its eastern end on the Alaskan Peninsula stands on old continental crust, while the Aleutian Islands are on relatively young oceanic lithosphere. Like most island arcs, it has a line of non-volcanic islands and a structural ridge off-shore from the volcanic chain of the Alaskan mainland. A well-defined Benioff zone dips below the arc at an angle of about forty-five degrees. A trench extends along the entire length of the Aleutian Islands, and, owing to the curvature of the arc with respect to the motion of the northern Pacific plate, the angle of incidence ranges from nearly perpendicular in the eastern part to parallel near the western extremities. The corresponding rates of convergence range from about 5.5 cm per year along the Alaskan Peninsula to zero at the western end of the arc. Subduction began about 70 million years ago, and magmatism has continued in an episodic fashion for most of the Cenozoic era. Thus, something of

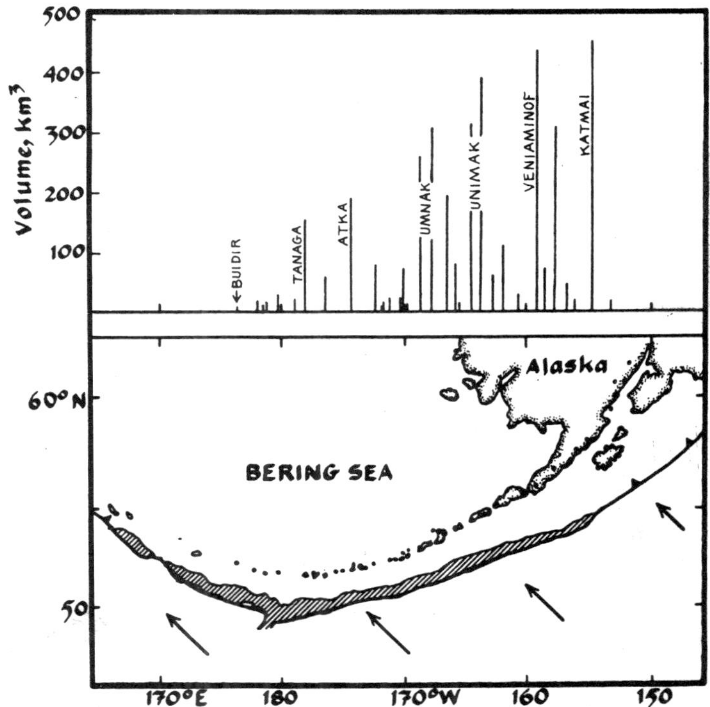

Figure 9–13 The Aleutian Islands are a prolongation of the volcanic range of the Alaskan Peninsula and are an excellent example of a belt that passes from a continental margin to an island arc. When the volumes erupted from the volcanoes are plotted according to their position along the length of the Aleutian Arc, they tend to decrease from east to west as the rate of subduction becomes less, owing to the decreasing angle of convergence. This relationship is strong evidence that the amount of magma generated in the arc is a direct function of the amount of subducted oceanic crust. (After B. D. Marsh, 1982, The Aleutians, *Andesites*, R. S. Thorpe, ed., 99–114.)

the order of 500 to 1,000 km^3 of oceanic lithosphere has been subducted for each cubic kilometer erupted during this period.

The detailed geologic history of the arc is poorly known, particularly in the more remote islands, but the broad elements of the stratigraphic sequence have been determined from studies of the major eastern islands. The section consists of three major volcanic units. The oldest of these, the Finger Bay Series, is a thick section of highly altered lavas and pyroclastic sediments, probably of early Eocene age. The overlying Andrews Bay strata consist of marine volcanoclastic beds, believed to be of middle to late Eocene age. No important Tertiary units of younger age have been recognized on land; the Recent volcanic series, which has been laid down in less than three million years (mostly in the last million years), is separated from the Eocene units by an unconformity representing all of middle and late Tertiary time.

A more complete record has been obtained from marine sediments offshore. It shows that volcanism was renewed at the beginning of the Miocene and continued with especially strong pulses about fifteen and ten million years ago. Thus, the present volcanoes stand on islands that were probably Tertiary volcanic centers and were subjected to repeated uplift and erosion. In the eastern part of the chain, some of these centers are marked by sub-volcanic plutons that have been correlated in age with an early Miocene episode of volcanism about thirty million years ago.

This pattern of multiple episodes of similar activity in the same locations through a large part of Cenozoic time is in contrast to the record in the Cascades, where volcanism shifted from place to place and seldom had a strong linear distribution. The episodic character of the two regions was similar, however. In fact, periods of intense volcanism seem to have developed simultaneously, not only here but around much of the Pacific rim.

The modern volcanoes form an imposing chain parallel to the trench and about 110 km above the Benioff zone. Only two small volcanic centers stand behind the arc. The distance between the trench and volcanic front increases systematically from west to east, as one would expect from the change of strike relative to the direction of subduction and the greater amount of sediments scraped from the descending slab and accreted to the leading edge of the arc. Large volcanic centers are regularly spaced at intervals of sixty to seventy km along the entire arc, but the chain is segmented by offsets and minor changes of strike corresponding to a similar segmentation of the underlying Benioff zone. Volcanoes situated near these offsets tend to be more tholeiitic than those in other parts of the chain.

Although the most recent episode of activity has lasted less than three million years, the total volume erupted during that period is estimated at 4,700 km^3. The distribution of this volume (Fig. 9–13) has a remarkably regular relation to the position of volcanoes along the arc. This, together with a weak correlation between the volumes of volcanic products and the spacing of centers along the arc, suggests that the intensity of volcanism is a function of the angle of plate convergence. Whether this is due to the amount of subducted lithosphere or to the energy associated with under-thrusting is less clear.

The Recent volcanic centers have evolved from broad shields composed mainly of thin basaltic lavas to high composite cones of andesite with large proportions of pyroclastic material. Greater volumes of silica-rich pyroclastic rocks have been erupted from volcanoes on the Alaskan Peninsula than from those on islands of the Aleutian chain. Many of the former develop calderas in their mature stages and erupt rhyolitic lavas and tephra. Although the eruptive vents migrate, they tend to remain within five to ten kilometers of the summit. As in many andesitic volcanoes, magmas discharged from vents on the lower flanks of large cones tend to be basaltic, while those from higher elevations are more differentiated.

SHALLOW DIFFERENTIATION

Compared to the large volumes of relatively homogeneous magma erupted from most oceanic volcanoes, the products of orogenic volcanoes have smaller volumes and differ in composition from one eruption to another, often in irregular ways. During the main stages of growth it is rare to see an andesitic volcano produce a series of progressively more differentiated lavas that can be related to steady differentiation. Instead, they often revert to more primitive compositions, even in the course of a single eruption. These irregularities indicate that the magma is stored and differentiated in small, shallow reservoirs, possibly a network of dikes and sills, rather than a single large chamber.

Plutonic intrusions several kilometers across can be seen in many eroded composite volcanoes where multiple stocks have stoped their way upward near the axis of the central conduit. Although they send out dikes and sills that may have reached the surface, it is unclear whether all of these bodies were reservoirs in which magma differentiated during intervals between eruptions. They seem to have played this role in at least some volcanoes. The dimensions of calderas resulting from sudden discharges of large amounts of magma indicate that large bodies can evolve at shallow depths while volcanoes are still potentially active.

One of the notable peculiarities of calc-alkaline volcanism is the relatively large volumes of highly differentiated magmas that evolve in short periods of time in many large, mature, volcanic centers. Another is the close association of magmas of contrasting compositions erupted from the same or closely related vents or in single outpourings of compositionally graded liquids. The degrees of differentiation are too great, the volumes too large, and the time intervals too brief for these differentiates to be produced by progressive fractional crystallization of the kind seen, for example, in layered intrusions. Moreover, the bimodality of many igneous calc-alkaline suites shows that they differentiate in ways that enable the undifferentiated magma to erupt together with the products of its own crystallization (Figs. 9-5 and 9-12).

Volcanologists observe that, during their long intervals of repose, mature volcanoes tend to evolve felsic magmas in the uppermost levels of their reservoirs, and the longer the interval between eruptions, the greater the volume and explosivity of the first liquid to be discharged.

This behavior may be the result of a process of differentiation based on the mechanism of liquid fractionation outlined in chapter five. When crystallization or melting at a wall entails a preferential concentration of heavy components in the crystalline phases, a buoyant boundary layer may develop, and this layer may rise to accumulate as a gravitationally stable unit overlying the main body of denser, more basic magma (Fig. 9–14). Such a process seems to offer an attractive explanation for sharply zoned magmas, such as that discharged during the great caldera-forming eruption responsible for Crater Lake (Fig. 9–15).

Similar effects would be expected if dense mafic magma melts more felsic wall rocks, as seems to have happened in the case of Paricutin Volcano described later in this chapter. Note that in this case, however, the light, differentiated magma was not the first to be erupted but followed the denser mafic lavas. This seeming anomaly has been explained as a result of the mechanics of withdrawal from a chamber in which light, viscous magma overlies a heavier, more fluid one (Fig. 9–16). When magmas of differing properties rise through a channel tapping a compositionally zoned reservoir of this kind, the lower liquid tends to be drawn up and enters the central part of the conduit. If the lower liquid is less viscous, as it is in this case, it flows more rapidly, and, even though it is denser and starts at a lower level, it can reach the surface before the more viscous differentiated liquid. As the rate of discharge declines, the draw-up diminishes, and the lighter, more viscous liquid is able to escape without entraining the lower part of the reservoir.

EXPERIMENTAL STUDIES OF CALC-ALKALINE ROCKS

Most of the compositional features of orogenic magmas of the tholeiitic type can be explained in terms of shallow melting or fractionation of the same minerals—plagioclase, olivine, augite, and magnetite—that account for the compositions of tholeiitic magmas elsewhere. It is more difficult to explain differentiation of andesitic magmas of calc-alkaline compositions by fractionation of this same assemblage of minerals. The problem is best illustrated by comparing the temperatures

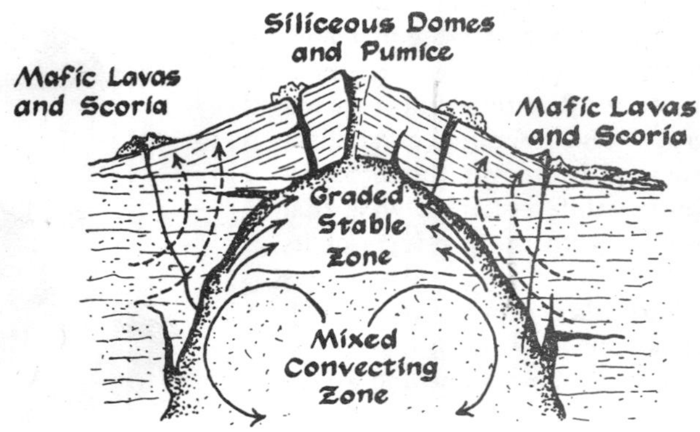

Figure 9–14 The concentrations of light components near the margins of shallow calc-alkaline intrusions may produce a buoyant boundary layer of differentiated magma that rises and accumulates in a compositionally zoned body of siliceous magma. Eruptions from different parts of the intrusion could account for the association of mafic and felsic rocks erupted from the summits and flanks of large andesitic volcanoes. The diagram is schematic and not to scale.

(a)

Figure 9–15 The siliceous pumice discharged during the great caldera-forming eruption responsible for Crater Lake is compositionally graded through most of its thickness, but changes abruptly to a hornblende-rich scoria near the top of the section. The magma appears to have been erupted continuously from a zoned magma chamber in which the siliceous magma at the top was the first to be discharged and the dark scoria was part of a denser, more mafic magma below. (Photograph by the Oregon State Highway Department.) (b) The size, depth, and zonation of the magma chamber have been reconstructed from chemical and experimental studies. (Constructed from data of J. L. Ritchey, 1980, *Jour. Volc. Geoth. Res.* 7:373–386; and R. L. Smith, 1979, *Geol. Soc. Amer. Spec. Paper 180* 5–27.)

(b)

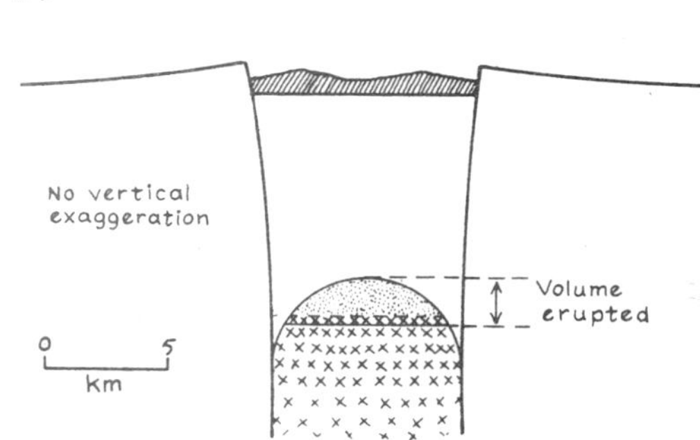

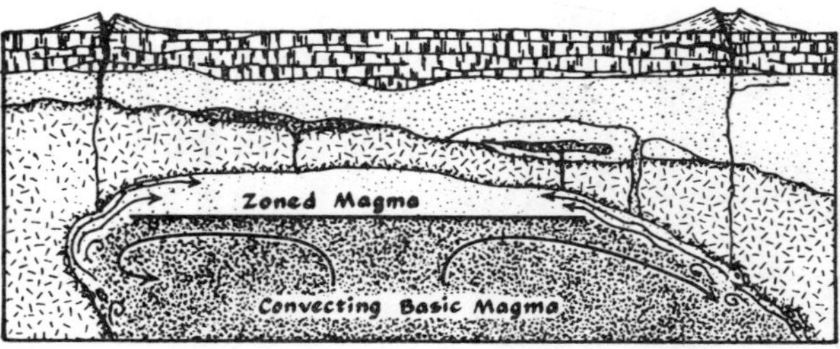

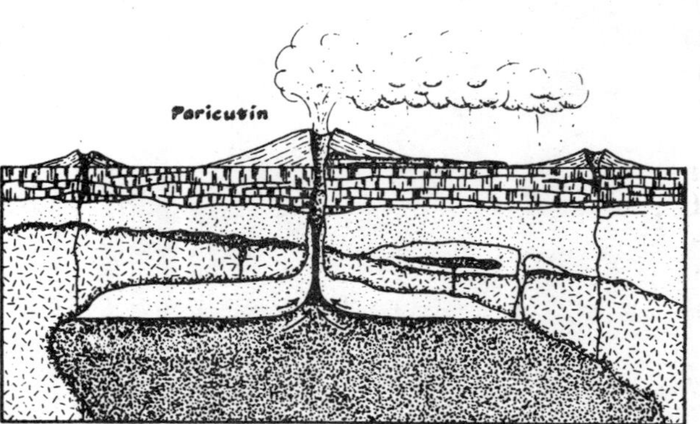

Figure 9–16 Before the Paricutin volcano erupted in 1943, a silica-enriched liquid, resulting from melting and assimilation of crustal rocks, is thought to have accumulated above the denser parental magma. Tapping of these two zones led to more rapid rise of the denser but less viscous lower magma and later eruption of a more silica-rich fraction when the rate of discharge declined.

at which these minerals crystallize in andesites with those at which they crystallize from the basic magmas from which andesites are thought to be derived.

Table 9–2 shows the temperatures of crystallization of plagioclase, olivine, and augite from three typical calc-alkaline rocks at atmospheric pressure. Note that, unlike the examples of tholeiitic rocks in chapter eight, the minerals begin to crystallize at extraordinarily high temperatures and over a wide range. Moreover, the liquidus temperature of plagioclase *increases* going from basalt to dacite. It is obvious that, if the three rocks represent co-genetic liquids, they could not have been produced by crystal fractionation of these same minerals under the conditions at which their liquidus temperatures were determined. Some basic aspect of the melting experiments must have been different from the conditions under which the natural system evolves, for otherwise it is impossible to account for the high liquidus temperatures of plagioclase and their marked increase with differentiation. In addition, we need to explain two other characteristics of calc-alkaline series, namely the lack of strong enrichment of iron and the correspondingly greater enrichment of alumina and silica. We shall examine each of these features in turn.

Large proportions of plagioclase

The anomalously high liquidus temperatures of minerals, especially plagioclase, could have two explanations. They could be due to addition of phenocrysts derived from other liquids, or to some component that lowered the liquidus temperatures of the original magma and left the system after the magma attained its present composition but before the sample was collected and remelted in the laboratory. The regularity of the bulk compositions of calc-alkaline rocks, especially andesites, together with other factors we shall note later, indicate that porphyritic samples do indeed represent liquid compositions. This leaves the alternative possibility that something has been lost. An obvious candidate for such a "lost" component would be a volatile, such as water.

As is normally the case when another component is added, water lowers the temperatures of crystallization of all anhydrous minerals (Fig. 4–18). Moreover, the amount by which liquidus temperatures are lowered differs from one mineral to another. As the simple system diopside-anorthite illustrates (Fig. 9–17), the liquidus temperature of plagioclase is depressed much more than that of a mafic mineral, such as pyroxene. Note that the liquidus curves of both minerals are lower at 10 kilobars water pressure than at atmospheric pressure, and, owing to the greater depression of the liquidus curve of anorthite, the eutectic composition is shifted to higher anorthite contents. A magma precipitating these minerals at an elevated water pressure would be more plagioclase-rich, but if raised to a shallower level with less pressure of water, the same composition would be far below its low-pressure liquidus and would crystallize large amounts of plagioclase before pyroxene. This is exactly what was observed in the low-pressure melting carried out on the natural rocks cited in Table 9–2.

The amount of water required to change the liquidus temperatures of plagioclase at elevated pressures is not large—probably less than one weight percent H_2O. A small initial concentration in a basaltic magma must increase as crystallization advances and the water is concentrated in smaller and smaller amounts of liquid. Thus, even though water contents of basaltic magmas are not great, they could affect the stability relations of plagioclase, and this effect would increase with differentiation, as the data in Table 9–2 seem to require.

Water affects not only the amount of plagioclase but its composition as well. Note in Figure 9–17a that at constant temperature and elevated pressure, a dry magma, L_A, would be in equilibrium with crystals of composition X_A, and on rising to the surface (P = 1 bar) the compositions would shift to L_B and X_B respectively, and crystals would be reversely zoned to more anorthitic rims. A wet magma, on the other hand, would have the composition L_C and An-rich crystals,

Table 9–2 Liquidus temperatures of calc-alkaline rocks determined by melting natural rocks at atmospheric pressure. (From G. M. Brown and J. F. Schairer, 1971, *Geol. Soc. Amer. Mem.* 130:139–157.)

		Liquidus Temperatures		
Sample	**SiO_2**	**Plagioclase**	**Olivine**	**Augite**
Olivine Basalt	50.5	1215°	1185°	1175°
Andesite	60.7	1255°	—	1180°
Dacite	69.9	1275°	—	1180°

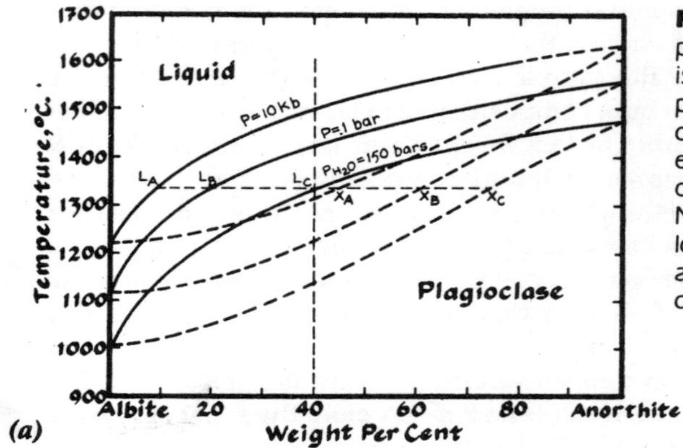

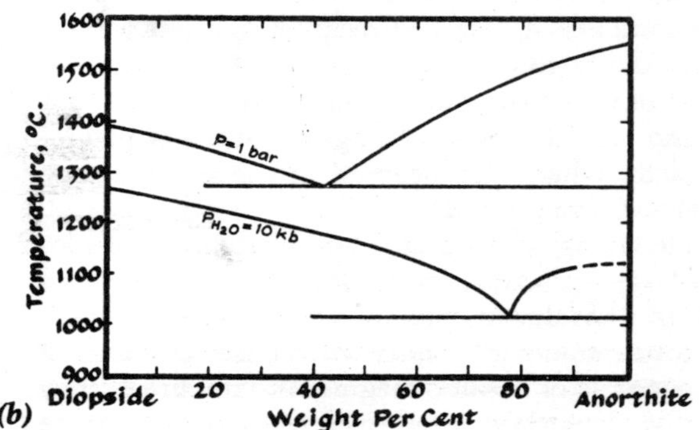

Figure 9–17 The effect of water pressure on the plagioclase system (a) is the opposite of that of dry load pressure; it lowers the temperatures of both the liquidus and solidus. The effect of water pressure on plagioclase is greater than on pyroxene (b). Note that the liquidus of anorthite is lowered more than that of diopside, and the eutectic is shifted to more anorthite-rich compositions.

X_C; on losing water as it rises, this liquid would produce crystals zoned to more *albitic* compositions. It must be remembered, of course, that the binary system portrayed here is highly simplified, and the form of the liquidus and solidus curves can be very different in more complex systems (Fig. 4–5).

Lack of iron enrichment

A simple way to explain a lack of iron enrichment during differentiation of any series of magmas is to postulate early crystallization of large amounts of an iron oxide mineral, such as magnetite. Experiments with iron-bearing systems described in chapter four show that the field of magnetite expands greatly with increasing oxidation. It overruns that of olivine, preventing liquids from evolving toward high iron enrichment and diverting the course of liquids toward greater silica contents. This effect seems particularly appropriate for calc-alkaline rocks formed in the oxidizing environment of the crust.

Magnetite is a common mineral in many basaltic lavas, particularly those of island arcs. It is less common, however, in andesites and other intermediate to

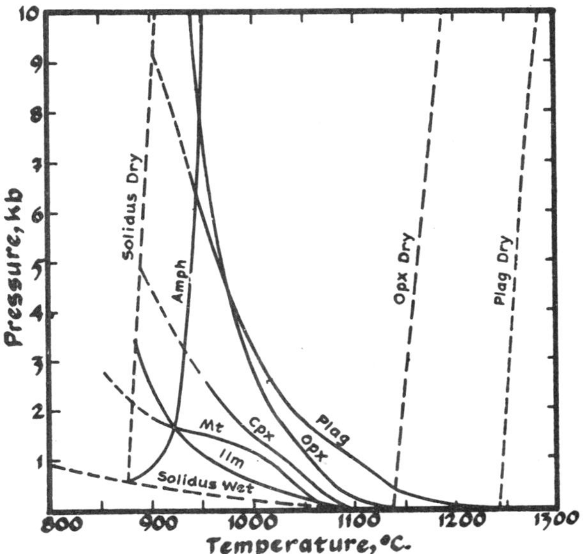

Figure 9–18 Stability relations of the principal phases of an andesite from Mount Hood, Oregon, as functions of temperature and water pressure. (After Eggler & Burnham, 1973, *Geol. Soc. Amer. Bull.* 84:2517–2532.)

silicic calc-alkaline lavas or as an important mineral in plutonic rocks of equivalent compositions. Melting experiments carried out on natural andesites at elevated water pressures show that magnetite becomes less important as calc-alkaline magmas differentiate and are enriched in water. Figure 9–18 summarizes results of a study of the phase relations of an andesite of Mount Hood, Oregon, over a range of water pressures up to ten kilobars. Again, the effect of water is to lower the liquidus temperatures of anhydrous minerals, particularly plagioclase, while raising that of the hydrous mineral, amphibole. At pressures of about seven kilobars, plagioclase, hypersthene, and amphibole all have nearly the same liquidus temperature of about 950°C. Note that the liquidus temperatures of magnetite and ilmentite are also lowered by water pressure, but these iron-oxide minerals are not liquidus phases at any water pressure or geologically reasonable oxygen fugacity. Above about two kilobars, they are replaced by amphibole.

The amount of water required to stabilize amphibole in place of magnetite is not great, especially at the relatively low liquidus temperatures of andesites. Common hornblendes contain large proportions of both ferric and ferrous iron, and they normally have a lower silica content than the calc-alkaline liquids in which they crystallize. It appears reasonable, therefore, that amphibole, rather than magnetite, could limit iron enrichment in the middle stages of differentiation of calc-alkaline magmas.

Enrichment of silica

Although the compositions of liquids cannot be estimated directly from Figure 9–18, the effect of elevated water pressure on the silica content of liquids can be seen in a relatively simple three-component system, such as forsterite-pyroxene-silica, illustrated in Figure 9–19. Comparison of the stability fields at high pressure under dry conditions with those at an equivalent pressure wet shows that all the main phase boundaries are shifted toward higher silica contents. Note in particular that the invariant point, E, is shifted to R across the pyroxene join toward the silica corner of the triangle. Unlike the effect of pressure under dry conditions, which increases the stability of enstatite relative to olivine (chapter eight), high pressures of water have the opposite effect; the stability range of olivine increases relative to pyroxene.

The consequences of this difference can be appreciated by comparing the compositions of liquids that would evolve under the two conditions, low pressure dry and high pressure wet. The compositions of basaltic liquids produced by melting a mantle consisting of olivine and two pyroxenes, corresponding to points E and R, do not differ greatly, but subsequent cooling and crystallization would cause the liquid evolving at higher water pressures to follow a much longer course of differentiation ending at a final composition greatly enriched in silica. The analogy to calc-alkaline rocks is seen if the compositions of natural calc-alkaline rocks are plotted on the same diagram (Fig. 9–19a). Apart from a slight divergence resulting, no doubt, from the effects of the additional components of natural melts, the course of the calc-alkaline magmas is close to the simplified system at elevated water pressure. An even closer approach to natural rocks is achieved if plagioclase is added to the same system (Fig. 9–19b). Amphibole appears as a stable liquidus mineral in the region of the cotectic between enstatite and diopside.

These effects offer a possible explanation for some of the differences between tholeiitic and calc-alkaline series and for the close link between the latter and subduction. Although the tholeiitic and calc-alkaline series have very similar parental basalts and are commonly found in close association, different conditions of differentiation cause them to evolve along very different trends. The same or very similar basalts can evolve along paths leading to a tholeiitic or calc-alkaline trend depending on the depth and amount of water present where they differentiate.

Tholeiitic-calc-alkaline transitions

We have already noted that differentiation of tholeiitic magmas is easily explained as the result of fractionation of plagioclase, olivine, augite, and titaniferous magnetite. As the mass-balance calculation in Table 7–5 illustrates, the major elements seem to fit such a scheme fairly well. But a similar calculation for the corresponding rocks of a calc-alkaline suite (Table 9–3) shows that the same minerals, if fractionated in slightly different proportions, could also produce a calc-alkaline andesite. The fit would be even better if hypersthene were included as a possible phase.

What these calculations show is that more than one mathematical solution can be found for the mass balance of major elements if enough minerals are used in the calculation. As the Phase Rule would predict, the larger the number of

Table 9–3 Test of derivation of natural calc-alkaline andesite from calc-alkaline basalt by fractionating two different assemblages of minerals. The calculation is carried out by the method illustrated in chapter seven; compositions of the magmas are taken from Table 9–1. In solution 1, the minerals fractionated are olivine, plagioclase, augite, and titaniferous magnetite, while in solution 2 they are plagioclase and hornblende.

	Solution 1 Liquids & Crystals		Solution 2 Liquid & Crystals	
Weight Proportions:	CA-B	1.000	CA-B	1.000
	−OLIV	−0.060	−AN50	−0.392
	−AN70	−0.276	−HORN	−0.195
	−AUG	−0.130	= CA-A	0.406
	−TI-MT	−0.045		
	= CA-A	0.480		

Chemical Composition:

	Major Elements			
	Daughter Analysis	Daughter Calculated	Daughter Analysis	Daughter Calculated
SiO_2	60.4	59.70	60.4	59.87
TiO_2	0.90	0.42	0.90	0.85
Al_2O_3	17.5	17.35	17.5	17.35
FeO*	6.4	6.52	6.4	6.41
MgO	2.8	2.88	2.8	2.70
CaO	6.2	6.36	6.2	6.15
Na_2O	4.3	5.57	4.3	4.20
K_2O	1.20	1.50	1.20	1.48
Sum of R Squares	1.735		0.073	

	Trace Elements					
	Bulk D	Observed	Predicted	Bulk D	Observed	Predicted
Ni	2.01	65	39	1.43	65	71
Cr	8.02	85	0	1.84	85	59
Sr	0.90	490	449	1.16	490	366
Rb	0.07	16	23	0.07	16	19
Ba	0.30	360	353	0.05	360	374

phases, the greater the degree of freedom in such a calculation and the easier it is to achieve a mathematically satisfactory solution. But these calculations, since they are unconstrained by phase relations, are useful only in the sense that they illustrate mathematical possibilities; they tell us nothing about the true crystal-liquid relations responsible for evolution of a liquid.

More meaningful, perhaps, are the calculated effects on the abundances of trace elements. Note that a somewhat better, though still far from perfect, fit is obtained for the key included and excluded elements by fractionating plagioclase and hornblende rather than plagioclase, olivine, augite, and magnetite. But again, this is only permissive evidence. It is one thing to contrive calculated frac-

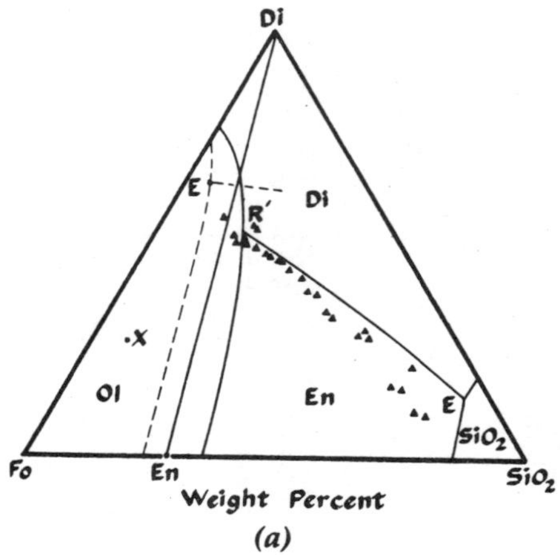

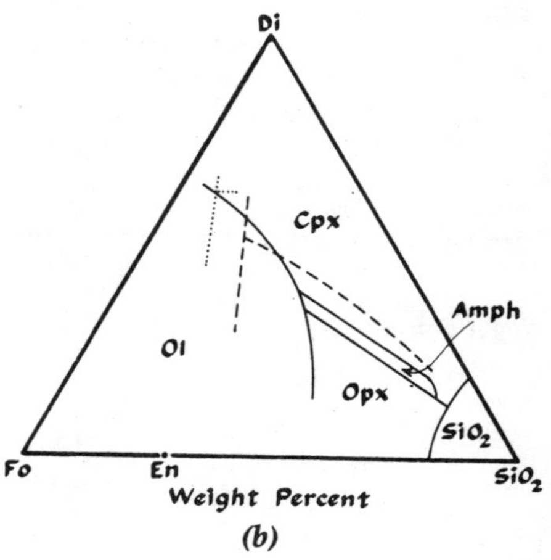

Figure 9–19 (a) The system diopside-forsterite-silica at twenty kbars water pressure illustrates the shift of compositions to greater silica contents with increased water pressure. Phase boundaries under dry conditions are indicated by broken lines. The compositions of calc-alkaline rocks from the Oregon Cascades (triangles) fall close to the two-pyroxene cotectic for twenty kbars and extend from basaltic andesites near the invariant point at R to rhyolites at a eutectic near the SiO_2 corner of the diagram. (b) When anorthite is added to the system, a field of amphibole appears in the middle range of compositions between the pyroxenes. At the same time, the boundaries shift toward SiO_2, and compositions of liquids come closer to calc-alkaline rocks. Fields are projected from anorthite, which is a stable phase throughout the system. Twenty kbar field boundaries for dry and wet conditions in (a) are shown by dotted and dashed lines respectively.

tionation schemes in the laboratory and quite another to prove them in the field. For example, we have already noted that hornblende is very rare in calc-alkaline basalts, and assimilation of crustal rocks could also alter trace-element abundances.

Reactions during rise through the mantle

Tholeiitic melts that re-equilibrate as they rise through the overlying mantle may change composition in a way that could alter their trend of differentiation to one resembling that of calc-alkaline magmas. As noted in our discussion of melting relations of oceanic basalts in chapter eight, melts rising to shallower depths are not in equilibrium with the same minerals as they were at greater pressures. Owing to expansion of the fields of olivine and plagioclase at the expense of pyroxene, the effect of decreasing pressure causes a rising liquid to be displaced from the low-pressure pseudo-invariant point (Fig. 9–20a) in such a way that it falls well within the field of olivine. Thus, a basaltic magma that equilibrates thermally with wall rocks as it rises will crystallize olivine but will be under-saturated with enstatite and tend to react with it. The effect of this exchange would be to increase the rate of enrichment of silica. At the same time, such a reaction could reduce the rate of enrichment of iron and produce a trend resembling that of common calc-alka-

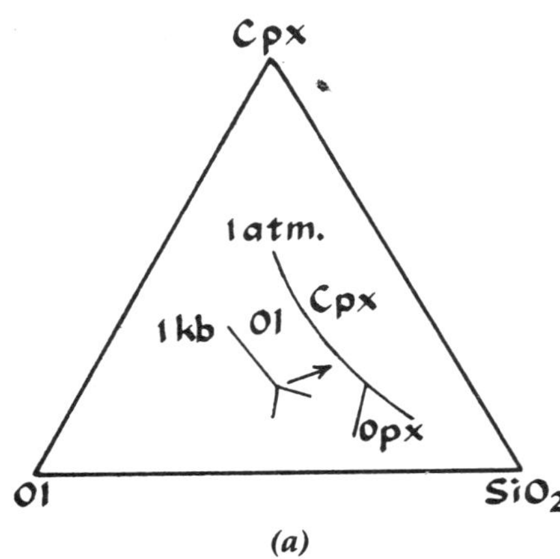

(a)

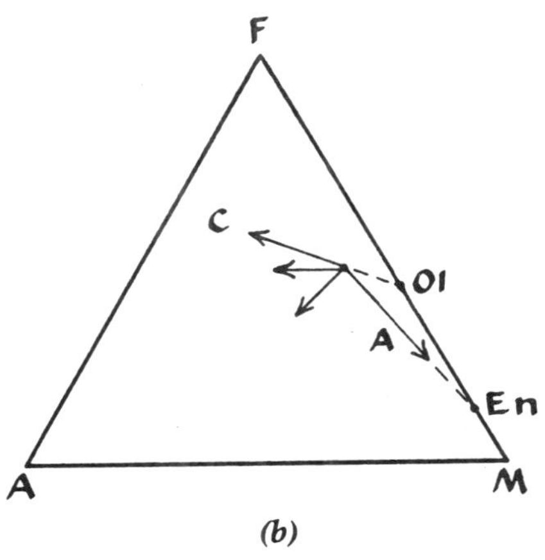

(b)

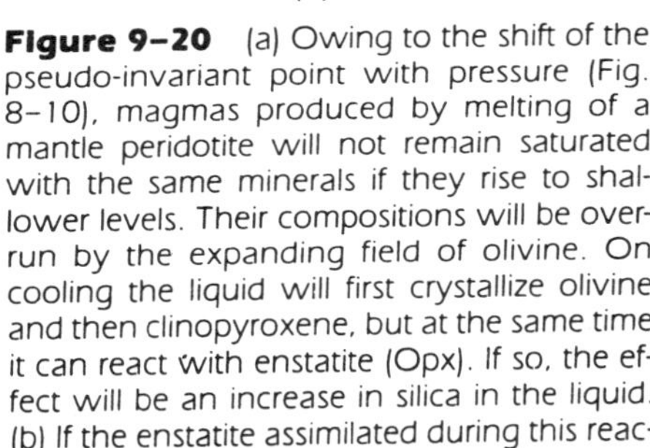

Figure 9–20 (a) Owing to the shift of the pseudo-invariant point with pressure (Fig. 8–10), magmas produced by melting of a mantle peridotite will not remain saturated with the same minerals if they rise to shallower levels. Their compositions will be overrun by the expanding field of olivine. On cooling the liquid will first crystallize olivine and then clinopyroxene, but at the same time it can react with enstatite (Opx). If so, the effect will be an increase in silica in the liquid. (b) If the enstatite assimilated during this reaction is the residue of earlier melting it would have a larger Mg-Fe ratio than the crystallizing olivine, and the effect of reaction would be to decrease the rate of enrichment of iron. Depending on the proportions of crystallized olivine and absorbed enstatite, the course of the liquid will be intermediate between that due to crystallization ("C") or assimilation ("A") alone. A detailed discussion of this effect has been given by P. B. Kelemen (1990, *Jour. Petrol.* 31:51–134.)

line magmas. The magnesium-iron ratio of the enstatite in residual mantle lherzolites or harzburgites is much more magnesian than that of either a differentiating basaltic liquid or the olivine it is crystallizing. Hence, assimilation of enstatite has the effect of reducing the rate of iron enrichment from what it would be if olivine were crystallizing without reaction (Fig. 9–20b).

This simple reaction offers a potentially important explanation for the difference between the calc-alkaline and tholeiitic trends. It is not clear, however, why the effect should be confined to mature subduction-related environments or why, under some conditions, the magmas of island arcs and continental margins change from tholeiitic to calc-alkaline.

ORIGINS OF CALC-ALKALINE MAGMAS

There is scarcely any petrogenetic scheme that has not at some time been invoked to explain the compositional features and geological occurrences of andesites. Despite decades of intense research much still remains to be learned about their origins. One reason for this is the complex physical and petrochemical relations of these rocks to a tectonic environment that is still only dimly understood. Unlike other rock series, the magmas evolve in dynamic conditions that are difficult to evaluate in terms of simple models based on equilibrium phase relations.

It was long thought that calc-alkaline rocks were simply products of tholeiitic magmas that had been contaminated by continental crust. Because andesite, the most distinctive member of the calc-alkaline series, is typical of regions where continental crust can be assimilated, it seemed obvious that tholeiitic magma rising through tens of kilometers of sialic rocks could scarcely reach the surface without being highly contaminated. The only question was how this came about. Andesites could result from basaltic magmas that melt the crust and then mix with the resulting silica-rich liquid, or they could evolve by crystal fractionation concurrent with assimilation.

This question came to the forefront in the 1920s, when a lively debate broke out between N. L. Bowen and C. N. Fenner over the origin of the calc-alkaline rocks in and around Katmai Volcano on the Alaskan Peninsula. Fenner visited the region shortly after the great eruption of 1912 had poured seven cubic kilometers of rhyolitic ignimbrites into the Valley of Ten Thousand Smokes. Near the base of Mount Katmai he observed a spectacular group of hybrid rocks, similar to the sample illustrated in Figure 5–13, and deduced that very hot rhyolitic magma of the main eruptive unit had melted and mingled with older mafic lavas in the interior of Mount Katmai. He went on to propose that mixing of two liquids, one mafic and the other felsic, could have produced the full range of intermediate compositions found elsewhere in the same region.

As support for this interpretation, Fenner pointed to the linear compositional variations of the rocks and argued that crystal fractionation would not produce such a trend (Fig. 9–21a). As we noted in chapter five, crystal fractionation normally produces non-linear variations, because the compositions and proportions of minerals being removed are constantly changing as crystallization advances. Fenner also drew attention to the lack of strong iron enrichment normally seen in intermediate differentiates, such as those of western Scotland or basic intrusions.

Bowen responded by pointing out that melting of mafic rocks by a more evolved magma, such as rhyolite, was thermodynamically absurd. The enormous amount of heat required to melt the mafic rock would not be available unless the rhyolite were superheated to an unrealistic degree. Even in the unlikely event that the rhyolitic magmas were originally superheated, i.e., at temperatures far above that at which they would begin to crystallize, the difference between the heat capacities of silicates (about 0.3 calories per gram) and their heats of fusion (about 80 calories per gram) is so great that a mafic rock caught up in superheated rhyolite would absorb so much heat that it could yield only trivial amounts of liquid.

Bowen went on to argue that Fenner's linear variations resulted from plotting compositions that had been altered by accumulation of phenocrysts and that if only aphyric rocks were used (Fig. 9–21b), the trends were slightly curved and could be explained by crystal fractionation. This argument seemed valid at the time, but it is now thought that most porphyritic calc-alkaline rocks do in fact approach liquid compositions.

But even if the trends of major-element variations were indeed curved, as

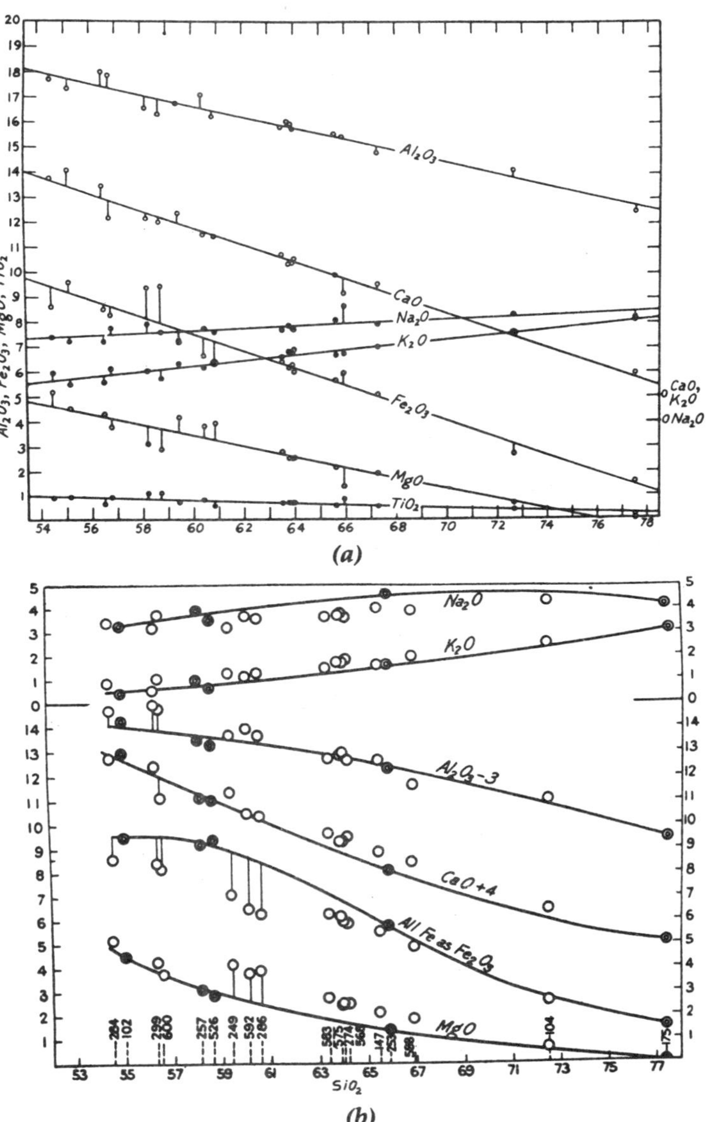

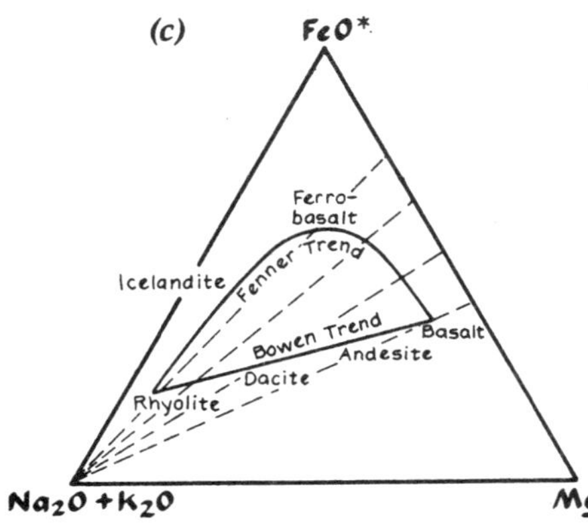

Figure 9–21 The Harker diagram shown in (a) is Fenner's original plot of the compositions of rocks from the Katmai region. Fenner inferred that their variations were linear and that they resulted from mixing of two end-members, one rich and the other poor in silica. The diagram in (b) is Bowen's interpretation of the same data. He disregarded all porphyritic rocks (open circles) and argued that those without phenocrysts (double circles) defined curved lines of the kind that would be expected for a series related by crystal fractionation. Here we have an example of how two petrologists, if they are determined to do so, can use the same data to support directly opposing conclusions. The basic differences in their interpretations can best be illustrated by an AFM diagram (c) showing the iron enrichment, or "Fenner trend," common in tholeiitic series, which Fenner considered typical of liquids related by crystal fractionation. He attributed the straighter "Bowen trend" of calc-alkaline rocks to mixing. Note that the trends associated with the two names are the opposite of those the two individuals saw in the rocks of Katmai.

Bowen maintained, they did not rule out other processes, such as combined crystal fractionation and assimilation. As we noted in chapter three, assimilation need not alter the trends of a liquid line of descent; it only changes the proportions of end products. So many of the geological relations of andesites seem to point to interaction between basic magma and crustal rocks that many geologists concluded that Fenner's scheme was simply backwards. It was more logical that mafic, high-temperature magmas assimilate crustal rocks to produce intermediate magmas of andesitic compositions. A number of observations lend support to this reasoning.

The role of crustal assimilation

The fact that calc-alkaline andesites are not erupted from volcanoes in the deep oceanic basins but are found along continental margins or in island arcs where subduction is thought to carry crustal material below the volcanic chains is impressive evidence that the distinctive character of the rocks is in some way a result of interaction between mantle-derived basaltic magma and more felsic components of the crust.

A number of detailed studies of calc-alkaline suites have shown how this process might operate. One of the most influential of these was a study by R. E. Wilcox of the lavas discharged by the Mexican volcano Paricutin between 1943 and 1952. During that period, 1.4 cubic kilometers of compositionally graded magma were discharged under conditions that permitted close observations and continual sampling. Silica contents of the lava increased from 54 percent in the first flows discharged in 1943 to over 60 percent at the close of the eruption nine years later (Fig. 9–22). At the same time, olivine decreased in abundance and developed reaction rims of pyroxene, while hypersthene became more abundant. These progressive changes in the composition of the lava can be explained by a combination of fractionation of the observed phenocrysts and assimilation of xenoliths of granitic rocks found in all stages of melting and incorporation into their host. Using a mass-balance calculation to relate the compositions of analyzed rocks and the minerals they contain, it is possible to show that the progressive variations in the major and trace elements are consistent with simultaneous fractional crystallization and assimilation of granitic basement rocks. The heat liberated by crystallizing minerals, by itself, would be insufficient to melt the necessary quantity of xenoliths, but it is reasonable to postulate that additional heat could be contributed by a larger body of convecting magma at greater depth and that no superheat would be required for the basalt to assimilate the requisite amount of granitic material.

Compositional evidence of crustal assimilation

At first glance, it might seem a simple matter to determine the degree to which such a process of assimilation might account for most of the compositional features of calc-alkaline rocks. For example, by examining long volcanic chains like the Alaskan-Aleutian Arc that cross from one type of crust to another, one can

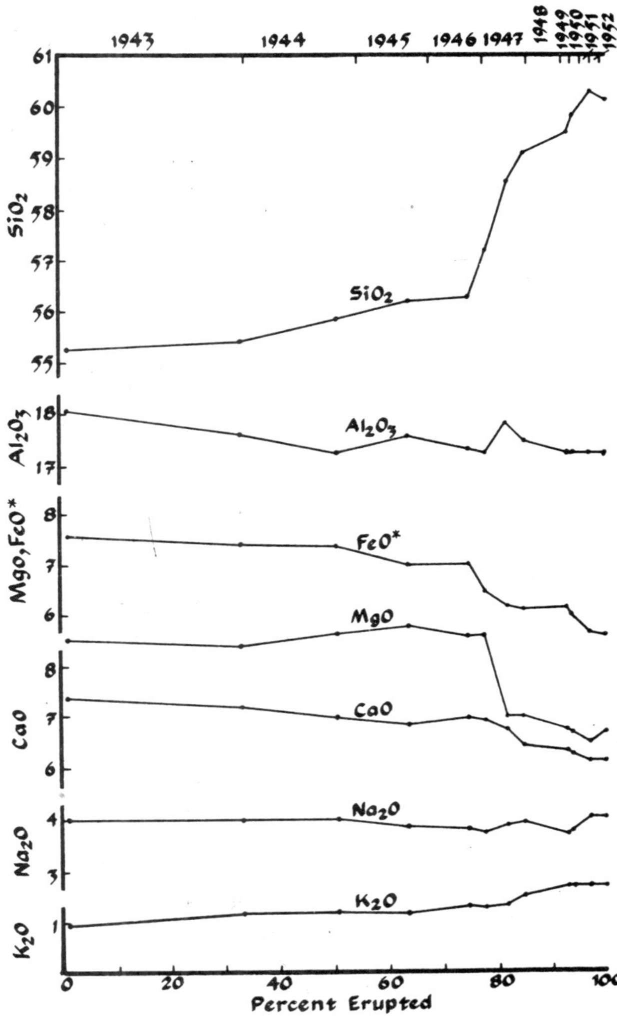

Figure 9–22 Compositional variations of the lavas of Parícutin Volcano during its continuous activity between 1943 and 1952. Note that the rate of eruption, as shown by the upper scale, declined with time and that the most silica-rich magma was the last to appear.

compare lavas from volcanoes on thick continental sialic crust with those erupted where the underlying section consists entirely of basic igneous rocks or volcanic sediments that differ little from the magmas passing through them. This test has been applied to several volcanic arcs, and in every case the lavas of volcanoes on thick continental crust are found to have major-element trends of differentiation indistinguishable from those on oceanic crust; assimilation, if it has played a role, has produced no obvious compositional difference in the rocks. On closer scrutiny, however, this observation proves to be less conclusive than it at first appears.

Consider first the compositions of crustal rocks and how they compare with the magmas in which they are being assimilated. If the crustal material has an unusual composition rich in components that are alien to common magmas, even small amounts of contamination may have very conspicuous effects. For example, when the Mexican volcano El Chichon erupted with such violence in 1981, the ejecta contained small crystals of the sulfate mineral anhydrite, a phase that is very rare in igneous rocks. This anhydrite is easily traced to the thick section of evaporites underlying the volcano. Another volcano, Concepcion, near the southern end of Lake Nicaragua, is underlain by Cretaceous sediments so rich in phosphates that they are a potential source of commercial fertilizer. The lavas of Concepcion contain extraordinarily large crystals of the phosphorus-bearing mineral, apatite, that must be a product of contamination by the sediments through which the magma rises.

Minerals like anhydrite or large crystals of apatite are conspicuous anomalies in calc-alkaline rocks. But if the assimilated material consists of felsic metamorphic or plutonic rocks of more common compositions, its contribution is much less obvious. Elements, such as silicon and the alkalies, that are normally enriched during igneous differentiation are also concentrated in the continental crust, and it is difficult to say whether these components are gained from assimilation or from differentiation; either process has the same effect.

Another consideration is inherent in the basic phase relations governing assimilation. Even if a magma were contaminated with rocks, such as limestone or clay shales, with bulk compositions far from those of common igneous rocks, the added components, such as CaO, Al_2O_3, and SiO_2, are the same as those entering minerals that normally crystallize at some stage of cooling of the magma. In such circumstances the effects of assimilation may be concealed by the way in which the magma responds to addition of large amounts of these components. So long as crystal-liquid relations control the course of differentiation, the major-element compositions of evolving liquids are constrained to follow a liquid line of descent that cannot deviate far from that defined by crystal fractionation.

As we noted in chapter 5, the principal effect of assimilation of crustal material added to a crystallizing magma is to change the proportions of end products; the major-element compositions of liquids may remain essentially unchanged. A basaltic magma contaminated with limestone or aluminous shales, for example, reacts with the xenolithic debris to form more of the same minerals, such as augite and anorthite, with which the magma is already saturated. If equilibrium is approached during this process, the effect of addition of foreign rocks is absorbed by increased crystallization of minerals that remove the added components, and the liquid evolves along a path that differs little from one it would have followed had assimilation not occurred. Although the proportions of liquid and crystalline residue will be altered, the magmas erupted at the surface would have major-element compositions and trends of differentiation consistent with normal crystal fractionation. Thus, if the effects of assimilation are to be detected, the evidence is not likely to be found in trends of differentiation. Instead, one should expect to find it reflected in the relative volumes of differentiated rocks. Magmas that assimilate large amounts of felsic continental crust should produce proportionately larger proportions of rock types, such as andesite, dacite, or rhyolite, that are richer in the components of continental lithosphere than those rising through mafic crustal rocks of oceanic character.

A test of this kind can be applied to the volcanic chain of the Cascade Range. It will be recalled that the northern and southern ends of the range are underlain by thick sections of metamorphic and plutonic rocks, whereas the crust in the central part of the belt seems to be largely oceanic in character. Although the trends of differentiation are found to be nearly the same from one end of the range to the other, the relative proportions of rock types differ widely. As we saw earlier, andesites and more differentiated rocks are relatively more abundant where magmas have risen through a thick sialic section.

But even this evidence, impressive as it is, may not be conclusive proof of wholesale assimilation, for the differences in proportions of rock types could have a much simpler explanation. Magmas passing through thick sections of cool continental crust must lose heat and crystallize on the way to the surface. Moreover, they rise more slowly through light continental rocks, and basic magmas, being denser than many shallow crustal rocks, may never reach the surface. Thus the continental crust may form a thermal barrier and "density trap" that inhibits dense mafic magmas of high temperatures from rising unaltered through cooler crustal rocks of low density. The volcanoes should produce lavas of smaller volumes and more evolved compositions, and this is true regardless of how much assimilation takes place. If so, differences in proportions of rock types may be due not so much to assimilation as to the physical limitations on the rise of magma through continental crust.

Isotopic evidence

What is needed to resolve this dilemma is a geochemical tracer that can serve as a measure of crustal contamination without being affected by differentiation. A distinctive component that has different concentrations in the mantle or continental crust but is insensitive to subsequent crystal fractionation would afford a way of detecting the relative contributions of the crust and mantle, no matter how the magma may have evolved. The isotopes of certain elements, such as strontium and lead, can provide just such a clue, because they have different concentrations in rocks of the crust and mantle but enter igneous minerals in amounts that are independent of their isotopic character.

Strontium has several isotopes of which one, ^{87}Sr, is produced from radioactive decay of ^{87}Rb. The other isotopes of Sr, including ^{86}Sr, are not radiogenic and do not change with time. Rubidium, like other alkalies, is a lithophile element and is strongly enriched in continental crust. Its radioactive isotope, ^{87}Rb, decays to ^{87}Sr with a half life of 5×10^{10} years. Hence, the ratio of ^{87}Sr to common nonradiogenic ^{86}Sr increases with time.

Because they are older and contain more Rb, continental crustal rocks have been enriched in the ratio $^{87}Sr/^{86}Sr$ to a greater degree than have rocks of the mantle or oceanic crust. We assume that at the time of formation of the earth the isotopes of strontium were uniformly distributed, so that even though the Sr contents of the rocks of the earth may have differed, their initial isotopic ratios were the same. Any process producing differences in the concentration of Rb in one part of the earth would with time lead to a corresponding difference in the amount of ^{87}Sr and hence in the ratio $^{87}Sr/^{86}Sr$.

Formation of continental crust was a process of this kind. It entailed strong enrichment of all lithophile elements, including Rb, in the upper crust, and this redistribution of Rb has led in turn to a greater rate of increase in the isotopic ratio of Sr, as ^{87}Rb decayed to ^{87}Sr (Fig. 9–23). The result of this gradual evolution can best be seen in old continental rocks, which now have ratios of the order of .713 to .725, whereas mantle-derived rocks, such as the basaltic lavas of oceanic volcanoes, have lower ratios, normally between .701 and .704. The differences between these ratios may seem small, but they are significant in terms of the precision of modern analytical techniques, and, more important, they impart detectable differences to magmas that result from a combination of both mantle-derived and crustal strontium. In this way the isotopic character of Sr can provide a measure of the contribution of continental crust to andesitic magmas.

The isotopic ratio of a contaminated magma depends not only on the ratios of the initial magma and contaminant but also on their total concentrations of Sr, as well as any loss to fractionated crystals. The amount of Sr in a contaminated magma (CM) can be calculated from a simple mass balance

$$(M + C - F)(Sr)_{CM} = M(Sr)_M + C(Sr)_C - F(Sr)_F \qquad (9\text{–}1)$$

where M and C are the weight fractions of original magma and contaminating material, and F is the amount of any crystals removed by fractionation. Sr_{CM}, Sr_M, etc., are the Sr contents in parts per million of Sr in the contaminated magma and the various added or subtracted components. The isotopic ratio of the contaminated magma results from the combined weighted contributions of strontium from both the original magma and its contaminant in the proportions of their strontium contents and isotopic ratios. The equation expressing this relation is

$$(M + C - F)\,Sr_{CM}\left[\frac{^{87}Sr}{^{86}Sr}\right]_{CM} = M\,Sr_M\left[\frac{^{87}Sr}{^{86}Sr}\right]_M + C\,Sr_C\left[\frac{^{87}Sr}{^{86}Sr}\right]_C - F\,Sr_F\left[\frac{^{87}Sr}{^{86}Sr}\right]_F \qquad (9\text{–}2)$$

where $^{87}Sr/^{86}Sr$ is the isotopic ratio of each of the components CM, M, C, and F.

In the case of Paricutin, a mass-balance calculation indicated that the amount of assimilated crustal material required to explain the major elements of the andesites was about 10 percent. The calculated amount of concurrent crystallization was negligible, probably because the crystals remained as phenocrysts. The basic lavas contain about 556 ppm Sr; felsic rocks, on the other hand, have much less, the average for the xenoliths and basement rocks at Paricutin being about 227 ppm Sr. The amount of Sr in the andesite should then be

$$Sr_{CM} = (0.9)(556) + (.1)(227) = 523 \text{ ppm}$$

This is consistent with the measured Sr contents of the most differentiated andesites, which range between 511 and 556 ppm.

The isotopic ratios of the most basic and most differentiated lavas are 0.7037

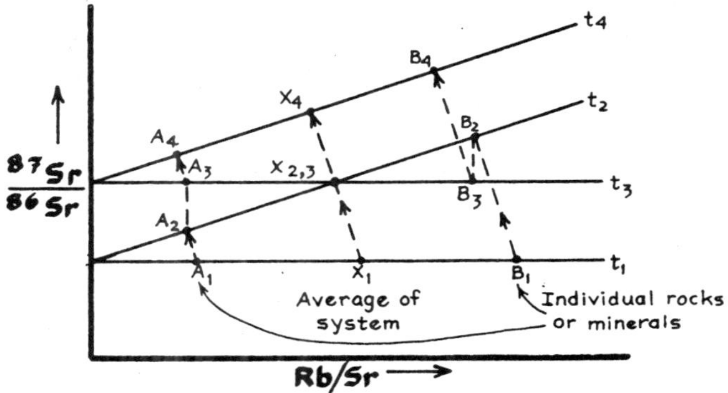

Figure 9–23 A plot of Sr isotopes against the ratio of Rb to Sr shows the individual effects of age and composition on isotopic ratios. If left to evolve, rocks or minerals of differing Rb/Sr ratios will increase in $^{87}Sr/^{86}Sr$ by amounts that are directly proportional to time and their Rb contents. At time t_2 they will define a line or "isochron" with a slope that is a direct function of age. At high temperatures, the minerals in a rock may re-equilibrate and take on a more uniform ratio, even though their Rb/Sr still differ. After a rock is "reset" in this way at time t_3, ^{87}Rb continues to decay, and the Sr ratio will again evolve from its new baseline to give another isochron at time t_4 that is a measure of time elapsed since the last "setting of the clock." If the rock is then melted and the liquid differentiates to a series of compositions, only the Rb/Sr ratio is affected. More differentiated compositions will be richer in Rb and poorer in Sr, but their Sr ratios will be the same until more time elapses and more ^{87}Rb decays to ^{87}Sr.

and 0.7043 respectively. Although this difference seems small, it requires assimilation of crustal material with a much larger ratio:

$$(523)(0.7043) = .9(556)(0.7037) + .1(227)(^{87}Sr/^{86}Sr)_C$$

$$(^{87}Sr/^{86}Sr)_C = 0.7144$$

Because the crustal rocks have much less Sr than the initial magma and contribute a proportionately small part to the andesite, they must have much larger isotopic ratios to have any conspicuous effect.

This example illustrates the factors that must be taken into account if Sr isotopes are to be used as a test of crustal assimilation. Because the Sr contents of mafic magmas are so much greater than those of felsic rocks, assimilation will be apparent only if the crustal rocks have large isotopic ratios or contribute very large proportions of Sr to the contaminated magma. These limitations probably explain why Sr isotopes are often found to give ambiguous results. In the Cascade Range, for example, the Sr ratios of andesites vary as much in a single volcano as they do throughout the chain as a whole, and no systematic difference is observed between the Sr in volcanoes standing on thick continental crust and those in regions where such crust is thin or totally absent. It is possible, of course, that the crust under the Cascades is too young or too poor in radiogenic Sr to leave a strong imprint, but similar relations are seen in other regions, such as the Andes, where the continental crust is thick, old, and rich in ^{87}Sr. Taken as a whole, the andesites of continental margins have Sr ratios that are statistically greater than those of island arcs, but the differences are so small and irregular that they do not seem to indicate more than minor sporadic contamination of magmas that are derived predominantly from sources in the mantle.

Continental crust is not, of course, the only possible source of crustal material capable of affecting the compositions of andesites. A contribution could also come from sediments subducted in trenches and carried down to depths below the volcanic arc.

THE ROLE OF SUBDUCTED CRUST

Just as we see that "all the rivers run into the sea; yet the sea is not full," we also know that sediments have long been eroded from the continents, and yet oceans are still deep and continents stand high above them. Continental material entering the oceans, either as solid erosional debris or soluble products of weathering, must in some way be returned to the continents. Otherwise, continents could not persist as they do through long periods of geologic time.

This remarkable balance can be achieved in two ways. As oceanic lithosphere converges on zones of subduction, light sediments may be scraped from the oceanic lithosphere and form an accreting wedge on the leading edge of the continent. Or they may be subducted along with the rest of the descending slab, melt, and rise into the overlying lithosphere. Magmas generated in this way would complete the cycle by returning to the continents in the form of orogenic lavas, pyroclastic rocks, and plutons.

Several attempts have been made to measure the volumes of youthful sediments along the inner sides of trenches, in order to compare them with the huge volumes that would be brought there on a converging oceanic plate. In this way it would be possible to determine whether some part of the volume has been subducted. Although the calculations are imprecise and interpretations are a matter of dispute, no large discrepancy has been found, and one must fall back on other lines of reasoning.

Sediments entering trenches have two distinct components, one a direct influx composed mainly of clastic turbidites from the adjacent continent or island arc and another composed of pelagic sediments laid down in the interior of the ocean basins as layer one of the oceanic crust. Terrigenous clastic material of the first type is less likely to be subducted; most appears to be added to the continental shelf and outer non-volcanic arc. But pelagic sediments, consisting mainly of calcareous oozes, wind-blown dust, and chemical precipitates that blanket the deep ocean floor, are notably scarce in the accreted wedges of continents. One simple way of accounting for their rarity is to assume they are subducted in proportionately greater amounts than terrigenous sediments.

One place to test the role of subducted crust would be in island arcs where continental rocks are absent from the basement directly under the volcanoes, and a direct input from that source can be ruled out. If, in addition, the character of sediments entering the trench differs along the axis of the arc, it should be possible to see their effect in spatial variations of the compositions of corresponding parts of the chain of volcanoes.

One such arc, the Lesser Antilles, is entirely on oceanic crust, but it has an asymmetrical trench. The southern part receives sediments from the adjacent continent of South America, while the northern part has only pelagic sediments from the Atlantic Ocean floor and volcanic debris from nearby volcanic islands. The volcanoes adjacent to the trench do not differ markedly from one end of the chain to another, but those nearer the continent tend to be richer in potassium and other lithophile components as would be expected if a greater proportion of continental material is being subducted in the south. It appears, therefore, that at least some terrigenous sediments are subducted and become incorporated in calc-alkaline magmas.

The isotopic character of subduction-related magmas provides additional evidence. The lavas of island arcs differ from oceanic basalts in their isotopic ratios of strontium and neodymium; they diverge from the "mantle array" toward higher $^{87}Sr/^{86}Sr$, but nearly constant Nd ratios. This trend could result from the effect of altered subducted oceanic crust, including both basalts and marine sediments, on the magmas generated beneath the arcs. The Sr ratio of modern seawater, about 0.709, is substantially greater than that of modern mid-ocean-ridge basalts, because radiogenic ^{87}Sr is carried into the oceans by rivers draining ancient, Rb-rich rocks of the continents. But the neodymium content of seawater is very small, owing to the short residence time of the rare-earth elements in the oceans. Hence, when seawater is circulated through the upper oceanic crust by hydrothermal systems at the ridges, ocean-floor basalts and sediments take on more radiogenic Sr while retaining their original Nd ratio. If this material is subducted and contributes to the magmas of island arcs, it should cause magmas to have greater Sr ratios but unchanged Nd. What is actually observed is far from clear-cut (Fig. 9–24). With so many other possible contributions of Nd, the effect of abyssal sediments, if there is any, is hard to distinguish.

Beryllium-boron tracers

Another radioactive isotope, beryllium-10, has been used more successfully to trace subducted sediments. ^{10}Be, which is produced in the atmosphere by the effect of cosmic rays on oxygen and nitrogen, is absorbed in the oceans and adheres to clays deposited on the seafloor. Having a half-life of only 1.5 million

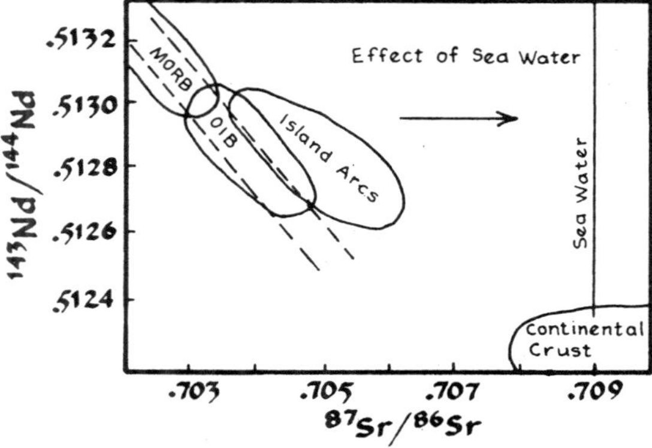

Figure 9–24 The distribution of Nd and Sr isotopes in lavas of island arc does not follow the "mantle array" defined by oceanic basalts but diverges toward larger Sr ratios. Part of this shift may be attributable to the effect of seawater, which imparts its signature to hydrothermally altered submarine rocks. Although Sr is an abundant constituent of seawater, the rare-earth elements are present in much smaller concentration and have little or no effect on the Nd ratios of sediments or altered submarine lavas. This could account for the shift of island arc values to higher Sr ratios. Note, however, that assimilation of continental crust could do the same.

years, only a small part is left after the ten million years or so required for a subducted slab to descend from a trench to a region below a volcanic chain. Nevertheless, the remaining amount of the isotope can serve as a measure of the rates at which sediments are carried down and returned to the surface in magmas. The amount of ^{10}Be in the lavas of subduction-related volcanoes is too great to have come from the mantle or old crustal rocks, where this isotope has long since disappeared.

In practice, the absolute amount of this isotope in rocks (a few million atoms per gram) is too small to be measured accurately. It is possible, however, to measure relative amounts of the beryllium isotopes with great precision. Thus, by measuring the ratio of ^{10}Be to the more abundant stable isotope, ^{9}Be, the proportion of the former in the total amount of Be can be accurately determined.

Because ^{10}Be declines with time, this ratio cannot, by itself, be used as a measure of the contribution of oceanic sediments or of the rates they are being subducted unless it can be related to another component of sediments that does not decay with time. Boron is such an element. Because it is abundant in sediments but not in the mantle, it can be used to estimate the amount of the total sedimentary contribution. Then, by plotting the ratio B/Be against $^{10}Be/Be$, the combined effects of volume and rates of subduction can be seen.

When this is done (Fig. 9–25), data for individual volcanic arcs tend to fall on straight lines between two major components. Mantle rocks with small ^{10}Be-Be and B-Be ratios fall in the lower left corner of the diagram, because they have little boron and any ^{10}Be they may have had has long since decayed. Fluids from the subducted plate, being a complex combination of seawater and components distilled from oceanic crust of different ages and compositions, form a broad field in the upper-right part of the diagram.

The linear distribution of points along the line for a given region indicates that the process by which these components enter magmas is one of simple addition. But it is difficult to reconcile this with the wide range of possible compositions of slab-derived fluids. The data are much more regular than those for other

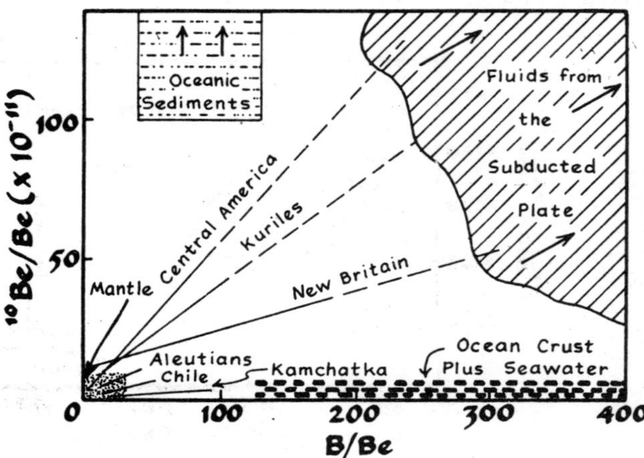

Figure 9–25 Relations of beryllium and boron in subduction-related magmas to the ratios of the same components in subducted oceanic sediments, crust, and mantle. The measured values for lavas in individual chains of volcanoes fall along well-defined mixing lines between mantle compositions and those inferred for fluids distilled from subducted sediments. They cannot be the result of direct melting of oceanic crust or of sediments alone but must have a component that is the result of fractional distillation of boron and beryllium from the subducted slab. (The diagram is the result of work by Louis Brown, W. P. Leeman, and others as summarized in *Yearbook 88* of the Carnegie Institution of Washington, 111–118.)

components, such as potassium or the isotopes of Nd and Sr, that could reflect the contribution of sediments to calc-alkaline magmas.

The relative enrichment of boron in subduction-related lavas indicates that the magmas are not the result of simple melting of oceanic sediments; if they were, boron and beryllium would enter the melts in their original proportions. It seems more likely that magmas incorporate a fluid that is derived from the oceanic crust in some way that takes proportionately more boron than beryllium. The strong linear trends for individual arcs suggest that these elements may be fractionated during distillation by amounts that are governed by thermodynamic conditions and that these are essentially constant in a given subduction zone.

GENERATION AND RISE OF SUBDUCTION-RELATED MAGMAS

The spacing of volcanoes along island arcs and continental margins indicates that magmas accumulate along a linear source until they reach a critical mass and begin to rise as buoyant diapirs. The regular spacing of large cones along the axis of a volcanic front can be related to the gravitational instability of light, partly molten, mantle rocks under a denser asthenosphere (Fig. 9-26). The spacing normal to the axis indicates that the greatest proportion of magma is produced just below the volcanic front; little or no melting takes place above shallower parts of the Benioff zone, and only minor amounts come from the deeper region

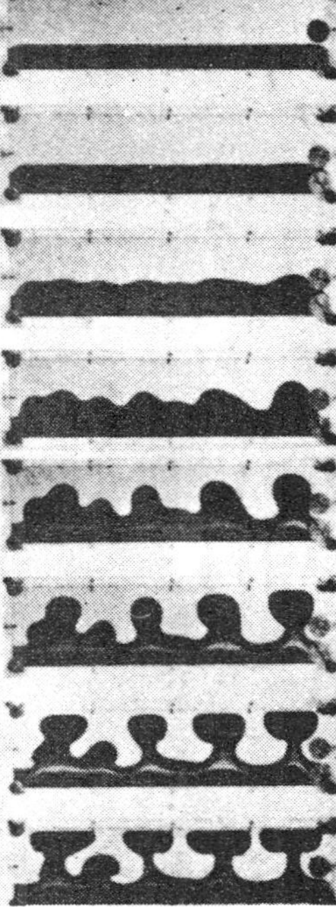

Figure 9-26 Melt generated along a line beneath the volcanic front is gravitationally unstable and will tend to rise as a series of nearly equally spaced plumes. This sequence of photographs by H. Ramberg shows a model in which a lighter liquid that has an initially even distribution (top) forms a wave-like surface and rises as separate plumes (bottom).

behind the front. Thus the zone of magma generation seems to be a long, narrow zone or prism in either the slab or in the overlying wedge of mantle.

Magmas generated in this environment pose an apparent paradox in that they come from regions in which cold subducted lithosphere should have the effect of drastically depressing the temperature of the mantle. Of the various mechanisms for generating magmas outlined in chapter seven, only two could be effective under such conditions. The first derives heat from the mechanical energy of subduction; the second lowers melting temperatures by introducing subducted material into the mantle.

The strong seismicity concentrated in Benioff zones testifies to the large amounts of mechanical energy released along the upper part of the descending plate. If part of this energy were expended in frictional heating of the subducted lithosphere and adjacent mantle, it could raise the temperature enough to cause melting. The distribution of earthquakes supports this interpretation. Most Benioff zones have fewer deep earthquakes directly beneath the main volcanic axis, and this deficiency could be the result of melting and lowering of the shear strength of rocks at that particular depth.

One way in which mechanical energy may be converted to heat in these zones is by the "thermal runaway" effect mentioned in chapter seven. If the rate of conduction to the cooler adjacent rocks is smaller than that of heat generation, temperatures will be highest near the locus of maximum deformation. The added heat reduces the strength of the sheared rocks and causes further deformation to be channeled into a progressively narrower zone where the rocks are hottest. This concentration of shear energy also localizes the heat production and further reduces the strength and viscosity of the rocks.

Depending on the nature of the driving force, this focusing effect could have either a positive or negative feedback. Under conditions of constant stress, the result would be to concentrate a fixed input of energy in a progressively smaller volume of rock, and the amount of melting would increase accordingly. A condition of constant strain, however, has the opposite effect. The decreasing viscosity of the heated zone reduces the resistance to a constant rate of deformation, so that the amount of heat produced by viscous dissipation declines and levels off at a slower rate. The conditions in subduction zones are probably intermediate between these to limiting cases. The more or less steady rates of subduction measured in most Benioff zones indicate that the regime is closer to one of constant strain, whereas, the episodic nature of volcanism suggests constant stress with periodic thermal runaway.

An alternative mechanism is based on the fluxing effect of volatile components expelled from the descending slab. We saw in the preceding section that boron and beryllium provide strong evidence that fluids driven out of sediments and hydrothermally altered basalts could play an important role in melting. The lithospheric plate descending to regions of higher pressure and temperatures beneath the volcanic arc must re-equilibrate with its new surroundings, and, as it does so, pore water that has not already been expelled by compaction would be incorporated into hydrous minerals that, in turn, become unstable as temperature and pressure increase. Depending on their individual stability limits, these

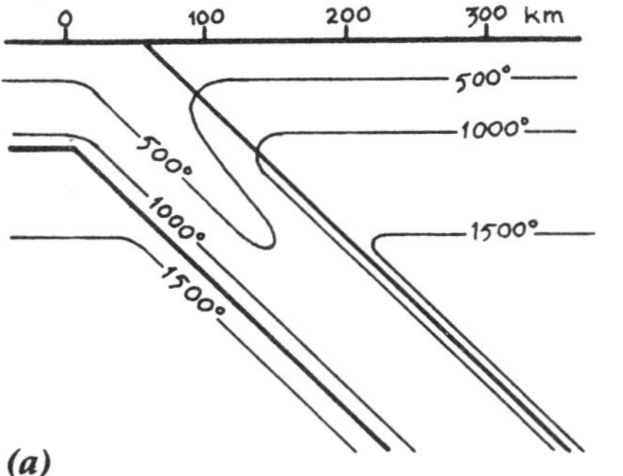

(a)

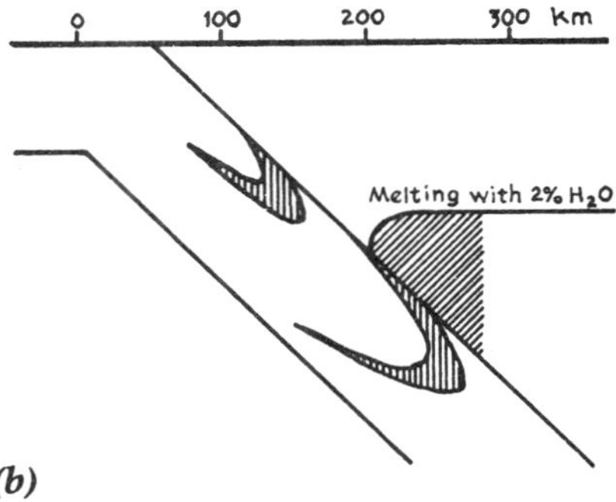

(b)

Figure 9–27 (a) Calculated distribution of temperature in a descending slab of oceanic lithosphere. (After D. T. Griggs, 1972, in *The Nature of the Solid Earth*, E. G. Robertson, ed., McGraw-Hill.) (b) Stability limits of the principal hydrous minerals in a slab of subducted oceanic crust. The upper zone of vertical ruling indicates the region in which the temperature and pressure would cause serpentine, clay, and hornblende to break down; the lower zone indicates the stability limits of the Mg-rich mica, phlogopite. The upper zone lies approximately below the positions of coast ranges (or non-volcanic outer arcs), whereas the lower zone is below the inner uplifted blocks and volcanic fronts (Figs. 9–2 and 9–10). A possible melting curve is shown for mantle rocks with about 2 percent water. The diagonally ruled area indicates the region in which breakdown of phlogopite might produce enough magma to mobilize diapirs under the volcanic front. At shallower depths where temperatures are lower, rising fluids would hydrate the mantle rocks and cause a volumetric expansion and elevation of the surface. (After Fyfe, W. S. and A. R. McBirney, 1975, *Amer. Jour. Sci.*, 275-A:285–297.)

hydrous minerals may persist to differing levels. Clays, chlorite, and serpentine break down at relatively low temperatures and reach only shallow depths (Fig. 9-27), but amphibole can survive somewhat longer, and the magnesium-rich mica, phlogopite, can reach the greatest depth of all. Thus, as the slab descends, a series of reactions may take place as each assemblage becomes unstable and is replaced by a new one of higher density. As the ultimate stability limits of hydrous minerals are reached, water must be released along with other components, such as silica and alkalies, that are soluble in water at elevated temperatures and pressures. In this way, the descending slab would be progressively dehydrated and partly depleted of its sialic components. And if these components rise into hotter levels above the slab, they could lower the melting temperature of the mantle and generate magmas solely by flux-melting without a net addition of heat. According to this hypothesis, the volcanic front stands above a level of the mantle wedge where the temperature reaches a threshold level above which an influx of fluids can trigger melting. The depth and rate of melting will depend in large part on the rate at which volatile components are supplied by subduction and diffuse into the hotter overlying rocks.

In the first of these mechanisms, thermal energy is derived from mechanical forces driving the descending slab; in the second, it is drawn from the stored heat of the overlying mantle. The first mechanism would continue to produce magma, possibly in pulses, but at undiminished rates so long as subduction continues. Flux-melting, on the other hand, draws on stored heat and will decline with time unless the source region is renewed by convective flow in the mantle above the subducted slab.

In the Cascade Range, the only region for which we have even limited data on the rates of volcanism over an extended period, the temporal decline of Cenozoic magmatism suggests flux melting of a source that is static or nearly so. This conclusion depends, however, on an assumption that the rate of subduction was constant for the same period, and this is difficult to verify. The correlation between the angle of subduction and volumes of magmas produced in the Alaskan and Aleutian arc is probably more meaningful. It lends strong support to a mechanism closely tied to the rate of subduction. This link could be through the rate at which sediments are subducted, but it could also be through the amount of shear energy converted to heat.

Certain trace elements provide a way of distinguishing between these two possibilities. If the mantle wedge melts as a result of volatile fluxing, the proportions of incompatible elements contributed to the melt along with the volatile phase should reflect their relative solubilties in hydrous solutions derived from the subducted slab. The solubilities of lithophile elements at elevated temperatures and pressures differ widely; they vary chiefly according to their ionic potential, the ratio of charge to ionic radius. Small ions with large charges, such as Ti, Zr, U, Th, Nb and Ta, commonly referred to as high-field-strength elements (HFSE) have much lower solubilities than large-ion lithophile elements (LILE) with lower charges. The latter include elements like Cs, Rb, K, Ba, Sr, and Pb. The rare-earth elements are intermediate between these two extremes. If melting is triggered by an influx of hydrous fluids that carry these trace elements in solution, the ratio of LILE to HFSE of the melt should be elevated relative to that of other mantle-derived magmas, such as mid-ocean ridge basalts. We noted early in this chapter that one of the distinctive marks of orogenic magmas is their relatively low Ti contents. They are also notable for their concentrations of rare-earths which, except in the case of K-rich series of the continental interiors, are very low. The LIL elements, on the other hand, tend to be more abundant in subduction-related magmas than in oceanic lavas of similar silica contents. The ratio Ba/La of orogenic rocks, for example, normally exceeds 15, whereas it averages only 4 in normal MORB. Similar contrasts are seen in ratios of LILE to HFSE, such as Ba/Th or Rb/Nb. All of these geochemical characteristics are consistent with a volatile flux contributing proportionately greater amounts of incompatible elements having high solubilities in hydrous solutions. In the final chapter we shall examine these relations in other tectonic settings and see that they seem to be consistent on a global scale.

SELECTED REFERENCES

Gill, J. 1981. *Orogenic Andesites and Plate Tectonics*. Springer-Verlag, 390 pp. A very detailed survey of orogenic rocks, including both tholeiitic and calc-alkaline types, with strong emphasis on trace-element geochemistry.

Grove, T. M., and R. J. Kinzler. 1986. Petrogenesis of andesites. *Ann. Rev. Earth &*

Planet. Sci. 14:417–454. A review of recent experimental work on differentiation of calc-alkaline and tholeiitic andesites.

McBirney, A. R., ed. 1969. Proceedings of the Andesite conference. *Bull. 65, Oregon Dept. Geol. Min. Indust.*, 193 pp. Though somewhat outdated by more recent work, this volume contains a number of classic papers, presenting in concise form many of the basic concepts that have been proposed to explain calc-alkaline andesites.

Thorpe, R. S., ed. 1982. *Andesites*. John Wiley, 724 pp. An especially broad and comprehensive compilation of papers dealing with the geology and petrology of andesitic volcanism.

10

GRANITIC PLUTONS AND SILICEOUS IGNIMBRITES

THE LARGE, INTRUSIVE BODIES of deeply eroded orogenic terranes can be thought of as the deeper roots of the volcanic belts described in the preceding chapter. The great majority have many of the chemical characteristics of calc-alkaline volcanic rocks, particularly in regions of thick continental crust, but plutonic rocks of intermediate to high silica contents are relatively more abundant than in their volcanic counterparts. It is mainly this last feature that distinguishes these plutons from the large gabbroic intrusions discussed in chapter six.

We refer to such rocks loosely as "granites" or "granitoids," even though they usually encompass a broader range of compositions than granite in the strict compositional sense. The dual usage of the term "granite" as both a general term for any more-or-less leucocratic, coarse-grained rock and as a name for a specific composition can be confusing but is probably too deeply ingrained to be changed. In most instances, the intended meaning is evident from its context.

Many of the attributes of plutonic rocks, particularly their large volumes of felsic compositions, also characterize the great sheets of rhyolitic and dacitic pyroclastic rocks, mainly ignimbrites, erupted in interior regions of continents. In fact, many siliceous ignimbrites have been traced to sources in shallow intrusions of similar compositions. This is not to say that all plutons had a volcanic expression at the surface, nor that all large, eruptive sheets come from plutonic intrusions, but the two are so often closely related and gradational one into the other that one can scarcely doubt their common origin.

Several broad categories of felsic plutonic rocks can be distinguished on the basis of their chemical and mineralogical compositions, tectonic settings, and ages.

PETROGRAPHIC AND MINERALOGICAL CLASSIFICATIONS

Of the various types of plutonic rocks listed in chapter two, we are concerned here with only those in the silica-saturated upper part of Figure 2–1. The series quartz diorite-tonalite-granodiorite-granite encompasses over 90 percent of the volume of most batholithic rocks, just as the equivalent volcanic rocks, andesite-dacite-rhyodacite-rhyolite make up all but a minor fraction of the large ignimbrite sheets.

Mineral assemblages and textures

Felsic plutonic rocks owe the large sizes of their crystals to slow cooling and the effects of volatiles, mainly water, that facilitate growth. Their microscopic textures (Fig. 10–1) differ from those of more mafic rocks in layered intrusions. Very few granitic plutons have fine-grained margins. Layering is much less common and limited almost entirely to thin, wispy streaks of dark minerals near the margins. Strong modal contrasts are rare, and cumulate textures are almost unknown. Instead, the principal minerals—feldspar, quartz, hornblende, and micas—tend to form anhedral grains in mosaic intergrowths. Porphyritic textures, which are rare in gabbros and peridotites, are very common in granites. Subhedral megacrysts of potassium feldspar may exceed five or ten centimeters in length. Many of these large crystals have inclusions of other minerals.

Though less diverse than their volcanic counterparts, plutonic rocks have a great variety of textures, reflecting their different conditions of crystallization. Hypidiomorphic-granular textures (Fig. 4–24a), which are so common in plutonic rocks, record the mutual spatial accommodations of crystals in their most stable forms as they interfere with one another during growth. How much of their form is due to recrystallization at sub-solidus conditions is difficult to say,

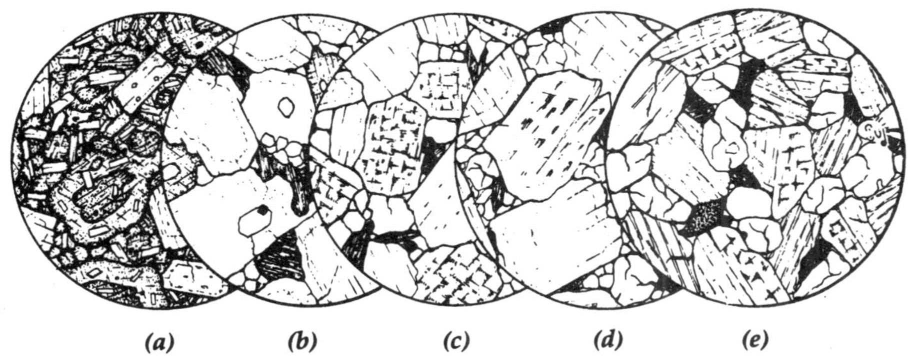

Figure 10–1 Textures of some common plutonic rocks. (a) Pyroxene hornblende gabbro from the Peninsula Batholith of Baja California. Hornblende appears to have replaced much of the earlier pyroxene. (b) Tonalite with hornblende, biotite, andesine, quartz, and minor alkali feldspar, Italian Alps. (c) Granodiorite from northern Nicaragua with quartz, oligoclase, and microcline. Biotite and hornblende are the main mafic minerals. (d) Subsolvus granite from the Precambrian shield of South Africa. About equal parts of quartz, perthitic orthoclase, and oligoclase zoned to albite, with lesser amounts of biotite, and accessory apatite. (e) Hypersolvus granite from the Isle of Skye, Scotland. A single feldspar has exsolved into two sub-equal parts of K-feldspar and sodic plagioclase. The most abundant dark mineral is the sodic amphibole, riebeckite.

but it is doubtful whether many of the textures of slowly cooled plutonic rocks are those of crystals grown directly from a liquid.

The granophyric textures so common in siliceous rocks of differentiated basic intrusions are rare in granitic plutons. Instead, coarser intergrowths of quartz and alkali feldspar may give the rock a *graphic* texture in which the crystallographic planes of the crystals have controlled the orientations of co-precipitated quartz and feldspar. Equally common are *myrmekitic* textures in which worm-like blebs of quartz and possibly plagioclase have formed within larger crystals of feldspar, usually orthoclase. All three of these textures—granophyric, graphic, and myrmekitic—result from crystallization of a eutectic composition consisting of quartz and alkali feldspars.

Feldspars and quartz account for well over half of the mode of felsic plutonic rocks. Pyroxenes and other anhydrous minerals are less common than amphibole and biotite. They are confined chiefly to rocks that crystallized at low water pressures. Though most common in shallow intrusions, pyroxenes are also typical of dry, high-pressure conditions. Muscovite rarely crystallizes from granitic melts at water pressures less than about five kilobars. It is found only in rocks with normative corundum, i.e, with an excess of alumina over the amount needed for feldspars.

Sub-solvus and hypersolvus granites

The character of the alkali feldspars is one of the most useful and widely applicable guides to the conditions of crystallization. We noted in chapter four that at low water pressures the system albite-orthoclase has a minimum between the two solid-solution series, and at sub-solidus temperatures a solvus limits the amount of solid solution between the two end-members (Fig. 4–6). It will be recalled that crystallization at low water pressures produces a single feldspar of intermediate composition, which, on cooling to the two-feldspar solvus, may exsolve into two forms, one rich in albite and the other in potassium feldspar. The result is a patchy intergrowth of two feldspars in a single grain. At increased water pressures, the solidus curves are lowered until they intersect the solvus, and instead of precipitating a single feldspar that exsolves only after an interval of sub-solidus cooling, separate sodic and potassic feldspars crystallize initially from the melt and quickly start to exsolve their counterpart to form perthite or antiperthite respectively.

These relations can be used to divide granitic rocks into two broad groups. *Sub-solvus granites* crystallized at elevated water pressures have two separate alkali feldspars (Fig. 10–1d); *hypersolvus granites* crystallized at a lower water pressure have a single feldspar (Fig. 10–1e). In either case the feldspars may show exsolution.

A distinctive type of hypersolvus granites with *rapakivi* textures is distinguished by large, rounded phenocrysts of alkali feldspar overgrown with plagioclase, normally oligoclase or andesine. Most have two generations of alkali feldspar and quartz. These unusual rocks are largely confined to Precambrian shield areas. They are thought to owe their textures to low-temperature recrystallization under shallow, possibly sub-volcanic, conditions.

Sanidine and other high-temperature alkali feldspars are confined to the very shallowest intrusions and to contact zones that have been heated to high temperatures by basic magma. The low-temperature potassium feldspar, microcline, is found in granites that have recrystallized under metamorphic conditions: it is not stable at magmatic temperatures.

Accessory minerals

Other minerals, such as tourmaline, zircon, topaz, or allanite, are common accessories and may be particularly distinctive of the granites and rhyolites of certain regions where the magmas contain anomalously large amounts of boron, zirconium, fluorine, or cerium. Carbonates, sulfides, and oxides of iron, copper, zinc, lead, tin, molybdenum, and other metals may either be disseminated or concentrated in veins or pods in and around an intrusion. Some of these components are introduced along with water, carbon dioxide, sulfur, and chlorine from surrounding rocks by hydrothermal solutions circulating through the plutons after they have solidified; others are inherent in the original magma and concentrated by late-stage processes of differentiation.

Pegmatites

Special mention must be made of the extraordinary group of very coarse-grained rocks, pegmatites, that form dikes and pod-like segregations in many granitic plutons and metamorphic rocks. Although they differ widely in form and composition, most pegmatites form at late stages, probably after the main mass of magma has crystallized and a hydrous fluid has formed a separate phase. Individual crystals reach enormous sizes, with single feldspars as large as 2 by 3.5 by 9 meters and micas 4 meters thick and 10 meters across.

Although most pegmatites are simply very coarse-grained rocks with compositions similar to those of normal granites, certain rare types are extraordinarily enriched in the elements concentrated in late-crystallizing granitic liquids. The high solubility of silica, alkalies, and other elements in this water-rich fluid enhances transfer and concentration of residual components, including rare and economically important elements, such as lithium, cesium, beryllium, tin, niobium, zirconium, uranium, thorium, boron, phosphorus, and fluorine. Many rare minerals, including beryl ($Be_3Al_2Si_6O_{18}$), the lithium pyroxene spodumene ($LiAlSi_2O_6$), and certain gemstones, such as aquamarine, are found mainly, if not exclusively, in pegmatites.

Siliceous volcanic rocks

At the opposite extreme of grain size from pegmatites are the glassy, volcanic counterparts of granitic rocks. All but a small fraction of these are pyroclastic rocks laid down either as pumiceous air-fall deposits or as ignimbrites. Viscous crystal-rich domes of dacite or rhyolite may be extruded in relatively small volumes, but voluminous lavas of these compositions are all but unknown.

Though sometimes referred to as "ash-flow tuffs," ignimbrites are composed of fragmental debris with a much greater size range than ash, and they do not necessarily form indurated rocks, as the word "tuff" implies. They are laid down by hot pyroclastic flows, typically of large volume, that move across the surface with great mobility and speed. Most are thought to be erupted from fissures along the boundary faults of large calderas, but no eruptions on this scale have been observed in historic times, and much of what is written about them is necessarily conjectural. Though infrequent on a historical scale, they were common in the recent geological past, especially during the middle Tertiary, when vast areas of the western United States, Mexico, Honduras, and the western slopes of the Andes were blanketed with sheets covering thousands of square kilometers to thicknesses of hundreds of meters.

One of the closest historic analogs, the 1912 eruption from Novarupta near the base of Mount Katmai, Alaska, flooded the Valley of Ten Thousand Smokes with about seven cubic kilometers of rhyolitic pumice. Though large by historic standards, the volume is small beside that of many prehistoric eruptions, in many of which individual sheets exceed a thousand cubic kilometers. The cumulative volumes discharged from the Taupo calderas of New Zealand and from the San Juan calderas of Colorado exceed 10,000 km^3. The total volumes of these vast sheets is at least comparable to that of flood basalts.

Most large-scale pyroclastic rocks are rhyolites, quartz latites, or dacites; only a few are andesites, and hardly any are basalts. Phenocryst contents range from nil to nearly half the volume of the rock. The matrix is made up of myriads of glass shards formed by disruption of highly vesiculated pumice. Depending on temperature, thickness, and volatile contents, these fragments of glass may be loose and porous or welded into a denser, compacted mass (Fig. 10–2). The fragmental shards of glass tend to be more welded with depth. Under normal conditions, temperatures on the order of 500 to 600°C are required for welding, but in the presence of abundant water vapor pumice fragments may be softened and fused into layers or lenses of dense, black glass.

Many ignimbrites, perhaps the majority, are compositionally zoned with a basal part more differentiated than the overlying section. These compositional variations appear to be inherited from stratified magma chambers tapped from the top downward in essentially uninterrupted outpourings.

CHEMICAL AND TECTONIC CLASSIFICATIONS

A confusing number of classification schemes have been proposed for granites. Some are based on tectonic settings or timing with respect to orogenic events. Others are based on the inferred source rocks or the mechanism of magma generation, and still others are a combination of two or more of these elements. For our present purposes, it will suffice to consider only the most generally accepted classifications.

Chemical classifications

It can be seen from Tables 2–1 and 2–2 that the chemical compositions of the common felsic plutonic rocks, quartz diorite through granite, are close to those

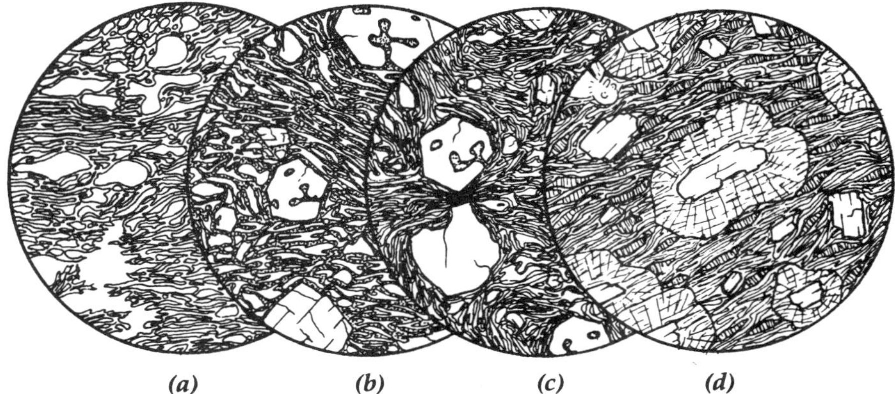

Figure 10–2 The textures of a series of specimens from a single ignimbrite sheet in central Honduras show progressive compaction with depth. (a) is from near the top, while (b) and (c) are from about five and two meters above the base, respectively. In (c), the shards have been partly remelted under the effects of high temperature and trapped water vapor to form lenticular "fiamme" of dense black glass. In (d), devitrification has produced radiating spherulites that have grown outward from centers around phenocrysts and across the original shards of glass.

of calc-alkaline volcanic rocks. Plutonic rocks of orogenic batholiths and continental interiors differ from the siliceous differentiates of other environments primarily in their greater contents of potassium and other large-ion lithophile components. Those with enough potassium to have subequal amounts of plagioclase and potassium feldspar can be assigned to a high-potassium series (Fig. 9–8) of which latites and quartz latites are the most common volcanic members.

In this respect, felsic continental rocks differ from the plagiogranites of oceanic environments and ophiolites. The latter lack the potassium feldspar that is so conspicuous in their calc-alkaline equivalents. Usually referred to broadly as *trondhjemites,* they are also common in ancient continental shields, island arcs, and other regions of thin crust. The distinction between trondhjemitic and calc-alkaline series is shown most clearly in their contrasting trends of enrichment of alkalies (Fig. 10-3a).

Though found in both continental and oceanic settings, trondhjemitic rocks of these two environments have subtle differences. Continental trondhjemites normally have in excess of 14.5 to 15 percent Al_2O_3 and in many cases normative corundum, C (Al_2O_3), whereas equivalent oceanic rocks have less than that amount of Al_2O_3 and are diopside normative. Another difference is in their proportions of rare-earth elements. Continental varieties are relatively enriched in the light rare-earth elements, whereas oceanic rocks have much flatter patterns (Fig. 10–3b).

Most granitic rocks can be assigned either to an "S-type" derived from sedimentary or metasedimentary source rocks or to an "I-type" produced by melting rocks that are dominantly igneous. The most conspicuous compositional differences are in their alumina contents and concentrations of certain trace elements inherited from their sources. Like continental trondhjemites, granites produced by melting of sedimentary rocks have more alumina than can be accommodated

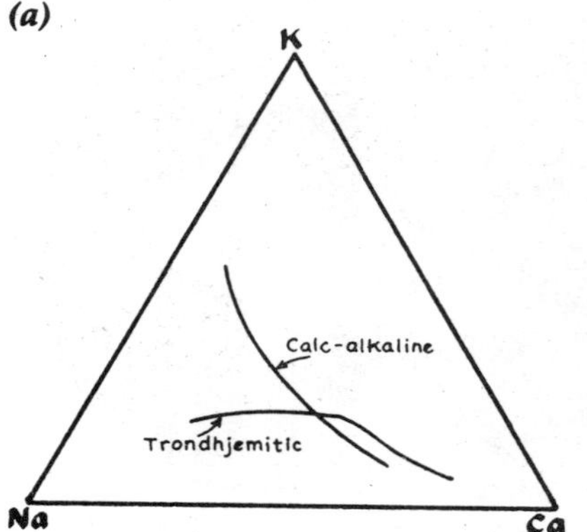

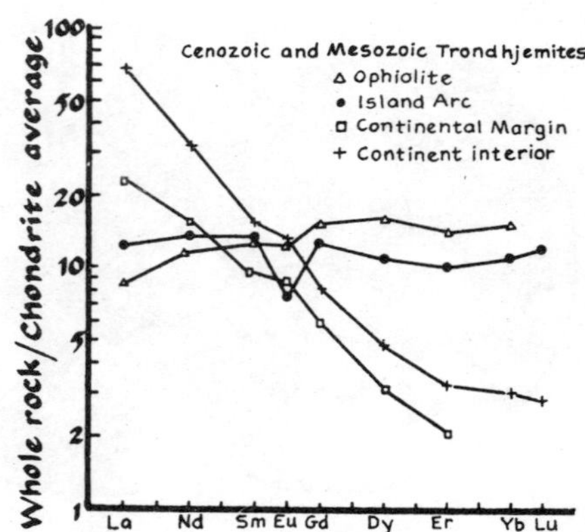

Figure 10–3 (a) Trondhjemitic series are best characterized by their normative feldspar, which become more albitic with differentiation than those of calc-alkaline granitic series. (After F. Barker and J. G. Arth, 1976, *Geology* 4:596–600.) (b) Continental trondhjemites have rare-earth element abundances that, when normalized to chondritic meteorites, are relatively enriched in light REE. Oceanic rocks of similar major-element compositions, such as plagiogranites of ophiolite complexes and island arcs, have flatter curves. (After J. G. Arth, 1979, in *Trondhjemites, Dacites, and Related Rocks*, F. Barker, ed., Elsevier, 123–132.)

in feldspars. The excess is expressed as normative corundum. The I-type has normative diopside. The former is also richer in transition metals and in several lithophile elements, such as Ba, Rb, Th, and light REE.

Tectonic classifications

Granites can be grouped into two broad categories, *orogenic* and *anorogenic*, based on whether or not the rocks are associated with an orogenic event. The former has at least two sub-types, *syntectonic* and *post-orogenic*, but a *late-orogenic* type has also been proposed.

Syntectonic granites are uncommon, especially in orogenic systems undergoing strong deformation. Most appear only when compressional forces are weak, but a few have been generated by thrusting of hot, deep-seated metamorphic rocks over cooler, water-rich horizons. They have strong fabrics produced by deformation in the plastic state. Late-orogenic granites include most of the large batholithic belts, such as the cordilleran system of North and South America. They resemble calc-alkaline volcanic rocks with which they undoubtedly share a common origin. Post-orogenic granites are said to result from relief of pressure on crustal rocks that have been deeply buried during a preceding orogenic event. They are very heterogeneous, as would be expected if they result from a combination of older crustal rocks and subduction-related igneous material produced during earlier stages of plate convergence.

Anorogenic plutonic intrusions tend to have a much wider diversity of rocks types, including anorthosites, rapakivi granites, and both alkaline and peralkaline rocks. We shall reserve them for special attention in the chapter that follows.

Table 10–1 compiles the salient chemical features of the felsic plutonic and volcanic rocks discussed in this chapter.

CRUSTAL ENVIRONMENT AND INTERNAL STRUCTURE

Siliceous magmas are intruded at a wide range of crustal levels. Their forms and cooling histories are determined mainly by the physical and chemical contrasts between the magmas and the environment into which they are emplaced. Shal-

Table 10–1 Chemical compositions of some special types of plutonic and siliceous volcanic rocks discussed in this chapter. Analyses of a broader spectrum of compositions are given in Table 2–2.

	1. S-type Granite	2. I-type Granite	3. Archean Trondhjemite	4. Massif Anorthosite	Bishop Tuff 5. Early	Bishop Tuff 6. Late
SiO_2	73.48	64.89	68.38	53.29	77.4	75.5
TiO_2	0.22	0.48	0.23	0.34	0.07	0.21
Al_2O_3	13.41	14.85	16.39	26.42	12.3	13.0
Fe_2O^*	1.87	5.24	1.97	2.44	0.7	1.1
MnO	0.04	0.10	0.03	0.03	0.03	0.02
MgO	0.71	2.73	1.00	1.09	0.01	0.25
CaO	1.70	5.51	1.75	10.26	0.45	0.95
Na_2O	2.63	1.83	7.09	4.32	3.9	3.35
K_2O	4.63	2.55	0.78	0.91	4.8	5.55
P_2O_5	0.08	0.09	0.08	0.10	0.01	0.06
Trace Elements (ppm)						
Rb	336	126	11	—	190	95
Zr	100	109	127	—	85	140
Sr	97	127	554	—	5	110
Ba	350	355	609	—	<10	465
Th	19	14	—	—	21	13
U	6	2	—	—	7	3
Nb	10	8	5	—	>25	<5
Y	33	Y	—	—	25	12
La	23	23	—	—	19	61
Ce	49	49	—	—	45	98
Molecular Norms						
Ap	0.17	0.20	0.17	0.21	0.02	0.13
Il	0.32	0.69	0.32	0.47	0.10	0.30
Mt	0.30	0.86	0.31	0.38	0.11	0.18
Or	28.13	15.64	4.62	5.33	28.68	32.83
Ab	24.29	17.06	63.82	38.44	35.42	30.39
An	8.14	25.72	8.18	49.56	1.90	4.23
Di	—	1.64	—	0.19	0.23	0.11
Hy	4.10	13.06	4.88	5.39	0.73	1.72
C	1.32	—	0.98	—	—	—
Q	33.24	25.14	16.72	0.04	32.81	30.12

1 and 2. S- and I-type granites, (B.W. Chappell, 1984, *Phil. Trans. Roy. Soc. London*, A310: 693–707).
3. Trondhjemite, (J. Tarney, B. Weaver, and S. A. Drury, 1979, in *Trondhjemites, dacites, and related rocks*, F. Barker, ed., p. 287.)
4. Massif-type anorthosite, (B. F. Windley, 1973, *Geol. Soc. South Africa, Spec. Pub. 3*, 319–332.)
5 and 6. Early- and late-stage rhyolites of the Bishop tuff, (W. Hildreth, 1979, *Geol. Soc. Amer. Spec. Paper 180*, 43–75.)

low bodies have textures and contact relations reflecting a strong temperature contrast with their surroundings; deep-seated granites have more gradational boundaries, especially where their host rocks are regionally metamorphosed crustal rocks of felsic compositions. These different settings or levels of emplacement can be divided into three broad zones. The deepest, the *catazone*, is exposed only in deeply eroded terranes of high-grade metamorphic rocks (Fig. 10–4a). They have margins with a concordant foliation that merges into surrounding gneisses with similar mineral assemblages. Some must have formed at or near their present level under *ultrametamorphic* conditions, i.e., close to the melting temperatures of siliceous crustal rocks. Others appear to have been emplaced as diapirs rising into a ductile crust with temperatures and physical properties approaching those of the magma.

In the *mesozone*, magmatic and metamorphic rocks are more easily distinguished, both in texture and mineralogy (Fig. 10–4b). Contacts may be concordant, as in the catazone, but most are sharply cross-cutting, often with abundant angular blocks from the roof in the margins. The plutons tend to have less internal structure, but many are compositionally zoned, both vertically and concentrically.

Shallowest of all are the plutons that have risen to the *epizone* within a few kilometers of the surface (Fig. 10–4c). Typical of these are the stocks and ring-complexes emplaced in brittle sedimentary or volcanic country rocks. Many are associated with contemporary volcanism. They have narrow zones of contact metamorphism, and many are hosts of economic mineral deposits associated with extensive alteration by hydrothermal solutions that circulated through the intrusions and their wall rocks. The contacts are sharply discordant. Dikes and sills penetrate the wall rocks, dislodging blocks of all sizes. The margins are often crowded with xenoliths.

The depths assigned to these three zones are imprecise. They depend less on pressure than on the thermal gradient and physical contrast between the magma and the environment into which it is intruded. Shallow epizonal bodies are thermally and rheologically disharmonious with their surroundings, whereas the contrast between catazonal plutons and the rocks they intrude may be detectable only in gradational differences of bulk composition, mineralogy, and texture.

Finally, we should add to this series a fourth category, the volcanic zone, in which magmas have breached the surface and solidified at atmospheric temperatures and pressures. The form of these eruptive bodies is governed by the structure of their vents and by the topography on which they are laid down. Much depends on the volume, mode of eruption, and physical properties of the magma. The vents from which most large ignimbrites and air-fall pyroclastic deposits were discharged are marked by broad, circular, or elliptical calderas that collapsed into an evacuated magma reservoir. Yellowstone, Wyoming, and Long Valley, California, are notable examples.

Cooling and crystallization

The rate of solidification of granitic plutons can vary within wide limits. In addition to the depth and temperature contrast between the magma and wall rocks,

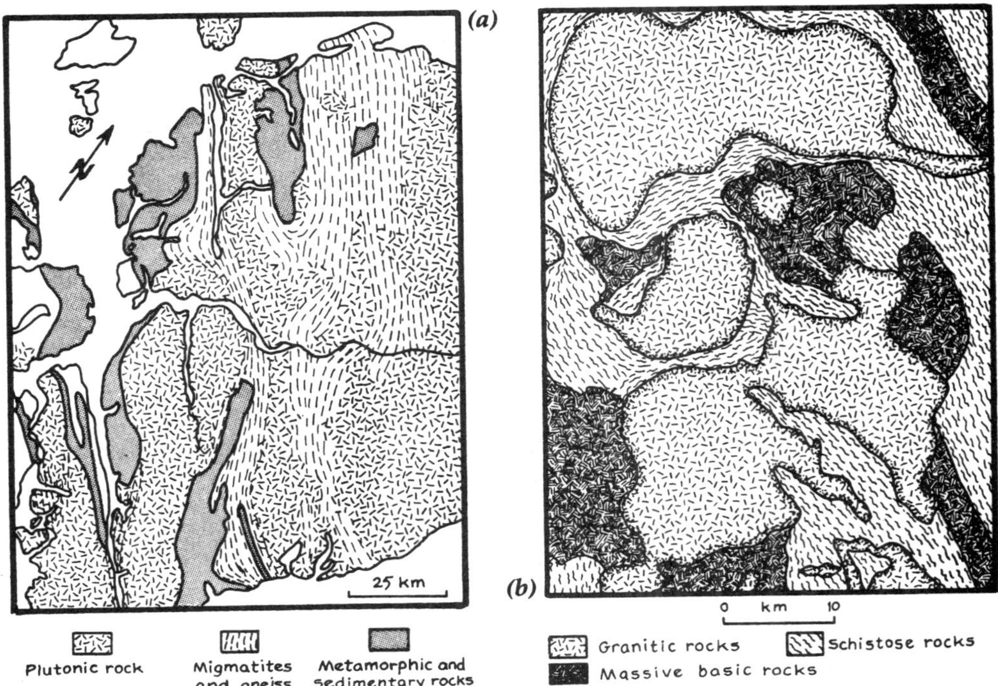

Figure 10–4 Environments of plutonic rocks. (a) A deep level of erosion is illustrated by this simplified map of the Mesozoic batholith of British Columbia. Note the concordance between the "tad pole" shapes of the granites and their surrounding metamorphic rocks. (After W. W. Hutchison, 1970, *Can. Jour. Earth Sci.* 7:376–405.) (b) Plutons exposed at intermediate depths are exemplified by this simplified map of part of the Sierra Nevada Batholith of California. Note the cross-cutting relations and more equidimensional forms of the intrusions. (After Bidwell Bar Quadrangle, U. S. Geol. Surv.) (c) Typical structures at the shallowest levels of intrusion are shown by this example from the coastal batholith of Peru. Note the fault-controlled structures and ring-like intrusions in close association with volcanic rocks. (Compiled from various maps, including those of J. S. Myers, 1975, *Bull. Geol. Soc. Amer.* 86:1209–1220, and M. A. Bussell, W. S. Pitcher, and P. A. Wilson, 1976, *Can. Jour. Earth Sci.* 13:1020–1030.)

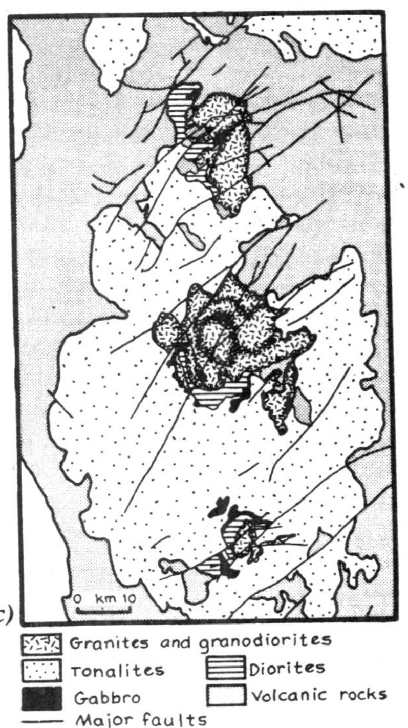

several less obvious factors govern the rate of heat loss to the surroundings. The mineral assemblage of the wall rocks, for example, can have an important effect on the temperature gradient and, hence, the rates of conductive heat transfer. Just as the latent heat of crystallization tends to retard the rate of cooling during crystallization, endothermic reactions in contact-metamorphic zones have the opposite effect; they buffer temperatures and retard the rise of temperature gradients into the walls.

Internal convection of the magma and external convection of a hydrothermal system both increase the rate of heat transfer. Their effect is to compress the isotherms around the lower levels where cool hydrothermal solutions flow radially inward and to widen them closer to the surface where the heated water flows upward and outward. This effect is reinforced by convection of the magma, if hot currents rise in the center and descend near the margins. Both forms of convective heat transfer are limited, however, by the much slower rate at which heat is conducted through the contact zone separating the two systems.

The cooling history of some plutons can be modeled by using the metamorphic zoning in wall rocks to establish maximum isotherms reached during the cooling history of an intrusion. In most cases where this has been done, it has been found that the dominant rate-controlling process is conduction. Because of this, the rate of convection within granitic intrusions is probably very sluggish. Similarly, the rate of convection of the hydrothermal system is limited by the rate of conductive heat transfer across the margins.

Internal structure

Although they are rarely layered, most granitic plutons have some sort of compositional zoning. Several types are illustrated in Figure 10–5.

Sharply bounded zones may represent successive intrusions (Fig. 10–5a) of progressively more differentiated magma, each more or less in the core of a less differentiated predecessor. In other cases (Fig. 10–5b) new magma may intrude along steep ring dikes at the same time that a central block of the roof subsides. The compositional relations in this situation tend to be more discordant than those of the first. The nature of the wall rocks of some intrusions (Fig. 10–5c) has been found to be reflected in subtle ways in the character of the adjacent rocks. Zoning from this effect is diffuse and gradational.

A body of magma crystallizing inward from its walls (Fig. 10–5d) tends to evolve in composition inward, and, so long as the magma is stable, the changing composition is normally seen only in modal and mineralogical changes with few if any marked discontinuities. In some instances, however, the orderly sequence of inward crystallization may be disrupted. If the differentiating liquid becomes more felsic and lighter than the overlying rocks, it may become gravitationally unstable and rise into its roof. Or new magma may be injected, possibly triggering volcanic eruptions and altering the temperature, composition, and sequence of crystallization of the remaining magma. If these events cause the magma to exsolve its volatile components, the phase relations of the remaining liquid will suddenly change and may bring on an abrupt increase in the rate of crystalliza-

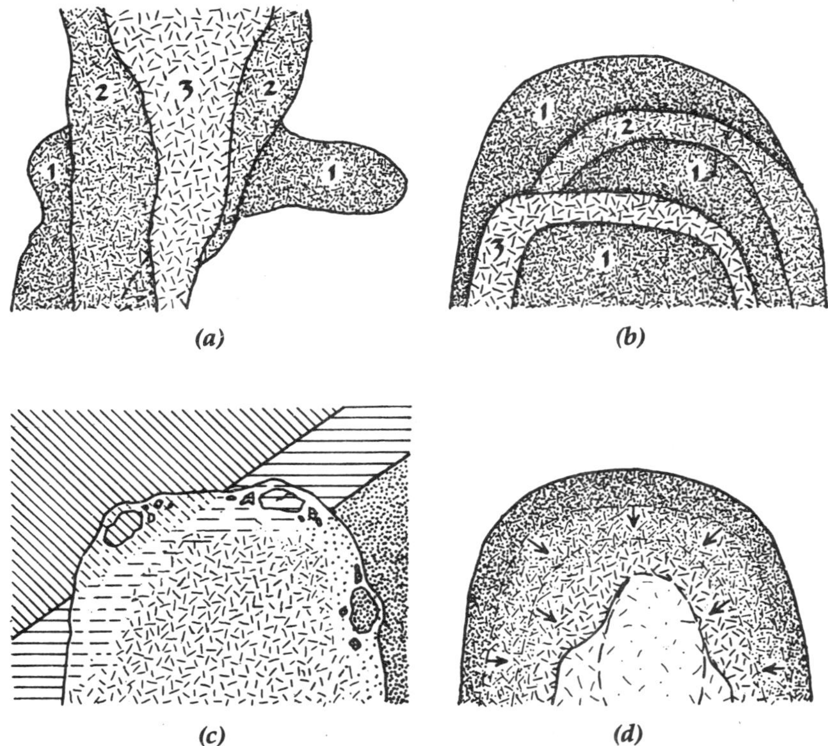

Figure 10–5 Zoning in granitic plutons may result from (a) successive cross-cutting intrusions, (b) subsidence of earlier rocks and injection of "bell-jar" intrusions or ring dikes, (c) contamination by different wall rocks, or (d) inward crystallization and differentiation. In the last case, the late-stage liquids may become lighter than the overlying rocks and rise into them.

tion. To decipher these various effects in a pluton that had a long and complex history requires careful, detailed studies and may be an impossible task if, as is often the case, much of the evidence has been lost to erosion.

TECTONIC SETTINGS

Large bodies of felsic rocks, either plutonic or volcanic, are confined mainly to the continents. The most notable, if not the only, exception is the series of Tertiary rhyolites in Iceland. Though small by the standards of continental ignimbrites, the Icelandic bodies are vastly larger than the small felsic lavas and intrusions on other oceanic islands. For many years it was widely believed that these rhyolites proved that Iceland was underlain by continental crust, but a more likely explanation, as we shall see shortly, is that they owe their origin to melting of an unusual type of oceanic lithosphere under the Icelandic Plateau.

Continental plutonic rocks are found in three types of structural settings. Most older bodies, such as those of the Precambrian greenstone belts and early Paleozoic metamorphic terranes, are scattered over wide areas of the continental shields. This is in contrast to younger plutons, especially those of the circum-Pacific region, which are concentrated near the continental margins. Some of the latter are in broad composite belts formed by multiple intrusive episodes; others consist of small, scattered intrusions, but most seem to have been close to convergent plate boundaries. In this respect they differ from the third group, made up of clusters or swarms of plutons well within the continental interior. This last group is thought to be a continental expression of intra-plate hot spots.

Convergent continental margins

The most extensive plutonic rocks on the American continents are those of the Cordilleran system near to the Pacific continental margins. The long episode of circum-Pacific plutonism lasting through most of the Mesozoic and Cenozoic was one of the great magmatic events of the earth's history. It must have been related in some way to a major event in the tectonic evolution of the present Pacific Ocean. Batholiths rose into rocks of all ages and lithologic character, with little regard for major differences in the local structure or degree of metamorphism. The structural differences seen in individual segments of the Cordilleran batholiths are not due to their crustal environment so much as their depths of erosion. The coastal batholith of British Columbia, for example, is set in high-grade metamorphic rocks of the catazone (Fig. 10–4a), whereas the batholiths of the western Sierra Nevada intruded shallower rocks, mostly within the greenschist facies of metamorphism (Fig. 10–4b), and the coastal batholith of Peru is exposed at an even shallower level of brittle, weakly metamorphosed, sedimentary and volcanic rocks (Fig. 10–4c).

Most of this enormous mass of granitic rocks was intruded in pulses between 225 and 18 million years ago. Few of these episodes coincided with major orogenic events, but many occurred during subsequent periods of uplift and erosion after compressive forces were relaxed. In some instances volcanism preceded plutonism, in others it followed, and in some the two were essentially contemporaneous. No simple reason has been found to explain why some periods are dominated by plutonism and others by volcanism.

The transition from plutonism to volcanism is shown most clearly in the coastal batholith of Peru. A belt of plutons, up to 65 kilometers wide and over 2,400 kilometers long, was intruded as more then 800 separate plutons over a period of about seventy or eighty million years (110 to 30 m.y. ago).

Swarms of intrusions ranging in size from centimeter-wide dikes to plutons tens of kilometers across came in at intervals of ten or twenty million years. Each intrusive pulse consists of a spatially-restricted group of consanguinous magmas that seems to stem from a separate parent. Starting with gabbro, they tend to become more felsic with time, and the average compositions of successive batches of magma have proportionately smaller volumes of gabbro and relatively more of granite.

No continuity is seen from one segment of the belt to another; magmas of differing compositions were intruded simultaneously in widely separated parts of the system. The impression gained from detailed radiometric dating and cross-cutting field relations in a given swarm of intrusions is that batches of magma formed at intervals of 18 million years or so. Individual intrusions took as long as seven million years or so to crystallize at depths of five or ten kilometers but much less in shallow, sub-volcanic bodies. Taken as a whole, the dominant pattern through the period of plutonism is one of diminishing volumes and lateral extent of the intrusions with time. In this respect the evolution of the plutonic belt resembles that of the volcanic belt of the Cascade system where widespread voluminous volcanism of the early Tertiary episodes became more restricted in distribution and less intense with time. Compositionally, however, the trend toward increasing proportions of felsic rocks in the plutonic series differs from that of the Cascades, where successive episodes tend to have greater proportions of more mafic rocks.

Within an individual sequence of plutonic intrusions, early gabbroic bodies are tabular or lens-shaped, whereas later, more felsic bodies took narrower and more steep-sided forms (Fig. 10-6). Most of the plutons seem to have been emplaced by stoping. Dikes can be traced from the plutons into the walls and roof where they wedged apart blocks that then sank and made room for the rising magma. In places, large blocks are seen to have settled through the magma to accumulate on the floor of the intrusion. Not all of the xenoliths are from the surrounding walls; some of the more mafic types could be the refractory residue

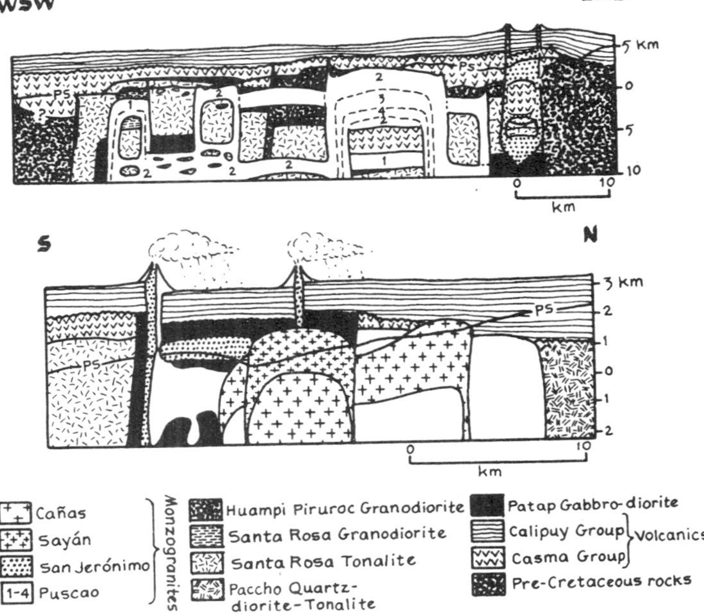

Figure 10–6 Schematic sections through the coastal batholith of Peru showing postulated relationship between intrusive and extrusive rocks. The present erosion surface is indicated by the lines labeled PS. (After J. S. Myers, 1975, *Bull. Geol. Soc. Amer.* 86:1209–1220, and M. A. Bussell, W. S. Pitcher, and P. A. Wilson, 1976, *Can. Jour. Earth Sci.* 13:1020–1030.)

of melting. Despite the abundance of various types of xenoliths, they seem to have had little effect on the composition of the magma.

The shallowest plutons were emplaced along ring fractures around a central block of the roof that subsided to make room for the new mass of magma. They are thought to have been expressed at the surface by large calderas. Great volumes of dacitic and rhyolitic ignimbrites poured from fissures in and around these calderas, and in some instances plutons continued to rise and intrude their own volcanic ejecta.

The magmas belong to the I-type derived from igneous sources with only a subordinate contribution from sedimentary sources. They include compositions ranging from gabbro to leucogranite. Except in the shallowest, sub-volcanic stocks, the felsic members are sub-solvus types with two discrete alkali feldspars.

The gabbroic rocks initially crystallized plagioclase and pyroxene, but most were later amphibolitized by influxes of volatiles, partly from later intrusions but mainly from the surrounding rocks. The original igneous crystals are replaced by new assemblages with metamorphic textures (Fig. 10–1a). Subsequent intrusions consistently follow an order of increasing silica content starting with quartz diorite, then evolving through tonalite and granodiorite to monzonite-granite, and finally rocks intermediate between syenite and granite. These successive magmas tend to be nested in zoned bodies that continued to differentiate as they crystallized from the floor upward and inward from the walls. Crystal sizes decrease upward, possibly because of loss of volatiles from the upper levels of the magma.

Compositional trends have much in common with those of orogenic volcanic rocks, such as the suites from continental margins discussed in chapter 9. The early gabbroic rocks have an independent trend (Fig. 10–7) not unlike the early tholeiitic rocks of volcanic series. They seem to have evolved by fractionation of pyroxene, plagioclase, and olivine. The later granitic rocks are distinctly calc-alkaline, with hornblende becoming more important than pyroxene, just as it does in comparable volcanic rocks.

Granites in zones of continental collision

Granitic batholiths are by no means confined to active continental margins, but even among those that are well within the continental interior, the great majority are thought to have been near converging plate boundaries when they were emplaced. When plate convergence culminates in collision of two continents, the intense crustal deformation that ensues may be accompanied by plutonism, but the scale is small compared to that of other settings. Plutons form only under unusual conditions and generally in relatively small volumes. The Alps and Himalayas are the main modern examples.

The two main intrusive complexes of the Alps, the plutons of Ademello and Bregaglia-Iorio, were emplaced during a brief period of extension in the Oligocene, immediately following the main period of compression when the African plate collided with Europe. They rose into small, fault-bounded areas of tension

Figure 10–7 AMF diagram for rocks of the coastal batholith of Peru. The early gabbroic rocks of each batch of magma define a compositional trend that differs from that of the more felsic gabbroic rocks. Relations such as these could arise from melting of a compositionally zoned lithosphere in the manner illustrated in Figure 10–21.

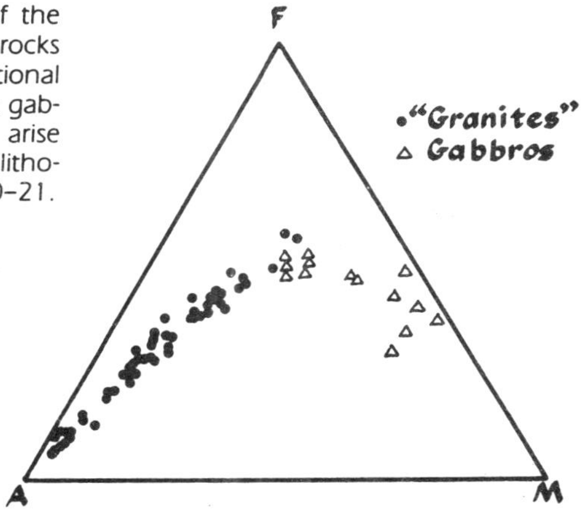

close to the Insubric Line marking the boundary between the two plates. The activity ended abruptly when compression was renewed in the Miocene.

The plutons are composed chiefly of felsic calc-alkaline rocks, including adamellites, monzonites, and tonalites that take their names from localities in the Italian Alps. The earliest intrusions were very mafic hornblende gabbros, which soon gave way to larger volumes of increasingly differentiated rocks. Small differences in the proportions of hydrous and anhydrous minerals precipitated in the early stages of differentiation led to two distinct trends, much as they did in the Coastal Batholith of Peru.

In the case of the Himalayas, granitic rocks have been produced at two stages of the collisional event when India converged on Asia. The first, a *syntectonic* group generated during the period of strong deformation, resulted from thrusting of hot metamorphic rocks over colder rocks of lower metamorphic grade (Fig. 10–8). Fluids driven out during heating of the lower unit rose into the overlying rocks, lowered their melting temperature, and triggered melting. The magmas are typical of the S-type derived from sedimentary source rocks.

A younger group, which appeared after relaxation of the main compressional forces, forms a separate group of *post-orogenic* intrusions more like those of the Alps. The magmas, which are of both the S- and I-types, come from greater depths, possibly from deeply buried sedimentary and igneous rocks. Over-thickening of the zone of maximum compression is thought to result in a condition of isostatic instability that leads to upwelling and thinning of the depressed crust. This brings hot crustal material to levels of lower pressure where it begins to melt and rise as dikes and diapirs through high-grade metamorphic rocks of the catazone. Though commonly marked by flow-related foliation, the granites have less tectonic fabric than those generated above thrust sheets.

Continental rifting and hotspots

Regions of crustal extension are normally associated with fissure eruptions of basaltic lavas, but many have produced equal or greater volumes of felsic vol-

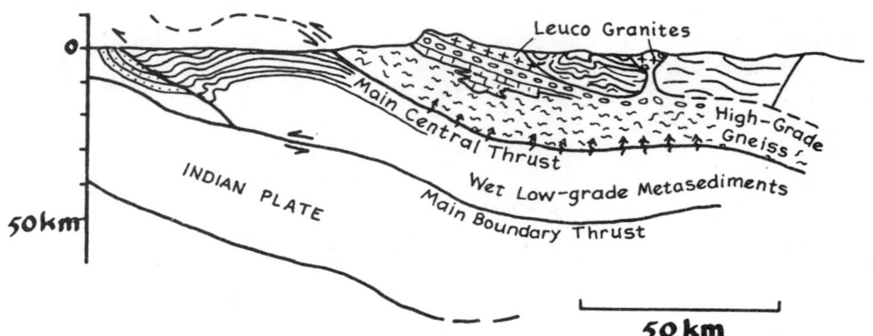

Figure 10–8 Syntectonic granites of the Himalayan Mountains result from thrusting of high-grade gneisses over wet, low-grade meta-sediments. Water and other volatile components from the underlying unit infiltrated up into the hotter thrust sheet triggering partial melting at temperatures of about 700°C. Melting continued for more than ten million years, while the heterogenous melts intruded as irregular sills and diapirs at depths of 10 to 15 km. (Adapted from C. France-Lanord and P. Le Fort, 1988, Trans. Roy. Soc. Edinburgh, *Earth Sci.* 79:183–195.)

canic rocks. In places, such as the Great Basin of the western United States and large areas of Mexico and Central America, basalts are quite subordinate to great sheets of siliceous ignimbrites. Unlike flood basalts, however, most of the felsic magmas are not discharged from long, linear fissures but from central sources marked by calderas and dome complexes.

Mention has already been made of the large caldera complexes, such as that of Yellowstone, that have no apparent relation to orogenic belts or continental rifting. Some of these have been attributed to hotspots in which the mantle sources underlie thick continental lithosphere. Others are thought to result from direct melting of the subcontinental lithosphere with no contribution from a hotspot.

In North America, the most common manifestation of intracontinental siliceous magmatism is volcanic, but on other continents it is plutonic. At least part of the difference must be due to depths of erosion. Only rarely are both the volcanic and plutonic rocks exposed in the same region. A notable exception is the cluster of large calderas and related volcanic rocks situated over a complex of Tertiary granitic intrusions in the San Juan Mountains of Colorado (Fig. 10–9).

The igneous history of the San Juan region has been divided into three stages extending through most of middle and late Tertiary time. Activity began about 35 million years ago with eruptions of lavas and breccias from large, central-vent volcanoes. The products of this stage were mainly andesites with subordinate amounts of more siliceous rocks (Fig. 10–10). About 30 million years ago, the volume of eruptions increased dramatically. Enormous pyroclastic flows issued from fissure vents to cover an area of about 25,000 km^3. More than sixteen major sheets of dacite and rhyolite are associated with a cluster of at least four-

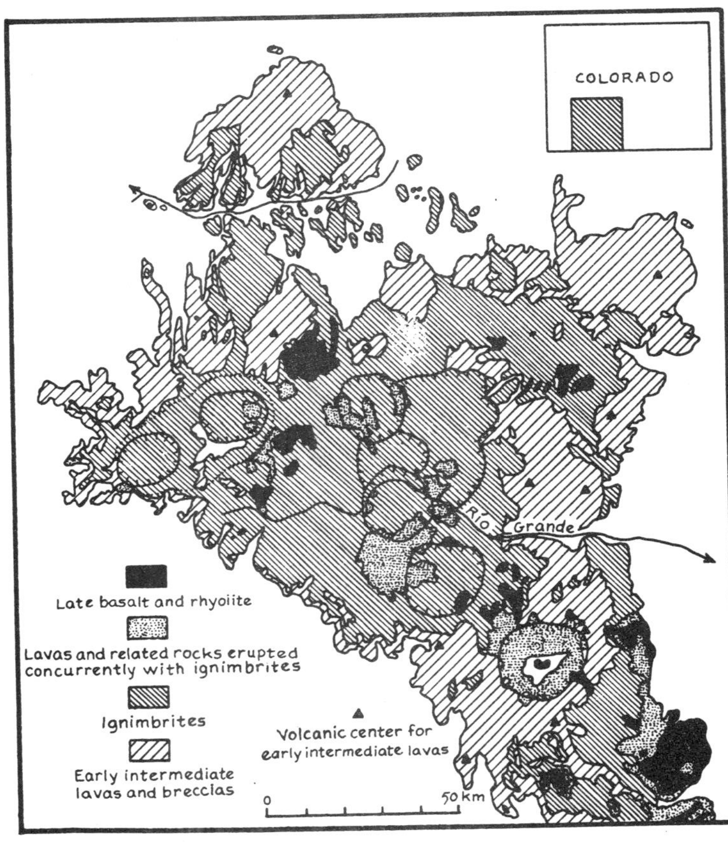

Figure 10–9 Generalized geologic map of the San Juan region of Colorado showing the distribution of calderas and principal volcanic rocks. (After P. W. Lipman et al., 1970, *Geol. Soc. Amer. Bull.* 81:2329–2352.)

teen calderas averaging about 20 km in diameter. Single sheets spread over as much as 15,000 km^2, reached local thicknesses of over a kilometer, and had volumes as great as 3,000 km^3. Intermediate lavas were largely restricted to areas in and around calderas. They are petrographically similar to the rocks erupted from central-vent volcanoes during the preceding period but were distinctly subordinate to the siliceous pyroclastic rocks. Activity declined rapidly, and at about the same time the eastern part of the field was faulted and tilted as a consequence of formation of the adjacent Rio Grande Rift.

This tectonic event ushered in a new and entirely different period of igneous activity marked by bimodal eruptions of basaltic lavas and rhyolitic domes and tephra. Compared to the preceding episode, the volumes of magma were relatively small. They came from widely scattered vents that seem to have little relation, either structurally or genetically, to the earlier events. Most likely they were part of the widespread bimodal volcanism that accompanied crustal extension throughout the Great Basin in late Cenozoic time.

Despite its conspicuous discontinuities, both in time and composition, the magmatic suite as a whole forms a coherent calc-alkaline series. Petrochemical

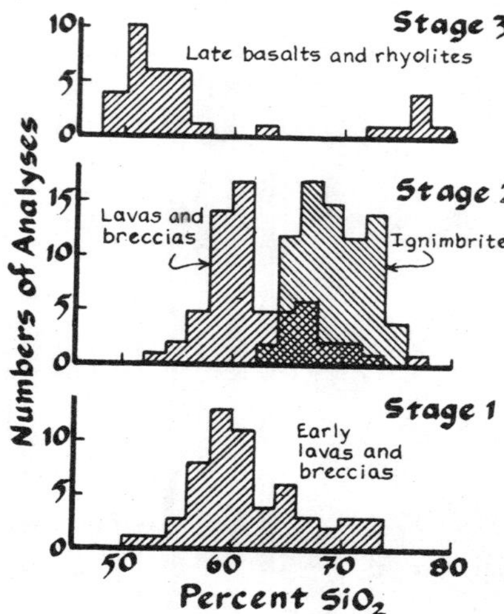

Figure 10–10 Proportions of rocks erupted during the three main episodes of igneous activity in the San Juan Complex. Note the progressive divergence of compositions with time. The third, most recent episode is thought to be related to more widespread regional tectonic events and has a wider distribution than the other two. (Adapted from P. W. Lipman et al., 1970, *Geol. Soc. Amer. Bull.* 81:2329–2352.)

differences are confined mainly to trace elements and isotopic ratios. In each eruptive sequence, remarkably large volumes were discharged in what must have been very short intervals of time. Without historic examples to judge by, the duration of the huge eruptions responsible for each ignimbrite sheet can only be guessed, but they could not have lasted more than weeks or months. The thick cooling units must have been discharged in single, continuous eruptions, for they have few if any erosional discontinuities or other signs of depositional breaks. In this sense, they resemble flood basalts, for despite their obvious differences in composition and eruptive behavior, they had comparable volumes and tectonic settings.

PLUTONIC ROCKS OF PRECAMBRIAN AGES

We noted in the opening chapter that certain types of igneous rocks are very characteristic of ancient continental shield areas and that some are confined almost entirely to such settings. The ultramafic komatiites are a conspicuous example. Two others, trondhjemites and anorthosites, are at the opposite end of the compositional spectrum (Fig. 10–11).

Archean trondhjemites

Though by no means confined to the Precambrian, the distinctive group of plutonic rocks known as trondhjemites is very common in Archean terranes, such as those of the Canadian Shield. As mentioned earlier, they are more sodic than most other granitic rocks (Fig. 10–3a) and have little or no K-feldspar. When these plutons were formed the continents lacked the large amounts of mature sediments, such as quartzose sands and aluminous clays, that developed only

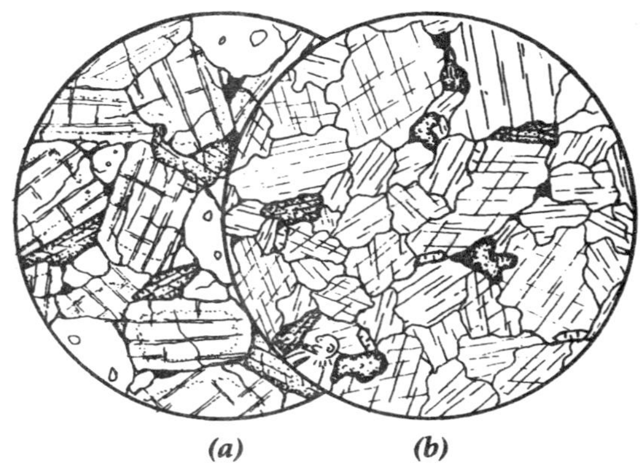

Figure 10–11 (a) A Precambrian trondhjemite from the Canadian Shield consists mainly of quartz and oligoclase but little if any K-feldspar. Hornblende is the principal mafic mineral, but sphene is an important accessory. (b) Anorthosite from the Adirondack Mountains of New York consists of labradorite with very subordinate amounts of pyroxene, ilmenite, garnet, and apatite.

after repeated cycles of weathering, erosion, and redeposition. There is little likelihood, therefore, that they could be the result of melting of sialic crust. On the other hand, weathering and erosions of these early plutons may have contributed much of the quartz that subsequently accumulated in continental sediments.

Many trondhjemitic plutons form the cores of thick volcanic complexes composed originally of basalt but now altered to low- to medium-grade metamorphic rocks, mainly greenstones and amphibolites. The trondhjemitic magmas could be partial melts of this basaltic crust. Downwarping, under the thick local accumulations of volcanic rocks, may have depressed the crust to levels where it was first amphibolitized, then partially melted and mobilized in the steep thermal gradient that is thought to have characterized the crust in Archean time. As we shall see shortly, partial melting of amphibole-rich mafic rocks can yield liquids rich in silica and with large ratios of sodium to potassium. Moreover, the abundance patterns of the rare-earth elements in trondhjemites are symptomatic of liquids in equilibrium with amphibole (Fig. 10–3b).

Younger felsic rocks of a similar sodic character are found mainly in tholeiitic suites of oceanic environments. We have already noted the rhyolites of Iceland and the plagiogranites of ophiolitic complexes; other examples are reported from island arcs and along the oceanic sides of calc-alkaline batholiths. The main feature all these regions have in common is an environment of oceanic or immature continental crust and steep thermal gradients.

Anorthosites

Another variety of plutonic rocks confined almost exclusively to the Precambrian is anorthosite, a singular rock consisting primarily of plagioclase (Fig. 10–11b). Often referred to as *massif-type anorthosites,* they differ from the stratiform anorthosites in gabbroic intrusions like the Stillwater and Bushveld complexes in that they are not interlayered with more mafic rocks. Instead, they form broadly lenticular or domical bodies of almost uniform compositions.

What makes these rocks so unusual is their total lack of aphyric volcanic equivalents. Although some very plagioclase-phyric basalts approach them in bulk composition, lavas that can be shown to have been true liquids of anorthositic compositions are unknown. Another puzzling feature is their restricted distribution in time and space. They are found almost exclusively in anorogenic terranes in a broad belt extending from the southwestern United States to Labrador and, on the other side of the Atlantic, through Norway and Sweden. A smaller group has been identified in the southern hemisphere. Without exception, the ages of all these bodies lie between 1.7 and 1.1 billion years with many close to 1.4 billion years.

Plagioclase, which accounts for at least 85 percent of their volume, is typically in the range of An-40 to An-60, in contrast to values of An-65 to An-85 in large, layered intrusions. Hypersthene and augite are the most common mafic minerals, and ilmenite and apatite are important accessories. Associated rocks include gabbro, usually the hypersthene-bearing variety, norite, that typically forms gradational margins around a central core of more leucocratic rocks composed of the same minerals. In fact, most anorthosites have compositions that are consistent with simple addition of plagioclase crystals to a noritic liquid. Thus, apart from their unusual proportions of plagioclase, they are sub-alkaline rocks with many affinities to tholeiitic magmas derived from a shallow, depleted mantle. If they interacted with the continental crust, it was only to a minor degree, for their trace-element contents and isotopic ratios are inconsistent with measurable amounts of assimilation.

Depths of emplacement of these bodies were probably between five and twenty-five kilometers; none has been shown to have approached the surface. Their temperatures must have been exceptionally high and their water contents low, for their contact aureoles show the effect of high temperatures but little evidence of hydrothermal fluids. These properties point to what must have been a condition unique in the earth's history, when a much steeper thermal gradient caused dry melting at shallow levels below a thin continental crust.

How this process produced rocks so rich in plagioclase is difficult to say. Most explanations appeal to unusual accumulations of plagioclase from magmas originally of more mafic compositions, but how so much plagioclase can be fractionated without corresponding amounts of mafic minerals is a mystery. The greatest proportion of plagioclase that could be precipitated from a normal, mantle-derived magma is of the order of 60 percent. To produce the much greater concentrations in anorthosites requires disposal of proportionate amounts of mafic minerals in some hidden part of the system.

Anorthosites deserve much more study than they have received, not just because they are petrologic curiosities but because they could reveal much about the early thermal and chemical evolution of the mantle and continental crust.

THE GRANITE SYSTEM

The phase relations of what is loosely referred to as the "Granite System" lie within the silica-saturated part of what Bowen aptly referred to as "Petrogeny's Residua System" (Figs. 7–4 and 10–12). As used by Bowen, the name was meant

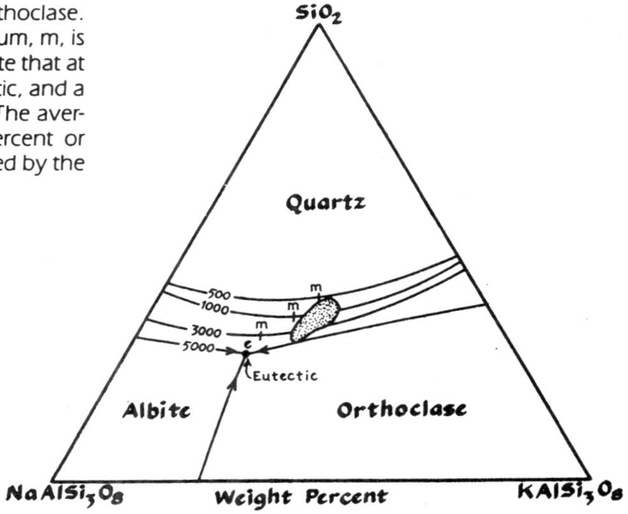

Figure 10–12 The granite system, quartz-albite-orthoclase. The quartz-feldspar boundary and temperature minimum, m, is shown for 0.5, 1, 3, and 5 kilobars water pressure. Note that at 5 kilobars the temperature minimum becomes a eutectic, and a cotectic line separates the fields of the two feldspars. The average composition of granitic rocks containing 80 percent or more of the three end-member components is indicated by the shaded oval area.

to imply that the phases come from the last liquid residue of crystal fractionation, not the refractory solid residue of melting. Though an oversimplification of natural systems, it is the basic starting point for understanding felsic magmas. Here we are concerned only with silica-saturated magmas and confine our attention to the part of the system above the feldspar join, Ab-Or, which is a thermal divide separating these rocks from feldspathoidal compositions below (Fig. 7–4). The latter are dealt with in the chapter that follows.

Unlike mafic magmas, which evolve primarily through fractionation of anhydrous ferromagnesian minerals and calcic plagioclase, the compositions of felsic magmas are governed mainly by crystallization of the alkali feldspars, quartz, and the hydrous minerals mica and amphibole. In their simplest form, rocks that are loosely referred to as "granitic" can be treated in terms of three components, quartz, albite, and orthoclase, that make up 80 percent or more of their normative or modal compositions. The close correspondence (Fig. 10–12) of the compositions of granitic rocks to the region of minimum temperature in the phase diagram for quartz and alkali feldspar is consistent with the supposition that the rocks are either the last products of differentiation or the first products of melting of a mineralogical assemblage dominated by these three mineral components.

Crystallization and melting under hyper-solvus conditions

Few, if any, magmas precipitate quartz before feldspar, and most crystallize plagioclase before potassium feldspar. Hence, the great majority of natural liquids will fall in the lower left part of the triangle. On crystallizing they follow a course across the feldspar field toward the quartz-feldspar boundary. A typical path of such a liquid is illustrated schematically in Figure 10–13b. Because both alkali feldspars form solid-solution series, the course of crystallization of liquids crossing the lower part of the diagram is not linear but curved and cannot be predicted

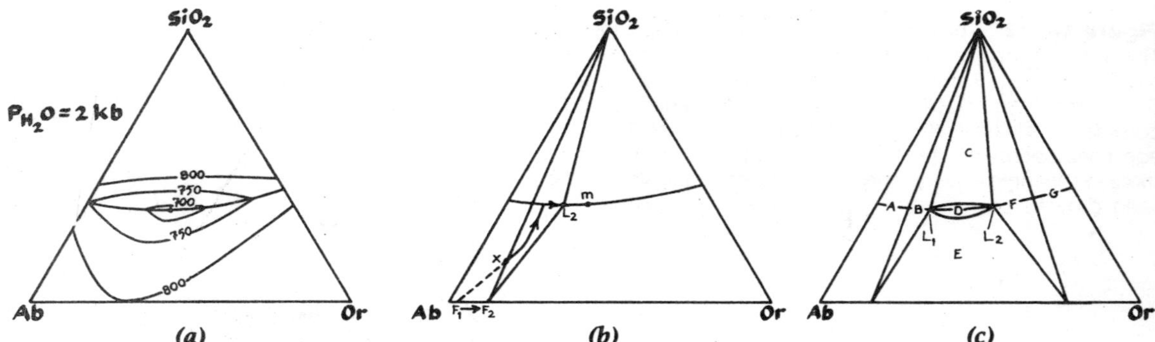

Figure 10–13 (a) The hypersolvus granite system at 2 kilobars water pressure. The numbered curves are contours of temperature on the liquidus surfaces. (b) shows a typical path of a liquid, X, that first crystallizes in the albite field and evolves with complete reaction. When the liquid reaches L_2, the bulk composition can be made up entirely of quartz and the equilibrium feldspar, F_2, and the liquid is consumed without reaching the temperature minimum at m. (c) is a constant temperature section at 700°C. The system is divided into various fields corresponding to bulk compositions that would have the following phase assemblages at that temperature.

A — sodic feldspar and quartz without liquid,
B — sodic feldspar, quartz, and liquid L_1,
C — quartz and liquid on the SiO_2-rich contour,
D — all liquid,
E — feldspar and liquid on the SiO_2-poor contour,
F — potassic feldspar, quartz, and liquid, L_2,
G — potassic feldspar and quartz without liquid.

exactly without knowing more about the composition of coexisting crystals and liquids.

The point m where the temperature of liquid-crystal assemblages reaches a minimum is not a true eutectic for hypersolvus conditions. Only liquids with a narrow range of intermediate compositions will crystallize under equilibrium conditions at the temperature and composition of that point. We saw the reason for this when we considered binary solid-solution series in chapter three and the alkali feldspar system in chapter four. Because it is not a eutectic, differentiating liquids reach point m only with extreme fractionation.

The same principles hold for melting. Under hypersolvus conditions, the first product of melting of crustal rocks with compositions consisting mainly of quartz and alkali feldspar may not be a liquid close to the composition m. As we noted when considering solid-solution series, the liquids that evolve during crystallization are not necessarily the same as those produced by melting. Much depends on the degree of fractionation and equilibration of crystals and liquid as the process advances. The same principles apply to crystallization and melting in the granite system. If, on cooling, a liquid X continues to equilibrate with its coexisting solid-solution minerals, its course is arrested when the composition of the crystals reaches that of the original starting liquid. Without equilibration, the liquid will continue to evolve until it reaches the composition and temperature of the system at m. But if a mineral assemblage consisting of unzoned crystals having the same bulk composition X is heated, no liquid appears at the temperature minimium at m but only at some higher temperature at which the crystals are in equilibrium with a liquid of different composition, such as L_2.

Figure 10–13c illustrates the main possibilities for a given temperature. Depending on the bulk composition, the system can consist of liquid and quartz, liquid and Na-feldspar, all liquid, liquid and K-feldspar, liquid without crystals, or crystals without liquid. The liquid composition differs according to the temperature and the mineral phases present, and the trend of liquid compositions must differ for every bulk composition, whether the process is one of crystallization or melting.

Crystallization and melting under sub-solvus conditions

In a multi-phase assemblage, the effects of water pressure will, as we saw in the preceding chapter (Fig. 9–14b), differ according to the nature of the individual phases, and, depending on the properties of each mineral, the compositions of liquids shift to include more or less of the different crystalline phases with which they are in equilibrium. For dry conditions, the compositions of melts in the granite system are not greatly altered by greater pressure, but with increasing water pressure the liquidus temperature of albite is depressed more than that of quartz or orthoclase, and the composition of the minimum melting temperature (point m in Fig. 10–12) is shifted in the direction of the albite corner of the diagram.

At the same time, we have seen that increasing water pressure causes the solvus in the alkali-feldspar system to intersect the solidus and the temperature minimum to becomes a true eutectic. As a result, the minimum, m, in the three-component system (Fig. 10–12) becomes a eutectic, and a cotectic divides the lower part of the system into two fields, one for each of the alkali feldspars.

Under these conditions the behavior is more restricted, and a broader range of compositions differentiate or melt to form liquids of the minimum-melting composition. The course of a liquid composition during crystallization or melting is simplified by the cotectic nature of the boundary between the two feldspars. A liquid initially crystallizing a sodic feldspar follows a curved path across the field of that mineral until it intersects the boundary with potassium feldspar or quartz. It then descends to the eutectic, where all three phases crystallize together. An opposite course is followed on melting.

Effects of anorthite

The four-component system, quartz-albite-orthoclase-anorthite, can be represented by a tetrahedron (Fig. 10–14) having anorthite at its apex and as its base the granite system of Figure 10–12. The front face is the familiar feldspar system, plagioclase-orthoclase. The line separating the field of quartz from that of feldspar in the granite system is now a surface extending into the interior of the tetrahedron roughly parallel to the front face and inclined to the base. From the sub-solvus feldspar cotectic, a curved surface extends back into the interior until it intersects the plane bounding the quartz volume.

Because most natural magmas precipitate plagioclase before quartz or potas-

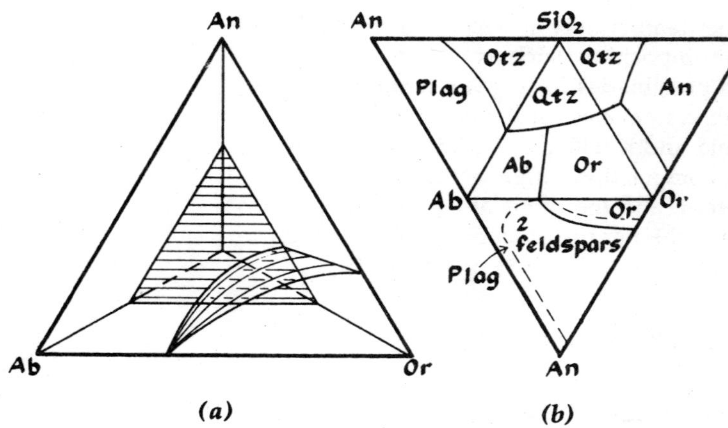

Figure 10–14 The sub-solvus system Ab-Or-SiO_2-An at elevated water pressures is shown schematically in (a) as a tetrahedron with anorthite at its apex and the granite system from Figure 10–12 as its base. The surfaces bounding the volume of quartz, plagioclase, and K-feldspar are exaggerated to show their geometric relations. In (b), the tetrahedron has been unfolded to show the three-component systems of the four faces of the three-dimensional diagram.

sium feldspar, their initial compositions must lie in the volume defined by the plagioclase edge of the tetrahedron and the two saturation surfaces for quartz and potassium feldspar (Fig. 10–15). On crystallizing, their compositions move away from plagioclase along a curved path as the crystals become more albitic. The path of the liquid will intersect one or the other of the two saturation surfaces and begin to precipitate quartz or potassium feldspar along with plagioclase. Then, moving along one of these surfaces, it eventually reaches the intersection with the second, and all three phases—plagioclase, quartz, and potassium feldspar—crystallize together as the liquid follows the cotectic line of intersection down toward the base of the tetrahedron.

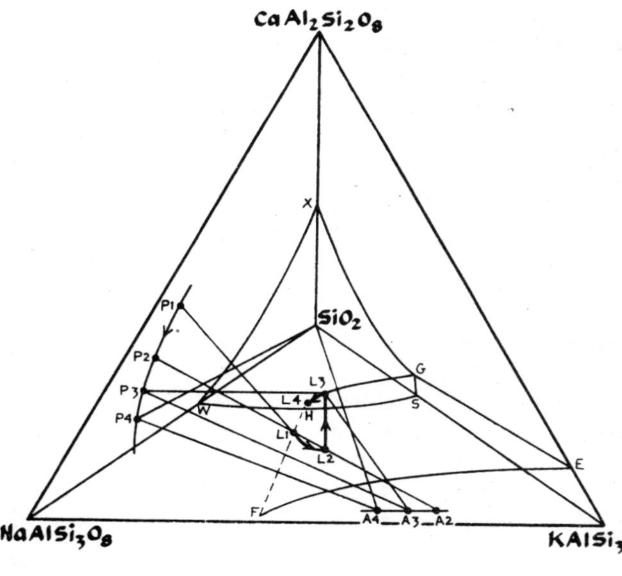

Figure 10–15 The course of crystal and liquid compositions of a magma that first crystallizes plagioclase in the system An-Ab-Or-SiO_2 at elevated water pressures. The initial liquid, L_1, in the interior of the tetrahedron, first crystallizes plagioclase of composition P_1 (on the front face of the tetrahedron) and follows a curved path away from plagioclase until it intersects the two-feldspar surface at L_2. Alkali feldspar A_2 (on the front face) begins to crystallize along with plagioclase, which has now reached composition P_2, and the liquid moves away from these feldspars along the curved surface until it reaches the silica-feldspar surface at L_3. Quartz now begins to crystallize along with feldspars (now with compositions P_3 and A_3), and the liquid then descends to an end point at L_4. (After I. S. E. Carmichael et al., 1974, *Igneous Petrology*, McGraw-Hill, 739 pp.)

In treating felsic rocks in terms of only quartz and alkali feldspar, as we did in the preceding section, the anorthite component was ignored, and compositions falling within the interior of the four-component system were in effect projected from the anorthite corner to the base of the tetrahedron. If the anorthite content is small, this may not introduce a major error, but if it accounts for more than 10 percent or so of the total, the effect can be misleading. Note that any composition on the plagioclase-quartz cotectic surface GH, i.e., a liquid crystallizing quartz, orthoclase, and plagioclase simultaneously, falls within the quartz field when projected along a line from the anorthite corner through the point representing the liquid composition to the basal triangle. The apparent effect of increasing anorthite content, when projected in this way, is just the opposite of increasing water pressure on the simpler three-component system. Thus, the combined effects of water and anorthite result in a range of possible compositions for the temperature minimum, m, that is an almost linear trend across the central part of the diagram. Without knowing the anorthite content, it is difficult to say to what degree the position of m is due to one effect or the other.

Another effect of this projection is to place the composition of liquids in equilibrium with both quartz and plagioclase in the quartz field of the simpler quartz-alkali feldspar system. This gives the false impression that the liquid is saturated with quartz but not with feldspar. A composition that, in the simple granite system, might appear to be the result of advanced melting of a very quartz-rich crustal rock may in fact be a normal igneous composition with enough anorthitic plagioclase to place it well above the base of the tetrahdron. This pitfall has misled more than one petrologist. It is a trap to beware of when dealing not only with granites but with any complex natural system in which one attempts to interpret compositional trends in terms of a simplified diagram that ignores other components of the rocks.

Hydrous mafic minerals

Thus far we have assumed compositions composed solely of quartz and feldspar and have ignored mafic components and hydrous minerals. From what was seen in chapter nine when we considered the role of water in systems such as diopside-forsterite-silica (Fig. 9–16), one would anticipate that the effect of water pressure on mafic compositions will be to produce liquids that are systematically more silica-rich than under anhydrous conditions. This is no less true when amphibole or biotite are stable phases, for most of these minerals have low silica contents and in most instances are equivalent to an assemblage that includes a silica-deficient mineral, such as nepheline or leucite. Hence, any melt in equilibrium with these minerals will be more silica-rich than one formed from partial melting of an equivalent anhydrous assemblage.

The stability relations of the hydrous minerals, biotite, muscovite, and hornblende, are a function of temperature, water pressure, and oxygen fugacity, and in contrast to anhydrous minerals, which melt at lower temperatures with increasing water pressures, hydrous minerals can have the opposite relation.

When superimposed on a single diagram, such as one for a typical granodiorite (Fig. 10–16), the stability limits of the hydrous and anhydrous minerals form crossing curves, and the order of crystallization or disappearance of minerals with cooling or heating will differ according to the pressure, water content, and oxidation state under which the process takes place. Such a magma, if cooling at high water pressure, would first crystallize the hydrous minerals, hornblende and biotite, then plagioclase with increasing albite content, and finally the granitic end-members, quartz, orthoclase, and albite, at temperatures just above the solidus. The same liquid crystallizing at a shallow depth or with less water would first crystallize pyroxene, but on further cooling the pyroxene might alter to an amphibole (uralite), and the feldspars might be altered to a mica, such as sericite. This mineral assemblage is common in shallow, sub-volcanic stocks.

Consider next what might happen to such a magma if it rises to erupt at the surface. The hydrous minerals formed at depth would become unstable, and exsolution of water would cause the magma to vesiculate. If the initial temperature were low, anhydrous minerals could crystallize, even at constant temperature, because a loss of water pressure raises their temperatures of crystallization, and the magma might freeze before reaching the surface.

Effects of a hydrous vapor phase

Having said virtually nothing about the vapor phase since we last touched on it in chapter three, this is an appropriate place to examine some of the ways in which the volatile components of magmas behave during cooling and cystallization. To do this, it will be helpful to look at a few basic principles of liquid-vapor systems and how they apply to magmas.

At the outset, it must be emphasized that when we speak of a volatile component, such as water, no distinction can be made between the vapor and a hydrous liquid phase at the temperatures and pressures of subsurface magmatic systems. Because the effect of increasing temperature on the liquid phase is to decrease its density, and the effect of pressure on the vapor phase is the reverse (Fig. 10–17a), the densities of the liquid and vapor converge, and beyond a certain condition, known as the critical point, the liquid and vapor are no longer

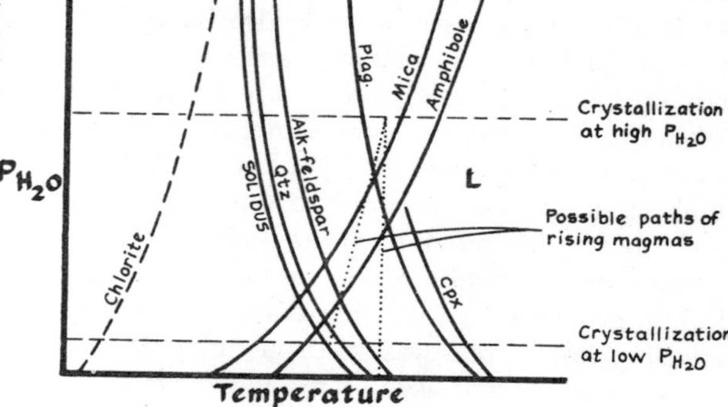

Figure 10–16 Stability relations of phases in a granodiorite as functions of temperature and water pressure. See text for a discussion of the possible courses of crystallization.

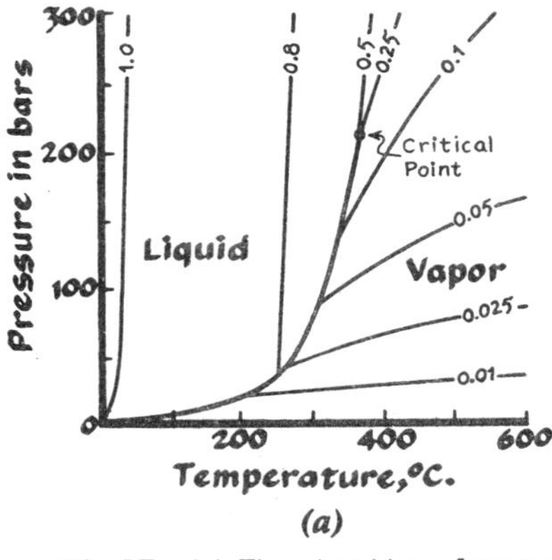

(a)

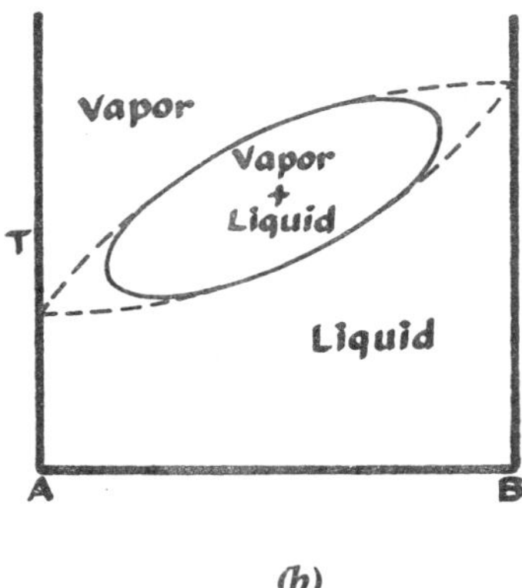

(b)

Figure 10–17 (a) The densities of water and steam, shown by light, numbered lines, vary directly with pressure and inversely with temperature in such a way that the densities of the two phases converge on common values, and above the critical point (C.P.) at 374°C and 221 bars the distinction between the liquid and vapor phases disappears, and properties are gradational. (b) Vapor-liquid relations for two components with differing vapor pressures resemble those for liquid-solid relations. The component with the low boiling temperature and high vapor pressure is more concentrated in the vapor than in the liquid phase. If both components are above their critical temperatures, the distinction between the vapor and liquid is gradational for compositions near the end-members.

separated by an abrupt difference in properties. The critical point of pure H_2O is only 221 bars and 374°C, and those of other magmatic gases are even lower, so it is clear that a high-temperature gas phase at any depth greater than a kilometer or so must be *supercritical*. That is to say, it has no well-defined boiling temperature but rather a continuous range of density. We may still refer to this fluid as a vapor phase, however, in order to distinguish it from silicate liquids, which, under most conditions, have physical properties different from those of H_2O-rich fluids.

In granitic systems, however, these differences are not great. Supercritical hydrous fluids are excellent solvents, capable of dissolving silica, alkalies, and other components, so that the vapor phase is composed of more than the components one normally thinks of as volatiles. Fluids containing large amounts of these components have properties approaching those of silicate melts, and the difference between a hydrous fluid with dissolved silicates and a silicate melt with dissolved volatiles becomes a narrow one.

A magmatic vapor phase can be thought of as consisting of two sets of components, those like water that have low boiling temperatures and high vapor pressures and those like silica that have very high boiling temperatures and low vapor pressures. Their phase relations are analogous to those of two miscible liquids of different volatilities, say water and alcohol (Fig. 10–17b). Their phase diagram at constant pressure has a form similar to the liquidus-solidus loop of solid-solution series. The component with the low boiling temperature (high vapor pressure) is preferentially enriched in the vapor. With falling temperature, a given intermediate composition does not change directly to a liquid but passes through an intermediate range of vapor + liquid, just as a liquid passes through a region of liquid + solid in crystallizing a solid solution in a "condensed" system.

The liquid-vapor loop in Figure 10–17b differs from the liquid-solid loop for a silicate solid solution in that the curves do not converge at the end-member compositions. Instead, the vapor passes gradually into the liquid at the two ends, because in those regions the critical conditions are exceeded for corresponding end-member components, and the boundary between the liquid and vapor is entirely gradational. Owing to the fact that each of the components has its own critical temperature and pressure, the system does not have a unique critical point but rather a curved boundary at each end. The student may find it instructive to show how this can be deduced from the Phase Rule.

With this general background, we can turn now to a system closer to natural melts, and see how a vapor phase may behave during crystallization of a magma. The system water-albite (Fig. 10–18) will serve to show most of the important relations. Taking water as the component with the low boiling temperature and high vapor pressure and albite as the one with the opposite properties, the vapor-liquid relations would be like those in Figure 10–17b. (The boiling temperature of albite is so high that it is meaningless in terms of natural conditions and is not shown.) The liquid-solid relations are depicted schematically as a sloping curve. Theoretically, there could be a eutectic close to the H_2O end of the diagram, where a small amount of albite would lower the freezing temperature of ice, but the solubility of albite in water is so low that this can be ignored. The middle part of the curve overlaps with the vapor-liquid region, so that superposition of the diagrams results in a combined set of phase relations, which shows the basic elements of the entire three-phase system.

Take, for example, a magma of composition X at an initial temperature, T_1. Two phases are present, a liquid of composition X_L and a more H_2O-rich vapor of

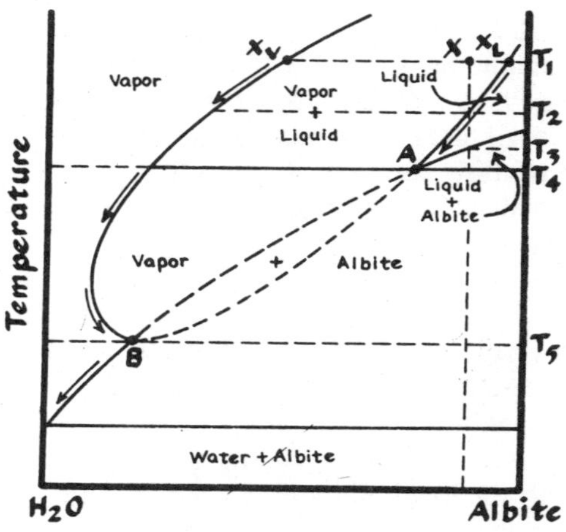

Figure 10–18 Schematic diagram for the H_2O-albite system. See text for discussion.

composition X_V. As the magma cools, the solubility of water in the liquid increases, and the proportion of vapor will diminish at the same time that the amount of liquid increases. At temperature T_2 all the vapor has disappeared and only a single phase, a liquid of composition X, remains. On further cooling, crystals of albite appear at T_3, and at temperature T_4 an H_2O-rich vapor phase reappears. Note the three-phase invariant point at A. The system cannot decline in temperature below this point until all of the liquid is gone, but once that happens albite continues to crystallize from the vapor phase. (The amount of albite crystallized in this interval is less than indicated by the diagram, which, in order to show the relations more clearly, exaggerates the compositional differences.) Note that in the lower part of this interval albite is redissolved, and the concentration in the vapor phase increases again until a second invariant point, B, is reached at T_5. Thereafter, albite crystallizes again.

Many pegmatites are thought to crystallize under conditions similar to those portrayed by the albite-water system, particularly in the lower temperature range where the vapor phase is rich in H_2O. The low viscosity and great solvent power of the fluid enhance its mobility and ability to transport components that have been concentrated in the late stages of crystallization of large bodies of magma. The high water content also facilitates growth of very large crystals.

GENERATION AND RISE THROUGH THE CRUST

The effect of increasing load pressure on melting or crystallization is, as we saw in the case of basalts, to raise the temperature of crystal-liquid equilibrium by amounts that are mainly a function of the difference between the specific volume of the solid and liquid. Because the specific volume of the liquid is greater than that of the solid, the change of volume on melting, ΔV, is positive, and the Clapeyron equation,

$$\frac{dT}{dP} = \frac{T\Delta V}{\Delta H}$$

shows that the slope of the liquidus curve is also positive, and its temperature increases with pressure (Fig. 10–19b). Increasing water pressure has the opposite effect. It lowers the melting temperature, because the combined volume of an anhydrous solid and water vapor is greater than that of the liquid with water in solution, and ΔV is negative. The temperature of the liquidus curve must therefore decrease with increasing water pressure, and two limiting cases can be defined, one for dry melting or crystallization in which the T-P curve is positive, and another for wet condtions that has a negative slope. To see how melting might proceed under such conditions, consider a hypothetical crustal source with a composition within the middle range of the granite system, so that the first melt has a composition at the eutectic in Figure 10–12.

The relative amounts of melt and crystals during melting or crystallization are strongly dependent on the solubility of water in the liquid. The amount of water the liquid can dissolve increases with increasing water pressure (again be-

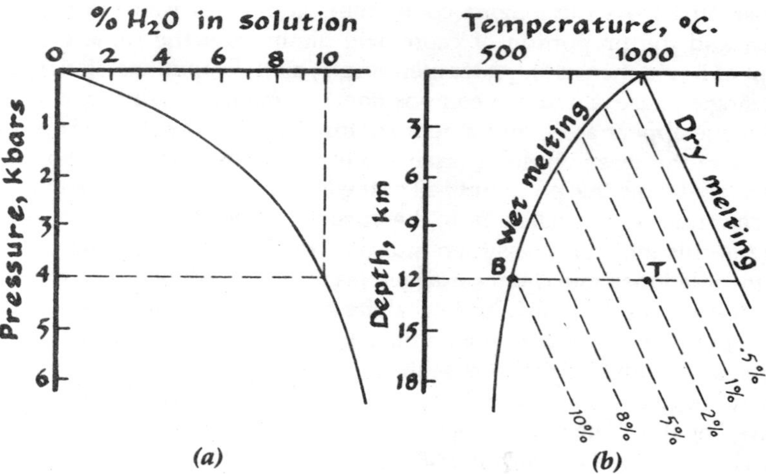

(a) (b)

Figure 10–19 (a) The solubility of water in granitic liquids, assuming that water pressure is equal to load pressure at the depths indicated on the vertical axis. (b) The melting curves of granite as functions of pressure, temperature, and water content. See text for discussion.

cause the volume of melt plus water vapor is much greater than that of the melt with water in solution). A typical solubility curve is shown in Figure 10–19a. The amount of water dissolved in the liquid on the wet-melting curve in Figure 10–19b corresponds to saturation for the prevailing pressure, while on the dry curve, of course, it is nil, and between the two curves is a region in which the liquid has an intermediate temperature and water content.

A rock having a water content equivalent to its solubility at the prevailing pressure would melt completely at the temperature corresponding to the water pressure on the wet-melting curve. But if it has less water—the more likely situation in nature—it will begin to melt on the wet curve (where the first liquid would be saturated), but it will melt only as far as is required to saturate the liquid at that temperature and eliminate the vapor phase. At this point ΔV changes from negative to positive, and to attain further melting the temperature must rise, and the liquid must become poorer in dissolved water. For example, a rock with 2 percent water at a depth of 12 km will begin to melt at a temperature, B, of about 600°C. If the solubility of H_2O at this pressure is 10 percent, melting will proceed at the minimum temperature, B, until 20 percent of the rock is liquid and all the H_2O is dissolved. The rock would be completely melted only if it were heated to a temperature, T, of about 1000°C.

A wide range of melting could result if the pressure of water increases with depth, and the geothermal gradient rises above the melting curves in the manner shown schematically in Figure 10–20a. The range of melting starting at the uppermost intersection of the geothermal gradient with the wet melting curve extends down the gradient with increasing amounts of liquid until the entire rock

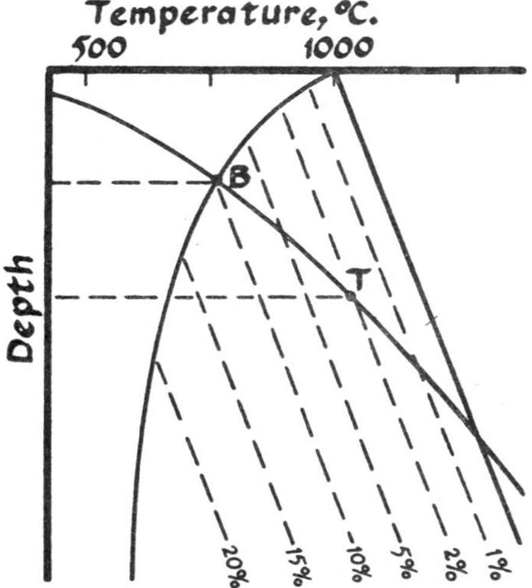

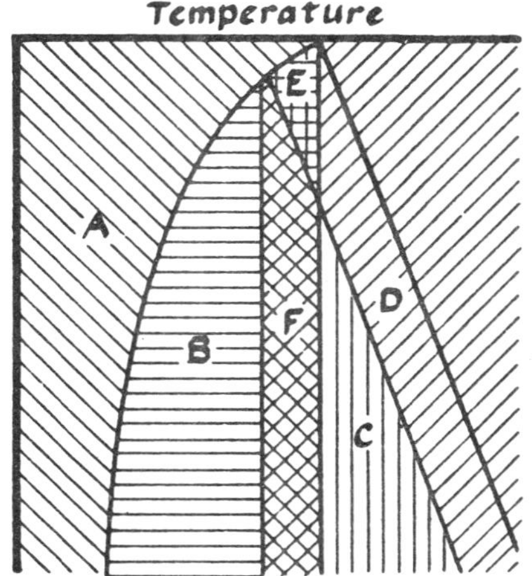

Figure 10–20 (a) Schematic illustration of the melting relations of granite with 2 percent H_2O in a geothermal gradient. Melting begins at point B, where the geothermal gradient first intersects the curve for wet melting, and increases with depth until the rock is totally melted at point T, where the thermal gradient reaches the melting curve for the water content of the rock. (Adapted from O. F. Tuttle and N. L. Bowen, 1958, *Geol. Soc. Amer. Mem. 74*.) (b) Regimes in which differing effects would be observed when magmas generated from a rock with 2 percent H_2O rise toward the surface.

A. No melting.
B. Partial melting; on rising, a crystal-liquid mixture first absorbs crystals and then grows larger ones.
C. Partial melting; on rising, the crystal-liquid mixture would be entirely liquid and superheated at the surface if no heat is lost en route.
D. Total melting; the liquid would reach the surface superheated if no heat were lost en route.
E. Total melting; the liquid begins to crystallize before reaching the surface.
F. The relations in field F are left for the student to deduce.

In nature, the presence of other components and the cooling effects of decompression and heat losses to the surroundings will modify this basic outline.

would be melted at the depth where the temperature reaches the melting curve corresponding to the total water content of the rock.

If a parcel of granitic magma were saturated with water at a temperature corresponding to the wet melting curve at some depth and then were to rise to a level of lower pressure, the solubility of water would decline, the magma would exsolve water vapor, and the melt would begin to crystallize. It can be seen from the negative slope of the wet melting curve that if such a magma did not rise in temperature during ascent, it would crystallize completely. The heat of crystallization might contribute to a somewhat higher temperature and enable the liquid to follow the melting curve to lower pressures, but it is doubtful whether this would be enough to offset the strong quenching effect of exsolving water. A second magma starting at the same depth but on the dry melting curve would have little or no water and an initially higher temperature. On rising to a level of lower pressure it enters a field above its liquidus and would be superheated. Adiabatic cooling (about 0.2 or 0.3 degrees per kilometer) would be insufficient to prevent the magma from becoming superheated, but loss of heat to the surroundings becomes increasingly important as the magma enters the cooler rocks of the crust.

Between these limiting cases we can distinguish several types of intermediate behavior. The diagram in Figure 10–20b is divided into six general zones, each characterized by a particular sequence of melting or crystallization that could result in different petrographic features if the magmas rose to a shallow level or erupted volcanically.

These examples assume the pressure of water to be equal to the total load pressure at any given depth and have been highly simplified in order to illustrate certain basic relations. In reality, conditions must be more complex. In nature, the pressure of water is probably less than the total load pressure, and, as we saw in chapter five (Fig. 5–14), under such conditions the solubility of water is less than when the two are equal. The amount of water a magma contains under such conditions is a function not only of the pressure of water, which tends to cause water to enter the magma, but also of load presure, which tends to squeeze it out. Thus, the water content can increase with falling load pressure, and magmas saturated at depth may become undersaturated and absorb water as they rise.

Melting of a layered lithosphere

Melting of a compositionally layered lower crust and upper mantle could result in a relationship similar to the one we considered in discussing generation of basaltic magmas in chapter seven (Fig. 7–14). Each compositionally different layer would have its own melting temperature and, on partial melting, would yield liquids of differing compositions. A rise of temperature along the geothermal gradient might result in an intersection with these different melting curves in the manner illustrated in Figure 10–21. Depending on the order in which the different layers begin to melt, it would be possible to produce magmas of different compositions as the cusp of each melting curve is intersected by the rising thermal gradient. Such a relation may account for the association of tholeiitic and calc-alkaline magmas in orogenic igneous suites. It could also explain how magmas derived from the mantle can be closely associated in time and space with magmas produced by melting of the crust.

MELTING BEHAVIOR OF NATURAL ROCKS

The foregoing outline of melting behavior in the granite system shows that the compositions of source rocks will have a marked effect on the way natural melts are produced. This is seen most clearly in comparing the "S" and "I" types of granites derived by partial fusion of sources consisting of sedimentary or igneous rocks (Table 10–1).

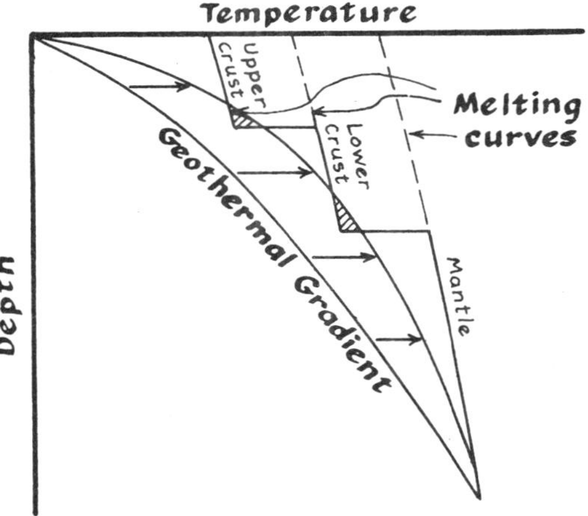

Figure 10–21 Schematic relations between a geothermal gradient and melting curves of a layered lithosphere. Because the lithosphere becomes more mafic with depth, each compositional zone must have its own melting curve, and a rising geothermal gradient first intersects the lower ends of these melting curves in such a way as to produce first one liquid and then another, in an order that depends on the relative slopes of the melting curves and geothermal gradient.

Melting of sedimentary and meta-sedimentary rocks

The problem of generating large volumes of siliceous magmas is greatly reduced if the source rock has a composition that is already close to that of granite. This, together with the commonly observed association of orogenic plutons with thick, deeply buried, and intensely metamorphosed sedimentary rocks supports the idea that many granites are the products of *anatexis*, as the process of melting continental crust is called. Although the principles of melting for such rocks are often thought of as the reverse of crystallization in the granite system, the process is altered somewhat by the compositions and mineral assemblages of sedimentary and equivalent metamorphic rocks that tend to diverge from the granite system. Most thick accumulations of continental sediments are *pelitic;* that is, they contain large proportions of clay and quartz. Most have such large amounts of these minerals that they are at least as rich in silicon, aluminum, and potassium as are granites. Unlike many granites, however, they have much less sodium than potassium.

Most sediments and their metamorphic equivalents contain large proportions of hydrous minerals, such as muscovite, biotite, and amphibole, that have a strong effect on melting behavior. Depending on their compositions and depths of burial, melting proceeds in multiple stages, each of which is governed by the effects of increasing temperature on a particular assemblage of minerals. The way in which melting advances is illustrated schematically in Figure 10–22a, which shows the sequence of changes that accompany an increase of temperature at constant pressure. Curve (1) depicts the upper stability limit of an assemblage that includes a hydrous mineral, H, in the presence of water vapor. On crossing this curve the assemblage goes to a melt, M_S, that is saturated with water. All of the hydrous mineral disappears, and the water vapor is completely dissolved in the melt. Of course, if water is present in excess of the amount that can be dissolved in the melt, a vapor phase will still remain. The same assemblage with a hydrous mineral but without a separate vapor phase will be stable to a higher

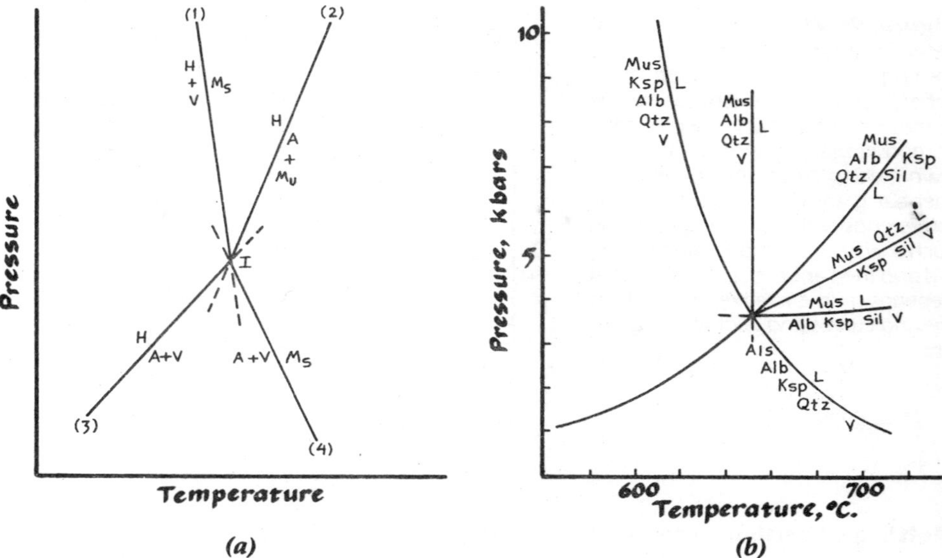

Figure 10–22 Stability limits and melting curves for hydrous and anhydrous minerals in the crust. The four curves in the schematic diagram (a) illustrate the principles explained in the text. H stands for a hydrous mineral, A for an anhydrous one; M_s for a melt saturated with water, M_u for an undersaturated one. V is water vapor. The more complex natural system (b) has basically the same form but is complicated by the greater number of possible minerals. Mus is muscovite, Ksp is potassium-rich alkali feldspar, Alb is albite, Qtz is quartz, Sil is sillimanite, and L is liquid. (Part (b) is adapted from Thompson and Algor, 1977, *Contrib. Miner. Petrol.* 63:247–269.)

temperature corresponding to curve (2) and will break down to one or more anhydrous minerals, A, and a melt, M_U, that is undersaturated with water. Melting of this kind is sometimes referred to as *dehydration melting*.

Conditions differ at pressures below that of the invariant point, I, because in this region the temperatures at which hydrous minerals break down are below the melting curve. In fact, the pressure of point I is the minimum pressure at which the hydrous mineral can coexist with any melt, whether it is saturated with water or not. Note that on curve (3), the low-pressure equivalent of (2), the hydrous mineral goes to an anhydrous equivalent plus water vapor; no melt is produced. If these products continue to rise in temperature and reach curve (4), they will produce a melt that is saturated with water. This last form of melting is exactly the same as the one discussed in the previous section.

The form of these curves for common minerals in pelitic rocks is shown in part (b) of the same figure.

Melting of mafic igneous and meta-igneous rocks

The long-held notion that the only way to produce significant amounts of siliceous magma is to melt siliceous rocks is not strictly true. Under the right conditions, a silica-rich melt can be produced from almost any common multi-

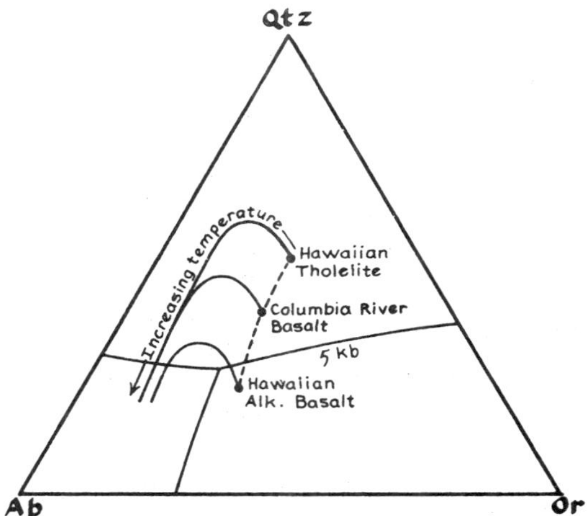

Figure 10–23 Liquids produced by partial melting of basalt at five kilobars water pressure. Compositions have been plotted in terms of their normative quartz, albite, and orthoclase. At the conditions of melting, the residue is mainly amphibole and plagioclase. The solid curves show the effects of progressive melting of three basalts. The points connected by the broken line show the compositions of the first liquids produced by melting of basalts with different degrees of silica saturation. (After R. T. Helz, 1976, *Jour. Petrol.* 17:139–193.)

component crustal rock, even a basalt. The compositions of liquids produced by partial melting of rocks as mafic as common basalt can be very siliceous, if the rocks are rich in hornblende or biotite. The amount of such liquids, of course, is severely limited by the bulk composition of the source.

Typical liquids produced experimentally by partial melting of various types of basalts under elevated water pressures are shown on the diagram for the granite system at five kilobars water pressure (Fig. 10–23). Note that most first melts fall in the quartz field, and their positions are more or less where one would expect them to be if the mineral assemblage includes abundant amorthite. Moreover, basalts of different compositions ranging from quartz tholeiites to nepheline basanites would have initial melts with compositions falling close to the line defined by the temperature minimum with varying water pressure. It is curious, and somewhat frustrating, that so many of the effects we have examined, including fractionation of plagioclase, varying water pressure, differing anorthite contents, and now the composition of mafic assemblages, all produce trends of liquid compositions that are almost indistinguishable, at least in terms of the end-members of the granite system.

With progressive melting of an amphibole-rich source rock, liquid compositions first become poorer in normative orthoclase. This is because so much of that component enters the first melt that little is left in the solid, and further melting simply dilutes the initial concentration. Thereafter, silica contents decline as more amphibole enters the melt. We shall note shortly that these trends are in accord with the compositions and geological occurrence of the group of sodium-rich felsic rocks collectively referred to as trondhjemites.

CRYSTALLIZATION AND DIFFERENTIATION IN THE CRUST

By the time plutons are uplifted and exposed by erosion, long after all traces of magma have solidified, all that one can examine are the cold, dissected remains of what was once a large magmatic intrusion. A petrologist attempting to reconstruct the life of such a body is in much the same position as a surgeon would be if he had studied only cadavers without ever having examined the anatomy of a healthy, living organism.

The volcanic counterparts of siliceous plutonic rocks pose the opposite problem. The nature of the magma is preserved, but one has no hope of seeing the magma chamber from which it came. In a sense, ignimbrites are simply "unroofed batholiths" in that they are derived from the gas-rich upper levels of plutons that have breached the surface. Thus, volcanic rocks record the conditions at the instant a magma was "from its womb untimely ripp'd." The sudden interruption of solidification and differentiation prevents re-equilibration at lower temperatures and preserves a clear record of the crystal-liquid relations at the instant the magma erupted. By integrating information from these huge volcanic magmas with observations of granitic plutons, one can reconstruct a composite picture of how siliceous magmas evolve.

The Long Valley Caldera of southeastern California (Fig. 10–24a) is an exceptionally well-studied and instructive example in which this has been done. One of a chain of volcanic centers close to the eastern front of the Sierra Nevada Range, Long Valley has long been the scene of recurrent activity, including an eruption 700,000 years ago of 170 cubic kilometers of rhyolite known as the Bishop Tuff.

Some idea of the size and form of the magma chamber can be inferred from geophysical measurements and the surface expression of the caldera. The zoning and temporal variations of the magma have been deduced from the ages, compositions, and spatial distribution of its eruptive units. The picture that emerges is one of a large, compositionally stratified intrusion with the form shown in Figure 10–24b. Similar patterns have been deduced for other bodies that have discharged compositionally zoned magmas (Fig. 10–25).

Using the temperature-dependent compositions of iron-titanium oxide minerals (Fig. 4–16), the temperature of the magma has been shown to have increased from about 720 °C for the first magma erupted to about 790 °C for the last. Although it varied by only about 2 weight percent SiO_2, the magma was compositionally zoned from the first to last erupted liquids (Table 10–1). The first magma, which presumably occupied the uppermost part of the reservoir, was enriched in most incompatible elements, such as Rb, U, Th, Nb, Y, and the heavy rare-earths, relative to the last magma discharged from lower levels. But it is poorer in some incompatible elements, such as Ba, Zr, P, Ce, and the light rare-earths, which are normally enriched by crystal fractionation. Although the liquid fraction of the magma was isotopically inhomogeneous, the Sr 87-86 ratio is in the range of only 0.706 to 0.709. It seems unlikely, therefore, that the trace-element variations could be due to large amounts of crustal assimilation. Ba was probably depleted by crystallization of sanidine, which takes in large amounts of that element. The accessory minerals, allanite, apatite, and zircon, though present in only small amounts, take in large amounts of other incompatible elements and deplete the liquid in the light rare-earth more than the heavy.

Part of the compositional zoning can probably be attributed to inward crystallization and fractionation of light liquids during sidewall crystallization (Fig. 9–14),

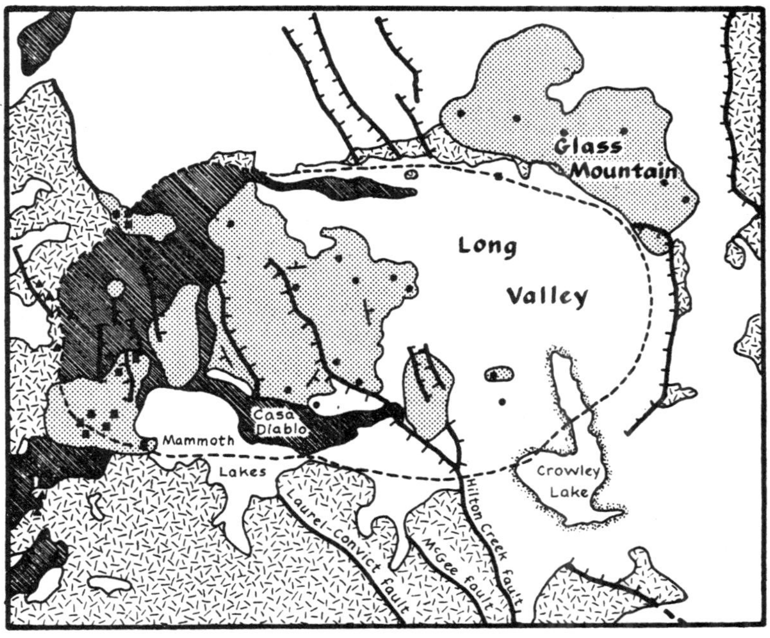

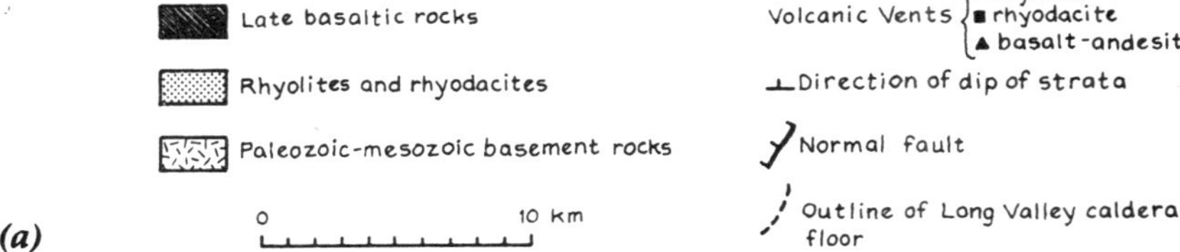

(a)

Figure 10–24 (a) Simplified geologic map of Long Valley Caldera, California. (b) Schematic section through the magma body under Long Valley as it has been inferred from the ages, spatial relations, compositions of eruptive units, and geophysical studies. (After R. A. Bailey, G. E. Dalrymple, and M. A. Lanphere, 1976, *Jour. Geoph. Res.* 81:725–744, and R. A. Bailey, personal communication.)

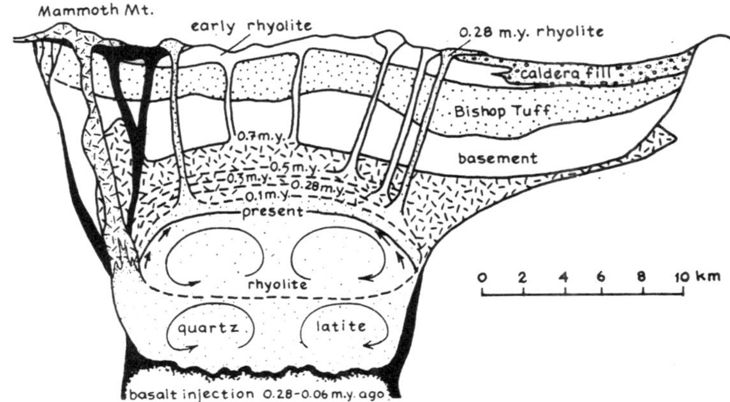

(b)

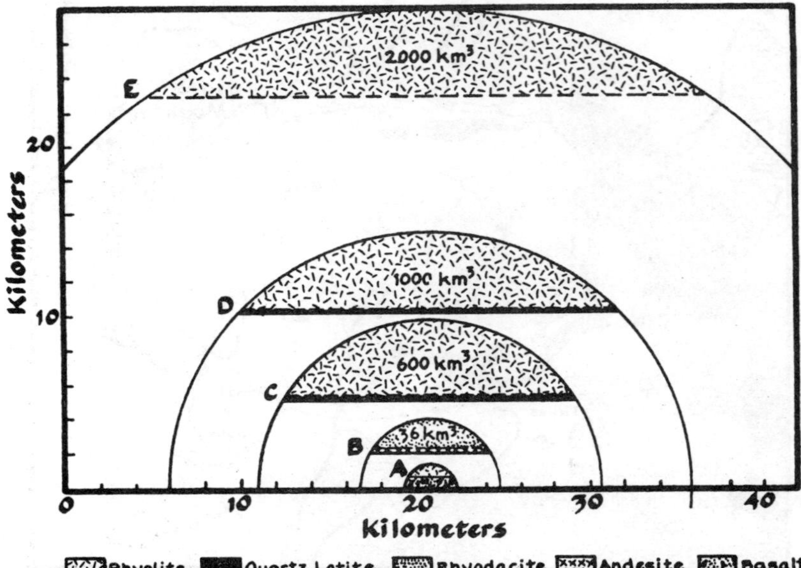

Figure 10–25 Schematic vertical sections through zoned and multicycled magma chambers inferred from the erupted volumes derived from the upper zones of hemispherical bodies of magma with the diameters of their associated calderas. Section A is for the Askja Caldera of northern Iceland and consists of rhyolitic magma directly overlying basalt. B depicts the magma of Mt. Mazama that erupted to form the caldera of Crater Lake, as illustrated in Figure 9–15. C represents the magma under the Valles and Toledo calderas of New Mexico just before eruption of the Bandelier Tuff. The upper zone is graded from rhyolite at the top to quartz latite and overlies much more basic magma. D corresponds to the approximate volumes of magma erupted during two cycles of Timber Mountain Caldera, Nevada. The upper unit is zoned from high-silica rhyolite at the top to quartz latite. Section E represents the system under the Yellowstone region about 600,000 years ago, just before formation of the Yellowstone Caldera. The upper zone consists of weakly zoned, high-silica rhyolite. Note that with increasing size, the contrast between the compositions of the units tends to become less pronounced. (After R. L. Smith, 1979, *Geol. Soc. Amer. Spec. Paper 180*, 5–27.)

but density stratification of successive intrusions is at least equally important. As the magma evolves, new injections of denser, less-differentiated liquids would tend to pond at the base. Although it is difficult to know how much each of these mechanisms contributes to the zoning, there is little doubt that periodic intrusions of fresh magma prolong the life of the magma by balancing losses to volcanic eruptions and cooling; the lifetimes of these systems are much longer than the times required for cooling and crystallization of a single pulse of magma.

ORIGINS OF GRANITIC AND RHYOLITIC MAGMAS

The "Granite Problem"

Granitic and siliceous volcanic suites that are notably deficient in intermediate compositions but have disproportionately large volumes of extreme differentiates present an obvious problem if one is to attribute their huge volumes to conventional crystal fractionation of basaltic magma. They would require crystallization of parent bodies of impossibly large dimensions.

It is mainly to surmount this volume problem that most explanations for large masses of felsic magma dismiss the possibility of differentiation from mafic magmas and, instead, call on melting of crustal rocks that are already enriched in silica, alumina, and alkalies by surficial processes. This inference is logical, in view of the almost total restriction of large bodies of siliceous rocks to continental settings and their scarcity in regions of oceanic lithosphere. As mechanisms for concentrating lithophile elements, the processes of weathering, erosion, and sedimentation, though slow, are far more efficient than those of magmatic differentiation. So, by postulating that crustal rocks are the sources of siliceous magmas, the problem of generating large volumes of granite and rhyolite are greatly reduced.

Geological support for this reasoning is not hard to find. Orogenic granites are typically associated with thick piles of sediments that accumulated in rapidly subsiding geosynclines where they seem to result from deep burial and heating that culminates in upheaval and large-scale plutonism. It cannot be coincidental that the times required for anatexis of a thickening crust, several tens of millions of years, are comparable to the time elapsed between orogenies.

Crustal melting and generation of magmas has been well-documented in many high-grade, metamorphic terranes. In some instances this process results in mobilization of what was clearly a magma; in others, crustal rocks seem to have been converted to granites, more or less in place, by a process of "ultrametamorphism" that transforms meta-sediments of varied compositions into homogeneous, coarse-grained, felsic rocks with textures and compositions very similar to those of magmatic granites. This process of *granitization* involves wholesale compositional changes and exchange of mafic and felsic components over distances of tens or even hundreds of meters. In the past, some of the more extreme advocates of this interpretation maintained that the process takes place entirely in the solid state, but more recent work indicates that a melt of some sort is indispensible.

Two strong arguments can be offered in support of a process in which crustal rocks are granitized. The first is based on examples of metamorphic rocks that can be seen to grade imperceptively into rocks that to all intents and purposes are granites but retain a "ghost stratigraphy" inherited from individual horizons in the layered rocks from which they are derived. In some cases, distinctive layers of amphibolite, quartzite, and marble project along strike from a metamorphic sequence into the interior of an otherwise homogeneous granite. Owing to their extreme compositions, these metamorphic remnants are more resistant to granitization and persist long after more pelitic rocks have been totally transformed. In other instances the granitic rocks have only subtle textural differences but retain zones with anomalous concentrations of trace elements inherited from an earlier, metasedimentary protolith.

A second argument is a geometrical one based on the so-called "room problem." Because granitic bodies occupy such enormous volumes, they could not be intruded without a corresponding displacement of surrounding rocks. In many cases, assimilation, stoping, or plastic deformation of the walls and roof can account for much of the room required for granitic intrusions, but in others the evidence for displacement of this magnitude is not always obvious. It seemed logical, therefore, to explain the emplacement of large plutons, not as introductions of great volumes of new magma, but as a simple redistribution of the components of the crust.

Although some form of granitization can, or indeed must, take place at deep crustal levels where the boundary between metamorphism and crustal melting becomes indistinct, the process requires at least enough melting to mobilize the magma and give it a mineralogical and chemical character consistent with crystal-liquid phase relations. The close resemblances of many high-grade metamorphic rocks to granites of magmatic origin may not mean that granites have a metamorphic origin but rather that they have cooled under similar conditions that led to recrystallization and loss of their original magmatic textures. The temperatures and pressures at which granitic liquids crystallize are so close to those of high-grade metamorphism that any division between magmatic and metamorphic processes becomes vague and somewhat artificial.

The fact that granites have compositions consistent with experimentally determined phase relations implies that they crystallize under conditions approaching equilibrium, but it says nothing about how they reach that state. As we have seen time and again in earlier chapters, a magma can arrive at a particular mineralogical composition by any of a number of routes, including crystal fractionation, partial melting, assimilation, and mixing; phase relations alone offer little evidence of how it reached that state. To resolve this question one must rely on a variety of clues, both geological and geochemical.

GEOLOGICAL AND GEOCHEMICAL EVIDENCE

Of the many detailed field studies that have contributed to our understanding of granite, one of the most noteworthy was focused on an area in County Donegal in northwestern Ireland, where an extraordinary cluster of well-exposed granitic bodies spans the entire spectrum from catazonal plutons associated with high-grade metamorphism to epizonal intrusions and sub-volcanic stocks (Fig. 10–26). H. H. Read, together with his students and co-workers, recognized an evolutionary sequence or "granite series" that encompasses a continuous series of structural and mineralogical relations. With increasing degrees of melting, magmas were generated, mobilized, and separated from their refractory residue, then rose diapirically to shallower levels. Examples of all stages of this process were identified within a remarkably small area.

The oldest of the granites is the Thorr Tonalite, a large, irregularly shaped body that intruded metasedimentary rocks of diverse lithologies. It contains rafts and xenoliths of all sizes torn from its roof and walls and has converted many of these older rocks to migmatites with differing degrees of textural and compositional homogenization. The main Donegal Granite (Fig. 10–26b), more properly a granodiorite, is structurally gradational into the surrounding metamorphic

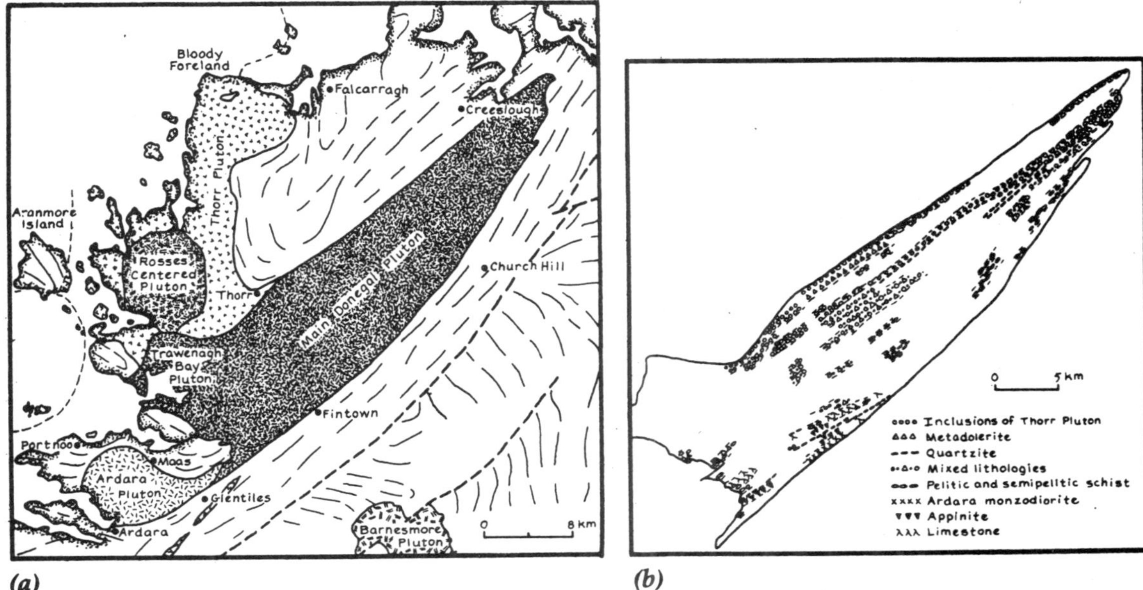

Figure 10–26 (a) Generalized map of Donegal, northwestern Ireland, showing the spatial relations of the main granites. (b) is a more detailed map of the Main Donegal Granite showing ghost stratigraphy inherited from granitized metasedimentary rocks. (c) The Ardara pluton illustrates the early stages of mobilization of granitic magma in a zone of plastic deformation. (d) The Rosses Centered Complex is interpreted as a nested set of shallow intrusions. (After a compilation by W. S. Pitcher and A. R. Berger, *Geology of Donegal*, Wiley Interscience, 435 pp.)

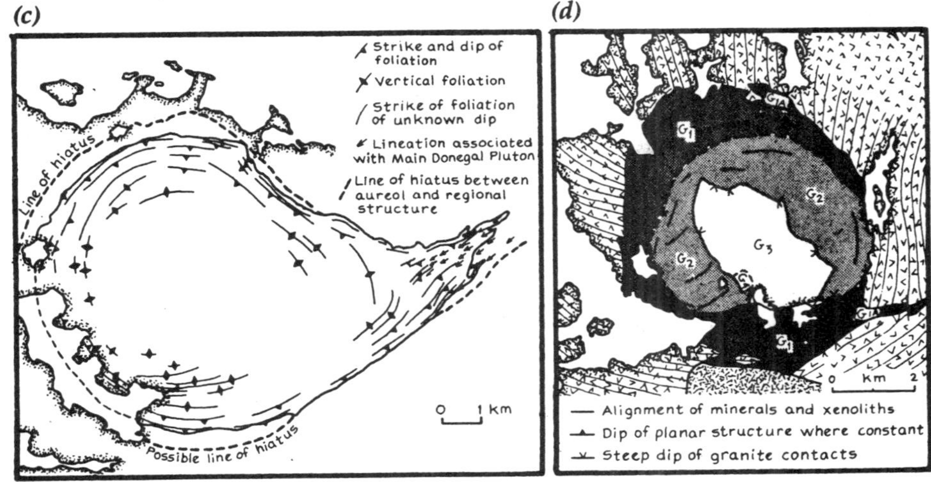

rocks and retains a remarkable ghost stratigraphy in the form of layers of quartzite, metadiorite, and schist extending along strike from the granodiorite into adjacent metamorphic units. Because of their more refractory compositions, these layers were more resistant to granitization by wedges of magma that appear to have intruded them from greater depths. The Ardara Pluton (Fig. 10–26c) contains fewer inhomogeneities and, from its curious pod-like form and flow-induced foliation, can be seen to have been intruded plastically, pushing aside the adjacent rocks to take on a tadpole-like shape. The Rosses Ring Complex (Fig. 10–26d) illustrates a more advanced stage of rise into shallower structural levels. It truncates adjacent units and has sharply defined concentric zones produced by successive intrusive pulses.

Those parts of this series that grade into metamorphic rocks can be seen to have been melted and partly mobilized. The melting did not result so much from deep burial as from heat supplied by magmas rising from deeper levels. The thermal gradients inferred from the widths of the metamorphic zones around deep-seated granites are much steeper than they would be if they resulted from deep burial. Moreover, some of the intrusive bodies are geochemically distinct from the rocks they intrude and must come either from differentiation of a more basic magma or from direct melting of a deeper source in the lower crust or upper mantle. Thus, only a small part of the granite has a local origin in the metamorphic rocks; by far the greater part comes from greater depths.

To sort out the relative contributions of crustal and mantle components to such rocks is a formidable task, as we shall see if we follow the attempts to do this with the granites of one of the Scottish Tertiary igneous centers discussed in chapter seven (Fig. 10–27). Although the rocks are in an unusual tectonic setting, they are well suited for this purpose, because they have been used as a petrologic testing ground for virtually every possible geochemical tool of igneous petrology.

Rare-earth elements

Among the trace components of granites, the rare-earth elements (REE) are especially useful, because they vary in abundance by very large factors and are fractionated in different ways by individual minerals. In addition, they are relatively unaffected by the hydrothermal processes that often redistribute other components of granitic rocks.

The range of REE abundances of eleven Scottish granites are shown in Figure 10–28, together with corresponding data for basement rocks and basalts from the same region on the Isle of Skye. If we look first for possible evidence of crustal anatexis and compare the granites with the Lewisian gneiss and Torridonian sandstones from which they could be derived, Figure 10–28a shows that the two groups have no overlap. The granites could not be products of anything approaching total melting of the basement in a closed system; that much is clear.

It could be argued, of course, that they are partial melts, because in such a process the REE would be enriched in the liquid fraction by an amount that varies inversely with the proportion of melt. Note, however, that the amount of enrichment is not uniform. The relative degrees of enrichment of the light and heavy elements depend on the identities of the residual crystalline phases, which have differing distribution coefficients relative to a liquid. The fact that the granites tend to be relatively less enriched in the light REE than the basement is difficult to reconcile with partial melting, because all common residual minerals that are likely to be left by partial melting of felsic crustal rocks would tend to increase the light elements in the liquid more than heavy ones (Fig. 5–24). If anything, the opposite seems to be true of the rocks of Skye. Hence, if crustal rocks contributed anything to the granites, it was either a very small amount or it was a material unlike the exposed basement and had an anomalous REE pattern.

Comparing the granites with their associated basalts (Fig. 10–28b), we note that although the granites are richer in the REE, there is a substantial range of overlap between the two sets of data. This lends support to the interpretation of the granites as differentiates of more basic magmas. Just as in partial melting, liquids produced by crystal fractionation tend to be enriched in the REE, particularly at the light end of the series. The two sets of data could be interpreted as a continuum in which the REE in the granites have been enriched by differentiation of the more mafic magmas. Moreover, the proportion of light REE increases with progressive differentiation, just as one would expect if pyroxene or hornblende had been fractionated. The negative Eu anomaly indicates that plagioclase was among the fractionated phases.

Strontium Isotopes

We have already seen from our consideration of calc-alkaline volcanic rocks in chapter nine how the Rb-Sr system has been used to evaluate the contribution of crustal material to andesitic magmas. The same system can be used to even greater effect in studying granites and rhyolites. The Rb-rich Precambrian basement rocks underlying the Tertiary igneous centers of Skye have $^{87}Sr/^{86}Sr$ ratios of the order of 0.720 or more. Thus their strontium is much more radiogenic than that of the basalts and should produce a marked contrast between magmas produced by melting of crustal rocks and those coming from the mantle. When the various igneous rocks of Skye were analyzed and the ratios recalculated to their initial values at the time of crystallization about 53 million years ago, they were found to fall into two distinct groups. Granites, granophyres, and rhyolites have larger ratios than the basalts and ultramafic rocks, and a histogram (Fig. 10–29) shows two separate populations with virtually no overlap. The difference is much greater than the possible margin of error in the analytical data.

What is surprising is not that the isotopic ratios differ but that they differ so little. The Sr ratios of the granites, though larger than those of the basalts, are much less than would be expected from source rocks with ratios of 0.720 or more. If they are partial melts their ratios should be at least as large, and under some conditions they could be much greater. The reason for this can be seen by

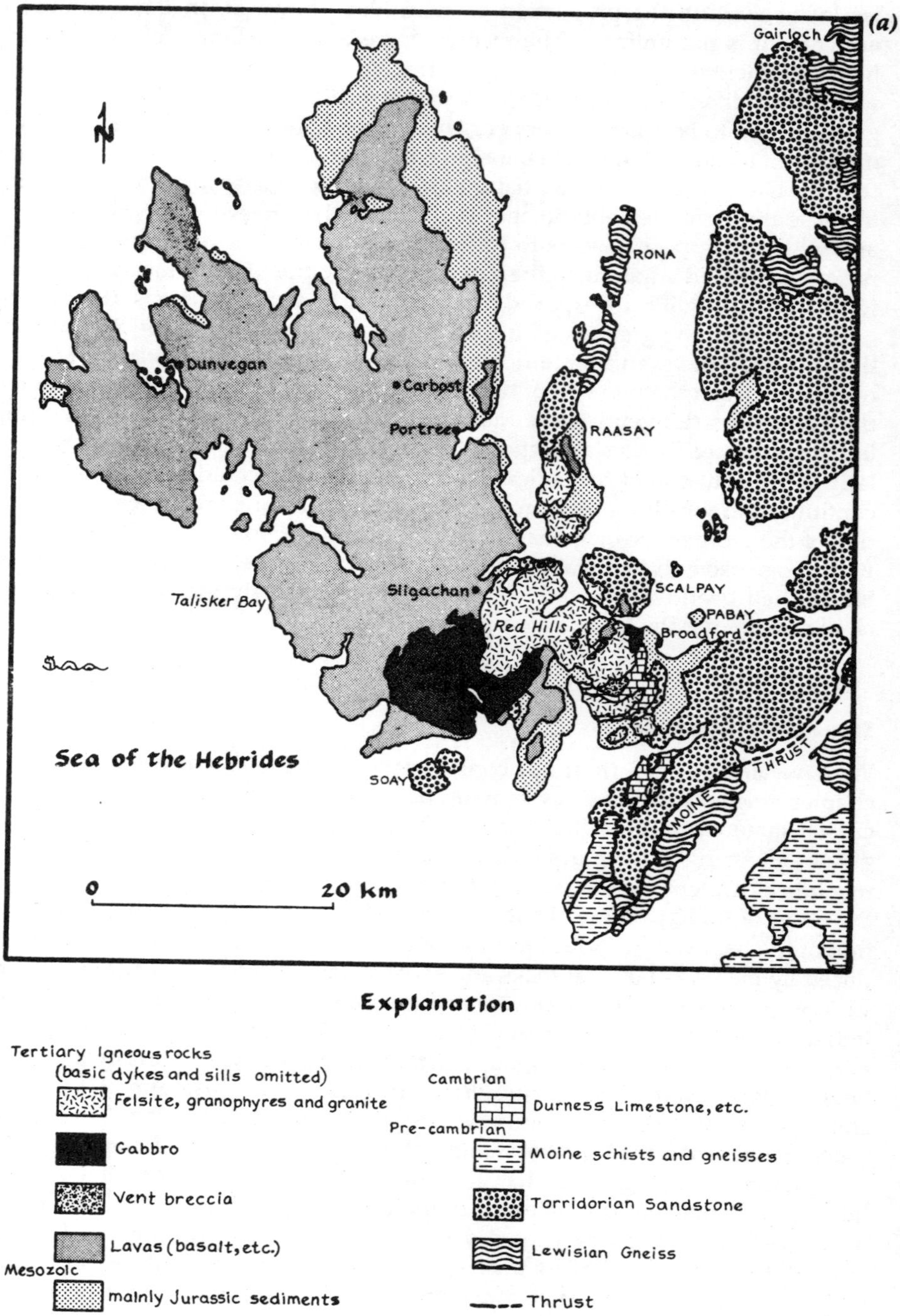

(a)

Gairloch

N

RONA

Dunvegan

Carbost

Portree

RAASAY

Sligachan

Talisker Bay

Red Hills

SCALPAY

PABAY

Broadford

Sea of the Hebrides

SOAY

MOINE THRUST

0 20 km

Explanation

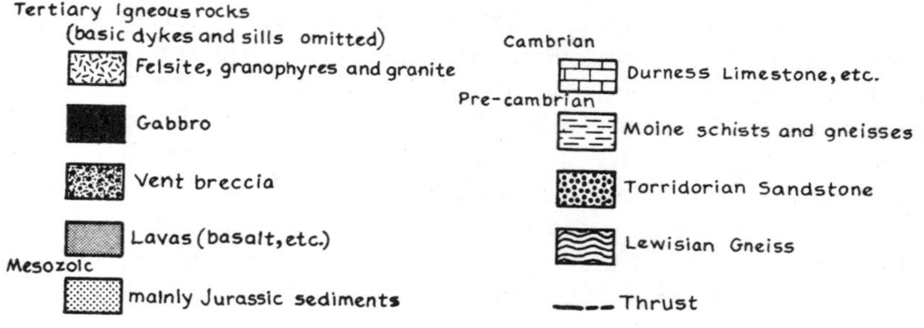

Figure 10–27 (a) Simplified geologic map of the central complex of Skye. Note that the rocks are essentially a bimodal association of basaltic and granitic compositions. (b) A schematic section illustrating subsurface structures inferred from surface exposures and geophysical measurements. Also shown is the pattern of convective circulation of meteoric water after the intrusion had solidified.

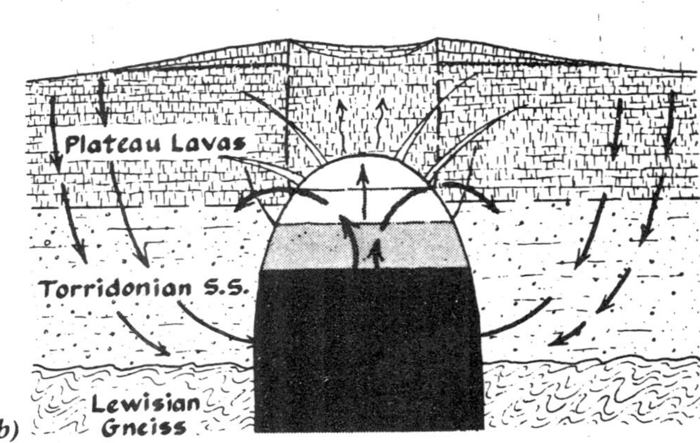

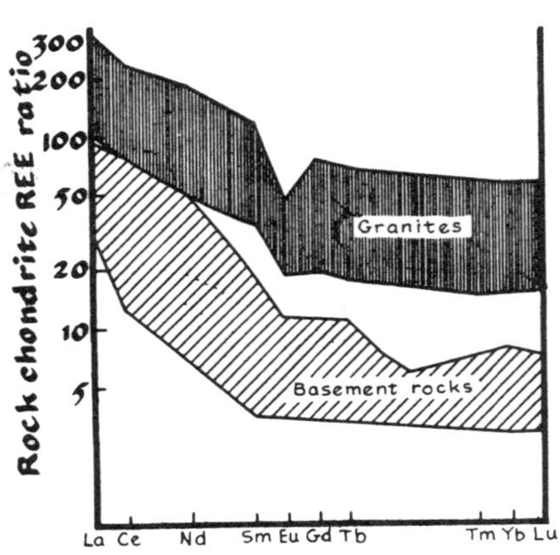

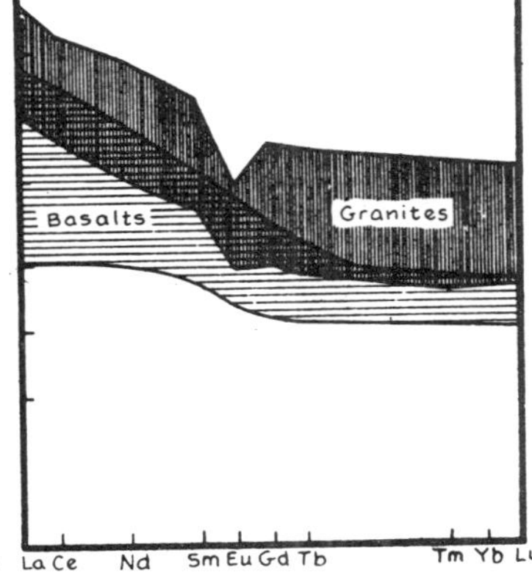

Figure 10–28 REE distribution patterns for granites of Skye (vertical ruling), Lewisian and Torridonian basement rocks (diagonal ruling), and basaltic lavas and dikes (horizontal ruling). (After *Igneous Case Study*, The Open University, 1980.)

Figure 10–29 Histogram of initial $^{87}Sr/^{86}Sr$ ratios for rocks and minerals of Skye. The average ratio of the exposed basement rocks in the same region is 0.720. (Modified from a figure in *Igneous Case Study*, The Open University, 1976.)

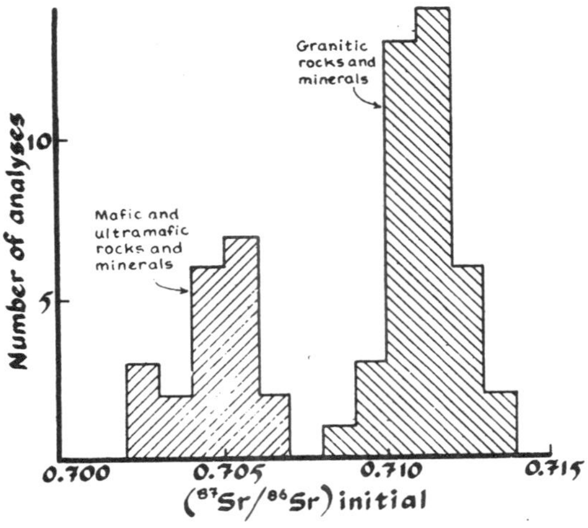

examining where the radiogenic Sr resides in the rocks and how it is partitioned into early melts.

When the individual minerals in ancient metamorphic and plutonic rocks are analyzed separately, they are found to have Sr ratios that differ greatly according to their individual Rb/Sr ratios (Fig. 9–23; Table 10–2). Micas and potassium feldspars, which have proportionately more Rb and less Sr, with time develop proportionately more radiogenic Sr. We saw in an earlier section (Fig. 10–16) that these same minerals are among the first phases to break down or melt with rising temperature. Hence, the first melts produced by rapid melting of a source containing rubidium-rich minerals could have strontium ratios that are more radiogenic than that of the original source rock.

This effect can be seen in the glassy fractions of basement xenoliths in basalts. An example from a late Cenozoic basaltic lava in Arizona contains several percent of black, magnetite-rich glass formed by partial melting when the felsic xenolith was immersed in the basalt. While the Sr ratio of the entire xenolith was found to be only 0.7060, that of the glass was 0.7231. This impressive enrichment, together with the large amount of magnetite in the glass, suggests that the glass was an early liquid produced by breakdown of biotite.

It is doubtful whether such large differences would be preserved during a prolonged period of heating prior to melting of the basement under Skye. More likely, the minerals would re-equilibrate before large amounts of melt could be produced. But, if micas break down early in the heating process, the water-rich solutions released from the rock could carry large concentrations of soluble components, including Sr, into any nearby magma. Because granites and rhyolites have very low absolute abundances of strontium, a small amount of contamination with ^{87}Sr from such a source would cause a marked increase in the ratio of isotopes in the magmas. Other isotopic systems seem to confirm that this is indeed what happened in the case of the Skye granites.

Neodymium Isotopes

It will be recalled that the systematics of the rare-earth elements, samarium (Sm) and neodymium (Nd), resemble in some respects those of rubidium and strontium (Appendix D). ^{143}Nd is produced by alpha decay of ^{147}Sm, just as ^{87}Sr is produced by beta decay of ^{87}Rb. For purposes of comparison, the radiogenic isotope is compared to the non-radiogenic isotope ^{144}Nd, just as ^{87}Sr is to ^{86}Sr. Thus, the ratio ^{143}Nd/^{144}Nd will be greater in rocks derived from sources with large Sm/Nd ratios. Basalts and mantle rocks tend to have relatively large ratios of Sm to Nd; i.e., they are relatively depleted in light REE. Crustal rocks, such as the Lewisian gneiss of Scotland, are quite different; they have relatively small Sm/Nd ratios and are enriched in the light REE. As a consequence, the ^{143}Nd/^{144}Nd ratio of granite derived from felsic continental basement rocks should be relatively small compared to contemporaneous mantle-derived rocks. Conversely, a large ratio would indicate derivation from a mantle source or basalt.

Table 10–2 Rb-Sr data for the individual minerals in a gneiss and granite, both of Paleozoic age. The enrichment of radiogenic Sr is a function of the Rb-Sr ratio and time. If either rock were heated rapidly to temperatures at which the micas begin to break down they could release hydrous fluids with very large isotopic ratios. When melting begins, the $^{87}Sr/^{86}Sr$ ratio of the first liquid would be very large but would decrease with time and more advanced melting and eventually approach that of the parent rock. Note that the biotite in the granite is relatively depleted in Rb and $^{87}Sr/^{86}Sr$ compared to that in the gneiss. Under the microscope, the mineral is seen to have partly broken down, perhaps as a result of mild alteration that affected only that mineral. The radiogenic Sr it lost could have contributed to raising the isotopic ratio of a nearby rock or magma. (After P. Pushkar, A. R. McBirney, and A. M. Kudo, 1972, *Bull. Volc.* 35:265–294.)

	Rb (ppm)	Sr (ppm)	Rb/Sr	$^{87}Sr/^{86}Sr$
Gneiss				
Total Rock	178	68.8	2.59	.7453 ± .0007
Muscovite	347	26.3	13.2	.8012 ± .0012
Biotite	620	12.7	48.8	.8426 ± .0007
Microcline	133	232	.582	.7411 ± .0009
Granite				
Bulk rock	267	82.7	3.23	.7395 ± .0010
Muscovite	960	36.3	26.30	1.1472 ± .0011
Biotite	137	50.9	2.69	.7200 ± .0013
Microcline	660	148	4.46	.7511 ± .0004
Plagioclase and Quartz	52.5	28	1.88	.7270 ± .0007

Note that the Nd isotopic enrichment and depletion relations are the reverse of those for Sr. Rb has a much lower abundance in basalts and other mafic rocks than it does in crustal rocks; Sr is only moderately lower. Crust with large Rb/Sr ratios will thus have greater $^{87}Sr/^{86}Sr$ ratios, while those of the mantle and basalts derived from it will be less. Hence, the ratio $^{87}Sr/^{86}Sr$ should vary inversely with $^{143}Nd/^{144}Nd$ in contemporary magma sources, even though both ratios increase with time. When the ratios of Nd are plotted against those of Sr (Fig. 10–30), most suites of related rocks define lines with negative slopes. This is why mantle-derived volcanic rocks of the oceans fall on the "mantle array" seen in chapter eight (Fig. 8–12). Oceanic rocks have a relatively small amount of variation along this line because they differ little in their Rb/Sr and Sm/Nd ratios, but a much wider range is found in crustal rocks, such as those forming the metamorphic basement under western Scotland.

The $^{143}Nd/^{144}Nd$ ratios of the granites of Skye are about 0.5115 and fall between those of the Lewisian gneiss (about 0.5110) and young basalts (about 0.5125). When these values are plotted against the ratios of Sr isotopes in the same rocks, they fall in distinct fields. Note that the spread of values for the granites is consistent with mixing of the basalt with Lewisian basement rocks having relatively large $^{87}Sr/^{86}Sr$ ratios. The proportions contributed by the basement, calculated by a simple mass balance, are indicated by the numbers along the mixing curve. Note that between 30 and 60 percent of the Nd and Sr in the granite appears to be from the basement rock.

This conclusion based on the radiogenic isotopes seems to conflict with the deduction, drawn from the rare-earth elements alone, that the granites have little if any crustal component. The apparent anomaly might be explained by postulating fractionation of a mineral relatively rich in the light REE. Although none of the common minerals of granites have the appropriate patterns to do this, certain REE-rich accessory minerals, such as sphene, apatite, and allanite, could effect these changes, provided they were fractionated in large enough amounts. Another more plausible possibility is the one suggested by the strontium, namely that the isotopic ratios of the granites do not result from melting or wholesale assimilation of crust but from contamination by fluids released by breakdown of hydrous minerals in the basement wall rocks.

Lead Isotopes

The isotopes of lead afford yet another way of detecting crustal contamination, but they can yield much more information than either strontium or neodymium. The isotopes of most use are those produced by radioactive decay of uranium (Appendix D). Like rubidium, uranium and lead are strongly concentrated in the continental crust. The two important isotopes, ^{235}U and ^{238}U, decay with long half-lives to ^{207}Pb and ^{206}Pb respectively. Just as the isotope ^{86}Sr is used as a reference for the abundance of radiogenic ^{87}Sr, ^{204}Pb, a non-radiogenic isotope of lead, is used as a reference for radiogenic ^{207}Pb and ^{206}Pb.

Because ^{207}Pb and ^{206}Pb are produced at different rates, and the rates change

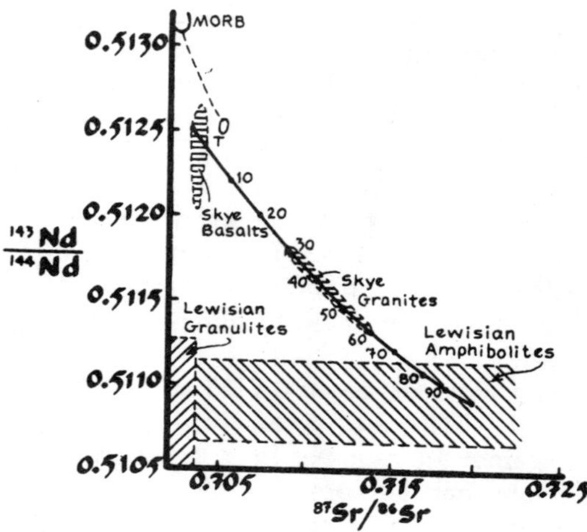

Figure 10–30 Relations between the isotopic ratios of Nd and Sr for rocks of Skye. Also shown is a typical trend for basalts of mid-ocean ridges (MORB) and other oceanic rocks (T). (After a compilation by R. S. Thorpe and P. W. Francis, 1979, *Origins of Granitic Batholiths: Geochemical Evidence*, M. P. Atherton and J. Tarney, eds., Shiva Publ. Co., 65–75.)

with time, a curved line will result when their ratios to ^{204}Pb are plotted against each other, as they are in the growth curve shown in Figure 10–31a. Note that the ratio $^{207}Pb/^{204}Pb$ increases at a diminishing rate compared to $^{206}Pb/^{204}Pb$. This change reflects the different half-lives and initial abundances of the uranium isotopes from which the leads evolve. Such a growth curve will have the same form for all lead produced from a source having the same ratio of the parental uranium isotopes, ^{235}U and ^{238}U. When the lead ratios of rocks of mantle origin are corrected for age and plotted against one another, they fall close to a curve of this form. Igneous rocks of different provinces have slightly different growth curves, indicating that mantle sources are not entirely homogeneous.

These relations can be used in a number of ways. First, one can measure the ages of certain types of igneous rocks by simply determining where their lead ratios fall on the growth curve. Second, they can be used to determine whether the lead in a given rock or mineral has come direcly from depleted mantle or has

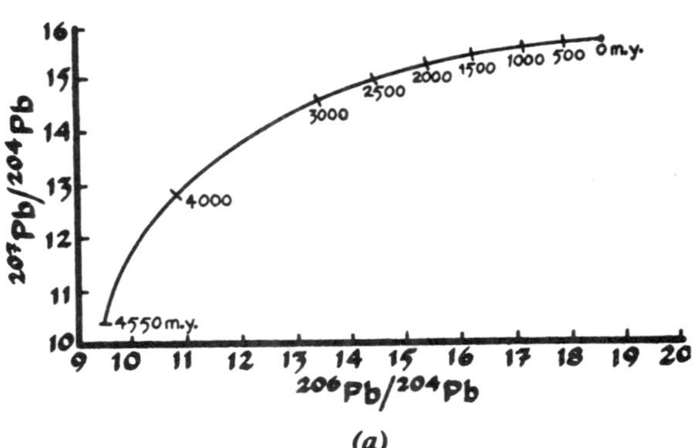

(a)

Figure 10–31 (a) Growth curve for lead isotopic ratios in mantle-derived igneous rocks. Numbers indicate ages in millions of years. The leads from basalts differ slightly from one province to another but have growth curves of this same form. (b) An enlarged section of the growth curve in (a) showing the principal rocks of Skye. (After *Igneous Case Study*, The Open University, 1976.)

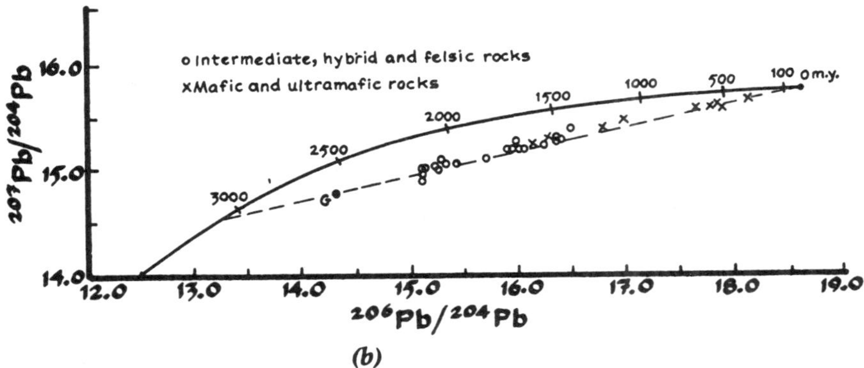

(b)

evolved in the upper crust or lithosphere. Once separated from the mantle, the proportions of uranium and lead in a rock produced by partial melting and other processes, including weathering, erosion, and mixture with other rocks, may differ from those responsible for the normal growth curve. Hence, the lead in such a rock will evolve in different ways and will not fall on the same curve as rocks derived directly from the mantle.

If an ancient crustal rock with a composition displaced from the growth curve is incorporated into a younger magma, the lead of the contaminated magma is no longer like that of the mantle. Its composition is the result of mixing two leads, one from the mantle and another from the contaminant. Figure 10-31b illustrates the measured ratios for a variety of Tertiary igneous rocks from Skye. Note that they fall on a remarkably linear cord, one end of which intersects the growth curve at a point corresponding to the time of igneous activity 53 million years ago. The average composition of the metamorphic Lewisian complex also falls on this line at point G. (The position of this point on the concave side of the growth curve is thought to result from deep-seated crustal processes that removed large amounts of the lithophile elements, including U, about 3,000 million years ago.)

Skye granites have lead with compositions closer to that of the average Lewisian gneiss than do intermediate and mafic rocks. Thus the spread of compositions is consistent with differing contributions of lead from the metamorphic complex to lead derived from the mantle at the time the magmas rose through the crust.

Note that mafic and even ultramafic rocks have also been contaminated with lead from a U-depleted source, even though they show no other evidence of assimilation. Because their lead contents are very small, the amount of lead required to change the ratios in these rocks is also small. The granites, however, have much greater absolute concentrations of lead, and to attain their present ratios they would have to gain proportionately greater amounts from the metamorphic crustal rocks.

Oxygen Isotopes

In weighing data such as these, it is important to bear in mind that the rocks we map and sample in the field have had complex histories, and the magmatic processes ending with crystallization were not necessarily the last chapter of their life story. Interpretations of isotopic relations of the granites of Skye illustrate this lesson very well.

Shortly after the results obtained from lead and strontium had been presented and petrologists had accepted the conclusion that crustal rocks had played an important role in the genesis of the granites of Skye, another study was initiated to determine the effects of hydrothermal alteration on the isotopic character of oxygen in the same rocks. We have already noted in chapter six that circulation of meteoric water through shallow intrusions has the effect of exchanging oxygen and that this results in a lowering of the ratio of ^{18}O to ^{16}O. This same effect was found in the rocks of Skye (Fig. 10–32). Large quantities of hot, meteoric water must have moved through the rocks. Hydrothermal waters are known to carry as much as 100 ppm Pb and 750 ppm Sr scavenged from the rocks through which the water flows. Hence, if oxygen, the most abundant element in the rocks, is exchanged with hydrothermal solutions, why not lead and strontium as well? Only minute amounts would have to be selectively dissolved from the metamorphic and sedimentary basement and deposited in the igneous rocks to produce the observed isotopic compositions.

If hydrothermal solutions had contributed lead to the rocks we would expect the effect on the Pb ratios to be greatest in rocks with the smallest initial lead contents, namely rocks of mafic composition and with the smallest oxygen ratios. The fact that no such correlation is seen suggests that the amount of contamination with hydrothermal lead has not been great. Nevertheless, the problem of subsolidus alteration is one that should always be kept in mind, especially in dealing with large intrusions that have cooled in or near a zone of hydrothermal circulation.

GRANITES AND CRUSTAL EVOLUTION

The conclusion we are left with after this examination of the rocks of Skye is that granites were not produced by partial melting of the metamorphic basement but of some deeper level. The magmas interacted to differing degrees with the continental crust through which they rose, but they acquired their essential character from more basic, less radiogenic rocks.

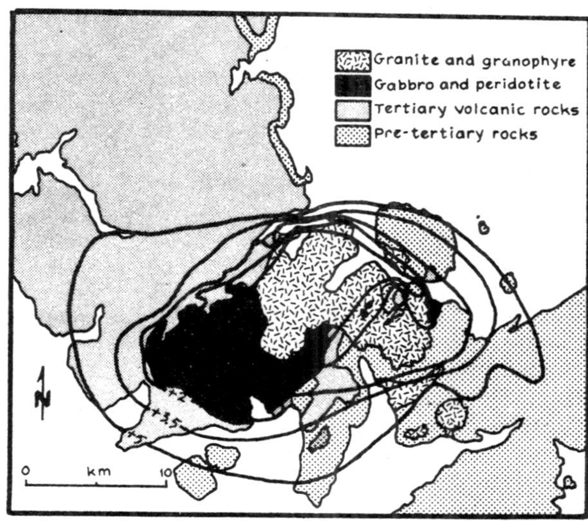

Figure 10–32 Zoning of oxygen isotopic ratios resulting from circulation of meteoric water in a hydrothermal system that continued long after the main bodies of magma had solidified. (After R. W. Forester and H. P. Taylor, Jr., 1977, *Amer. Jour. Sci.* 277:136–177.)

It was long assumed that voluminous felsic magmas could only be produced by melting of crustal rocks of similar composition. While many are indeed directly traceable to crustal sources, others clearly are not. Although all are rich in silica and other lithophile components, many have isotopic ratios that are not notably radiogenic, and minor amounts of contamination could account for any small excess over the ratios of mantle-derived basalts.

One might well ask why, if siliceous magmas are not necessarily products of anatectic melting of continental sediments, are they confined to continental settings? The answer, of course, is that they are not. The voluminous rhyolites of Iceland, though unique, are highly instructive, for they demonstrate that such magmas can be produced in the absence of continental crust provided certain special conditions prevail.

The amount of rhyolite that can be derived directly from a mantle peridotite is, of course, trivial. We have seen, however, that rhyolitic liquids can be produced in substantial volumes by melting of basalts at elevated water pressures. Thus, an appropriate lithosphere, namely one of amphibolitic character, could be a suitable source rock, whether the overlying crust is oceanic or continental. We noted in the opening chapter that the long-term compositional stability of the continents could not be maintained unless the contribution of mantle-derived basic magmas were balanced by comparable additions of more felsic material. Though the process is indirect and much slower than it was during the early history of the earth, the mantle continues to contribute felsic material to the continents.

Before considering these relations on a global scale, we should examine one final group of igneous rocks, the highly alkaline and related series that are the topic of the chapter that follows.

SELECTED REFERENCES

Atherton, M. P., and J. Tarney, eds. 1979. *Origins of Granite Batholiths: Geochemical Evidence*. Shiva Publ. Co., 148 pp. A collection of papers dealing with geochemical studies of granitic rocks with strong emphasis on isotopes and rare-earth elements.

Brown, P. E., ed. 1988. *The Origin of Granites*, Trans. Roy. Soc. Edinburgh. 79: pts 2 & 3. Proceedings of a symposium on siliceous plutonic and volcanic magmas. Includes several excellent summaries of recent work.

Chapin, C. E., and W. E. Elston, eds. 1979. *Ash-Flow Tuffs*. Geol. Soc. Amer. Spec. Paper 180, 211 pp. A compilation of papers dealing with many aspects of siliceous ignimbrites. The papers have an unusually good balance of geological and geochemical topics.

Pitcher, W. S., and A. R. Berger. 1972. *The Geology of Donegal: A Study of Granite Emplacement and Unroofing*. Wiley Interscience, 435 pp. A summary of detailed studies of a series of plutons illustrating a wide range of structural and mineralogical relations ranging from ultrametamorphism to a high-level ring complex. The work in Donegal had a great influence on many basic concepts of granitic magmatism.

The Open University. 1976. *Igneous Case Study, The Tertiary Igneous Rocks of Skye, NW Scotland*. Open Univ. Press, 88 pp. A very thorough and lucidly presented survey of the evolution of igneous rocks of one of the Tertiary igneous centers of western Scotland. Contains illustrative problems suitable for independent study by students with two or three years of geology.

Tuttle, O. F., and N. L. Bowen. 1958. *Origin of Granite in the Light of Experimental Studies in the System* $NaAlSi^3O^8$*-*$KAlSi^3O^8$*-*SiO^2*-*H^2O. Geol. Soc. Amer. Memoir 74, 153 pp. An early account of experimental work on the simple "Granite System" and how it pertains to plutonic rocks. This classic work marked a turning point in interpretations of granitic rocks.

11

ALKALINE ROCKS OF CONTINENTAL INTERIORS

THE PREVIOUS CHAPTER dealt with a wide range of silica-saturated continental rocks, mainly in orogenic settings. We turn now to a more diverse group of continental rocks, mostly of alkaline compositions, that occur in the interior regions of continents, far from the orogenic belts of convergent plate boundaries. Although some are associated with continental rifting, many of these rocks have no distinctive tectonic environment. Indeed, if they have anything in common, it is their tendency to appear in widely differing settings that seem to have little relationship to their unusual compositions.

For this reason, it is easier to group these rocks according to their compositions than their geologic relations. The main types are best distinguished by their relative concentrations of three components, Na, K, and Ca, and each of these groups may be relatively poor in SiO_2, Al_2O_3, or both.

Unlike oceanic suites in which sodium is the dominant alkali and Na_2O/K_2O is rarely less than 2.0, continental suites have a much greater range of alkali ratios, and either sodium or potassium may be more abundant. Moreover, some of these rocks, especially sodic types, contain abnormally large amounts of calcium. In some of the latter, this element is in calcite; in others it appears as one of a group of calcium-alumina silicates, such as melilite or the calcium-bearing olivine, monticellite.

Each of these Na-, K-, or Ca-rich types may be deficient in SiO_2, in which case they are *alkaline* in the sense that their composition is "critically undersaturated" with silica and yields Ne in the norm. Or they may be deficient in Al_2O_3, in which case they are *peralkaline* in the sense that alkalies are exceptionally enriched with respect to Al_2O_3 but not necessarily SiO_2. That is, they have a molecular excess of $Na_2O + K_2O$ over Al_2O_3, so that the alumina content is insufficient to accommodate all the alkalies in normative feldspars.

Taken as a whole, the rocks span an especially wide range between felsic and ultramafic end-members, but individual groups may have a very limited range of differentiation. One group, the *lamprophyres*, includes a great variety of very mafic alkaline compositions that fit no scheme of differentiation or genetic lineage. Some are associated with calc-alkaline plutonic rocks, others with alkaline and peralkaline series, and still others have no clear petrologic or tectonic association of any kind.

It must be emphasized that the various divisions of these rocks are gradational one into the other, and any classification, either compositional or genetic, is simply an artificial device to aid in recognizing certain common associations. The limitations of these classifications will become evident as we consider each of the various groups in turn.

ALKALINE AND PERALKALINE SERIES

Alkali-silica relations

Many continental alkaline series share certain of the distinguishing marks of their oceanic counterparts. Some resemble the familiar Hawaiian alkaline series of alkali olivine basalt-hawaiite-mugearite-benmoreite-trachyte in that they straddle the division between hypersthene-normative and nepheline-normative compositions. In the more alkaline series, basanites have differentiated through feldspathoidal intermediate rocks to phonolites not unlike the Tahitian rocks. But continental suites tend to include rocks of more extreme compositions, such as *nephelinites* and *leucitites*, with very abundant Na or K feldspathoids but little or no feldspar. And unlike most oceanic suites, continental alkaline rocks form a wider spectrum between end-members that are highly enriched in either sodium or potassium.

Thus, one can think of a continuum including sodic rocks of various degrees of alkalinity or peralkalinity at one end and a corresponding potassic series at the other. Between these two extremes is a large intermediate group in which roughly equal proportions of the alkalies are reflected in two separate feldspars, one plagioclase and the other anorthoclase, sanidine, or orthoclase. These two-feldspar rocks, loosely referred to as *trachytic*, include rocks that have been called *trachybasalts*, *latites* (or *trachyandesites*), *tristanites*, and *trachytes*. (Note that the use of the term trachyte in this sense implies nothing about the degree of silica saturation, as it does when used to refer to differentiated rocks with less than about 10 percent normative Q and no normative Ne.) Some varieties contain small amounts of modal leucite.

Alkali ratios tend to vary widely with differentiation, even in a single series (Fig. 11-1). A common tendency is for series initially rich in either sodium or potassium to converge with differentiation on felsic end-members with more nearly equal amounts of the two alkalies, as would be expected if the liquids were descending toward a eutectic-like end-member. Looking again at "petrogeny's residua system" (Figs. 11-2 and 11-3) and noting especially the range extending from the granitic rocks of the preceding chapter into that of more silica-poor compositions considered here, we find that the felsic differentiates of alkaline magmas fall in a thermal valley crossing the central part of the diagram. Ignoring for the moment the field of leucite, consider only the region of the thermal trough. Note that syenites and trachytes occupy an area near the feldspar join where compositions have little or no normative quartz or feldspathoid. Silica-deficient nepheline syenites and phonolites have compositions below this join close to a minimum on the cotectic boundary between the feldspars and felspathoids.

The course of a differentiating liquid that crystallizes alkali feldspars along

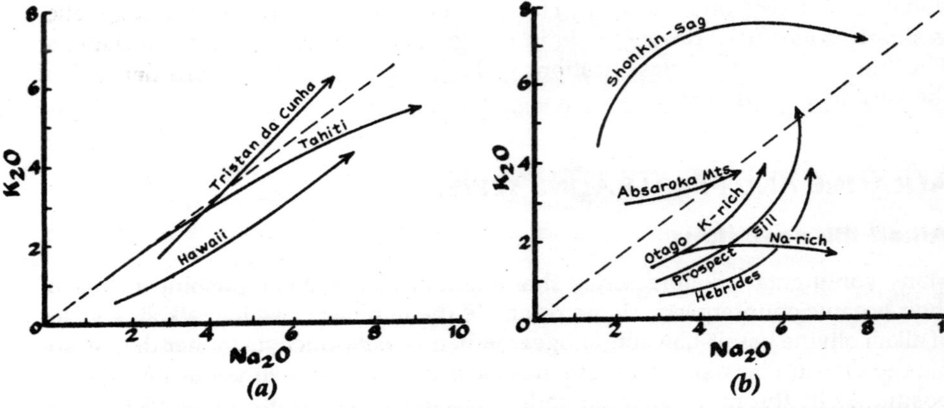

Figure 11–1 Variations of alkali ratios in some typical oceanic (a) and continental (b) alkaline series. (Hawaiian curve after H. S. Yoder, Jr. and F. Chayes, 1982, *Carnegie Inst. Washington Yrbk.* 81:309–314.)

the Ab-Or join should diverge from that line and descend along curved paths away from feldspar and toward one side or the other of a thermal trough. Depending on which side of the saddle it starts on, it should continue to either of two temperature minima. The nature of this divide is shown more clearly by a section down the axis of the thermal trough (Fig. 11–3). Any liquid with an initial composition on the silica-saturated side of the divide should become richer in SiO_2 and evolve toward a granitic composition; liquids even slightly undersaturated should descend toward the low-SiO_2 minimum. In nature, however, many series straddle this divide and stubbornly refuse to descend to either of the two minima.

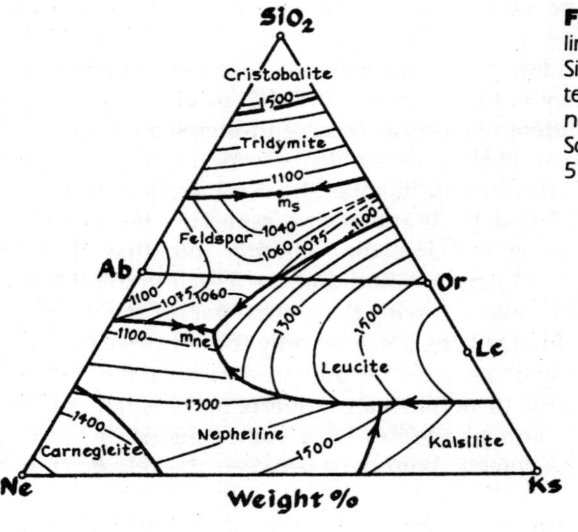

Figure 11–2 The system nepheline-kalsilite-silica ($NaAlSiO_4$-$KAlSiO_4$-SiO_2). Carnegieite is the high-temperature form of nepheline; it is not found in nature. (After J. F. Schairer, 1950, *Jour. Geol.* 58:512–517.)

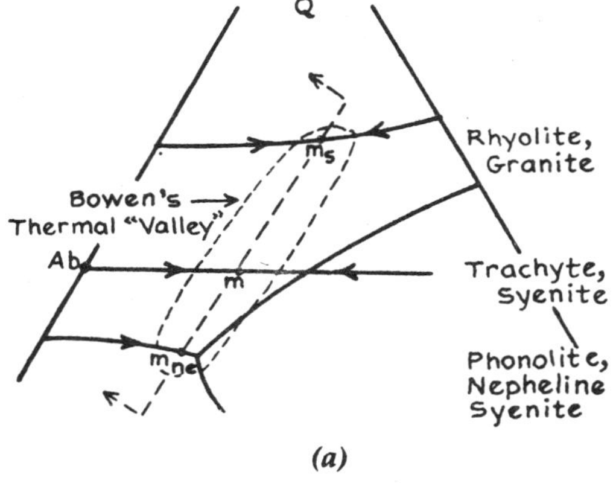

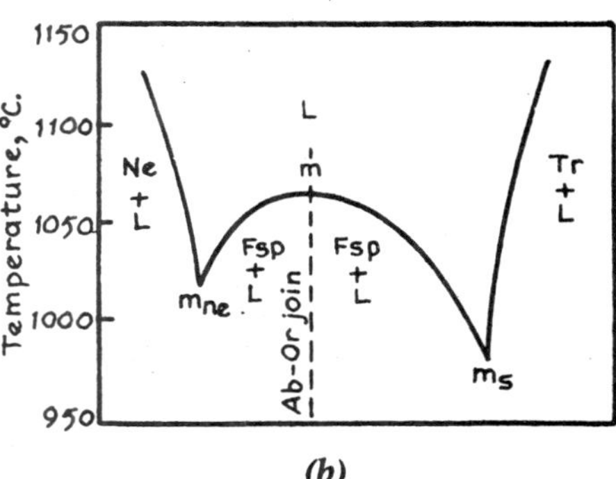

Figure 11–3 (a) The thermal valley defined by the minima in the system Ne-Ks-SiO_2 in Figure 11–2. The section shown in (b) passes through the compositions of felsic differentiates of alkaline, transitional, and sub-alkaline series. These fall in the lower, middle, and upper parts of the valley shown in (a) and on the left, middle, and right of the section in (b).

Alkali-alumina relations

The peralkalinity that is so characteristic of many continental series results from a relation between alkalies and alumina that is in some ways similar to that between alkalies and silica. Depending on how the amount of alumina is related to that required for the feldspars or feldspathoids, a rock is said to be *peraluminous*, *metaluminous*, or *peralkaline*.

In *peraluminous* rocks, molecular $Al_2O_3 > Na_2O + K_2O + CaO$. This excess is expressed in the norm as corundum, Al_2O_3, and in the rocks by minerals such as mica or garnet. In *metaluminous* rocks, molecular $Na_2O + K_2O + CaO > Al_2O_3 > Na_2O + K_2O$, and the norm has both anorthite and diopside. This group includes most of the common sub-alkaline magmas as well as the great majority of oceanic alkaline rocks. In *peralkaline* rocks, molecular $Na_2O + K_2O > Al_2O_3$ and, as a result, part of the Na_2O is assigned to normative acmite (Ac – $NaFeSi_2O_6$) and, in rocks very rich in Na or K, to sodium or potassium metasilicate (Ns – Na_2SiO_3 and Ks – K_2SiO_3 respectively). In natural assemblages, the excess alkalies enter pyroxene, amphibole, and other minerals in which iron and titanium take the place of aluminum.

Note that these relations do not necessarily entail a deficiency of silica; peraluminous, metaluminous, or peralkaline rocks may be saturated or undersaturated with silica and may have normative Ne, Hy, or Q. Q-normative felsic peralkaline rocks are sometimes referred to as *comendites* or *pantellerites*, but the use of these names to characterize such a rock series can be somewhat misleading. Defined originally on the basis of petrographic characteristics, the names have been applied so loosely to rocks of various chemical compositions that modern usage has tended to avoid them in favor of the more general term, peralkaline rhyolite.

Differences in the amount of alumina are closely reflected by the proportions of feldspars and mafic minerals in modal assemblages. Note that anorthite, $CaAl_2Si_2O_8$, contains twice as much aluminum as the alkali feldspars, (Na,K)$AlSi_3O_8$. Because all liquids crystallize feldspar that is relatively richer in anorthite, and hence Al, than their coexisting liquid, it follows that at the same time the liquid is enriched in Na and Si it is also impoverished in both Al and Ca. Hence, crystallization of plagioclase should cause derivative liquids to become relatively depleted in Al and hence potentially peralkaline. This is true, of course, only if feldspar is the dominant crystallizing mineral. If a ferromagnesian mineral, such as augite, that contains Ca but little Al crystallizes in abundance, its removal may offset this "plagioclase effect" and impede depletion of Al as was pointed out in Figure 5–15. Thus, whether a given magma follows a peralkaline trend or not depends chiefly on the proportions of feldspar and ferromagnesian minerals in the fractionating assemblage.

ALKALINE AND PERALKALINE SERIES OF CONTINENTAL RIFTS

A few examples of alkaline and peralkaline rocks of widely differing ages will serve to illustrate the salient features of these magmas in continental extensional environments. Starting with the presently active East African Rift and then turning to the progressively older Oslo Graben and Gardar Province of Greenland, the characteristics these rocks share can be traced through almost the entire span of post-Archean time.

East Africa

The largest and perhaps the most varied province of Cenozoic continental volcanism is the one extending from the Red Sea and Afar Depression through Ethiopia and the rift valleys of East Africa as far as southwestern Tanzania (Fig. 11–4). Another zone of Jurassic and Cretaceous magmatism, also associated with rifting, extends farther south into Mozambique and Zambia.

The most active part of this region today is that of the Afar Depression in Ethiopia where floods of alkaline basalt issue from fissures along an active rift extending southward from a junction with the Red Sea. Starting in Eocene time and continuing with few interruptions down to the present, floods of magma covered what are now the broad slopes of the Ethiopian Plateau. Most of the activity prior to the main period of uplift took the form of fissure eruptions of both basalt and siliceous ignimbrites but changed during the late Miocene and Pliocene to shield-building eruptions of basalt and closely associated rhyolite and phonolite. In the Plio-Pleistocene, explosive eruptions of siliceous magma were confined mainly to the axis of the rift, while basalts poured out on the adjacent plateau. The current activity in the rift produces both basalt and rhyolite, with the latter accounting for an unusually large proportion, perhaps as much as 25 percent of the volume of eruptive rocks. Representative compositions are given in Table 11–1.

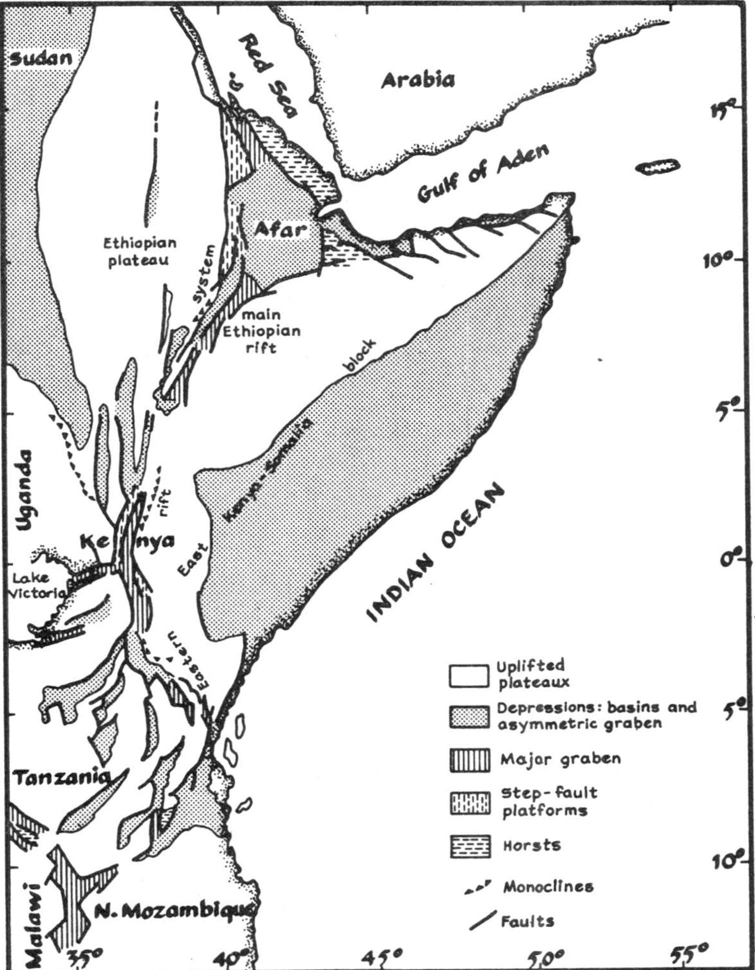

Figure 11–4 General map of the East African Rift zone.

This activity in the northern part of the system differs from that farther south in Kenya and Tanzania, where the Tertiary activity produced much less basalt but relatively greater proportions of differentiated magmas, including very fluid sheets of flood trachytes and phonolites that spread from vents on the floor and margins of the rift. In the eastern or Gregory Rift, the rocks tend to be sodic, whereas volcanoes along the western branch have produced some of the most potassic lavas known. Of the total of 220,000 cubic kilometers of Cenozoic volcanic rocks in the region of the Kenya Rift, about half is phonolite, trachyte, and rhyolite, and many of the central volcanoes consist almost exclusively of these highly differentiated rocks. Basalts are rare throughout the late Cenozoic series, especially in the central part of the rift.

Table 11-1 Chemical compositions of some characteristic rocks of a peralkaline series from the Afar Rift, Ethiopia. (From F. Barberi et al., 1975, *Jour. Petr.* 16:22–56.)

	1.	2.	3.	4.	5.	6.	7.
SiO_2	48.36	47.00	56.81	59.44	65.02	69.91	72.11
TiO_2	1.92	3.10	1.76	1.82	0.36	0.43	0.38
Al_2O_3	15.34	13.26	13.88	15.00	14.88	13.14	9.35
Fe_2O_3	2.42	7.82	0.70	2.02	1.75	2.83	2.30
FeO	7.75	8.22	9.37	5.45	3.48	1.53	3.80
MnO	0.17	0.19	0.29	0.21	0.13	0.14	0.21
MgO	7.83	4.84	2.13	1.76	0.04	0.01	<0.01
CaO	12.04	8.62	5.04	4.00	1.34	0.71	0.34
Na_2O	2.42	3.70	5.00	4.97	5.90	5.95	5.74
K_2O	0.63	1.55	2.15	3.27	4.30	4.52	4.40
P_2O_5	0.32	0.59	0.72	0.48	0.04	0.01	0.02
Trace Elements (ppm)							
Ni	33	10	6	9	2	2	8
Cr	291	18	6	49	56	—	77
Ba	—	541	408	715	736	652	<10
Rb	13	33	49	79	106	111	147
Sr	343	462	360	323	60	24	3
La	19.9	48.7	60.0	80.8	111.5	—	159.5
Sm	—	10.6	16.6	13.8	17.4	—	27.0
Lu	0.3	0.4	1.0	0.9	1.4	—	2.0
Molecular Norms							
Ap	0.68	1.28	1.55	1.02	0.09	0.02	0.04
Il	2.71	4.48	2.53	2.59	0.51	0.60	0.54
Mt	2.56	8.49	0.75	2.15	1.87	0.44	—
Or	3.77	9.51	13.10	19.70	25.97	26.86	26.57
Ab	21.99	34.50	46.29	45.51	54.15	45.28	25.59
An	29.49	15.57	9.36	9.14	1.45	—	—
Di	23.08	19.86	9.25	6.32	4.06	2.78	1.27
Hy	7.81	3.22	13.84	6.72	2.04	0.35	5.18
Ol	7.90	3.09	—	—	—	—	—
Q	—	—	3.33	6.84	9.86	16.90	28.58
Ac	—	—	—	—	—	6.77	6.55
Ns	—	—	—	—	—	—	5.67

1. Olivine basalt 2. Ferro-basalt 3. Dark trachyte 4. Oversaturated trachyte 5. Alkali rhyolite 6. Pantellerite or peralkaline rhyolite 7. Comendite or peralkaline rhyolite

Although most of the differentiated rocks are peralkaline, the great variety of lavas, ignimbrites, and tephra have a range of compositions rarely found in such close association (Fig. 11-5). Individual Quaternary volcanoes along the axis of the Gregory Rift of Kenya and Tanzania are composed almost entirely of phonolite (e.g., Suswa), trachyte (Menengai), or peralkaline rhyolite (near Lake Naivasha). Still others, such as Kilimar.jaro, Mt. Kenya, and the large Pliocene center of Mt. Olokisalie in south-central Kenya, have produced a variety of series

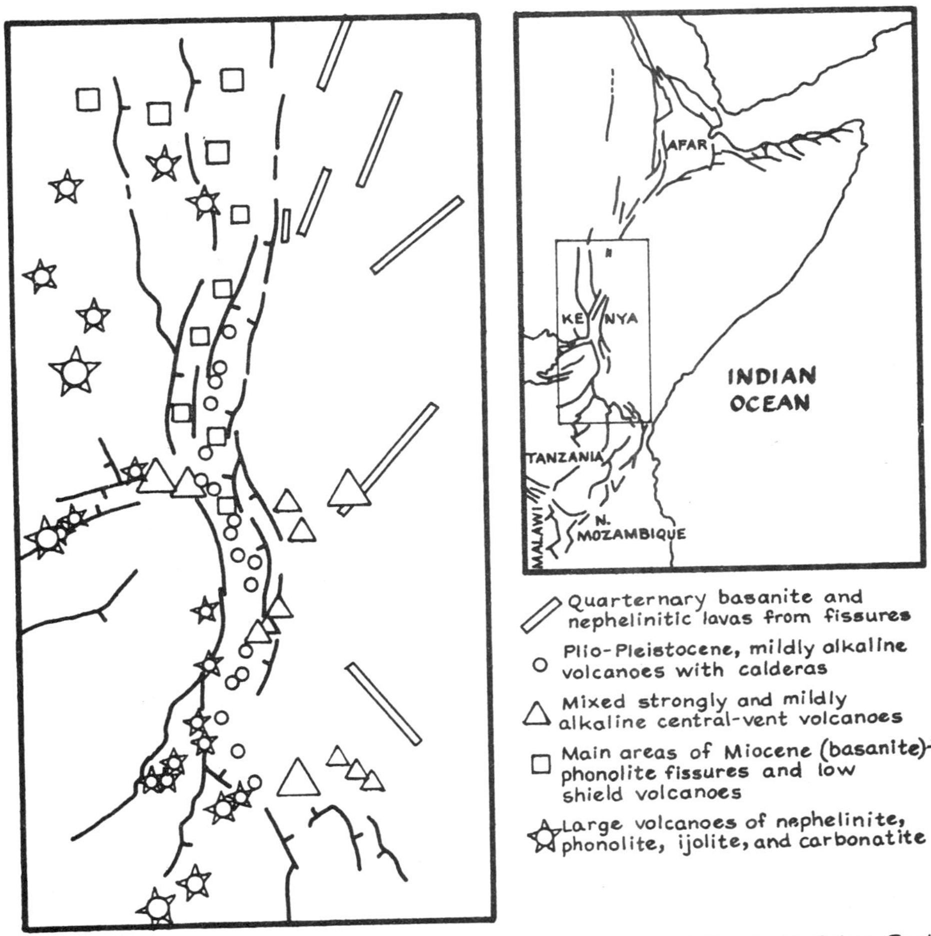

Figure 11–5 Map of the Western Rift of Kenya showing the distribution of different types of volcanoes with respect to major structural features. (After B. H. Baker, *Geol. Soc. Amer. Spec. Paper 136* and unpublished work.)

mixed in seemingly random fashion throughout the eruptive sequence. The rocks of Mt. Olokasalie form at least three distinct trends with differing degrees of silica saturation, one hypersthene-normative, one mildly alkaline (with a few percent normative Ne), and a third that is much more strongly undersaturated in silica and includes rocks with more than 7 percent normative nepheline.

The petrologic identity of each of these series is well-defined by the different trends of their large-ion lithophile elements (LILE) with differentiation (Fig. 11-6). Silica, which is such a useful measure of differentiation in most other types of rocks, can be misleading in the highly alkaline series, for it may increase non-linearly or even reverse its trend and decline in the latest stages of differenti-

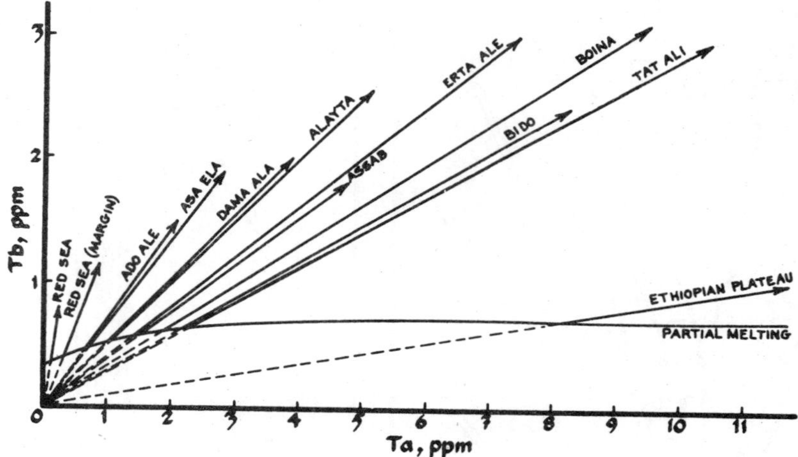

Figure 11–6 Variations of the excluded elements. Tb and Ta, in volcanic rocks of the Red Sea, Afar Depression, and Ethiopian Plateau. Rocks erupted from each volcanic center show linear correlations between the two elements, as would be expected for fractional crystallization of magmas having the Tb/Ta ratios along a curve defined by differing degrees of partial melting of a source that is common for the entire region. Compare with Figure 5–23. (After G. Ferrara and M. Treuil, 1974, *Bull. Volc.* 38:548–574.)

ation. The incompatible elements, which are so plentiful in these rocks, provide much better indices of differentiation.

The parental magmas of each individual series can be explained as products of differing degrees of partial melting, whereas their differentiated series evolve along separate trends governed by crystal fractionation (Fig. 11–7). But the huge volumes of phonolitic and trachytic magma and paucity of basalts seem to demand a special mechanism of differentiation. We shall return to consider this problem in a later section.

The Oslo Graben

A close plutonic counterpart to the East African volcanic series can be seen in the Oslo Graben of southern Norway (Fig. 11–8). Although volcanic rocks are still preserved in a number of thick sections of felsic ignimbrites, the roots from which they were erupted are also visible in a cluster of calderas and subvolcanic intrusions.

The volcanic series consists of an early group of basaltic lavas, apparently the products of fissure eruptions, followed by large volumes of differentiated lavas and ignimbrites. The lavas were given the local name *rhomb porphyries* because of their prominent feldspar phenocrysts, but are more generally classified as trachyandesites and latites. Their moderately high potassium content, which in some of the more felsic rocks exceeds sodium, is responsible for the prominence of the alkali feldspar that is so characteristic of these rocks. A few rhyolitic lavas

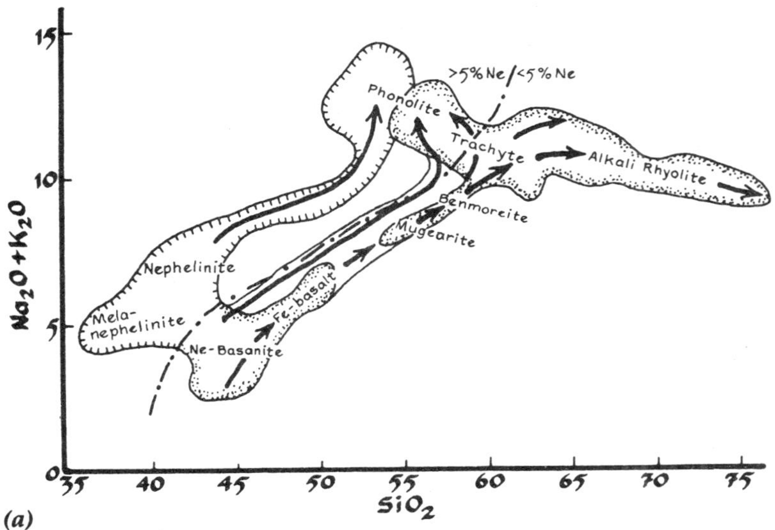

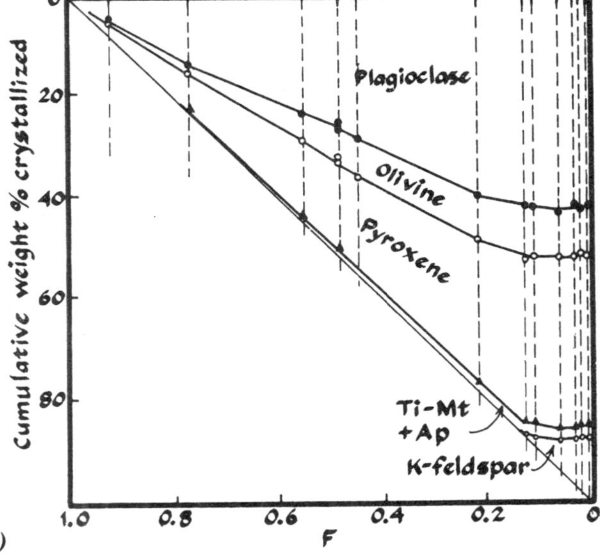

Figure 11–7 Variations of alkalies and silica in the major volcanic series of the Kenya Rift system of Figure 11–5. The heavy dashed line with dots separates rocks with greater than and less than 5 percent normative nepheline. (After B. H. Baker, 1987, *Alkaline Igneous Rocks*, Geol. Soc. Spec. Publ. No. 30, 293–312.) (b) Cumulative weight percentages of minerals fractionated from a parental basaltic magma to produce the various differentiated rocks of the basalt-benmoreite-trachyte series in (a). F is the fraction of liquid represented by individual rocks. Calculations are based on the method illustrated in Table 7–4. (After B. H. Baker *et al.*, 1977, *Contr. Mineral. Petr.* 64:303–332.)

are found in the upper parts of the section, but like basalts they are very subordinate in volume to intermediate rocks.

The intrusive rocks have been divided into two groups, one making up a series of subvolcanic gabbroic and dioritic sills and pipes that must have fed many of the lavas erupted early in the history of the region, and the other a cluster of plutonic stocks and ring dikes of syenitic and granitic compositions. Various forms of potassium-rich feldspar appear in all but the most basic compo-

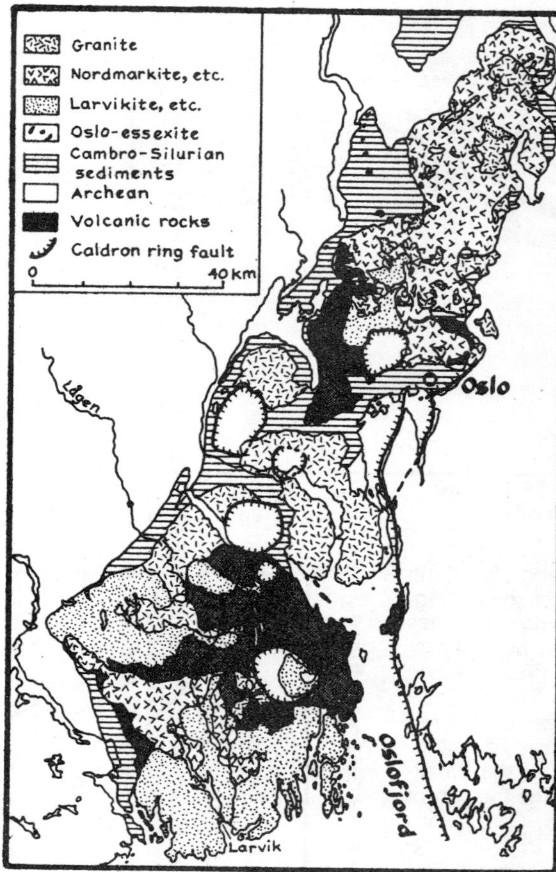

Figure 11–8 Generalized map of the Oslo region of southern Norway. (After C. Oftedahl, 1978, *Jour. Volc. Geoth. Res.* 3:343–371, with modifications from other work by the same author.)

sitions. Even some of the gabbros contain enough potassium feldspar to deserve the name *essexite,* and in the felsic plutonic rocks alkali-feldspar is dominant over plagioclase and may even be the sole feldspar. By far the most voluminous member of the series is a varied group of augite syenites (*larvikites*), which are plutonic equivalents of the rhomb porphyries. Some of these contain quartz, others nepheline.

Depending on whether the feldspars are a sub-solvus assemblage of two feldspars, oligoclase and alkali feldspar, or a single hypersolvus micropherthite, these rocks have very different appearances, both in hand specimen and under the microscope (Fig. 11–9). The perthitic variety is a beautiful, dark-bluish rock in which the feldspar has a *schiller* structure, giving it a spectacular, satiny sheen. A popular ornamental stone, it is commonly seen in the facing of hotels and bars, particularly those aspiring to an affluent clientele.

With progressive differentiation, larvikites give way to two divergent series. One becomes progressively oversaturated with SiO_2 as it follows a trend through

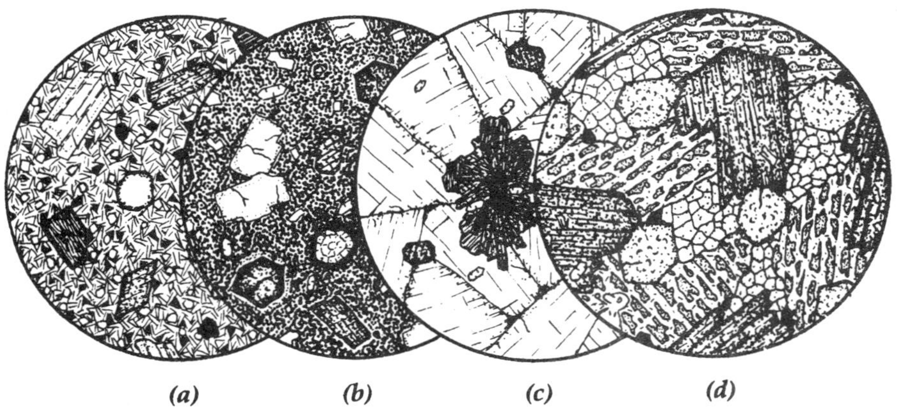

Figure 11–9 Petrographic features of some characteristic continental alkaline and peralkaline rocks. (a) A phonolite of Puy de Dôme, central France, consists of phenocrysts of albite, sodalite, Na-pyroxene, amphibole, biotite, and titaniferous magnetite in a groundmass of sanidine, albite, clinopyroxene, apatite, magnetite, and analcite. (b) A nephelinite lava from Tanzania contains phenocrysts of nepheline, Na-pyroxene, melanite garnet, and apatite in a nearly opaque groundmass. Vesicles are filled with zeolites and calcite. (c) Larvikite from Larvik, Norway, consists of about 80 percent combined alkali feldspar and oligoclase, the remainder being made up of clusters of Ti-augite, biotite, amphibole, and unusually abundant apatite. (d) Kakortokite from the Ilimaussaq Intrusion of southern Greenland contains the zirconium silicate, eudialyte (nearly equant grains of high relief), together with alkali feldspar, Na-amphibole, augite, and nepheline. (Diameter of fields 3 mm.)

single-feldspar syenites (*nordmarkites*) close to the boundary of silica saturation, before passing into biotite-bearing hypersolvus granites. A second branch grades into nepheline-rich rocks that, with increasing amounts of alkali feldspar, reach the composition of nepheline syenite. The silica-rich branch is volumetrically most important; nepheline syenite amounts to less than one percent of the total mass of exposed rock. The divergent trends are closely related to the thermal divide in the residua system illustrated in Figures 11–2 and 11–3. Magmas that were initially saturated with silica descended toward the granitic minimum, while those that were more silica-deficient followed the opposite course.

The Gardar Province of southwestern Greenland

A similar structural setting seems to have been the focus of another complex of highly alkaline rocks near the southwestern edge of the Greenland icecap. A northeast-trending graben cutting very ancient felsic plutonic and metamorphic rocks still preserves remnants of a Proterozoic volcanic series, mainly basaltic, that appears to have been fed by a group of dikes trending parallel to the boundary faults of the down-dropped block. Cutting across these structures are several large dikes and irregularly shaped stocks composed of an extraordinary group of plutonic rocks ranging in composition from granite to nepheline syenite.

Although most of the volcanic series has been stripped away by erosion, the subvolcanic feeders of the system are still preserved. They extend from basanites through hawaiites and mugearites into a divergent series of phonolite, trachyte, and sodic rhyolite (Fig. 11–10). A few small intrusions of lamprophyre, carbonatite, and related rocks came in, apparently at a late stage.

Many of the phonolites and rhyolites are peralkaline; all are hypersolvus in that they contain only a single feldspar. Mafic rocks are distinctly subordinate and are common only in early dikes. Some contain megacrysts of plagioclase and xenoliths of anorthosite indicating that plagioclase crystallized in abundance and must have had a strong influence on the trends of differentiation, but the way in which critically undersaturated mafic liquids differentiated to silica-saturated rhyolites and granites is unclear. Small bodies, such as dikes and volcanic necks, have relatively greater alkali contents than larger, more slowly cooled intrusions, indicating that volatile components were retained under conditions of rapid cooling but, during slow crystallization, escaped into the surrounding rocks to produce broad metasomatic aureoles.

Perhaps the most remarkable feature of the peralkaline intrusive rocks, apart from their rich concentrations of lithophile elements, is the structural relations of the differentiated plutonic series. The Ilimuassaq intrusion, for example, consists of a group of syenites that appear to have differentiated from a single body of

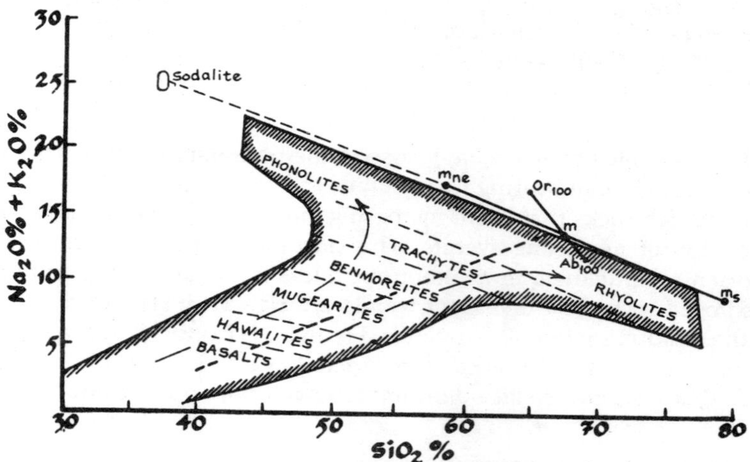

Figure 11–10 Alkali-silica diagram showing compositional relations of rocks of the Gardar Province of southern Greenland. Note that the felsic differentiates diverge into a broad series ranging from nepheline phonolites and syenites to rhyolites and granites. As in the African rocks (Fig. 11–7) the silica contents of the phonlitic series declines in the later stages of differentiation while that of the rhyolitic series increases. The upper compositional limit follows close to the alkali-silica ratio of the thermal valley in the residua system, indicated by the line m_{ne}–m_s from Figure 11–3. The dashed diagonal line down the axis of the main trend of compositions separates compositions that are critically undersaturated (above) from those with normative hypersthene (below). (After B. G. J. Upton, 1974, *The Alkaline Rocks*, H. Sorensen, ed., 221–238.)

magma, having a form somewhat like that of the Skaergaard intrusion. The original magma had the composition of a peralkaline phonolite and crystallized as augite syenite in a border group along the roof and margins of the intrusion. The interior of the body differentiated into three main divisions analogous to the Upper Border Series, Layered Series, and Sandwich Horizon of the Skaergaard (Fig. 11–11). Composed mainly of differing proportions of sodalite, aegirine, arfvedsonite, alkali feldspar, and the bright red zirconium silicate, eudialite, the rocks have suitably improbable names: *naujaite, kakortokite,* and *lujavrite*. The first of these forms the Upper Border Series and consists of up to 80 percent sodalite that accumulated by flotation. The kakortokite, a spectacular red and black rock consisting of alkali feldspar, aegirine, amphibole, and eudialite, has very well-developed layering and is thought to have accumulated on the floor. At middle levels are the lujavrites, representing the last residual magma left by crystallization of the other two groups, much as the Sandwich Horizon of the Skaergaard was, but forming a much thicker unit. The mechanism of crystal fractionation is uncertain. Some of the structural features, such as spectacular layering and foundered blocks from the roof, point to gravitational segregation, but conflicting density relations and anomalous compositional variations indicate that other processes may have been important. Feldspar was certainly the most important fractionating mineral, and, as we shall note shortly, could account for at least some of the compositional variations of the major units.

Mantle origins of rift-related rocks

Continental rifts resemble mid-ocean ridges in the sense that both are extensional zones where magma can be produced by decompression of upwelling asthenosphere (Fig. 8–11). Even though the asthenosphere is overlain by thick

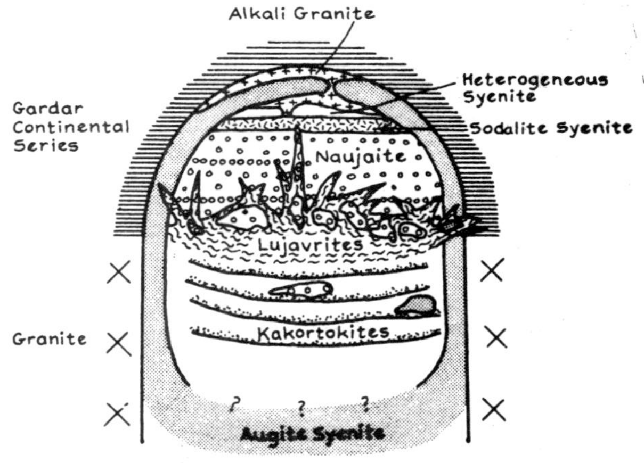

Figure 11–11 Schematic diagram showing the inferred relations between the principal units of the Ilimaussaq intrusion of southern Greenland. The augite syenite encasing the main body was the first unit to crystallize. The heterogeneous syenites, along with a sodalite-rich variety (known as *foyaite*) seem to have accumulated buoyant crystals by flotation at the same time that the lower kakortokites formed on the floor. The naujaites of the upper series then crystallized, possibly from a liquid overlying the denser magma from which the kakortokites were formed on the floor, but fragments of solid naujaite were dense enough to settle into the lower units along with blocks of augite syenite from the roof. The last liquid to crystallize in the core formed lujavrites, which have extensively invaded the overlying rocks. At some time during this long sequence, alkali granites of unknown origin intruded the upper margins of the intrusion. The vertical scale has been exaggerated by about three times to show the relations more clearly. (After J. Ferguson, 1964, *Medd. om Gron.* 172:5–82.)

continental lithosphere, the compositions of the primary rift-related basalts are largely independent of the continental environment.

This is shown most clearly in a chain of small oceanic islands and continental volcanoes extending from the Gulf of Guinea directly across the continental shelf into the active Cameroon line on the West African mainland (Fig. 11–12). The chain is thought to be related to the Benue trough, a Cretaceous rift that has drifted about 300 km northwest of the presently active zone. The basalts erupted along the oceanic sector of this line are essentially identical to those erupted on the continent. Although they vary widely in composition, the variations are consistent from one end to the other, and any basalt found in one sector can be matched by an identical one in the other.

If the basalts are products of the same asthenosphere as mid-ocean ridge basalts they must be the result of much smaller degrees of melting. To obtain basalts with the observed concentrations of alkalies and incompatible elements from such a source, the fraction of melt could not be more than one percent. The problem is alleviated somewhat if we accept a certain amount of inhomogeneity in the the asthenosphere. As we noted in chapter eight, the basalts of oceanic ridges owe their uniformity to collection and homogenization of large amounts of magma; where smaller volumes are discharged from off-axis volcanoes, the com-

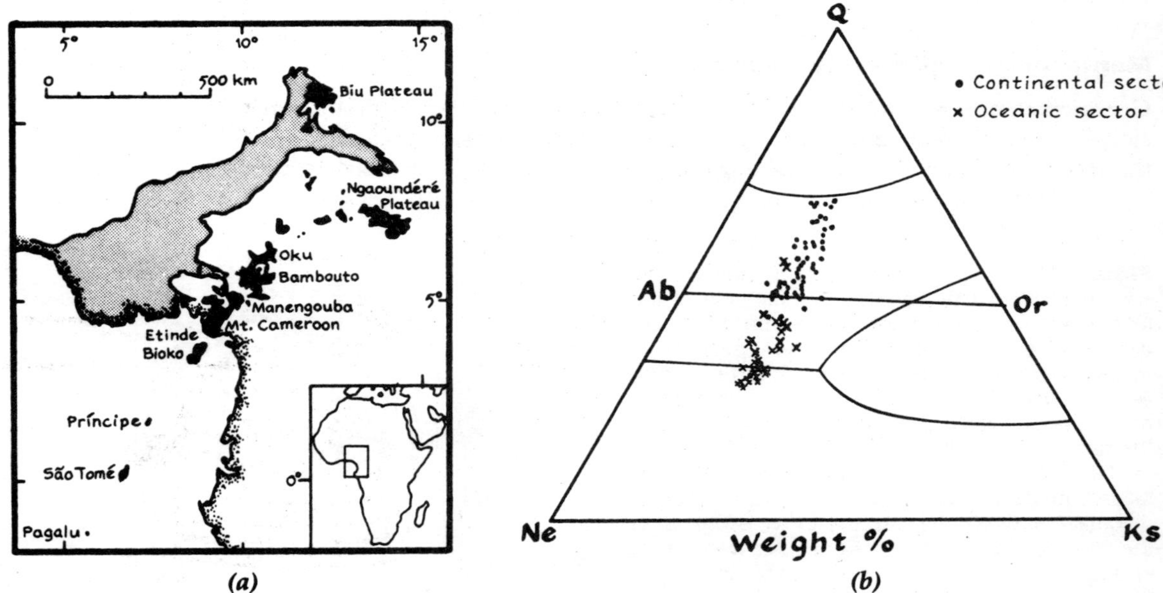

Figure 11–12 Location (a) and alkali-silica variations (b) of volcanic rocks of the West African rift system passing from the Cameroon line across the continental shelf and into the deep ocean basin. Although the basalts of the oceanic and continental sections are essentially the same, the oceanic magmas follow a trend toward phonolite, while those of the continental setting diverge toward increasing silica enrichment. (After J. G. Fitton, 1987, *Alkaline Igneous Rocks*, Geol. Soc. Spec. Publ. No. 30, 273–291.)

positions are less uniform. It was concluded that under these conditions, the enriched parts of the asthenosphere are the first to melt, and the first liquids are more enriched in incompatible elements than a larger volume of melt at the ridge axis where these components are diluted and local variations are averaged out. The small volumes of highly varied basalt erupted from volcanoes of the Cameroon line may have a similar explanation.

Throughout the chain, differentiated lavas make up a large proportion of the volume. They define a forked trend on an alkali-silica diagram very much like that of East Africa and other purely continental suites. With few exceptions, the oceanic magmas evolve to phonolite and the continental magmas to rhyolite (Fig. 11–12b). The normal trend seems to have been toward increasing alkalinity, but contamination of the early and intermediate magmas with siliceous crust appears to have deflected the liquid toward the silica-enrichment side of the thermal divide.

Differentiation of peralkaline magmas

In each of these examples, the late-stage divergence toward alkaline, subalkaline, or peralkaline liquids conforms to what might be expected from a system with a thermal divide, such as that of Q-Ne-Ks (Figs. 11–2 and 11–3). In any system of this kind, small differences in the compositions of parental magmas and the conditions of crystal fractionation are greatly magnified in the final products of strong differentiation. Feldspar, since it is the most important phase in felsic liquids, has the greatest effect on concentrations of alumina, alkalies, and silica and must play a major role in determining whether individual series are enriched or depleted in these elements.

The importance of feldspars in the evolution of peralkaline magmas suggests that water pressure was initially high but at some stage fell sharply, causing disproportionate amounts of that phase to crystallize. Although it is not known how this came about, it is possible to draw certain inferences about the physical mechanisms of differentiation.

The mineral assemblages responsible for the observed trends are those that would be stable at relatively shallow depths in the crust; little deep-seated differentiation is called for. But the large proportions of felsic magmas and their contemporaneous association with more basic magmas seem to require a mechanism similar to that proposed for similar relations in calc-alkaline differentiates and siliceous ignimbrites. The effects of these processes are seen in volcanic complexes in which the eruptive sequences and spatial relations of the magmas have been determined from the field relations of eruptive units. Two examples from western Europe are especially instructive.

The Quaternary volcanic center of Laacher See produced some of the most extreme alkaline compositions of all the many vents along the axis of the Rhine Graben. A large, explosive eruption about 11,000 years ago laid down five cubic kilometers of pumice over an area extending from the Baltic Sea to northern Italy. The first phase of the eruption produced a crystal-poor phonolite rich in volatile and incompatible elements and accounting for about 85 percent of the total volume (Fig. 11–13). This was closely followed by more crystal-rich phonolite of somewhat more mafic composition, which is thought to have come from a lower level in the reservoir. The final products were a hybrid group of very crystal-rich ejecta formed by mixing of phonolitic and more mafic components. The disequilibrium features in this last magma are so marked that they must have developed during the turbulent discharge, for they are too great to have persisted for long in a high-temperature magma chamber. The compositional relations are consistent with crystallization of the observed phenocrysts and segregation of the differentiated liquid into the uppermost cupola of a vertically zoned intrusion.

The form of such a body may be indicated by the evidence seen in Puy de Dôme, a late Pleistocene to Recent complex of lavas and steep-sided domes near the center of a belt of youthful volcanic centers just west of the Rhône Valley in central France (Fig. 11–14). Compositions range from basalt to siliceous trachyte,

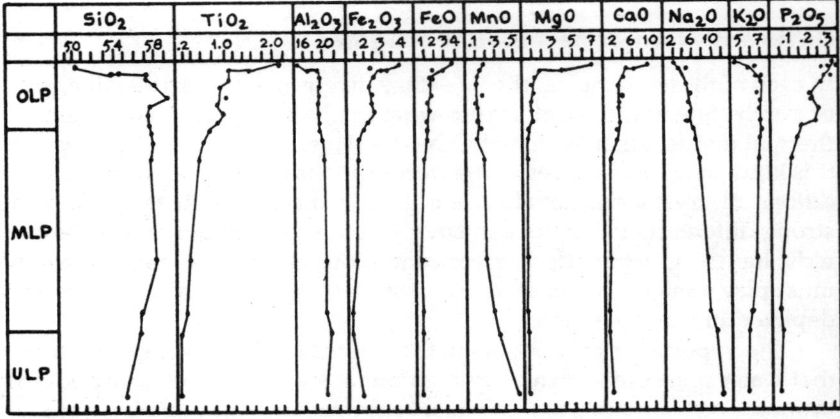

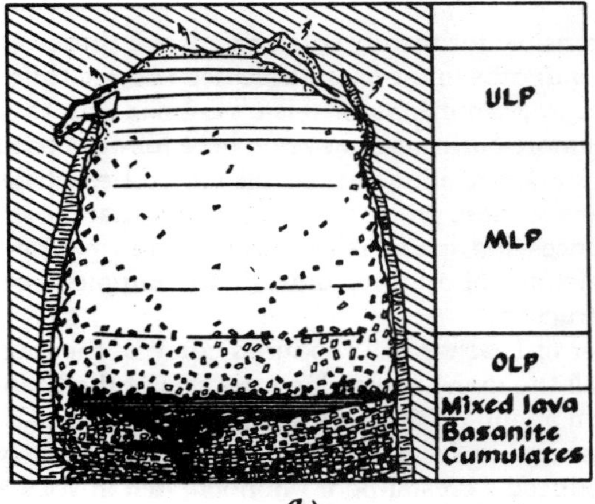

Figure 11–13 (a) Variations of compositions of phonolitic tephra erupted explosively from the zoned magma chamber from the volcanic vent of Laacher See in Western Germany. (b) is a schematic illustration of what the zone magma chamber may have been like immediately prior to eruption. (Adapted from G. Wörner and H. U. Schmincke, pers. comm.)

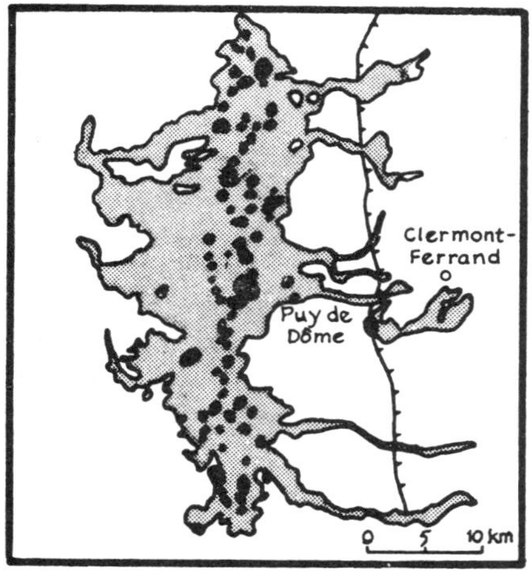

(a)

Figure 11–14 (a) The alkaline complex of Puy de Dôme lies on the rim of a graben just east of a line of Pliocene volcanoes in central France. (b) A schematic section through the complex shows a hypothetical relationship between the different extrusive units and a shallow zoned magma chamber. The degree of differentiation of the units is indicated by the darkness of the shading, the lightest being the most felsic. (a) after R. Brousse, 1963, *C. R. Soc. Savantes,* 88 ème Sess., Clermont-Ferrand, 93–114. (b) has been modified from original diagram of Y. K. Bentor, 1954, *Bull Serv. Carte Geol. France* 52:373–806.)

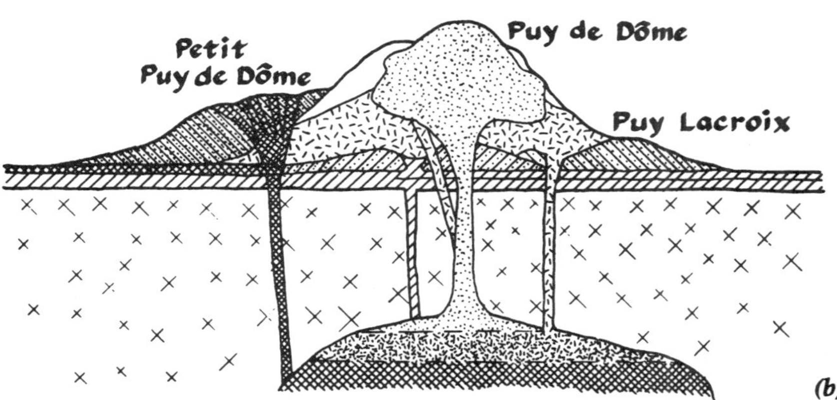

(b)

with the more felsic magmas coming last from vents near the center of the complex. One of several hypotheses offered for the temporal and spatial relations of the eruptive sequence postulates a broad, shallow intrusion, the upper part of which melted and assimilated the granitic basement rocks to form a strongly zoned magma. Whatever the origins of the compositional differences, they seem to have resulted in a vertically zoned body not unlike those proposed as sources for similarly graded magmas elsewhere. Eruptions tapping the upper levels could have supplied the highly differentiated magmas, whereas magmas drawn from lower parts of the same body supplied the denser, more mafic compositions.

CARBONATITES AND RELATED ROCKS

Of all the unusual rocks of continental alkaline complexes, none are more remarkable than magmatic carbonate rocks and the host of alkali-rich and silica-poor rocks with which they are associated. Until the middle of this century many petrologists maintained that carbonatites did not even arise from mantle sources but rather from limestones or dolomites mobilized in the continental crust. Their true magmatic origin was effectively demonstrated when it was shown that carbonatites contain alkalies, P, Ti, Ba, Sr, Nb, Zr, Th, Ce, REE, and other trace elements in concentrations much too great to be derived from common sediments. Their isotopic ratios of oxygen, carbon, and strontium are also distinctly mantle-like. If any question still lingered after these geochemical studies, it disappeared in 1960 when the volcano Oldoinyo L'Engai in Tanzania erupted carbonatite magma with all the morphological aspects of pahoehoe lava. Since that time it has erupted on several occasions when it could be closely observed and sampled. The lavas were seen to have exceptionally low viscosities, even though the measured temperature ranged between 491 and 544°C.

Carbonatites, as their name implies, are composed largely of carbonates of Ca, Mg, Na, and Fe; no potassium-rich carbonatite has ever been reported. Typical accessories are apatite, magnetite, and rare minerals, such as monazite and pyrochlore, which, in high concentrations, are economic sources of the rare-earth elements and several rare metals. True carbonatites range between almost pure calcite at one extreme and sodium carbonate at the other. They normally contain only minor amounts of silica (Table 11–2). Those with greater proportions of silicate minerals grade on the one hand into a series of Ca-rich rocks characterized by the mineral melilite and on the other into a Na-rich *ijolite* series with widely ranging proportions of nepheline (Fig. 11–15). Even though these series are gradational and divisions between them are somewhat artificial, it is helpful to see how the two main trends vary with changing proportions of their constituent minerals.

Melilite-bearing rocks

Pure melilite, it will be recalled, is a solid-solution mineral with two end-members, akermanite ($Ca_2MgSi_2O_7$) and gehlenite ($Ca_2Al_2SiO_7$), but in igneous rocks another component, $CaNaAlSi_2O_7$, also enters the mineral. It is convenient to think of these components as equivalents of silica-deficient diopside or anorthite and albite with an extra CaO. Indeed, reaction between basaltic magmas and calcite can lead to melilite replacing plagioclase and pyroxene in just this way. Experimental work has shown that melilite is precipitated together with olivine, usually the Ca-rich variety monticellite, from liquids very rich in Ca and Na but poor in SiO_2.

No useful purpose would be served by elaborating on more than the main members of the diverse family of melilite-bearing rocks. Typical of many are the *alnoites*, which can be thought of as rocks intermediate between carbonatites and mafic-potassium-rich basalts. In addition to melilite, they contain biotite, olivine, pyroxene, calcite, lesser amounts of chromium- and titanium-rich minerals, and a dark-brown, titaniferous andradite garnet called *melanite*. The alnoites of Ile Cadieux, Quebec, are especially notable, for they contain two forms of olivine, one a common magnesium-iron type and the other the calcium-magnesium vari-

Table 11–2 Some examples of the chemical compositions of carbonatites, alnoite, ijolites, and melilite-bearing rocks. The two carbonatite analyses illustrate sodium-rich and calcium-rich compositions (1 and 2 respectively).

	1.	2.	3.	4.	5.
SiO_2	0.16	1.07	33.26	37.29	39.92
TiO_2	0.02	0.10	2.15	3.46	2.80
Al_2O_3	—	0.44	5.90	14.41	6.60
Fe_2O_3	0.28	1.88	5.30	4.23	8.90
FeO	—	—	6.54	6.10	5.89
MnO	0.38	0.45	0.15	0.32	0.22
MgO	0.38	0.46	26.41	4.15	12.59
CaO	14.02	52.77	14.47	13.69	15.71
Na_2O	32.22	0.08	1.23	5.61	1.19
K_2O	8.38	0.03	0.82	4.22	0.86
H_2O+	0.56	—	1.91	0.69	2.71
H_2O-	—	3.03	0.09	0.04	1.15
P_2O_5	0.85	1.43	0.76	0.77	0.47
SrO	1.42	0.79	—	1.06	—
BaO	1.39	0.16	0.08	0.22	—
CO_2	31.55	37.19	1.10	3.29	—
Cl	3.40	—	—	0.33	—
F	2.50	—	—	0.32	—
SO_3	4.43	—	0.22	6.07	—

1. Sodium carbonate lava, 1988 eruption of Oldoinyo Lengai Volcano, Tanzania. (J. Keller and M. Kraft, 1990, *Bull. Volc.* 52:629–645.)
2. Carbonititic dike, Kaiserstuhl alkaline complex, Rhine Graben, Germany. (J. Keller, 1981, *Jour. Volc. Geoth. Res.* 9:423–431.)
3. Monticellite alnoite, Isle Cadieux. (N. L. Bowen, 1922, *Amer. Jour. Sci.* 203:1–34.)
4. Ijolite, Magnet Cove, Arkansas. (R. L. Erickson and L. V. Blade, 1963, *U. S. Geol. Surv. Prof. Paper 425*.)
5. Olivine-melilite-nepheline lava, Kisingiri, Kenya. (M. J. Le Bas, 1977, *Carbonatite-Nephelinite Volcanism*. Wiley, 347 pp.)

ety, monticellite ($CaMgSiO_4$). The latter has been shown experimentally to be the product of subsolidus reaction between normal olivine and melilite to form augite and monticellite.

Melilite and feldspar seem to be mutually exclusive in igneous rocks, for they are never found together. For example, volcanic varieties of melilite-rich rocks, the melilitites, contain no feldspar but only melilite, augite, and various titanium-rich minerals; olivine, biotite, nepheline, and leucite are other possible phases. As these assemblages suggest, the melilitic rocks may be either sodic or potassic, but the latter are less common.

The ijolite series

In several continental provinces, such as Magnet Cove, Arkansas, the Monteregian Hills of Quebec, and Kisingiri in western Kenya, carbonatites are closely associated with and gradational into the series of nephelinic rocks referred to

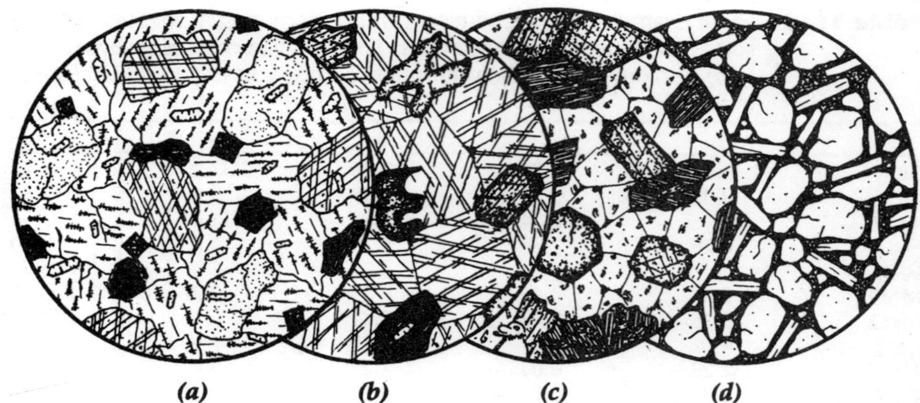

Figure 11–15 Petrographic features of melilitic rocks, ijolites, and carbonatites. (a) Okaite from the Oka Complex of Quebec contains very abundant melilite with lesser amounts of green biotite, calcite, nepheline, perovskite, apatite, and magnetite. (b) Monticellite carbonatite, also from the Oka Complex, consists mainly of calcite, but monticellite,. pyroxene, melanite, and apatite are also important. (c) A mafic variety of ijolite from Oldoinyo L'engai, Tanzania, contains bright green aegirine-augite, nepheline, melanite, green biotite, apatite, and sphene. (d) A carbonatite lava erupted from the same volcano in 1960 consists mainly of sodium carbonate. Rounded clots of phonolitic composition are believed to have exsolved as an immiscible liquid as the magma rose in the conduit of the volcano.

collectively as *ijolites* (Fig. 11–15). Again, depending on their proportions of minerals, these range from leucocratic nephelinites, consisting of nepheline and only minor amounts of pyroxene, to melanocratic pyroxenites. Nepheline is the dominant felsic mineral, leucite being much less common, whereas either titaniferous augite or aegirine-augite is the most important mafic component. But a wide variety of other mafic minerals is very characteristic. The rare but beautiful *jacupirangites*, for example, are a petrographer's delight. They contain only minor amounts of nepheline but are composed chiefly of bright green aegirine-augite rimmed with purple titaniferous augite and intergrown with differing amounts of magnetite-ilmenite, biotite, melanite, olivine, calcite, apatite, barkevikite, perovskite, pyrite, and zeolites. Some varieties contain melilite and others wollastonite.

While ijolites are characteristically sodic, they grade into a corresponding group of potassic rocks of more gabbroic composition, known as *essexites*. Like ijolites, the latter contain abundant nepheline, but it is accompanied by K-feldspar, and titaniferous augite and amphibole are more characteristic than aegirine. Essexites are found in many of the same clusters of igneous complexes as ijolites, but they are more commonly associated with and gradational into plagioclase-bearing rocks of more common gabbroic and syenitic types.

Geological relations

Although recorded in ninety or so localities throughout the world, carbonatites, melilitic rocks, and ijolites tend to occur in small bodies more than half of which are in the eastern and southern parts of Africa. Though characteristic of continental rifting, they are not confined to the continents; carbonatites are reported from the oceanic islands of the Cape Verde Archipelago in the eastern part of the Atlantic Ocean. The most familiar examples in North America, mentioned already in the preceding section, are illustrated in Figure 11–16.

The eruptive centers have no visible relation to crustal structures. Nor do they define linear trends with regular progressions of ages, as would be expected if they were produced at hotspots.

Most intrusive bodies are ring-complexes emplaced at shallow levels as volcanic vents. Their form is typically that of a concentrically zoned cylindrical or conical pipe. The examples from the Monteregian province illustrate the great variety of rock types found in closely associated bodies of a single district. The structural relations and origins of the radial zonation of these various units have been interpreted in almost as many different ways as there are rock types. In the case of the Monteregian pipes, the contacts with surrounding rocks are sharp and clearly cross-cutting, and their internal structure has been attributed in some cases to successive intrusions and in others to inward crystallization and differentiation.

Many of these ring-complexes, particularly those with cores of carbonatite, show clear evidence that the outer zones and wall rocks have been strongly altered by volatile-rich fluids. A classic example is the Fen Complex (Fig. 11–17) that intrudes Precambrian basement rocks just west of the Oslo Graben in southern Norway. The central carbonate core, originally interpreted as altered limestone, consists of calcite, dolomite, ankerite, and hematite with small bodies of brecciated kimberlite, all of which appear to have been emplaced explosively in a series of violent volcanic eruptions. This core is surrounded by a succession of zones that pass first into mixed carbonates and felspathoidal rocks of the alnoite variety, then into various types of ijolites and an outer ring of nepheline syenite or phonolite. The granitic gneisses of the walls have been transformed by wholesale metasomatic alteration resulting, no doubt, from fluids emanating from the intrusion. This process is referred to as *fenitization*, and the syenitic rocks it produced are called *fenites*, after this locality where they were first described. The fenites are essentially syenites that tend to be nepheline-rich close to the intrusion and progressively more silica-saturated outward until they give way to a zone of fractured but otherwise unaltered gneiss.

The relation between these ring-complexes and volcanic vents can be seen in the deeply eroded cone of Napak in Uganda where a nearly circular plug of carbonatite is surrounded by ijolitic rocks. Only parts of the flanks of the volcano are still preserved; they are composed mainly of nephelinitic tuffs and lavas. But the core of the volcano contains a zoned assemblage very much like that of the Fen Complex.

Petrologic relations

It is clear that volatile components are an important part of alkaline magmas. The effects of carbon dioxide, chlorine, and fluorine are pervasive, not only in the mineral assemblages but also in alteration zones in and around intrusions.

(a)

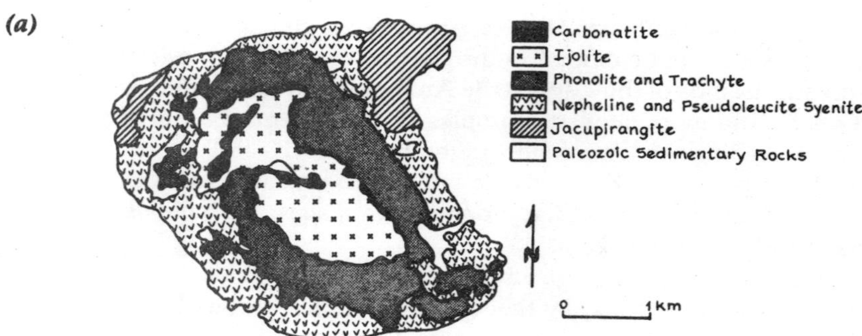

(b)

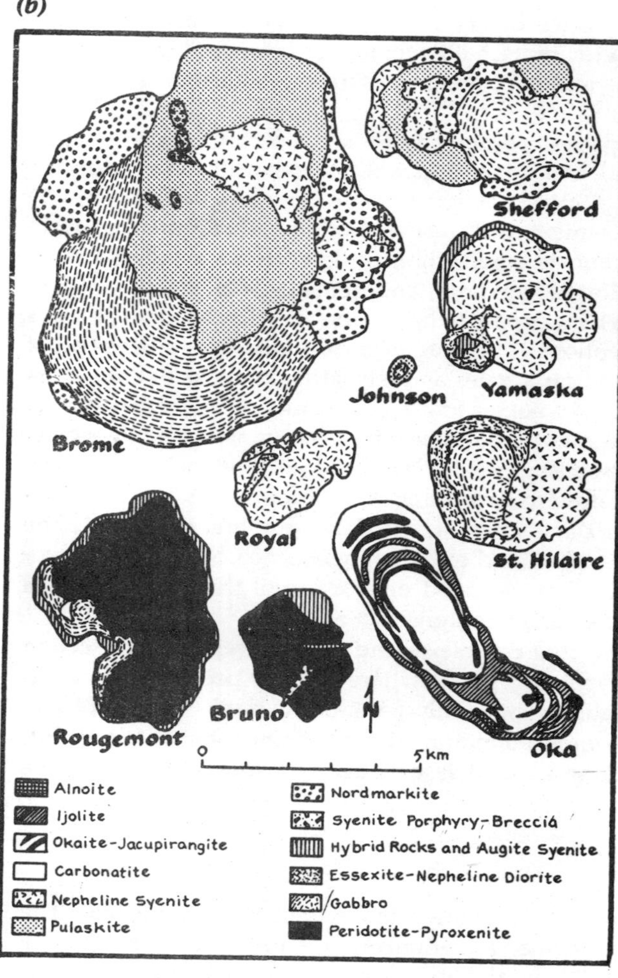

Figure 11–16 (a) Simplified geological map of the Magnet Cove Complex of Arkansas (After R. L. Erickson and L. V. Blade, 1963, *U.S. Geol. Surv. Prof. Paper 425*.) (b) General features of the main Monteregian intrusions of Quebec. (After compilation by A. R. Philpotts, 1974, *The Alkaline Rocks*, H. Sorensen, ed. 293–310.)

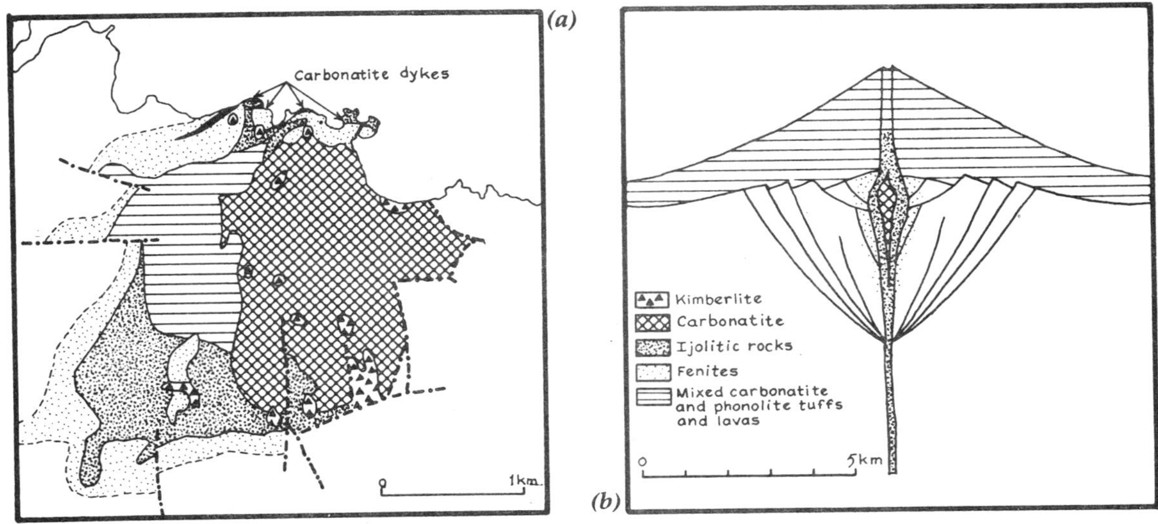

Figure 11–17 (a) Simplified map of the Fen Complex of southern Norway. (After E. Saether, 1957, Kong. Norske Fidensk, Skr., No. 1.) (b) A schematic diagram showing possible relations between such a ring-complex and the structure of carbonatite volcanoes, such as those of East Africa. (After E. A. Middlemost, 1974, *Lithos*, 7:255–275.)

The very low viscosities and explosive character of the magmas are certainly due to their large concentrations of dissolved volatiles. The amounts of these volatiles are too great to be the result of residual concentration by crystal fractionation; they must have been inherent in the magmas at their origin, and they may have been further concentrated in the upper zones of shallow magma chambers.

As the fenites clearly show, volatile transfer must have led to metasomatic alteration of some of the rocks while they were in the crystalline state. But other structural and textural aspects of the rocks have been interpreted as evidence that volatiles can be exchanged in magmas that are still largely if not completely liquid. Perhaps the most controversial of these are the round felsic clots or *ocelli* commonly found in a matrix of mafic minerals. Advocates of gaseous transfer propose a process in which the magma vesiculates on rising, then cools so that the gas pressure in the vesicles declines and a partial vacuum is created that draws a vapor-rich fluid into the vesicle. A second explanation, supported by a growing body of experimental evidence, is that the ocelli were a separate phase exsolved not as a gas but as an immiscible liquid.

The role of liquid immiscibility is particularly well demonstrated in CO_3-rich alkaline liquids. The system Na_2O-CaO-SiO_2-Al_2O_3-CO_2, shown here in Figure 11–18, has a large, two-liquid field at elevated pressures and at most geologically reasonable temperatures. It corresponds remarkably well to the associations found in assemblages of carbonatites and highly undersaturated alkaline rocks. The volcano Oldavai L'Engai mentioned earlier is a vivid example. It erupts lavas and tephra consisting essentially of sodium carbonate but with clots of silicates

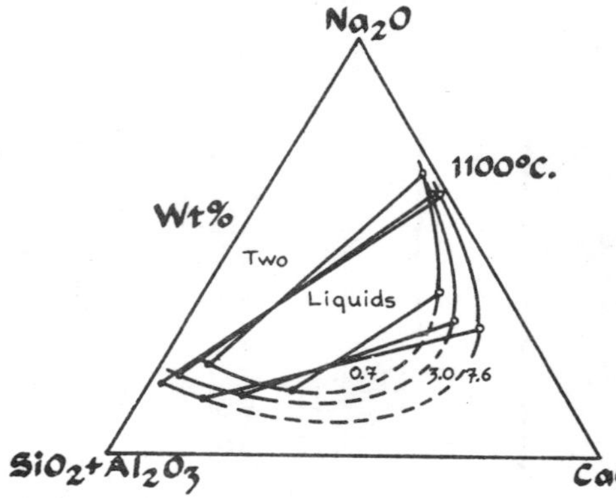

Figure 11–18 The system Na_2O-SiO_2-Al_2O_3-CaO-CO_2 at 1,100°C. Pressure of CO_2 (in kbars) is indicated by the numbers on the curves bounding the two-liquid field. Note that the tie lines connecting compositions of coexisting liquids rotate with increasing pressure, so that one becomes richer in CaO while the other becomes richer in SiO_2 and Al_2O_3. The first can be thought of as equivalent to calcium carbonate liquids and the latter to alumino-silicate melts. (After I. C. Freestone and D. L. Hamilton, 1980, *Contr. Mineral. Petrol.* 73:105–117.)

having the composition of sodic phonolite. Before this immiscible relation was recognized, it was believed that the carbonates were derived from evaporites in the beds of nearby Lake Natron, but several geochemical aspects of the evaporites, particularly their carbon isotopic ratios and fluorine contents, show that the reverse is more likely. The carbonatites erupted from the volcano, being very soluble in rainwater, are quickly dissolved and carried into the groundwater system from whence they are transported via hot springs back to the surface. Over centuries they have accumulated to saturation levels and precipitated in thick evaporite deposits known as *trona*. This process of "meteoric differentiation" leaves insoluble silicates residually enriched in the structure of the volcano and gives the impression that only nephelinitic tephra have been erupted.

LAMPROPHYRES

Closely related to the silica-poor and alkali-rich group just discussed is another broad series of mafic and ultramafic alkaline rocks known collectively as lamprophyres. Though more common as minor associates of other rock types than as a genetic series of their own, they share a number of singular features setting them apart from most other rocks. Almost all are hypabyssal porphyritic rocks without plutonic equivalents. They are found almost exclusively in continental settings, mostly in the deep interior regions of cratons but also in orogenic plutonic belts, where they form dikes, sills, or volcanic pipes. Some have been discharged as coarse heterogeneous tephra or, more rarely, as small flows of dense lava.

Early studies of lamprophyres resulted in a complex classification and nomenclature based on their diverse modal assemblages, but most recent work has placed greater emphasis on their chemical and petrologic characteristics. Four or five main groups are distinguished (Fig. 11–19). Two of these, the calc-alkaline and alkaline lamprophyres, will be discussed here. Ultramafic (melilite-bearing) lamprophyes and *lamproites* (mafic ultrapotassic rocks) are dealt with elsewhere in this same chapter. Kimberlites are closely related to lamprophyres and are

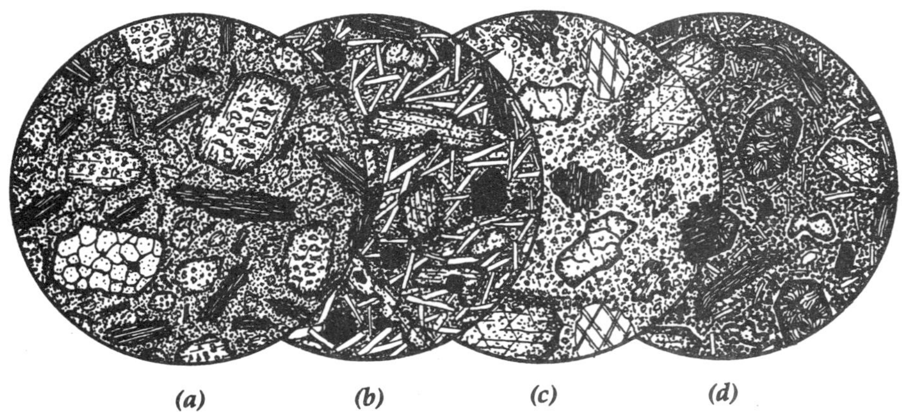

(a) (b) (c) (d)

Figure 11–19 Petrographic features of lamprophyres and kimberlite. (a) A calc-alkaline biotite lamprophyre (minette) from a volcanic neck in the Navajo region of Arizona contains reddish-brown biotite with oxidized rims, zoned augite, orthoclase, magnetite, and abundant accessory apatite. A small altered xenolith of granitic basement rock is shown at the left edge. (b) An alkaline lamprophyre (camptonite) from the Oregon Coast Range contains phenocrysts of dark-brown barkevikite, Ti-augite, and olivine in a groundmass rich in andesine and apatite. (c) An alnoite from the Oka Complex of Quebec has phenocrysts of biotite, augite, and olivine in a matrix of melilite, carbonates, perovskite, magnetite, and apatite. (d) A kimberlite from the Premier Diamond Pipe of South Africa consists of serpentinized olivine, phlogopite, ilmenite, garnet, and altered rock fragments in a turbid groundmass of calcite, serpentine, and clay.

commonly thought of as members of the same clan, but they have such special importance that they are best treated separately.

Calc-alkaline lamprophyres are typically found in orogenic systems, most often as late-stage dikes cutting felsic plutonic rocks of dioritic to granitic compositions. Their SiO_2 content normally exceeds 48 percent, and they contain more K_2O than Na_2O. In these respects, calc-alkaline lamprophyres are gradational into the potassic sub-alkaline series discussed earlier. But for their greater contents of water and carbonates, their compositions would differ little from those of mafic shoshonitic lavas. The principal petrographic types are broadly distinguished as *biotite lamprophyres* and *hornblende lamprophyres* according to the nature of the dominant mafic mineral. If the main feldspar is potassic, the former are referred to as *minettes*, if plagioclase, *kersantites*. The equivalent hornblende-rich rocks are *vogesites* and *spessartites*, respectively. In most instances, however, the feldspar is fine-grained and so thoroughly altered that its identification is at best uncertain. All common types may contain diopsidic augite, serpentinized olivine, apatite, iron oxides, and carbonates. Though most contain both normative and modal olivine, quartz may be common, particularly in the groundmass of biotite-rich types. This is due not so much to a greater Si_2O content, but to the large amount of K_2O that enters the silica-poor micas and leaves the remaining assemblage more silica rich than it would be if orthoclase were formed.

Alkaline lamprophyres are common associates of nepheline syenites and carbonatites, chiefly in stable continental interiors and rifts where they may be associated with ultramafic lamprophyres and lamproites. Having less than 48 percent SiO_2 and large amounts of Na_2O, they typically contain 5 to 10 percent normative Ne. Like the calc-alkaline group, they can be divided according to their principal mafic minerals and feldspar, but the amphibole is the brown sodic variety, barkevikite, or the darker brown to black Ti-rich kaersutite. Biotite, though a common constituent, is less important than Ti-augite. The amphibole-rich *camptonites* normally have labradorite in the groundmass, but the augite-rich *monchiquites* contain little or no feldspar. Instead, their groundmass consists of analcite, nepheline, or pale glass of phonolitic composition. These seem to be textural variations reflecting differing degrees of crystallization of the groundmass rather than inherently different chemical compositions. Other common constituent minerals of the alkaline lamprophyres are olivine, iron-oxides, apatite, zeolites, and carbonates, normally dolomite. A few containing melilite and abundant carbonates are gradational into ultramafic types, such as the alnoites mentioned in a previous section.

One example of a lamprophyre province will serve to illustrate the relations found in many others. The Navajo-Hopi region of northeastern Arizona was the scene of many small, highly explosive volcanic eruptions during Pliocene time. Today only lava-capped mesas and towering remnants of volcanic necks (Fig. 11–20) remain of what was once a volcanic field covering thousands of square kilometers. Although in close proximity, two sub-fields have very distinct lamprophyres, one calc-alkaline and the other alkaline. The rocks of the Navajo region are mainly minettes crowded with xenoliths from all levels of the crust. Those of the adjacent Hopi region are more sodic. They are mainly monchiquites and a gradational series of related rocks, including analcite basanites and olivine-

Figure 11–20 An eroded volcanic neck of the Navajo region, Arizona. These towering columns were cores of Miocene volcanoes that erupted lamprophyres and lamproites over much of northeastern Arizona and adjacent parts of Utah and New Mexico.

augite basalts. The crustal xenoliths that choke most of the Navajo pipes are much scarcer in the more sodic rocks of the Hopi region.

Early interpretations drew mainly on the abundance of biotite-rich plutonic and metamorphic basement rocks to explain the unusual potassium contents of the Navajo rocks. Breakdown of biotite heated at shallow levels by their host magma could release a hydrous, potassium-rich fluid that would add many of the essential ingredients of the calc-alkaline lamprophyres, including the volatile components responsible for their explosive eruption. Although assimilation of this kind must have been important, especially for the Navajo minettes, it is not a satisfactory explanation for the alkaline Hopi lamprophyres or for ultra-potassic rocks in general. A deeper origin is needed for the latter group that shows much less evidence for strong contamination. Some of the possibilities can be seen from studies of kimberlites, another group of potassic alkaline rocks that has been studied in greater detail.

KIMBERLITES

Though closely akin to the alkaline lamprophyres, kimberlites are distinctive enough in their associations, geologic occurrence, and petrological importance to merit a special identity of their own. They are volatile-rich, potassic, ultramafic rocks that have risen from deep origins to form dikes, sills, and volcanic pipes, many of them diamondiferous.

Kimberlites are found in the southern and western parts of the African continent, Quebec, Siberia, India, Brazil, and the eastern and central United States. None is known from the oceans. Few are of Precambrian age; they seem to have become more abundant with time. In southern Africa they have reappeared repeatedly in the same provinces at intervals of hundreds of millions of years. Though often cited as examples of continental hotspots, their distribution is not linear except on a local scale, and their scattered recurrence in nearby regions, even after long periods of drift, indicates that the magmas originate in the continental lithosphere, not in the underlying mantle.

Thanks to their economic importance, diamond pipes have been explored and studied in minute detail. Three main zones are recognized (Fig. 11–21). In most places the shallow "crater zone" has long since been removed by erosion, but the underlying "diatreme zone," which extends to depths of a kilometer or two, has been explored in most of the deeper mines. It is typically a highly brecciated and deeply weathered steep-sided pipe formed by explosive boring through the shallow crust. It rises from a "root zone" in which the shape tends to be more dike-like and vesiculation less intense. The preservation of sedimentary xenoliths indicates that temperatures of the shallow, brecciated horizons were unusually low, but the dikes and sills at greater depths were emplaced at higher temperatures; they are also more homogeneous and less contaminated.

Brecciated kimberlites are difficult rocks to study, owing to the deep weathering and hydrothermal alteration that have altered the minerals to clay and serpentine. Their compositions and textural forms differ widely, even in a single

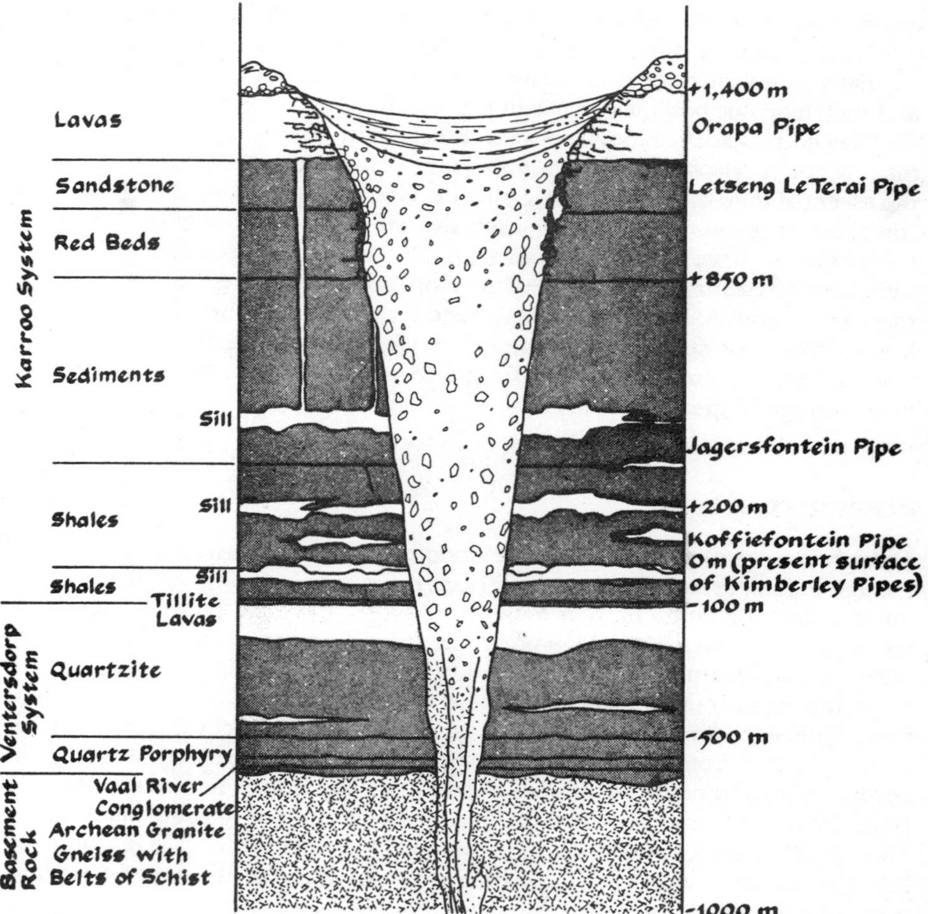

Figure 11–21 Diagrammatic section of a kimberlite pipe based on the relations found in South African diamond mines. The pipes are of Cretaceous age and have been eroded and weathered to differing depths. The narrow feeder consists of multiple, unvesiculated, dike-like bodies of differing composition. (After K. G. Cox, 1978, *Sc. Amer.* 238:120–132.)

body. The most common petrographic type (Fig. 11–19d) is porphyritic with large amounts of serpentinized olivine, clay, and carbonates, and widely differing proportions of phlogopite, purplish pyrope-rich garnet, ilmenite, chrome diopside, apatite, spinel, perovskite, and monticellite. Some of these minerals are phenocrysts, but many of the largest crystals are xenocrysts far out of equilibrium with their host.

Bulk chemical compositions are similar to those of potassic peridotites. SiO_2 rarely exceeds about 33 percent, but Al_2O_3, TiO_2, P_2O_5, and alkali contents are greater than those of other ultramafic rocks. The ratio K_2O/Na_2O is normally greater than 2.0 and may reach 5.0 or more. Differences in their isotopic ratios and trace element concentrations indicate that most kimberlites are mixtures of magmas derived from at least two distinct sources. One end-member of this spectrum is rich in mica; the other is not.

In some respects, kimberlites resemble the carbonatites with which they are closely associated in some of the ring complexes described earlier. They contain many of the same minerals, and their characteristic trace-element patterns are similar. But whereas carbonatites are more characteristic of continental rifting, kimberlites are found mainly in tectonically stable regions. Kimberlitic dikes associated with carbonatite ring complexes are small and lack the variety of xenoliths so characteristic of diamond pipes.

In addition to diamonds, kimberlites contain a wealth of exotic xenoliths and xenocrysts. The compositions of the large megacrysts of olivine, pyroxenes, garnet, and ilmenite are far from uniform. Some could be in equilibrium with each other, but others seem to have more complex origins. In many ways the ultramafic xenoliths resemble those found in basaltic magmas (chapter eight), but garnet lherzolites and eclogites are much more common in kimberlites, and the most common depleted type is harzburgite rather than wehrlite. Two textural varieties have been distinguished (Figs. 7–18e and f), one granular and the other highly deformed. In the latter, the mineral grains are intensely crushed and sheared, and much of the olivine has shadowy "kink bands" resulting from deformation of their crystal lattice. Pyroxene shows less deformation, garnet the least of all.

Eclogites consisting of pyrope garnet and a sodium-rich pyroxene, omphacite, are especially intriguing, because some have the bulk chemical composition of common basalts but the high-pressure mineral assemblages of mantle rocks. Their origins are a matter of speculation. They could be products of high-pressure crystallization of basaltic liquids or, alternatively, older rocks brought to mantle depths and recrystallized to a mineral assemblage stable at elevated pressures. Their ages, as determined radiometrically, are generally greater than those of their host, and their isotopic compositions indicate that they could not have been in equilibrium with either the kimberlitic magma or the ultramafic inclusions in the same pipes.

Depths of origin

The xenoliths found in diamond pipes must come from many levels of the crust and mantle. An estimate of the minimum depths tapped by kimberlites can be gained from the experimentally determined stability relations of the two forms of carbon, graphite and diamond (Fig. 11–22). Note that when the diamond-graphite curve is compared to the estimated geothermal gradient for continents, the two are seen to intersect at pressures of about 35 kbars.

The pressures at which quartz inverts to coesite, which have been determined in the same way as those for diamond, define a similar though somewhat shallower range of depth, and minute inclusions found in a few diamonds show that coesite was the stable form of SiO_2. If these two polymorphic transitions, one for carbon and the other for silica, are projected to the calculated geothermal

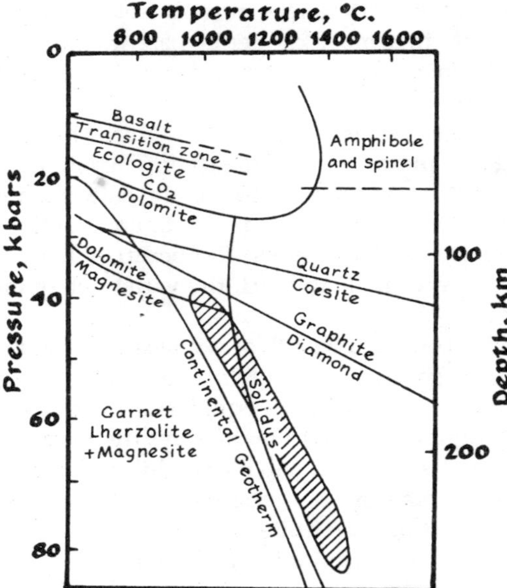

Figure 11–22 Pressure-temperature relations of the various phases found in kimberlites can be related to the earth's geothermal gradient to define the range of depths from which kimberlites must rise. The diagonally ruled area is the range of temperatures and pressures determined from the compositions of pyroxenes in ultramafic nodules, as shown in Figure 7–20. Also shown is the solidus curve for a garnet lherzolite in the presence of a CO_2-rich fluid. (Solidus curve is taken from D. Canil and C. M. Scarfe, 1990, *Jour. Geoph. Res.* 95:15805–15816.)

gradient, they place the minimum depth at around 100 km. The maximum depth to which coesite would be the stable form of SiO_2 is about 250 to 300 km. The absence of the higher-pressure polymorph, stishovite, may place an upper limit on pressure, but it is possible that stishovite inverts to coesite on relief of pressure.

It will be recalled from chapter seven that the compositions of coexisting pyroxenes in ultramafic inclusions can be used to estimate the depths and temperatures at which peridotites last equilibrated in the mantle (Figs. 7–20 and 7–21). The garnet lherzolites in kimberites define a range of temperatures and pressures (Fig. 11–22) that differ slightly from one pipe to another but indicate temperatures close to, but slightly above, the geothermal gradient estimated independently from heat-flow measurements. Inclusions from the shallowest range of depths have undeformed granular textures, whereas almost all those from the greatest depths are highly sheared, as would be expected if they come from the asthenosphere.

The experimentally determined solidus for garnet lherzolite in the presence of a CO_2-rich fluid is shown in the same figure. Note the sharp inflection where the solidus is intersected by a curve marking an abrupt increase of the solubility of CO_2. At this depth carbonate becomes a stable subsolidus phase. The compositions of the liquids produced by melting in the range of fifty to seventy kbars are found to be very similar to those of natural kimberlites but only within this interval; at shallower depths, liquids are more like melililites, and at greater depths they have more MgO than natural melts. This part of the solidus curve corresponds fairly closely to the range of temperatures and pressures estimated from the pyroxenes in ultramafic xenoliths brought up in kimberlite pipes. Thus kimberlitic magmas must originate in a "window" between depths of about 150 and 250 km corresponding to the approximate depth of the base of the continental lithosphere.

Melting could be triggered when the solidus temperature is lowered either by upwelling of the mantle or by an influx of a fluid rich in CO_2 and H_2O. The resulting decrease of density may cause the magma to rise diapirically, and because the solidus at this depth has a positive slope that is steeper than the adiabatic gradient, the amount of melt would increase upward. Amphibole, phlogopite, and carbonates, which become unstable at temperatures only slightly above the solidus, would contribute H_2O and CO_2 to the rising liquid. On reaching a depth of about 80 km where the solubility of CO_2 decreases abruptly, the magma suddenly exsolve a volatile phase that greatly accelerates its rise. The highly explosive nature of most alkaline magmas, particularly kimberlites, must be due to this effect.

MELTING RELATIONS AT HIGH PRESSURES

Most recent attempts to understand the origins of kimberlites and related magmas have focused on the role of volatile components at high pressures. It has become increasingly clear that H_2O and CO_2, which are such important constituents of these magmas, must have played a key role in their generation and rise to the surface.

As we have seen in earlier chapters, water has a pronounced effect on melting (Fig. 11-23). Note that the solidus temperature where melting begins is greatly reduced by pressures of H_2O up to about twenty kbars, but at greater pressures it increases again. Because the compressibility of the vapor phase is so much greater than that of the solid, the sign of $\Delta V_{melting}$ is eventually reversed.

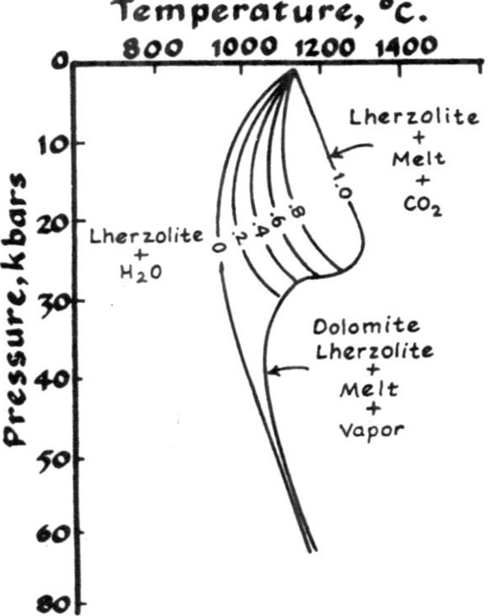

Figure 11-23 Effects of pressure of H_2O and CO_2 on the melting of peridotite. The solidus curve is shown for different proportions of CO_2 and H_2O. The sharp inflection occurs close to the pressure at which the carbonate mineral, dolomite, becomes a stable phase. The intersection of the carbonate stability curve with the solidus migrates according to the proportions of CO_2, as indicated by numbers corresponding to the ratio of CO_2 to $CO_2 + H_2O$. (After P. J. Wyllie, 1979, *Amer. Min.* 64:469–500.)

Increasing pressure of CO_2, on the other hand, has an initial effect of increasing the solidus temperature, because CO_2 has such low solubility in the liquid that ΔV is positive. At pressures greater than about twenty kbars, however, this condition begins to disappear; the solubility of CO_2 increases rapidly, probably as a result of a pressure-induced change in the structure of the liquid that causes CO_2 to take the form of $(CO_3)^{2-}$.

The melting relations of lherzolite in the presence of fluids with differing proportions of CO_2 and H_2O are illustrated in Figure 11-23. Note that at pressures below the stability range of carbonates, H_2O lowers the solidus much more than CO_2, but at greater pressures the effect changes abruptly, because CO_2 goes into carbonate and the fluid becomes proportionately richer in H_2O. Addition of phlogopite to the system does not change the basic form of the melting relations.

The amount of water contained in the hydrous minerals of peridotites is strictly limited by the bulk composition of the rock. Although amphibole can contain up to 2 or 3 percent H_2O, the amount of amphibole is restricted by the major elements to about 15 percent of the total mineral assemblage. Hence H_2O is limited to well under 0.5 percent. Moreover, the stability range of amphibole does not extend to very high temperatures and pressures; it becomes unstable at about the same pressure as spinel, and little if any can be present close to the solidus at depths greater than 100 km or so. The stability range of phlogopite is much greater, but the amount of H_2O in phlogopite is limited by the K_2O content of the rock. Because phlogopite requires about 10 percent of this essential component and takes in only 4 percent H_2O, a peridotite with a K_2O content of 0.1 percent can contain only 0.04 percent H_2O if phlogopite is the only hydrous mineral.

The limitations on CO_2 are less severe, because the major elements needed to form carbonates are present in greater amounts, and the CO_2 content of the carbonates is also greater. At pressures greater than about fifteen to twenty-five kilobars CO_2 combines with olivine and pyroxene to form dolomite, according to the reaction

$$\underset{\text{Carbon dioxide}}{2CO_2} + \underset{\text{Forsterite}}{2Mg_2SiO_4} + \underset{\text{Diopside}}{CaMgSi_2O_6} \rightarrow \underset{\text{Dolomite}}{CaMg(CO_3)_2} + \underset{\text{Enstatite}}{2Mg_2Si_2O_6} \quad (11\text{–}1)$$

and at pressures of thirty to forty kilobars, enstatite and dolomite go to magnesite and diopside:

$$\underset{\text{Enstatite}}{Mg_2Si_2O_6} + \underset{\text{Dolomite}}{CaMg(CO_3)_2} \rightarrow \underset{\text{Diopside}}{CaMgSi_2O_6} + \underset{\text{Magnesite}}{2MgCO_3} \quad (11\text{–}2)$$

Thus the mantle is theoretically capable of storing large amounts of CO_2 in the form of carbonate minerals at depths below 100 km or so. It is uncertain how much carbonate is contained in mantle peridotites; very little dolomite or magnesite is found in mantle xenoliths. Carbonates are certainly subordinate to silicate minerals, so it is doubtful whether the amount of dolomite or magnesite would be limited by the bulk composition, and CO_2 in the form of carbonates is probably more abundant at high pressures than H_2O in phlogopite.

The phase relations of a mantle lherzolite in the presence of small amounts of

H_2O and CO_2 are illustrated in Figure 11–24a. The temperature of the solidus drops sharply where carbonate becomes stable, and a second sharp inflection around twenty-five kbars marks the depth where amphibole reaches its upper stability limit, and phlogopite becomes the stable hydrous phase. Thereafter, the temperature of the solidus continues to increase.

The compositions of potassic and carbonatitic liquids on the solidus (Fig. 11–24b) define an orderly progression of compositions with increasing pressure. The principal effect is to produce melts that are, first, increasingly silica-deficient and alkaline, then more carbonate-rich and alkali-poor. Note that the pressures at which the liquid compositions cross the series of field boundaries are less with CO_2 saturation than in the absence of a volatile phase. Although Figure 11–24b was constructed from the phase relations in a potassic system, the trend for sodic compositions has been shown to be similar. The general sequence is probably qualitatively valid for most natural magmas.

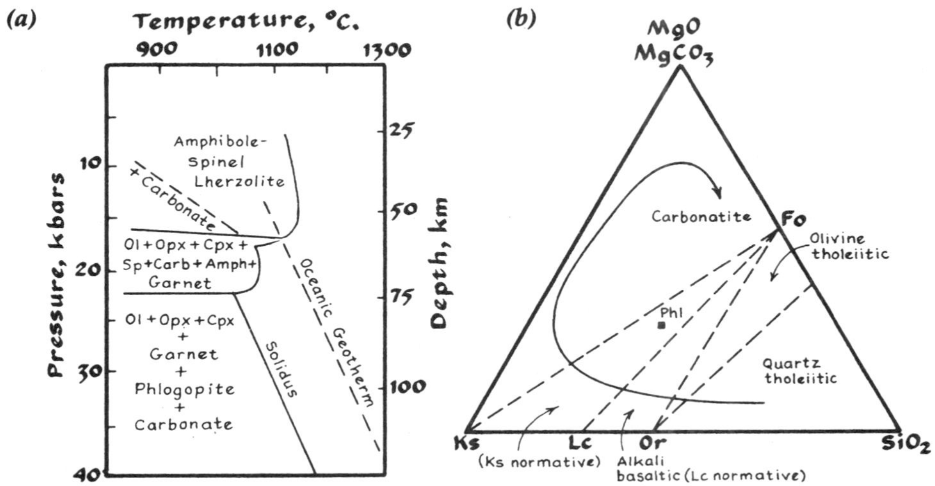

Figure 11–24 (a) Phase relations of lherzolite in the presence of H_2O and CO_2. Molar $CO_2/(CO_2 + H_2O) = 0.5$. Note that the solidus has two inflections, one at the stability limit for carbonate and another for amphibole. The kimberlite solidus in Figure 11–22 has only one, because H_2O was not a component in the experimental system. The absence of H_2O also causes the temperature to be higher. The oceanic geotherm shown here is for lithosphere that is 30 m.y. old. The continental geotherm would be well below the solidus. (After M. Olafsson and D. H. Eggler, 1983, *Earth Planet. Sci. Ltrs.* 64:305–315.) (b) The general trend of potassic liquids with increasing pressure, indicated by an arrow, is essentially the same with or without H_2O and CO_2, but the pressures at which the liquids cross the field boundaries and differ:

Boundaries of liquids	Pressures of transitions Volatile-free	CO₂-saturated
Hy to Lc	19 kbars	14 kbars
Lc to Ks	34.5 "	27.5 "
Ks to $MgCO_3$-	—	>29 "

(Adapted from R. F. Wendlandt and D. H. Eggler, 1980, *Amer. Jour. Sci.* 280:385–420.)

ULTRAPOTASSIC SERIES

Like their sodic counterparts, highly potassic rocks have a number of unusual features that set them apart from all other rock series. Although an abundance of potassium may be expressed in a variety of minerals, the most characteristic is leucite, (K,Na)$AlSi_2O_6$, or *pseudoleucite,* a faintly birefringent intergrowth of nepheline, K-feldspar, and analcite formed from leucite on cooling. Whereas all rocks with modal nepheline are critically undersaturated in silica, rocks containing the potassic feldspathoid, leucite, may be alkaline, sub-alkaline, or peralkaline. This difference is the result of two factors. The first is simply the greater silica content of leucite. Unlike nepheline, (Na,K)$AlSiO_4$, which contains only 40 to 44 percent SiO_2, leucite, (K,Na)$AlSi_2O_6$, contains an additional SiO_2 and about 54 percent silica. The second reason is related to the incongruent melting of potassium feldspar. Melting of sanidine or orthoclase at low pressures does not yield a liquid of its own composition, but leucite and a liquid somewhat richer in SiO_2 than feldspar (Fig. 11–25a). The relations are much like those of enstatite, which melts incongruently to forsterite and a liquid richer in SiO_2 than pyroxene. Thus, if a liquid that is not undersaturated in SiO_2 precipitates leucite, the remaining liquid can become quartz-normative.

As can be seen from the system Ne-Ks-Q (Fig. 11–25b), the leucite field contracts with increasing water pressures, so that the incongruent melting of the potassium feldspar disappears at pressures slightly in excess of two kbars. At the same time, the temperature minimum at m_{ne} becomes a true eutectic, just as the corresponding minimum, m_s, is in the silica-saturated part of the system (Fig. 10–12). The field of leucite, though smaller, persists up to water pressures of about 8.4 kbars and even higher under dry conditions.

Thus, even though it is a feldspathoid, leucite does not necessarily indicate the same degree of silica deficiency as nepheline, for many rocks with modal leucite do not have that mineral in their norm. For this reason, a distinction is often made between leucite-bearing rocks that are critically undersaturated in SiO_2, i.e., those with normative Ne, and those that are not alkaline in the strict sense of the term. For example, leucite-bearing basalts that contain olivine are usually distinguished from those that do not. Because the former are more likely to be undersaturated with silica, they are called *leucite basanites,* whereas the latter are referred to as *leucite tephrites.* A similar distinction is made between felsic, leucite-rich rocks containing normative hypersthene and those with modal or normative nepheline. The former are given the name *leucite trachytes,* the latter *leucite phonolites.*

The potassic equivalent of nepheline is kalsilite (named from the first five letters of its chemical formula, $KAlSiO_4$). The mineral, which is optically indistinguishable from nepheline, has been reported from only two provinces, the Western Rift of Africa and Italy.

Volcanic potassic suites

Some of the first potassic lavas to attract scientific attention were the leucite-rich products of Vesuvius, the volcano responsible for the destruction of Pompeii in A.D. 79. Although it is now known that these lavas are not, as was once thought,

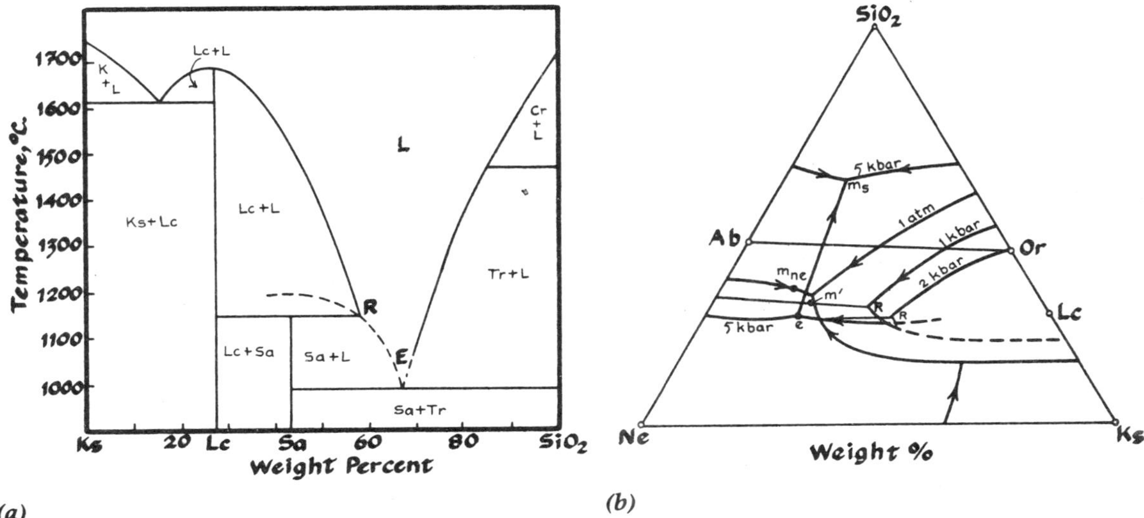

(a) *(b)*

Figure 11–25 (a) The system kalsilite ($KAlSiO_4$)-silica resembles that of forsterite-silica in that the intermediate compound, sanidine, melts incongruently to a more silica-poor phase, leucite, and a more silica-rich liquid. (After J. F. Schairer and N. L. Bowen, 1955, *Amer. Jour. Sci.* 253:681–746.) (b) The effect of increasing water pressure on the system nepheline-kalsilite-silica of Figure 11–2 is to reduce the field of leucite, as shown by the boundaries retreating toward the right side of the triangle. At the same time, the boundary between the feldspars and feldspathoids moves farther from silica and the minimum on this boundary eventually becomes a eutectic. (After compilation by J. Gittins, 1979, *The Evolution of the Igneous Rocks: Fiftieth Anniversary Perspectives*, H. S. Yoder, Jr., ed., 351–390.)

unique to the Roman province of central Italy, leucitic rocks are found in only a few scattered localities outside the Mediterranean. Examples (Figure 11–26) are known from the western United States, Africa, Australia, and Indonesia, but all these occurrences are small and isolated.

If one can speak of such diverse suites as "types" when some occur in only a single, small locality, it is possible to divide potassic rocks into three very broad types, alkaline, peralkaline, and sub-alkaline, on the basis of their relative contents of alkalies, silica, and alumina.

Alkaline potassic rocks are, by definition, critically undersaturated in SiO_2; that is, they have nepheline in their norm. The leucitic lavas of the Western Rift of East Africa are perhaps the most important example. They are so rich in potassium and deficient in silica that, in addition to leucite, they contain kalsilite, as well as olivine, nepheline, melilite, biotite, and the usual accessories of these minerals, perovskite and apatite. Typical chemical compositions are illustrated in Table 11–3. Even the most mafic varieties, such as *ugandite*, are exceptionally rich in Ba, Sr, Zr, and REE, as well as TiO_2 and P_2O_5. The name *lamproite* is used as a general term for mafic varieties consisting mainly of phlogopite, Ca-pyroxene or

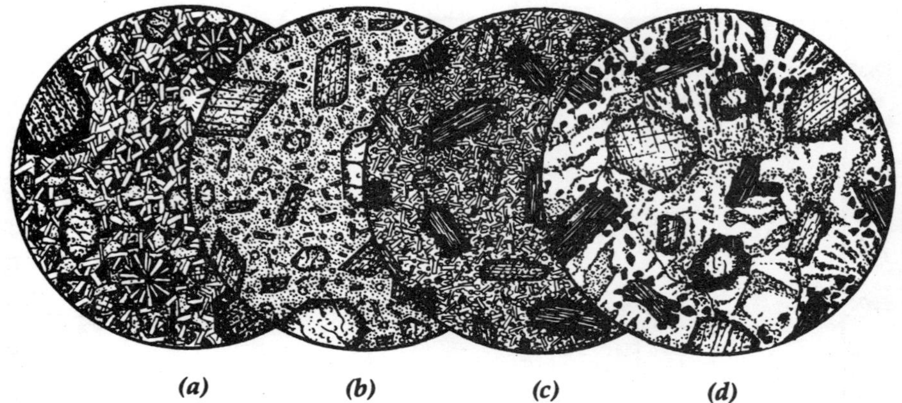

(a) (b) (c) (d)

Figure 11–26 Petrographic features of ultra-potassic rocks. (a) A leucite basanite from Muhavura Volcano, Rwanda, consists of phenocrysts of olivine and zoned Ti-augite in a groundmass rich in small crystals of leucite. (b) Ugandite is a similar rock in that it consists mainly of leucite, augite, and olivine but has a sodium-rich groundmass and is more mafic. (c) Wyomingite from the Leucite Hills, Wyoming, contains phenocrysts of titaniferous phlogopite and slender crystals of greenish augite in a groundmass rich in leucite. (d) Shonkinite from the Shonkin Sag intrusion, Montana, consists mainly of sanidine, augite, biotite, olivine, iron-titanium oxides, and minor nepheline and apatite. (Diameter of fields 3 mm.)

Table 11–3 Chemical compositions of characteristic types of mafic potassic alkaline rocks. The following normative minerals may be unfamiliar: Tn-sphene ($CaTiSiO_5$), Ru-rutile (TiO_2), Lc-leucite ($KAlSi_2O_6$), Ks-potassium metasilicate (K_2SiO_3), Ns-sodium metasilicate (Na_2SiO_3), Hm-hematite (Fe_2O_3), Cm-chromite (Cr_2FeO_4), Hl-halite (NaCl), Fl-fluorite (CaF_2). Pv-perovskite ($CaTiO_3$). (See Appendix A.)

	1.	2.	3.	4.	5.	6.	7.	8.
SiO_2	44.08	38.05	41.63	47.67	49.86	53.99	55.02	56.26
TiO_2	1.85	3.84	4.94	1.13	0.76	1.06	2.39	2.54
Al_2O_3	9.93	9.85	7.99	18.14	11.07	17.82	11.10	10.13
Fe_2O_3	3.07	8.41	5.60	0.63	3.64	5.16	3.20	3.56
FeO	8.12	2.80	4.96	6.48	5.52	2.94	1.51	0.83
MnO	0.17	0.21	0.16	—	0.17	0.12	0.06	0.06
MgO	20.34	13.55	16.09	4.19	14.60	4.25	7.12	8.05
CaO	8.77	13.90	10.19	9.01	8.38	6.15	4.80	3.84
Na_2O	1.55	1.31	0.68	2.78	1.96	3.30	1.39	1.29
K_2O	1.74	3.02	7.33	7.47	3.54	4.53	11.58	12.00
P_2O_5	0.37	0.95	0.44	0.50	0.50	0.68	1.83	1.46
CO_2	—	1.47	—	—	—	—	—	—
Cl	—	—	—	—	—	—	0.03	—
F	—	0.27	—	—	—	—	0.50	—
Cr_2O_3	—	0.02	—	—	—	—	0.10	—
SrO	—	0.24	—	—	—	—	0.24	—
BaO	—	0.27	—	—	—	—	1.23	—

Table 11–3 (Cont.)

	Molecular Norms							
Ap	0.75	2.13	0.91	1.05	1.02	1.42	4.11	3.03
Il	2.49	4.71	6.80	1.57	1.03	1.48	2.32	1.37
Tn	—	—	—	—	—	—	0.82	3.22
Pv	—	—	—	—	—	—	0.37	—
Ru	—	—	—	—	—	—	0.45	—
Mt	3.10	—	1.56	0.66	3.72	4.90	—	—
Hm	—	5.93	1.67	—	—	0.33	—	0.16
Or	9.94	0.62	—	13.52	20.44	26.78	58.90	54.92
Ab	4.77	—	—	—	15.00	29.65	—	—
An	14.50	12.22	—	15.09	10.71	20.44	—	—
Di	20.18	33.66	37.72	21.37	21.39	4.51	12.29	3.27
Hy	—	—	—	—	—	9.49	—	20.45
Ol	39.05	5.76	18.80	6.81	25.36	—	9.73	0.81
Ne	5.21	7.14	0.18	15.11	1.32	—	—	—
Ac	—	—	4.59	—	—	—	8.67	9.20
Lc	—	13.94	8.31	24.80	—	—	—	—
Kp	—	—	19.45	—	—	—	—	—
Ks	—	—	—	—	—	—	2.28	4.65
Ns	—	—	—	—	—	—	0.26	—
Q	—	—	—	—	—	1.00	—	—
Cc	—	3.76	—	—	—	—	—	—
Hl	—	—	—	—	—	—	0.17	—
Fl	—	0.36	—	—	—	—	0.58	—
Cm	—	0.01	—	—	—	—	0.07	—

1. Olivine ugandite, Uganda. (A. Holmes and F. Harwood, 1937, *Mem. Geol. Surv. Uganda*, 3.)
2. Katungite, Uganda. (A. D. Edgar and M. Arima, 1981, *N. Jb. Miner. Mh.* 12:539–552.)
3. Biotite mafurite, Uganda. (A. Holmes, 1942, *Min. Mag.* 26:197–217.)
4. Leucite tephrite, 1872 lava of Vesuvius. (H. S. Washington, 1906, *Carnegie Inst. Washington, Publ.* 57.)
5. Absarokite, Absaroka Mts., Montana. (D. E. Gest and A. R. McBirney, 1979, *Jour. Volc. Geoth. Res.* 6:85–104.)
6. Shoshonite, Absaroka Mts., Montana. (D. E. Gest and A. R. McBirney, 1979, *Jour. Volc. Geoth. Res.* 6:85–104.)
7. Average wyomingite, Leucite Hills, Montana. (Th. G. Sahama, 1974, *The Alkaline Rocks*, H. Sorensen, ed., 96–109.)
8. Average orendite, Leucite Hills, Montana. (Th. G. Sahama, 1974, *The Alkaline Rocks*, H. Sorensen, ed., 96–109.)

amphibole, olivine, leucite, and sanidine but without primary plagioclase, melilite, kalsilite, nepheline, or melanite.

Peralkaline potassic rocks are exemplified by the lavas of the Leucite Hills, Wyoming. Though highly potassic and rich in leucite, they are not strongly undersaturated in SiO_2. Their deficiency of alumina is reflected in the norm, not only as acmite but also as potassium metasilicate, Ks, a normative mineral with the formula K_2SiO_3. (Ks is calculated from the K and Si remaining after both Al and Fe^{3+} have been exhausted. Although its normative designation is Ks, it should not be confused with kalsilite ($KAlSiO_4$), which, unfortunately, is often abbreviated Ks on phase diagrams. The designation for normative kalsilite is Kp after its polymorphic form, kaliophilite.)

The normative mineral Ks is not a modal component of these rocks. Instead, the lavas are unusually rich in phlogopite. *Wyomingites*, for example, are essentially phlogopite-rich leucite tephrites; similar rocks with abundant sanidine in their groundmass are called *orendites*. The sanidine in the latter is an interesting manifestation of the peralkaline potassic character of the rocks. It is rich in ferric iron, which substitutes for Al in the feldspar lattice, and in that sense it is analogous to acmite, the sodium-ferric iron-pyroxene that characterizes peralkaline sodic rocks.

Sub-alkaline potassic rocks may have ratios of K_2O to Na_2O ranging from less than 1.0 to 6.0 or more. Those with smaller ratios may be gradational into the more common types of rock series. In chapter nine, for example, we noted that certain subalkaline series of the continental interiors are somewhat more potassic than the common calc-alkaline series of continental margins (Fig. 10–8) and that they define a "high-K series" consisting of trachybasalts, trachyandesites, and latites, all distinguished petrographically by modal alkali feldspars, usually sanidine or orthoclase. In most respects, these rocks follow the same trends of differentiation as normal calc-alkaline rocks.

Though these mildly potassic calc-alkaline rocks are sometimes said to be *shoshonitic*, true *shoshonites* are richer in alkalies, particularly K_2O, and contain leucite. They are essentially basaltic rocks composed of olivine and augite phenocrysts in a groundmass of orthoclase-rimmed labradorite, olivine, and leucite. With increasing amounts of olivine, they grade into *absarokites*, and with increasing silica into *banakites*. Their compositions are characterized by large concentrations of Ba, Rb, Sr, and most large-ion lithophile elements.

Differentiation of ultra-potassic magmas

Trends of differentiation in these highly potassic series are difficult to define and almost impossible to explain. In many cases, felsic alkaline magmas occur alone or in a bimodal association with mafic rocks and few if any intermediate compositions. Only rarely is the range of compositions extensive, and in most provinces where basic, intermediate, and felsic rocks are found in close association, their genetic relations are obscure.

The problem is well-illustrated by a rare example of a differentiated potassic intrusion, the Shonkin Sag laccolith in the Highwood Mountains of Montana (Fig. 11–27). Some forty to seventy meters thick, the body has chilled upper and lower margins that grade into medium- to coarse-grained mafic rocks consisting mainly of augite, sanidine, and olivine, with subordinate biotite, titaniferous magnetite, apatite, zeolites, carbonates, and differing amounts of pseudoleucite and minor nepheline. The main mafic mineral, pyroxene, ranges in composition from Ca-rich augite to Na-rich acmite. Sphene and the dark-brown, iron-rich garnet, melanite, are common accessories. These rocks, called *shonkinites* after the Indian name for the Highwood Mountains, encase a core of sanidine-rich syenite. The lower part of the latter is pegmatitic and intermediate in composition between the underlying shonkinite and a more differentiated syenite above. All the rocks are strongly undersaturated with normative Ne reaching values of nearly 30 percent in the syenites, but most of the modal nepheline seems to have been altered to zeolites. The minerals of both the shonkinite and syenite have

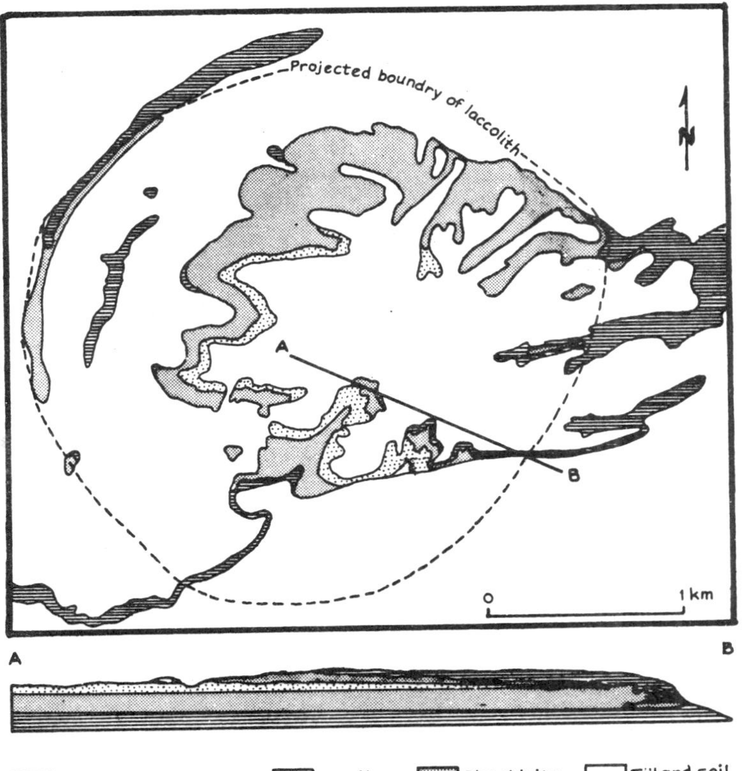

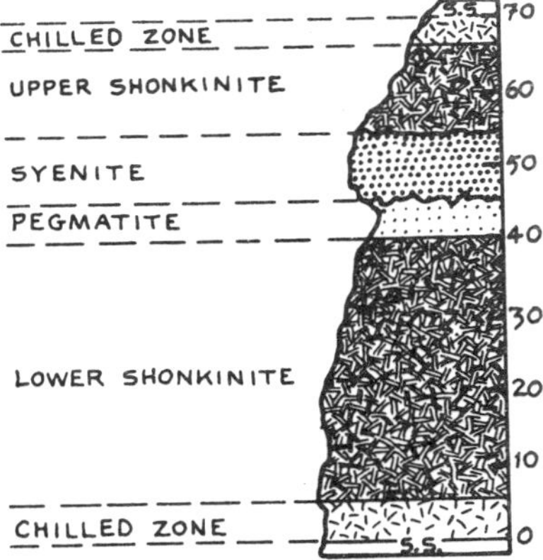

Figure 11–27 Simplified map and cross section through the Shonkin Sag Laccolith of Montana. (Map after C. S. Hurlbut, Jr. and D. Griggs, 1939, *Bull. Geol. Soc. Amer.* 50:1043–1112; section after G. C. Kendrick and C. L. Edmond, 1981, *Geology* 9:615–619.)

similar compositions, and the differences between the two rock types is mainly in the proportions, rather than the compositions of dark and light minerals.

The manner in which the body differentiated is difficult to explain in terms of any conventional scheme of crystal fractionation. The chilled margin contains abundant phenocrysts of what is now pseudoleucite and lesser amounts of biotite, so we can assume that both minerals were stable phases in the magma at the time of intrusion. In the more slowly cooled interior, pseudoleucite gives way to sanidine, as would be expected if the early formed crystals reacted with the liquid on cooling. But when the compositional variations of the various units from the chilled margin to the syenitic core are plotted on a diagram for the system Q-Ne-Kp, they define a nearly linear series (Fig. 11–28a). It must be remembered, of course, that in such a plot the mafic components have been ignored, so that the bulk compositions are projected from outside the triangle. It is instructive, nevertheless, to compare the observed trends with those that would result from crystal fractionation (Fig. 11–28b).

Note that a potassium-rich liquid, such as X, crystallizing initially in the leucite field, should follow a curved course away from the composition of leucite

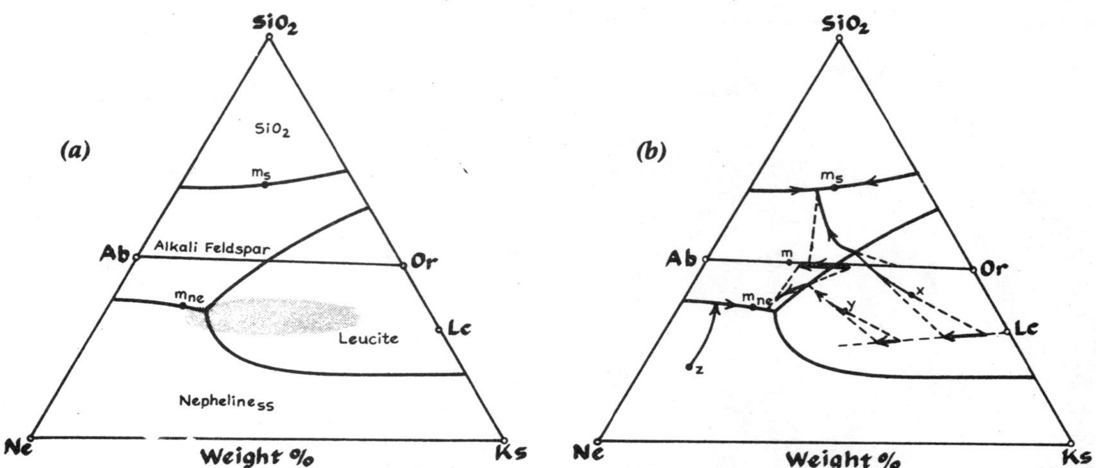

Figure 11–28 (a) The compositions of rocks of the Shonkin Sag Laccolith plotted in the same system as Figure 11–24(a). (After W. P. Nash and J. F. G. Wilkinson, 1970, *Contr. Mineral. Petrol.* 25:241–269.) (b) Trends of various liquids crystallizing in the silica-deficient part of the system Ne-Ks-Q. (After S. A. Morse, 1980, *Basalts and Phase Diagrams*.)

that becomes increasingly sodic with falling temperature. On reaching that part of the boundary of the leucite field that is a peritectic, i.e., the part above the feldspar join, the remaining liquid may react with the leucite crystals to form K-feldspar, or, if no reaction takes place, continue to descend toward the granite minimum at m_s. A more sodic liquid, such as Y, reaches the leucite field boundary below the feldspar join, where it is a cotectic. It then precipitates leucite together with K-feldspar, and descends toward the other low-temperature end-point at m_{ne}. An even more sodic liquid, such as Z, falls in the field of primary crystallization of nepheline, and its course on cooling would be away from the composition of that mineral. The evolving liquid will eventually reach the nepheline-feldspar boundary and descend along it toward m_{ne}.

The rocks of Shonkin Sag follow none of these trends. Instead, they fall along a line between the composition of leucite and that of the eutectic at m_{ne}. Because of their proximity to the trace of the reaction point R as it advances along the feldspar join with falling pressure (Fig. 11–25b), the rock compositions might be explained as the result of loss of water during degassing of the intrusion were it not for the fact that loss of a water-rich volatile phase causes R to migrate in the opposite direction, increasing the leucite field and tending to stabilize that mineral. As already noted, sanidine, not leucite, is the stable phase in the late syenitic rocks. Alternatively, if the amount of water had increased, owing, perhaps, to concentration of the volatile components in a diminishing volume of liquid, temperature would also have to increase if the composition of the liquid were to follow the point R toward the right and away from the minimum at m_{ne}.

The fact that the variations correspond to differing proportions of minerals in a matrix of nearly constant phonolitic composition suggests that the differentiated rocks are simply products of gravitational segregation of crystals. Leucite, being very light, might float and accumulate in the upper levels of the reservoir, but leucite is not notably more abundant at the top of the intrusion than it is on the floor.

Another possibility is that volatile transfer was responsible for the differing proportions of K_2O and Na_2O. It was proposed many years ago, for example, that the potassic character of the leucitic lavas of Vesuvius results from selective partitioning of Na into a volatile phase. The volatiles escape into a hydrothermal system that is manifested in sodium-rich hotsprings and fumaroles on the flanks of the volcano. This selective loss of sodium would leave the magma relatively enriched in K.

In the case of the Shonkin Sag, the extensive hydrothermal alteration of the rocks and the wide variation of their alkali ratios lend credence to this interpretation. Evidence of a vapor phase is found in the abundance of zeolites, carbonates, and other products of hydrothermal alteration. Moreover, the proportions of Na and K are consistent with the experimentally determined partitioning of alkalies between feldspars and hydrothermal solutions. The composition of a hydrous vapor phase in equilibrium with alkali feldspars is very sensitive to the composition of the feldspar with which it is in equilibrium (Fig. 11–29). It tends to be much richer in sodium than all but the most sodic feldpars. If the feldspars of the rocks plotted in Fig. 11–28a have approximately the same ratios of alkalies as the bulk rocks, a vapor in equilibrium with them would be much richer in sodium and, if separated and deposited in a cooler part of the system, they could effect a marked change of the bulk composition of the remaining crystalline assemblage. Thus a vapor phase may be an effective means of fractionating alkalies, and the observed variations may have less to do with crystal-liquid fractionation than with alkali transfer in a vapor phase exsolved during late stages of cooling.

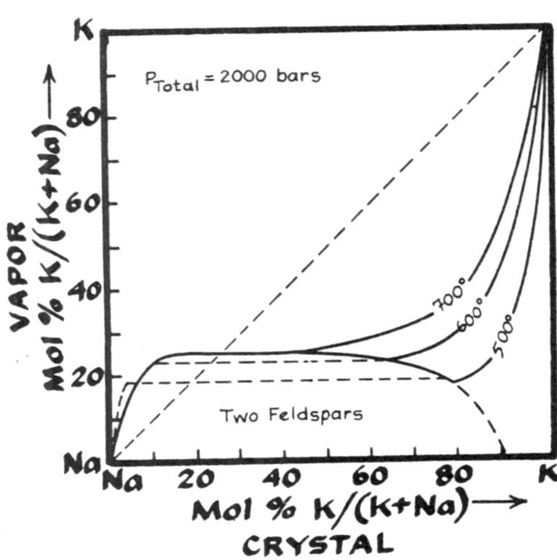

Figure 11–29 The ratio of Na to K in a vapor phase containing alkali chlorides, shown on the vertical axis, is sensitive to that of coexisting alkali feldspar, shown on the horizontal axis. The data shown here are for a total pressure of 2,000 bars and a concentration of 2 mole percent total alkali chlorides in the vapor phase. At this pressure the feldspar solvus limits the range of compositions of the alkali feldspars (Fig. 4–6b). Note that for a broad range of feldspar compositions, the composition of the vapor phase, shown by the curves labeled for temperature, is much richer in sodium than coexisting K-feldspars. Because of these differences, a chloride-rich vapor phase could be an effective agent of fractionation of alkalies. (After P. M. Orville, 1963, *Amer. Jour. Sci.* 261:201–237.)

Another explanation of the linear compositional variations would relate the syenites and shonkinites to two immiscible liquids that separated during the middle and late stages of cooling. This interpretation, which was favored by early geologists who examined the body late in the last century, fell into disfavor when N. L. Bowen convinced many American geologists that immiscibility was an unlikely explanation for differentiation of magmas. More recently, however, immiscibility has been shown to be a very real feature of many alkaline liquids, and the fact that the two main rocks of the laccolith contain very similar minerals in different modal proportions is consistent with such a relationship.

MANTLE ORIGINS OF INTRA-PLATE ALKALINE MAGMAS

Highly alkaline magmas, particularly the potassic varieties, have only recently been accepted as primary melts of the mantle. They were long considered to be the result of assimilation of continental crust or even the products of partial melting of metamorphic rocks rich in biotite or hornblende. Even though very similar rocks were found on oceanic islands, it was argued that these islands must be underlain by ancient continental crust. We now know that this is impossible.

The volcanic islands of Tristan da Cunha and Gough lie close to the Mid-Atlantic Ridge in the South Atlantic, and both have unusually potassic alkaline rocks. The lavas of Tristan da Cunha, for example, include leucite basanites rich in Rb, Ba, Sr, and Nb; those of Gough are somewhat less potassic but are no less enriched in lithophile elements. The occurrence of carbonatites in the Cape Verde islands was mentioned earlier. Trinidade and Fernando da Noronha, two tiny islands in the western part of the South Atlantic, have nephelinitic lavas and sodalite phonolites that differ in only minor ways from those of East Africa. Xenoliths in the volcanic rocks of Trinidade include coarse-grained rocks similar to mafic varieties of ijolite, such as jacupirangites.

Thus there is no question that intra-plate alkaline magmas with these unusual compositions are derived from the mantle and do not require continental lithosphere to account for their unusual compositions. How then are they produced? As we saw in chapter seven, the common types of oceanic basalts are readily explained as the products of differing degrees of melting garnet lherzolite. Getting highly potassic magmas, nephelinites, melililites, and the like from such a source is something else; some other factor must contribute to the compositions of mafic melts that have large amounts of MgO and yet are unusually rich in alkalies and incompatible elements.

High-pressure experiments in which reasonable mantle source rocks, such as garnet- or spinel-lherzolite, are partially melted under a wide range of conditions, fail to yield potassic liquids undersaturated in SiO_2. Moreover, when liquids of these compositions are crystallized at high pressures their near-liquidus phases do not include all the essential minerals of normal mantle peridotites—olivine, two pyroxenes, and spinel or garnet. Each composition is found to have different liquidus minerals that crystallize over a wide range of conditions, including temperature, pressure, and contents of CO_2 and H_2O. In short, there is no simple way in which these magmas could be produced by melting of normal mantle.

One can gain insights into the nature of the source rocks and conditions of melting by comparing the minerals that crystallize from the lavas in high-pressure experiments with those of ultramafic rocks found as inclusions in the same lavas. An especially thorough study of this kind was conducted on a suite of highly potassic lavas and associated ultramafic inclusions from the Western Rift of Africa. The lavas are from the ugandite-katungite-mafurite series mentioned in an earlier section (Table 11–3). They have brought to the surface a variety of mafic and ultramafic nodules, but the most common types consist mainly of clinopyroxene, phlogopite, and minor Fe-Ti oxides, sphene, and apatite. They have little or no garnet or olivine and have cross-cutting veins and other textural features suggestive of metasomatic recrystallization.

When the potassic lavas were melted and recrystallized at high pressures in the presence of a water-rich volatile phase, the liquidus phases were found to be the same as those in the nodules, namely Ca-rich pyroxene, phlogopite, and a Fe-Ti oxide. Olivine was an additional mineral in some but not all compositions. These results showed that the liquids would have been in equilibrium with a deep source consisting of the same principal minerals found in their associated ultramafic inclusions but not those of normal lherzolites. This conclusion was confirmed by partially melting an ultramafic assemblage with the composition of the average phlogopite-bearing nodule. The liquids obtained in this way have compositions, though not identical, at least very similar to those of the lavas (Table 11–4.) Moreover, the changes in composition of the liquid with progressive degrees of melting corresponded in a crude fashion to the variations in the series of lavas.

Though experiments of this kind have yet to explore the full range of possible melting conditions, they indicate that under certain conditions the lavas could be derived by partial melting of ultramafic rocks of appropriate compositions. The combination of compositions and melting conditions determined in each set of experiments is unique to an individual lava; each type seems to require different melting conditions and source rocks, few of which correspond to normal mantle compositions. While the phase equilibria seem to explain the association of various types of intra-plate alkaline magmas, they leave unanswered the question of how the source rocks were altered mineralogically and enriched in elements that are normally only minor constituents of the mantle.

Mantle metasomatism

We have already noted that an increase of CO_2 and H_2O can lead to major mineralogical changes, and it is not difficult to imagine these reactions taking place when a volatile-rich fluid or melt invades normal mantle peridotites in advance of a front of melting. A loss of garnet, spinel, olivine, and orthopyroxene and an increase of clinopyroxene and either phlogopite or amphibole is consistent with the effects one would expect from addition of CO_2 and H_2O. Note that both reactions defined by equations 11–1 and 11–2 yield clinopyroxene at the expense of

Table 11–4 Partial melting at thirty kbars of an assemblage of clinopyroxene, phlogopite, and minor T-magnetite, sphene, and apatite corresponding to the average composition of ultramafic nodules (No. 1) erupted from volcanoes in the Katwe-Kikorongo and Bunyaruguru district of southwestern Uganda resulted in liquids with the composition shown in column 2. The composition at 25 percent melting is close to that of the average lava in the same district (3). The amount of melt increased from about 20 percent at 1,225° to about 30 percent at 1,250°C. (After F. E. Lloyd, M. Arima, and A. D. Edgar, 1985, *Contrib. Mineral. Petrol.* 91:321–329.)

	1.	2.	3.
SiO_2	40.20	39.9	37.1
TiO_2	4.92	5.28	5.55
Al_2O_3	7.27	7.84	6.78
Fe_2O_3	6.69	—	—
FeO	7.12	11.5*	11.9*
MnO	0.09	0.21	0.18
MgO	12.60	10.15	10.1
CaO	12.21	12.35	12.4
Na_2O	1.21	1.95	1.56
K_2O	1.21	4.96	4.06
H_2O+	1.49	2.27	—
CO_2	0.98	0.76	—
P_2O_5	0.70	0.98	1.41
F	0.15	—	—
Cl	<0.02	—	—

* All iron reported as FeO.

olivine and orthopyroxene. Increased activity of H_2O or K can lead to formation of amphibole or phlogopite at the expense of garnet, spinel, and olivine. Thus the minerals that are conspicuously absent from the mantle xenoliths are those that would be destablized by an increase of CO_2 and H_2O.

In addition to these mineralogical changes, the bulk compositions of ultramafic inclusions in highly alkaline magmas show increased abundances of K, Na, Al, F, S, Cl, Ca, Ti, Fe, Rb, Y, Zr, Nb, Ba, and REE. It is thought that these are introduced as part of the same process. Fluids rich in CO_2 and H_2O at mantle temperatures and pressures are powerful solvents capable of dissolving large amounts of alkalies. For example, at pressures between 10 and 30 kbars and temperatures of 1,050 to 1,100°C, such fluids can dissolve as much as 25 weight percent K_2O. It is interesting to note that the solubilty of Na is lower than that of K at high pressures, because pressure causes the former to enter omphacite, a sodic clinopyroxene that is stable under these conditions. Hence fluids are likely to have large K/Na ratios at deep levels, whereas the reverse would be true at shallow depths. This may account, at least in part, for the marked differences of enrichment of the two alkalies in magmas.

The physical mechanisms by which these metasomatic effects come about are poorly understood. Whether the active agent is a fluid or a silicate melt may be largely a question of semantics, for under these conditions the distinction between the two is ill-defined. Having low viscosities and densities, both are highly mobile and should migrate with ease through a crystalline matrix; they would outpace more mafic melts in a rising zone of melting. If the source of the fluid is a crystallizing intrusion or a zone of progressive melting, it may not be able to alter large volumes. The mass required to effect wholesale changes is so great that in these cases the process must operate on a local scale, such as an aureole at the leading edge of an advancing front of melting or along veins where the effect is limited to narrow selvages of the walls. If the source is a convecting asthenosphere giving up mobile components to the lithosphere, the scale of the effect may be vastly greater.

An interesting consequence of the latter possibility is its potential for generating felsic magmas. One of the most puzzling aspects of peralkaline and alkaline magmatism is the relatively large proportion of highly differentiated rocks and the scarcity of intermediate compositions. We noted earlier the trachytes and phonolites that make up such a large proportion of the Tertiary sequence of the East African Rift. Similar though perhaps less extreme examples are to be found in many intraplate provinces, both continental and oceanic. The embarrassingly large proportions of extreme differentiates are difficult to explain in terms of conventional crystal fractionation of basalt, but they present no obstacle if one postulates melting of a separate source that has been greatly enriched metasomatically in felsic components and incompatible trace elements.

Figure 11–30 illustrates how this may come about. Small amounts of early melts rising along a geotherm will encounter the stability fields of several alkali-rich felsic minerals at depths of 80 to 100 km and pressures near 25 kbars. These phases include kalsilite, jadeite, sanidine, nepheline, and, of course, amphibole. They will crystallize these minerals, and if the process continues, it could contribute enough of these essential components to serve as a later source of felsic magma. The sharp inflections of the solidus at these same depth provide a favorable condition for accumulation and later melting, either by a rise of temperature or decrease of pressure. The greater abundance of voluminous felsic alkaline magmas in regions underlain by old continental lithosphere indicates that the process of enrichment proceeds slowly on a regional scale.

Mantle sources of enriched magmas

The magmatic processes we have been considering have an important bearing on the continuing differentiation of the earth outlined in the opening chapter. If the elements that are characteristically enriched in alkaline magmas are derived almost entirely from mantle sources, as all we have learned about them indicates, they involve a selective transfer of lithophile elements contributing to the long-term evolution of the crust and mantle.

The basic nature of this process remains to be resolved. It may be one that recycles crustal material and maintains a more or less constant balance in the earth as a whole, or it may be part of the continuing segregation of lithophile components from the mantle into the crust.

This problem is similar and no doubt related to the one raised by oceanic

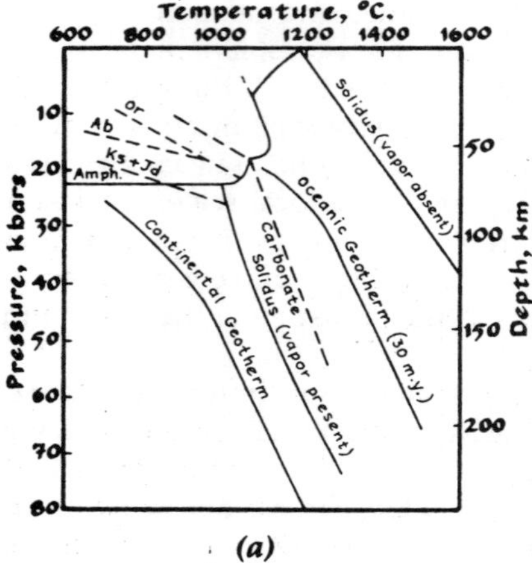

(a)

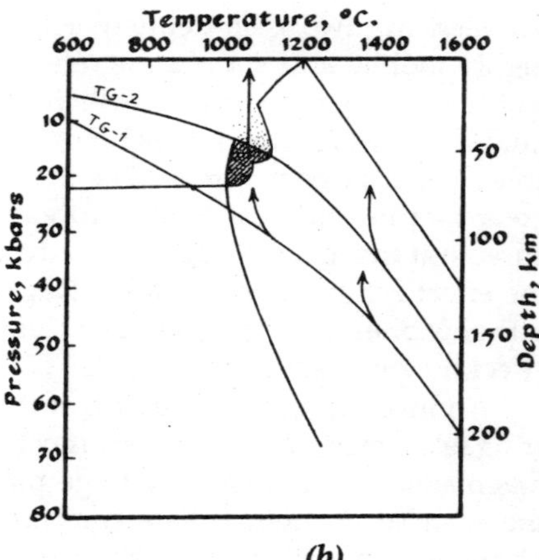

(b)

Figure 11–30 (a) Stability fields of felsic minerals in the low-pressure regime of the systems illustrated in Figure 11–24a. The names of the phases are written on the stable sides of their limiting curves. (Adapted from D. K. Bailey, 1987, *Alkaline Igneous Rocks*, Geol. Soc. Spec. Publ. No. 30, 1-13.) (b) As explained in chapter ten (Fig. 10-20), melting along a thermal gradient, such as TG-1 would produce volatile-rich liquids at shallow depths and progressively more advanced melting at deeper levels. The low-density, low-viscosity melts produced at the uppermost levels may rise and encounter the stability fields of amphibole and felsic minerals in the stippled region. They will accumulate and create an enriched zone from which felsic liquids could be generated by a later rise of the thermal gradient (TG-2). Magmas produced by melting of this assemblage in the diagonally ruled region can have very felsic compositions (Fig. 10–23) and could erupt together or alternately with more mafic magmas coming from greater depths.

hotspots. There, too, mantle-derived magmas contribute incompatible elements to the crust from sources with geochemical characteristics very different from those tapped at mid-ocean ridges. While most petrologists would agree that the sources of these lithophile components lie somewhere beneath the asthenosphere, there is little agreement on their nature or origin. Some advocate recycling between the crust and mantle via subduction of oceanic lithosphere; others assign an important role to an enriched lower mantle that has continued to be a source of lithophile components through much of geologic time. We have already noted (in chapter eight) that the diverse character of intra-plate oceanic basalts must reflect mantle inhomogeneities on a scale ranging from broad regional provinces down to local domains with dimensions measured in meters. On a small scale, we saw that even within a single seamount, lava flows may differ, both isotopically and in their trace-element patterns. On a global scale, the intra-plate magmas erupted in the southern hemisphere are consistently more enriched in incompatible elements that those of the northern hemisphere.

If these inhomogeneities stem from parts of the mantle that were not depleted by an earlier melting event, their distribution would be consistent with the smaller proportions of continental crust in the southern hemisphere, but they could also reflect crustal material returned to the mantle via subduction. In discussing the calc-alkaline magmas of orogenic systems, we found convincing evidence that at least part of the crustal component of subducted plates returns to the continents in the form of calc-alkaline magmas, but beyond that nothing more was said of the fate of the remaining oceanic lithosphere that continues to descend into the mantle. Fragments of basaltic crust and remnants of subducted sediments may continue to descend and form a deep reservoir that later serves as a source for hotspot magmas.

Depending on one's preferred convective model for the earth, this subducted material could accumulate at the 670 km discontinuity at the base of the upper mantle, or it could continue to the base of the mantle (Fig. 1–8). In the first case, magma could be generated by heat coming from the lower mantle and from potassium and other heat-producing elements contained in the subducted material itself. At the core-mantle boundary, it could be produced by heat released from the interior of the core or from exothermic reactions between molten nickel-iron and silicate minerals.

It would seem that, with all the petrologic and geochemical tools at our disposal, it would be a simple matter to distinguish between inhomogeneities due to subducted lithosphere and those due to residual primordial material. In theory, the rare gases in basalts should be able to do this. It is thought that they provide a way of identifying magmas coming from a source not completely degassed or previously tapped by melting processes. The noble gases in lavas differ in proportions and isotopic ratios from those of the atmosphere, in some instances by very large factors. Helium is a good example. This gas had a primordial isotopic ratio of ^{3}He to ^{4}He of about 1.4×10^{-4}, whereas the ratio for the modern atmosphere is two orders of magnitude smaller. This difference is due to the increase with time of ^{4}He (as a result of decay of U and Th) relative to non-radiogenic ^{3}He. Degassing of radiogenic ^{4}He from crustal rocks rich in U and Th causes it to accumulate in the atmosphere.

The isotopic ratios of He in oceanic basalts have been found to be about ten to thirty times greater than that of the atmosphere. Those of MORB tend to be fairly constant at the lower end of this range, but intra-plate lavas are much more varied from one locality to another and even within a single hotspot chain. These results, though still difficult to interpret, indicate that the mantle has not completely expelled its primordial He and that degassing has not been uniform, at least at the levels tapped by hotspots. If volcanism is the main mechanism of degassing, we can infer that intra-plate magmas are derived, at least in part, from inhomogeneities of the primitive mantle. It is doubtful that He could be retained by subducted crustal rocks long enough to return to the mantle.

Other geochemical factors, however, indicate that subducted lithosphere does in fact contribute to these magmas. The isotopic ratios of Sr, Nd, and Pb can be used to define at least three enriched components found in differing proportions in most intra-plate magmas (Figure 11–31). One of these is distinguished by unusually radiogenic Pb (^{206}Pb/^{204}Pb > 20.5) derived from sources with elevated ratios of ^{238}U to ^{204}Pb. This group is usually referred to as HIMU after the term μ that is used for this ratio (Appendix D, Fig. D–2). Two other groups, EMI and EMII, are both products of enriched mantle. Both of the latter must have unusual amounts of large-ion lithophile elements and light REE giving the magmas elevated ratios of ^{87}Sr/^{86}Sr and low ratios of ^{143}Nd/^{144}Nd, but this characteristic is more pronounced in EMII ($^{87}Sr/^{86}SR > 0.7065$) than it is in EMI ($^{87}Sr/^{86}Sr$ = 0.7050 to 0.7055). With the exception of MORB, the isotopic character of all the major types of basalt can be accounted for as combinations of components from groups fall close to the mantle array defined by Sr and Nd (Fig. 8–12.)

The characteristics of these three components have been explained as the results of changes that are thought to take place during dehydration of the subducted lithosphere. The behavior of incompatible trace elements during this process would be governed in large part by the solubilities of these elements in a hydrous vapor-phase. Solubilities vary inversely with ionic potential (the ratio of valence to ionic radius), so that high-field-strength elements (HFSE), such U, Th, Nb, and Ta, are less soluble than large-ion lithophile elements (LILE), such as Cs, Rb, K, Ba, and Sr. Thus, dehydration of the upper part of a subducted slab should result in a loss to the more soluble LILE and residual enrichment of less soluble elements, such as Nb and Ta. Relative to the original mid-ocean ridge basalt, the dehydrated basalt would have small LILE/HFSE ratios, and these ratios should be retained even after the basalt is converted to eclogite. If the elements have very small distribution coefficients, their ratios should not be greatly altered by subsequent partial melting or shallow differentiation.

The parent nuclides of radiogenic Pb, U, and Th have large ionic potentials (U^{4+} 4.5, U^{6+} 8.2, and Th^{4+} 4.3); whereas that of lead is much smaller, about 1.7. The ratios of U and Th, which are retained, to Pb, which will be prefentially lost from subducted lithosphere, will therefore be increased, and as the radioactive isotopes of U and Th decay, the dehydrated rocks will take on the isotopic character of HIMU. This effect will also be evident in low ratios of LILE, such as Ba and Rb to HFSE, such as Th and Nb.

These same ratios are distinctly larger in basalts with a large component of the EMI-type source, because the abundances of HFSE are proportionately lower. Ba, an element that is strongly enriched in pelagic sediments, is especially abundant in basalts of this type. This, together with somewhat more radiogenic Sr ratios, has been taken as evidence that this component comes from the subducted part of layer one of the oceanic crust. Because the abundances of HFSE

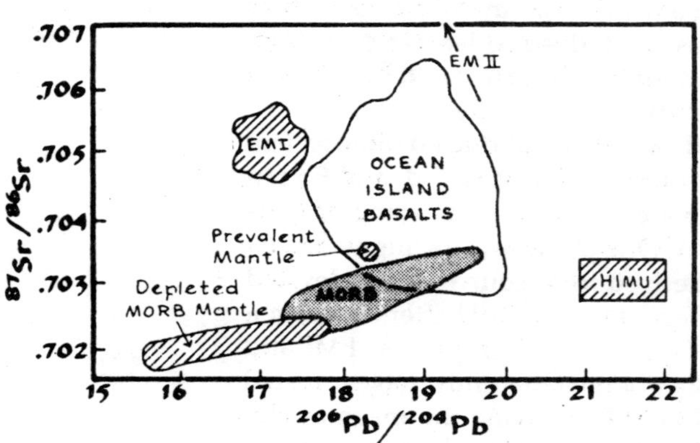

Figure 11–31 Several mantle sources of basalts can be identified by their isotopic ratios of Pb, Sr, and Nd. Two of these (EM-I and EM-II) are more enriched in lithophile elements than the "prevalent mantle"; the high-μ component (HIMU) is distinguished by an unusually large ratio of U to Pb. Note that most ocean-island basalts can be explained as combinations of different proportions of magmas from these three components. Mid-ocean-ridge basalts (MORB) are derived from mantle sources that have been depleted by one or more earlier melting events. (Adapted from A. Zindler and S. Hart, 1986, *Ann. Rev. Earth Planet. Sci.*, 14:493–571.)

are very low in seawater, pelagic sediments absorb relatively less of these insoluble elements. The EMII component is similar and commonly gradational into EMI. It contains much less Ba but more radiogenic Sr and, for this reason, is thought to reflect the contribution of terrigenous sediments eroded from the continents and mixed with pelagic material in trenches.

It is probably unrealistic to expect clearly identifiable patterns in these relations. Melts from mantle inhomogeneities due to subducted crust must be mixtures of all these components and perhaps others as well. Their trace-element ratios may be altered by differing degrees of partial melting, and their isotopic ratios will vary with age. Moreover, the interpretations outlined here are based on very limited analytical data and may very well be discredited as more mantle-derived basalts are studied. Whatever the merits of these hypotheses, however, they illustrate the fascinating lines of current work and clearly demonstrate the opportunities for future research.

SELECTED REFERENCES

Bonin, B. 1986. *Ring Complex Granites and Anorogenic Magmatism.* North Oxford Academic, 188 pp. A concise, well-presented survey of an important group of continental intrusive rocks.

Dawson, J. B. 1980. *Kimberlites and Their Xenoliths.* Springer-Verlag, 252 pp. A very thorough treatment of the occurrence, compositions, and modern genetic theories of kimberlites.

Fitton, J. G., and B. G. J. Upton, eds. 1987. *Alkaline Igneous Rocks*. Geol. Soc. Spec. Publ. No. 30., 568 pp. By far the most comprehensive and up-to-date compilation of outstanding papers on all aspects of alkaline rocks. The numerous reviews of broad topics are unusually informative and lucid.

Le Bas, M. J. 1977. *Carbonatite-Nephelinite Volcanism.* Wiley, 347 pp. A detailed account of carbonatites and related rocks with emphasis on those of Kenya but with discussions of general petrogenetic relations.

Pasteris, J. D. 1984. Kimberlites: complex mantle melts. *Ann. Rev. Earth Planet. Sci.* 12:133–153. A concise summary of recent work on kimberlites with a useful bibliography of relevant literature.

Sorensen, H., ed. 1974. *The Alkaline Rocks.* Wiley Interscience, 622 pp. A comprehensive survey of nearly all types of alkaline and peralkaline rocks presented in a collection of review papers. Though some sections are outdated, the book contains a vast amount of useful information.

APPENDIX A

Calculation of Normative Minerals

The principles of normative calculations are discussed in chapter two of the text. The procedure given here is for the "Molecular" or "Barth-Niggli" norm. The values obtained can be converted to a CIPW norm by multiplying the proportions of minerals by their molecular weights and recalculating to 100 percent. Note that abbreviations for minerals of the molecular norm are capitalized, whereas those of the CIPW norm are not.

Normative Minerals

Mineral	Symbol	Chemical Formula	Formula Wt.
Acmite	Ac	$Na_2O \cdot Fe_2O_3 \cdot 4SiO_2$	462
Albite	Ab	$Na_2O \cdot Al_2O_3 \cdot 6SiO_2$	524
Anorthite	An	$CaO \cdot Al_2O_3 \cdot 2SiO_2$	278
Apatite	Ap	$3.3CaO \cdot P_2O_5$	310
Calcite	Cc	$CaO \cdot CO_2$	100
Chromite	Cm	$FeO \cdot Cr_2O_3$	224
Corundum	C	Al_2O_3	102
Diopside	Di	$CaO \cdot (Mg,Fe)O \cdot SiO_2$	217–248*
Fluorite	Fl	CaF_2	78.1
Halite	Hl	$NaCl$	58.4
Hematite	Hm	Fe_2O_3	160
Hypersthene	Hy	$2(Mg,Fe)O \cdot 2SiO_2$	200–264*
Ilmenite	Il	$FeO \cdot TiO_2$	152
Kaliophilite	Kp	$K_2O \cdot Al_2O_3 \cdot 2SiO_2$	316
K-metasilicate	Ks	$K_2O \cdot SiO_2$	154
Leucite	Lc	$K_2O \cdot Al_2O_3 \cdot 4SiO_2$	436
Magnetite	Mt	$FeO \cdot Fe_2O_3$	232
Nepheline	Ne	$Na_2O \cdot Al_2O_3 \cdot 2SiO_2$	284
Na-metasilicate	Ns	$Na_2O \cdot SiO_2$	122
Olivine	Ol	$2(Mg,Fe)O \cdot SiO_2$	141–204*
Orthoclase	Or	$K_2O \cdot Al_2O_3 \cdot 3SiO_2$	556
Pyrite	Pr	FeS_2	120
Quartz	Q	SiO_2	60.1
Rutile	Ru	TiO_2	79.9
Sodium carbonate	Nc	$Na_2O \cdot CO_2$	106
Sphene	Tn	$CaO \cdot TiO_2 \cdot SiO_2$	196
Wollastonite	Wo	$CaO \cdot SiO_2$	116
Zircon	Z	$ZrO_3 \cdot SiO_2$	183

* Two values are given for the molecular weights of solid-solution ferromagnesian minerals, the first for the Mg component and the second for its Fe counterpart.

The following procedure is a condensed version that does not include all possible components but illustrates the basic principles of the calculation.

A. *Calculating cation percentages.*

1. Divide each weight percentage except H_2O by the equivalent weight of the oxide based on a single cation (e.g., $AlO_{1.5}$ rather than Al_2O_3).
2. Multiply each number thus obtained by 1,000.
3. Find the total of all the products of step 2, divide each by this total, and multiply by 100. The proportions obtained in this way should sum to 100.

B. *Calculating provisional norms.*
In the following steps, it is necessary to maintain a running balance of the amount of each component left after assigning portions of it to the various normative minerals.

1. Calcite is formed from CO_2 and an equal amount of Ca.
2. Apatite is formed from P and 1.67 times this amount of Ca.
3. Pyrite is formed from S and 0.5 times this amount of Fe^{+2}.
4. Ilmentite is formed from Ti and an equal amount of Fe^{+2}.
5. The alkali feldspars are formed provisionally from K and Na, each being combined with an equal amount of Al and 3 times as much Si to form Or and Ab, respectively.
6. a. If there is an excess of Al over K + Na, it is assigned to An by combining the remaining Al with an equal amount of Si and half as much Ca.
   b. If there is not enough Ca to combine with Al in this way to make An, the excess Al is assigned to C.
7. a. If in 5 there is an excess of Na over Al, it is combined with an equal amount of Fe^{+3} and twice as much Si to make Ac.
   b. If there is an excess of Fe^{+3} over Na, it is combined with half as much Fe^{+2} to make Mt.
   c. If there is not enough Fe^{+2} to utilize all the Fe^{+3}, the remaining Fe^{+3} is assigned to Hm.
   d. Any remaining Fe^{+2} is combined with Mg and Mn and thereafter treated as FM.
8. Di is formed from the Ca left from 1, 2, and 6a by combining it with an equal amount of FM and twice as much Si.
9. Hy is formed by combining the FM remaining from 8 with an equal amount of Si.

C. *Balancing Si.*
Having assigned all the cations to provisional normative minerals, we next consider the distribution of Si.

10. a. If an excess of Si remains, it is assigned to Q.
    b. If there is a deficiency of Si, minerals of lesser silica content must be substituted, either wholly or in part. First, Hy is converted to Ol according to the equation:

$$4\ \text{Hy} = 3\ \text{Ol} + 1\ \text{Q}$$

where Q is the amount of the deficiency of Si.
    c. If all Hy has been changed to Ol, and Si is still deficient, Ab is converted to Ne according to the equation:

$$5\ \text{Ab} = 3\ \text{Ne} + 2\ \text{Q}$$

where Q is now the deficiency of Si remaining after 10b.
    d. If this still leaves a deficiency of Si, Or is converted to Lc according to the equation:

$$5\ \text{Or} = 4\ \text{Lc} + 1\ \text{Q}$$

where Q is the deficiency remaining after 10c.
    e. In rare cases, there is not enough Si to form Lc. Then Kp is formed as follows:

$$4\ \text{Lc} = 3\ \text{Kp} + 1\ \text{Q}$$

EXAMPLE

A. *Calculation of cation percentages.*

Oxide	Wt. %	Mol. Wt.	C.P. × 1000	Cation %
SiO_2	49.10	60.09	817	46.0
TiO_2	3.59	79.90	45	2.5
Al_2O_3	16.21	50.99	318	17.9
Fe_2O_3	2.87	79.85	36	2.0
FeO	6.84	71.85	95	5.3
MnO	0.05	70.94	1	0.1
MgO	5.04	40.31	125	7.0
CaO	8.90	56.08	159	9.0
Na_2O	3.53	30.99	114	6.4
K_2O	2.76	47.10	59	3.3
P_2O_5	0.54	70.98	8	0.5
			1777	100.0

B. *Calculation of Norm.*

	Provisional	Final
1. Analysis has no CO_2, so go to 2.		
2. Ap = 0.5 P + 1.67 × 0.5 Ca =	1.3	1.3
3. Analysis has no S, so go to 4		
4. Il = 2.5 Ti + 2.5 Fe^{+2} =	5.0	5.0
5. Or = 3.3 K + 3.3 Al + 3 × 3.3 Si =	16.5	16.5
Ab = 6.4 Na + 6.4 Al + 3 × 6.4 Si =	32.0 − 4.8	27.2
6. a. An = 4.1 Ca + 8.2 Al + 8.2 Si =	20.5	20.5
7. b. Mt = 2.0 Fe^{+3} + 1.0 Fe^{+2}	3.0	3.0
c. FM = 12.4 − 2.5 − 1.0 = 8.9		
8. Di = 4.1 Ca + 4.1 FM + 8.2 Si =	16.4	16.4
9. Hy = 8.9 FM + 8.9 Si =	17.8 − 17.8	0.0
10. b. Ol = 17.8 − 2.4 =		7.2
c. 4.8 Ab = 2.9 Ne + 1.9 Si =		2.9

RUNNING BALANCE

Si	=	46.0 − 9.9 − 19.2 − 8.2 − 4.1 − 1.8 − 7.1 − 2.4 + 1.9	=	0
Ti	=	2.5 − 2.5	=	0
Al	=	17.9 − 3.3 − 6.4 − 8.3	=	0
Fe^{+3}	=	2.0 − 2.0	=	0
Fe^{+2}	=	5.3 − 2.5 − 1.0 − 1.8	=	0
Mn	=	0.1 − 0.1	=	0
Mg	=	7.0 − 7.0	=	0
Ca	=	9.0 − 0.8 − 4.1 − 4.1	=	0
Na	=	6.4 − 6.4	=	0
K	=	3.3 − 3.3	=	0
P	=	0.5 − 0.5	=	0

APPENDIX B

Calculations of Densities and Viscosities of Silicate Melts

DENSITY

The calculation given below is based on the method of Bottinga and Weill (1970, *Amer. J. Sci.* 269:169–182) but uses more recently determined values of molar volumes. The original analysis, in weight percent, is recalculated to molecular proportions water-free in the manner explained in Appendix A but without renormalizing to 100 percent. T = (temperature in °C − 1400) × 10^{-5}

$$\begin{aligned}
Z1 &= SiO_2 \times 27.03 \\
Z2 &= TiO_2 \times 22.6 \times (1 + T \times 26.7) \\
Z3 &= AlO_{1.5} \times 36.63/2 \times (1 + T \times 14.7) \\
Z4 &= FeO_{1.5} \times 43.73/2 \times (1 + T \times 12.2) \\
Z5 &= (FeO + MnO) \times 13.85 \times (1 + T \times 31.2) \\
Z6 &= MgO \times 11.43 \times (1 + T \times 9.4) \\
Z7 &= CaO \times 16.32 \times (1 + T \times 38.4) \\
Z8 &= NaO_{0.5} \times 14.39 \times (1 + T \times 23.5) \\
Z9 &= KO_{0.5} \times 22.965 \times (1 + T \times 24.9) \\
\text{Density} &= 100 / (Z1 + Z2 + Z3 + Z4 + Z5 + Z6 + Z7 + Z8 + Z9)
\end{aligned}$$

VISCOSITY

The calculation below is based on the method of H. R. Shaw (1972, *Amer. J. Sci.* 272:870–893). It gives the viscosity, η, of crystal-free silicate melts in poise in log units. Weight percentages of oxide components are first recalculated to 100 percent, then converted to cation proportions. Temperature (T) is in degrees K.

$$\begin{aligned}
SI &= SiO_2 / 60.0843 \\
TI &= TiO_2 / 79.8988 \\
AL &= Al_2O_3 / 50.9806 \\
F3 &= Fe_2O_3 / 79.8461 \\
F2 &= FeO / 71.8461
\end{aligned}$$

MN = MnO / 70.9374
MG = MgO / 40.3044
CA = CaO / 56.9895
NA = Na_2O / 30.9895
K = K_2O / 47.0980
H = H_2O / 18.0152
P = P_2O_5 / 70.9723
Normalize to 100
FM = F3 + F2 + MN + MG
NK = N + K
C = SI + TI + AL + FM + CA + (NK + P)/2 + H
Q1 = AL × 6.7
Q2 = FM × 3.4
Q3 = (CA + TI) × 4.5
Q4 = NK × 1.4
Q5 = H × 2
QT = (Q1 + Q2 + Q3 + Q4 + Q5) × SI/C
X = (QT/(1 − SI/C) × (10000/T − 1.5)) − 6.4
Log η = X/2.303, η = eX

The viscosity of partly crystallized magmas can be estimated from the following empirical equation (McBirney and Murase, 1984, *Ann. Rev. Earth Planet. Sci.*, 12: 337 and Murase, McBirney, and Melson, 1985, *Jour. Volc. Geoth. Res.*, 24: 193).

$$\log \eta_{eff} = \log \eta_o + \frac{0.019D_m}{(1/\phi)^{-1/3} - 1}$$

Where:

η_{eff} = the effective viscosity of the liquid and crystals,
η_o = the viscosity of the liquid alone,
D_m = the mean diameter of the crystals in microns, and
ϕ = the volume fraction of crystals.

APPENDIX C

Error Functions

The two error functions most commonly used in calculations of thermal or chemical diffusion are given in the table below. Others are given in standard references, such as J. Crank, 1967, *Mathematics of Diffusion,* Oxford Press.

x	*erf x*	*erfc x*	*x*	*erf x*	*erfc x*
0	0	1.0	0	0	1.0
0.05	0.056372	0.943628	1.1	0.880205	0.119795
0.1	0.112463	0.887537	1.2	0.910314	0.089686
0.15	0.167996	0.832004	1.3	0.934008	0.065992
0.2	0.222703	0.777297	1.4	0.952285	0.047715
0.25	0.276326	0.723674	1.5	0.966105	0.033895
0.3	0.328627	0.671373	1.6	0.976348	0.023652
0.35	0.379382	0.620618	1.7	0.983790	0.016210
0.4	0.428392	0.571608	1.8	0.989091	0.010909
0.45	0.475482	0.524518	1.9	0.992790	0.007210
0.5	0.520500	0.479500	2.0	0.995322	0.004678
0.55	0.563323	0.436677	2.1	0.997021	0.002979
0.6	0.603856	0.396144	2.2	0.998137	0.001863
0.65	0.642029	0.357971	2.3	0.998857	0.001143
0.7	0.677801	0.322199	2.4	0.999311	0.000689
0.75	0.711156	0.288844	2.5	0.999593	0.000407
0.8	0.742101	0.257899	2.6	0.999764	0.000236
0.85	0.770668	0.229332	2.7	0.999866	0.000134
0.9	0.796908	0.203092	2.8	0.999925	0.000075
0.95	0.820891	0.179109	2.9	0.999959	0.000041
1.0	0.842701	0.157299	3.0	0.999978	0.000022

APPENDIX D

Mathematical Functions of Radiogenic Isotopes

As noted in the text, the decay of radioactive elements is useful not only for determining the ages of rocks and minerals; it also yields useful information about the evolution of the crust and mantle and the origins of magmas.

Three isotopic systems are currently of special interest to petrologists: rubidium-strontium, uranium-thorium-lead, and samarium-neodymium. Basic equations governing all three are illustrated by the rubidium-strontium system that was described briefly in chapter nine. Strontium has several isotopes, one of which, ^{87}Sr, is produced by decay of ^{87}Rb. Its abundance is measured relative to another isotope, ^{86}Sr, which is stable and is not derived from decay of another element. The rate of decay of any unstable parent nuclide, such as ^{87}Rb, is proportional to the number of atoms remaining at any time, t.

$$\frac{dN}{dt} = -\lambda N \qquad (1)$$

where the decay constant, λ, is the statistical proportion of atoms that decay in a given unit of time. The minus sign indicates that the number of atoms decreases with time. Integrating (1) we get

$$-\ln N = \lambda t + C \qquad (2)$$

where C is the constant of integration. At $t = 0$,

$$C = -\ln N_0 \qquad (3)$$

where N_0 is the initial number of atoms in a system such as a rock or mineral. Therefore,

$$-\ln N = \lambda t - \ln N_0,$$

$$\ln \frac{N}{N_0} = -\lambda t,$$

$$\frac{N}{N_0} = e^{-\lambda t}, \text{ and}$$

$$N = N_0\, e^{-\lambda t} \qquad (4)$$

This is the standard equation for decay of any radioactive nuclide. The elapsed time at which $n = 0.5\ N_0$ is defined as the half-life of the parent, $t_{1/2}$, and the relation between t and λ in (4) is

$$t_{1/2} = 0.693/\lambda$$

Since the half-life of ^{87}Rb is about 48.8×10^9 years, λ has a value of 1.42×10^{-11} per year.

Because decay is an atom-for-atom process, the initial number of atoms of ^{87}Rb is equal to the present number plus the number of new radiogenic atoms, $^{87}Sr^*$, produced by decay during time t. (4) can be written

$$^{87}Rb = (^{87}Rb + {}^{87}Sr^*)e^{-\lambda t} \qquad (5)$$

or, rearranging,

$$^{87}Sr^* = {}^{87}Rb(e^{\lambda t} - 1) \qquad (6)$$

The total amount of ^{87}Sr is the sum of the original amount, $^{87}Sr_0$, and the amount produced by decay in time t:

$$^{87}Sr = {}^{87}Sr_0 + {}^{87}Sr^* \qquad (7)$$

Combining (6) and (7) gives

$$^{87}Sr = {}^{87}Sr_0 + {}^{87}Rb(e^{\lambda t} - 1) \qquad (8)$$

The required data are obtained by mass spectrometery, a technique capable of measuring only isotopic ratios. Therefore, the quantities are converted to ratios by dividing by ^{86}Sr, which is constant and tends to have the same order of abundance as ^{87}Sr. Thus, we have

$$\frac{^{87}Sr}{^{86}Sr} = \left[\frac{^{87}Sr}{^{86}Sr}\right]_0 + \frac{^{87}Rb}{^{86}Sr}(e^{\lambda t} - 1) \qquad (9)$$

Because the small values of λ make exponential terms negligible, the last term, when expanded, reduces to

$$(e^{\lambda t} - 1) = 1 + \lambda t + (\lambda t)^2/2 + \ldots\ldots -1 = \lambda t$$

Thus (9) becomes

$$\frac{^{87}Sr}{^{86}Sr} = \left[\frac{^{87}Sr}{^{86}Sr}\right]_0 + \frac{^{87}Rb}{^{86}Sr}\lambda t \qquad (10)$$

In most analytical procedures, the absolute abundances of Rb and Sr are measured in parts per million by weight, whereas in (1) they are in numbers of atoms. Their weights can be converted to proportions of atoms by dividing each by its atomic weight. (The atomic weights vary with the proportions of isotopes and, for precise calculations, must be calculated for the specific sample.) At a given time, such as the present, the proportion of ^{87}Rb in total Rb is essentially constant at 27.83 percent. Owing to radiogenic variability, the proportion of ^{87}Sr differs slightly from one sample to another, but it is typically about 9.87 percent. Therefore,

$$\left[\frac{^{87}Rb}{^{86}Sr}\right]_{atomic} = \left[\frac{Rb}{Sr}\right]_{wt.} \times \frac{87.62}{85.47} \times \frac{.2783}{.0987} = 2.89 \left[\frac{Rb}{Sr}\right]_{wt.} \quad (11)$$

By inserting this factor and multiplying it by the value of λ, (10) can be rewritten as

$$\frac{^{87}Sr}{^{86}Sr} = \left[\frac{^{87}Sr}{^{86}Sr}\right]_0 + 4.018 \times 10^{-11} \frac{RB}{Sr} t \quad (12)$$

which is the equation for a straight line (Fig. 9–22) with its origin at the initial ratio $(^{87}Sr/^{86}Sr)_0$ and a slope proportional to t.

It can be seen that the ratio $^{87}Sr/^{86}Sr$ increases with time by an amount that is directly proportional to the ratio of the parent-to-daughter elements, of Rb/Sr. A series of rocks or minerals that initially have the same ratio of Sr isotopes but different Rb/Sr ratios will evolve, as shown in Figure D–1, to new isotopic ratios that define a straight line known as an *isochron*.

If two or more co-magmatic rocks have compositions that define such a line when their isotopic ratios are plotted against Rb/Sr, they could be interpreted as having evolved to their present isotopic ratios over the period of time defined by the isochron. If the rocks are old, one can calculate the isotopic ratio they had at the time they were erupted by substituting their known age in the decay equation and solving for the initial ratio. If this correction results in a flat line, i.e., a zero age, then the magmas would be interpreted as having evolved in an isotopically uniform reservoir in which they differentiated shortly before erupting. If the line still has a slope, however, it could be interpreted in two ways. It could indicate that the magmas evolved independently and, after differentiating, remained isolated from one another for a corresponding period of time before they were erupted. But a similar linear array of compositions could also result from simple mixing of two end-members, one with low ratios of the isotopes and Rb/Sr and the other with high ratios. Such a relation would be a "pseudo-isochron" and would reflect the amount of mixing rather than elapsed time.

The other isotopic systems, U/Th-Pb and Sm-Nd, evolve in similar ways. The

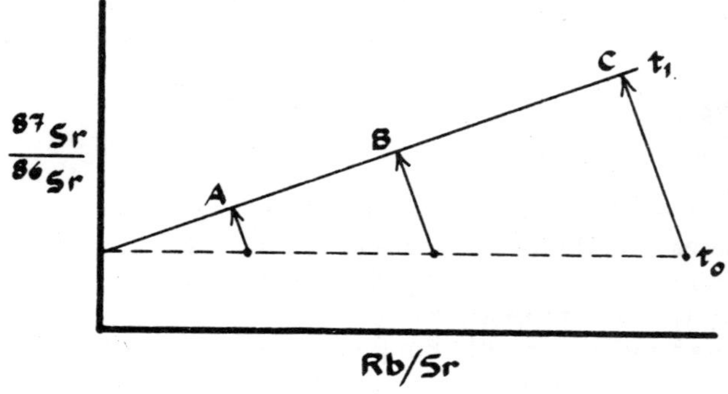

Figure D–1 The rate of increase of $^{87}Sr/^{86}Sr$ is directly proportional to the ratio of Rb to Sr (specifically $^{87}Rb/^{86}Sr$), so that, with time, a series of rocks or minerals with diferrent Rb and Sr contents will evolve Sr isotopic ratios defining a straight line. As shown in Figure 9–20, homogenization of the Sr by reheating may reset the isotopic ratios to a uniform value without changing their Rb/Sr ratios, so that further decay of Rb would lead to a subsequent isochron that would be a measure of the time elapsed since the secondary event occurred. Note that a linear array of points on such a diagram may not necessarily be a true isochron; it could also result from mixing. An intermediate value, such as B, could be produced from end-members A and C.

rare-earth element samarium-147 (^{147}Sm) decays to another rare earth (^{143}Nd) with a half-life of 106 billion years (l = 6.34×10^{-12}), and the abundance of ^{143}Nd is compared to that of the essentially stable isotope, ^{144}Nd, just as ^{87}Sr is measured relative to ^{86}Sr. Pb, however, has three radiogenic isotopes, ^{206}Pb derived from ^{238}U, ^{207}Pb from ^{235}U, and ^{208}Pb from ^{232}Th. Each of these nuclides has its own decay curve with time. As explained in chapter ten, the abundances of the radiogenic isotopes of Pb are normally compared to that of the stable, non-radiogenic isotope ^{204}Pb, and, when the ratios are plotted against each other, they define curves that reflect the differing half-lives and changing abundances of the two parent isotopes of U (Figs. D–2 and 10–31). ^{207}Pb has increased only slightly in the last four billion years, because much of its parent, ^{235}U, decayed early in the earth's history.

Because the parent/daughter ratios of the mantle are not uniform, the growth curves of the Pb isotopes differ from one region to another, and these differences cause the igneous rocks of one province to differ more or less systematically from those of another. At any given time, however, the isotopic ratios of Pb from sources with different parent/daughter ratios would define an isochron, just as they do for Sr. As Figure D–2 shows, the present isochron (often referred to as

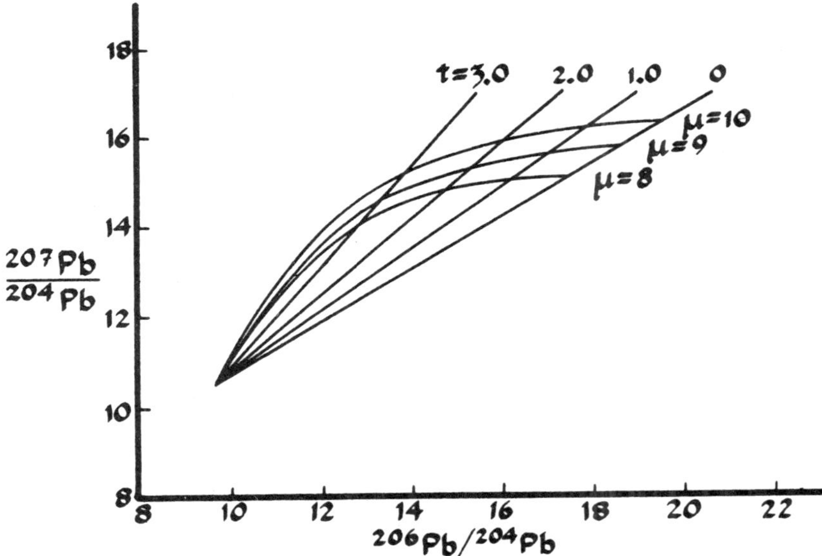

Figure D–2 When the ratios of ^{207}Pb and ^{206}Pb to the non-radiogenic isotope ^{204}Pb are plotted, they define a curve with a slope that varies according to the changing parent/daughter ratios. The ratio of ^{238}U to ^{204}Pb, which determines the rate of increase of $^{206}Pb/^{204}Pb$, is referred to as μ. The ratio of ^{235}U to ^{205}Pb, which governs the rate of increase of $^{207}Pb/^{204}Pb$, has a value of $\mu/137.8$. Thus the rates of increase of both radiogenic isotopes can be related to μ, and, as illustrated by the curves for different values of this factor, the evolution of the isotopes with time would have a different curve according to μ. Note that points on two or more curves at a given time define a straight line or isochron; the specific zero-age isochron for the present day is called the "Geochron."

the zero-age isochron for the earth, or the "Geochron") should govern the lead ratios of modern, mantle-derived rocks. Unfortunately, they do not always do so. Other events in the earth's history appear to have redistributed U and Pb at different times and by different amounts, so that the isotopic character of a given suite of rocks tends to be governed by the history of the crust and mantle in a particular region.

The Nd system resembles that of Sr but is in a sense complementary. With time, the ratio of ^{143}Nd to ^{144}Nd increases as ^{147}Sm decays to ^{143}Nd with a decay constant, λ, of $6.54 \times 10^{-12}\ yr^{-1}$. The rate of increase of the Nd ratio is a direct function of the relative amounts of Sm and Nd, but in this case the parent-daughter ratio, Sm/Nd, is smaller in crustal rocks than in the mantle (even though the absolute abundances of both of these rare-earth elements are greater in the crust). In a similar way, the ratio of Sm to Nd is smaller in partial melts than in their source rocks, whereas the opposite is true of Rb/Sr.

The isotopic ratios of Nd and Sr are often compared by relating them to standard values, which are normally taken as the estimated ratios for the bulk earth. For $^{143}Nd/^{144}Nd$ this is 0.51264, and for $^{87}Sr/^{86}Sr$ it is taken as 0.7047. Ratios are reported in terms of ϵ_{Nd} and ϵ_{Sr}, the fractional deviation from the reference value in units of 0.01 percent. Thus, for neodymium:

$$\epsilon_{Nd} = \left[\frac{(^{143}Nd/^{144}Nd)_{SAMPLE}}{0.51264} - 1\right] \times 10^4$$

and for strontium:

$$\epsilon_{Sr} = \left[\frac{(^{87}Sr/^{86}Sr)_{SAMPLE}}{0.7047} - 1\right] \times 10^4$$

APPENDIX E

(a) Symbols and Physical Constants

- A — area, cm^2
- a — activity
- C_P — heat capacity at constant pressure, ≈ 0.3 cal/deg g
- D — chemical diffusivity, 10^{-5} to 10^{-8} cm^2/sec; also bulk distribution coefficient
- DI — Differentiation Index = 1/3 Si − Mg − Ca + K = 0.1606 SiO_2 − 0.603 MgO − 0.715 CaO + 0.830 K_2O
- F — degrees of freedom or fraction of liquid
- f — fugacity
- G — Gibbs free energy, cal/mole deg
- g — acceleration of gravity, 980.6 cm/sec^2
- ΔH_F — heat of fusion or crystallization, $\approx$ 60–100 cal/g
- km — kilometers
- K_d — distribution coefficient, concentration in the solid relative to concentration in a coexisting liquid
- K — thermal conductivity, $\approx 3 \times 10^{-3}$ cal/cm deg sec
- k — thermal diffusivity, $K/\rho C_P$, $\approx 4 \times 10^{-3}$ cm^2/sec
- P — pressure, bars or kilobars; distribution coefficient for proportions of phases entering melts
- ppm — parts per million
- R — gas constant, 1.9872 cal/mole deg
- S — entropy, cal/mole deg
- ss — solid solution
- T — temperature, deg. Celsius (C) or Kelvin (K)
- t — time, sec
- U — velocity, cm/sec
- V — volume, cm^3, or specific volume, cm^3/g
- X — weight, molar or weight fraction; also a hypothetical composition
- α — coefficient of thermal expansion, $\approx 3 \times 10^{-5}$ deg^{-1}
- β — compressibility, solid $\approx 1.5 \times 10^{-6}$ bar^{-1}, liquid $\approx 7 \times 10^{-6}$ bar^{-1}
- γ — activity coefficient
- η — viscosity, poise, 10^2 to 10^5 g/cm sec
- ν — kinematic viscosity, η/ρ, 10^2 to 10^4 cm^2/sec
- μ — chemical potential, cal/mole
- ρ — density, g/cm^3

(b) Abbreviations of Minerals

Ab	albite	Fs	ferrosilite	MATS	Mg-tschermak molecule
An	anorthite	Gt	garnet	Lc	leucite
c	corundum	Hb	hornblende	Mt	magnetite
CATS	Ca-tschermak molecule	Hd	hedenbergite	Ne	nepheline
Ap	apatite	Hy	hypersthene	Ol	olivine
Di	diopside	Il	ilmenite	Or	orthoclase
En	enstatite	Jd	jadeite	Q	quartz
Fa	fayalite	Ks	kalsilite	Wo	wollastonite
Fo	forsterite	Kp	kaliophilite		

(c) Atomic and molecular weights and radii of the major and minor elements most commonly used in petrologic calculations. Oxide weights, where appropriate, are given for the single-cation formula.

Element	Charge	Atomic Radius	Atomic Wt. Wt.	Molecular Wt. of Oxide
Si	+4	0.42	28.09	60.09
Ti	+4	0.68	47.90	79.90
Al	+3	0.51	26.98	50.99
Fe	+3	0.64	55.85	79.85
Fe	+2	0.74	55.85	71.85
Mn	+2	0.80	54.94	70.94
Mg	+2	0.66	24.31	40.31
Ca	+2	0.99	40.08	56.08
Na	+1	0.97	22.99	30.99
K	+1	1.33	39.10	47.10
P	+5	0.35	30.97	70.98
H	+1	1.54	1.01	9.01
C	+4	0.16	12.01	44.01
Ba	+2	1.34	137.33	153.33
Cr	+3	0.63	52.00	76.00
Ni	+2	0.69	58.70	74.70
Rb	+1	1.47	85.47	93.47
Sr	+2	1.12	87.62	103.62
Zr	+4	0.79	91.22	123.22
F	−1	1.33	19.00	—
Cl	−1	1.81	35.45	—
S	−2	1.84	32.06	—
S	+4	0.37	32.06	64.06

APPENDIX F

Units and Conversion Factors

The units used throughout this text are the standard "CGS" system based on centimeters, grams, seconds, and calories. The "SI" system, introduced in 1974, has a different set of units for force (newtons), stress (pascals), energy (joules), and power (watts).

ENERGY

1 gram calorie	$= 4.1840 \times 10^7$ ergs = 4.184 joules
	= 42.685 kg cm = 41.84 bar cm^3
1 kilocalorie	= 1000 g cal
1 erg	$= 1$ g cm^2/sec^2 = 1 dyne cm
	$= 0.239901 \times 10^{-7}$ g cal
1 joule (J)	$= 1 \times 10^7$ ergs = 1 kg m^2 = 1 N m
	= 0.239 gram-calories (at 20°C)

FORCE

1 dyne	= 1 g cm/sec^2 = 10^{-5}N
1 newton (N)	= 1 kg m/sec^2 = 10^5 dyne = 1 J/m

PRESSURE

1 bar	= 10^6 dyne/cm^2
	= 101.972 k Pa = 1.01972×10^5 N/m^2
	= 10^6 g/cm sec^2 = 0.9869 atm
	= 1.020 kg/cm^2
1 atmosphere	= 1.0133 bars = 1033.2 g/cm^2
1 km seawater	= 100 bars
1 km mantle	= 0.3 kbars (density ≈ 3.3 g/cm^3)
1 kilobar (kbar)	= 1000 bars = 1.020×10^6 g/cm^2
	= 3.5 km depth of mantle, 3.3 g/cm^3
	= 0.102 GPa
1 pascal (Pa)	= 1 kg/m sec^2 = 1 N/m^2
1 gigapascal (GPa)	= 10.2 kbars

LENGTH

1 kilometer	$= 10^5$ cm
1 micron (μ)	$= 1 \times 10^{-4}$ cm
1 Angstrom (Å)	$= 1 \times 10^{-8}$ cm

TIME

1 year	$= 3.1536 \times 10^7$ sec.

TEMPERATURE

degrees Kelvin (K) = degrees Celsius (C) + 273

HEAT

1 calorie (cal) = 4.184 joules

HEAT FLOW

1 heat flow unit (HFU) = 1×10^{-6} cal/cm^2 sec
= 4.19×10^{-2} W/m^2

VISCOSITY

1 poise = 1 g/cm sec = 0.1 Pa sec

KINEMATIC VISCOSITY

1 stoke = 1 cm^2/sec = 1 poise / density

APPENDIX G

Distribution Coefficients and Normalizing Factors

(a) Typical partition coefficients of trace elements between crystals and liquids. (Mainly from J. G. Arth, 1976, *Jour. Res. U. S. Geol. Surv.*, 4: 41–47, and D. R. and S. P. MacCaskie, unpubl. manuscript.)

Basaltic Liquids

Element	Oliv	Opx	Cpx	Amph	Garnet	Spinel	Plag	Mica
Ni	4-10*	8.3	2.5	6,0	0.5	5.0	0.05	7.6
Cr	0.2	2.0	11.5	5.2	2.0	10.0	0.06	7.0
Co	3.9	2.4	1.0	6.5	3.2	2.0	0.05	1.1
Sc	0.2	1.2	2.7	3.5	3.4	2.0	0.03	3.0
Sr	0.01	0.003	0.11	0.6	<0.1	<0.1	2.1	0.1
Ba	0.02	0.05	0.02	0.4	<0.1	<0.1	0.38	<0.1
Rb	0.02	0.006	0.03	0.4	<0.1	<0.1	0.09	2.0

*The value for Ni in olivine varies with oxygen fugacity from about 4 near the wustite-magnetite buffer to 10 approaching the fayalite-magnetite-quartz buffer.

Rhyolitic Liquids

Element	Opx	Cpx	Amph	K-Feld	Biotite	Phlogopite	Plag
K	<0.1	<0.1	0.08	—	—	—	0.1
Rb	<0.1	<0.1	0.14	0.3	4.1	0.9	0.04
Sr	<0.1	0.5	0.02	3.9	0.17	0.7	4.4
Ba	0.09	0.1	0.10	4.6	9.7	15.3	0.3

(b) Distribution coefficients for trace elements in coexisting mafic and felsic immiscible liquids. Ranges of values given are for the weight ratio of the element in the mafic liquid to the amount in a co-existing felsic liquid. (After E. B. Watson, 1976, *Contrib. Min. Petrol.*, 56: 119–134.)

Ba	1.37–1.63	Mn	2.86– 3.09
Ca	1.79–3.14	P	8.34–13.33
Cr	3.22–4.29	Sr	1.33– 1.84
Cs	0.30–0.31	Sm	4.19– 5.15
La	3.70–4.31	Ta	4.18– 4.42
Lu	4.18–7.13	Ti	2.87– 3.32
Mg	2.04–2.23	Zr	2.28– 2.54

(c) Distribution coefficients for trace elements in immiscible sulfide liquids coexisting with liquids of basaltic composition. Values are weight ratios of the concentration in the sulfide to the concentration in the basaltic liquid. (After V. Rajamani and A. J. Naldrett, 1978, *Econ. Geol.*, 478: 82–93.)

	Olivine Basalt	Basalt 1255 °C	Basalt 1305 °C	Andesite 1255 °C
Ni	231	274	257	460
Cu	333	245	180	243
Co	n.d.	80	61	n.d.

(d) Abundances of rare-earth elements in the Leedey chondritic meteorite. Dividing the abundances in other rocks by these amounts yields normalized values that plot as smoother curves that are more readily compared and interpreted. (After Masuda *et al.*, 1973, *Geoch. Cosmoch. Acta* 37:234–248 and G. G. Goles, pers. comm. Atomic radii are for six-coordination and are taken from Whittaker and Muntus, 1970, *Geoch. Cosmoch. Acta*, 34:945–956.)

Atomic No.	Element	Ionic Radius (Å)	Symbol	Abundance
57	Lanthanum	1.13	La	0.330
58	Cerium	1.09	Ce	0.880
59	Praseodymium	1.08	Pr	0.112
60	Neodymium	1.06	Nd	0.600
62	Samarium	1.04	Sm	0.181
63	Europium	1.03	Eu	0.069
64	Gadolinium	1.02	Gd	0.249
65	Terbium	1.00	Tb	0.047
66	Dysprosium	0.99	Dy	0.325
67	Holmium	0.98	Ho	0.070
68	Erbium	0.97	Er	0.200
69	Thulium	0.96	Tm	0.030
70	Ytterbium	0.95	Yb	0.200
71	Lutetium	0.94	Lu	0.034

(e) Standard values for normalizing minor and trace elements in spidergrams. (After J. A. Pearce, 1983, in *Continental Basalts and Mantle Xenoliths*, Hawksworth and Norry, eds., Shiva Publ., and Pearce *et al.*, 1987, *Phil. Trans. Roy. Soc. London* A300:299–317. Values for La, Lu, and Ni from G. G. Goles, pers. comm.) Values are in parts per million except for K_2O, P_2O_5, and TiO_2, which are in weight percent of the oxide. A more extensive table of average abundances in rocks commonly used as reference standards is given in (f).

Element	Abundance	Element	Abundance	Element	Abundance
Sr	120	K_2O	0.15	Rb	2
Ba	20	Th	0.2	Ta	0.18
Nb	3.5	La	3.8	Ce	10
P_2O_5	0.12	Zr	90	Hf	2.4
Sm	3.3	TiO_2	1.5	Y	30
Yb	3.4	Lu	0.52	Sc	40
Cr	250	Ni	150		

(f) Element concentrations (in ppm) for chondrites, normal- and enriched-type mid-ocean-ridge basalts (N- and E-MORB), and ocean island basalt (OIB). (After S. S. Sun and W. F. McDonough, 1989, *Magmatism in the Ocean Basins*, A. D. Saunders and M. J. Norry, eds., *Geol. Soc. Amer. Spec. Publ. No. 42*, 313–345.)

Element	C1 Chondrite	Primitive mantle	N-type MORB	E-type MORB	OIB
Cs	0.188	0.032	0.0070	0.063	0.387
Tl	0.140	0.005	0.0014	0.013	0.077
Rb	2.32	0.635	0.56	5.04	31.0
Ba	2.41	6.989	6.30	57	350
W	0.095	0.020	0.010	0.092	0.560
Th	0.029	0.085	0.120	0.60	4.00
U	0.008	0.021	0.047	0.18	1.02
Nb	0.246	0.713	2.33	8.30	48.0
Ta	0.014	0.041	0.132	0.47	2.70
K	545	250	600	2100	12000
La	0.237	0.687	2.50	6.30	37.0
Ce	0.612	1.775	7.50	15.0	80.0
Pb	2.47	0.185	0.30	0.60	3.20
Pr	0.095	0.276	1.32	2.05	9.70
Mo	0.92	0.063	0.31	0.47	2.40
Sr	7.26	21.1	90	155	660
P	1220	95	510	620	2700
Nd	0.467	1.354	7.30	9.00	38.5
F	60.7	26	210	250	1150
Sm	0.153	0.444	2.63	2.60	10.0
Zr	3.87	11.2	74	73	280
Hf	0.1066	0.309	2.05	2.03	7.80
Eu	0.058	0.168	1.02	0.91	3.00
Sn	1.72	0.170	1.1	0.91	3.00
Sb	0.16	0.005	0.01	0.01	0.03
Ti	445	1300	7600	6000	17200
Gd	0.2055	0.596	3.680	2.970	7.620
Tb	0.0374	0.108	0.670	0.530	1.050
Dy	0.2540	0.737	4.550	3.550	5.600
Li	1.57	1.60	4.3	3.5	5.6
Y	1.57	4.55	28	22	29
Ho	0.0566	0.164	1.01	0.790	1.06
Er	0.1655	0.480	2.97	2.31	2.62
Tm	0.0255	0.074	0.456	0.356	0.350
Yb	0.170	0.493	3.05	2.37	2.16
Lu	0.0254	0.074	0.455	0.354	0.300

APPENDIX H

Glossary of Rock Names

The brief definitions given here are for general use and quick reference. More precise definitions can be found in the text and in standard references, such as:

Irvine, T. N., and W. R. A. Baragar, 1971, A guide to the chemical classification of common volcanic rocks, *Can. Jour. Earth Sci.* 8:523–548.

Holmes, Arthur, 1920, *The nomenclature of petrology*. Allen & Unwin, 284 pp. Reprinted in 1972 by Hafner Publ. Co.

Streckeisen, A., 1978, Classification and nomenclature of volcanic rocks, lamprophyres, carbonatites and melilitic rocks. *Neues Jahrb. Miner. Abhandl.* 134:1–14.

Absarokite: a potassium-rich, olivine basalt characterized by plagioclase rimmed with orthoclase; leucite may also be present. With decreasing olivine grades into shoshonite.

Achondrite: a stony meteorite that lacks chondules. Most are coarser-grained than chondrites, and they contain little if any metallic nickel-iron. Many are aggregates of fragments, but of all the types of meteorites they are most like terrestrial rocks.

Adamellite: see quartz monzonite.

Alaskite: leuco-granite, normally with a granular texture and less than a few percent mafic minerals.

Alkali dolerite: dolerite with normative nepheline and other characteristics of alkaline basalts; often differentiate to small pods or veins of syenite.

Alnoite: a silica-poor alkaline lamprophyre, normally with melilite; phlogopite, olivine, carbonates, and perovskite are common constituents.

Andesite: a calc-alkaline volcanic rock with 53 to 63 percent SiO_2 and a color index of less than 30; andesite with 53 to 57 percent SiO_2 is usually referred to as basaltic andesite.

Ankaramite: basalt, normally of alkaline character, with abundant large phenocrysts of augite and olivine.

Anorthosite: a plutonic rock consisting almost solely of plagioclase, normally labradorite. One type of anorthosite is found in large, layered intrusions, another in unstratified plutons, or "massifs."

Aplite: a fine-grained, felsic rock often found in shallow dikes and sills. Textures referred to as "aplitic" are granular or "sugary" with few of the crystals showing well-developed crystal faces.

Banakite: a potassic volcanic rock similar to shoshonite but with more silica—usually more than 57 percent SiO_2.

Basanite: basalt with a modal feldspathoid,

normally nepheline. Leucite basanite must also contain olivine; otherwise it is a tephrite.

Benmoreite: a mildly alkaline rock intermediate between mugearite and trachyte, normally with nearly equal amounts of alkali feldspar and andesine or oligoclase.

Boninite: an unusually Mg-rich andesite with little or no feldspar.

Calc-alkaline: a type of sub-alkaline magma series characterized in the middle stages of differentiation by andesites. Chemical compositions are hypersthene-normative, have little iron enrichment in the middle stages of differentiation, and generally have more than 16.5 percent Al_2O_3.

Camptonite: an amphibole-rich alkaline lamprophyre.

Carbonatite: a magma or igneous rock consisting mainly of carbonates. The most common minerals are calcite, magnesite, and sodium carbonate.

Chondrite: a common type of stony meteorite characterized by chondrules in a fine-grained matrix of silicate minerals and metallic nickel-iron. Their compositions differ somewhat, but on average they are probably close to the original, undifferentiated compositions of the terrestrial planets.

Chondrule: a spherical grain or aggregate, often with radially oriented crystals of olivine and pyroxene, found in many stony meteorites. Chondrules are thought to have formed from silicate droplets during accretion of the parent body of meteorites.

Chromitite: a rock composed mainly of chromite.

Comendite: a peralkaline rhyolite containing a sodic pyroxene or amphibole. Similar to pantellerite, but more felsic and richer in silica, though not necessarily alkalies.

Dacite: a felsic, sub-alkaline rock with 63 to 68 or 69 percent SiO_2, a color index less than 20, and at least 10 percent normative or modal quartz.

Diabase: See dolerite.

Diorite: an intermediate plutonic rock (color index usually between 40 and 30) in which neither quartz nor alkali feldspar account for more than 10 percent of the volume.

Dolerite: a medium-grained, hypabyssal rock of basaltic composition; commonly found in dikes and sills. In America, synonymous with diabase.

Dunite: a coarse-grained, ultramafic rock composed primarily of olivine.

Eclogite: a high-pressure assemblage of sodic pyroxene (omphacite) and pyrope-rich garnet. Ca-poor pyroxene and olivine may also be present but are not major constituents. The bulk chemical composition is similar to that of basalt.

Essexite: an alkaline gabbro having orthoclase as an essential constituent.

Eucrite: gabbro consisting of calcium-rich plagioclase (bytownite or anorthite), augite, and olivine.

Ferro-basalt: a basalt, normally tholeiitic, that has evolved to a high degree of iron enrichment with more than 12 percent total iron oxides.

Ferro-gabbro: the plutonic equivalent of ferro-basalt.

Gabbro: a coarse-grained rock of basaltic composition composed of calcic plagioclase, pyroxene, and possibly olivine, opaque oxides, and hornblende.

Granite: a felsic, plutonic rock consisting of about equal parts quartz, potassium feldspar, and sodic plagioclase. The name is also used as a general term for all leucocratic, silica-rich, plutonic rocks.

Granodiorite: a felsic, plutonic rock similar to granite but with less potassium feldspar (less than a third of the total feldspar) and a higher color index (usually between 20 and 30).

Granophyre: a medium- to fine-grained felsic rock of rhyolitic composition; commonly found as differentiates of hypabyssal intrusions. Textures referred to as "granophyric" are characterized by intimate intergrowths of quartz and alkali feldspar.

Harzburgite: a coarse-grained, ultramafic rock composed primarily of olivine and enstatite or bronzite; "saxonite" is considered synonymous with harzburgite, but some petrologists reserve the former for harzburgites containing opaque oxide minerals.

Hawaiite: an andesine-basalt with normative nepheline.

Icelandite: an intermediate member of the tholeiitic series similar to andesite but with more iron and less alumina (usually <16.5 percent Al_2O_3); associated with oceanic and other types of anorogenic sub-alkaline series.

Ignimbrite: a fragmental volcanic rock laid down by a pyroclastic flow; most are siliceous, and many are welded, but these are not essential elements of the definition.

Ijolite: an alkaline, plutonic rock consisting chiefly of nepheline and aegirine-augite, normally without feldspar; most contain a variety of other minerals, such as melanite, apatite, green biotite, sphene, and calcite.

Jacupirangite: a mafic variety of ijolite.

Kakortokite: a nepheline syenite containing the red zirconium mineral, eudialyte, and a sodic pyroxene, usually acmite.

Katungite: a melilite-bearing, ultra-potassic, volcanic rock, usually with olivine and minor amounts of leucite but no augite.

Kersantite: a calc-alkaline lamprophyre with biotite and plagioclase.

Komatiite: an ultramafic lava consisting almost entirely of olivine and pyroxene and characterized by acicular crystals that grew rapidly from the low-viscosity, high-temperature melt to give the rock a distinctive "spinifex" texture.

Lahar: a type of fragmental volcanic material deposited by debris flows; characterized by unsorted clasts with a wide range of sizes and compositions.

Lamproite: a general term for mafic volcanic or hypabyssal ultra-potassic rocks.

Lamprophyre: a diverse group of mafic hypabyssal or volcanic rocks, normally rich in alkalies, hydrous phases, P_2O_5, CO_2, and certain minor or trace elements, such as Ti, Ba, and Sr. Some varieties lack feldspar.

Larvikite: an augite syenite characterized by coarse plagioclase with brilliant schiller structure.

Latite: a sub-alkaline, volcanic rock of intermediate silica content containing potassium feldspar; a potassic variety of andesite.

Leucitite: a rock consisting mainly of leucite and pyroxene and usually lacking feldspar.

Leucogranite: a granite of very low color index (<10).

Lherzolite: a peridotite consisting of olivine, diopsidic augite, enstatite, and possibly spinel or garnet.

Lujavrite: a textural variety of kakortokite distinguished by slender plagioclase and acicular pyroxene.

Mafurite: an ultra-potassic rock consisting chiefly of kalsilite, olivine, and augite; with increasing silica grades into leucitite.

Maskelynite: isotropic plagioclase formed by intense shock. Found in meteorites and terrestrial rocks shocked by impact or a nuclear explosion.

Melilitite: a rock containing at least 50 percent melilite.

Metaluminous: a magma or igneous rock in which molecular $Na_2O + K_2O + CaO > Al_2O_3 > Na_2O + K_2O$.

Migmatite: a composite rock composed of igneous-looking crystals and metamorphic minerals of similar mineralogical composition; may be formed by ultrametamorphism or proximity to a magma.

Minette: a calc-alkaline lamprophyre with biotite and potassium feldspar.

Monchiquite: an alkaline lamprophyre rich in augite but with little or no feldspar.

Monzonite: a plutonic rock of intermediate color index and sub-equal alkali feldspar and plagioclase; has less than 10 percent quartz.

Mugearite: an oligoclase basalt, usually with normative nepheline.

Naujaite: a sodalite-rich nepheline syenite with microcline, albite, acmite, and a sodic amphibole.

Nephelinite: a nepheline-rich rock lacking feldspar but normally containing sodic or titaniferous pyroxene.

Nordmarkite: a quartz-bearing alkali syenite, usually with biotite and aegirine.

Norite: a type of gabbro containing hypersthene and labradorite; augite and iron-oxide minerals are also possible phases.

Okaite: a very silica-poor alkaline rock consisting mainly of melilite, hauyne, Ti-biotite, and a wide variety of accessory minerals.

Ophiolite: a collective name applied to basalts, gabbros, ultramafic rocks, and pelagic sediments that were originally part of the oceanic lithosphere.

Orendite: a leucite-bearing volcanic rock rich in diopsidic augite and phlogopite; unlike wyomingite, its groundmass contains sanidine.

Palagonite: hydratated basaltic glass, usually with a golden orange color, formed by subaqueous or subglacial eruptions.

Pantellerite: a peralkaline rhyolite with sodic pyroxene or amphibole; slightly less felsic than comendite.

Pegmatite: any very coarse-grained igneous rock.

Peralkaline: a magma or igneous rock in which molecular $Na_2O + K_2O > Al_2O_3$; can be identified by acmite (Ac) in the norm.

Peraluminous: a magma or igneous rock in which molecular $Al_2O_3 > Na_2O + K_2O + CaO$; can be identified by corundum (C) in the norm.

Peridotite: an ultramafic, plutonic rock consisting of at least 90 percent combined olivine and pyroxene.

Plagiogranite: a felsic, plutonic rock consisting mainly of quartz and sodic plagioclase but lacking K-feldspar; syn. trondhjemite.

Phonolite: a felsic, alkaline rock composed of alkali feldspar (typically anorthoclase or sanidine) and nepheline; the volcanic or hypabysssal equivalent of nepheline syenite.

Pulaskite: a leucocratic syenite with perthitic or antiperthitic feldspar.

Quartz monzonite: a monzonite with 10 to 20 percent quartz; also called adamellite.

Rhyodacite: a volcanic rock intermediate between dacite and rhyolite.

Rhyolite: a felsic, volcanic rock with more than 68 percent SiO_2; broadly equivalent to granite.

Saxonite: see harzburgite.

Seriate: a texture in which the crystals have a continuous, gradational range of sizes.

Shonkinite: a potassium-rich, mafic syenite consisting mainly of sanidine, augite, biotite, olivine, apatite, and zeolitized nepheline.

Shoshonite: a potassium-rich basalt characterized by plagioclase rimmed with orthoclase; leucite may also be present.

Siderite: a type of meteorite composed mainly of native nickel-iron, commonly with minor amounts of the iron sulfide, troilite. Also a mineral with the composition $FeCO_3$.

Siderolite: a stony-iron meteorite composed of crystals of olivine or pyroxene in a matrix of metallic nickel-iron.

Sideromelane: clear, basaltic glass.

Sovite: a leucocratic, coarse-grained carbonatite.

Spessartite: a calc-alkaline lamprophyre containing hornblende and plagioclase.

Syenite: a felsic, plutonic rock with subequal amounts of sodic plagioclase and K-feldspar, but less than 10 percent quartz.

Tachylite: opaque basaltic glass.

Tephra: a general term for all types of pyroclastic deposits.

Tephrite: a leucite basalt lacking olivine.

Teschenite: analcite dolerite.

Tholeiite: a type of subalkaline magma characterized by normative hypersthene and strong iron enrichment in the middle stages of differentiation. The same name is applied to the basaltic parent of such a series.

Tonalite: a plutonic rock in which more than 90 percent of the feldspar is plagioclase, and quartz accounts for at least 15 percent of the volume; gradational into trondhjemite with decreasing color index.

Trachyandesite: an intermediate volcanic rock with abundant plagioclase, usually andesine, and at least 10 percent alkali feldspar; intermediate between andesite and latite. The name is not favored in modern usage.

Trachybasalt: a variety of weakly alkaline basalt containing abundant plagioclase, usually labradorite, and at least 10 percent alkali feldspar; has little or no feldspathoid.

Trachyte: a felsic, volcanic rock with no nepheline and less than 10 percent quartz or tridymite; the volcanic or hypabyssal equivalent of syenite.

Tristanite: an intermediate member of the potassic alkaline series.

Troctolite: a gabbroic rock rich in calcic plagioclase and containing olivine but little or no pyroxene.

Trondhjemite: a felsic, plutonic rock with sodic plagioclase and quartz but little or no K-feldspar; syn. plagiogranite.

Ugandite: a leucite-bearing, silica-deficient, potassic volcanic rock rich in mafic minerals, mainly olivine, Ti-augite, and Ti-magnetite.

Uralite: a pale green amphibole, commonly the product of alteration of pyroxene.

Vogesite: a calc-alkaline lamprophyre containing hornblende and potassium feldspar.

Websterite: an ultramafic plutonic rock composed primarily of Ca-rich and Ca-poor pyroxene and little or no olivine; plagioclase, spinel, or garnet may be present in accessory amounts.

Wyomingite: a potassic volcanic rock with phenocrysts of phlogopite and possibly diopsidic augite in a leucite-rich groundmass.

Xenocryst: a crystal of foreign origin included in a magma or igneous rock.

Xenolith: a rock of foreign origin included in a magma or igneous rock.

Illustrative Problems

Chapter 1

1–1. In calculating the average composition of the mantle by subtracting the average composition of the crust and core from that of an average chondritic meteorite, it was assumed that most elements, except Fe, Ni, and S, are totally excluded from the core. The recent discovery of an iron meteorite containing a K-rich mineral has led to speculation that the behavior of this element may differ at very high pressures; it may become more like the metals that enter sulfide minerals, such as troilite. Because the pressure in the earth's core is much greater than it was in the parent body of the meteorites, this could have a significant effect on the partitioning of K in the earth. This possibility has special importance, because K is an important source of radiogenic heat, and its distribution would have a major influence on the temperature gradients and convective behavior of the core and mantle.

Calculate the K content of the mantle assuming that the core has a small amount of K, say 0.01 wt. percent. To do this, use the values given below for the volumes, densities, and K contents of the major units of the earth and chondritic meteorites.

	Volume km^3 × 10^9	Density g cm^{-3}	K wt. %
Chondrites	—	—	0.10
Core	175	10.7	0.01
Crust	15	2.8	1.42
Oceans	1.372	1.03	0.00038
Mantle	892	4.5	?

Consider your result in terms of the data in Table 1–1 and comment on their compatibility. If it is true that the core has more K than we have hitherto assumed; and the mantle has less, how might this influence ideas about the depths at which basaltic magmas originate?

1–2. Taking the estimated global rates of magmatism given in Table 1–3 and assuming the magma has an average density of 2.8 g cm^{-3}, estimate the amount of heat required to produce magma at the estimated present rate if the heat of fusion is 100 cal g^{-1}. The heat produced by radiogenic heat sources in the mantle can be calculated from the values in Table 1–2 and the density and volume of the mantle given in the preceding problem. Compare the heat produced in the mantle with the amount just calculated from present rates of magmatism. How do these results affect the conclusion reached in the preceding problem?

Chapter 2

The major oxide components of a chemical analysis are normally reported in weight percent and listed in the conventional order shown in the example below. Although the values are usually given to two decimal places, this is not an accurate reflection of the reliability of the determinations for all components. If the relative error, or "fractional uncertainty" (the ratio of the possible error to an absolute abundance), is about the same for all components, those with large abundances, such as SiO_2 and Al_2O_3, would be accurate to fewer decimal places than a minor component, such as K_2O. Moreover, the analytical techniques by which SiO_2 and Al_2O_3 are determined tend to be less precise than those for other components, such as MgO and the alkalies. But, because it is awkward to use analyses in which all the oxides are not given with the same number of decimal places, it is conventional practice to report them in a uniform way. The difference between the total and 100 percent is made up mainly by minor constituents, such as CO_2 and trace elements. It also reflects the precision of the analysis. Totals less than about 98 percent and more than 100 percent are, in most instances, the result of inaccurate determinations.

H_2O+ is the amount of water dissolved in glass or contained in the structure of hydrous minerals; it is measured by determining the weight loss when the sample is finely ground and heated to a high temperature, usually above 700°C. H_2O- is moisture absorbed on the surfaces of grains; it can be driven out of the sample at a temperature of 110°C. Large amounts of water, especially H_2O+, may indicate that the sample is weathered. A large proportion of Fe_2O_3 is another characteristic of alteration.

2–1. Using the method outlined in Appendix A, calculate a molecular norm for the following composition.

SiO_2	46.17
TiO_2	1.95
Al_2O_3	15.96
Fe_2O_3	2.23
FeO	8.26
MnO	0.19
MgO	10.11
CaO	10.32

Na_2O	2.91
K_2O	0.50
H_2O+	0.30
H_2O-	0.50
P_2O_5	0.20
Total	99.60

2–2. (a) Using the procedures in Appendix B, calculate the density and viscosity of a crystal-free liquid with this same composition, assuming a temperature of 1,200°C and 0.30 weight percent H_2O.

(b) Calculate the viscosity again assuming the magma contains 10 volume percent crystals.

2–3. A number of lines of evidence indicate that the magmas erupted from the volcanoes of Hawaii come from a reservoir at depths of about 50 km. For example, earthquakes are sometimes observed to start near that depth and become shallower until magma erupts at the surface. Moreover, the estimated geothermal gradient of the oceanic mantle approaches the melting temperature at about that same depth.

If basaltic magma rises from its own buoyancy, the maximum height to which it can rise may be determined by the hydrostatic balance between the pressure of the overlying lithosphere on the source region and the weight of a column of magma reaching the summit of the volcano. The weight of the volcano and sea water are usually neglected.

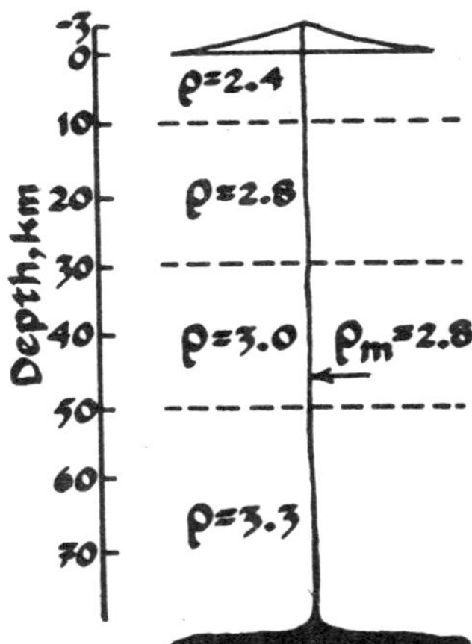

(a) Assuming the densities given for the magma and various components of the mantle and crust shown in the diagram, calculate the depth, h, at which such a column of magma would be in equilibrium with the lithostatic pressure, ρgh, on the mantle reservoir.

(b) The depth calculated in (a) is that at which the column of magma would just be in balance, but additional pressure is required to drive this column through the long channel, as shown by equation 2–18 in the text. If a rate of discharge of 3.1416 cubic meters per second is measured during an eruption, what additional depth would be required to drive the magma to the surface if the conduit is assumed to be a pipe with a uniform radius of one meter and the viscosity of the magma is 500 poise?

(c) It has been observed that magma can stand at a constant level in a lava lake in Kilauea volcano at the same time that magma is erupted from the nearby summit of Mauna Loa, 3,000 m higher. What could one deduce from this observation?

(d) In these calculations, it has been assumed that the density of the magma at the surface, 2.8 g cm^{-3}, does not change with depth, but this cannot be correct, because the increased pressure and temperature in the mantle will both have an effect, one tending to increase density and the other to decrease it. In order to see how serious this factor might be, calculate the density of the basaltic magma at a depth of 50 km (15 kb). Assume the basalt is at its melting temperature, which is 1,200°C at the surface and increases with pressure at a rate of 0.01°C per bar. Typical values for the coefficients of thermal expansion and compressibility for silicate melts are 3×10^{-5} per degree and 7×10^{-6} per bar, respectively.

Chapter 3

3–1. Using the accompanying diagram for the binary system forsterite-silica:

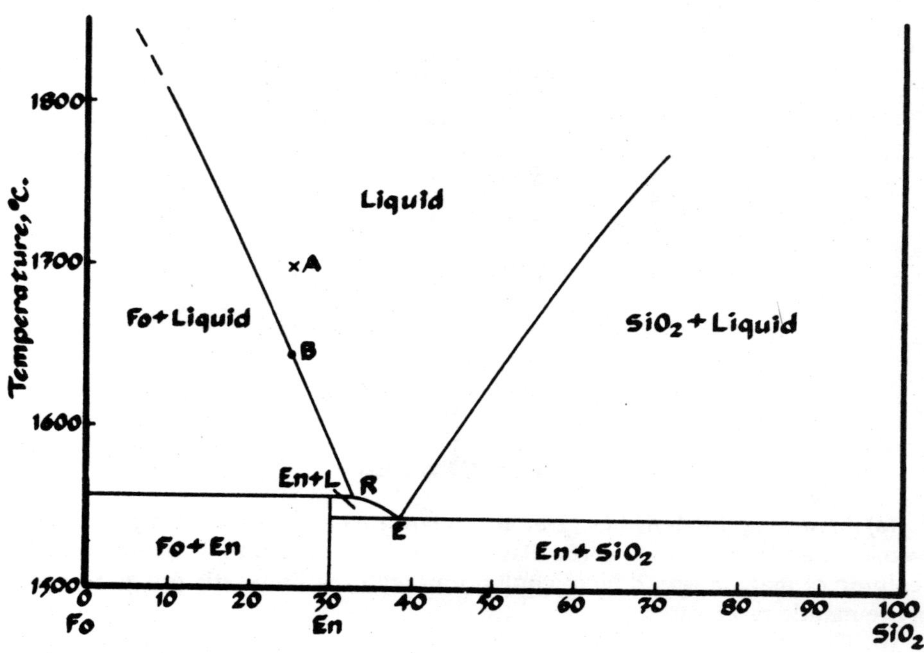

(a) Trace two courses of crystallization of a liquid "A" with an initial temperature of 1,700°C and 75 percent forsterite through its successive stages of cooling, and at each major change give its temperature, composition of the liquid (in percent of the SiO_2 component), and the proportions of all phases present at that point. Do this for two cases, first assuming complete reaction and second for perfect fractionation (no reaction).

(b) Draw a hypothetical cooling curve for the liquid (temperature vs. time) and identify the changes of slope corresponding to the points tabulated in part a. Assume constant heat loss.

3–2. Using the ternary diagram for the system anorthite-forsterite-silica given here and in Figure 4–13b, indicate all sub-fields having distinct orders of crystallization, reaction, or both. For each field, tabulate in concise form the order of precipitation or reaction. Note in particular the field of spinel ($MgAl_2O_4$). Although the composition of this mineral lies outside the triangle, it is the liquidus phase of compositions near the midpoint on the Fo-An join. What does this tell you about the four-phase point where Fo, An, and Sp can coexist with a liquid? In your answer, write the equations expressing this relationship.

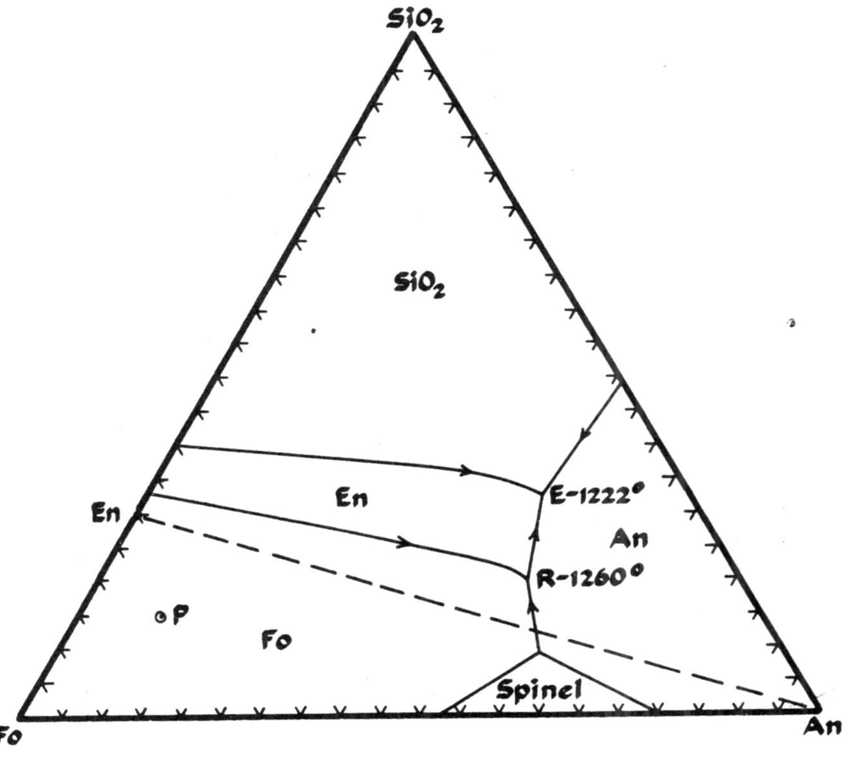

3–3. Assume that a certain horizon in the earth's mantle consists of feldspathic peridotite with an initial temperature of 1,000°C and the bulk composition of point "P" on the accompanying diagram. A local increase in the heat-flow from greater depth causes the temperature to rise. Assume that heat is added at a constant rate of 1.0×10^{-6} cal g^{-1} sec^{-1}. The heat capacity of the peridotite in both its solid and liquid forms is 0.3 cal g^{-1}, and the heat of fusion (and reaction) of a composition corresponding to the point "R" is 100 cal g^{-1}.

After a period of slightly more than three years (1,115 days to be exact), an earthquake occurs, and the liquid fraction is separated from the solid and intruded as a dike in a remote part of the system. What is the mineral composition of (a) the dike and (b) the refractory residue in the original layer?

The temperature in the layer continues to rise and eventually reaches a maximum of 1,800°C, then declines rapidly to 1,000°C with no reaction during crystallization. What will be the final mineral composition of the layer?

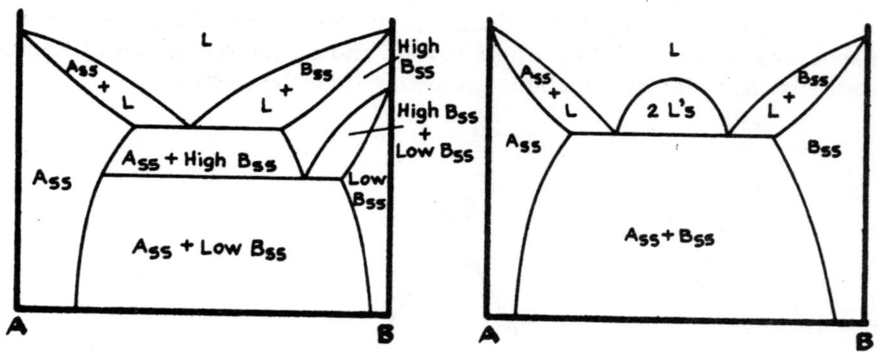

3–4. The two phase diagrams shown here depict the phase relations for minerals having limited mutual solid solution. The binary system on the left has a phase, B, with two polymorphic forms; the one on the right has a field of liquid immiscibility. Examine the diagrams and, by use of the Phase Rule, test whether or not the diagrams are compatible with the principles of phase equilibria.

Chapter 4

4–1. An experimentalist undertaking a reconnaissance study of the phase relations of two minerals, A and B, knows that the melting temperature of pure A is 1,125°C and pure B is 1,200°C. Both minerals are able to take in limited solid solution of the other, and they are commonly seen intimately intergrown in slowly cooled igneous rocks. B has two forms, B_H, which is stable above 800°C in the pure form, and B_L, which is stable at lower temperatures. As in all such minerals, the high-temperature polymorph can take more A into solid solution at a given temperature than can the low-temperature form.

A series of samples of glass with compositions intermediate between the pure end-members are held at various temperatures in a furnace until they reach equilibrium. They are then quenched and examined under a microscope. The results of these runs are tabulated below. Compositions are given in percent A. "GL" indicates liquid quenched to glass.

T, °C	A_{90}	A_{80}	A_{60}	A_{40}	A_{20}	A_{10}
1050°	A+GL	GL	GL	GL+B_H	GL+B_H	B_H
900°	A	A+GL	B_H+GL	GL+B_H	B_H	B_H
600°	A	A+B_H	A+B_H	A+B_H	B_H+B_L	B_L
300°	A	A+B_L	—	—	A+B_L	B_L

Using the outline below, plot the probable form of the phase diagram. Indicate boundaries of the fields for the various crystalline forms and liquid.

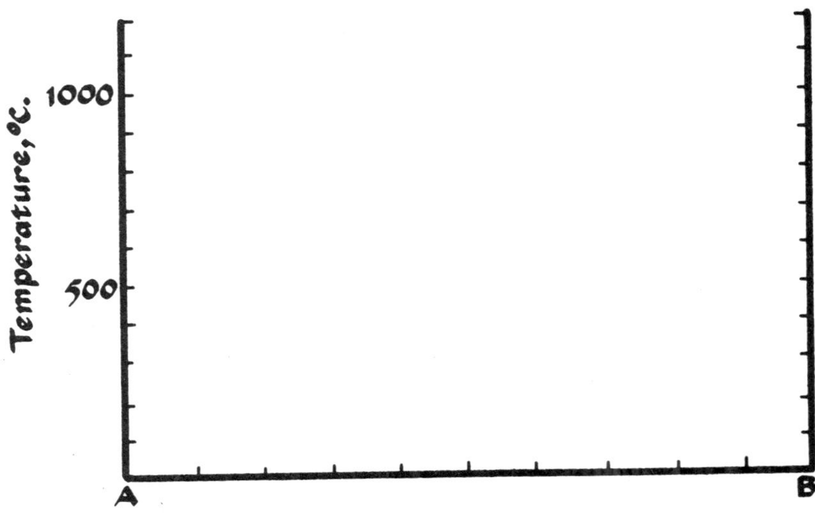

4-2. Two minerals, A and B, have an intermediate compound, AB, with equal parts of the two end-members (i.e., 50–50 A and B). Listed below are the melting temperatures, T_M, heats of fusion, ΔH_F, and differences of molar volume between solid and liquid, ΔV, for each phase. Note that the units for ΔH_F are in kilocalories per mole, corresponding to the units of ΔV, which are cm^3 per mole.

	T_M, °K	ΔH_M, kcal/mol	ΔV, cm^3/mol
A	2172	16.06	1.77
B	2001	1.97	.31
AB	1752	47.19	19.30

(a) Calculate and plot the liquidus curves for the system A-B, assuming ideal liquids with no heats of mixing.

(b) Calculate the liquidus curves for the same system at 10 kbars assuming that ΔH_F and ΔV_F do not vary with pressure.

(c) If a liquid formed by melting of a mixture of A and AB at 10 kbars were to rise to the surface and lose heat without reacting chemically with its surroundings, what changes would occur during its rise and subsequent cooling under equilibrium conditions?

Chapter 5

5–1. A useful method of studying the genetic relations of a series of igneous rocks is to examine their trends on variation diagrams. Depending on the nature of the rocks and what one is trying to learn about them, any of a variety of diagrams can be used. Two of the most common types are the Harker and AMF diagrams. In the former, various oxide components are plotted against SiO_2. In the latter, the ratio $Na_2O + K_2O : MgO : FeO + .9Fe_2O_3$ is plotted on a triangular diagram.

OCEANIC SERIES

SiO_2	48.34	49.42	51.03	53.74	56.65	61.87	66.94	70.43
TiO_2	1.93	2.11	2.41	2.21	1.84	1.26	1.02	0.56
Al_2O_3	13.57	13.72	14.54	15.01	13.92	12.45	12.07	12.58
Fe_2O_3	2.11	2.98	3.45	3.75	1.90	2.10	1.24	1.32
FeO	7.73	9.17	10.22	9.40	8.26	4.49	2.92	1.88
MnO	0.25	0.32	0.47	0.38	0.21	0.41	0.08	0.23
MgO	9.23	6.42	3.81	2.52	2.08	1.41	0.98	0.54
CaO	10.91	11.22	9.50	7.48	6.11	4.98	3.28	2.34
Na_2O	2.31	2.66	2.71	2.82	3.23	3.91	4.32	4.51
K_2O	0.59	0.74	1.19	1.78	2.37	2.89	3.18	4.03
H_2O+	0.48	0.43	0.31	0.21	1.54	1.56	1.90	1.33
H_2O-	0.32	0.37	0.12	0.19	0.38	0.74	0.82	0.47
P_2O_5	0.40	0.52	1.03	0.81	0.62	0.53	0.28	0.10
Total	98.17	100.08	100.79	100.30	99.11	98.33	99.04	99.32

OROGENIC SERIES

SiO_2	48.60	50.68	53.50	58.32	60.85	63.81	69.36	72.41
TiO_2	1.30	1.22	1.10	0.92	0.86	0.38	0.31	0.18
Al_2O_3	17.95	17.85	17.65	16.77	16.10	15.67	15.67	14.60
Fe_2O_3	1.84	1.68	2.01	2.08	2.18	2.11	0.88	0.24
FeO	8.65	7.76	6.50	4.33	3.24	2.15	1.53	1.26
MnO	0.30	0.32	0.29	0.21	0.20	0.09	0.11	0.04
MgO	6.73	6.12	5.42	3.73	3.01	2.28	1.14	0.18
CaO	10.65	9.67	7.43	6.17	5.85	4.97	3.17	2.35
Na_2O	2.47	2.70	3.48	3.92	3.97	4.08	4.06	4.15
K_2O	0.25	0.68	0.73	0.98	1.30	1.96	3.02	4.10
H_2O+	0.30	1.98	0.82	0.67	0.98	0.98	0.37	0.28
H_2O-	0.25	0.38	0.12	0.07	0.30	0.82	0.31	0.13
P_2O_5	0.08	0.23	0.30	0.42	0.45	0.28	0.31	0.23
Total	99.66	98.87	99.75	99.29	100.11	99.58	99.80	100.15

(a) Chemical analyses for two sub-alkaline series of rocks are given in the accompanying table. One is an oceanic series, and the other is from a orogenic volcanic province. Plot these on Harker and AMF diagrams and draw smooth trend lines, making a visual fit through the points. Plot both series on the same AMF diagram but use separate sheets for the two Harker diagrams. In the former, plot the sum of alkalies rather than separate values of Na_2O and K_2O, and use total iron oxide, ($FeO^* = FeO + .9Fe_2O_3$). Ignore H_2O. Reference to the criteria given in Figure 2–4(b) will show that one is tholeiitic and the other calc-alkaline.

(b) Assuming the most mafic (silica-poor) basalt is closest to the parental magma for the orogenic rocks, draw from each of its points on the Harker diagram an arrow to indicate the effect of subtraction of plagioclase from this first liquid, assuming the composition given below.

	Plagioclase	Augite	Olivine	Magnetite	Ilmenite
SiO_2	50.5	51.3	39.2	—	—
TiO_2	—	—	—	—	52.7
Al_2O_3	31.7	—	—	—	—
FeO^*	—	6.1	13.3	100.0	49.3
MgO	—	21.3	47.5	—	—
CaO	14.4	21.3	—	—	—
Na_2O	3.2	—	—	—	—
K_2O	0.3	—	—	—	—

(c) If the minerals listed above are separated in weight proportions of 58 percent plagioclase, 17 percent augite, 12 percent olivine, 10 percent magnetite, and 3 percent ilmenite, would the resulting effect correspond to the observed trend of differentiation? To answer this, reduce the mineral assemblage to a bulk composition with the appropriate proportions of the components, and plot the effect on each oxide in the Harker diagram, just as you did for plagioclase alone.

(d) Assuming that similar minerals were fractionated from the oceanic series, what was their order of precipitation, and at what stage did the effect of each mineral become apparent?

5–2. Another way of producing intermediate magmas is by mixing liquids of different compositions, possibly by injecting a new, more primitive magma into a reservoir already occupied by a magma that has evolved to a more advanced state. Consider two hypothetical liquids, L_1 and L_2, at different points on a curved cotectic, such as the one shown in the accompanying figure. Note that, because the cotectic is not straight, a mixture of sub-equal parts of L_1 and L_2 would not fall on the cotectic but on its concave side in a part of the field of olivine, where the saturation temperature is above the temperature on the three-phase cotectic. Assume the two liquids equilibrate thermally while being thoroughly and quickly mixed by a process such as the one described in Figure 5–13. Describe the effects of mixing by drawing schematic sections through the diagram to trace the changes of temperature and composition of the resulting liquid.

Do this for three conditions:

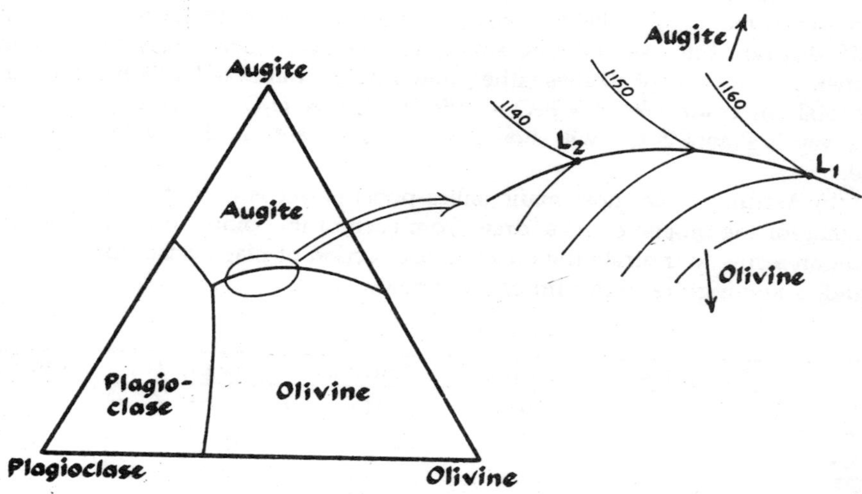

1. A crystal-free mixed liquid that does not react with its walls or earlier crystallized minerals and does not exchange heat with its surroundings;
2. The same liquid but with slow, steady heat loss to its surroundings; and
3. A liquid containing suspended crystals of both olivine and pyroxene slowly cools and equilibrates.

5–3. Three trace elements that are commonly used to test the effects of crystal fractionation are Ni, Sr, and Rb. Ni is strongly partitioned into olivine, but does not enter significantly into other minerals, and for that reason it is useful for testing whether olivine has been removed. Sr tends to be fractionated by plagioclase but is excluded to differing degrees by other minerals. Rb is largely excluded from all the common minerals of basalts. Distribution coefficients are given in Table A of Appendix G. Assuming the proportions of phases fractionated from a basaltic parent were found by mass-balance calculations to have been:

Olivine	10%
Augite	25%
Hypersthene	12%
Plagioclase	50%
Magnetite	3%

and the proportion of a derivative andesitic liquid is 30 percent of that of the basalt, what would be the Ni, Sr, and Rb contents of the andesite if the original basalt contained 27 ppm Ni, 135 ppm Sr, and 12 ppm Rb? Test the two extreme values for the distribution coefficient of olivine.

5–4. Assume a lava lake with a depth of 100 m consists of basaltic magma with a density of 2.7 g cm^{-3}, heat capacity of 0.3 cal g^{-1} deg^{-1}, and an initial temperature of 1,200 °C. Thermal conductivity is 4×10^{-3} cal cm^{-1} deg^{-1} sec^{-1}.

(a) Calculate the thickness and temperature profile in the crust, first after one year and then after five years, assuming that heat is radiated to the atmosphere and cooling is so rapid that the crust is largely glass, i.e., the heat of crystallization can be ignored. Take the temperature of the surface as 30 °C and the base of the crust as the level where the temperature reaches 1,100 °C and viscosity changes sharply.

(b) Cooling of the base of the lava lake differs from that of the crust in that the underlying rocks are not at a constant temperature but become hotter as they gain heat from the lava. Moreover, their thermal properties are different because they are already below their solidus temperature, whereas the magma is giving up its heat of crystallization as it cools. Assume that the lava gives up a heat of crystallization of 100 cal per gram through a temperature interval of 300°, and that the thermal conductivity of both the lava and underlying rocks is 4×10^{-3} cal cm^{-1} deg^{-1} sec^{-1}. The temperature at the contact can be taken as the mean between the initial temperature of the lava, 1,200°, and the ground, 20 °C. Calculate the temperature profile in the ground and base of the lava after one year.

(c) Two crystals are growing in the lava illustrated in Figure 5–2. One is olivine, Fo_{80}, and the other labradorite, An_{60}, and both have radii of half a millimeter at a level five meters below the surface. If the lava has the composition of the most basic basalt in the first table of problem 5–1, what is the likely fate of the crystals?

(d) The preceding calculation makes a number of simplifying assumptions. List additional refinements that could be added to make the calculation more realistic, and predict the effect each might have on the solution.

Chapter 6

6–1. In attempting to interpret the origins and field relations of igneous rocks, it is important to bear in mind certain limitations inherent in most of the numerical data used in quantitative interpretations. All measurements, be they simply strikes and dips measured with a Brunton compass or thermodynamic and experimental data determined with sophisticated laboratory instruments, are subject to unavoidable errors, and, before accepting them, one must evaluate the magnitude and effects of their uncertainties. Contrary to the impression one might get from much of the modern literature, there is little correlation between the reliability, or even the usefulness, of scientific data and the cost entailed in getting it.

The following rules can be used to estimate the magnitude of possible errors in calculations based on measured physical values. Uncertainties in measurements may be related to a single source of error, such as the limitations of an instrument that is used to measure all values in the same way. Or they may be independent of one another if the measurement of each value involves a variety of unrelated sources of possible error. If the best estimates for the values of a series of quantities, X, Y, . . U, and W are obtained in such a way that the uncertainties, of each, dX, dY, . . dU, and dW, are the result of similar measurements, all with the same sources of error, then the cumulative error in Q, a value obtained from addition or subtraction of these values, is additive.

$$Q = X + Y + \ldots . - U - W$$

$$dQ = dX + dY \ldots + dU + dW$$

For example, the total uncertainty in the algebraic sum of a series of measurements of distance, weight, time, etc. is the sum of the uncertainties in all the individual measurements, because each was obtained using the same measuring device subject to the same uncertainty. If Q is the product or quotient obtained from multiplication or division of values obtained in this way, the uncertainty in Q is equal to the sum of the fractional uncertainties or relative errors in each measurement, X/dX, Y/dY, etc.

$$Q = XY \ldots . \times U/W$$

$$dQ = X/dX + Y/dY \ldots + U/dU + W/dW$$

A calculation of area from two linear measurements of length and width would have an uncertainty equal to the sum of the fractional uncertainty in each measurement.

In the case of thermodynamic data, most values are obtained by measurements with many possible sources of uncertainty, few of which are related to each other, and the error associated with one term is not necessarily related to the same source of error as that in the others. For example, a measurement of the heat of fusion of a mineral involves uncertainties in the measuring device, preparation of the sample, and the possible exchange of heat between the container (calorimeter) and its surroundings. Uncertainty propagated through a calculation using values with unrelated or random uncertainties of this kind are determined by the following rules.

For addition or subtraction, where:

$$x = au + bv \quad \text{or} \quad x = au - bv$$

and

$$s_x^2 = a^2 s_u^2 + b^2 s_v^2$$

where a, b, and c are constants, and s is the uncertainty in x, u, etc. For multiplication of division,

$$\frac{s_x^2}{x^2} = \frac{s_u^2}{u^2} + \frac{s_v^2}{v^2}$$

(The derivation of these rules, as well as clear explanations of their application to problems in physics and thermodynamics, can be found in J. R. Taylor, 1982, *An Introduction to Error Analysis,* University Science Books, 270 p., and G. M. Anderson, 1977, Uncertainties in calculations involving thermodynamic data, *MAC Short Course in Applications of Thermodynamics to Petrology and Ore Deposits,* H. Greenwood, ed., 199–215.)

Consider again the calculation of temperature and pressure from the mineral associations in the Sandwich Horizon of the Skaergaard intrusion in chapter six (Fig. 6–31). In order to relate the silica minerals to the change from Fe-wollastonite to hedenbergite, it was necessary to calculate the effect of pressure on the temperature of the quartz-tridymite inversion by means of the Clapeyron equation. The precision of the measurement of the temperature of this reaction at atmospheric pressure is given as 3 °C. The method used to determine the heat of reaction, ΔH_R, is based on the differences in the heats of formation of the two minerals:

$$\Delta H_R = H_{QUARTZ} - H_{TRIDYMITE}$$

The experimentally determined values for the latter are:

$$H_{QUARTZ} = -3.622 \div .004 \text{ kcal/g}$$

$$H_{TRIDYMITE} = -3.609 \div .0095 \text{ kcal/g}$$

Assuming that these are the only sources of uncertainty in the calculation, determine the possible error in the estimated depth of the Sandwich Horizon.

Chapter 7

7–1. The reservoir under ridges and large, mature volcanoes must be periodically recharged with new magma, so that the mass discharged to the surface is continually replaced by a new influx. Under such conditions, each renewal would partly reset the earlier magma back to a more primitive composition. In the case of oceanic ridges, the reservoirs are thought to maintain almost constant volumes with the losses to crystallization and discharge to lavas and dikes being balanced periodically by equal amount of new magma. As explained in the text, differentiation under these conditions is very different from that of a closed system. This problem is designed to illustrate these differences.

(a) Assume a reservoir of constant volume under an oceanic spreading axis in which, during each cycle, 0.10 parts are crystallized, 0.05 are discharged as lavas and dikes, and these are replaced by 0.15 parts new magma. For each of two elements, one included (D = 5) and another excluded (D = 0.1), each with an initial abundance of 100 ppm, plot the concentrations in the reservoir for enough cycles to determine the nature of the variations and abundances when the system approaches a steady state. In doing this, plot the abundance of one element against the other in the manner shown in Figure 8–9.

(b) Examine these relations and show how, all other things being equal, the compositions of magmas of a fast-spreading ridge would differ from those where the proportion of magma discharged as lavas and dikes to that crystallized would be smaller, and the influx of new magma crystallized would be correspondingly less. This can be done most directly by utilizing the equation for the steady-state concentration, C_{ss}, where the number of cycles approaches infinity.

(c) Starting with the same initial composition, calculate the concentrations of the two elements in a closed system evolving by Rayleigh-type crystal fractionation. Compare the results by plotting on the same diagram used in (a) the concentrations at .9, .8, .7, and .6 parts remaining liquid.

(d) The behavior of trace elements in such a system is quite different from that of the major elements, because the distribution coefficients of the latter are much closer to unity. Compare, for example, the enrichment of Fe ($D \approx 0.8$) and the depletion of Mg ($D \approx 2$) in basaltic liquids evolving in these two types of systems.

Chapter 8

8–1. A distinction can sometimes be made between a series of liquids produced by differing degrees of melting and crystal fractionation by examining the relations of two trace elements, one that is almost totally excluded ($D = 0.001$ or less) and another that is also excluded but slightly less effectively ($D \approx .01$). When these highly and moderately "magmaphile" elements, designated H and M respectively, are plotted on a diagram for the ratio H/M vs. H, they may define different slopes depending on how they evolved. The way this comes about is well-illustrated by the behavior of the two rare-earth elements, Ce and Sm, at different degrees of partial melting and Rayleigh-type crystal fractionation.

(a) Taking the bulk distribution coefficients of Ce and Sm as 0.001 and 0.01 respectively, calculate the amounts of each element in liquids produced by 1, 2, 4, 8, 16, and 32 percent melting of a source rock containing 2 ppm Ce and .41 ppm Sm. Plot the results on a diagram for H/M vs. H. Then calculate the abundances of the same elements for liquids that evolve from crystal fractionation of the 4 percent melt, taking fractions of remaining liquid as .9, .8, .7, .6, and .5. Plot your results on the same diagram.

(b) Kohala volcano, at the northwestern corner of the island of Hawaii, has a sequence of tholeiitic, transitional, and alkaline lavas that have the abundances of Ce and Sm tabulated below. Judging from the relations seen in part (a), how could these data be interpreted in terms of their compositional relations to the stratigraphic sequence? The samples are listed in stratigraphic order.

Rock type	Ce, ppm	Sm, ppm
Top alk. basalt	157.0	12.9
alk. basalt	110.0	11.1
alk. basalt	43.9	6.6
alk. basalt	51.9	8.2
alk. basalt	204.0	20.8
trans. basalt	142.0	14.5
trans. basalt	53.1	7.5
trans. basalt	70.3	11.0
trans. basalt	41.7	7.4
tholeiite	20.4	4.4
tholeiite	18.8	4.0
tholeiite	24.5	4.9
Base tholeiite	24.6	4.9

(Adapted from data of Feigenson et al., 1983, *Contrib. Mineral. Petrol.* 84:390.)

Chapter 9

9–1. Petrologists long argued whether the straight-line variations so typical of calc-alkaline series result from fractionation of early-formed crystals, assimilation of siliceous crustal rocks, or a combination of both. The compositions given below represent four possible members of such a series. The high-alumina basalt and andesite are lavas forming a Central American volcano, and the crustal xenolith and gabbro are fragments ejected during strong explosive eruptions. The object of this problem is to evaluate the possible relations of these components both chemically and thermally.

	Chemical Compositions			
	1	2	3	4
SiO_2	51.04	59.67	74.58	45.35
TiO_2	1.43	0.77	0.33	0.88
Al_2O_3	20.42	17.42	17.55	20.42
Fe_2O_3	1.51	2.78	0.12	6.62
FeO	6.68	3.39	1.92	4.81
MnO	0.13	0.10	0.05	0.06
MgO	4.94	2.87	1.56	6.06
CaO	9.28	5.97	0.78	13.15
Na_2O	3.47	3.84	0.36	1.30
K_2O	0.71	2.00	2.21	0.09
H_2O+	0.12	0.74	0.16	0.33
H_2O-	0.03	0.17	0.24	0.70
P_2O_5	0.17	0.14	0.05	tr.
Total	99.93	99.86	99.91	99.77
	Molecular Norms			
Ap	0.34	0.26	0.10	—
Il	1.98	1.08	0.46	0.94
Mt	1.58	2.94	0.14	7.09
Or	4.20	12.00	13.55	0.55
Ab	31.10	34.90	3.35	11.95
An	37.98	24.68	3.75	51.05
C	—	—	14.97	—
Di	5.48	3.64	—	12.92
Hy	12.06	8.68	7.14	13.28
O	13.30	—	—	—
Q	—	11.93	56.59	2.22

1. High-alumina olvine basalt
2. Hypersthene-augite andesite
3. Thermally metamorphosed xenolith
4. Gabbroic (or noritic) xenolith

(a) Calculate the chemical composition of:

1. the smallest amount of material that would have to be subtracted from the basalt to make the andesite by crystal fractionation, and

2. the smallest amount of material that would have to be added to the basalt to make the andesite by contamination. It is not necessary to calculate your components closer than the nearest tenth of a percent by weight. You can do this

graphically if you plot the oxides against SiO_2 with a scale of 1 cm = 1 percent SiO_2 for the horizontal axis. All your results will fall between 45 and 75 percent SiO_2. Use total iron as FeO* by multiplying $Fe_2O_3 \times 0.9$ and adding to FeO. By plotting $Al_2O_3 - 10$ rather than total Al_2O_3, it will be easier to keep it on the graph, and by plotting $P_2O_5 \times 10$ you will obtain a better slope.

(b) Calculate the normative compositions for the two solutions obtained above. In doing this, recalculate FeO* from part (a) back to FeO and Fe_2O_3 by assuming a uniform ratio of $Fe_2O_3/FeO = 0.5$ for both compositions. Compare the subtracted material with the gabbro and added material with the crustal xenolith. Judging from the composition of the crustal xenolith, what might the original rock have been?

(c) What are the minimum amounts by weight relative to that of the original basaltic magma that would have to be added or subtracted?

(d) Would it be chemically and thermally feasible to produce the andesite by crystallizing half of the original mass of basalt while adding to it a quarter of its original mass in crustal material? Assume the basalt remains at a temperature close to 1,100°C, and the heat of crystallization (100 cal g^{-1}) goes to raising the temperature of the crustal material from 700° to 1,100°C and melting it. Take the heat capacity of the crustal material as .25 cal deg^{-1} g^{-1} and its heat of fusion (or reaction) as 100 cal g^{-1}.

9–2. A shale deposited during Ordovician time, 450 m. y. ago, had an initial $^{87}Sr/^{86}Sr$ ratio of 0.715 and concentrations of Rb and Sr of 150 and 70.5 ppm, respectively. A basaltic magma of a Quaternary volcano assimilates a proportion of the shale (now a phyllite) equivalent to half the mass of the magma. The fresh basalt has a $^{87}Sr/^{86}Sr$ ratio of 0.704 and a strontium content of 475 ppm.

(a) Calculate the $^{87}Sr/^{86}Sr$ ratio of the contaminated basalt assuming a decay constant of 4.256×10^{-11} for ^{87}Rb and perfect isotopic equilibration.

(b) If the contaminated rock was found to have a strontium content of 225 ppm, was the process of assimilation a closed system? If not, what could have happened?

9–3. A few years ago, a group of geochemists published a paper in which they asserted that the evidence of certain trace elements ruled out the possibility that andesites could be derived from basalts by crystal fractionation. They found that calc-alkaline basalts have an average vanadium content of about 250 ppm and andesites about 175 ppm. Because magnetite is very rich in V (about 6,000 ppm), they reasoned that each weight percent of magnetite removed from the basalt would reduce the V content of the liquid by 60 ppm, and since mass-balance calculations, such as the one carried out in problem 9–1, indicate that between 3 and 4 percent magnetite had to be removed to bring the iron content down to that of an andesite, the andesite should have less than 70 ppm V. Because it has much more than this amount, they reasoned that the andesite could not result from crystal fractionation.

There was a basic flaw in this reasoning; the calculation ignored the effects of fractionating other minerals. If they contain little or no V, other fractionated minerals have the effect of reducing other components while concentrating the remaining V in a smaller amount of the derivative liquid. Assume that the mass of andesite is 30 percent of that of the original basalt and that V goes only into magnetite. What is the correct amount of magnetite that would have to be fractionated to account for the V content of the andesite?

Chapter 10

10–1. In discussing the origin of the Tertiary granites of Scotland, it was noted that their oxygen isotopes are a mixture derived from both mantle and surficial sources. The granites could either have been altered by meteoric water circulating through them after emplacement, or the magmas could be derived from crustal rocks that had equilibrated with surface water at some earlier time. In the case of the granites of Skye, the concentric zoning (Fig. 10–30) and the fact that the oxygen ratios differ from mineral to mineral indicate that the effect is due to hydrothermal alteration. Because plagioclase alters more readily than quartz, its oxygen is shifted to lower ratios than other minerals. If the magma had acquired its oxygen ratio before it crystallized, all the minerals would have a nearly uniform character.

Because oxygen accounts for about 50 weight percent of igneous rocks, the amount of water required to change the ratio of a granite is very large. The amount can be estimated from a simple mass balance of the following form.

O in granite × initial ratio of granite +
O in water × initial ratio of water =
O in granite × final ratio of granite +
O in water × final ratio of water

The granite is roughly half oxygen by weight and has a density of about 2.5, whereas the water is about 90 weight percent oxygen and has a density of 1.0. Assume the granite has an outcrop area of 400 km^2 and is altered to a depth of 2 km. Take its initial ratio of ^{18}O as that of common igneous rocks, +5, and the final ratio as that of the rocks today, about 0. The isotopic ratio of the meteoric water was about −10, and the hydrothermal water discharged in warm springs would have been about −5.

Calculate the volume of water required by this budget of oxygen; then, in order to put your answer into perspective, compare the required volume to the precipitation (say 100 cm per year) over the area of the hydrothermal system (about 2,500 km^2) during the cooling time of the intrusion. If only 10 percent of the rainfall went through the rock, how long would it take to supply the needed oxygen?

10–2. Consider next a granite that derived its isotopic ratio from a magmatic source consisting of two components, one a mantle-derived basalt and the other an assemblage of crustal rocks, and assume that the isotopes were thoroughly mixed and equilibrated in the magma. As stated in the text, the effect of mixing on the abundances of major elements is to produce straight-line variations, such as those in the Harker diagram shown in Figure 9–21a, but this generality does not apply to ratios of components, such as isotopes. The latter define hyperbolas on most mixing diagrams. The reason for this can be illustrated by a simple example using isotopic ratios of strontium and oxygen.

(a) Examine the effect of mixing a basaltic magma, such as the one associated with the Tertiary granites of Skye, with metamorphosed crustal rocks. Assume that the basalt has a typical mantle ratio of $^{87}Sr/^{86}Sr = .703$ and a Sr content of 300 ppm, but the crustal material has a ratio of .735 and 100 ppm Sr. A typical $\delta^{18}O$ value for uncontaminated basalt is +5, whereas that of the crustal rock at Skye is about +19. Oxygen can be assumed to account for about half of each of these components.

First plot the Sr and O isotopic ratios against the fraction of crustal material in a series of mixtures of basalt with various proportions of crust. (A convenient scale is 2 units ^{18}O = .004 units $^{87}Sr/^{86}Sr$ = 0.1 parts crust.)

The preceding plots show how the different absolute abundances in the two end-member components of mixing can cause the ratio to deviate widely from a straight line, even though a plot of individual components would be linear. It is the differing abundances of Sr in the two components of the mixture that cause the compositions to define a curve; oxygen, since it has about the same abundance in both end-members, varies linearly.

(b) Simple calculations such as these assume mixing in a closed system and are, of course, unrealistic. In nature, the heat absorbed in assimilating crustal material probably leads to an equivalent amount of crystallization, as illustrated in part (d) of problem 9–1. In the case of a component, such as Sr, which tends to be strongly fractionated into plagioclase, this results in a further effect on the composition of the contaminated liquid. Repeat the previous calculation for various amounts of assimilation, but this time assume that the crustal material is added to the basalt and that this addition is balanced by crystallization of a plagioclase-rich assemblage with a mass equal to that of the assimilated rock. (For example, 0.1 parts crust + 1.0 parts basalt − 0.1 parts crystals = 1.0 parts contaminated magma.) In this way, the mass of the magma remains unchanged. Assume the crystals have a bulk Sr content twice that of the basalt (i.e., the ratio of the Sr in crystals to Sr in the remaining basalt is always 2.0) and that they separate before the basalt mixes with the added crust. In this way, the crystals would take their isotopic ratio and Sr content from the magma only.

Chapter 11

11–1. A possible explanation for the unusual concentrations of K and other lithophile components in continental alkaline rocks is that these components may be selectively absorbed from the crustal rocks through which the magmas rise. If a mantle-derived basalt is exposed to crustal rocks, the amount of the individual components it will absorb depends on a number of factors, such as time, the ratio of the mass of the magma to the surface area of the crustal rock, the diffusivities and activities of the component in the rocks and magma, and the amount of convective stirring of the magma. For example, a magma is much more easily contaminated by xenoliths, even if they eventually settle out, than by wall rocks, because the former provide a larger surface area. Moreover, they quickly rise to high temperatures, and this increases diffusivity and reaction rates.

Experimental studies (E. B. Watson, 1982, *Contrib. Mineral. Petrol.* 80:73–87) show that some minor and trace elements, such as K, high-valence lithophile elements, and rare earths, diffuse much more rapidly than silica and other essential components of crustal rocks. With sufficient time, of course, the magma and crustal material would be totally mixed and reach a uniform mineral composition, but in the time required for magma to rise through the crust, equilibrium might not be achieved.

In order to appreciate the potential effects of selective contamination, assume that a basaltic magma with 0.1 wt. percent K_2O and 50 percent SiO_2 rises by turbulent flow through crustal rocks with 2.5 and 70 percent K_2O and SiO_2, respectively. The diffusivities of these components at high temperatures are estimated at 5×10^{-7} and 3×10^{-10} cm^2 sec^{-1} respectively. Suppose that the magma carries 10 percent xenoliths with an average radius of 50 cm. The diffusion of components between a sphere and a well-stirred medium of limited volume is governed by the principles outlined in chapter two, but the equations for calculating the rates of transfer are very complex. Fortunately, curves have been calculated to facilitate the solution (J. Crank, 1967, *The Mathematics of Diffusion*, Oxford Univ. Press). The relevant curve for this problem, reproduced in the accompanying diagram, shows the amount of a component, M_t, transferred in time t, relative to M_∞, the amount of the component when the system reaches equilibrium, as a function of diffusivity, D, time, and the radius of the sphere, r.

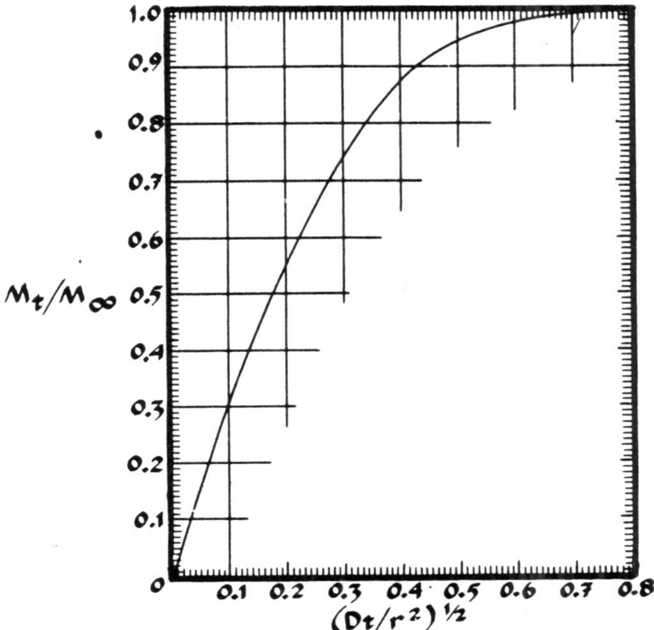

Calculate curves for the K_2O and SiO_2 concentrations of the basalt as a function of time up to ten years. This can be done by determining concentrations at 0.1, 0.5, 1, 5, and 10 years. Then comment on the possible relevance of such a process of selective contamination as an explanation for potassic magmas, such as those in Table 11-3 of the text. Can you think of any common component of the crust that could provide potassium and silica in appropriate proportions to a basalt and produce the leucite tephrite of Vesuvius with 47.67 percent SiO_2 and 7.47 percent K_2O? If so, test it.

11–2. High-pressure melting experiments of the kind described in the text showed that a melt with a composition close to that of a katungite lava can be produced by 25 percent melting of a metasomatized phlogopite clinopyroxenite. The amount of each phase going into the melt can be calculated by converting the liquid composition to the appropriate normative minerals in a manner similar to that illustrated in Appendix A. The amount of each phase in the xenolith is known from a modal analysis. These values are shown below together with abundances of selected trace elements.

	Katungite	Xenolith
Ca-rich pyroxene	52	53
phlogopite	24	35
apatite	3	2
sphene	6	4
Ti-magnetite	15	6
Rb	126	84
Sr	2127	519
Ba	1781	1146
La	162	90
Ni	142	34

The high-pressure partition coefficients for these minerals and elements are poorly known, especially for crystal-liquid relations in the presence of a volatile phase, but the following are reasonable estimates.

	Cpx	Phl	Ap	Sph	Ti-mgt	Oliv
Rb	.03	2	.01	.01	.001	.001
Sr	.1	.2	5	.2	.001	.001
Ba	.005	2	.01	.2	.001	.001
La	.06	.02	5	8	.001	.001
Ni	.6	.8	.8	.5	6	12

Compare the observed trace elements concentrations with those predicted for the melting relations. Would the results be improved if:

(1) the fraction of melting were less, say 15 percent?
(2) the source rock contained olivine?

(3) the source rock contained more sphene?
(4) the volatile phase carries lithophile and rare-earth elements?
(5) a small amount of melt had been extracted from the source during an earlier stage of melting?

11–3. Another mechanism that has been proposed to account for potassic lavas is zone refining (chapter five). The partitioning of trace elements in this process is governed by the equation:

$$\frac{C_L}{C_O} = \frac{1}{D} + \left[\frac{1}{D} - 1\right] e^{-nD}$$

where C_O is the concentration of an element in the original rock, C_L is the concentration in the liquid, D is the bulk distribution coefficient, and n is the number of equivalent volumes of solid through which the zones of melt rises. Test this mechanism assuming the liquid rises through 5, 10, 25, 50, 75, and 100 equivalent volumes of a peridotite with the same composition as in 11–2 and compare the results with those obtained by the other mechanisms.

INDEX